REVISE AQA A LEVEL
Psychology
REVISION
GUIDE AND WORKBOOK

Series Consultant: Harry Smith

Authors: Sarah Middleton, Anna Cave, Susan Harty and Sally White

Our study resources are the smart choice for those studying AQA A Level Psychology. This book will help you to:

- **Organise** your study with the one-topic-per-page format
- **Speed up** your revision with summary notes in short, memorable chunks
- **Track** your revision progress with at-a-glance check boxes
- **Check** your understanding and exam skills with worked examples
- **Develop** your exam technique with exam-style practice questions and full answers.

> **For the full range of Pearson revision titles across KS2, KS3, GCSE, Functional Skills, AS/A Level and BTEC visit:**
> www.pearsonschools.co.uk/revise

Contents

4.1.1 Social influence

1 Types of conformity
2 The Asch study
3 Variables affecting conformity
4 The Stanford Prison experiment
5 Milgram's study of obedience
6 Explanations for obedience
7 Situational variables
8 Obedience: dispositional explanation
9 Resistance to social influence
10 Resisting social influence through social support
11 Minority influence
12 How social influences affect social change
13 Exam skills 1
14 Exam skills 2
15 Exam skills 3
16 Exam-style practice 1
17 Exam-style practice 2

4.1.2 Memory

18 The multi-store model
19 The sensory register
20 Short-term memory
21 Long-term memory
22 The working memory model
23 Types of long-term memory
24 Explanations of forgetting: interference
25 Cue-dependent forgetting
26 Misleading information
27 Anxiety
28 The cognitive interview
29 Exam skills 1
30 Exam skills 2
31 Exam skills 3
32 Exam-style practice 1
33 Exam-style practice 2

4.1.3 Attachment

34 Caregiver–infant interactions
35 Stages of attachment development
36 The role of the father
37 Animal studies of attachment
38 Learning theory of attachment
39 Bowlby's monotropic theory
40 Ainsworth's 'Strange Situation'
41 Cultural variations in attachment
42 Bowlby: maternal deprivation
43 Romanian orphan studies
44 The influence on later relationships
45 Exam skills 1
46 Exam skills 2
47 Exam skills 3
48 Exam-style practice 1
49 Exam-style practice 2

4.1.4 Psychopathology

50 Definitions of abnormality 1
51 Definitions of abnormality 2
52 Phobias
53 Depression
54 Obsessive compulsive disorder
55 The two-process model of phobias
56 Behavioural treatments for phobias
57 Beck's negative triad
58 Ellis's ABC model
59 Treating depression
60 Biological explanations of OCD
61 Biological treatments of OCD
62 Exam skills 1
63 Exam skills 2
64 Exam-style practice 1
65 Exam-style practice 2

4.2.1 Approaches

66 Origins of psychology
67 Classical conditioning
68 Operant conditioning
69 Social learning theory
70 The cognitive approach
71 The biological approach
72 The psychodynamic approach
73 Humanistic psychology
74 Humanistic therapy
75 Comparison of approaches 1
76 Comparison of approaches 2
77 Exam skills 1
78 Exam skills 2
79 Exam skills 3
80 Exam-style practice 1
81 Exam-style practice 2
82 Exam-style practice 3

4.2.2 Biopsychology

83 Divisions of the nervous system
84 Neurons and synaptic transmission
85 Endocrine system
86 Localisation of function in the brain
87 Lateralisation and split-brain research
88 Plasticity and functional recovery
89 Ways of studying the brain
90 Biological rhythms
91 Endogenous pacemakers and exogenous zeitgebers
92 Exam skills 1
93 Exam skills 2
94 Exam-style-practice 1
95 Exam-style practice 2

4.2.3 Research methods

96 Experiments
97 Observational techniques
98 Self-report techniques
99 Correlations
100 Case studies and content analysis
101 Aims and hypotheses
102 Variables
103 Sampling techniques
104 Experimental design and control
105 Observational design
106 Ethics in research
107 Peer review
108 Implications of psychological research for the economy
109 Validity and reliability
110 Features of science
111 Report writing
112 Types of data
113 Descriptive statistics

114 Maths skills
115 Displaying data
116 Distributions
117 Levels of measurement
118 Inferential testing 1
119 Inferential testing 2
120 Using critical value tables
121 Exam skills 1
122 Exam skills 2
123 Exam skills 3
124 Exam skills 4
125 Exam-style practice 1
126 Exam-style practice 2
127 Exam-style practice 3

4.3.1 Issues and debates
128 Gender bias
129 Cultural bias
130 Free will and determinism
131 Nature–nurture
132 Reductionism and holism
133 Idiographic and nomothetic
134 Ethical implications of research
135 Exam skills 1
136 Exam skills 2
137 Exam-style practice 1
138 Exam-style practice 2

4.3.2 Relationships
139 Evolutionary explanations
140 Self-disclosure
141 Physical attractiveness
142 Filter theory
143 Social exchange theory
144 Equity theory
145 Rusbult's investment model
146 Duck's model of breakdown
147 Virtual relationships and self-disclosure
148 Absence of gating
149 Parasocial relationships
150 Absorption–addiction model
151 Attachment theory explanation
152 Exam skills 1
153 Exam skills 2
154 Exam-style practice 1
155 Exam-style practice 2

4.3.3 Gender
156 Sex-role stereotypes
157 Androgyny
158 Chromosomes and hormones
159 Klinefelter's syndrome

160 Turner's syndrome
161 Kohlberg's theory of gender development
162 Gender schema theory
163 Freud's psychoanalytic theory
164 Social learning theory
165 Influence of culture
166 Influence of media
167 Social explanations for GID
168 Biological explanations for GID
169 Exam skills 1
170 Exam skills 2
171 Exam-style practice 1
172 Exam-style practice 2

4.3.4 Cognition and development
173 Piaget's theory of cognitive development
174 Piaget: Sensorimotor stage
175 Piaget: Pre-operational stage
176 Piaget: Concrete operational stage
177 Piaget: Formal operational stage
178 Vygotsky's theory of cognitive development
179 Zone of proximal development
180 Baillargeon: early infant abilities
181 Social cognition: Selman
182 Theory of mind
183 Theory of mind and autism
184 Mirror neurons
185 Exam skills 1
186 Exam skills 2
187 Exam-style practice 1
188 Exam-style practice 2

4.3.5 Schizophrenia
189 Classification of schizophrenia
190 Reliability of diagnosis
191 Validity of diagnosis
192 Co-morbidity
193 Culture bias
194 Gender bias
195 Symptom overlap
196 Genetic explanation for schizophrenia
197 The dopamine hypothesis
198 Neural correlates
199 Family dysfunction explanation
200 Cognitive explanations

201 Dysfunctional thought processing
202 Drug therapy
203 Cognitive behaviour therapy
204 Family therapy
205 Token economies
206 Interactionist approach
207 Exam skills 1
208 Exam skills 2
209 Exam-style practice 1
210 Exam-style practice 2

4.3.6 Eating behaviour
211 Food preferences: evolutionary explanations
212 Food preferences: learning experiences
213 Neural and hormonal mechanisms
214 Anorexia nervosa
215 Anorexia: family systems theory
216 Anorexia: social learning theory
217 Anorexia: cognitive theory
218 Obesity
219 Obesity: psychological explanations
220 Success and failure of dieting
221 Exam skills 1
222 Exam skills 2
223 Exam-style practice 1
224 Exam-style practice 2

4.3.7 Stress
225 General adaption syndrome
226 Sympathomedullary pathway
227 Hypothalamic-pituitary-adrenal system
228 Immunosuppression
229 Cardiovascular disorders
230 Life changes and daily hassles
231 Workplace stress
232 Self-report scales
233 Physiological measures of stress
234 Types A, B and C personality
235 Hardiness
236 Drug therapy
237 Stress inoculation therapy
238 Biofeedback
239 Gender differences
240 Social support

241 Exam skills 1
242 Exam skills 2
243 Exam-style practice 1
244 Exam-style practice 2

4.3.8 Aggression
245 Neural and hormonal mechanisms
246 Genetic factors
247 Ethology
248 Evolutionary explanations
249 Deindividuation and frustration
250 Social learning theory
251 Institutional aggression
252 Media influences
253 Exam skills 1
254 Exam skills 2
255 Exam-style practice 1
256 Exam-style practice 2

4.3.9 Forensic psychology
257 Defining crime
258 Offender profiling: top-drown
259 Offender profiling: bottom-up
260 Historical explanation for crime

261 Genetic explanation
262 Neural explanation
263 Eysenck's theory of the criminal personality
264 Cognitive explanations for crime
265 Cognitive distortions
266 Psychodynamic explanations
267 Custodial sentencing
268 Recidivism
269 Behaviour modification and rehabilitation
270 Anger management
271 Exam skills 1
272 Exam skills 2
273 Exam-style practice 1
274 Exam-style practice 2

4.3.10 Addiction
275 What is addiction?
276 Risk factors
277 Nicotine and neurochemicals
278 Nicotine and learning theory
279 Gambling and learning theory
280 Gambling and cognitive theory

281 Reducing addictions: drug therapies
282 Behavioural intervention
283 Cognitive behavioural therapy
284 Theory of planned behaviour
285 Prochaska's model of behaviour change
286 Exam skills 1
287 Exam skills 2
288 Exam-style practice 1
289 Exam-style practice 2

290 ANSWERS

. . . .

A small bit of small print
AQA publishes Sample Assessment Material and the Specification on its website. This is the official content and this book should be used in conjunction with it. The exam-style questions asked in this book have been written to help you practise every topic. Remember: the real exam questions may not look like this.

Types of conformity

You need to know the two explanations for conformity and the three types of conformity that explain social influence. An **influence** is a process where people agree or disagree about appropriate behaviours and maintain or change social norms accordingly.

Normative social influence (NSI)

In this influence people conform because they **fear being isolated** and want to be part of a group. Others are seen as having the power to approve or disapprove of us. The conflict between our private beliefs and what we feel we have to say out loud leads to **compliance** but this could just be temporary while in the presence of the group.

Informational social influence (ISI)

Wanting to be correct (do the right thing) in the presence of others is a powerful influence. The **need for certainty** makes us seek information to reinforce our perception of a situation, so we look to see what other people are doing. We then compare ourselves with others and **internalise** their beliefs as ours.

Compliance

When someone asks us to do something we might comply with their request. We might agree to do someone a favour for example. Compliance could be viewed as a first step towards **internalisation**. However, we might agree in public but disagree in private.

Internalisation

When someone truly takes on the beliefs and attitudes of a group, they internalise them and they become their own beliefs. They have effectively conformed. They agree both publicly and privately with the group.

Identification

Sometimes we feel that a part of our identity is belonging to a group. We value that feeling and publicly respect and follow the attitudes and behaviour of the group. We may still disagree with some aspects of the group behaviour in private.

> Types of conformity

The rise of the selfie illustrates our need to identify with significant others.

Why we conform

Conformity serves a valuable social purpose. It helps social interaction to happen smoothly and allows us to predict what other people will do.

In schools and prisons it allows a small minority of staff to manage a large majority of students and prisoners without problems as long as the students and prisoners conform to their social roles.

Prisoners cooperate with guards to allow a prison to run safely.

Now try this

Which type of influence leads to true conformity?

The Asch study

Key study In 1955, Solomon Asch conducted a series of laboratory experiments to investigate the degree to which individuals would conform to the majority who gave obviously wrong answers. You need to know why Asch carried out such a seemingly simple experiment on conformity.

Aim

Asch wanted to measure the strength of the conformity effect using an unambiguous task.

In the task, the participant has to say which of lines A, B or C matches the stimulus line (X).

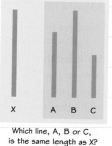

X   A   B   C

Which line, A, B or C, is the same length as X?

Procedure

Between seven and nine confederates sat in a line or semicircle. Asch gave naïve participants a seemingly obvious task – to match vertical lines on a card. On the first two trials the confederates gave the right answers but on the third they gave the wrong answer. The **dependent variable** was who would conform to the confederates and give the wrong answer having heard their answers first.

Results

- The naïve participants conformed to the wrong answer 36.8% of the time when alone with the confederates over 12 trials; 25% never conformed.

- There was also a control trial with no confederates to check the task was unambiguous. Mistakes were made 1% of the time – far less than under the experimental condition.

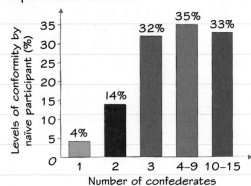

Levels of conformity by naïve participant (%)

4% 14% 32% 35% 33%

Number of confederates: 1 2 3 4–9 10–15

Conclusions

Some individuals' judgements/decisions are influenced by majority opinion – even when the majority opinion is obviously wrong. Although 36.8% is not the majority, participants conformed at least once to the majority 75% of the time.

Asch gave three reasons why 36.8% conformed.

1 Distortion of perception – they came to see the lines the same way as the majority.

2 Distortion of judgement – they doubted their judgement and went with the majority.

3 Distortion of action – they agreed in public but not privately (they complied).

The graph shows that three confederates were critical to getting conformity, after this there was little difference.

Evaluation

- 👍 **Reliability:** Asch used a standardised procedure which means that the findings can be replicated, increasing their reliability.

- 👍 **Internal validity:** There was no ambiguity in the task and therefore he was measuring conformity and not people's ability to perceive small differences in length, giving it internal validity.

- 👍 Because the answers were obvious, Asch's study shows the impact of the majority.

- 👎 **External validity:** The set-up was artificial and the task an odd thing to be discussing around a table, thus it lacks external validity or mundane realism.

- 👎 **Ethics:** The participants were deceived as they thought it was a visual perception task.

- 👎 Bogdonoff et al. (1961) found that participants in an Asch-type study had greatly increased levels of **autonomic arousal** (linked to stress), suggesting they were in a conflict situation possibly causing psychological harm.

- 👎 Perrin and Spencer (1980, 1981) found that engineering students were much less compliant. Look at page 3 for a summary of the results and conclusions of this study.

Now try this

Which **two** of the following are types of conformity?

A Agentic state   **B** Compliance   **C** Group size   **D** Identification   **E** Unanimity

Variables affecting conformity

Asch identified a number of **situational variables** that influence levels of conformity. These include group size, unanimity versus social support from a fellow dissenter and task difficulty. You need to know how these affect conformity.

Group size

Asch's research indicated that a majority of three was enough to create conformity (see the graph in the Results section on page 2). So, the rate of conformity increased as the size of the majority influence increased, but only to a certain point. After that there was very little difference.

Unanimity vs social support

If the naïve participant had a fellow dissenter, he would be more likely to resist the majority and conformity fell to a quarter of the original level. However, if the naïve participant had a fellow dissenter and then lost him, he would be more likely to conform. This type of conformity was more likely to be **internalisation** because he would have **identified** more strongly with someone who originally shared his opinion.

Task difficulty

Asch made the difference between the lines less obvious in one variation and found that as task difficulty increased, so did conformity. This suggests the **informational influence** was at work.

⤴ Extend   Recent research

You can extend your knowledge by looking at more recent research which has identified other variables, including individual differences, confidence and expertise, support for normative influence and conformity to roles.

Individual differences

Eagly and Carli (1981) in a meta-analysis of 145 conformity studies found inconsistent differences in conformity between genders. The biggest effect came from studies where there was pressure from an audience. In this case, females were more conformist. Male researchers are more likely to find females more conformist, possibly because they design studies more suited to men.

Becker (1986) found that women conformed more than men in public settings but not when their opinions were kept private.

Confidence and expertise

Perrin and Spencer (1980, 1981) repeated Asch's study with engineering students. Conformity was much lower. This could be because they had more confidence in making exact judgements and a more critical outlook.

Support for normative influence

Schultz et al. (2007) found that when hotel guests saw a message saying that 75% of guests reused their towels, they used far fewer new towels themselves.

Conformity to roles

Zimbardo found strong conformity to roles in his prison experiment in 1973. There was very little dissent among the guards over the treatment of prisoners. Some prisoners did try to rebel but were overcome and then became compliant.

At **Abu Ghraib**, however, many US soldiers were involved in the torture and abuse of Iraqi prisoners. Zimbardo believed that the behaviour of the guards in this prison was a result of situational factors such as poor training and boredom. They abused the power they held in their role.

Now try this

Outline **two** types of conformity which look at situational factors.

The Stanford Prison experiment

Key study The Stanford Prison experiment investigated conformity to **social roles**, using the roles of prisoner and prison guard. Haney, Banks and Zimbardo's (1973) **aim** was to assess how strongly an individual conforms to their role. Zimbardo played the role of prison governor and as such made day-to-day decisions about the running of the prison.

Sample

21 male volunteer college students were drawn from a pool of 75 and paid $15 a day. They were checked for mental and physical health and randomly divided into prisoners and guards.

Method

Using a **controlled observation**, a realistic mock prison was created at Stanford University.

Results

- Prisoners quickly became passive and negative in their attitudes while the guards became more active.

- Five prisoners had to be released because of extreme reactions to the situation but the rest endured the study until it was ended after six days.

- The guards showed **pathology of power**, meaning that they enjoyed the absolute control they had over the prisoners. This was exhibited by many actions such as making toilet visits a privilege and making the prisoners do press-ups.

Procedure

Guards arrived first, set up the prison and decided the rules. They were not allowed to use physical violence. They worked shifts and went home in between. The prisoners were arrested by real police, taken to the station where they were finger-printed and then taken blindfolded to the mock prison. They were randomly allocated to the cells and were all strangers.

The uniforms of both groups were designed to **de-individuate** (anonymise) the students. Smocks and numbers for the prisoners, dark mirrored glasses for the guards.

Conclusions

The fake prison situation can create a realistic role play to study the relationships between prisoners and guards and its destructive effect on human nature.

Haney et al. also believed they had shown how normal people are changed by the prison situation to show extreme reactions, supporting Zimbardo's **situational hypothesis** (see below). As a consequence, he went on to campaign for prison reform.

Evaluation

👍 **Control:** This was high in this observation, where everything was filmed and recorded.

👍 **Consent:** This was given but participants were not fully informed. For example, prisoners were not aware they would be arrested at home.

👎 **Ecological validity:** Real prisons are worse; this was a clearly artificial setting and so it lacks validity.

👎 **Ethics:** There were severe reactions by the prisoners. Although there was **a very thorough debrief** afterwards, Haney et al. failed to **protect** participants.

👎 **Observer bias:** Zimbardo has since admitted he lost his objectivity as the prison governor and got too involved.

👎 Not all the participants showed conformity to their role. Some maintained their identity and resistance.

Situational vs dispositional hypothesis

Haney et al.'s research in 1973 tested the **situational** versus the **dispositional** hypothesis. At the time, the popular view was that criminals were bad by nature or disposition and therefore they needed correction, and harsh prisons were the way to do this. Zimbardo believed the opposite – bad situations such as prisons could create bad behaviour and improving prisons would improve prisoners.

Reicher and Haslam's **BBC prison experiment** in 2006 challenged this view and said that it was the strength of the **social identity** with the role that led to the formation of a group identity. In their study, it was the prisoners who were the stronger group.

Now try this

Identify and briefly discuss **two** reasons why people have criticised Haney et al.'s prison study.

Milgram's study of obedience

Key study Moving from an **autonomous state**, where you are in control of your own actions, to being in a state of mind where you are ready to obey another (in an **agentic state**) is called **agentic shift**. In Milgram's original experiment in 1963, there was a **gradual commitment to the experimenter** and a **buffer** (a wall) between the teacher and the learner. The **authority figure** was dressed in a grey lab coat. The setting conveyed trust and authority, which increased obedience.

Aim

To investigate obedience to an authority figure using a laboratory-based procedure.

The experimenter has four prompts to use if the teacher is reluctant to continue. 'Please continue', etc.

The learner (a confederate) is appearing to be ever more distressed while pretending to be shocked.

Experimenter   Teacher

Learner

Naïve participants draw lots to be the teacher or learner and always end up as the teacher.

The teacher has to read one half of a word pair and the learner supplies the other half. Once in a while, the learner gets it wrong and gets a shock.

The Milgram experiment set-up and procedure

Procedure

A sample of 40 men answered a newspaper advertisement to volunteer for the experiment. The laboratory was set up as above. The prompts from the experimenter created the **independent variable**, and the **dependent variable** was how far in volts the participant would go to shock the learner. The experimenter wore a grey lab coat to accent his legitimate authority. The voltage levels went up in 15 volt increments to a maximum of 450 volts, creating a **gradual commitment**. The learner gave predetermined recorded responses, gradually increasing in panic.

Results

- Signs of extreme tension in most participants, including one who had a seizure.
- All participants went up to 300 volts.
- 14 defied the experimenter after this point (remaining **autonomous**).
- 26 obeyed to the end and gave 450 volts (agentic **shift**).

Conclusion

People are surprisingly obedient to authority even when being told to inflict pain for no good reason. Agency theory appears to work in this scenario.

Evaluation

👍 **Internal validity:** Milgram appeared to have created a situation which the participants believed to be true as evidenced by their strong reactions.

👍 **Ethics:** His debrief was very thorough and 84% of participants said they were pleased to have taken part.

👎 **Informed consent:** There was no **informed consent**, and the participants were very stressed and not **protected**, although they met the unharmed learner at the end.

👎 **Low ecological or external validity:** The task did not reflect real life obedience.

An alternative explanation and evaluation

Haslam and Reicher (2012) used social identity theory to explain Milgram's findings. They said that group identification occurs in the experiment as the participants identify with the experimenter and the science behind the experiment. They agree with the prompts 'it is important for the experiment that you continue' because they have bought into the group they have become a part of. However, the last command 'you have no other choice' produces refusal because there is no additional rationale, although 26 obeyed even after hearing this.

Now try this

What is meant by an autonomous state? How does it affect obedience?

Explanations for obedience

You need to know two explanations for why people obey orders in various situations.

Agency theory

Milgram (1974) believed that we exist in two different states.

 In the **autonomous state** we show **free will** and make our own choices and decisions.

 In the **agentic state** we follow instructions from someone we perceive has **legitimate authority** over us such as a teacher or police officer. We learn this through socialisation.

When we are asked to do something we do not like or that is immoral or unjust, we experience **moral strain** and feel uncomfortable and stressed. However, once we have shifted into an obedient state we feel relieved of the strain and displace responsibility onto the authority figure.

Legitimacy of authority

Milgram believed that society is **hierarchical** – people are ranked from top to bottom, and naturally obey those who are higher up the order than themselves. This happens because children are **socialised** to obey their parents and teachers from an early age. An army is a strong hierarchy and soldiers are trained to obey orders without question.

My Lai

During the Vietnam War, American soldiers entered the village of My Lai and were ordered by their lieutenant to shoot the inhabitants. They killed everyone, even small children. Later, when on trial, they said they were 'just obeying orders'. The soldiers were no longer **autonomous** but **agents** of the army. The responsibility for the massacre rested on the United States.

🔍 Key study — Evidence for agency theory

Aim: Hofling et al. (1966) used the hospital hierarchy to test obedience in nurses.

Procedure: A confederate doctor rang a ward and asked the nurse to give twice the marked safe dose of an unknown drug 'Astroten' to a patient.

Results: 21 out of 22 nurses obeyed the orders against the hospital rules. When a control group of 22 nurses were asked what they would have done, they denied they would have acted without proper authorisation in writing.

Conclusion: Hofling concluded that the power hierarchy in hospitals was a bigger influence on nurses than following hospital rules.

🔍 Key study — Evidence against agency theory

Aim: Rank and Jacobsen (1977) wanted to challenge Hofling's findings.

Procedure: They repeated Hofling et al.'s (1966) experiment, using valium (a familiar drug) at three times the recommended dose. When the researcher pretending to be a doctor telephoned, he had a familiar name and the nurses were able to discuss the order with other nurses before carrying it out.

Result: Only 2 out of 18 nurses followed the order.

Conclusion: The increased realism of the experiment, and the discussion with a colleague, lowered obedience rates in exactly the same way that Milgram's addition of a dissenting confederate had done.

Evaluation

👍 Both studies have high ecological validity as they used a naturalistic setting.

👍 Both studies have great application in that hospital procedures have since been tightened up.

Evaluation: evidence against agency theory

👎 It does not explain individual differences.

👎 Autonomy and agency are concepts that are hard to measure and define and they vary depending on the situation.

👎 It does not explain why some people are more motivated to follow certain people more than others who have equal authority.

 Now try this

Apply agency theory to explain why a Year 9 pupil is more likely to obey instructions from a head teacher than from a classroom assistant when asked to pick up litter in front of his/her mates.

Situational variables

Milgram went on to investigate many more variables. The three you need to know are **proximity**, **location** and **uniform**. They are all variations on the original experiment, using the same basic set-up or paradigm shown on page 2, and they look at **external** or **situational explanations for obedience**.

Proximity of the learner

Proximity increases awareness of obeying an order. A task is harder if you can see the person you are hurting.

Voice feedback condition: The teacher and learner are in separate rooms. The teacher can hear the learner through the wall but does not see him. The teacher obedience to experimenter rate is 65%.

Proximity condition: Both teacher and learner are in the same room. The obedience rate falls to 40%.

Touch proximity condition: The teacher has to force the learner's hand onto the plate for a shock. The obedience rate falls to 30%.

Proximity of the authority figure

If the person giving orders is right next to you, it is harder to disobey them.

Baseline condition: The experimenter is only a few feet away from the teacher. The obedience level is 65%.

Experimenter absent condition: The experimenter leaves the room and gives his instructions to the teacher over the phone. The obedience level falls to 22.5% and teachers tend to lie about the level of shocks they have given to the learner.

Location

The location of the experiment can alter the level of obedience.

Baseline condition: Milgram ran the study at the prestigious Yale University. The obedience level is 65%.

Rundown office block condition: Milgram gets a private company to run the same study in Bridgeport, Connecticut, in a rundown office block. The obedience rate falls to 48%.

This shows that being in a prestigious setting increases **legitimate authority**. Yale University is well regarded. Any research carried out there is seen as important and participants' willingness to be helpful increases. An office block location makes the research appear less important, and is a strange context for a learning experiment.

Uniform

Wearing a uniform can increase the perception of authority.

Baseline condition: The experimenter wears a grey lab coat. The obedience level is 65%.

Non-uniform condition (the ordinary man condition): Three people arrive at the laboratory; two are confederates in normal dress. They draw lots. One becomes the 'new' experimenter as the real experimenter makes an excuse and leaves. The naïve participant was the teacher. The third person is the learner. The replacement experimenter in normal dress has little influence. In the absence of the 'real' experimenter, the learner himself prompts the teacher to increase the shocks by saying it could help him to remember. The obedience level is only 20%, and the participants need a lot of prompting to get to this level.

Evaluation

- Highly standardised and controlled experiments are very reliable.
- Qualitative and quantitative data were collected, making the research credible and scientific.
- Samples were all from the same area with very few women included so were not representative of obedience in the whole population.
- The sample was self-selected by advertisement so the participants were more likely to follow orders.
- The situation may not have convinced the participants. Recent research from Perry (2012) has challenged Milgram's findings and procedures, suggesting more knew it was a hoax set-up and that Milgram exaggerated his results.

Now try this

How could you apply the situational variables above to increase obedience in a school?

Think about how classrooms are designed and laid out for proximity, how they are decorated and furnished for location, and what students, teachers and head teachers wear for uniform.

Obedience: dispositional explanation

Key study In 1950, Adorno et al. proposed there was an **authoritarian personality**. This type of person was hostile towards other ethnic groups, had no time for weakness and was servile towards authority. Therefore your personality (an individual difference) could make you more obedient. Adorno used Freudian methods to find unconscious motives in his sample. The dispositional explanation is an **internal** explanation for obedience.

Aim

To investigate the authoritarian personality.

Procedure

A sample of 2000 American participants agreed or disagreed with statements on a six-point Likert scale so that researchers could determine their attitudes towards religious and ethnic minorities, their views on politics and economics, and their moral values. Adorno believed certain attitudes represented the authoritarian personality.

About 100 were then interviewed in depth, including questions on upbringing. His sample included the most and least prejudiced from the scales (see Adorno's scales and sample statements).

Results

Adorno found correlations between his scales, showing the strength of the generalised prejudice in his sample. The highest correlations were between anti-Semitism and ethnocentrism (.80) and ethnocentrism and fascism (.65), showing that a dislike of foreigners was linked to anti-Jewish and Nazi sympathisers.

These individuals had developed an 'us and them' mentality. These characteristics of the authoritarian personality make them hostile to all non-conventional people and they believe in power and toughness and the rule of law.

Conclusion

Children who grow up in a harsh disciplinarian family may repress their hostility towards their parents and seem to idolise them. In later life they act in a submissive way towards authority figures.

Their repressed hostility towards their parents is displaced onto non-threatening minority groups as prejudice and discrimination.

Note that the language used in Adorno's work is that of the 1950s and reflects the society of the time, where widespread prejudice and discrimination against ethnic minorities and homosexuals was the norm.

Adorno's scales and sample statements

To measure the strength of participants' prejudice, they were asked how much they agreed with certain propositions. For example:

✓ **Anti-Semitism** (AS) – Could they imagine marrying a Jew?

✓ **Ethnocentrism** (E) – Even though Negroes have rights should they stay in their own district?

✓ **Political and economic conservatism** (PEC) – Should a child learn the value of money early in life?

✓ **Potentiality for fascism** – This had its own subset of nine personality dimensions. (Fascism is an ideology where people believe in the superiority of one race over another and want to 'cleanse' their nation of undesirable members.)

Potentiality for fascism (F) scale

✓ **Conventionalism** – Are obedience and respect for authority the most important virtues?

✓ **Power and toughness** – Can people be divided into the weak and the strong?

✓ **Sex** – Should homosexuals be punished?

Evaluation

🖓 The **response set** had problems as all the statements invited agreement despite giving the option to disagree.

🖓 The interviews were biased because the interviewer knew the F-scale dimensions.

🖓 It cannot explain the sudden attitude shift we see towards groups such as refugees or the prejudice of huge groups at once, and may represent Adorno's personal bias as an exiled Jew living through the Second World War.

🖓 Rokeach (1960) showed that the F-scale only measured right-wing authoritarianism. It was politically biased.

🖓 Social identity theory is a more convincing explanation of obedience.

Now try this

How does the authoritarian personality explain why a person might be more obedient?

Resistance to social influence

Not all of Asch's (1955) and Milgram's (1963) participants behaved as expected. This suggests that some people are more resistant to social influence than others.

Locus of control (LoC)

This concept was identified by Rotter (1966) and can be used to explain resistance to social influence. It refers to how much people believe they are in control of their own lives. To measure your LoC, you complete scales that force you to choose between two extremes on a scale of 1–10. For example, 'there is no such thing as fate or destiny' or 'life is a game of chance'.

Internal locus and obedience

A person with an **internal locus of control** believes they are always responsible for their behaviour. Because of this, they are likely to seek more information before following orders.

A person with an internal LoC has greater self-confidence and self-belief so is more likely to be a leader themselves and hence feel more confident to challenge authority.

🔍 Key study Age

Chubb et al. (1997), in a longitudinal study of 174 Grade 9 students, found that they got less external each year as their confidence grew over a four-year period. However, other researchers have found that LoC remains stable until old age, when people tend to become more external.

External locus and obedience

A person with an **external locus of control** sees their life as being controlled by luck, chance or by others – especially others with more power. They are therefore more likely to obey an authority figure.

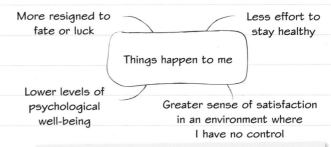

An external locus of control may relate to **learned helplessness**, a behaviour in which a person puts up with endless discomfort or distress because they feel unable to escape from it.

🔍 Key study Males vs females

Sherman et al. (2007) summarised two decades of research and found that males are more likely to have an internal LoC. They are more likely to become leaders.

Females are more likely to seek links with others rather than behave independently. However, women who are internal locus do better in the workplace than those who are external locus.

Evaluation

👍 The LoC self-report inventory has been standardised and used over vast samples, increasing its validity.

👍 Avtgis (1998) used a meta-analysis to investigate LoC and conformity. Results showed that those with an internal locus were more resistant to persuasion and less likely to conform.

👍 Holland (1967) showed that internal locus people showed greater resistance to authority in a replication of Milgram's 1963 study.

👎 Twenge et al. (2004) found that external locus people have increased in number over time but resistance to authority has increased as well, which sheds some doubt on the concept.

Now try this

As an internal locus of control gets more likely as you get older, this suggests it is learned. Suggest how a person could learn to be less external and more internal locus.

Resisting social influence through social support

🔍 **Key study** When authority is seen to act unjustly, there is often rebellion by people who together form a protest group. This small-scale rebellion can escalate into mass protests against governments, for example. You will have seen this in anti-war protests and anti-austerity marches.

Gamson et al. (1982): The MHRC set-up

A group of strangers is hired individually by a large company (MHRC) to perform a discussion group on camera. After accepting the job, they discover that the company is acting wrongly in their eyes. However, they are asked to be **agents** of the company by agreeing to carry out some tasks. The situation unfolds gradually and at three points in time the **authority** requests specific acts of wrong doing.

1 In total, 261 people answered an advert asking them to take part in research. They were paid $10 and they consented to being recorded on film.

2 In 33 groups of around eight or nine, they arrived at a hotel and began the discussion. The experimenter left when they started.

3 They discussed a case of unfair dismissal. The employee had been sacked for cohabiting with his partner (he was a bad example) and questioning company pricing.

4 The experimenters had prompts to get the groups to continue. 'We find we get better discussion if three people take another viewpoint.'

5 **Early protest:** After a while, three people were asked to argue the pro-company view that he deserved to go for cohabiting with his partner and he should not have gone public with his revelations about pricing.

Late protest: Then three more were asked to comply.

Finally, they were asked to sign a release form consenting for their views to be used in court.

🔍 **Key study** **The MHRC set up**

Results: In 16 out of the 33 groups, one-third of participants rebelled when asked to take the company view in the early protest phase.

In two cases, they would go no further.

Typical comments

F mumbled, 'I mean, I'll take the money, but this is the most ludicrous afternoon...'

'I think we should object on principle.'

R added, 'I know one thing: it's against my personal thing to try to, uh, go against my own ideas.'

In all, 23 out of 33 groups rebelled and 14 groups refused to sign the release form.

Conclusion: Having support from others increases resistance to orders, especially if the orders are seen as unjust.

Evaluation

👍 It had ecological validity as the participants believed in the set-up in the hotel conference room.

👍 It had internal validity as the participant responses showed they believed the task.

👍 It had strong results, showing the effect of a supportive minority.

👎 The ethics are questionable, lots of deception and stress was caused to the participants.

👎 The original intention of using 80 groups had to be abandoned after the researchers saw that the level of emotion put the participants at risk. The research is therefore incomplete.

Now try this

Why did the participants in this study resist the agentic state?

You could consider whether the company was a legitimate authority, whether the experimenter was present in the discussion and the nature of the task.

Minority influence

Sometimes a strong minority or an individual can sway public opinion and change previously held attitudes. Think, for example, of the Gay Rights Movement, the Suffragettes or Nelson Mandela.

Conversion theory

This suggests that when a minority has informational social influence over the majority by providing new information and challenges to the majority, it can convert the majority to the new ideas or beliefs.

Consistency

For a minority to effect change, it has to be consistent in its message between the people in the group (**synchronic consistency**) and over time (**diachronic consistency**).

Commitment

People who show commitment to a cause through strong actions and personal suffering are more likely to be believed.

Flexibility

Minorities who are consistent but inflexible are less persuasive. Rigidly sticking to the same arguments is unappealing, and a degree of flexibility is a more successful style.

The effect of a defector

Clark (2001) used the *Twelve Angry Men* paradigm to investigate the impact of jury verdicts.

Participants acting as jurors were more influenced by minority opinion when they thought they had defected from the majority. Their arguments were more effective because they were viewed as independent.

🔍 Key study Moscovici et al. (1969)

Aim: To examine the effect of a consistent minority on the majority using an unambiguous task.

Procedure: Groups of four naïve participants and two confederates were asked to estimate the colour of 36 slides. All the slides were blue but the brightness was varied by adding filters. In one condition, the two confederates (the **consistent minority**) called the slides green on **all** trials in the hearing of the naïve participants. In another condition, the minority varied the consistency of their responses. The control group was not exposed to the minority.

Results: The naïve participants agreed that blue was green on 8.42% of the trials and 32% said the slides were green at least once in the consistent condition. In the **inconsistent condition**, only 1.25% gave green responses compared to the control group, who gave just two 'wrong' answers (0.25%).

Conclusion: These results are small changes, but they are significant. They show that a minority can sway the majority even when absent as long as consistency is maintained.

Internalisation

Majority influence is qualitatively different to minority influence. With majority influence, participants comply publicly in order to save face, which is called the **normative influence**. In minority influence, the attitude shift is **internalised**.

In **Martin et al.' study (2003)** participants heard a minority group agree with an initial point of view while a second group heard the same point from a majority. Martin found that people think more deeply into a minority message – this has a lasting effect and is more convincing.

Application

Juries are an example of where a minority can sway a majority by forcing more discussion over the evidence. Nemeth (2005) has shown that getting discussion to take place with a dissenting voice gives minorities more influence. When a case is taken point by point, the evidence is often not as convincing as first thought, and the majority gradually agree with the minority.

> You need to be able to give an example of how minority influence occurs in real life.

Evaluation

🔺 These studies used artificial laboratory experiments so lack ecological validity and internal validity.

🔺 There is an ethical issue of deceit as they were told it was a visual perception task.

👍 In another condition, Moscovici found that getting his participants to write their answers privately after exposure to the minority view maintained the conformity effect even in its absence.

Now try this

What is meant by minority influence?

How social influences affect social change

Social change occurs when society or a significant part of society changes its views and adopts new behaviours as the 'norm'. You need to know **two** examples of how social influences affect change.

Minority influence – a consistent minority challenges beliefs

Terrorist acts committed by the IRA in Northern Ireland over many years **drew attention** to their argument and eventually forced round-table discussions and power sharing in government.

The IRA showed **consistency** and **persistence** in their message to have a united Ireland. This caused a **cognitive conflict** in society. People were forced to consider their own views.

Supporters of the argument for unity would **internalise this minority position** and be ultimately ready to kill for it. This **augmented** their position.

The snowball effect meant that more people had to take sides, and at the time it seemed normal to have bombings and reprisals. These individuals **conformed to the idea** that this was a rightful fight.

Majority influence – the power of the majority to establish norms

The ban on smoking in public places in 2007 and the **obedience** of smokers in following it has led to a fall in smoking. This is an example of a **social norms intervention**.

People thought that after the ban more smokers would light-up at home, but this does not seem to have happened. Equally, a study looking at children's exposure to second-hand smoking in England (1996–2007) found that exposure levels had declined by nearly 70%. It seems that the unacceptability of smoking in public led to **conformity** and **obedience** in private.

This example of a new law shows how the **majority influence** of non-smokers led to a social change in the minority smoking group.

Evaluation

🖎 The timescale for minority influence to work is often very long because groups tend to conform to the majority position.

For example, the fight for women's suffrage took nearly 60 years from beginning to end.

🖎 Being perceived as extreme limits the influence of minorities in the early stages. For example, Greenpeace was seen as an extreme movement in their first campaigns against whaling.

🖎 Social norms interventions using the majority influence can sometimes backfire, encouraging those who already behave in a socially acceptable way to conform to the majority and drop their high standards. For example, Schulz et al. (2007) found that in getting high-energy users to use less power, those already using less increased their usage.

🖎 Violent minorities such as the IRA used destruction and fear to try to influence the majority.

It's against the law

The new ban on smoking in cars with children will depend on obedience because it will be difficult to police.

Nemeth's (1987) theory of minority influence

Charlan Nemeth suggested that that the minority and majority influence lead to different types of thinking, which she called her convergent–divergent theory.

This theory states that the minority who dissent stimulate thought that is broader and takes in more information. This leads to better decisions and more creative solutions (divergent thinking). On the other hand, people expect to agree with the majority and when they don't, they find themselves stressed, so they narrow their thinking and become more convergent thinkers.

Nemeth pointed to Nobel prize winners such as Roger Sperry, a researcher who showed us how the brain functions, as being great examples of divergent minority thinkers who have led advances in science and society.

Now try this

What is meant by social change?

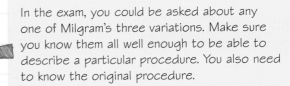
Exam skills 1

AO1 questions require you to describe, outline, name or identify. With these questions, do not evaluate or discuss as it is a waste of your time. However, watch out for questions that mix AO1 and AO2/AO3 requirements.

Worked example

Outline the procedure used by Milgram (1963) in his 'ordinary man' variation. **(4 marks)**

In the <u>baseline</u> condition the experimenter wore a grey lab coat. In this case, obedience was 65% up to 450 volts. The non-uniform condition is called the ordinary man condition. In this variation, three people arrived at the laboratory; two were <u>confederates</u> in normal dress. They drew lots. One of the confederates became the experimenter because the actual experimenter quickly made an excuse and left. The <u>naïve participant</u> was the teacher. The third person was the confederate learner. In the absence of the 'real' experimenter, the learner himself prompted the teacher to increase the shocks by saying it could help him to remember. In this way, Milgram tested whether having authority indicated by a 'uniform' (the grey lab coat in the original study) affected obedience.

In the exam, you could be asked about any one of Milgram's three variations. Make sure you know them all well enough to be able to describe a particular procedure. You also need to know the original procedure.

There are four marks available for this question, so you should make four points.

To do well, you need to give a clear and coherent outline of the procedure. Make sure your answer is in a logical sequence and give relevant details of the methods and test conditions used.

Make sure you use specialist terminology in your explanation.

Worked example

Outline the procedure for Haney et al.'s (1973) Stanford Prison experiment. **(4 marks)**

In the basement corridor of Stanford University, Haney et al. created a mock prison. Using volunteer students who drew lots to role play guards or prisoners, the researchers recreated life in a prison. All participants gave consent to be part of the study, but the prisoners were collected by police from their homes without warning (this was not part of the consent form), fingerprinted and strip-searched. They were then taken to the jail and locked up. The guards drew up the rules and enforced their rule over the prisoners. Both groups were de-individuated by wearing either a guard's uniform or a prisoner's smock. The guards got the prisoners to do demeaning tasks and roll calls, and used punishments. The whole experiment was filmed and Zimbardo was the prison governor. The experiment lasted six days and was then called off because of the reactions of the participants.

The challenge here is keeping it brief. The same applies if you were asked for Milgram's original procedure. Think: Where? How? Who? When? What did they have to do? What were the instructions?

Exam skills 2

AO2 questions require you to apply your knowledge and understanding in different contexts or when handling data. This is often done with a scenario. Sometimes a question scenario or stem will allow you to use more than one aspect of a topic. In this case, **conformity** and **obedience**, which are both social influence processes.

Worked example

In an attempt to lose weight, many dieters turn to weight loss classes.

Using your knowledge of social influence processes, explain why these are often more successful than dieting alone. **(4 marks)**

By attending a weight loss class such as Weight Watchers, dieters have to reveal their weekly progress to the group and listen to advice from the leader. Within the group, there will be **majority pressure** to conform to the progress of the others by keeping up with the weight loss programme. It will be hard not to comply under the pressure, particularly if the others make a lot of progress. This is quite like the Asch paradigm, where his participants heard the answers of the others before giving their own. They described feeling the pressure not to be rejected by the group. In addition, the class leader has some **legitimate authority** over the dieter who will want to obey instructions to follow the diet. The dieter will be in an **agentic state** because they want to follow the class leader. There may even be prompts to follow the weight loss instructions, as seen in Milgram's research.

People who try to diet alone at home are free from conformity pressure and are **autonomous**. This may make it harder to stick to the diet.

> Note the use of '**processes**' in this question – you are being directed to use more than one. You must also link to the stem or the scenario in your answer.

> You need to give a clear explanation of how social influence processes might affect dieters. Make sure you refer to the example of joining weight loss classes in your answer and give relevant examples. Aim to use specialist terminology where possible.

> This is a good answer because it is relevant throughout and clearly applies concepts and understanding of social influences:
> - Reference is made several times to dieting and weight loss classes.
> - Two possible explanations are offered.
> - There is effective use of terminology (shown in bold).

> Think about conformity to social roles for this question. What is special about a uniform? Think about Haney et al.'s (1973) Stanford Prison experiment study.

Worked example

A school has been having problems with the behaviour of its pupils. A new head teacher was appointed and the first thing she did was to smarten up the school uniform and bring back blazers.

Using your knowledge of social influence processes, explain why this should work to improve the behaviour of the pupils. **(4 marks)**

Bringing in a uniform will work to improve behaviour because it will de-individuate the pupils, meaning that they will lose the sense of their own identity and become one of many. Haney et al. found that putting their participants in uniform helped them play the roles of guards and prisoners. The resistance of the prisoners was less because they were in smocks, flip-flops and no underwear, and they had a number, not a name. The head teacher wants the pupils to be in an agentic state as described by Milgram in his obedience experiment in 1963, so that they will obey instructions from staff. This is more likely if they are less autonomous. Wearing their own chosen clothes increases autonomy and makes them more likely to resist authority.

Exam skills 3

Some questions on the exam paper will test your application of knowledge (AO2 skills). They will use a scenario or stem which can be explained by something you have learned in that section. You would be expected to refer to the scenario in your answer.

Worked example

Energy bills that inform users of how they compare with others in the same street or neighbourhood are currently being trialled in parts of the UK. The expectation is that this will lead to lower usage of electricity.

Does this demonstrate normative social influence (NSI) or informational social influence (ISI)? Explain your answer.   **(4 marks)**

This demonstrates the normative social influence (NSI). When people see that most people in their street use less electricity than they do, they will feel outside the 'norm' and then feel a bit uncomfortable. The intention is to use the **majority influence** to change attitudes to excessive use of power. **Asch** showed that one-third of people will conform to a majority influence most of the time and three-quarters will do it once. Other researchers such as **Schultz et al. (2007)** have found that exposure to other people's behaviour can manipulate people to behave more responsibly. Shultz left messages in hotel rooms saying that 75% of guess re-used their towels and found use of new towels fell by 25%. In this case, knowing that most people use less electricity should lead to a fall in consumption.

This stem/scenario is a trigger for you to think: *Why would knowing what other people are doing lead to a change in your behaviour?*

This question directs you to two possibilities. To get it right, you need to be clear about the difference between NSI and ISI. Have a look at page 1 for a reminder about the explanations for conformity.

This answer correctly applies normative social influence to explain why the use of sample energy bills should work and includes good use of evidence.

- A link is made to the stem several times.
- The right terminology is used (shown in bold).
- Detailed knowledge is demonstrated by quoting relevant research evidence.

This is how a typical bill would look to encourage normative social influence, leading to a reduction in consumption.

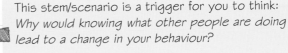

Last month neighbour comparison
You used **36% less** electricity than your efficient neighbours

You	▇
Efficient neighbours	▇▇
All neighbours	▇▇▇▇▇▇

How you're doing:

▶ **GREAT**   ☺ ☺ ☺
Good   ☺ ☺
More than average   ☺

Worked example

A school prefect has started a book club at lunchtime for younger pupils. At first only three pupils came, but now there are over 40 Year 7s reading books. Using your psychological knowledge of social influence, explain why this is happening.   **(4 marks)**

Once three pupils came to the book club more followed because three was the critical number found to create a majority by Asch in his conformity experiments (1955). These three students would have talked to others about how they enjoyed the club and as a majority influence they would persuade others to join. Once the others came along they would enjoy it too and their attitude to reading would gradually change from compliance to a group of friends to internalising a positive attitude towards reading.

There is a clue in the number three, which was the critical number that Asch found increased conformity. Also think about the internalisation of the new attitude towards reading books.

Had a go ☐   Nearly there ☐   Nailed it! ☐

Exam-style practice 1

Practise for Paper 1 of your A level exam with these exam-style questions. There are answers on page 290.

1 Which of the following is a definition of the normative social influence?
   Shade **one** box only.

   A We agree with the majority because we want to be right.   ⬭

   B We agree with the majority because we want to be accepted.   ⬭

   C ~~We disagree with the minority because we want to be autonomous.~~   ⬭ ⬅

   D We agree with the majority for an easy life.   ⬭

   (1 mark)

   > **Normative social influence** is about the **majority** so C can be ruled out.

2 Briefly outline Asch's (1955) findings on group size.

   (3 marks)

   > Try to make **two** points about his findings in this variation. Knowing the **percentages** is an added strength.

3 Read the item and then answer the question that follows.

   > Adorno et al. (1950) used scales to test for the authoritarian personality. Participants had to rate their agreement with each item on a six-point scale from 'agree strongly' to 'disagree strongly'. He then looked for correlations between the scales. The highest agreement agreement was between anti-Semitism and ethnocentrism (.80) and ethnocentrism and fascism (.65).

   Using your knowledge of psychology, explain **one** strength and **one** weakness of his **methodology**.

   (6 marks)

   > Think about the **nature** of correlational data. Think about **objectivity** and **subjectivity**. Think about using **statistics** to test findings. Note that **only methodological points** will count here.

   > Answers should be accurate and detailed with effective evaluation of the methods used and use specialist terminology.

4 Social groups form an important part of our daily lives. Within these groups pressures exist which encourage the individual to comply with the group's viewpoint. This influence, which creates social conformity, is known as 'majority influence' and is the dominant process of social control. However, there also exists a 'minority influence', which emerges from a small subsection of the group and is a dynamic force for social change.

   Outline **two** characteristics of minorities which can bring about dynamic change in society.

   (4 marks)

   > Choose two that you can illustrate with examples.

5 Skinny jeans have been given a health warning after a woman had to be cut out of them after developing compartment syndrome.

   Explain how social influence affects social change (in this case a fashion trend).

   (6 marks)

   > You can use both minority and majority influence to answer this question.

6 Briefly describe **two** social norms you use on a daily basis.   **(2 marks)**

   > This could be anything, keep it simple.

Exam-style practice 2

Practise for Paper 1 of your A level exam with these exam-style questions. There are answers on pages 290–291.

7 Using evidence, describe **and** evaluate **two** explanations of resistance to social influence.   **(16 marks)**

> The two explanations need to be balanced in content. Note the instruction to use **evidence** – studies must be quoted. It is good to have studies to use in support of the explanations and against them. In evaluation, try to cover **methodological points**, such as validity or reliability, and **application points** such as usefulness.
>
> Also think about time; allow about 20 minutes for a 16-mark question on the basis of roughly one mark a minute, including some reading, thinking and planning time.

8 Some people think conformity is a bad thing. Briefly explain why conformity might be helpful.   **(2 marks)**

> Think about the applications of the obedience research to answer this.

9 What is meant by unanimity?   **(1 mark)**

> This is a simple definition question.

10 Describe the procedure for Asch's study of conformity to a majority.   **(4 marks)**

> A procedure is like the recipe for what the participants had to do in the study.

11 Insert the letter for the correct definitions in the table to explain Asch's experimental conclusions.

Distortion of perception	
Distortion of judgement	
Distortion of action	

   A They agreed in public but not in private.

   B They doubted their decision and went with the majority.

   C They came to see the lines in the same way as the majority.

> If you know one, try to work the rest out by a process of elimination.

> When discussing limitations try using issues like determinism, generalisability and application as well as the supporting or challenging research.

12 Discuss **two** limitations of agency theory as an explanation of obedience.   **(6 marks)**

> This question needs you to make clear links to the actions of the participants who obeyed and those who did not.

13 Explain how the theory of locus of control could be used to understand the behaviour of Milgram's participants.   **(4 marks)**

The multi-store model

The multi-store model (MSM) of memory was introduced in 1968 by Atkinson and Shiffrin as a cognitive explanation of memory. The MSM uses the analogy of a computer and the concepts of encoding, storage and retrieval to understand memory. It includes the concept of three separate memory stores that were first identified by Hermann Ebbinghaus in the 1880s.

Stimuli reach the sensory register from the *haptic*, *iconic*, *echoic*, *olfactory* and *gustatory* senses.

The rehearsal loop maintains the information in the STM for long enough to retain it and for a LTM to form, e.g. to remember a number.

We select what to pay atten- tion to and pass this on to the STM.

The store represents knowledge and experience. It feeds back (yellow arrow) what to pay attention to, i.e. what is worth rehearsing in STM.

The MSM, showing how information flows through a series of three permanent storage systems – the **sensory register (SR)**, the **short-term memory (STM)** and the **long-term memory (LTM)** – like data through a computer processor.

| Sensory register | → | Short-term memory (STM) | ⇐ | Long-term memory (LTM) |

Most information is lost immediately through forgetting.

Retrieval and use of the memory or loss and forgetting.

Evidence for the MSM

This comes from evidence for the existence of separate stores and for rehearsal. Neuroimaging has supported the distinction between a separate STM and LTM. Talmi et al. (2005) gave participants 12 items to remember and then asked them to recall words from the beginning (using LTM) or end (using STM) of the list. They found that the medial temporal lobe of the brain was used for the early items and the right inferior parietal lobe for the late items. These findings lend support to the model since these two areas of the brain do not overlap.

Evidence for STM

Miller (1956), Peterson and Peterson (1959) and Baddeley (1966) have all conducted studies that have supported STM as a separate store (see page 20).

Evidence for LTM

The LTM is now known to have different types of memory and it uses different types of processing from STM (see page 23). Baddeley (1966) found that participants mixed up words with similar meaning when they were using their LTM (he tested this using a delayed recall condition). This shows that LTM uses semantic processing (see page 21) whereas STM uses acoustic processing (see page 20).

Rehearsal

Rehearsal is thought to be important because participants prevented from rehearsing in any experimental memory task show a drop in performance (see Peterson and Peterson, 1959, on page 20). However, in real life, we clearly remember things we have not rehearsed because they are meaningful.

Evaluation

👍 Studies on coding, capacity and duration in STM (see page 20) and LTM (see page 21) have shown research evidence for separate stores.

👍 Case studies of stroke patients have supported the existence of separate stores depending on where the damage occurred.

👍 The case study of HM (see page 23) who lost his hippocampus in an operation leaving him unable to learn new things in LTM while retaining the ability to remember short strings of digits in STM indicates there are two separate stores.

👎 More recent research using scanning techniques is showing that the idea of just three stores is too simple. There are LTMs for episodic, procedural and semantic memory (see page 23) and scans can show that these are distinctively different.

👎 Retaining information in LTM is not just done by rehearsing. In 2003, Raaijmakers and Shiffrin included elaboration as a type of rehearsal in response to criticisms of the model.

Now try this

Outline evidence that supports Atkinson and Shiffrin's (1968) multi-store model of memory.

The sensory register

The sensory register (SR) continually receives input from all our senses and is the first storage system in the multi-store model (MSM) of memory (see page 18). It contains all the information that we attend to consciously or subconsciously.

Coding in the SR

Information in the SR is coded by the nervous system as action potentials stimulating different parts of the brain depending on which sense has received it. For example, sense receptors in the back of the eye code visual signals. The ears receive sound waves, which stimulate receptors in the inner ear. These are fleeting signals lasting fractions of a second. Each sensory input has a separate sensory store:

- *echoic* for sound
- *iconic* for vision
- *gustatory* for taste
- *olfactory* for smell
- *haptic* for touch.

🔍 Key study Crowder (1993)

Crowder found that information stayed for only a few milliseconds in the iconic store but for several seconds in the echoic store, suggesting that they are different. Recent research has suggested that memory for speech, including lip movements, is a key part of the function of the SR.

The phenomenon of persistence of vision is an example of the iconic sensory store. This is when you see an afterimage for a fraction of a second once the original stimulation has moved on, giving an illusion of continuous movement.

Capacity of the SR

Each sensory memory store has a large capacity. It is ever changing as we move around in the world and experience vast amounts of stimuli.

Evaluation

🖋 It is hard to investigate a sensory memory store without creating highly artificial controlled experiments. In the future, neuroscience may give the answers more readily.

🔍 Key study Sperling (1960)

R	S	T	V
H	B	X	U
J	N	E	P

Sperling grid

Sperling flashed a 3 × 4 grid of letters onto a screen for one-twentieth of a second. He then asked participants to recall the letters of one row. He sounded different tones – high, medium or low – to indicate which row had to be recalled. Recall was good (up to 75%), showing that participants had the capacity to recall the whole grid.

Duration of the SR

Different sensory memory stores appear to have different durations. However, almost all decay quickly because the brain needs to respond to live stimulation constantly.

Evaluation

🖋 There is probably an evolutionary explanation in that too many remembered stimuli would require too much processing and slow us down. We are therefore highly selective about what we pay attention to.

🔍 Key study Triesman (1964)

Triesman presented identical auditory messages to each ear with a slight delay. Participants noticed whether the messages were the same if the delay was two seconds or less but no longer, suggesting this was the duration of the store, at least for auditory stimuli.

The capacity of the iconic store is thought to be less. This may be so that we can perceive tiny movements in the visual field as each movement of the eye (a saccade) refreshes the image.

Now try this

What is meant by the terms 'coding', 'capacity' and 'duration'?

Had a look ☐ Nearly there ☐ Nailed it! ☐

Short-term memory

The second memory store in the MSM described on page 18 is **short-term memory (STM)**. Research has shown it to be separate from long-term memory (LTM) and different in terms of coding, capacity and duration.

Coding in STM

Coding is the process by which the brain stores information from the senses, first via the SR and then in one of three ways in the STM:

- **visually** – remembering images
- **acoustically** – remembering sounds and words
- **semantically** – remembering the meanings of things.

 Baddeley (1966)

Baddeley discovered that coding in STM is mainly acoustic. He gave participants acoustically similar words to learn in one condition and compared the recall with other groups given dissimilar words. He found that the similar-sounding words were least well recalled (10%), with the other lists recalled between 60% and 80%. He suggested that this shows coding is acoustic because of the confusion caused when coding the words.

Capacity of STM

The capacity of the STM is limited to between five and nine items. However, we use **chunking** to increase capacity.

When we chunk information we find a common link or meaning between a set of numbers or letters. You might chunk your phone number into two or three chunks instead of remembering nine separate digits, for example.

Miller (1956) and Jacobs (1887)

'The magical number seven, plus or minus two' was the memorable title of Miller's work. He suggested the average span for letters and numbers was seven, but that this could be increased by chunking.

In 1887, Jacobs used the **digit span method** to find the limits of STM. He found a mean of 9.3 for numbers and 7.3 for letters.

```
5 9 0
4 8 6 1
7 3 0 9 4
2 4 9 6 5 8
1 4 6 8 2 4 5
3 9 2 1 5 7 6 0
6 2 5 7 3 9 1 8 4
0 6 3 8 9 4 1 7 2 5
```

The digit span method: each time, the participant has to recall a longer list of numbers or letters until they reach their limit.

Duration of STM

The duration of the STM is thought to be brief – a maximum of 30 seconds – but this can be extended by repetition or rehearsal. This is the function of the rehearsal loop in the MSM. It is the key process by which information flows from STM to LTM.

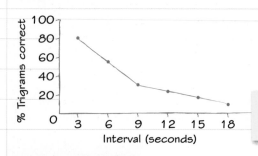

Peterson and Peterson (1959)

Peterson and Peterson used trigrams (a set of three consonants, such as ZFB) to test retention in STM. They got participants to learn the trigrams and then count backwards from a three-digit number until told to stop (to prevent rehearsal). They tested recall of the trigrams after 3, 6, 9, 12, 15 or 18 seconds, which they called the retention interval. They found that STM declined rapidly without the benefit of rehearsal.

Peterson and Peterson (1959) found that STM duration declined rapidly beyond 18 seconds.

Now try this

Give an example of an acoustically similar pair of words.

Long-term memory

Long-term memory (LTM) makes us who were are. It stores information over long periods of time. Throughout our lives, LTM allows us to remember important people, our daily existence and our knowledge base. Research shows that there are several different types of LTM (see page 23).

Coding in LTM

This is how the brain stores information for long-term access:

- **Visual** – remembering places, faces
- **Acoustic** – remembering songs, voices
- **Semantic** – the main way information is remembered in LTM is through its meaning.

Craik and Lockhart (1972) showed that the deeper information is processed, the better it will be remembered. Semantic processing gives the deepest processing and best recall.

 Frost (1972)

Frost used a free recall task to show that participants used both visual and semantic coding. This depended on whether they were expecting to recall or recognise visually or semantically categorised pictures or picture names. He found that parallel access of visual and semantic memory codes occurred. When *recognition* is expected, a visual cue provides faster access; when expecting *recall*, verbal access is more efficient. This demonstrates that separate coding occurs.

Capacity of LTM

The capacity of LTM is thought to be unlimited, depending on individual differences. However, decay, interference and illness may result in the loss of information.

 Ramscar (2014)

Dr Michael Ramscar of Tübingen University 'trained' computers to mimic elderly people's brains. He found that as the computers 'aged' by acquiring more and more information, they slowed down. The research suggests that human brains slow down because they are filling with information. An elderly person has to sift through much more knowledge to find a name or date, which appears to make them slow.

Ramscar's (2014) research suggests that older people take longer to recall facts because they have to sift through more information, reflecting their storage capacity.

Duration of LTM

There appears to be no upper limit and many people remember people, events and facts for a whole lifetime.

Evaluation

🔖 The research evidence is largely from laboratory experiments, testing memory recall under strictly controlled conditions. In real life, we recall information surrounded by cues and interference. The findings are therefore limited in mundane realism.

 Bahrick et al. (1975)

Bahrick et al. asked people to put names to faces from their school yearbook. Those who had left 48 years previously were very accurate (70%). They were less accurate in the free-recall condition in which they had to recall their peers without seeing the yearbook (30%). This shows that memory for faces is very good, but that recognition is easier than recall. Most of the time we use recognition, which could explain why straight recall of facts in exams is more challenging.

Now try this

Outline a piece of research that describes how information is coded in long-term memory.

The working memory model

Baddeley and Hitch (1974) thought that STM is more complex than Atkinson and Shiffrin (1968) had proposed. They felt that in STM more pieces of information are held simultaneously for a few seconds while the brain decides what is relevant or not. They called this **working memory**. There are four main components and they all code information differently.

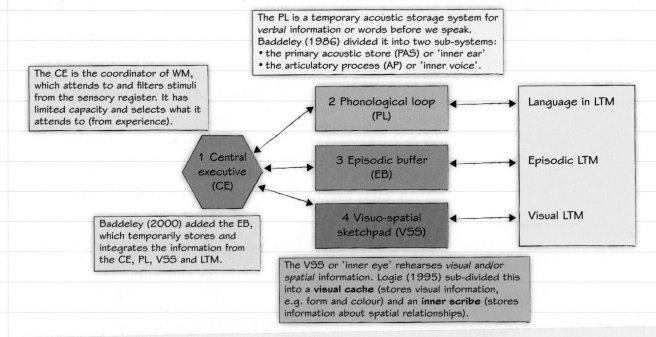

The CE is the coordinator of WM, which attends to and filters stimuli from the sensory register. It has limited capacity and selects what it attends to (from experience).

The PL is a temporary acoustic storage system for *verbal* information or words before we speak. Baddeley (1986) divided it into two sub-systems:
• the primary acoustic store (PAS) or 'inner ear'
• the articulatory process (AP) or 'inner voice'.

Baddeley (2000) added the EB, which temporarily stores and integrates the information from the CE, PL, VSS and LTM.

The VSS or 'inner eye' rehearses visual and/or *spatial* information. Logie (1995) sub-divided this into a **visual cache** (stores visual information, e.g. form and colour) and an **inner scribe** (stores information about spatial relationships).

Baddeley and Hitch suggested that we consciously focus attention on a task, such as playing chess, using information from the senses. The **CE** directs attention to the parts of the stimuli that are relevant. The **PL** and **VSS** are 'slave' systems to the CE and complement each other in processing sound and vision. Our 'inner ear' and 'inner eye' are necessary for making each move in the game.

Research support for the PL

Baddeley et al. (1975) demonstrated the **word length effect** by asking participants to remember long or short words in lists. They could hold fewer long words in the PL, which lasts about two seconds, because each word occupied so much memory space. However, if they had to speak out loud while learning the short word list, they had similar problems because the PL was kept busy by speech and the advantage of learning short words ended.

Research support for the VSS

Gathercole and Baddeley (1993) asked participants to track a moving light at the same time as describing the angles on a letter F (both using the VSS). They compared their performance with participants simultaneously doing a verbal and visual task (using the PL and VSS). When both tasks involved the VSS, performance dropped, but when the two separate systems were in use, participants found it easier. This suggests there are two separate components to the model.

The problem of the CE

As yet no one has been able to pin down a part of the brain that could be the CE. It is possible that future research will show a neural basis for selective attention, but at present it is still a mystery.

Dual task experiments

Until recently, much of the evidence for the model came from dual task experiments where participants were asked to do two things at once. These are highly artificial experiments and lack mundane realism. Scanning evidence is now replacing them as a technique.

Now try this

Draw and label a diagram of the working memory model.

Types of long-term memory

Different types of LTM can be conscious, unconscious or automatic.

Research has shown that there are several types of LTM.

Long-term memory → Explicit (conscious recall) → Episodic memory / Semantic memory

Long-term memory → Implicit (unconscious recall) → Procedural memory

Episodic memory

These are memories of events in life. They are usually processed deeply because they have meaning and emotional content. It requires some conscious effort to recall them.

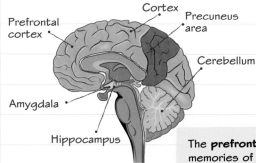

Labels: Prefrontal cortex, Cortex, Precuneus area, Cerebellum, Amygdala, Hippocampus

Key study: Clinical evidence: HM and Clive Wearing

Both retained procedural memory but lost episodic memory for events in their lives.

HM had brain surgery for epilepsy, removing his hippocampus. It left him unable to retain new memories for more than a few minutes.

Clive Wearing suffered a viral infection of the brain, damaging his hippocampus. He retains the ability to play the piano but is unable to remember his wife for more than a few minutes.

The **prefrontal cortex** is involved in the initial coding, but the memories of different parts of an event are stored in the **visual, auditory** or **olfactory cortex** and linked by the **hippocampus**.

Semantic memory

These are memories that make up our knowledge. As we mature, we accumulate knowledge through facts, events and actions. We store those that have meaning for us, and it requires some conscious effort to recall them.

Key study: Neuro evidence

Using PET scans, Tulving et al. (1994) discovered that the left prefrontal cortex is involved in semantic memories, and the right prefrontal cortex in episodic memory.

Hassiblis et al. (2007) got participants to recall either true or imaginary experiences in an fMRI scanner. They found the anterior medial prefrontal cortex, the posterior cingulate cortex and the precuneus area of the brain were involved in true experiences but not in the imaginary ones.

Procedural memory

This is memory for how to do things, such as ride a bike, skip, skate, sew, knit. Once learnt, it is often automatic and requires little conscious effort to recall.

Key study: Korsakoff and Corkin (1960s–80s)

In a series of studies, Korsakoff and Corkin showed that patients with damage to the hippocampus (and therefore no long-term factual memory) could perform motor/spatial tasks just as well as a control group of healthy adults. This provides strong evidence that procedural memory is not associated with the hippocampus, where most other LTM is stored.

Evaluation

👍 Knowing that there are different types of LTM means more effective help for stroke patients or those being rehabilitated after surgery or injury.

👍 There is now strong evidence for different memory types with the availability of scanning technology. This has increased the reputation of psychology as a science.

👍 Case studies have provided valid in-depth insight into the problems of partial memory loss.

Now try this

Explain why Clive Wearing can still play the piano but does not realise he is playing the same piece of music over and over again.

23

Explanations of forgetting: interference

Forgetting is a retrieval failure when material stored in the LTM is lost temporarily or permanently despite conscious efforts to recall it. You need to know two explanations: **interference** and **retrieval failure** (see page 25). Interference occurs when information stored in memory cannot be recalled because other information blocks it.

Retroactive interference (RI)

Learning something new disrupts information already stored. For example, learning German and then learning French disrupts the memory of the German, so you would use a French word when you wanted to say a German one. So, RI works backwards. In other words:

- learn A then learn B
- try to remember A
- B interferes.

Proactive interference (PI)

PI works forwards in time. So, something already learned disrupts something you are trying to learn. For example, a familiar piece of music distracts you from learning a new tune. In other words:

- learn A then learn B
- try to remember B
- A interferes.

🔍 Key study McGeoch and McDonald (1931)

Six groups had to learn 10 adjectives perfectly. They then had to learn a new list that had a similar meaning (synonym), opposite meaning (antonym) or there were various controls such as nonsense syllables or a rest with no learning.

Results: Performance depended on which second list they experienced and whether it interfered with the learning of the adjectives. Those in the rest condition did best because there was no interference and those in the synonym condition performed poorly.

Conclusion: The similarity of the synonyms created greater interference, causing more forgetting.

Evaluation

👍 Lots of laboratory studies with high control and standardised procedures mean they are reliable findings.

👍 These findings are easily applied to real life and are useful in improving retention in memory by avoiding learning similar items at the same time.

👎 The tasks can be criticised for lacking in validity or mundane realism. For example, learning nonsense syllables is never done normally.

👎 It is not the most useful explanation of forgetting because the instances of interference are relatively rare.

🔍 Key study Ebbinghaus' serial position curve

In 1885, Ebbinghaus demonstrated the serial position curve effect, which shows how our memory operates when we try to recall a word list in any order.

Ebbinghaus taught himself to learn a list of words and then tried to recall them in free recall. He noticed that the words were recalled more accurately from the beginning and end of the original list, which he called the **primacy** and **recency effects**. This can be explained by interference effects.

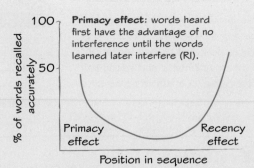

Primacy effect: words heard first have the advantage of no interference until the words learned later interfere (RI).

Recency effect: words heard last have an advantage of little RI but there could be PI.

Now try this

A teacher keeps calling her new student Elizabeth. Her actual name is Charlotte. Elizabeth is her older sister. Is this an example of RI or PI?

Cue-dependent forgetting

An absence of a cue can cause a **failure to retrieve** a memory from the LTM store. Cues can be **context** (from the situation) or **state** (from the physiological state a person is in) dependent. Tulving (1983) described the **encoding specificity principle**. He said that for a cue to be effective, it needs to be present when learning and recalling. If the cues are different, there will be a failure to retrieve the memory even though it is still in the LTM store.

Key study Evidence for cue-dependent forgetting (CDF)

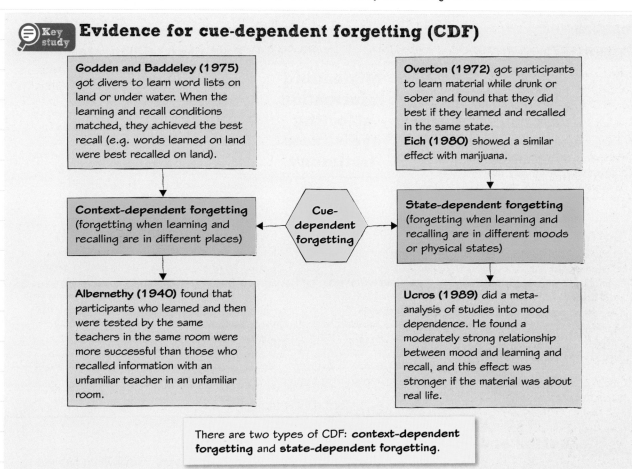

Godden and Baddeley (1975) got divers to learn word lists on land or under water. When the learning and recall conditions matched, they achieved the best recall (e.g. words learned on land were best recalled on land).

Overton (1972) got participants to learn material while drunk or sober and found that they did best if they learned and recalled in the same state.
Eich (1980) showed a similar effect with marijuana.

Context-dependent forgetting (forgetting when learning and recalling are in different places)

Cue-dependent forgetting

State-dependent forgetting (forgetting when learning and recalling are in different moods or physical states)

Albernethy (1940) found that participants who learned and then were tested by the same teachers in the same room were more successful than those who recalled information with an unfamiliar teacher in an unfamiliar room.

Ucros (1989) did a meta-analysis of studies into mood dependence. He found a moderately strong relationship between mood and learning and recall, and this effect was stronger if the material was about real life.

There are two types of CDF: **context-dependent forgetting** and **state-dependent forgetting**.

Evaluation

- 👎 Much laboratory research, which lacks mundane realism. Real-life memories are likely to have multiple cues when coding and recall.

- 👎 Getting participants drunk or high for a research purpose is wrong ethically even with the consent of participants. The substances are potentially harmful.

- 👍 The findings actually explain why most forgetting occurs in LTM and relate to the levels of processing theory described by Craik and Lockhart (1972), where the greater the elaboration of material to be remembered, the better the recall.

Application

Cue-dependent forgetting can explain:
- ✓ why we often forget what we went to fetch once we leave the room we started the thought process in
- ✓ why students find multiple choice a more friendly type of testing; the questions are acting as cues to recall
- ✓ why crime reconstructions help witnesses in remembering the events of a crime.

Now try this

Recent research has shown that chewing gum while learning and recalling could enhance performance. Is this state- or context-dependent learning?

Misleading information

Leading questions and **post-event discussion** are two factors that can affect the accuracy of eyewitness testimony. Both have been extensively researched. You need to know examples of each as factors that affect eyewitness testimony.

 Key study

Leading questions

Such as, 'Did you see **the** broken glass?'
- **Response-bias explanation:** When a person gets a leading question it biases their response without changing the memory.
- **Memory substitution explanation:** When a person gets a leading question, it actually changes the stored memory.

Misleading information affecting eyewitness testimony

Post-event discussion

When witnesses discuss what they saw after a crime their memory can become contaminated by what others say or by misleading information. Witnesses must be kept apart until statements are taken to avoid this. In court, witnesses are not allowed to come into contact until the trial is finished. Seeing media coverage of the case would also affect their accuracy.

Loftus and Palmer (1974)

Students watched film clips of car crashes and then were asked how fast the cars were going when they: 'contacted', 'bumped', 'collided', 'hit' and 'smashed' into each other.

They found that the mean estimated speed increased depending on which description was used in the question, between contacted at 31.8 and smashed at 40.8 mph. This showed the effect of the leading question.

Loftus and Pickrell (1995)

Loftus and Pickrell found that they could plant false memories of being lost in a store aged 5 in their sample of 24 participants. Nearly 30% of the sample recalled being lost and were able to provide details purely from suggestion.

This suggests that memory is reconstructive and not like a video re-enactment.

 Extend ## Loftus and Pickrell (2003)

Further research by Loftus and Pickrell showed that a false memory could be created of a childhood visit to Disneyland.

Around 30% of participants recalled seeing Bugs Bunny at Disneyland, which is impossible because he is not a Disney character.

This time, Loftus and Pickrell were able to plant the false memory by using a picture of a fake advert. This is a more subtle way of suggesting the memory but equally effective.

Evaluation

👍 This research is very useful when applied to the criminal justice system and it has led to improvements in procedures.

👎 Early research was very artificial and laboratory-based. For example, the Loftus car crash work used police crash videos lasting a few seconds and had limited samples (psychology students) so was lacking in validity and generalisability.

👎 This research could be abused to plant suggestions, for example, by advertisers to make people buy their products.

Now try this

What is the difference between the response-bias explanation and the memory substitution explanation for the effect of leading questions?

Anxiety

Anxiety also affects eyewitness accuracy. Most witnesses to crimes are in an emotional state. You need to know how this affects the accuracy of **eyewitness testimony** (EWT).

The weapon focus effect

Loftus (1987) found that if a person is carrying a weapon, witnesses are more likely to look at it than at the face of a suspect. The presence of the gun increases anxiety, taking attention away from the perpetrator and leading to poorer EWT.

Pickel (1998) suggested it was the unusualness of the gun that caused the weapon focus effect. He showed participants a man using scissors, a gun, a wallet or raw chicken either in a place they were expected to be or in an unusual place. Participants' recall of the man was poorest in the most unusual conditions. The unusual items would have increased arousal, causing a narrowing of focus away from the perpetrator.

> **Research into EWT and anxiety**

Christianson and Hubinette (1993)

In Sweden, 110 witnesses of 22 real-life bank robberies were interviewed 4–15 months after the robberies. Some had been onlookers or customers (low anxiety), and others were bank employees who had been directly threatened or subjected to violence during the robberies (high anxiety). The victims were 75% accurate in their recall of the robbers' clothing and behaviour, and the accuracy was still evident 15 months later. There was no difference between rated degree of emotion and number of details remembered.

Yuille and Cutshall (1986)

Yuille and Cutshall conducted a field experiment with 13 real-life witnesses to a shooting. They interviewed them four or five months after the crime and compared their report to police statements taken at the time. They were scored for number of details and how stressed they were on a seven-point scale. The witnesses who were the most stressed were 88% accurate compared with 75% accuracy of those who said they were not particularly stressed, showing that anxiety had **not affected memory**.

Models of arousal

According to the **Yerkes–Dodson model (1908)**, as arousal increases so does performance up to an optimum point. After this, it drops away. Therefore witnesses with low arousal should be poorer witnesses than those who have been a bit scared.

This idea was challenged by **Deffenbacher et al. (2004)** who said the catastrophe model by Fazey and Hardy (1988) was better at explaining witness accuracy in real-life situations, such as the studies above.

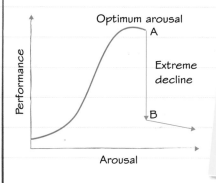

The graph shows the point of optimal arousal for both models and the catastrophic drop (from A to B) in performance as anxiety increases, which Fazey and Hardy (1988) describe.

Evaluation

👍 This research has added to our understanding of what happens to real-life witnesses and has increased their credibility in court even if they were scared at the time.

👍 Real-life studies are higher in ecological validity.

👎 It is very difficult to investigate anxiety and stay ethical other than using actual events. Even so, asking a person to recall the event could be distressing.

👎 Real-life studies lack the controls of laboratory experiments. Extraneous variables may interfere with the results. For example, witnesses could have discussed what they saw and altered their memory of the events.

👎 Research findings are contradictory and seem to vary depending on whether the crime was a violent one or not.

Now try this

Describe **one** piece of evidence that suggests that anxiety does not affect witness accuracy and **one** piece of evidence that suggests anxiety does reduce witness accuracy.

The cognitive interview

One technique used by police forces to improve eyewitness recall is the **cognitive interview (CI)**. It is based on cognitive research into memory and was devised by Fisher and Geiselman in 1984. It is an interview style that helps witnesses recall more details of crimes when giving statements to the police. You need to know the four stages and how it works.

The four stages of the CI

1 Report everything
The witness is first asked to recall all they can about the event without interruption. They are told to include every detail, even ones which seem irrelevant. Even if they are not sure, they should tell the officer recording the interview. This allows the interviewer to plan strategy for the rest of the interview.

Creating a mental picture enacts the encoding specificity principle, which states that recall is better when learning and recall states are similar.

The cognitive interview (1984)

2 Reinstate the context
The witness is encouraged to imagine themselves back in the context of the incident, so maybe late at night walking back from the pub. What was the weather like? What was the lighting like? Who was around? All these features will act as cues to recall.

3 Reverse the narrative order
Once the witness has described the events in chronological order, they are asked to recall it from the last thing that happened to the first. This can help to fill in gaps in the narrative.

Using multiple ways of retrieving the memories is based on the fact that memory is stored in multiple ways.

4 Change perspective
Lastly, they are asked to imagine what the scene would look like to someone on the other side of the street. What would they have seen? Heard? What would the offender have seen?

Evaluation

- Fisher and Geiselman (1985) found that the CI achieved more accurate detailed memories than the standard police interview.

- Kohnken et al. (1999) in a meta-analysis of 55 studies found that CIs produced both more accurate and less accurate details than the Standard Police Interview (SPI). Time passing reduced its effectiveness and there was no effect of age. Witnesses did best when personally involved and when interviewed soon after the event.

- All police forces are now trained in the technique.

- Tulving's (1973) encoding specificity theory underpins the CI. Both context- and state-dependent cues are involved in witnessing an event.

- It only works for some witnesses and some crimes.

The enhanced CI (ECI)

In 1987, Fisher and Geiselman included some extra features.

- The witness should control the flow of information, so no leading questions.

- Witnesses must not be distracted by interruptions when recalling.

- The witness should recall slowly and focus strongly on an image.

- Remind witnesses to report everything and not to guess.

The ECI is intended to build trust between the interviewer and witness and to reduce anxiety in the witness.

Evaluation of the ECI

- It has been developed for use with children and in clinical settings to get more information from patients.

- Coker (2013) found that the extra emphasis on focused mental imagery increased the accuracy of recall of facts compared to the CI.

- Witnesses may be more likely to confabulate memories (blend false and true memories) using this method.

- It requires the interviewer to be very good and well trained to be effective.

Now try this

Explain what is meant by the cognitive interview.

Exam skills 1

Long-answer questions ask you to create **arguments** as discussions or evaluations. This takes practice, but a suggestion to help you is given below. This would apply to any question that goes beyond mere description (AO1). See also page 33.

Worked example

Discuss **two** factors that are known to affect the accuracy of eyewitness testimony.

(16 marks)

Table 1 The basics of a good argument

Point	One factor that affects the accuracy of eyewitness testimony is the sample. The samples used by researchers in the witness testimony studies lack generalisability.
Example	This is because the researchers use opportunity samples of their own students to carry out the research.
Evidence	Loftus and Palmer (1974) used their own psychology students to carry out their research into leading questions.
Explain	Therefore, we would have to be cautious when applying the findings to an actual courtroom.

Argument structure

You may have learned to construct your argument using either the **Point, Example, Comment (PEC)** method or the **Point, Example, Explain the first two (PEE)** method. These will give your essay a basic structure which is easy to follow. However, your answer will be better developed and demonstrate thorough understanding if you can use theoretical or practical **evidence** as well as reasons to back up your point.

Table 2 A more developed and stronger argument

Point	One factor that affects the accuracy of eyewitness testimony is the sample. The samples used by researchers in researching witness testimony lack generalisability.
Example	This is because the researchers use opportunity samples of their own students to carry out the research.
Evidence	Loftus and Palmer (1974) used their own psychology students to carry out their research into leading questions.
Evaluative comment	The problem with this is that psychology students who are getting credit for their degrees by taking part are likely to show uncharacteristic behaviour by perhaps being more willing to give the researchers the findings they want. This is because they will be familiar with experiments from their own reading and may be tuned in to any cues the researcher may unconsciously give, and also more likely to guess the researchers' aim. This is called showing demand characteristics, and demand characteristics tend to reduce the validity of any findings.
Conclusion	Therefore, we would have to be cautious when applying the findings to an actual courtroom because the findings may not be representative of a wider population and so could not be easily generalised.

Now you need to analyse or evaluate the evidence you have quoted.

Notice how the answer is contextualised by explaining the point using real world examples relevant to the actual sample in the study.

If you wanted to be really thorough in demonstrating your understanding and especially in a 'discuss' question, you could do this by using a counter-point or argument and then answering it. You could also add a contrasting piece of research carried out using a different methodology such as a field experiment.

Table 3 Counter-point

Counter-point	On the other hand, the researchers need the convenience of an opportunity sample to be able to complete their research in a reasonable time and within a limited budget. This also meant that Loftus and Palmer could conduct many variations of the independent variable to be sure their findings were reliable, but on balance, we would have to be cautious ...

Exam skills 2

Before reading these questions, remind yourself about the working memory model by Baddeley and Hitch (page 22) and the multi-store model by Atkinson and Shiffrin (page 18).

Worked example

A researcher wanted to find support for the working memory model. She asked one group of students to listen to some directions while looking at them on a map. A second group listened to the same directions while reading them. Using your knowledge of psychology, decide which group is likely to do best when asked to repeat the directions, and explain why it would support the model.

(4 marks)

First, ask yourself: *Why would one group do better than the other?* Then link this to the parts of the working memory model. Finally, explain why it would provide support for the model.

Make sure you read all of the question thoroughly and cover each part.

The group that heard the directions while following them on a map is likely to do best. This is because they would be using both the visuo-spatial sketchpad and the phonological loop in Baddeley and Hitch's model separately. This means that the central executive can allocate attention to both and maximise the ability of the short-term memory to recall the information. The other group will be using the phonological loop for both listening and reading (through the inner voice) and this will tend to overload this part of working memory, leading to a fall in performance. The fact that there will be a difference in the performance of both groups provides support for the model because it does suggest there are separate systems and limited attentional capacity, which has to be allocated as predicted by the model.

The student directly answers the first part of the question by clearly making a decision.

The student uses the correct parts of the model and shows understanding of how it works. In this case, the visuo-spatial sketchpad and the phonological loop.

Here the student has answered the final part of the question – 'explain' – by clearly linking to the working memory model.

You could use a quick diagram to help explain your answer.

One explanation of memory is the multi-store model. Some evidence for the model comes from case studies. Give **one** advantage and **one** disadvantage of using the case study method to demonstrate how memory works.

(4 marks)

Note the injunction to link your answer to memory explicitly. This is not just a question about the advantages and disadvantages of case studies, but about using the case study method to demonstrate how **memory** works.

An advantage of using case studies to provide evidence for the multi-store model is that individuals, such as HM and Clive Wearing, can be studied in great depth, conducting many experiments over years. This means that we can see both the short- and the long-term effects of memory loss and which parts of the brain are responsible for short- and long-term memory. Using these case studies has shown us that there are separate stores because the individuals do not lose both short- and long-term memory at the same time.

You could answer this with just one case study and detail how it supports the idea of separate stores.

A disadvantage of using case studies to find evidence for the model is that there are usually strong medical reasons for the loss of memory, such as surgery for epilepsy or virus infections. These could be confounding variables that are unique to the case history, and therefore do not generalise to a healthy brain.

Exam skills 3

Before looking at these questions, it would be helpful to revise explanations of forgetting, including interference on page 24 and cue-dependent forgetting on page 25.

Worked example

Outline **and** evaluate evidence that forgetting is cue-dependent.

(8 marks)

Cue-dependent forgetting is explained in two ways: through a change of context and a change of state. To investigate context-dependent forgetting, Godden and Baddeley (1975) got divers to learn word lists on dry land or under water. When the learning and recall conditions matched, they got the best recall, suggesting that keeping the context the same was beneficial through cues that existed in the environment.

To investigate state-dependent forgetting, Overton (1972) got participants to learn material while drunk or sober and found that they did best if they learned and recalled in the same state. Eich (1980) showed a similar effect with marijuana. The idea is that drugs or alcohol were also in some way acting as cues to recall through a change in mood state.

Godden and Baddeley's research can be criticised for lacking in external validity. They used two extremely different environments, dry land and under water, as their two contexts. It is very likely that forgetting would occur when transferring from one environment to the other, purely due to the time delay involved, unlike walking from one room into another, for example.

However, the research was very reliable because Godden and Baddeley had a standardised procedure, using tape recordings and strict timings to enable the divers to complete the task safely. The results are therefore objective and replicable.

Overton's and Eich's research is often criticised for its ethics in giving participants alcohol or drugs, although their participants were all over 21 and used to drinking alcohol or smoking marijuana. They also restricted them to moderate intoxication so that minimum harm was caused. Their findings were relevant to everyday life and had mundane realism for the participants.

Your answer should cover **context-** and **state-dependent forgetting**. One study of each is enough given the time constraints in an exam. Your evaluation should include the strengths and weaknesses of each.

Consider your time carefully. Aim for a mark a minute plus reading and thinking time, so allow around 10 minutes for an 8-mark question.

When outlining a study, aim to write one line for each of sample, procedure, findings and conclusions.

When evaluating, make a point, illustrate it with an example or evidence, and then explain the point fully.

Remember to include positive as well as the negative evaluations if applicable.

Command words

Outline means to describe briefly, writing about just the key points.

Evaluate literally means to look for value in the studies/evidence by weighing up their strengths and weaknesses.

Exam-style practice 1

Practise for Paper 1 of your A level exam with these exam-style questions. There are answers on page 292. Before looking at these questions, it would be helpful to revise eyewitness testimony.

1 Complete the following statement about the weapon focus effect. Shade **one** box only.

The weapons effect:

A   Improves recall of crimes where a weapon is present.   ◯

B   Improves recollection of the assailant with the weapon.   ◯

C   Causes the witness to pay less attention to their assailant.   ◯

~~D   Means that crimes with weapons are the most frightening~~   ◯

(1 mark)

> Multiple choice questions are designed to make you think. Use a logical approach and systematically rule out wrong answers.

> The anxiety experienced as a witness could be caused by factors other than weapons so D can be ruled out.

2 Complete the following statement about eyewitness testimony. Shade **one** box only.

Real-life studies of eyewitness testimony have shown that:

A   Witnesses who are anxious make inaccurate witness statements   ◯

B   Witnesses who are anxious make better witnesses.   ◯

~~C   Anxiety and accuracy of witnesses are not linked.~~   ◯

D   Real-life studies are more accurate.   ◯

(1 mark)

> Research has shown that anxiety and the accuracy of witnesses are linked so C can be ruled out.

3 How eyewitness testimony is investigated and which method is used has been shown to affect the accuracy of the witnesses. Identify **and** outline **two** ways that the research method used could affect the accuracy of the witnesses. **(4 marks)**

> This is a straightforward description question requiring just AO1 skills. Do not evaluate.

> Note the injunction to give **two** ways, not just one. In the exam, make sure you read the question carefully.

4 Mahima has witnessed an armed robbery at a post office and the police wish to interview her using the cognitive interview procedure. What can Mahima expect to happen when she is interviewed as a witness? **(4 marks)**

> This question is testing whether you know how the interview works. You should write a paragraph detailing the four components – report everything, reinstate the context, reverse the narrative order and change perspective.

5 What is the difference between the echoic store and the iconic store in sensory memory? **(1 mark)**

> This should be a single sentence answer.

Exam-style practice 2

Practise for Paper 1 of your A level exam with these exam-style questions. There are answers on page 292.

6   Outline **two** criticisms of the methods used to investigate STM.
                                                                      (4 marks)

> These are laboratory experiments so think about how you would criticise them.

7   Give **one** example of proactive interference and **one** example of retroactive interference.   **(2 marks)**

> A simple question but have your examples ready.

8   What is the encoding specificity principle?   **(2 marks)**

> Look back at cue-dependent forgetting for help with this.

9   Label the multi-store model of memory by Atkinson and Shiffrin (1968).   **(5 marks)**

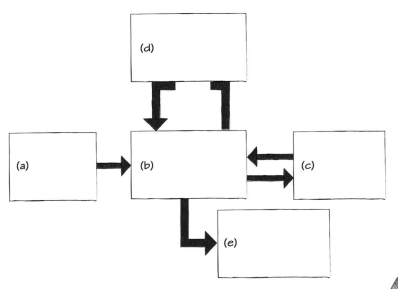

10 Give **one** advantage and **one** disadvantage of using laboratory studies to investigate memory.   **(4 marks)**

> Think about the difference between laboratory studies and real life memory.

11 Discuss how the accuracy of eyewitness testimony is affected by anxiety and the cognitive interview.   **(16 marks)**

> Remind yourself about these two factors by referring to pages 27 and 28, then try the answer. Memorise the relevant research evidence that you will quote.
>
> Then, think about the context of the question – you need to be talking about eyewitnesses all the way through.
>
> When answering the question, you will need to use a **point, example, explain** structure. You need to construct an argument with points made about what makes a witness more accurate or less accurate (see how to construct an argument on page 29). Support your points with examples from research evidence, citing the findings and conclusions, and ideally make some comparison points looking at methods used by the researchers and the generalisability of the findings.

Caregiver–infant interactions

You are required to know about the interactions between human caregivers and their infants that encourage the development of **attachment**. This is the enduring emotional bond between an infant and its caregiver. You must be able to describe and apply the terms **reciprocity** and **interactional synchrony**. These behaviours are present at birth and are thought to be universal as infants and carers all over the world routinely engage in them.

Reciprocity

The infant and their caregiver are able to reliably produce responses in each other.

> Infants have an innate ability to imitate carers' facial expressions, so if a carer smiles at the infant, the infant will smile back.

Interactional synchrony

The infant and carer coordinate their activity to form a type of conversation without language. This is characterised by turn-taking – when one has finished interacting they pause and the other takes over. For example, the baby might make noises while looking at the caregiver who waits for the baby to finish before using language to respond to the child, usually in caregiverese (see below).

Brazelton (1979) and Condon and Sander (1974)

Reciprocity is shown in Brazelton's 'frozen face' study where the infant becomes distressed if the mother stops reciprocating with them and adopts a passive face.

Interactional synchrony is shown by Condon and Sander who, in 1974, did a frame-by-frame analysis of mother–infant interactions and found clear evidence of turn-taking.

Other forms of caregiver–infant interactions

Mimicking	• Infants have an innate ability to copy facial expressions and simple hand gestures demonstrated by an adult in their first few weeks of life. This is consistent with a biological instinct to help form attachments. • Melzoff and Moore (1977) found that infants as young as 3 days old could mimic facial expressions. However, a recent large scale replication of this study by Oostenbroek (2016) found no evidence of imitation.
Caregiverese	• Adults interacting with young infants use a specific speech pattern and tone. It is higher pitched and similar to the patterns in songs. This allows infants to develop interactional synchrony by giving them access to simplified conversations. • Papousek et al. (1991) found caregiverese across many cultures, suggesting that it is instinctive behaviour by parents.
Bodily contact	• Physical contact such as skin to skin, especially in the period immediately after birth, helps to form and strengthen the bond between infant and caregiver. • Klaus and Kennell (1976) found that when babies were given extended physical contact with their mums immediately after birth they developed a stronger physical relationship compared to those denied such contact.

Now try this

Outline the ways in which interactions between caregiver and infant may lead to attachments being made.

Stages of attachment development

Babies will form more than one attachment, for example to their siblings and grandparents. You need to be able to describe the **stages of attachment** based on Schaffer and Emerson's (1964) study and chart the development of **multiple attachments**.

🔍 Key study: Schaffer and Emerson (1964)

Aim: To investigate the process by which attachments are formed.

Procedure: This was a longitudinal study of 60 newborn babies and their mums who lived in a working-class area of Glasgow. Mums and babies were visited in their homes once a month until the babies were 12 months old and then again at 18 months. The researchers conducted observations and interviewed the mums.

They measured attachment by the amount of **separation protest** and **stranger anxiety** (see Ainsworth, page 40).

Results:

- Separation protest was evident in most infants between six and eight months old.
- Stranger anxiety started about one month later.
- Strong attachments developed between babies and mums when the mums were very responsive and sensitive to the babies' needs.
- Most infants developed multiple attachments; at 18 months, 87% had at least two, with 31% having five or more attachments.
- For 39% of infants the primary attachment was not to their mother.

Schaffer's stages of attachment

Stage	Description
Pre-attachment (birth to three months)	Up to six weeks of age infants show little discrimination or preference for humans (asocial) but after that they show more interest in humans over other environmental stimuli. They start to smile at people's faces.
Indiscriminate attachment (three months to seven/eight months)	Infants can discriminate between familiar and unfamiliar faces, showing more social behaviour to familiar people but are still quite happy to let strangers hold them and look after them.
Discriminate attachment (seven/eight months and beyond)	Infants become attached to specific people and will show separation protest and stranger anxiety.
Multiple attachments (nine months and beyond)	Infants form strong emotional bonds with other caregivers and with siblings. Attachment to mum is strongest and stranger anxiety becomes less important.

Evaluation

👍 The longitudinal design of this study controlled for participant variables that might have affected the development of attachment.

👍 It also has ecological validity and mundane realism as the infants were monitored in their own homes, making their behaviour more natural than if observations were done in a lab.

👎 Due to the nature of the data collection by observation and self-report, it is possible that some element of subjective bias affected the data.

👎 Although the data broadly supported the stages of attachment there were large individual differences in the timing, as some infants developed them earlier than others.

Other research

✓ Carpenter (1975) found that infants younger than six weeks were able to distinguish their mum's face and voice, going against Schaffer's view that this did not happen until later.

✓ Fathers have been shown to have a role in the development of attachment, showing support for the idea of the development of multiple attachments rather than just one with the mum. For example, see Brown's (2010) findings described on page 36.

Now try this

Describe the behaviour of an infant in each of the four stages of attachment.

The role of the father

You need to be able to outline and evaluate the role of the father in the development of attachment. Traditionally, the father's role in child rearing has been to provide resources for the family; some have even argued that men are biologically unsuited to child rearing. However, with more mothers working outside the home, fathers are taking a larger role in parenting. Psychologists are interested in finding out whether fathers can form attachment bonds in the same way as mothers, and what the outcomes for children are with and without fathers.

Research on the role of the father

Most research has focused on mother–infant bonds, with some researchers suggesting that fathers take the role of playmate more than caregiver. Mothers build an early attachment with the child because they show **sensitive responsiveness**. This means that they are sensitive to the needs of the child and are quick to respond to them. The relationship with the father is sometimes different. Research shows that this is not necessarily biological, with several factors influencing how it develops.

- **Degree of sensitivity:** Fathers who show sensitivity to the needs of the infant develop more secure attachments (Lucassen, 2011).

Lucassen (2011) found that men who display sensitive responsiveness develop a more secure attachment with their children.

- The relationship between the father and mother affects attachment. The amount of **marital intimacy** between parents is important. Brown (2010) found that **supportive co-parenting** affects the type of attachment they have, with more supportive fathers developing more secure attachments than less supportive ones.

- **Type of attachment with own parents:** In families where the father is the caregiver, the attachment bond with their child is similar to the one they had with their own parents.

Evaluating whether fathers are different

- 👍 Geiger (1996) suggests that fathers serve a different purpose in the development of the child than mothers do, suggesting that fathers are more likely to be playmates and engage in stimulating activity.

- 👍 Lamb (1987) found that when children are happy they prefer interacting with their dads, but mums are preferred when they are not happy, suggesting different roles for each parent.

- 👍 Hardy (1999) found dads were not as good as mums in detecting distress in children.

- 👎 Lamb (1987) found that dads who were the sole carer were able to sense unhappiness in the child.

Evaluation

Application of psychology to the real world looks at the outcomes for the child of having a bond with their father.

- 👍 Secure attachment to the father has positive benefits for the child, including being able to form better social relationships and having more emotional control.

- 👎 Lack of a father has been shown to lead to negative outcomes such as higher risk-taking behaviour and aggression (especially in boys).

Now try this

Outline **one** way that research has suggested that the role of the father is different from that of the mother.

Animal studies of attachment

Animal studies have been conducted to provide controlled experiments to track the development of attachment in infants.

🔍 Key study Lorenz (1935)

1 Lorenz split a clutch of goose eggs so that half hatched under the mother and the other half were kept with Lorenz.

2 When they hatched, Lorenz imitated the noise made by a mother goose and observed the goslings.

3 To test that **imprinting** had occurred, Lorenz put both groups of goslings together under a cardboard box and then lifted the lid to see which 'mother' they would go to.

Results and conclusions:

When mixed under a cardboard box and then released, the goslings split into two groups and returned to either Lorenz or to their mother.

Lorenz concluded that geese **imprint** on the first moving object that they see during a 12–17 hour critical period after birth. This suggests that attachment is innate and imprinting takes place without any feeding taking place.

Imprinting has consequences both for short-term survival and for longer-term development.

🔍 Key study Harlow (1959)

1 Harlow raised infant monkeys in isolation with two surrogate 'mothers'. One surrogate was made of wire and the other was wire covered in cloth.

2 The infant monkeys were observed to see which of the two surrogates they spent the most time with and which they used as a safe base when deliberately frightened.

One of Harlow's monkeys feeding from the wire surrogates. These monkeys still imprinted on the cloth surrogate and used it as a 'safe base'. They spent most of their time on the cloth mother.

Results:

- Surrogates were physiologically equal: infants drank the same amount of milk and put on the same amount of weight.
- Surrogates were not psychologically equal: infants preferred the cloth mother.
- When exposed to a stressful situation, the infants used the cloth surrogate as a 'safe base'.
- Monkeys raised in isolation grew up to be unable to form social relationships with others.

Conclusions:

Attachment is not based on food as predicted by the learning approach (see page 38). Instead, Harlow's findings support the evolutionary theory of attachment (see page 39). It is the sense of comfort and security provided by the caregiver that is important rather than the provision of food. Furthermore, social contact is crucial for normal development.

Evaluation: Harlow

👍 This study advanced our understanding of the development of attachment.

👍 It supports change in maternity wards, hospitals and children's homes to ensure that children's emotional needs are met.

👍 As monkeys are genetically and behaviourally more similar to humans than other species are, the study adds validity to Lorenz's findings on geese.

👎 There are ethical issues in that severe emotional harm and distress was caused to the infant monkeys by their isolation.

👎 Longer-term effects were also seen, especially in relation to female monkeys being unable to care for their young.

👎 It is questionable whether this study helps us to understand anything about attachment and deprivation in human infants because human infants develop differently from monkeys, so the findings are not truly generalisable to humans.

Now try this

Explain the importance of contact between an infant and the mother or caregiver. Support the arguments you make with at least one of the studies described on this page.

Learning theory of attachment

Learning theory (behaviourism) is a **nurture-based theory** that suggests that infants **learn** to become attached to their caregivers. It is sometimes referred to as the **cupboard love theory** because it says that attachment depends on food provision. The two theories applied to attachment are **classical** and **operant conditioning**.

Classical conditioning

This occurs when a natural response to an environmental stimulus becomes associated with something else. In this case, the stimulus is food.

1   **Before learning**

unconditioned stimulus → unconditioned response

Example: food leads to satisfaction

2   **During learning**

unconditioned stimulus + neutral stimulus → unconditioned response

Example: food plus caregiver leads to satisfaction

3   **After learning**

Eventually the neutral stimulus acquires the power of the unconditioned stimulus and becomes a conditioned stimulus:

conditioned stimulus → conditioned response

Example: caregiver without food causes satisfaction

The food satisfies a need by removing hunger, and children learn to associate this nice feeling with the caregiver.

Operant conditioning

This is linked to **drive reduction** – an instinctive need that causes behaviour change.

For example:

- The baby feels hunger, which is a **negative drive state**.
- The primary caregiver feeds the baby and therefore reduces the negative drive state.

- The primary caregiver's presence is **negatively reinforced** by the reduction of hunger and the baby becomes attached to them.

Hungry baby in a negative drive state

Evaluation

👍 Operant conditioning has strong theoretical support as it has been demonstrated many times experimentally on animals. For example, see Pavlov (page 67) and Skinner (page 68).

👍 Dollard and Miller (1950) state that infants are fed 2000 times in their first year of life, usually by their primary caregiver. This is frequent enough for them to learn a conditioned response, adding mundane realism to the theory.

👎 Schaffer and Emerson (1964) show infants have multiple attachments where they form attachments to people who do not feed them, casting doubt on the theory (see page 35).

👎 Fox (1977) studied Israeli infants brought up in kibbutzim and cared for by a non-family member who feeds them. They still form strong attachments to their mothers.

👎 The theories offer simple explanations for complex behaviour. This makes them reductionist as they ignore many aspects of attachment such as the existence of different types.

👎 Drive reduction has limited explanatory value and fails to explain why we engage in behaviour that makes us feel anxious. For example, enjoying going on roller coasters or watching scary films.

👎 These theories cannot explain the evidence from Harlow (1959) as infant monkeys showed attachment to a cloth mother without food in preference to a wire mother with food (see page 37). In contrast, Bowlby's (1951) theory can explain animal and human research findings on attachment (see page 39).

Now try this

Explain the development of attachment using learning theory.

Bowlby's monotropic theory

🔍 Key study John Bowlby was influenced by the work of Lorenz (see page 37), which suggested that attachment behaviour was biologically programmed. Bowlby applied this idea to human infants. Bowlby's monotropic theory (1951, 1969, 1973) focuses on innate behaviour programmed by **evolution**, rather than by the environment as as suggested by classical or operant conditioning.

Bowlby's theory

- Attachment behaviours are pre-programmed in our genes in order to provide an adaptive advantage that increases survival.

- Infants who stay close to an adult caregiver (usually the biological mother) during the critical period of infancy will survive longer, be successful and ultimately pass on their genes.

This theory is on the **nature** side of the nature vs nurture debate, unlike the conditioning or cupboard love theories.

Other theories accept biological influences but argue that it is driven by the **personality** of the baby. Kagan (1984) said that difficult babies do not form the same quality of relationships as easy-going ones.

Attachment is based on forming a **monotropic** relationship with **one** special person (usually the biological mother).

This is an **innate** function designed to improve the baby's chances of survival.

This relationship forms an **internal working model** or pattern for how relationships work.

Babies are programmed to exhibit **social releasers** which are behaviours designed to attract attention and response from adults.

The relationship must form within the **critical period** of early infancy (up to 3 years old).

The **continuity hypothesis** states that the internal working model based on this relationship influences all future relationships.

Adult caregivers respond to social releasers through displays of **sensitive responsiveness** such as interactional synchrony (see page 34).

Adult caregivers show sensitive responsiveness.

Evaluation

- 🗨 The concept of a monotropic relationship is challenged by studies that show multiple attachments between infants and caregivers, such as Schaffer and Emerson's (1964) study (see page 35).

- 🗨 The critical period is challenged by studies that show children deprived of close relationships with adults during early infancy still go on to form good relationships later in life. For example, Koluchova's (1972) case study of the Czech twins (see page 43).

- 👍 Brazelton (1979) supported sensitive responsiveness, finding that both mothers and newborn babies imitated each other and if the mother ceased to respond the infant would be distressed and withdrawn.

- 👍 There is support for the continuity hypothesis from Hazan and Shaver (1987). They found a correlation between type of infant attachment and adult attachments, consistent with the internal working model (see page 44).

Now try this

Define the key terms that make up this theory, including sensitive responsiveness, critical period, monotropic relationship, social releasers, internal working model and continuity hypothesis.

Ainsworth's 'Strange Situation'

🔍 **Key study** Mary Ainsworth worked with Bowlby in the 1950s. She went on to further his theory by researching different attachment types and linking them to sensitive responsiveness. You need to be able to describe and evaluate her 1978 **Strange Situation Procedure (SSP)** in which she aimed to classify different attachment types.

Method

Mum and baby (9–18 months old) engaged in eight episodes of about three minutes each.

Episodes

1 Mum and baby play
2 Mum sits and baby plays
3 Stranger enters and talks to mum
4 Mum leaves, baby plays, stranger offers comfort if needed
5 Mum returns, offers comfort to baby, stranger leaves
6 Mum leaves, baby is alone
7 Stranger enters and offers comfort
8 Mum returns and offers comfort.

Data gathering

Researchers watched and recorded the behaviour of the baby, looking for proximity seeking or avoidance and contact maintenance or avoidance. They measured:

• the willingness of the infant to explore

• stranger anxiety

• separation protest

• reunion behaviour.

They were then able to make a judgement about the attachment type of each baby based on the behaviour shown, and classified them into one of three types of attachment.

Results

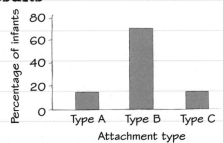

Percentage of infants showing each attachment type: 70% of the infants were classified as **Type B** (securely attached), with 15% classified as **Type A** (insecure-avoidant) and 15% **Type C** (insecure-resistant).

Conclusions

Ainsworth concluded there are three types of attachment.

Type A: Insecure-avoidant	Infants ignore mum and don't engage with her if she is present. They treat mum the same as a stranger and show most distress when left alone.
Type B: Secure	Happy when mum is there, distressed when not. They showed stranger anxiety, sought comfort from mum at reunion and quickly settled down.
Type C: Insecure-resistant	Infants did not settle well even with mum there. They were distressed when she left and would not be comforted on her return.

Evaluation

🌱 Bronfenbrenner (1979) argued that the SSP lacked ecological validity as infant behaviour at home would not show such strong attachments.

🌱 The strict controls used for the observation might have increased the likelihood of mums showing demand characteristics, thus causing a lack of mundane realism.

🌱 The SSP could be said to have caused psychological harm as the infants were distressed, but it is unlikely to have been lasting and such short separations are not uncommon for most infants.

👍 Ainsworth linked attachment type to sensitive responsiveness, suggesting that training parents to be more sensitive would be useful.

🌱 Main and Solomon (1986) found a fourth type, insecure-disorganised (type D), suggesting the original study was lacking in validity.

🌱 The SSP has been widely accepted as a good way to measure attachment but may not be valid for application in some cultures (see cross-cultural research on page 41).

Now try this

Evaluate the Strange Situation Procedure as a measure of attachment.

Cultural variations in attachment

If attachment is universal and develops from caregiver–infant interactions (such as sensitive responsiveness) then it should be seen across cultures despite different child-rearing practices.

Key study: Van Ijzendoorn and Kroonenberg (1988)

Aim: To compare research using the SSP in different cultures and to assess whether similar patterns of attachment emerged.

Procedure: A meta-analysis of 32 SSP studies from 8 countries. In total, 1990 mother–infant pairs from 32 different studies were used.

Results: Type B (secure) was the most common type in all cultures but there were differences across cultures.

Conclusions: In every culture the majority of children showed secure attachments. There were variations although the overall pattern matched Ainsworth's findings.

Results

Country	% secure	% insecure-avoidant	% insecure-resistant
W Germany	57	35	8
UK	75	22	3
USA	65	21	14
Netherlands	67	26	7
Sweden	74	22	4
Israel	64	7	29
Japan	68	5	27
China	50	25	25

Evaluation

👍 The use of a meta-analysis means that the sample size is large and should produce generalisable results.

👎 Different studies in the analysis might have had different interpretations of the children's behaviour, making some aspects of the data unreliable.

👎 Eighteen of the studies were done in USA and only one was done in China, biasing the data towards a western perspective.

Bigger differences were found **within** cultures than **between** them, so cultural differences are not based on nationality.

Issues of ethnocentrism

The SSP specifically measures separation distress, safe base and stranger anxiety, suggesting that these behaviours are consistent indicators of the attachment type of the child.

However, this has been accused of being an **imposed etic**, which is the application of ideas and concepts developed in one culture to measure and explain behaviour in another. Different cultures value different kinds of behaviour, therefore childrearing practices will reflect this, so a child's behaviour in the SSP is a reflection of culture more than attachment.

Further research from alternative cultures

Mali McMahon-True et al. (2001)	Korea Kyoung (2005)	Australia Malin (1997)
• studied mother and infant pairs in rural Africa • found that 67% were securely attached despite extended daytime care by grandmother • SSP found no Type A, 8% Type C and 25% Type D	• used SSP to compare mother and infant pairs in USA with Korea • found that the percentage of Type B infants was very similar even though there were differences in the way the mums and babies interacted	• studied Aboriginal children in rural areas • found significantly different child-rearing practices • SSP showed lack of secure attachment

McMahon-True et al. (2001) and Kyoung (2005) show that SSP might be applicable across cultures, but Malin (1997) shows that it is not valid when child-rearing is very different.

Now try this

Compare and contrast the results from China and Britain based on Van Ijzendoorn and Kroonenberg's (1988) findings.

Bowlby: maternal deprivation

Bowlby's (1951) theory of maternal deprivation is distinct from his monotropic theory. It focuses on the effects of the absence of a mother or primary caregiver rather than the benefits of having one.

Bowlby's theory

Bowlby's theory of maternal deprivation claims that disruption of the attachment bond between infant and caregiver during the critical period (see page 39), even if only relatively short term, can cause serious and permanent damage to the emotional, social and intellectual development of the child.

The length of separation between child and caregiver, and the age at which it happens, affect the outcome for the child. Bowlby said that deprivation (separation either long or short term) of the mother could lead to **affectionless psychopathy**. This is a personality style characterised by a lack of empathy with/for others.

 Real world **Bowlby's influence**

Bowlby's research had a big impact on **economic activity** in post-war Britain. It seemed to provide scientific evidence that 'a mother's place was in the home', suggesting that mums should not have jobs if they cared about the emotional well-being of their children. This then cleared the workplace for returning soldiers.

However, it also led to a revolution in how children were cared for during separations, long or short term, from their parents, ensuring continuity of care for the child. For example, it has led to mother and baby units being created in the prison system, where women who are given custodial sentences are housed in specialist units with their young babies.

Different lengths of separation have different outcomes for the child.

Types of separation

Short term	• Separations are temporary and don't last long; children go through protest, despair and detachment (PDD model) which changes the nature of the relationship with their caregiver. • Support for this comes from Robertson and Robertson (1971), who found evidence for the PDD model in cases where infants were separated from their mothers for a week or so.
Long term	• Separations due to parental death, divorce or imprisonment can lead to long-term, negative effects for the child. • Bifulco et al. (1992) studied women who had undergone separation for more than a year from their mothers or their mother had died, and found that they had a 10% increased risk of depression and/or anxiety disorders as adults. This risk was highest in those who experienced separation before the age of 6, consistent with the critical period.

Evaluation

👍 Evidence from several studies, such as Robertson and Robertson (1971), Bifulco (1992) and Bowlby (1944), supports the theory. All show an increased risk of emotional problems linked to separation in early childhood.

👍 For ethical reasons research tends to use the case study method, which is high in ecological validity as the data is based on real lives.

👎 Interpretation of the data from case studies may be prone to bias due to possible subjective interpretation of the information.

👎 Not all children react to separation in the same way, so it is possible that the reason some develop emotional problems is due to other factors besides maternal deprivation.

 Key study **Bowlby's (1944) study of juvenile 'thieves'**

Aim: To investigate whether the causes of juvenile delinquency could be linked to maternal deprivation.

Procedure: Using case histories of patients at a clinic where he worked, Bowlby identified 44 who had been referred because of theft and 44 controls; all were emotionally maladjusted. He looked for signs of affectionless psychopathy in both groups and for evidence of maternal deprivation.

Findings: 14 of the 44 juvenile thieves displayed affectionless psychopathy and none of the control group did; 86% of the affectionless thieves had frequent separations from their mothers in early childhood. Separations were much less common amongst the other thieves or the control group.

Conclusion: Early childhood separations are linked to emotional maladjustments later in life.

Now try this

Based on Bowlby's ideas, what advice should be given to a judge trying a case of a pregnant woman regarding a prison sentence?

Romanian orphan studies

You need to be able to describe and evaluate the Romanian orphan studies and the effects of **institutionalisation** (being brought up in a hospital or orphanage).

Privation

Privation describes the situation where an infant is denied the opportunity to form an attachment with a caregiver. While it is unethical to create a situation like this, there are cases where this occurs. Psychologists research these to draw conclusions about attachment.

After the fall of the Romanian dictator Ceaușescu in 1989, the world was shocked to see the awful conditions in which thousands of institutionalised children were kept. They had very little care and spent a lot of time in caged beds.

Key study Rutter (1998)

Aim: To see if the experience of privation as a young infant could be overcome by sensitive care following adoption.

Procedure: This was a longitudinal study.

- Rutter tracked the development of 165 Romanian orphans adopted into UK families; 111 of them were under 2 years old at the time of adoption, the rest were under 4.

- Rutter recruited a comparison group of 52 British children adopted before the age of six months.

- He assessed the children's physical and cognitive progress at the outset and then every four years.

Findings: At the outset, the Romanian children were behind the UK children on all measures. Four years later, he found that most of the Romanian children had caught up physically and cognitively (especially those adopted by the age of six months).

Conclusion: Privation of infants due to institutionalisation can be recovered from if given sensitive high-quality care.

Evaluation

🖒 There were no records of how the children were treated in the orphanages. Some may have been given more care than others, perhaps because they were more responsive to the staff, and this might have protected them from the effects of privation. These individual differences between children have not been taken into account.

👍 Rutter's results are consistent with other case studies, such as Koluchova (1972), of twin boys in former Czechoslovakia who were rescued from abuse and neglect at age 7 and given good-quality care. The boys recovered and went on to develop normal relationships as adults.

Further research

☑ O'Connor (1999) found that orphans frequently showed **disinhibited attachments** where they developed indiscriminate attachments to strangers. This was especially true for those who had spent a long time in the institution.

☑ Rutter (2001) followed up the Romanian orphans at age 6 and found many of them had attachment problems.

☑ Rutter (2007) reviewed the orphans at age 11 and found that many had no ill effects but 50% of those who were shown at age 6 to have disinhibited attachments were still doing so.

Institutionalisation: conclusions

- Effects can be reduced or removed by providing high-quality, sensitive care for the children, especially through early adoption.

- For some children, there are permanent effects such as inappropriate familiarity towards strangers and clingy attention-seeking behaviour (O'Connor, 1999).

- Quinton (1984) found that women brought up in care were more likely to have their own children put into care.

Now try this

Summarise the procedure and results of Rutter's (1998) study of adopted Romanian orphans.

The influence on later relationships

Bowlby's idea of the **internal working model** (see page 39) suggests that the primary attachment relationship in childhood will act as a template for all future relationships, influencing how secure they are. This is known as the **continuity hypothesis**. You need to know how early attachment is reflected in later relationships.

Childhood relationships

Children with secure attachments will have an internal working model that reflects this, and so will expect that others will be friendly. This affects their friendships as they are more likely to be open and trusting with others.

Evaluation of childhood relationships

👍 Sroufe (2005) found that infants classified as securely attached were much more socially competent, being less likely to be isolated and more empathetic. This suggests that such children will be advantaged later in life.

🔍 Key study **Hazan and Shaver (1987)**

Aim: To see if the primary attachment relationship with parents is reflected in **adult relationships**.

Procedure: 620 people answered a 'love quiz' published in a local newspaper in the USA. The questionnaire was designed to establish the type of attachment people had with their parents and then the types of relationships as adults.

The researchers analysed the data to classify past and future relationships into different attachment types. To review attachment types, see page 40.

Findings:

Securely attached children tended to have long-lasting relationships that were happy.

- People classed as insecure-avoidant in childhood were more likely to doubt that love would last.

- Those classed as insecure-resistant were particularly vulnerable to being lonely (although this was also true of insecure-avoidant to a lesser degree).

Conclusions: The **continuity hypothesis** is supported as there was a correlation between early attachment type and adult relationship.

Evaluation of continuity hypothesis

👍 Hazan and Shaver (1987) can be criticised for lacking generalisability. The sample was self-selected and two-thirds female, meaning they may be unrepresentative.

👍 However, many other studies show similar findings. Kirkpatrick and Davis (1994) studied dating couples and found a positive correlation between early attachment and satisfaction with their current relationship.

👍 Other studies show that insecure attachment in infancy influences adult relationship behaviour. Brennan and Shaver (1995) found children with insecure-avoidant relationships more likely to engage in casual sex as adults.

👍 This research is consistent with Harlow's (1959) findings (see page 37) that the adult monkeys could not easily form normal relationships, including with their own babies. Human research conducted by Quinton (1984) found that mothers who lacked a secure attachment in their childhood also tended to lack one with their own children.

👎 Research does not show a conclusive link between the internal working model and adult behaviour. Steele (1998) found only a small correlation between childhood and adult attachments.

Now try this

Evaluate the claims that early childhood attachment types affect future relationships.

Exam skills 1

Before you look at these questions, remind yourself about caregiver–infant interactions on page 34, stages of attachment on page 35 and the role of the father on page 36.

Worked example

Put the following stages of attachment in the correct order. The first one has been done for you.

(3 marks)

Table 1 Stages of attachment

Stage	Order
pre-attachment	1
multiple attachment	4
discriminate attachment	3
indiscriminate attachment	2

> In this type of question, you simply have to put the right number in the box to show you understand the order of the stages of attachment.

> It helps if you know the age of the child as it goes through each stage.

Worked example

Read the item and answer the question that follows.

Amy is 6 months old. She is a happy child but seems happiest when with her mum, Caroline. Specifically, she seems to engage in conversations where she waits for Caroline to finish talking to her before she responds by vocalising and smiling. When Amy smiles, Caroline smiles back.

Identify an example each of reciprocity and of interactional synchrony.

(2 marks)

Interactional synchrony is shown when Amy waits for Caroline to finish talking before she responds. Reciprocity is shown when Amy smiles and Caroline smiles back.

> Here, you need to identify examples of interactional synchrony and reciprocity. In other questions, you may be required to describe and apply them.

> Give your answer in full sentences, not bullet points.

Worked example

Some theorists have described fathers as a biological necessity but a social irrelevance.

Outline findings from research into the role of fathers in the development of attachment.

(6 marks)

Schaffer and Emerson (1964) found that infants were not as likely to show attachment to their dads as they do to their mums. Only 3% of infants had their fathers as first attachment compared with 65% who had their mothers.

Hermann (1994) found that dads are not as responsive to their infants. This will affect the development of an attachment relationship as it requires sensitive responsiveness. If dads are not as able to pick up cues they will not be as sensitive. However, Lamb (1987) found that in single parent families where the dad is the parent, they are more responsive to the distress of the infant. Lucassen (2011) found that men who do display sensitive responsiveness to their infants develop a more secure attachment.

> You are asked to focus on research findings, so you do not need to give any procedural detail of the studies. You are also asked for more than one study. Each finding must relate to fathers **and** attachment.

> The opening is appropriate and detailed and focused on the role of fathers.

> Hermann's study is relevant and linked to attachment.

> This is a good answer. It covers four studies, all of which are linked to attachment. A balanced account is provided with evidence that shows attachment with dads happens or that it is less likely to happen than it does with mums.

Exam skills 2

These are examples of some of the types of questions you might be asked on learning theory and attachment. Look at pages 37–39 to remind yourself about these topics.

Worked example

Read the item and then answer the question that follows.

Harry has noticed that his baby son Kye does not seem to respond to him in the same way as he does to his mum, Ayesha. Harry has been working long hours to bring in extra money and has had very little physical contact with his son, leaving all the feeding and caregiving to Ayesha.

Using concepts drawn from learning theory, explain why Kye might show more attachment to his mum than to his dad.

(4 marks)

Kye prefers his mum because she feeds him. Food is an unconditioned stimulus that brings about a pleasant feeling of relief from hunger (unconditioned response). Because Ayesha is feeding him, Kye associates her with the food and she becomes a conditioned stimulus, leading to pleasant feelings in the baby. Harry does not feed or look after Kye, so Kye has not learned to associate him with anything and therefore does not show pleasure in his company.

This is a rudimentary but relevant point, and so it is a good start.

This shows an appropriate use of **key terms**, which needs to be linked to Kye's behaviour.

The terms are now **linked** to explain the baby's feelings for his mother.

This is a good **explanation** that links why Kye shows more attachment to mum than to dad.

Here the student has used classical conditioning to answer the question. If the question was longer, it would be good to be able to add operant conditioning, using the key terms of positive and negative reinforcement.

Worked example

Evaluate learning theory as an explanation of attachment in infants.

(6 marks)

Animal studies do not support learning theory as an explanation for attachment. Harlow (1959) found that infant monkeys would attach to a surrogate wire mother covered in cloth in preference to a wire mother that contained milk, suggesting that attachment is based on comfort and love rather than as a result of having your physical needs such as provision of food met. Lorenz (1935) also showed that newly hatched geese instinctively attached to the first moving object they encountered, suggesting the behaviour is innate and not learned. Schaffer and Emerson (1964) found that infants form multiple attachments, including to those that do not feed them. This suggests that the emotional component is more important than a simple association between caregiver and the provision of food.

When **evaluating** any theory you should / could:

- provide evidence from research that supports and/or refutes it
- compare it with another theory that explains the same thing (e.g. Bowlby's 1969 monotropic theory) to successfully explain events in real life.

In all cases, you must ensure that you are using evaluative language and that you link the point directly back to an aspect of the theory.

This uses clear evaluative language to introduce the findings of three studies, outlines the findings effectively and concisely, and finally links back to the claim of learning theory. This is a good answer.

Exam skills 3

You need to know about Bowlby's two theories: **monotropy** and **deprivation**. Although there are overlapping concepts, they are distinct theories and you need to be able to explain these. Look at page 39 to find out about monotropy and page 42 for deprivation.

Worked example

Describe and evaluate Bowlby's monotropic theory of attachment.

(16 marks)

Bowlby believed that children need to form one important relationship during the critical period of early childhood. This is a monotropic relationship based on innate behaviour as children are born equipped to form such a relationship by using social releasers to attract attention from caregivers and make them respond to their needs. Caregivers display sensitive responsiveness to the infant's needs and in this way they build a relationship that goes on to act as an internal working model for future relationships. Bowlby suggested that this one important relationship will be a template for all others.

This theory is supported by animal studies such as Lorenz (1935) who found that geese show innate attachment behaviour, but geese are very different from human infants so may behave very differently. However, Harlow's (1959) research on rhesus monkeys show that monkeys, an animal more similar to humans, fail to form appropriate relationships in the future when they have no monotropic relationship in infancy, supporting the idea of the internal working model developing as a result of the attachment relationship. Human studies also show support for the theory. For example, Hazan and Shaver (1975) found that the type of attachment adults had as children was reflected in their adult relationship. This shows that Bowlby's idea that an internal working model is shaped by the attachment relationship is valid.

However, his claim that the child forms only one important relationship is challenged by Schaffer and Emerson (1964) who found that the vast majority of infants had multiple attachments beyond that with the primary caregiver. Further studies have found that even when deprived of a monotropic relationship during early childhood, children can recover if given appropriate care. For example, the Czech twins were not rescued and given care until they were 7, but both now have formed good relationships with others, suggesting that the critical period is not as important as Bowlby thought.

You should balance the description with the evaluation. However, evaluation points must be linked and expanded on, so this should take more time and space.

Apply AO1 **descriptive** skills to begin with. Start with the claim of the theory (infants have an innate mechanism that leads to attachment) and then describe and link the key concepts together to form the theory, including monotropy, social releasers, critical period, sensitive responsiveness and internal working model.

Effective use of **terminology** is a key feature of a top band essay. Make sure that you are using the terms appropriately throughout your answer.

For **evaluation**, a range of detailed and appropriate points should be made, backed up with examples or evidence. State whether the evidence supports or refutes the theory, then detail the findings and finally link this to the theory.

It is a good idea to include negative evaluation points as this provides a balanced answer, though it is not a requirement in this essay. You could be asked for strengths and weaknesses in other questions.

Remember: your answer should be clear, coherent and focused on Bowlby's monotropic theory.

Exam-style practice 1

Practise for Paper 1 of your A level exam with these exam-style questions. There are answers on pages 293–294. Before looking at these questions, it would be helpful to revise cultural variations in attachment.

1 Which of the following was found by Van Ijzendoorn and Kroonenberg (1988)? Shade **one** box only.

   A The least common form of attachment is secure across all cultures. ⬭

   B There were bigger differences within cultures than between them. ⬭

   C Japanese children showed high levels of insecure-avoidant attachment. ⬭

   D British children had the lowest levels of secure attachment. ⬭

   (1 mark)

> In the exam, make sure you read the instructions carefully. In this case, be careful to indicate only **one** answer.

2 Outline the findings of van Ijzendoorn and Kroonenberg's (1988) cross-cultural study of attachment types. **(4 marks)**

> This question asks you to focus on the **findings** of the study. You should broady consider the **results** and **conclusions** drawn from the research rather than going into a lot of detail.

3 Ainsworth and Bell (1978) developed the Strange Situation Procedure (SSP) in order to investigate and categorise different attachment styles. They used a controlled observation technique.

> You need to define **controlled observation** and provide sufficient information to gain both marks.

   (a) What is meant by a controlled observation? **(2 marks)**

> **Outline** means to briefly describe something, so identify the issue clearly and add limited detail.
>
> One issue you could consider is the **validity** of the technique in finding natural behaviour in the participants.

   (b) Identify **and** outline **one** issue (other than ethical) that might arise from the use of a controlled observation. **(2 marks)**

4 Outline the key behavioural characteristics of :

   (a) a securely attached infant. **(2 marks)**

   (b) an insecure avoidant infant. **(2 marks)**

   (c) an insecure resistant infant. **(2 marks)**

> For both marks you need to ensure that more than one characteristic is provided, or that you have done one in depth.

> Try to link the infant's behaviour to what happens at separation and reunion with the primary caregiver.

5 Discuss cross-cultural variations in attachment. **(16 marks)**

> An AO1 paragraph will feature details of the findings of appropriate studies, such as **Van Ijzendoorn and Kroonenberg (1988)**, and outline differences between cultures. It should include good use of terminology.
>
> AO3 paragraph(s) will outline explanations for the differences in attachment. You should focus on **evaluating** the study/ies, e.g. the use of the SSP may lead to ethnocentric bias, with a good **explanation** of why this may be the case by drawing on **examples** from different cultures.
>
> Further AO3 points could include the fact that Van Ijzendoorn and Kroonenberg found that there were more differences **within** cultures than there were **between** them, and why this might be a problem for the research.

Exam-style practice 2

Practise for Paper 1 of your A level exam with these exam-style questions. There are answers on page 294. Before looking at these questions, it would be helpful to revise the section on research methods.

6 Research into attachment relies heavily on the observational method.
Define the following terms.

(a) Event sampling
(b) Time sampling
(c) Covert observation **(3 marks)**

> This question calls for simple definitions. As each is for only one mark, these can be quite basic.

7 Schaffer and Emerson's (1964) Glasgow study aimed to track the development of attachment.

> This question requires you to **apply in context**. This means you must refer to an appropriate aspect of the Schaffer study.

(a) This study was longitudinal. Explain this term in the context of the study. **(2 marks)**

(b) How was the strength of the attachments measured in this study? **(2 marks)**

> Here, you need to show understanding of the results and how the researchers operationalised the dependent variable.

(c) Data was gathered by self-report and by interviews with the mothers. Explain **one** strength and **one** weakness of this method of data-gathering. **(4 marks)**

> There is no need to refer to the study in this case, as the question requires an **evaluation** of gathering self-report data via interviews. However, it would be entirely acceptable to use the study to **illustrate** your points.

8 Identify **and** outline problems that researchers might encounter when investigating very young infants. **(4 marks)**

> This question calls for more than one problem to be explained. You could focus on the **ethical issues** of studying children and the **issues of interpreting behaviour** of children in order to draw conclusions about the child's **motivations**.

9 According to Bowlby, 'motherlove in infancy is as important for psychological development as are vitamins and minerals for physical development'. Explain what Bowlby meant by this statement. **(6 marks)**

> This question is asking you to use **Bowlby's theory** to explain the importance of attachment relationships. A good answer will draw on research into both **monotropy** and **deprivation**.

Definitions of abnormality 1

In psychology, increasing attention is being paid to understanding the **differences between individuals**. Psychopathology looks at mental and behavioural disorders. Any behaviour that varies from the **social norm** is considered abnormal. You need to be able to explain and evaluate the **definitions of abnormality**.

Deviation from social norms

This explanation attempts to draw a line between what societies deem acceptable behaviour by their members and that which is seen as unacceptable or irrational. The behaviour has to go beyond eccentric and be seen to have a negative impact on a person's existence. It also has to persist so that the person is always behaving oddly.

Evaluation

👍 The behaviour is seen within a context so it can be judged more holistically. Being naked would be normal on a nudist beach but not in wider society.

👍 Definitions of abnormality can adapt with age. A toddler who bites another small child is naughty, but an adult who bites another is abnormal.

👍 The abnormal behaviour is visible to others. It helps to identify people who need help and gets them the right support.

👍 Deviation from social norms is an example of the **individual differences** approach, which looks at each individual in their own right without making generalisations.

👎 It is very subjective and depends on who is making the judgement. It could be a medical professional or someone using power to control those seen as threatening to society. The line between abnormality and illness is usually drawn when the person becomes a danger to themselves or others.

👎 The change in attitudes in any society is volatile and over time the change can be immense. Homosexuality was a crime until the 1960s and a mental disorder until 2000.

👎 Ethnocentric bias may affect perceptions of normality within a society that has ethnic minorities, or across cultures from East to West.

Statistical norms definition of abnormality

The standard deviation can be used to plot anyone's results on any test against the norm for that behaviour. For example, a person could take Beck's Depression Inventory (see page 57). Their score can then be compared to give the clinician a good idea of the severity of this person's mental illness.

Statistical abnormality is defined using the **normal distribution curve**. About 68% of the population lie between −1 and +1 standard deviation (SD) around the mean and are considered 'normal' people. People who fall between 1 and 2 SDs around the mean would be classed as unusual; those at the extremes (±3 SDs) would be abnormal.

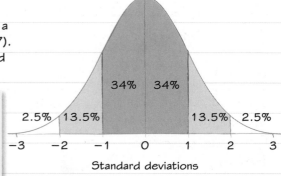

34% 34%

2.5% 13.5% 13.5% 2.5%

−3 −2 −1 0 1 2 3

Standard deviations

Evaluation

👍 It uses an objective point of two standard deviations to define abnormal behaviour.

👍 It is used to measure normal development in children against the normal percentile.

👍 It uses scores on well-established standardised tests so it is objective and more scientific.

👎 Some abnormal behaviour is desirable, such as genius level IQ.

👎 A person's scores (e.g. on a depression inventory) are based on self-reports. These are subjective despite the overall test being reliable.

👎 The definition does not consider any cultural factors that might be affecting behaviour.

Now try this

Explain how deviation from social norms can be used to diagnose someone as mentally ill.

Definitions of abnormality 2

The two definitions – **failure to function adequately** and **deviation from ideal mental health** – can be considered alongside each other. You need to know their similarities and differences.

 Key study ## Failure to function adequately

Rosenhan and Seligman's (1989) seven features of **personal dysfunction** describe when a person is unable to cope with ordinary life.

1 Personal distress – feeling upset

2 Maladaptive behaviour – behaving oddly

3 Unpredictability – erratic behaviour

4 Irrationality – doing illogical things

5 Observer discomfort – others don't like what we are doing

6 Violation of moral standards – breaking society's taboos

7 Unconventionality – not following normal standards

Clinical psychologists use the Global Assessment of Functioning (GAF) scale to assess the level of functioning on social, occupational and psychological levels.

Evaluation

👍 This puts the personal experience of the client at its heart.

👍 The GAF scale can be used to assess the severity of the condition.

👍 The list is of behaviours that can be seen by an observer – not cognitions, which would be invisible.

👎 Sometimes it is normal to be distressed, for example after bereavement.

👎 What is considered normal functioning depends on culture.

👎 It is subjective and depends on an observer's point of view.

 Real world ## Labelling

It is all too easy to put a label on someone who is behaving oddly or failing to cope. We might call them depressed or psychotic. These labels are useful in the clinician's surgery where they will be applied to provide the correct treatment. In the real world, however, they often have a stigma attached, affecting prospects of getting work and maybe forming and keeping relationships. Psychiatrists are justifiably cautious in diagnosing people because they know this is an issue.

 Key study ## Deviation from ideal mental health

Marie Jahoda (1958) suggested a set of criteria for ideal mental health. An absence of any of these healthy characteristics indicates that a person is abnormal, or **deviating from ideal mental health**.

1 We are symptom-free

2 We are rational

3 We are self-actualised (we have achieved our potential)

4 We are unstressed

5 We are realistic

6 We have good self-esteem

A mentally ill person would lack some or all of these characteristics.

Evaluation

👍 This is a holistic approach, looking at many variables.

👍 It is very positive and can be used to set goals for the person to achieve.

👎 It is subjective and not well-defined – what is a realistic view of the world?

👎 It varies over time and between cultures. For example, we see independence as healthy; collectivist cultures such as North Korea would not.

👎 Most people do not self-actualise but we would not say they are abnormal.

👎 Most people do not meet all the criteria but we would not say they are abnormal. So the definition cannot truly identify those who are abnormal.

Now try this

Outline **two** limitations of the deviation from mental health definition of abnormality.

Phobias

Phobias are classed as **anxiety disorders**. Anxiety is a natural response to a perceived threat, but a **phobia** is an irrational, persistent and extreme fear of something. It compels you to avoid it, despite reassurance that it is harmless. It goes beyond normal fear of real danger. You need to know how people feel, think and behave when they have this disorder.

Emotional

The phobic person has:
- feelings of panic or anxiety when in the presence of or in anticipation of meeting the feared object
- an immediate fear response, or a panic attack, cued by a specific situation or object.

Cognitive

These include:
- irrational thoughts – you are not in any danger but you believe you are
- resistance to logic – the facts do not convince you
- self-awareness – you know you have a phobia and you are being irrational
- cognitive distortion – seeing things as ugly when they are not.

Behavioural

These include:
- avoidance – running away
- freezing – an ancient response to a predator
- fainting – loss of blood pressure
- fight-or-flight response – a big adrenaline surge causing raised heart rate, nausea, breathing difficulties (see page 85).

Characteristics

A phobic person can have a high anxiety response to a feared object or situation.

DSM-5 categorisation of phobias

All phobias are characterised by an extreme and irrational response to a stimulus. The DSM-5 (see page 53) recognises three categories:

1 Specific phobia – phobia of an object such as an animal or insect

2 Social phobia – social anxiety, such as public speaking

3 Agoraphobia – fear of being outside in public places.

Prevalence of phobias in the population

Real world

The three most frequently occurring phobias with their prevalence in the population

social phobia, e.g. fear of public speaking	17.2%
agoraphobia (see below)	9.9%
specific phobia, e.g. arachnophobia (fear of spiders)	0.75%

(Source: *National Phobics Society survey 2005/06*)

Agoraphobia

Agoraphobia is a fear (phobia) of being in crowds or public places. When in these situations, the person must engage in avoidance behaviours to avoid the fear and/or a related panic attack. The diagnostic criteria for agoraphobia are listed in DSM-5.

Agoraphobia develops between the ages of 18 and 35 with either a sudden or gradual onset; two-thirds of sufferers are women. Most people develop agoraphobia after a spontaneous panic attack. It is the most disabling phobia and treatment is difficult.

Now try this

A fellow student has described feeling irrational fear when in the presence of spiders. Despite telling himself that they are harmless and knowing that he is being irrational, he is unable to stop the fear. He sees spiders as hideous and dangerous even when they are not. Which characteristics of phobias is he describing?

Depression

Depression is a long-term mood or **affective disorder** that severely disrupts daily functioning. It comes in several forms, the most common types being **unipolar** and **bipolar depression**. (The DSM-5 does not use these categories but they are still in common use with clinicians.)

Emotional

Sufferers may experience:
- feelings of sadness
- loss of interest in things usually enjoyable (anhedonia)
- feelings of emptiness
- feelings of hopelessness
- low self-esteem
- despair
- feelings of anger against the world or turned inwards.

Cognitive

Sufferers may experience:
- negative self-belief
- negative self-concept
- feelings of guilt
- recurrent thoughts of death or suicidal ideation.

Characteristics of major (unipolar) depression

Behavioural

These include:
- reduced activity and energy
- tiredness
- agitation
- restlessness
- sometimes wringing their hands or tearing at their skin
- sleeping too much or too little
- eating too much or too little.

With severe depression, a person loses all enjoyment of life. Angelina Jolie battled bouts of depression through her teenage years.

Features of depression

- Only 2% of the population experience a depressive episode without 'co-morbid' anxiety (occurring at the same time).
- Depression tends to recur in most people. More than half of people who have one episode of depression will have another, while those who have a second episode have a further relapse risk of 70%.
- After a third episode, the relapse risk is 90%.
- For about one in five people, the condition is chronic.

(Source: Mental Health Foundation 2007)

Bipolar depression

Bipolar depression is less common. Sufferers experience alternating manic episodes with high energy and reckless behaviour, delusions and 'highs' in addition to the symptoms of unipolar depression.

 Prevalence of depression in the UK

More women than men are affected. In a 2013 ONS report, 19% of people aged 16 and over reported symptoms of mild mental illness (including depression). Signs were reported by:
- 27% of divorced or separated respondents
- 20% of single respondent single
- 16% of married respondents or those in a civil partnership

(Source: ONS (2013), cited in BPS report 2013)

DSM-5 and ICD-10 criteria for major depression

The DSM (the American Psychiatric Association's Diagnostic and Statistical Manual of Mental Disorders) and WHO's ICD-10 are used to classify mental disorders using sets of diagnostic criteria. In general, for a diagnosis of major depression, symptoms as described above must be present almost every day for at least two weeks. Four symptoms present suggest mild depression, five or six symptoms suggest moderate depression, and seven or more – with or without psychotic symptoms – suggest severe depression.

Now try this

How are different levels of depression diagnosed?

Obsessive compulsive disorder

Obsessive compulsive disorder (OCD) is an anxiety disorder characterised by obsessive thoughts and repetitive compulsive behaviours. OCD usually begins in teenage years or early adulthood and appears to run in families, suggesting a genetic link. It is equally common in males and females.

Emotional

These may include:
- feelings of anxiety and distress generally about the condition
- feelings of embarrassment because clients know they are behaving oddly
- feelings of disgust at the thought of touching things if they are worried about germs. For example, touching a toilet.

Characteristics of OCD

Behavioural

- These involve compulsions, which are repetitive behaviours such as hand-washing, counting and praying. Sufferers feel that they have to perform these actions or something terrible will happen, and this creates anxiety.
- Compulsions reduce anxiety, so carrying out the behaviour is repeated over and over again.
- The behaviours intrude on normal life, and when bad can prevent a person carrying out daily activities, such as going to work.

Cognitive

- Obsessions, which are the thoughts sufferers feel, are intrusive and dominating. They may also be frightening. For example, a person may obsess that they left a door or window open and that someone will get in and attack them.
- The sufferer can recognise that their thoughts are irrational or unreasonable.
- They may be hyper-vigilant, always looking for disasters that could happen.

People with trichotillomania compulsively pull out their hair

DSM-5 categories of OCD

The DSM-5 diagnostic system recognises several disorders characterised by obsessional thinking and compulsive behaviour, including:

- ✓ OCD as described on this page
- ✓ trichotillomania – compulsive hair pulling
- ✓ hoarding disorder – compulsive keeping of possessions and random objects and distress on parting with them
- ✓ excoriation disorder – compulsive skin-picking.

🌐 Real world Prevalence of OCD

In the UK, current estimates suggest that 12 out of every 1000 people will have OCD. This means 1.2 per cent of the total population is affected. More importantly, almost 50 per cent of OCD cases, a very high proportion, will fall in the 'severe' category. Cases considered 'mild' constitute less than a quarter of the total presented. These numbers have led to suggestions that nearly 2–3% of patients visiting their GPs suffer from OCD.

(Based on *OCD-UK 2013*)

Extend Contributory factors

Genetic: OCD is a highly heritable condition.

Neurobiological: Characteristic neuropsychological profiles have been found in children and adults who are diagnosed with OCD.

Environmental: The role of environmental factors remains unclear, with conflicting evidence regarding environmental triggers such as social isolation and physical abuse.

Individual: Personality traits such as perfectionism, rigidity, high personal expectations and low self-esteem are considered risk factors.

(Source: *Clinical review GP online May 2015*)

Now try this

Describe **one** example of an obsession and **one** example of a compulsion suffered by a person with OCD.

The two-process model of phobias

The two processes in the model are **classical conditioning (CC)** and **operant conditioning (OC)**. Both have been used to explain how phobias form. Behaviourists explain all phobias as learned through association or an experience (CC) and maintained through reinforcement (OC). You need to know how each plays a part in initiating and maintaining a phobia.

Classical conditioning (CC)

A phobia is **initiated** by an association between a neutral stimulus and a feared object. The feared object is the unconditioned stimulus. Over just one (if it is frightening enough) or several pairings, the person will learn a phobia of the neutral stimulus, which then becomes the conditioned stimulus. Remind yourself of Pavlov's (1927) work classically conditioning dogs (see page 67).

Operant conditioning (OC)

A fear is **maintained** by negative reinforcement. Escaping or avoiding the feared object is rewarding, so you keep on doing it. There is also the possibility that being frightened gets attention, which could be positively reinforcing. See page 68 for more on reinforcement in operant conditioning.

Sleeping with the light on is a way of avoiding a fear of the dark. The light acts as a positive reinforcer and maintains the phobia.

🔍 Key study   Little Albert

John Watson and Rosalie Rayner (1920) created a phobia in Albert.

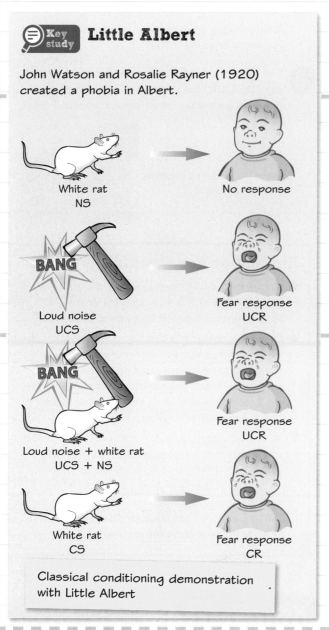

White rat
NS
→ No response

Loud noise
UCS
→ Fear response
UCR

Loud noise + white rat
UCS + NS
→ Fear response
UCR

White rat
CS
→ Fear response
CR

Classical conditioning demonstration with Little Albert

⤴ Extend   Biological preparedness

Biological preparedness is another explanation from an evolutionary perspective. This idea sees us as being prepared to avoid those things that could have harmed us in our evolutionary past such as snakes and spiders. These ancient fears or instincts are still within us today. Hence, we are far more likely to develop phobias of creatures rather than cars, even though cars are more likely to hurt us. For more on the role of evolution, see page 71.

Evaluation

👍 A phobic person often knows of a specific incident that started the phobia, lending support to classical conditioning.

👎 However, as this is not always the case, biological preparedness or modelling could be a better answer.

👍 The application of this model to therapy through systematic desensitisation and flooding lend support to it.

👎 It ignores cognitive factors such as selective attention to the phobic stimulus, irrational beliefs and cognitive distortions.

Now try this

Describe **one** alternative explanation for phobias.

 This could be social learning theory (see page 69) as well as biological preparedness.

Behavioural treatments for phobias

Systematic desensitisation (SD)

SD was developed by Wolpe in 1958 and is now the main behaviourist treatment for phobias. Phobic people typically avoid the feared stimulus. SD teaches the client to **relax** and then progressively face a **hierarchy** of fears (see below). The client associates the positive feelings of relaxation with the feared object.

This treatment is based on the principles of classical conditioning (see page 67).

How SD works

Over many sessions the therapist and client meet and work through the therapy. It requires commitment and determination to be successful.

1 The client is taught progressive relaxation techniques (working round muscle groups and relaxing them one by one).

2 The therapist and client construct a hierarchy of fears about the object, from the least to most feared representation. These are then imagined by the client.

3 The client starts with the least feared representation and uses a fear thermometer to indicate how relaxed they feel in its presence.

4 The client moves up the hierarchy, slowly relaxing at each stage.

5 They face the most feared representation successfully.

Steps 2–5

Fear ⟶ · Time ⟶

Flooding

Flooding was invented by Thomas Stampfl in 1967. This approach attempts to remove phobias by directly facing them. It floods the client with the fear while supporting them in lowering their arousal until they feel calm in the presence of the feared object or place.

This treatment is based on the classical conditioning principles of association (see page 67).

How flooding works

1 The client is taught progressive relaxation techniques until successful.

　　Alternatively they may be put into a light hypnotic trance.

2 The client is faced with their most feared situation with the therapist and over one long session learns to lower their panic and relax.

London Zoo offers hypnosis for arachnophobias.

Evaluation for flooding

👍 Cheaper than SD and quicker. Wolpe (1960) drove a girl with a fear of cars around for four hours until her panic was eradicated.

👍 Evidence suggests the two treatments are equally effective. For example, Craske et al. (2008) reviewed several studies that tested this and found little difference. Thus, on a cost–benefit analysis, flooding would be the treatment of choice.

👎 It can be seen as quite unethical even if the client has consented, and could be badly tolerated. If the client is unable to stick with it until the fear is eradicated, it could actually make them worse. Clients often go on to develop new phobias, so anxiety is transferred rather than cured.

Evaluation for SD

👍 It works for those who can learn to relax and imagine their fears while doing so.

👍 It works best with the actual object, such as tiny spiders, working up to the tarantula.

👍 The 'Little Peter' (Jones, 1924) case study supports SD when he successfully reversed a phobia of a white rabbit using food rewards. Little Peter lost his fear of the rabbit gradually, eventually stroking him on his lap.

👎 It works well for simple phobias but not so well for agoraphobia or social phobia.

👎 It is more ethical than flooding but may still cause distress.

Now try this

Outline systematic desensitisation as a treatment for a phobia.

Beck's negative triad

You need to know how depression is explained from a **cognitive perspective**. There are two theorists, Beck (1987) and Ellis (1957). Although they take slightly different approaches, they both see depression as rooted in faulty thinking. Ellis's model of depression is explained on page 58.

 Key study ## Beck's (1987) model

All these negative thoughts are **automatic** regardless of reality.

| **Negative views of the world** |
| 'No-one likes me because I am so worthless. People avoid me.' |

Beck's cognitive theory sees depressed people thinking in a **negative triad** of core beliefs and automatic thoughts.

| **Negative views of the self** |
| 'I am just pointless.' |
| 'I am worthless.' |

| **Negative views of the future** |
| 'I am always going to be like this, nothing will change.' |

The cognitive approach sees depression as being the result of developing poor coping mechanisms through upbringing. **Negative thinking** is triggered later by a stressor, which could be exams, family break-up or bereavement. Personality factors interact with the stressor. The negative thinking is not the cause but it perpetuates the depression through creating negative self-schemas (packets of information and ideas gained through experience).

Evaluation

👍 In a review of 180 articles, Ernst (1985) reported 91% supported Beck's theory and 9% did not. Of these, 150 specifically supported the cognitive triad idea within the theory.

👍 Boury et al. (2001) found Beck's depression inventory scores significantly correlated with automatic thoughts and number of core beliefs, supporting Beck's assumptions that negative thought content characterises depression.

👍 Bates et al. (1999) got 79 non-depressed individuals to read lots of self-statements that were negative (experimental group) or neutral (control group). The negative statements created

a depressed mood state, supporting the idea that exposure to negativity affects mood.

👎 Does not explain all types of depression such as bipolar disorder (see page 53).

👎 Someone with major depression may not feel sad and may experience psychosis, which suggests another cause.

👎 The evidence linking negative thinking to depression is correlational. There is a relationship between inventory scores and the level of depression but this is not causal evidence. There could be an inherited biological or genetic predisposition to depression in the family, for example.

 ## Cognitive biases

Cognitive biases are thinking errors seen in depressed people, which perpetuate their illness.

- **Black or white thinking** – no grey areas, everything has to be perfect or we are a failure.

- **Overgeneralising** – a person may see a single, unpleasant event as part of a never-ending pattern of defeat.

- **Blaming** – we hold other people responsible for our pain or we blame ourselves. In reality, there is no blame.

- **'Shoulds'** – 'I really should exercise. I shouldn't be so lazy.' You don't exercise and then you feel angry with yourself.

 ## Beck's depression inventory (BDI-II)

The inventory has 21 groups of statements. This self-report is used diagnostically by doctors to assess the seriousness of the depression. Here is an example:

Item 7: Self-dislike
0 I feel the same about myself as ever
1 I have lost confidence in myself
2 I am disappointed in myself
3 I dislike myself

Scores up to 30 cover mild to moderate depression. Scores over 30 are severe depression.

Now try this

Outline Beck's negative triad.

Ellis's ABC model

A second **cognitive** explanation for depression is Ellis's (1962) **ABC model**. In this model, **activating events** are situations in which **irrational thoughts** are triggered. For Ellis, an irrational thought is one that stops us feeling happy and content.

Ellis's (1962) ABC model

Ellis's explanation from a cognitive approach also sees irrational thinking as the root cause of maintaining a depressed state. If you were not depressed, you would not think like this. The cognitive approach is based on scientific principles and can be objectively tested. For example, clients with depression have been shown to selectively attend to negative stimuli.

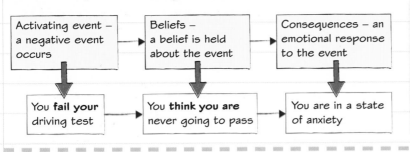

Activating event – a negative event occurs	→	Beliefs – a belief is held about the event	→	Consequences – an emotional response to the event
↓		↓		↓
You **fail your** driving test	→	You **think you are** never going to pass	→	You are in a state of anxiety

Unlike Beck's model where negative thinking is automatic, Ellis sees **activating events** as having consequences. These are affected by our beliefs. Not everyone will think like this. It depends on the level of the emotional response in the consequence whether this will trigger depression.

Evaluation

👍 Many people become depressed because of events such as marriage breakdown, loss of a job or baby or failure in an exam. This is called a **reactive depression** and the model works well.

👍 Ellis's idea of irrational beliefs can be used in cognitive behavioural therapy (CBT) where it is powerful and effective (see page 59). This suggests he is right about how depression is caused.

🖐 It does not explain all types of depression (see page 53). Major (unipolar) depressions often have no obvious trigger.

🖐 It cannot explain why some people experience psychotic symptoms when depressed. Bipolar depression is sometimes associated with psychosis in which people experience hallucinations or hear voices.

🖐 It does not really account for why people often recover on their own, without therapy, over time.

⤴Extend Internal and external locus of control (LoC)

People with an internal LoC believe that only they are responsible for their successes and failures, no one else. External locus people trust to luck or see fate having a hand in their lives. See page 9 for more about LoC.

Twenge et al. (2004) conducted a meta-analysis of 97 samples of college students ($n = 18\,310$). They concluded that college students in 2002 had a more external LoC than 80% of college students in the early 1960s. They found that externality is correlated with poor school achievement, helplessness and depression. Cognitive theory would predict that being fatalistic would tend to breed negative thoughts about your chances in life.

⤴Extend Findings from neuroscience

Using fMRI scans of 27 females, Beevers et al. (2010) found that different brain areas were active in patients with low levels of depression than those with high levels of depression when presented with happy or sad faces. There was no difference when looking at neutral stimuli.

They concluded that people with depression have difficulty activating areas of the brain associated with cognitive control of emotional information in the lateral prefrontal cortex and superior parietal regions. This would support Ellis's ideas that depression pre-sets people to think negatively.

Now try this

Identify **one** difference and **one** similarity between Beck's model and Ellis's explanation of how depression occurs.

Treating depression

Cognitive behavioural therapy (CBT) is the most widely used and well-researched cognitive treatment for depression. For each of the cognitive explanations, Beck and Ellis have a treatment therapy that is slightly different but would still be described as CBT. CBT is effective because it works on both thoughts and behaviour together.

Beck's cognitive therapy (CBT)

This attempts to identify the automatic thoughts that drive depression.

Abnormal behaviour is caused by disordered **automatic** thought processes relating to the **negative triad**.

⬇

Clients identify irrational thoughts with the therapist called **cognitive biases**, such as:
- **overgeneralisation** – sweeping generalisation about one failure meaning constant failure
- **minimising and maximising** – minimising successes and maximising failures.

⬇

The therapist offers alternatives and challenges the automatic thoughts. For example, the therapist might ask: 'Where is the evidence for the belief? Is it logical to think like that and is it helpful to think like that?'

⬇

Client as scientist – clients are set tasks to record when they enjoyed something or when someone gave them a compliment.
This is to get the client a more rational view of their lives.

⬇

Behavioural activation is used where the client is encouraged to take small steps to increase their level of enjoyable activities.

Ellis's rational emotive behaviour therapy (REBT)

This attempts to challenge irrational thoughts.

Abnormal behaviour is caused by people's view of things.

⬇

Ellis identifies 11 **musturbatory** beliefs that are emotionally damaging. For example:
- 'I must be loved'
- 'I must be excellent in all respects'.
Trying to live up to these ideals is stressful.

⬇

The therapist challenges these beliefs through **reframing** – suggesting more realistic and positive ways of looking at life events.

⬇

Clients practise positive and optimistic thinking. There are usually around 12 sessions. In this education phase, clients learn about the links between their thoughts, emotions and behaviour.

⬇

Behavioural activation and pleasant event scheduling is used to get the client out and about again, such as planning a trip to the cinema. Goals are set to boost self-esteem where the therapist is confident the client will succeed. These involve challenging negative beliefs such as thinking they could not manage a bus journey by actually doing one.

Support for the effectiveness of cognitive behavioural treatments

- 👍 March et al. (2007) compared CBT with antidepressant drug therapy alone and then together. They found that after 36 weeks, 81% of the CBT group, 81% of the antidepressant group and 86% of the combined group of 327 depressed adolescents were significantly improved.

- 👍 CBT works relatively fast and is therefore cost-effective but it relies on well-trained therapists for its effectiveness.

Points against the effectiveness of cognitive treatments

- 👎 Ethics of protection – Ellis advocated a strongly challenging approach; not all clients could take this.

- 👎 We do not really know whether irrational thinking is the cause or the effect of depression. There is a correlation and that is all.

- 👎 Embling (2002) showed that not all depressed clients benefit from CBT. Personality factors such as perfectionism and external locus of control can hinder its effectiveness.

Now try this

Outline Ellis's rational emotive behaviour therapy (REBT) as it would be experienced by a depressed client.

Biological explanations of OCD

The biological approach emphasises the role of abnormal physical functions in explaining behaviour, in this case OCD. Two possible biological explanations are **genetic transmission** and **damage to neural mechanisms**. You need to be able to describe, evaluate and apply these explanations.

Genetic explanations

OCD appears to run in families. Research over the years with twin and family studies has put its heritability at around 45%. See van Grootheest et al. (2005) below.

The **diathesis-stress model** suggests that there may be characteristics that are inherited then switched on by a stressful event later in life.

Several genes have been identified as relevant; they are called **candidate genes**.
For example, OCD may be associated with a rare combination of two mutations within the human serotonin transporter gene (hSERT).

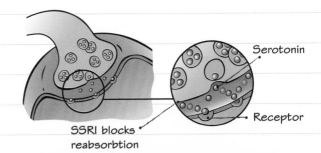

Serotonin

SSRI blocks reabsorbtion

Receptor

Low levels of serotonin at the synapse are known to create low mood. As in depression, using SSRIs (see page 61) can improve the condition because they block the reuptake of serotonin, increasing the level in the synapse.

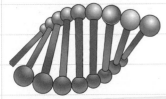

An illustration of a mutation on the hSERT gene. When the two mutations appear together, a significantly lower amount of serotonin is available within the synapse than is seen with either one of the mutations alone. This results in greater biochemical effects and more severe symptoms.

Neural explanations

Dopamine and serotonin are two neurotransmitters (see page 84) whose levels affect our mood. These are implicated in OCD.

The frontal lobes are involved in planning and decision-making. It is seen that activity levels in this part of the brain are increased as the client obsessively thinks about their worries and plans their rituals.

Szymanski (2012) reported that there is some evidence that throat infections through streptococcal bacteria create sudden onset of OCD symptoms through damage to neural systems. This can be treated and cured by antibiotics given promptly.

Evidence: the influence of genes

👍 In a meta-analysis of 28 twin studies by van Grootheest et al. (2005), findings showed that the genetic influences ranged from 45% to 65% in children, and in adults it was 27% to 47% heritable.

👍 Using gene mapping, Samuels et al. (2007) found that there was a genetic link with hoarding behaviour.

👎 There are so many genes implicated as 'candidates' for OCD there is unlikely to be a clear picture of genetic influence.

👎 Twin studies can be flawed because monozygotic (MZ) twins usually share a lot of similar environments as well as genes so it is hard to separate the genetic influences from the environmental ones.

Evidence: neural influence

👍 Hu (2006) compared serotonin activity in sufferers and non-sufferers. He found serotonin levels to be lower in OCD clients, supporting the idea that low levels of serotonin are implicated in OCD.

👍 Some antidepressants work as serotonin reuptake inhibitors meaning that higher levels of serotonin are left in the synapse. These drugs are effective against the anxiety of some OCD sufferers, suggesting that serotonin is implicated.

👎 We do not know whether brain and neural changes cause OCD or whether they are the result of OCD.

👎 We do not know how genes may interact with neural transmission to cause the symptoms of anxiety and OCD. Research is still in its infancy.

Now try this

Give **one** criticism of genetic explanations and **one** criticism of neural explanations of OCD.

Biological treatments of OCD

Biological treatments of OCD and other illnesses use **drug therapy** (sometimes called pharmacotherapy) to correct the **abnormal levels of serotonin**. Biological explanations of OCD have a lot of support and so it is likely that biological treatments will be effective.

How drug therapy works

Selective serotonin reuptake inhibitors (SSRIs) are the standard treatment for OCD. It is thought that people with OCD have lower levels of serotonin than normal.

When an action potential is triggered, the serotonin that is stored in vesicles in the pre-synaptic neuron is released into the synapse. It travels across the synapse and locks into its receptor cells. These then change electrical potential and send the message onwards. Serotonin keeps us feeling calm and in a stable mood.

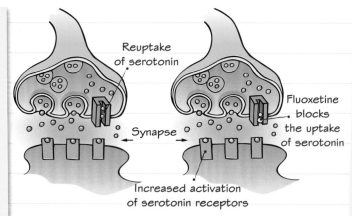

Reuptake of serotonin

Synapse

Fluoxetine blocks the uptake of serotonin

Increased activation of serotonin receptors

SSRIs (e.g. fluoxetine) block the reuptake of surplus serotonin, allowing it to accumulate in the synapse so the OCD sufferer gets back to normal levels. It takes around two weeks for levels to change and usually about six weeks for the client to feel the effects.

Evaluation

🚩 Side effects are serious for some with an increase in suicidal thoughts in the initial few weeks of the treatment, particularly in young people.

🚩 Some cause weight gain and heart arrhythmias and a loss of libido, causing people to stop taking them.

🚩 Non-biological, cognitive group CBT sessions of two hours over 10 weeks have better remission. (Source: NICE guidelines evidence, 2014)*

👍 Treatment-resistant cases are offered antipsychotic drugs in combination with SSRIs. This appears to help.

👍 Drug therapy is quick and easy to administer compared to waiting for CBT. It is also cheaper and a GP can administer it. It is not a cure but it manages the symptoms.

*The 'National Institute for Health and Care Excellence' (NICE) guidelines are used in the UK to advise doctors on evidence-based treatments.

Evidence

In a meta-review of 17 studies that used SSRIs with OCD patients, Soomro et al. (2008) found them to be more effective than placebos in the short-term (three months later).

Current NICE guidelines (2014) say SSRIs should be prescribed after failure of a course of CBT or jointly with CBT as it is equally effective.

 Extend ## Randomised controlled trials (RCTs)

All drug treatments should be tested in a **double-blind randomised** trial to be convincing. First, baseline data is collected from a group of patients so that any improvement is measurable. Next, the researchers match the active drug with an identical looking but inactive placebo. The doctors who then administer the drug and the placebo, and the clients who receive them, have no idea which they are getting – it is random and prepared by another researcher. Finally, at the end of the trial, the two groups are compared for improvement.

This type of research is the gold standard of science, free from bias and experimenter effects. However, the effect of the placebo grows over time as patients increase their belief in any medicine working. This means that the active drugs have to be more than 70% effective to beat the effect of the placebo.

Now try this

Evaluate the use of drug therapy to control OCD.

Exam skills 1

Before attempting these questions, remind yourself about how **abnormality** is defined (see pages 50 and 51).

Worked example

Which of the following is the statistical definition of abnormality? Shade **one** box only.

A Uses government statistics to understand how much mental illness there is in the country. ◯

B Uses percentages to decide who is abnormal. ◯

C Uses the normal distribution to decide who is abnormal. ●

~~**D** Uses the Mann-Whitney test to decide who is abnormal.~~ ◯

(1 mark)

> A good way to learn definitions is to make flash cards as you go along. Team up with a friend and test each other.

> You should know that the Mann-Whitney test is not used for defining abnormality so should be able to rule it out.

Worked example

Discuss two or more ways that abnormality has been defined. **(16 marks)**

> To tackle this question, a **quick essay plan** would be very helpful.

Essay plan

1 Outline the first definition of abnormality (e.g. the statistical norms definition).

2 Give an example of how it is used.

3 Give an argument in favour of this definition using an issue with evidence.

4 Give an argument against the definition with evidence.

5 Suggest an alternative way of defining abnormality (e.g. the social norms definition).

6 Repeat steps 2–4.

7 Compare or contrast with the first definition, using an issue.

8 Contextualise commentary using real world examples and relevant research evidence

9 Conclusion.

> You can give context and support to your explanation by using examples or research evidence.

> This is a good opening to the essay because it gets straight to the point. The definition is clearly explained and an example further clarifies the point being made.

Abnormality has been defined in various ways, one of which is the statistical definition. This looks at the normal distribution and standard deviation to decide who falls outside of the majority.

Around 68% of people fall within one standard deviation and 95% within two standard deviations. Outside this, scores are seen as abnormal. If the scores were about intelligence, for example, the mean is taken as 100 and a standard deviation is 15. So, if your IQ was over 130 or under 70, you would be abnormal by this definition.

The advantage of this definition is ...

Normal distribution curve

34% 34%
2.5% 13.5%   13.5% 2.5%
−3 −2 −1 0 1 2 3
Standard deviations

> You could also sketch the normal distribution curve to help explain your answer. Correctly labelled, it can demonstrate your understanding and clarify your thinking when you explain it.

> You would now need to choose an **issue** to focus on and make your point. Good issues to use for this essay include **validity, cultural relativism, objectivity vs subjectivity, psychology as a science** and **usefulness**. Use the DSM-5 criteria as evidence with an example.

Exam skills 2

These questions look at **evaluation skills**, using evidence to support the points being made. Notice that the description part is really brief as this will not be credited. To prepare for evaluation questions, practise using issues with studies and theories.

Worked example

Evaluate the evidence for a genetic cause for OCD. **(4 marks)**

The evidence for a genetic cause for OCD comes from twin studies such as the meta-analysis of 28 twin studies by van Grootheest et al. (2005). Their findings showed that the genetic influences ranged from 45% to 65% in children and in adults it was 27% to 47% heritable.

However, twin studies can be flawed because monozygotic (MZ) twins usually share a lot of similar environments as well as genes. It is therefore hard to separate the genetic influences from the environmental ones unless the twins were separated at birth. This is very rare, which means we cannot be certain the OCD is inherited. It could be learnt because the environment is shared.

Modern research uses <u>gene mapping</u>. Samuels et al. (2007) found that there was a genetic link with hoarding behaviour. There are, however, so many genes implicated as 'candidates' for OCD, that there is unlikely to be a clear picture of genetic influence in the near future.

To do well, try to make up to four points linked to the evidence for a genetic cause for OCD.

You need to know that twin studies are used to provide the evidence for a genetic basis for OCD and discuss how strong the evidence is.

Here the student has highlighted that there are **confounding variables** with twin studies.

This is a good point and shows that gene mapping is now being used to find the genes responsible.

Remember to look at **both sides** of the argument. Here, the student has correctly pointed out that there are so many implicated genes we might never know how it all works.

Worked example

<u>Discuss</u> **two** <u>limitations</u> of drug therapy for treating OCD. **(6 marks)**

Drug therapy for OCD involves treatment with SSRIs, such as fluoxetine, initially. It works to increase levels of serotonin, relieving the patient's anxiety. Unfortunately, a limitation is that side effects are serious for some, with an increase in suicidal thoughts in the initial few weeks of the treatment, particularly in young people. Some also cause weight gain and heart arrhythmias and a loss of libido, causing people to stop taking them before they have had an effect.

A second limitation is that SSRIs are not as effective as non-biological group cognitive behavioural therapy (CBT). According to NICE guidelines, CBT should involve sessions of two hours over 10 weeks, and these have no side effects. However, there is a shortage of CBT therapists and long waiting lists, so it is usually quicker and cheaper to take the SSRIs. CBT is better in the long term because it changes patients' thinking and behaviour, whereas drug treatments just treat symptoms.

Command words in a question

A **discussion** involves presenting the key points and saying why they are key points.

Limitations means you discuss the negatives without the positives.

Here the student leads the reader into the answer by clearly talking about two limitations.

The student has used **key terms** effectively, clearly showing their knowledge of the subject.

Make sure your answer is clear and effective, coherent and organised.

Exam-style practice 1

Practise for Paper 1 of your A level exam with these exam-style questions. There are answers on pages 295–296. Before attempting these questions, remind yourself about phobias.

1   Your friend Becky has trypanophobia (a fear of injections).

    (a) Describe the emotional and behavioural characteristics she might experience.   **(4 marks)**

> This is a straightforward describe question. You should write a paragraph and aim to make four good points covering both characteristics. Do not just list the characteristics.

    (b) Briefly outline **one** weakness of systematic desensitisation to treat trypanophobia.   **(3 marks)**

> Think about the **practicalities** of this treatment. How far up the **anxiety hierarchy** could you realistically go? How could you keep it **ethical**?

    (c) Evaluate one alternative treatment from the behaviourist approach which Becky could use to overcome her phobia.
   (3 marks)

> Try to make **three** points: think about **cost-effectiveness**, this particular **type** of phobia and **trauma**.

2   Outline the behavioural characteristics of OCD.   **(4 marks)**

> Notice it's just the behavioural characteristics that are required.

3   (a) Explain the two-process model of phobias.   **(4 marks)**

> When explaining it is very useful to use an example.

    (b) Evaluate the two-process model of phobias. In your answer you must make one comparison with an alternative explanation for how phobias develop.   **(6 marks)**

> Your alternative is biological and so you could consider the nature/nurture debate as part of your answer.

4   Joe spent 13 years resisting drug treatments to manage his depression. He often said, "there has to be a way other than medication to beat this condition!" Multiple times, he rolled the dice by stopping the medication without telling his clinicians. He would be fine for a while and then, like clockwork, would be back in the hospital.

> You could use the problems of non-adherence to medical advice as one of your evaluation points.

    Outline and evaluate the alternative treatments Joe could have tried for his depression.   **(16 marks)**

> Allow about 20 minutes for a 16 mark question – roughly one mark a minute, including time to read and plan.

Exam-style practice 2

Practise for Paper 1 of your A level exam with these exam-style questions. There are answers on page 296. Before attempting these questions, remind yourself about phobias.

5 Explain one weakness of Beck's cognitive explanation of depression. **(2 marks)**

6 Read the item and then answer the questions that follow.

Table 1 shows fear scores for males and females who have a phobia of dogs, where 1 is least fear and 10 is most fear.

> **Maths skills** Read the section on methodology on page 113 to help you with this if you need it.

Table 1: Fear scores for males and females with a phobia of dogs

Male fear scores	Female fear scores
5	6
3	7
2	3
7	9
8	9
8	1
5	5
6	6
7	6
8	3

(a) In Table 1, $n = 10$. What does this mean? **(1 mark)**

(b) Calculate the mean, median and mode for each group. **(6 marks)**

(c) Identify the range of scores in the two conditions. **(1 mark)**

(d) What does the range tell us about the level of fear in the two groups? **(1 mark)**

> **Maths skills** Remember to take a calculator into the exam.

> Show your working and keep it neat. Look at page 113 to remind yourself about these descriptive statistics.

7 Outline one methodological and one practical problem with studying people with mental illnesses. **(6 marks)**

> Practical problems are those that face any researcher dealing with sensitive topics and people who may resist being studied.

Origins of psychology

Psychology has existed as a distinct area of study since around 1875 when Wilhelm Wundt, a German physician, established the first laboratory to study the human mind. Here we will look at how psychology has developed as an area of scientific research.

Wundt's approach

Wundt set up his laboratory in the University of Leipzig in 1875. His approach to studying the human mind was to focus on aspects of the mind that could be observed and measured in controlled conditions. Wundt used **introspection**, which is to study the functions of the mind by asking people to describe their own thoughts, feelings and experiences.

In 1879, Wundt developed the Institute of Experimental Psychology in the University of Leipzig, which became a centre purely for the experimental study of psychology.

Timeline of psychological developments

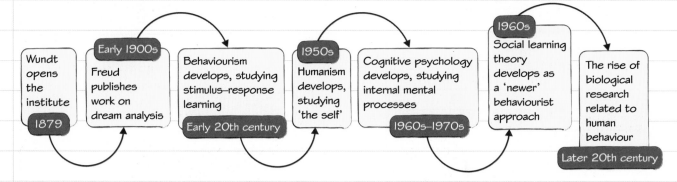

Wundt opens the institute — 1879

Early 1900s — Freud publishes work on dream analysis

Early 20th century — Behaviourism develops, studying stimulus–response learning

1950s — Humanism develops, studying 'the self'

1960s–1970s — Cognitive psychology develops, studying internal mental processes

1960s — Social learning theory develops as a 'newer' behaviourist approach

Later 20th century — The rise of biological research related to human behaviour

Psychology as a science

Wundt was the first person to suggest that the mind could be studied **empirically** using experiments. However, the concept of using **introspection** to gather data was criticised by researchers such as John B. Watson for being very **subjective**.

Watson began the **behaviourist movement**, studying observable stimulus–response behaviour in the early 20th century after speaking at Columbia University in 1913, which signalled the beginning of psychology as a science. His approach attempted to be more **objective** than Wundt's research.

Key terms

Control: being able to keep variables constant and isolate variables to look for cause and effect

Empirical: knowledge that is based on evidence

Hypothesis-testing: designing research to support an initial prediction

Objectivity: judgements made that are based on fact and are not open to interpretation

Replicability: research can be repeated and similar results can be found

Predictability: being able to prejudge what the outcome of research will be based on previous findings

Methods used in psychology

1. The **behaviourist approach**: This brought controlled, scientific research into psychology. These methods, such as **laboratory experiments**, are still widely used today.

2. **Cognitive psychology**: This developed as a way to quantify and study the internal processes of the mind by **testing hypotheses** in laboratories under **controlled conditions**.

3. The **biological approach**: The later development of the biological approach has seen further developments in methodology, such as the use of brain scans. Such developments add even more scientific methodology to the study of psychology.

Now try this

1 Explain the term 'introspection' as put forward by Wundt and outline one criticism of the concept of introspection.

2 Explain why it could be argued that psychology has emerged as a science.

Classical conditioning

Behaviourism is an example of a **learning approach** in psychology. It emphasises the role of the environment and experience in the learning of behaviours. Behaviourism describes only observable behaviour and uses methods such as laboratory experiments to gain control of variables and look for cause and effect relationships. Two examples of behaviourism are **classical conditioning** and **operant conditioning** (see page 68).

🔍 Key study — Classical conditioning

Classical conditioning is learning by association and was discovered by Ivan **Pavlov** in 1927. He found that if a new stimulus was paired many times with an existing stimulus–response, an association was made between the two stimuli. Pavlov found that dogs could be trained to salivate to the sound of a ringing bell. There are three key steps in Pavlov's study.

1 Before conditioning

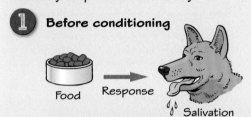

Food → Response → Salivation

Ringing bell → Response → No salivation

An **unconditioned stimulus** (the food) leads to an **unconditioned response** (salivation).

A **neutral stimulus** (ringing bell) produces **no response**.

2 During conditioning

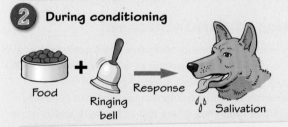

Food + Ringing bell → Response → Salivation

3 After conditioning

Ringing bell → Response → Salivation

Pairing a neutral stimulus with an unconditioned stimulus will create an **association** with the unconditioned response.

After regular pairing, the neutral stimulus will become a **conditioned stimulus** and will lead to its own **conditioned response**.

↥ Extend — Additional findings

Stimulus generalisation: Pavlov found that other stimuli similar to the conditioned stimulus (e.g. bells of different pitch and tone) will also lead to the conditioned response even though they have never been directly associated with the unconditioned stimulus.

Stimulus discrimination: If many different neutral stimuli are experienced, but only one is reliably paired with the unconditioned stimulus, there can be stimulus discrimination whereby only one specific stimulus will become the conditioned stimulus.

Temporal contiguity: The unconditioned stimulus and neutral stimulus have to be paired together at or around the same time for the association to be created.

Evaluation

👍 Most research is done in laboratories and is therefore reliable due to the high level of control possible.

👍 Classical conditioning has been used in developing treatments for mental illness such as systematic desensitisation to treat phobias, which has been found to be very effective.

👎 Classical conditioning ignores the role of biology in behaviour. Instead, it suggests everything stems from stimulus–response learning.

👎 Classical conditioning does not account for the role of cognition/thought in behaviour as this is not observable.

Now try this

1 Describe the process of classical conditioning.
2 Outline one assumption of the behaviourist approach in psychology.

Operant conditioning

Operant conditioning is another example of a behaviourist theory that also focuses on stimulus–response learning. Unlike classical conditioning where learning by association is emphasised, operant conditioning focuses on the role of learning from the consequences of our behaviour.

 Key study **Skinner's research**

B. F. Skinner conducted research placing rats into a cage that was specially designed to deliver food only when a lever was pressed by the rat. He found that the rats quickly learned to press the lever and would continue to do this until they were full.

Skinner conducted variations of the study. One used a box that administered a continuous electric shock under the rats' feet until the lever was pressed. Another variation delivered a shock to the rat when the lever was pressed. In both cases, the rats swiftly learned what would lead to the most positive consequence and would repeat that behaviour.

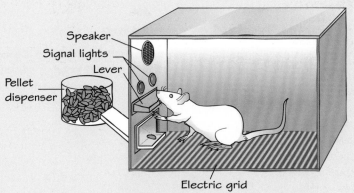

Skinner found rats could be trained to repeat or avoid behaviours by adapting the consequences of their actions to different stimuli such as buzzers, food and lights.

Operant conditioning

Operant conditioning is learning from the consequences of our behaviour. **Positive** and **negative reinforcements** mean we are more likely to repeat a behaviour, while **punishment** tends to prevent behaviour being repeated.

- Positive reinforcement is a reward as a positive consequence of the action.
- Negative reinforcement means removing something unpleasant as a positive consequence of an action.
- Punishment is a negative consequence of an action.

Schedules of reinforcement

Reinforcing every response (continuous reinforcement) is a useful way to establish the learning of a particular response, but is difficult to maintain over a long period of time. A **partial reinforcement schedule** would reinforce regularly (e.g. every 10th time they show the response) and is more easily maintained over time.

Types of punishment

Punishment can be **positive** where an unpleasant action is given as a consequence of behaviour, e.g. slapping the hand of a child when they play with a plug socket.

Punishment can also be **negative** where something pleasant is removed as a consequence of a behaviour, for example receiving a fine for parking in the wrong place.

Evaluation

👍 Evidence suggests that operant conditioning is an effective way for both humans and animals to learn. For example, schools use operant conditioning to shape student behaviour through rewards and punishments.

👍 Token economies, a form of therapy based on operant conditioning, have been shown to be effective for treating many different problematic behaviours, such as reducing aggressive behaviour in prisoners.

👎 Skinner's work was conducted on animals and has been criticised for then being applied to humans. One reason is that humans often have thoughts associated with learning that are not taken into account in this theory of learning.

👎 Much of the research took place on animals and exposed them to some unpleasant stimuli, which may breach ethical guidelines.

Now try this

Explain the difference between classical and operant conditioning.

Social learning theory

Social learning theory (SLT) is another example of a learning theory. It was first put forward by Albert Bandura in 1971 as an update to the older classical and operant conditioning theories. SLT emphasises the role of cognitive processes in learning, not just stimulus–response relationships.

Key concepts

SLT suggests we learn by observing others. If we see the behaviour of other people being reinforced (**vicarious reinforcement**) then we are influenced to **imitate** the behaviour. We pay particular attention to **role models** and learn from their behaviour because these are the people we **identify** with most. For example, children are prone to copying the behaviour of athletes or TV characters who they view as role models. When they see their behaviour being rewarded (e.g. athletes winning at events), they are even more likely to copy them.

Mediational processes

The role of **mediational processes** is in learning and 'doing' the behaviour seen. Behaviour is noticed by others (**attention**) and remembered (**retention**). Then, if there is a reward (**motivation**), the behaviour may be copied later (**reproduction**).

Bandura's research

During the 1960s, Bandura conducted research on the transmission of human behaviour through observation, i.e. copying what we see others do. His work was an extension of behaviourist theories because he accepted the role of learning in behaviour, but was also interested in how cognitive processes were involved.

🔍 Key study Bandura's (1961) Bobo doll experiments

Aim: To see if children would learn and imitate aggression from watching adult role models.

Procedure: Children observed either an adult role model being aggressive towards a Bobo doll, or a demonstration of non-aggressive behaviour towards the doll. The children were then exposed to mild frustration before being left in a room with a Bobo doll.

Results: Many of the children who saw the adult being aggressive went on to imitate the aggression on the doll. Less aggression was seen in the group who watched the non-aggressive adult behaviour.

Conclusion: Children exposed to aggressive role models are likely to imitate their behaviour.

A child imitating aggressive behaviour on a Bobo doll.

Evaluation

- 👍 SLT accepts that cognitive processes are involved in learning and it is not just an automatic process.

- 👍 There is a great deal of research evidence supporting the claim that we learn from the observation of others, for example, Bandura's Bobo doll studies from the 1960s.

- 👍 SLT can have useful applications. For example, social skills training aims to model positive behaviour to reduce criminal behaviour.

- 👎 SLT tends to ignore the role of biological factors in shaping behaviour.

- 👎 Much of the evidence to support SLT comes from laboratory studies. Thus it may explain behaviour in controlled settings but may not relate to real-life behaviour in the same way.

- 👎 SLT has been used to argue that violent media can increase violent behaviour, especially in children. However, some people argue that aggressive people are drawn to violent media as an outlet for their impulses.

Now try this

Explain the role of vicarious reinforcement in learning according to the social learning theory.

The cognitive approach

The cognitive approach began to emerge in the 1960s after researchers criticised the behaviourist approach for not taking into account internal mental processes in behaviour. This approach assumes that the internal processes of the mind (for example, our thought processes) should be studied using controlled laboratory studies.

Assumptions

The cognitive approach is based on two assumptions:

1. Internal processes can be studied in laboratories by inferring the actions of the mind from behaviour seen.

2. The human mind works like a computer, with input from the senses and output in the form of behaviour.

The role of schema

Schemas are unique 'packets' of information that we use to interpret our world. They come from experiences we have encountered and help us to predict what is going to happen in a new situation. This means they form the unique way we all interpret the world around us.

Theoretical models

The cognitive approach uses **theoretical models** to represent internal mental processes, such as the multi-store model as a representation of how memory works (look back at page 18 for more on this). This enables us to consider how the brain processes information by thinking in terms of different structures and what each of them does. By breaking down the processes into component parts, researchers can more easily test the individual elements of the theory.

Computer models

The cognitive approach has also used the development of computers to create **computer models** of mental processing.

Input		Processing		Output
Sensory information	Transfer	Sequence of mental operations	Transfer	Perceptions, memories, behaviours

We can use the analogy of the brain working like a computer – taking in information, processing it and then producing some form of output. For example, we touch something hot, process that it's hot and move our hand away.

Cognitive neuroscience

Recently, **cognitive neuroscience** has emerged as a new area of research. This is the scientific study of how different areas of the brain are involved in mental processes such as memory or perception. The use of brain scanning techniques such as **PET** or **fMRI** scans means it is now possible to see the function of the brain while different behaviours are being performed. For example, different areas of the brain have been found to activate when recalling episodic memories and procedural memories (see page 23).

Evaluation

👍 The cognitive approach is highly scientific because of the emphasis on controlled laboratory research in studying the mind.

👍 The cognitive approach has many useful applications, such as in treatments for depression and the development of artificial intelligence.

👎 It has been argued that the approach simplifies human behaviour too much because it ignores the role of human emotions and motivations in behaviour.

👎 Because cognitive research tends to take place in laboratories, it could be thought to lack validity as the processes studied may be artificial.

Now try this

1 Outline **two** assumptions of the cognitive approach in psychology.

2 Explain how cognitive neuroscience has emerged as an area of study in psychology.

3 Describe **two** criticisms of the cognitive approach in psychology.

The biological approach

The biological approach suggests that human behaviour is caused by biological factors, such as **genes**, **neurochemicals** and **physical structures** (the brain and nervous system).

Assumptions

The biological approach is based on three core assumptions:

1 A person's **central nervous system** (CNS) has a very strong influence on their behaviour.

2 The genetic make-up of individuals influences their behaviour. This may also relate to the influence of **evolution** on behaviour.

3 **Chemicals** present in the body, such as **hormones** and **neurotransmitters**, will influence behaviour.

Central nervous system (CNS)

The structure of the CNS – the **brain** and **spinal cord** – will influence a person's behaviour (see page 83 for more on the structure of the CNS). The CNS allows communication between the environment and the brain/body by passing messages throughout the body.

Chemicals in the body, such as neurotransmitters in the CNS, will influence the behaviours seen. For example, high levels of dopamine can lead to behavioural symptoms such as hearing imaginary voices in schizophrenics.

The role of genetics

The genetic make-up of individuals can have an influence on their behaviour. Psychologists have investigated genetic explanations for many human behaviours, including mental illnesses, personality and criminal behaviour.

Biological psychologists believe that the genes a person has from the moment they are conceived have a strong influence in determining the kind of person they will become. We can observe the influence of genes by studying **monozygotic (identical) twins** who share an identical genetic code. A high **concordance rate** or correlation between identical twins' behaviour may suggest a genetic component is involved. However, concordance rates will not be 100% as even though the **genotype** is the same, the **phenotype** of the twins will still be different.

Genotype and phenotype

A person's **genotype** refers to the actual genetic material that a person has (genetic make-up). Unless you have an identical twin, your genotype is unique to you.

A person's **phenotype** refers to the way the genes are expressed in the behaviour or physical appearance of an individual. The phenotype can be influenced by the environment. For example, you may have a genetic component that increases your risk of developing depression, but it will only develop if something in the environment triggers it.

Even identical twins will look or behave differently depending on environmental factors such as nutrition.

The role of evolution

Evolution is the process by which a species adapts to its environment. Genetic material is passed on through the generations of a species when the resulting behaviour will aid survival or, in some cases, reproduction. For example, a physical response to threat such as the fight-or-flight response (see page 85) could have evolved because those who were genetically programmed to show this behaviour were more likely to survive and pass on their genes.

Evaluation

👍 The biological approach has been tested using highly scientific methods such as brain scans and twin/family studies.

👍 It has many practical applications, such as the use of drugs to treat mental illness.

👎 It does not take into account the influence of the environment on behaviour – it looks purely at **nature** and ignores **nurture** as an influence.

👎 It assumes that certain biological factors determine particular behaviours and they cannot be changed.

Now try this

Explain the difference between genotype and phenotype.

The psychodynamic approach

The psychodynamic approach (the 'first force') was developed by Sigmund Freud in the late 19th century to explain personality, and it forms the basis of psychoanalytic therapy.

The role of the unconscious

Freud believed that a large part of the mind is not accessible (unconscious), yet is able to influence our behaviour.

Freud likened the mind to an iceberg. The unconscious mind contains information that the conscious mind would find uncomfortable, so is repressed by defence mechanisms to protect the person from anxiety.

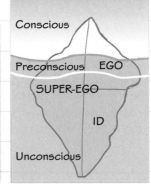

Conscious

Preconscious   EGO

SUPER-EGO

ID

Unconscious

Defence mechanisms

1 **Repression:** the unconscious diversion of unacceptable wishes and desires to protect the person. They do not go away and continue to influence our behaviour.

2 **Denial:** the refusal to accept reality in order to avoid psychological pain associated with it, e.g. a person might refuse to see that their partner is unfaithful even though to others it is obvious.

3 **Displacement:** the redirection of impulses away from the real target to safer ones.

Psychosexual stages

Freud proposed that the personality develops through a sequence of five developmental stages, each marked by conflicts and a different focus of psychological urges.

Age	Stage	Development
0–2 years	Oral	Focus on mouth; gratification achieved by feeding. Id is dominant.
2–3	Anal	Focus on anus; gratification gained by pooping. Ego develops through potty training.
3–6	Phallic	Focus on genitals; child passes through Oedipus or Electra stage; gender identity and superego develop.
6–12	Latency	Focus on developing relationships with others; the conflicts of previous three stages are repressed.
12+	Genital	Focus of sexual energy directed towards relationships with sexual partners.

Structure of personality

Freud proposed that our personalities consist of three distinct parts, which develop in childhood.

Id	Ego	Superego
Present from birth; unconscious; contains our primitive desires for sex and death. It demands immediate gratification.	Develops in the anal stage. It is the mediator between the id and reality, trying to get what the id wants but in a socially acceptable way.	Develops in the phallic stage; consists of the conscience and the ego ideal. This punishes us with guilt when we transgress the rules of society and pushes us to be good.

Evaluation of psychoanalysis

👍 First **talking** cure for psychological disorders.

👍 Uncovers the unconscious motivation for mental health issues.

👍 Widely used and successful.

👎 Accused of being sexist and overemphasising male sexuality.

👎 Culturally limited, as it was developed within Western society.

Now try this

Outline **one** contribution of the psychodynamic approach.

Humanistic psychology

Humanistic psychology was developed by Carl Rogers and Abraham Maslow in the 1950s.

The humanistic approach

Known as the 'third force' in psychology, humanistic psychology rejects the reductionist and deterministic views about human motivation and behaviour that arose from Freud's ideas (the 'first force', see page 72) and the early behaviourists (the 'second force', see pages 67–68).

This approach focuses on the **subjective** experience of being human, believing that every person is **unique**. The scientific method based on principles of reductionism is therefore not suited to the study of human experience.

The humanistic approach has led to the development of **counselling psychology** (see page 74).

Key ideas

The approach includes some basic assumptions.

1 Humans cannot be **reduced** to components.

2 Humans are all **unique**.

3 Humans are **conscious and aware** of themselves in the context of other people's reactions to them.

4 Humans have **free will** – the ability to make choices – and therefore have responsibility for their actions.

5 Humans are **purposeful and creative**; they have intention behind their behaviour.

Maslow's hierarchy of needs (1943, 1954)

Self-actualisation

Esteem

Love/Belonging

Safety

Physiological

Morality, creativity, spontaneity, problem-solving, lack of prejudice, acceptance of facts

Self-esteem, confidence, achievement, respect of others, respect by others

Friendship, family, sexual intimacy

Security of body, of employment, of resources, of morality, of the family, of health, of property

Breathing, food, water, sex, sleep, homeostasis, excretion

Maslow proposed that we are driven to be the best we can be, but this depends on having our needs met. Our basic needs are physiological and safety needs. Once these are met, our needs become more psychological. Only when these are also met are we able to achieve self-actualisation.

Self-actualisation

A core concept of the humanistic approach is that everyone has a drive to achieve **self-actualisation**. This is where you become the best person you can be and achieve your full potential as a human being.

Progress towards self-actualisation depends on lower-level needs being met. To maintain self-actualisation, these lower needs must continue to be met.

Self-actualisation is not the norm and most people do not achieve it.

Free will

Humanists argue that we are free to choose who we want to be (**free will**). In contrast, other approaches argue from a stance of **determinism** that who we are and who we become is pre-determined by other forces, such as nature (biology) or nurture (socialisation). For more on free will and determinism, see page 130.

Although the humanistic approach acknowledges the constraints set by nature and nurture, it still proposes that we have the subjective feeling of choice.

Now try this

1 What is meant by free will?
2 What is meant by determinism?

Humanistic therapy

Humanistic psychology led to the development of **counselling** as a form of therapy.

Conditions of worth

According to the theory, personal growth is hampered by experiencing **conditional positive regard** where, in order to get positive regard, the person has to meet certain requirements. For example, a child may feel that they can only receive approval from a parent when they are performing well at school.

Conditional positive regard limits the chances of achieving **self-actualisation** (see page 73), as the person is unlikely to achieve **congruence** because they feel their **ideal self** and their **self-concept** are different. **Client-centred therapy** aims to allow personal growth by providing **unconditional positive regard** where the client is accepted for who they are without judgement.

Client-centred therapy

The client–therapist relationship is of central importance to this therapy. The therapist must create conditions in which personal growth can take place. Personal growth depends on the client developing their own understanding of issues in their life and deciding for themselves how to overcome them.

The therapist is **non-directive** and seeks to reflect back to the client whatever the client discloses in a climate of trust and mutual regard. In this way, clients solve their own problems by examining them in a situation where the therapist provides empathy and unconditional positive regard.

Therapy focuses on the self

Rogers (1951) proposed that there are three selves which need to be integrated in order to feel good.

The self-concept – the self you think you are; this is similar to self-esteem.

The ideal self – the self you aspire to being.

The three selves

The real self – who you really are.

The aim of therapy is to explore issues that affect the balance between the selves. Only when there is balance can personal growth towards self-actualisation take place.

Congruence

Rogers stated that for self-actualisation to be possible, the person's selves must be **congruent**. This means that the self-concept, the ideal self and the real self should be the same or very similar to each other.

This is provided in a therapeutic setting by the therapist giving unconditional positive regard to the client. This allows the client to increase their self-esteem and adjust their sense of the ideal closer to the real self.

Evaluation

- 👍 Humanistic theory allows for personal growth and accepts the idea of free will, which seems intuitively correct – we all feel that we make choices.

- 👍 The therapy developed from humanism has been shown to be effective and is a good alternative to lengthy psychoanalysis or medication.

- 👎 The ideas central to the approach, such as the hierarchy of needs, have been criticised for being culturally biased towards individualistic cultures, and have limited usefulness in collectivist cultures.

- 👎 Because this approach acknowledges the subjectivity of experience, its claims are hard to test scientifically.

Now try this

Outline the role of congruence in humanistic therapy.

Comparison of approaches 1

To demonstrate your knowledge of approaches in psychology, you may be asked to draw comparisons between them. This is easiest to do based on the issues in psychology.

Determinism vs free will

For more on determinism and free will, see page 130.

Biological	Proposes that genes, biochemistry and brain structure have a strong influence on behaviour. These are things we do not choose and cannot easily change, so this approach is deterministic with limited opportunity for free will.
Cognitive	Information processing influences behaviour; as this is based on schema, which we can change, this approach argues for some element of free will.
Learning/ Behaviourist	Pure behaviourism argues that who we are is shaped by our environment and develops through stimulus–response learning, so is very deterministic. Social learning theory takes a softer view, arguing that we have a choice of role model.
Psychodynamic	Argues that behaviour is heavily influenced by our unconscious mind, which develops in early childhood and is beyond our control, so it is deterministic.
Humanistic	This is the only approach that proposes human beings have free will and can choose to behave however they want.

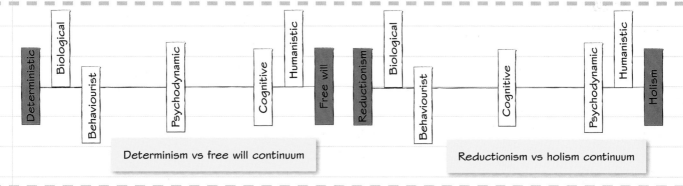

Determinism vs free will continuum

Reductionism vs holism continuum

Reductionism vs holism

For more on reductionism and holism, see page 132.

Biological	This approach is very reductionist as it explains behaviour as resulting from the interaction between simple biological mechanisms such as genes, neurotransmitters and brain structure.
Cognitive	Cognitive theories tend towards reductionism as they break down information processing into different functions such as memory or attention, when in fact the two are used together.
Learning/ Behaviourist	Operant and classical conditioning are very reductionist as they explain complex behaviour in terms of simple stimulus–response learning. Social learning theory is less reductionist as it includes cognitive processes that mediate between the environment and the person's learning.
Psychodynamic	Although not entirely holistic, as it advocates that much of our behaviour is governed by unconscious drives, it does take account of a range of influences that can affect how we think, feel and behave.
Humanistic	This approach is holistic. It believes people should be viewed as a whole, and rejects the idea that human behaviour can be broken down into components in any meaningful way.

Now try this

Compare **two** approaches in psychology according to their views about free will.

Comparison of approaches 2

Further issues on which approaches can be compared include the nature–nurture debate and the idiographic vs nomothetic debate.

Nature vs nurture debate

For more on the nature–nurture debate, see page 131.

Biological	This approach is strongly on the side of nature as it proposes that much of our behaviour is innate. However, it also accepts a role for nurture due to the plasticity of the brain – it will change as a result of environmental factors.
Cognitive	This approach accepts that both nature and nurture influence the development of information processing capability. Some cognitive mechanisms are innate but they are also shaped by experience.
Learning/ Behaviourist	This approach is firmly based in nurture. Behaviourists would argue that we are born a 'blank slate' with no predispositions imposed on us; all our behaviour is learned from the environment.
Psychodynamic	Psychodynamic theorists would argue for an interactionist approach between the innate drive of the id and the socialising influences of the parents, which affect the development of other parts of the personality.
Humanistic	This approach rejects the debate as not valid because the human condition cannot be broken down into specific influences. The drive to self-actualisation is regarded as innate although it is heavily influenced by social factors.

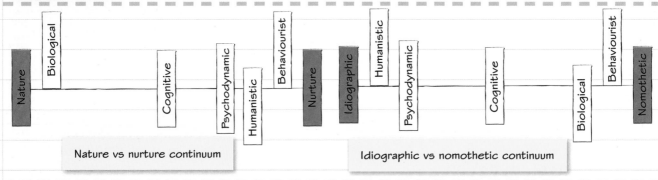

Nature vs nurture continuum

Idiographic vs nomothetic continuum

Idiographic vs nomothetic approaches

For more on idiographic and nomothetic approaches, see page 133.

Biological	Proposes general laws that apply universally based on common physiology. Individual differences can be explained by an understanding of the physiological aspects of the person.
Cognitive	Accepts that individuals differ in some aspects of their information processing but proposes that the general mechanisms underlying this are the same for all people.
Learning/ Behaviourist	Heavily nomothetic as it applies general laws of learning such as operant and classical conditioning across all species, not just humans. Social learning theory is more human-based but also nomothetic as it applies to all humans.
Psychodynamic	Contains nomothetic elements such as the structure of personality, but also recognises all humans as unique products of multiple influences. Therefore does not propose general explanations for specific behaviours.
Humanistic	Very idiographic as it considers everyone to be unique, although it could be argued that elements such as the hierarchy of needs apply to all people, so it is not entirely idiographic.

Now try this

Compare **two** approaches in terms of their stance in the idiographic vs nomothetic debate.

Exam skills 1

Before you look at these worked examples, remind yourself about the humanistic approach in psychology (see pages 73–74).

Worked example

Which one of the following terms matches this definition: 'when your ideal self matches your real self'? Shade **one** box only.

A Unconditional positive regard ◯

B Congruence ⬤

C Self-actualisation ◯

D Client-centred therapy ◯

(1 mark)

> Although this looks like it could be self-actualisation, to achieve this the person must first attain congruence. A person is congruent when the self-concept, the ideal self and the real self are the same or very similar to each other. Self-actualisation occurs when a person achieves their full potential as a human being, which few people achieve.

Worked example

Outline **two** basic principles of the humanistic approach.

(2 marks)

Humans cannot be reduced to the actions of component parts and must be viewed holistically.

Humans have free will and can make choices and take responsibility for their own actions.

> ### Command word: Outline
> **Outline** means to briefly describe something, so do not provide too much detail in your answer.

> This is a good answer. It gives enough detail but does not waste time and space on extra description.

Worked example

Describe Maslow's hierarchy of needs.

(4 marks)

Maslow (1954) proposes that our current motivation is governed by our position on the hierarchy of needs. We are motivated to meet our needs at each level before we can progress to the next level. So someone who has not met their needs for love and belongingness will not be motivated to fulfil their esteem needs until they have achieved the former.

Maslow proposed five levels of needs with physiological needs on the bottom, which includes things we need to stay alive. This is followed by safety needs, which are about feeling secure. Belongingness comes next, in which we feel part of a social group, then esteem, which includes self-respect. The final level is self-actualisation, which means becoming the best you can be.

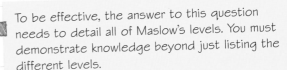

> To be effective, the answer to this question needs to detail all of Maslow's levels. You must demonstrate knowledge beyond just listing the different levels.
>
> You also need to describe the process. The whole point of the model is that people move up and down the hierarchy, so make sure this is included.

> This answer is more than a list as it gives information about each level. It is brief, but given the limited marks available it is adequate. It also explains the process of changing motivation.

Exam skills 2

Before you look at this worked example, remind yourself about the psychodynamic approach in psychology (see page 72).

Worked example

Discuss the psychodynamic approach as an explanation for human behaviour.

(16 marks)

According to Freud, our personality develops in stages during our early childhood and is made up of three interacting components. The id is an instinctive drive we are born with, often referred to as 'the pleasure principle'. The ego develops at around the age of 3 years and tries to satisfy the id in a socially acceptable way. The superego emerges at around the age of 6 years when the child resolves the complex issues associated with the phallic stage of development.

Our behaviour is the product of the ego's efforts to balance the needs of the id with the needs of the superego and protect our psyche from trauma and anxiety.

The validity of the approach is challenged as the unconscious processes are difficult to falsify through empirical research because we cannot directly access the unconscious mind. Therefore, the approach remains hypothetical.

Furthermore, most evidence for the theory comes from case studies, which lack generalisability as the people involved are usually unrepresentative. For example, Little Hans (1909), Freud's only child case study, came from a family of people interested in Freud's views. This was very atypical of the period.

Case study data can also be interpreted subjectively, making the evidence unreliable.

The ideas that form the theory are a product of Western civilisation, so it could be argued that it is **culturally biased**. Furthermore, it is **androcentric**, focusing on male sexuality as being of prime importance in the development of the psyche, largely ignoring the female experience.

However, it has led to successful therapy, such as psychoanalysis, and was one of the first humane treatments for people with psychological distress.

Command word: Discuss

When asked to 'discuss', you should first describe (AO1) and then evaluate (AO2/AO3) the topic, in this case the psychodynamic approach to human behaviour. Make sure you support your points with theoretical or practical examples.

It helps to separate your points into paragraphs. You can then see if your essay is focused and includes enough detail. Without a clear structure and delineation, this would be more difficult.

As the question is asking how the approach explains behaviour, and there are only 6 marks for the descriptive element, you do not need to go into detail about the psychosexual stages. Instead, focus on the drivers of behaviour, the id, the ego and the superego, and briefly outline their role and how they develop.

The evaluative section of this answer covers several issues associated with the approach. Issues with the case study method are carefully linked to the development of the theory, so are relevant here.

Rather than just listing lots of evaluation points, try to clearly elaborate the points that you make. This can be done by providing further research evidence, practical or real-world examples, or comparisons to other explanations of approaches that may contradict the cognitive approach's view.

There is good use of terminology throughout this answer. Reference is made to key issues in psychology, such as cultural bias and androcentrism.

A positive point is made at the end. Although it is only one point, it does highlight something good about the approach. Complete the answer by adding a comment about temporal validity as a mitigating point for the cultural bias evident in the theory.

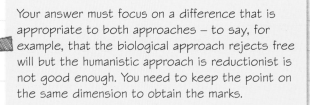
Exam skills 3

Before you look at these worked examples, remind yourself about the comparisons between approaches in psychology (see pages 75–76).

Worked example

Explain **two** differences between the biological approach and the humanistic approach.

(4 marks)

The biological approach takes a nomothetic stance as it proposes general laws that govern behaviour based on our physical make-up, whereas the humanistic approach rejects the idea of general laws and states that humans are all unique. Linked to this is the idea of determinism. The biological approach states that our behaviour is influenced by our genetic make-up which predisposes us to behave in a certain way, therefore denying free will. The humanistic approach rejects this view and says that we all have the freedom to choose how we behave and who we become.

> Your answer must focus on a difference that is appropriate to both approaches – to say, for example, that the biological approach rejects free will but the humanistic approach is reductionist is not good enough. You need to keep the point on the same dimension to obtain the marks.

> The answer picks two appropriate issues on which to compare the approaches. The level of detail and use of terminology are both good. The points made are clearly linked across approaches.

Worked example

Read the item and then answer the question that follows.

> Charlie argues with his friend James, saying that most of our behaviour is based on factors beyond our control and that we have no free will. James disagrees and suggests that we are all responsible for our own actions.

Explain the views of Charlie and James, using your knowledge of the approaches in psychology to inform your answer.

(4 marks)

Charlie is arguing for a deterministic view of human behaviour. He is therefore likely to be talking about a biological or behaviourist explanation, as both of these suggest that we are heavily influenced by things we cannot control. For example, the biological approach would state that our genes govern our behaviour, and the behaviourist would say it is our environment. On the other hand, James is arguing from a humanistic perspective, as only this approach really suggests that humans have free will to act in any way they choose.

> When you are given stimulus material, it is important that you use it. This question is asking you directly to explain the views of Charlie and James, so refer to them in your answer.

> This answer focuses more on Charlie's view. As fewer approaches would argue for complete free will, the degree of focus is appropriate in this case. The answer is relevant and is pitched at the right level of detail. The examples given are also useful. All the information provided is clearly linked to the stimulus material.

Exam-style practice 1

Practise for Paper 2 of your A level exam with these exam-style questions. There are answers on page 297. Before looking at these questions, it would be useful to revise the behaviourist approach in psychology.

1 Read the item and then answer the questions that follow.

> Dylan and Bartek have been involved in a fight at school and are talking to their head of year about what happened. Dylan admits that he started the fight after an argument over comments Bartek made about Dylan's sister. Bartek says this is the first time he has been in a fight, while Dylan has been in trouble before for fighting with other boys in his year. The head of year finds out from Dylan's parents that he spends every evening playing on his xBox, and his favourite games are shooting ones. Dylan has an older brother at the school who has been excluded several times for fighting. His parents are concerned about his behaviour, but as the fight occurred at school they want the punishment to be decided at school.

(a) Using your knowledge of learning approach explanations of behaviour, explain why Dylan may be showing a high level of aggression.   **(6 marks)**

(b) Define 'negative reinforcement' and give an example from Dylan's behaviour to illustrate your answer.   **(4 marks)**

2 What is meant by a schema?   **(2 marks)**

3 Describe how Skinner investigated operant conditioning.   **(3 marks)**

4 Explain one criticism of the concept of introspection as outlined by Wundt.   **(3 marks)**

5 In the following example, identify what the unconditioned stimulus is.

> Ella's mum wants her to stop biting her nails. She paints some fluid onto Ella's fingernails and when Ella puts her fingers into her mouth the taste of the fluid makes Ella feel nauseous. After a few days of wearing the fluid Ella's mum decides to not put any on and see what happens. She notices that Ella does not put her fingers to her mouth any more to chew her nails.

Is the unconditioned stimulus:

A the fluid   ⬭

B Ella's finger nails   ⬭

C Ella feeling nauseous   ⬭

D chewing her nails?

(1 mark)

When given a scenario to discuss, highlight or underline any hints or examples to help you answer the question. For example, reference is made to playing **violent video games**, which could be used to **explain Dylan's behaviour.**

List key terms associated with learning approaches as prompts for what to use in your answer.

Here, marks are likely to be divided between the **definition** and the **example**, so make sure both are clear and concise.

For both marks you should aim to give a clear definition of what a schema is, and then give a suitable example of a schema to illustrate this.

This question asks you to describe the procedure used to investigate operant conditioning in the work of Skinner. This would mean describing the use of the box and how reinforcements and punishments in response to pressing the levers were used to shape the behaviour of the animals.

For 3 marks there is a need to elaborate your answer making at least 3 linked points. Start by stating a key criticism of the concept of introspection such as that it might be subjective. After this you must then explain why introspection might be subjective and what problem this creates in the use of introspection in research.

Read the multiple choice question carefully and make sure you identify the correct part to illustrate the key term.

Remember the unconditioned stimulus is something that happens that produces a natural or reflex response

Exam-style practice 2

Practise for Paper 2 of your A level exam with these exam-style questions. There are answers on pages 297–298. Before looking at these questions, it would be useful to recap the biological approach section.

6　Which of these would be an assumption made by the biological approach?

　A　Internal mental processes influence behaviour　☐

　B　Behaviour is influenced by genetics　☐

　C　All humans have free will to become whatever they want　☐

　D　Humans can learn behaviour from observing others　☐

(1 mark)

> Read multiple choice questions really carefully. Sometimes many different answers COULD fit the question, but by thinking before you answer you will be less likely to make a mistake.
> Remember, the biological approach is all about biology influencing behaviour.

7　Which of the following researchers are associated with classical conditioning?

　A　Pavlov　☐

　B　Skinner　☐

　C　Bandura　☐

　D　Baddeley　☐

(1 mark)

> As the question asks you only to evaluate the approach, only AO3 marks will be available. This means that describing social learning theory will not gain you any marks. You should begin with an evaluative statement such as 'One criticism of social learning theory is….' to stop you describing.
>
> There will always be a 'breadth and depth trade-off' in a question like this. This means that you can choose to make lots of different evaluation points in less detail OR you can choose to do 2 or 3 in a lot of detail.

8　Evaluate social learning theory as an explanation for human behaviour.　**(6 marks)**

9　You have been asked to write a short newspaper article for homework on the work of Albert Bandura in developing social learning theory.

　Write an opening paragraph to introduce what Bandura did in his research and what the research evidence he found has told us about human behaviour.　**(4 marks)**

> You need to describe Bandura's research including the procedure and the results.
>
> As the question is contextualised as a newspaper article you should try to write your answer using language that is more accessible to the general public, making sure that any specialist psychological terms are clearly explained.

10　Define the term inference as it relates to the study of human behaviour by the cognitive approach.　**(2 marks)**

11　Outline **and** evaluate the biological approach to explaining human behaviour.　**(16 marks)**

> To infer means to make an assumption based on evidence. Explain how this would relate to the way cognitive psychologists study behaviour.

> Write a brief essay plan before you begin to structure your answer. When discussing the biological approach, consider the influence of **genes**, **biochemistry** and the **nervous system**.
>
> You are asked to **outline** the biological approach, which means you need to **describe** what the approach is about in psychology. To **evaluate** means you need to make a **judgement** on how valuable the biological approach is in psychology. This could include research evidence supporting the approach, and applications of the approach to the real world.
>
> Remember to write in continuous prose, using correct spelling, punctuation and grammar throughout.

Exam-style practice 3

Practise for Paper 2 of your A level exam with these exam-style questions. There are answers on page 298. Before looking at these questions, it would be good to review classical and operant conditioning (see pages 67–68), Wundt's technique of introspection (see page 66), and the cognitive (page 70) and biological (page 71) approaches in psychology.

1   Read the item and then answer the questions that follow.

> When Ananda was a small child, she and her brother, Mo, used to play hide-and-seek around the house. On one occasion Ananda hid in a cupboard in her bedroom while Mo tried to find her, but Mo got distracted by the TV and stopped looking for her. When Ananda realised he wasn't coming she tried to push open the cupboard door herself, but it was stuck and there was no handle on the inside. Ananda was very scared in the dark and began to scream and cry until her mum came to open the door and get her out. Ever since that event Ananda has had a fear of small spaces and likes to keep her bedroom door open when she sleeps.

(a) Using classical conditioning, explain why Ananda has developed a fear of small spaces, making reference to the above scenario.   **(4 marks)**

(b) Using operant conditioning, explain why Ananda avoids being in small spaces with closed doors.   **(2 marks)**

2   Outline what is meant by 'introspection'. Explain one limitation of using introspection to investigate human behaviour.
   (4 marks)

3   Briefly explain one limitation of the biological approach in psychology.   **(2 marks)**

> Always read the scenario carefully and look for hints about how to answer the question. It can be useful to underline or use a highlighter to pick out key words or phrases.

> Remember to use the correct terminology to match the explanation they are asking about. Explaining something using psychological knowledge means applying your understanding in the context of the scenario. Describing the theory or research with no reference to the scenario is not answering the question.

> Make sure you use Ananda's name in your answer because this shows you are using this scenario.

> To make this relate to operant conditioning, you should refer to some kind of reinforcement or punishment in your answer – whatever is relevant to the scenario you've been given.

> Start with a definition, making sure you know your key terms – 3 marks will be for a negative evaluation point.

> Use appropriate key terms in your answer, such as **reductionism**, and add some elaboration to extend the original point to claim all the marks.

Structuring answers

When asked to provide detail on **one point**, it is useful to think of how to **structure** your answer to be sure you include the detail that will enable you to get more than 1 mark for your response.

> 1 **State** the point to make   2 **Explain** what this means   3 **Elaborate** why this is relevant ⟶ This is a useful strategy

Divisions of the nervous system

Our nervous system is split into two parts: the **central nervous system (CNS)** and the **peripheral nervous system (PNS)**. The CNS is the brain and spinal cord and the PNS is the nerves outside the CNS. The role of the nervous system is to relay messages from the brain to the rest of the body to instruct it what to do.

Divisions of the nervous system

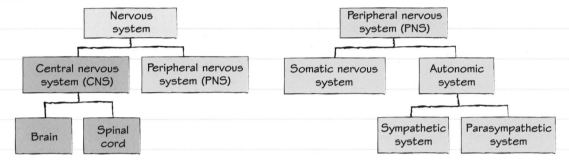

Function of the nervous system

The **brain** is involved in mental processing and it is in overall 'control' of body functions.

The **spinal cord** is responsible for passing messages from the brain to the rest of the body, and then transmitting messages back to the brain.

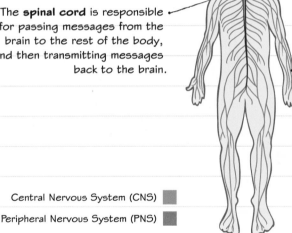

Central Nervous System (CNS) ▇

Peripheral Nervous System (PNS) ▇

In the **peripheral nervous system:**
- the **somatic nervous system** is responsible for passing messages to the brain from sensory organs, and from the brain to the muscles. It controls voluntary or conscious actions
- the **autonomic nervous system** controls the body's 'automatic' or involuntary actions such as breathing and heart rate. The autonomous functions of the body need to happen quickly rather than waiting for us to think about when to breathe or when our heart should beat.

The autonomic nervous system is divided into the **sympathetic nervous system (SNS)** and the **parasympathetic nervous system (PSNS)**.

The role of the SNS

The **SNS** is the body's alert system. It is involved in preparing the body to respond to threats (see page 85 for the fight-or-flight response).

The role of the PSNS

The **PSNS** is sometimes referred to as the 'rest and digest' system because its role is to relax the body by counteracting the effects of SNS activation.

SNS	PSNS
increased heart rate	decreased heart rate
reduced activity within the stomach	increased activity within the stomach
saliva production is inhibited	saliva production increased to aid digestion
pupil dilation/expansion	pupil contraction
relaxation of the bronchi of the lungs	constriction of the bronchi of the lungs
glucose (energy store in liver) is released	glucose is stored

Now try this

1 Explain the role of the sympathetic nervous system.
2 Briefly describe the role of the central nervous system.

Neurons and synaptic transmission

Neurons are cells in the nervous system that carry the nerve impulses around the body to control behaviour. Different types of neuron do different things by communicating messages between the brain and body through a process called **synaptic transmission.**

Structure of different neurons

sensory neurons carry messages from sense organs (e.g. eyes, nose) to the brain to be turned into meaningful information.

motor neurons carry messages to muscles and glands in order to produce responses.

relay neurons (or interneurons) allow communication between sensory and motor neurons.

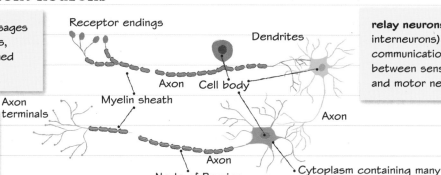

Synaptic transmission

Neurons communicate with each other by passing chemical messages across a **synapse** – the gap between two neurons. An electrical impulse is triggered in a neuron. This causes small **vesicles** containing **neurotransmitters** to travel down the neuron to the **terminal button**. The vesicles fuse with the outer membrane of the terminal button and release neurotransmitters into the **synaptic fluid** of the **synapse**. These neurotransmitters are then absorbed by **receptors** on the adjacent neuron and converted into an electrical impulse, or they are reabsorbed by the releasing neuron in a process called **reuptake**.

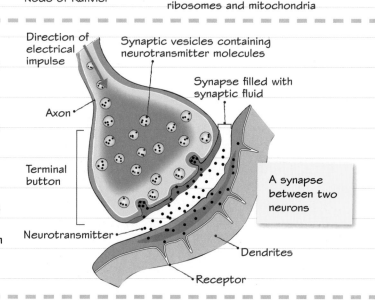

A synapse between two neurons

Functions of neurotransmitters

Neurotransmitters have specific functions. For example:

- **Dopamine** can be involved in our ability to pay attention to tasks as well as in our ability to learn from our experiences. In very high levels, dopamine has been linked to the symptoms of **schizophrenia**, such as hallucinations and delusions.

- **Serotonin** has been implicated in the expression and control of emotions. Serotonin levels are sometimes found to be low in people who are suffering with depression as a result.

Inhibitory and excitatory messages

When neurotransmitter messages have been passed across a synapse, they will be either **inhibitory** or **excitatory**.

- **Inhibitory** neurotransmitters calm down the brain and nervous system. For example, the brain produces GABA (gamma-aminobutyric acid) after periods of stress to return the body to a calm state.

- **Excitatory** neurotransmitters stimulate activity in areas of the brain. For example, caffeine can encourage dopamine to be released into synapses. This can make a person feel more alert and able to focus for a short period of time.

Now try this

1 Describe the process of synaptic transmission.
2 Explain the difference between a motor neuron and a sensory neuron.

Endocrine system

The **endocrine system** has a series of **glands** that release **hormones** throughout the body. The endocrine system works alongside the nervous system but at a much slower pace. The **fight-or-flight response** – a response to threat – is one reaction in the endocrine system.

The function of the endocrine system

Glands in the endocrine system produce chemicals (hormones) that are released into the blood. They travel around the body, stimulating organs and other body tissues into action. Hormones can influence many human behaviours.

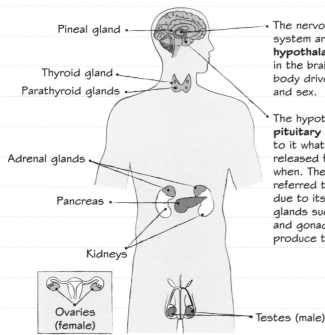

Pineal gland

Thyroid gland

Parathyroid glands

Adrenal glands

Pancreas

Kidneys

Ovaries (female)

Testes (male)

The nervous system and endocrine system are linked by the **hypothalamus** – a small structure in the brain that regulates a lot of body drives, such as hunger, thirst and sex.

The hypothalamus controls the **pituitary gland** by communicating to it what hormones need to be released from which glands, and when. The pituitary gland is often referred to as the 'master gland' due to its role in stimulating other glands such as the adrenal glands and gonads (testes/ovaries) to produce their own hormones.

The endocrine system

Fight-or-flight response

When faced with a potential threat in the environment, the nervous system will pass a message to the brain and then on to the rest of the body to alert it into action. This is believed to be a survival instinct as it happens without conscious awareness. The fight-or-flight response helps us to react quickly and prepares our body to stand and fight or to run away from the threat.

The stages in the fight-or-flight response

Step 1
- The **amygdala** (area of the brain for emotional behaviour and motivation) identifies a threat.
- The hypothalamus communicates the threat to the **sympathetic nervous system** (see page 83) to trigger a fast response.

Step 2
- The message travels down the SNS to the **adrenal medulla**.
- The adrenal medulla releases the hormone **adrenaline** into the bloodstream.

Step 3
- **Adrenaline** in the bloodstream will trigger the **fight-or-flight response**, preparing the body to stand and fight or to run away from the threat.
- The fight-or-flight response involves various physical changes such as increased heart rate, increased blood pressure, pupil dilation and increased muscle tension.

Step 4
- Once the adrenaline has started to wear off, the **parasympathetic nervous system** acts to bring the body back to its normal state.

Now try this

Explain the function of the endocrine system.

Localisation of function in the brain

The brain is the organ of behaviour. Psychologists study brains to find out how cognitive functions – such as memory – are organised in the brain.

Localisation of function

Motor cortex
This controls the muscles via the spinal cord. It is situated in the frontal lobes of both hemispheres. Different parts of the motor cortex control specific areas of the body. The cortex in the right hemisphere controls the left side of the body and the right side is controlled by the left hemisphere. The amount of cortex given over to areas of the body depends on how much complexity of movement is required. For example, more area is given over to hands as they are capable of complex movement.

Somatosensory cortex
This area is responsible for the sensation of touch. It is distributed across the parietal lobes and receives information from the opposite side of the body to the lobe. More area in the cortex is given over to areas of the body with a lot of sensory receptors, such as the fingers and the lips.

Visual centres
Many areas across the brain are involved in processing visual information. The main area for detecting patterns and processing information about moving objects is the visual cortex in the occipital lobe.

Front   Back

Broca's area
This area is one of the language areas and is involved in speech production. It is situated in the left hemisphere (in most people) close to the section of motor cortex that controls the mouth.

Wernicke's area
This is another language centre involved in language comprehension and anomia (difficulty accessing everyday words). It is situated near the junction of the left temporal and parietal lobes.

Auditory centres
These are located in the temporal lobes on both sides of the brain. Information from the ears is processed in different areas of the brain but ends up in the auditory cortex where it is recognised and responded to.

Evaluation

👍 Case studies on brain damage support the idea of some localisation of function. For example, cases of aphasia (loss of language) are associated with damage to Broca's area.

👎 The equipotentiality theory (first proposed by Lashley in 1929) suggests that, apart from motor and sensory functions, other cognitive functions are spread across brain areas rather than localised in one site.

👎 Lashley experimented on rats during the 1930s and 1940s, systematically removing different brain areas to locate the area responsible for memory. He found that it was the total amount of brain damage rather than the destruction of any one site that affected memory.

👎 Further challenges come from the fact that the brain can rewire itself after damage, to relocate functions to an undamaged area.

Now try this

Explain what 'localisation of function' is.

Lateralisation and split-brain research

You need to demonstrate knowledge and understanding of **hemispheric lateralisation** in the brain and **split-brain research**, such as Sperry (1968).

Hemispheric lateralisation

The brain consists of two hemispheres, which roughly mirror each other in terms of structure. Research shows that although they appear similar there are differences in terms of function located in each hemisphere. This is called **lateralisation**.

- The **left hemisphere** (in most people) is responsible for processing language (see Broca's and Wernicke's areas on page 86).

- The **right hemisphere** processes intuitive and spatial information (understanding the relationships of objects in space).

The hemispheres are connected by the **corpus callosum** – a bundle of fibres that act as a pathway for inter-hemispheric communication.

Split-brain research

In order to treat people with severe epilepsy that spreads from one hemisphere to the other, the corpus callosum is occasionally surgically severed so that the hemispheres are no longer connected, thus controlling the seizures. These cases are known as 'split-brain' patients.

This offers psychologists an ideal chance to study hemispheric lateralisation because of the way vision is organised.

Images that are presented to the left visual field are processed in the right hemisphere, whereas images presented to the right visual field are processed in the left hemisphere.

🔍 Key study Sperry (1968)

Aim: To investigate the functions of the left and right hemispheres of the brain in split-brain patients.

Procedure:

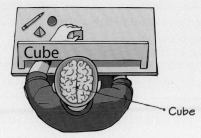

A specially designed apparatus was used to control the visual input to split-brain patients so that objects presented to them were only available to one hemisphere.

Results: Objects presented to the right visual field (processed in the left hemisphere) could be described using language. Objects presented to the left could not because the right hemisphere has no language centres. However, if asked to point out which object was seen from an array, the patient could point it out with their left hand (controlled by the right hemisphere).

An object projected to the left visual field is only recognised again when presented to that same field; it was not recognised if presented to the other field.

Conclusions: Research shows that the two hemispheres have different specialisations, confirming that language is a left hemisphere function.

Evaluation

- 👍 This is a natural experiment and it is the only ethical way to investigate the isolation of the hemispheres.

- 👍 The research is very useful as it shows lateralisation of function exists.

- 👎 Sperry's work was based on only a few patients who had experienced long-term problems with epilepsy. These factors might limit generalisability from this sample to the population.

Now try this

Outline what is meant by 'lateralisation of function', and explain how it may be tested.

Plasticity and functional recovery

Brain injury is serious and can change a person's life and personality. However, we know that in many cases it can be overcome through the brain's ability to 'rewire' itself around the damage, thus limiting or even counteracting the effect of the damage.

Plasticity

Neuroplasticity refers to the brain's ability to change throughout life and respond to environmental factors, including injury.

Plasticity occurs at different levels within the brain. At one extreme, it could involve the wholescale re-mapping of the cortical structures in the brain in response to major brain trauma. At the other extreme (and more usually), it happens at the level of individual neurons and synapses.

For example, synapses and neurons are re-organised by **environmental experience**. When you learn a new skill such as juggling, for example, areas of your brain change, but a lack of practice will reverse these changes.

Demonstrating plasticity

Synaptic pruning

As we age, neurons that do not transmit or receive information die in a process called **apoptosis**. This is a key feature of brain development in early childhood. As the brain adapts to its environment, it strengthens connective pathways that are being used and the weaker ones die through lack of use.

In response to damage

When an area of the brain is damaged, neighbouring neurons have reduced input. This actively stimulates other undamaged areas of the brain to compensate for the loss of function by creating new synapses to reroute the signals previously handled by the damaged areas.

Evaluation of claims for plasticity

- 👍 Rosenzweig et al. (1962) demonstrated that rats raised in an enriched, stimulating environment had increased cortical volume showing evidence of a greater number of synapses compared to rats raised in a wire cage without enrichment.

- 👍 Maguire et al. (2000) found that the hippocampal areas (involved in forming spatial memory) of the brains of London taxi drivers were larger than those of a control group. This was thought to be due to extensive learning of the routes around London affecting the brain.

- 👍 Evidence from case studies of functional recovery after trauma also adds validity to the claims for brain plasticity.

Functional recovery after trauma

This happens when brain function is rewired around a damaged area, usually following rehabilitation. This is affected by various factors:

- **Age:** the younger the person is when the damage occurs the more likely it is that functional recovery will happen.

- **Years spent in education:** people who have spent longer in education, e.g. university graduates, recover better than those who did not go to college.

- **Perseverance:** recovery from brain injury takes a lot of time and effort.

- **Gender:** some evidence suggests that women recover better from brain injury than men because their brain functions are not as lateralised in the first place.

Evaluation of functional recovery

- 👍 Marquez de la Plata et al. (2008) found that patients older than 40 years regained less function after treatment than younger patients. This is probably due to younger brains being more plastic than older brains.

- 👍 Under controlled conditions, Tajiri et al. (2013) showed that rats injected with stem cells near the site of the injury displayed evidence of neural recovery, whereas those given a control solution did not.

- 👎 Case studies frequently show functional recovery but have limited generalisability and, although high in mundane realism, lack the necessary control to scientifically validate the process.

Now try this

Outline the evidence for brain plasticity.

Ways of studying the brain

Brain scanning techniques

Functional magnetic resonance imaging (fMRI)
- People are placed in the fMRI scanner and asked to perform a cognitive function.
- The scanner detects increased oxygen use in the area of the brain that is activated.

Electroencephalogram (EEG)
- Electrodes placed on the scalp record broad patterns of electrical activity. This is used to detect anomalies or identify big changes in brainwave activity.

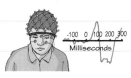

Event-related potentials (ERPs)
- These use the same equipment as EEGs.
- The person is asked to respond to specific stimuli. Over time, the researcher is able to cancel out all the background activity by finding the area that is consistently active.

Post-mortem examinations

The brain is examined after death. If the person displayed loss of cognitive functioning in life, a post-mortem could show lesions.

For example, Broca (1861) examined the brain of a patient without speech and found a lesion in the area now known as Broca's area. This method is used to understand psychopathologies such as Alzheimer's.

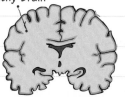 

Healthy brain   Unhealthy brain

A healthy brain is compared to one with Alzheimer's disease to understand the physiology of the disease.

Evaluation

	👍	👎
fMRI	It is reliable and objective.	It may only be measuring communication between parts of the brain, so may not be a valid measure of function.
EEG	Useful in clinical diagnosis, for example, in detecting epilepsy. Shows real-time data of a working brain.	Only provides a general picture of the activity of the surface of the brain.
ERP	It is possible to pinpoint localisation of function.	It takes a lot of time and effort to get any meaningful data.
Post-mortem	Provides a detailed anatomical analysis of brain structure that cannot be achieved by other methods.	Many variables could have caused the changes observed, so cause and effect conclusions may not be valid.

Now try this

Outline the similarities and differences between electroencephalograms (EEGs) and event-related potentials (ERPs).

Biological rhythms

Biological rhythms are regular cyclical changes in our biological systems. Rhythms repeat over different lengths of time.

Infradian rhythms

These last longer than 24 hours:

- monthly rhythms such as the human menstrual cycle
- annual rhythms such as seasonal affective disorder in humans.

Hibernation is an infradian rhythm in some non-human species.

Evaluation

🦴 There are large individual differences in the duration of rhythms, which may be due to biological causes or to external or exogenous factors that affect the onset of rhythms (see page 91).
For example, the onset of menstruation can be affected by exposure to pheromones released in the sweat of women at another stage of their cycle (Stern and McClintock, 1998).

Circadian rhythms

These last for 24 hours:

They are regulated by an internal pacemaker – the suprachiasmatic nucleus (SCN) – interacting with external pacemakers (zeitgebers).

- The sleep/wake cycle is a circadian rhythm (see page 91 for factors that affect this rhythm).
- Core body temperature has a circadian rhythm.
- Hormone release also follows a circadian rhythm (the release of melatonin at night encourages sleep).

Evaluation

👍 Free-running body clock experiments remove all external cues about time and monitor sleep/wake cycles. Siffre (1975) spent time in a deep cave and his bodily rhythms, including his sleep/wake cycle, were monitored. His natural circadian rhythm extended to around 25 hours but was still regular despite a lack of cues, showing the regulatory action of the SCN.

🦴 Other studies have shown big individual differences in the onset and duration of rhythms, suggesting that a purely biological explanation of the rhythm is too reductionist, as other factors play a part.

Ultradian rhythms

These are shorter than 24 hours (they repeat more than once a day).

- The stages of sleep are ultradian, as there is a repeating 90-minute cycle of brain activity that lasts throughout the sleep period.

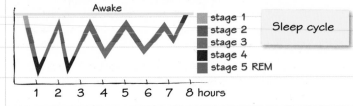

Awake

■ stage 1
■ stage 2
■ stage 3
■ stage 4
■ stage 5 REM

Sleep cycle

1 2 3 4 5 6 7 8 hours

- The Basic Rest–Activity Cycle (BRAC) applies to the waking state, proposing we are more or less alert on a 90-minute repeating cycle.

Evaluation

👍 There is strong evidence for the sleep cycle. EEGs (see page 89) monitor brainwaves as people sleep and show distinct stages in the sleep cycle that repeats several times a night.

🦴 Tucker et al. (2007), although broadly supportive of this finding, showed large individual differences in the duration of stages.

👍 Ericsson et al. (2006) found that expert violinists tended to practise in 90-minute sessions and then needed to nap to recover alertness, thus supporting BRAC.

Now try this

What is the difference between ultradian and infradian rhythms? Use examples to illustrate your answer.

Endogenous pacemakers and exogenous zeitgebers

The **sleep/wake cycle** is an example of a circadian rhythm. When and for how long we sleep is controlled by internal **endogenous** pacemakers and external or **exogenous** zeitgebers.

Endogenous pacemaker

The **suprachiasmatic nucleus** (SCN) – a small group of brain cells – is also known as the **body clock**. It is the main endogenous pacemaker.

- The SCN causes the **pineal gland** to release a hormone called **melatonin**. This happens when the **optic nerve** reduces its activity as night falls. Melatonin reduces brain activity and makes us sleepy.
- Melatonin production stops when activity on the optic nerve increases as daylight levels increase.

In the absence of exogenous cues (such as light levels), the SCN operates independently on a 25-hour or longer cycle. Our sleep/wake cycle is therefore longer than 24 hours when we are isolated from external time cues (zeitgebers).

The SCN is entrained by exogenous factors so that our sleep pattern follows a circadian or 24-hour rhythm.

> Light levels reset the body clock so it works to the circadian day/night cycle.

Entrainment

Our internal body clock is **entrained** by exogenous (external) factors, which synchronise our internal timekeeper with the external world.

The key exogenous factor that affects the sleep/wake cycle is light levels.

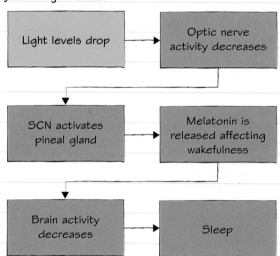

Other exogenous factors

Social cues, such as bedtime routines or mealtimes, are known to affect the cycle. The sleep/wake cycles of travellers synchronise more quickly if they engage in the activities of the new time zone, suggesting that these quicken entrainment and reset the body clock.

Evaluation

- 👍 Research in this area has led to the development of strategies to reduce the impact of shift work and jet lag. The manipulation of light levels, for example, allows shift workers to sleep when they would normally be awake.
- 👍 Siffre's (1975) cave study (see page 90) shows that the body clock maintains a regular sleep/wake cycle in the absence of all exogenous cues, supporting the view that a biological mechanism underlies this cycle.
- 👎 Free-running body clock studies, such as Siffre's, have few participants, thus limiting the generalisability of such studies.

- 👎 These studies are further criticised for using artificial light, which could affect the way the body clock works, and so lack ecological validity.
- 👍 Morgan (1995) removed the SCN from hamsters, obliterating the sleep/wake cycle. When SCN transplantation was done, they resumed a normal pattern, providing strong evidence that the SCN is the body clock.
- 👎 Extrapolation from animal studies may be limited due to the physiological differences between species.

Now try this

Outline the role of endogenous pacemakers on the sleep/wake cycle.

Exam skills 1

These exam-style questions require you to identify and explain. Before you look at them, have a look at page 85 to remind yourself about the human endocrine system, and page 83 for revision of the divisions of the nervous system.

Worked example

(a) Identify **one** hormone produced by the adrenal glands.

(1 mark)

Adrenaline

(b) Explain **one** role the hormone identified in part A has in human behaviour.

(3 marks)

Adrenaline is produced during periods of acute, or short-term, stress. It is a hormone that helps to prepare the body to cope with stress by triggering the fight-or-flight response. When adrenaline levels in the blood are high we might see an increase in heart rate, blood pressure, muscle tension and pupil dilation, which are all associated with preparing the body to fight the threat or run away from it.

Reading the question

With this kind of two-part question, it is really important to look at both parts before answering the question. Here, for example, you would have a choice of different hormones for part A. However, as part B is asking you to explain what the hormone does, it would make sense to name a hormone you know more about in part A, so that you can aim for more marks in part B.

As adrenaline is produced by the adrenal medulla, this is a relevant hormone released by the adrenal gland for part A. Another hormone you could have stated here would be **cortisol**, which is produced by the adrenal cortex.

This is a good, concise answer. The student states the function of adrenaline in the triggering of the fight-or-flight response and elaborates to provide more detail on the functions of the hormone. There is no need to say where the hormone adrenaline is produced as it is not part of the question asked.

Worked example

Explain the role of the autonomic nervous system.

(3 marks)

The autonomic nervous system is the part of the peripheral nervous system that is responsible for automatic nerve responses. The autonomic nervous system controls actions such as the beating of the heart and the functions of the lungs that require fast, involuntary reactions. These actions need to be made quickly without conscious thought, and this is what the autonomic nervous system can do.

Explaining the role of something means that you need to give some indication about what it is **and** what it does. It is really useful for you to use an example to illustrate this as it tells the examiner that you not only *know* what it is and what it does, but you also *understand* it.

Worked example

Describe one role of adrenaline in the fight-or-flight response.

(2 marks)

Adrenaline is released in periods of stress by preparing the body to fight a threat or run away. Adrenaline causes the heart rate and blood pressure to increase in order to pump more blood around the body faster to deliver oxygen to the muscles.

Describe questions will always require you to demonstrate knowledge in an accurate and detailed way, but make sure you take note of the number of marks available before answering. It can be tempting to write everything you know but if they are only offering 2 marks your answer should be brief.

Exam skills 2

Before you look at these worked examples, remind yourself about split-brain research (page 87) and biological rhythms (pages 90–91).

Worked example

Outline the procedure used in split-brain research.

(4 marks)

People with severe epilepsy sometimes have their corpus callosum severed, which disconnects the two hemispheres of the brain. Psychologists study these people to investigate how each hemisphere operates independently from the other. One way they do this is by presenting information to either the left or the right visual field by screening objects so they are only visible to one or other eye, causing one or other hemisphere to process the information. The patient is then tested to see if they can express in language what they experienced.

> This calls for quite a lot of detail about how the participants were tested. Answers must focus only on the procedure.

> This is a good answer because it focuses on the procedure rather than the findings. It details who was used in the research, how they tested them and how they recorded the results.

Worked example

Identify the type of biological rhythm from the following descriptions.

A   Repeats once every 24 hours.

B   Repeats less frequently than every 24 hours.

C   Repeats more frequently than every 24 hours.

(3 marks)

A Circadian
B Infradian
C Ultradian

> You need to be able to identify each type of rhythm by its frequency, as this is its defining factor. Make sure you read the question carefully as this can be phrased in different ways.

Worked example

Explain how endogenous **and** exogenous factors affect the sleep/wake cycle.

(6 marks)

The sleep/wake cycle is regulated by our endogenous body clock – the suprachiasmatic nucleus (SCN). The SCN receives information from the optic nerve about light levels (an exogenous factor) and signals the pineal gland to release or stop releasing the hormone melatonin. Low light levels reduce the activity on the optic nerve, which signals the SCN to trigger the pineal gland to produce melatonin. Melatonin reduces brain activity, which leads to sleep. When light levels increase, the optic nerve increases its firing rate and this signals the SCN to switch off the melatonin production, which increases brain activity and wakes us up. The sleep/wake cycle is synchronised to a circadian rhythm by the entrainment of the SCN to a 24-hour repeating pattern by the action of external factors.

> This question is asking you to explain the interaction between internal and external factors that govern the sleep/wake cycle. No evaluation is needed, but the answer must be firmly linked to the circadian sleep/wake rhythm.

> The answer includes the key terminology, especially in relation to endogenous factors.

> The answer clearly explains how internal or endogenous factors are influenced by external factors to promote or reduce sleepiness. The explanation is effective and focuses on how sleep is influenced by relevant factors.

Had a go ☐   Nearly there ☐   Nailed it! ☐

Exam-style practice 1

Practise for Paper 2 of your A level exam with these exam-style questions. There are answers on pages 298–299. Before looking at these questions, it would be good to review biopsychology.

1 Read the item and then answer the question that follows.

Alessio has woken up late and has to rush to school. When he arrives, he is challenged by the deputy head teacher who demands an explanation. When Alessio starts to talk he realises he is quite shaky, his hands are sweating and his heart is racing.

Using your knowledge of the fight-or-flight response, explain what is happening to Alessio. **(4 marks)**

> Simply describing the fight-or-flight response is not appropriate here. You need to **apply your knowledge** and understanding to what has happened to Alessio. It might help to use his name in your answer.

2 Label the divisions of the human nervous system, numbered 1–4, to complete the diagram. **(4 marks)**

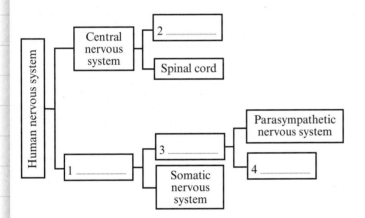

> Your answer should include the **key biological processes** in relation to Alessio's scenario. You could refer to the challenge from the deputy head as a potential threat and then go on to discuss how the nervous system will react to this. Key terms to consider would be **hypothalamus**, **adrenal medulla** and **adrenaline**.

> It is important that the labels go in the correct place and that the **correct terminology** and spellings have been used. You should double-check your answer when complete to make sure you have not made an error.

3 Describe the process of synaptic transmission **(4 marks)**

> Describing a 'process' means that you should be explaining what happens rather than just naming physical structures. Begin by stating that synaptic transmission is the passing of messages between 2 neurons across a synapse, and then go on to describe how this process happens.

4 Which part of a neuron binds to neurotransmitters after they have been released into the synapse?

A Axon ◯

B Terminal button ◯

C Soma ◯

D Receptor ◯

(1 mark)

> Make sure you can clearly draw and label a synapse and the three types of neuron. Many questions in Biopsychology are likely to require accurate knowledge of the structures involved and what they do.

5 Briefly outline the function of the pituitary gland in the endocrine system. **(2 marks)**

> Binding to neurotransmitters could also be referred to as 'receiving' the neurotransmitter.

> As this is only two marks, and asks for a brief outline, aim for no more than two sentences and focus on what the pituitary gland does rather than peripheral details like where it is.

Exam-style practice 2

Practise for Paper 2 of your A level exam with these exam-style questions. There are answers on page 299. Before looking at these questions, it would be good to review the localisation of function in the brain (page 86), brain plasticity and functional recovery (page 88), ways of investigating brain function (page 89) and endogenous and exogenous factors (page 91).

6 Outline **two or more** factors that might affect functional recovery following brain injury.   **(6 marks)**

> If you know two factors really well it is better to provide in depth detail on those than try to write about further factors.

7 What is meant by localisation of function?   **(2 marks)**

> For 2 marks, it would be useful to provide an example of a localised function along with a brief definition.

8 Read the item and then answer the question that follows.

> George has had a stroke that has left him unable to use spoken language. He understands what is said to him, but all he produces in response is a meaningless collection of words.

> You need to review your knowledge of Broca's and Wernicke's areas to explain the pattern of deficit experienced by George.

Using your knowledge of localisation of function, explain what has happened to George.   **(4 marks)**

9 Evaluate the claim that the brain is plastic.   **(4 marks)**

> This answer should focus on relevant evidence. For example, from case studies that show recovery after trauma.

10 Outline the key features of an electroencephalogram (EEG).   **(2 marks)**

> Explain what an EEG measures and detects, and how this is done.

11 Briefly evaluate the claim that endogenous factors control **one or more** biorhythms.   **(4 marks)**

> Focus on the sleep/wake cycle and use evidence to evaluate this claim. You might also consider the validity of the research evidence. A good answer will effectively link the evidence together.

Experiments

Experimental methods are often used in psychology as a way of conducting scientific research by testing the effect of a change on a specific measured behaviour. Experiments are a type of research method on their own, but not all research uses experimental methods, so **do not** refer to *all* studies as *experiments*.

Key features of experiments

In an experiment there are two key variables:

- the **independent variable (IV)** – the thing you change

- the **dependent variable (DV)** – the thing you measure.

For example, Milgram investigated the effect of changing situational variables, such as the setting of his 'shocking' study (IV), on the percentage of people willing to continue to 450 volts (DV). For more on Milgram's (1963) study of obedience, see page 5.

The overall aim of an experiment is to establish a **cause and effect** relationship between the IV and the DV.

Types of experiment

| Laboratory experiments |
- take place in a controlled setting, such as a laboratory
- the participants can be randomly allocated to conditions

| Field experiments |
- take place in participants' natural environments
- participants can be randomly allocated to conditions

| Natural experiments |
- can take place in laboratories or natural settings
- the IV is a variable which is controlled by someone other than the researcher. Often involves exploiting an event that is happening.

| Quasi experiments |
- can take place in laboratories or natural settings
- the IV is a variable that occurs naturally in the population and cannot be manipulated

Evaluating laboratory experiments

- 👍 It is possible to control the environment closely, making **replication** easier and increasing **reliability**.

- 👍 As participants are in an artificially controlled setting, they are more likely to know they are being studied, and therefore be able to **consent**.

- 👎 The environment is artificial, meaning that the behaviour seen may lack realism too.

- 👎 As participants know they are being observed, **demand characteristics** are more likely to influence their behaviour, so internal validity may be low. For more on demand characteristics, see page 102.

Evaluating field experiments

- 👍 As participants are in their natural environment, the behaviour seen is more likely to be realistic, thus increasing ecological validity.

- 👍 Participants may not know they are being studied, so they would be less prone to **demand characteristics**, improving experimental validity.

- 👎 The environment is less controlled so there is more chance of extraneous variables influencing the results.

- 👎 Participants may not be aware they are being studied meaning that gaining consent may be difficult.

Evaluating natural experiments

- 👍 The change or difference being investigated in the IV is not being controlled by the experimenter, meaning they are less likely to influence the data due to **experimenter bias**, thus increasing validity.

- 👍 As the IV is something that is actually happening, any changes in the DV are more likely to be realistic and not artificially created.

- 👎 As the experimenter cannot directly control the IV, they do not know how **reliable** the change is and therefore cannot infer cause and effect.

- 👎 The lack of control in changing the IV means that there is more chance of **confounding variables** influencing results (see page 102).

Evaluating quasi experiments

- 👍 The IV is a naturally occurring difference between people, meaning changes in the DV may have more realism than if the IV was artificially created.

- 👍 Participants are likely to be aware they are being studied, making consent easier to gain and so there may be fewer ethical issues.

- 👎 Quasi experiments can only be used where a naturally occurring difference between people can easily be identified, so they are difficult to set up.

- 👎 The task used to gather data for the DV may still be unrealistic, meaning that the data itself has little mundane realism.

Now try this

Explain the difference between a laboratory and a field experiment.

Observational techniques

These are used when psychologists want to know what people do. All types of observation involve the systematic watching and recording of target behaviour in order to see what actually happens. You need to know about the different types of observation. Each observation can be a mix of the different types. For example, it could be a covert, non-participant naturalistic observation.

Naturalistic or controlled

(1) **Naturalistic** observations are conducted in the real world in the location where the behaviour being studied takes place.

For example, Schaffer and Emerson studied infant attachments in their homes. For more on Schaffer and Emerson's (1964) study of attachments in infancy, see page 35.

(2) **Controlled** observations are conducted under laboratory conditions and often involve the researcher setting up a situation for the participants to interact with.

For example, Ainsworth's Strange Situation Procedure (SSP) studied infant attachment in the laboratory. For more on Ainsworth's (1978) SSP, see page 40.

Evaluation: control vs ecological validity

👍 As the amount of control increases, so does the reliability of the data measurement because the research is set up to watch for specific behaviour.

Reliability

Ecological validity

👎 However, this results in a loss of ecological validity because the participants are not in their natural environment and therefore their behaviour might be affected.

Participant and non-participant

(1) A **participant** observation involves the researcher becoming part of the group being observed. They can record the data openly (**overt**) or **covertly**, for example with cameras or when alone.

(2) A **non-participant** observation is done when the researcher is watching from outside the group being observed.

Non-participant observation through a one-way mirror in the SSP

Evaluation: recording data accurately

👎 Whatever type of observation is being conducted the data must be recorded accurately, usually in real time, and this creates problems especially when a lot of people are being observed simultaneously.

👎 Often this process is affected by **subjective bias** where different researchers might see the same behaviour but interpret it differently, affecting the reliability of the data.

👎 Accurate recording of data is difficult especially in a participant observation, when you are among the people being watched and cannot easily take notes.

Covert and overt

(1) A **covert** observation is one in which the participants do not know they are being observed.

For example, the nurses in Hofling's hospital study. For more on Hofling et al.'s (1966) obedience study, see page 6.

(2) An **overt** observation is one in which the participants are aware that they are being studied.

For example, Haney et al.'s (1973) Stanford Prison experiment used overt observation (see page 4).

Evaluation: ethical issues

👎 Covert observations cannot gain informed consent therefore could be regarded as unethical.

👎 In overt observations, consent can be obtained but this could affect the validity of the data as people then know they are being watched and may change their behaviour.

Now try this

1 What is the key feature of all observations?

2 What are the ethical issues associated with covert, naturalistic observations?

Self-report techniques

Surveys gather **self-report data**. Rather than the psychologist recording the behaviour they are interested in studying, they simply ask their participants questions. This can be done by **interviews** and **questionnaires**.

Interviews

These have been described as a 'conversation with a purpose' because they are normally done face to face (or perhaps by phone).

The organisation of the questions in interviews can vary (see 'Design of interviews' below).

> The interviewer asks the questions and records the data.

Questionnaires

These are usually paper-based but are being done more frequently in an online format. They consist of a series of questions, which can be set in different formats, and require the participant to give a written answer.

- **Open** questions allow the participant to answer in any way they choose, so they do not limit the possible responses. The data will be **qualitative**, as they describe what they think.

- **Closed** questions limit the possible responses by providing tick boxes or offering a scale to indicate agreement, such as a Likert scale. The data will be **quantitative**.

Strongly agree   Agree   Undecided   Disagree   Strongly disagree

An example of a Likert scale

Evaluation of interviews

- 👍 It is possible to get in-depth data from interviews that allow a meaningful exploration of individual views.

- 👎 It can be very time-consuming to gather the data as each participant will usually be interviewed on their own. This means that the sample size is likely to be small and therefore less generalisable to the population.

- 👎 The data will need to be transcribed to a written format and this takes time and effort.

- 👎 A common issue with interviews is that analysis of the data is subjective and open to a variety of interpretations so is less reliable.

Evaluation of questionnaires

- 👍 Large amounts of data can be gathered quickly by issuing a postal or online survey.

- 👍 Data from closed questions can be analysed quickly and comparisons made between variables.

- 👎 Social desirability bias can affect the validity of the data as participants answer the questions in such a way as to make them look good.

- 👎 Although the presentation of the questions is reliable as all participants get the same questions in the same way, there is no control over the situation in which they answer them and this can lead to unreliability in the data.

- 👎 Participants may not understand the questions or may not be honest in their answers, making the data less valid.

Design of interviews

Structured interviews – the questions are set in advance of the interview and the schedule of questions does not vary. These are best used when you need to make comparisons between participants by asking them the same questions.

Unstructured interviews – these are looser. There are questions but the interviewer can deviate from them and follow up an interesting answer which may take the interview in a different direction. These are best used when the research is exploratory and requires depth.

Questionnaire construction

- Questions need to be carefully constructed to make them clear and easy to understand; leading questions must be avoided.

- The order and presentation of the questions should be checked to ensure it is easily understood and not so long that it is too time-consuming.

- The type of data needed (quantitative or qualitative) dictates whether open or closed questions are used.

- A pilot study will check that the questions are reliable and valid for the research.

Now try this

What is self-report data?

Correlations

Technically, a correlation is a way of analysing data, rather than a research method in itself. A correlation is a way to test whether a relationship exists between two **co-variables**.

What is a correlation?

A **correlation** is a way to look for a relationship that may exist between two measured variables. *Do not* confuse this with experiments where one variable changes and the other is measured. The variables in a correlation are referred to as **co-variables** because they are not causally linked; instead they are two variables that may or may not be related to one another in some way.

Correlations can be conducted on **secondary data**, and often provide a useful starting point for psychological research. For more on secondary data, see page 112.

Positive correlation

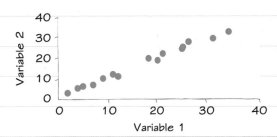

In a **positive correlation**, as one variable increases, so does the other. The closer the points on the scattergram are to forming a line at a 45° angle, the stronger the correlation.

Correlations can measure the **direction** and **strength** of any relationship between co-variables, and the data can easily be displayed on a **scattergram**.

Negative correlation

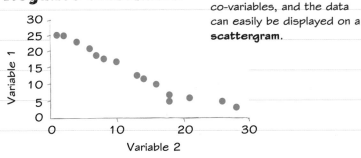

In a **negative correlation**, as one variable increases, the other decreases. The closer the points are to forming a straight or curved line, the stronger the correlation.

No correlation

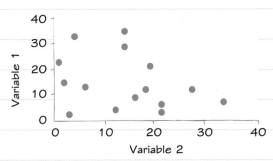

If points on a scattergram appear to have no particular arrangement (i.e. are scattered), then there may well be no relationship between them.

Correlation coefficient

The strength of a correlation can be measured by calculating the **correlation coefficient**, which is a number between −1 and +1.

- The closer the score is to −1, the stronger the negative correlation.
- The closer to +1, the stronger the positive correlation.
- A score of 0 would indicate no correlation.

Evaluation

👍 Correlations can be conducted quickly using **secondary data** as a way to investigate whether there may be a relationship between two variables worthy of further study using another research method.

👎 Correlations cannot give you information about **cause and effect** – they can only tell you a relationship exists, but not how or why.

👎 Correlations only measure relationships between two variables, but there may be unmeasured variables influencing the data that are not taken into account.

Now try this

1 Identify **one** psychological example of a positive correlation.

2 Explain **one** problem associated with conducting correlations in psychological research.

Case studies and content analysis

Case studies and **content analysis** are non-experimental techniques used to gather information. **Thematic analysis** and **coding** are analytical methods used to interpret qualitative data.

Case studies

- They aim to gather detailed information about a case, such as an individual, a specific group of people or an event.
- They use multiple methods, for example interviews and observations, to gather data.
- The data can be qualitative or quantitative, and it can include primary and/or secondary data (see page 112).
- They can be done fairly quickly or may take many years.

Evaluation

- 👍 The data gathered is detailed and in-depth, so more valid conclusions can be drawn.
- 👍 This method can be used to investigate events and behaviour that are rare or would be unethical to investigate by other means.
- 🔻 These studies can take a lot of time.
- 🔻 The sample is limited and not representative of the wider population.

Content analysis

- This is an indirect observation using pre-existing communications such as a magazine article or a TV programme.
- It involves a systematic examination of the material in order to determine meanings that underlie the content.
- This can be done by **thematic analysis**.

Evaluation

- 👍 Quite ethical as no people are being used in order to gather data.
- 👍 High in ecological validity as it analyses real communications.
- 🔻 Data collection may be subjective as it relies on the researcher's interpretation.
- 🔻 This method describes what is seen but does not explain the causes of it.

Thematic analysis

This is an analytic technique used to summarise key ideas from qualitative data gathered by methods such as interviews and case studies, and identifies patterns.

It is a 'bottom-up' process where the analysis of the data leads to the development of categories or themes that emerge from it.

1. The researcher gets familiar with the material, finds categories/themes and creates codes for analysis.

2. They then re-examine the data and code it according to the themes.

3. They review the themes by checking against the data.

4. The data is summarised by its themes and supported with data drawn from the transcript, such as verbatim quotes from an interview.

5. This is then written up as the data analysis.

Coding

This is the means by which qualitative data is summarised into meaningful units for analysis.

> Read data and identify themes to create categories related to the research aims

↓

> Sort the data according to the categories

↓

> Review the categories to ensure they are supported; if not, re-categorise and re-code

The coding process

For example, one category for an interview transcript on attitudes to people with mental health issues could be negative names for disorders; terms such as 'looney', 'mad' and 'bonkers' would then be coded in that category.

Now try this

Explain **one** strength and **one** limitation of using the case study technique.

Aims and hypotheses

When designing an experiment, you need to be clear from the start about what you are trying to find out, what you expect to happen and how your experiment will be set out to achieve this. Whether it is likely to 'work' or not is irrelevant. What is important is that the experiment sets out to test a specified **aim**. So careful planning from the outset is important.

Aims

When starting a study you should have a clear idea in mind of what it is you are setting out to investigate. The *purpose* of the study is also known as the **aim**, and it is a really important starting point to set the scene for the study. An aim should always be written as a statement – it is *not a prediction* of the outcome of the study.

For example, the aim of Loftus and Palmer's (1974) study could be phrased as:
To see if changing the verb used in a question on the speed of a car involved in an accident would affect the estimates of speed given by participants.
For more on Loftus and Palmer's (1974) car crash study, see page 26.

Hypotheses

Once the aim is clearly stated, you would then need to develop a **hypothesis** to predict the likely outcome of the experiment. The type of hypothesis you choose would depend on how much past research has already been done to inform the likely outcome of your experiment.

Null and alternative/experimental hypotheses

Scientific research begins with a **null hypothesis**. This states that there will be no effect of an independent variable on the dependent variable, or there will be no relationship between the two co-variables being tested.

The **alternative hypothesis** is a hypothesis that predicts that there will be some kind of significant outcome from the research. This would be phrased as a statement outlining what is expected to happen as a result of conducting the research. If we are doing an experimental study, this hypothesis can be referred to as the **experimental hypothesis**. Alternative hypotheses can be **directional (one-tailed)** or **non-directional (two-tailed)**.

---

1 Directional (one-tailed) hypothesis

A directional hypothesis states exactly what outcome is expected from the experiment, using comparative language to describe the expected outcome of each condition.

For example, in Loftus and Palmer's study, they could state:
Participants given the verb 'smashed' in the question will give significantly <u>higher</u> estimates of speed than participants given the verb 'contacted'.

A directional or one-tailed hypothesis is selected when previous research predicts a likely direction of the results.

2 Non-directional (two-tailed) hypothesis

A non-directional hypothesis states that there will be a difference in performance between the conditions in the experiment, but not what the difference will be.

For example, in Loftus and Palmer's study, a non-directional hypothesis would be:
*There will be a **difference** in the estimates of speed given by participants given different verbs in the questions.*

A non-directional or two-tailed hypothesis is chosen when previous research gives confounding results.

Now try this

1 Explain how an aim differs from a hypothesis.
2 Outline what is meant by a 'directional' hypothesis.

Variables

Variables are factors that can change or vary in some way during research. In your research, there may be some variables you want to change, some you want to keep the same and some that might change without you realising. The more you consider the possible variables in your research, and plan for how you can control interference from other variables, the better your chance of conducting a credible piece of research.

Manipulation and control of variables

In an experiment, the independent variable (IV) is **manipulated** by the researcher by making a change to it in one (or more) condition/s. This can then be compared to another condition of the IV to identify what effects can be measured in the dependent variable (DV).

In some experiments, a **control** condition may be included where no change of the IV is tested to compare to the other change/s.

Look at page 96 for a reminder about independent and dependent variables.

Operationalising variables

When changing IVs and measuring DVs, it is important that you clearly define exactly what the variables are. **Operationalising** variables means to define the variables and make them measurable and observable so that a cause-and-effect relationship can be seen.

For example, Loftus and Palmer operationalised their IV (changing the verb used in the question) by using the same question with five different verbs for five different groups of participants. This way, they could see whether the wording had any impact on the estimates of speed given. For more on Loftus and Palmer's (1974) car crash study, see page 26.

Extraneous variables

These are any variables other than the IV that could possibly influence the measurement of the DV and could include:

- **participant variables**, such as age or intelligence
- **situational variables**, such as the lighting levels in the laboratory
- **experimenter variables**, such as whether the researcher is male or female.

Confounding variables

If a variable has actually been found to have influenced the results of the research then it would be considered to have confounded the results.

For example, if you ended up with one condition full of participants with an excellent memory and compared them to a group with average memory, this would be a confounding variable if the DV was related to memory.

Demand characteristics

One factor that can influence results is if the participants are aware of what the researchers are looking for. This can lead to **demand characteristics** whereby the participants may confound the results by trying to either help the researcher support their hypothesis or deliberately 'mess up' the data.

If researchers deceive the participants by not telling them the aim of the research before they take part, this can help to prevent demand characteristics. However, this would have to be ethically justified. It is also possible to reduce demand characteristics by conducting an independent groups design (see page 104) so that participants are only exposed to one condition of an experiment. This makes it harder for them to predict the aim.

Investigator effects

The researcher's presence in the study can have an influence on the results gathered because they could unconsciously (or deliberately!) change the participants' behaviour. These **investigator effects** can be caused by anything from smiling more at some participants than others, to actively encouraging participants to say more in an interview if the answers they give do not suit the researcher's hypothesis.

One way of reducing investigator effects is to conduct a **double-blind** procedure. In this, the researcher *and* the participant are unaware of which condition of an experiment is being tested, meaning that the researcher cannot influence the results as they do not know what they are testing.

Now try this

Explain **one** way in which demand characteristics could be reduced in a psychological study.

Sampling techniques

The **target population** is the group of people that you are studying. This can be quite specific, for example people who work for a particular organisation, or it can be general, for example all people over the age of 16. In the majority of cases, it is impossible to study every individual in the target population so a **sample** is drawn to represent them. **Samples** are selected using different techniques.

Random sampling
Every member of the target population has an equal chance of being selected for the research. This can be done by picking names from a hat, or in larger target populations by putting names on a database and using a computer to randomly select the number required.

Opportunity sampling
The sample consists of whoever happens to be available at the time where the study is happening.

Systematic sampling
The researcher picks people according to a system, for example every fourth person is chosen.

Sampling techniques

Stratified sampling
The target population is broken down into its key demographic components (or strata) and participants are selected from each strata according to its relative size in the population

Target population

Strata

Stratified samples

Self-selecting sampling
Also known as **volunteer** sampling. The sample consists of people who choose to respond to a request for participants (often made through advertising).

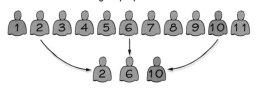

Target poplulation

① ② ③ ④ ⑤ ⑥ ⑦ ⑧ ⑨ ⑩ ⑪

② ⑥ ⑩

Sample (every 4th)

Evaluation

👍 Good samples must **represent** the target population and some methods are more likely to get a representative sample than others. This means that it is possible to **generalise** from the sample to the target population.

👍 They should not take too much time and **effort** as this will impact on the resources needed to do the study.

👍 They should rule out the possibility of researcher **bias** in the selection process where they choose people who might be likely to support their hypothesis. For example, if Milgram had chosen people that he knew to be obedient then he would have been guilty of researcher bias. For more on Milgram's (1963) study of obedience, see page 5.

The likely strengths and weaknesses of each sampling method

	Random	Stratified	Self-selecting	Opportunity	Systematic
representative	high	high	low	low	medium
effort	high	very high	low	low	medium
bias	very low	low	high	high	medium

Now try this

Explain the advantages of random and opportunity sampling.

Experimental design and control

When doing experiments you need to decide how to organise your sample of participants across the two (or more) conditions. This is what we call the **experimental design**. There are three types of experimental design – **independent groups**, **repeated measures** and **matched pairs**.

1 Independent groups

A B C D E   F G H I J

Condition A ≠ Condition B

Involves different groups doing each condition.

👍 Participants are less likely to guess the aim and change their behaviour accordingly.

👎 As the groups contain different people, their individual differences might influence the results.

2 Repeated measures

A B C D E   F G H I J

Condition A = Condition B

Involves one group doing all conditions.

👍 By using the same participants in all conditions, there are no **individual differences** to act as a **confounding variable**.

👎 By doing the experiment more than once in different conditions, the participants may be affected by **order effects**.

3 Matched pairs

A B C D E   F G H I J

Condition A ≠ Condition B

Different groups in each condition **but** the groups are matched on key factors.

👍 By matching the groups in each condition on key **participant variables**, the influence of individual differences should be significantly reduced.

👎 Despite some **control**, it is impossible to remove all individual differences.

Counterbalancing

The problem of order effects can be overcome by counterbalancing, also known as an ABBA design.
- The group of participants are split into two smaller groups.
- Half the participants do condition A then condition B, while the other half do condition B followed by condition A.
- This means the potential effects of doing one condition after another in a repeated measures design will be counteracted.

Random allocation

In an independent groups design, individual differences in each group can cause problems. To reduce the potential of bias, participants can be randomly allocated to one of the conditions. For example, the first 20 participants' names drawn from a hat are in condition I. The next 20 are in condition 2.

Control

Standardisation

Standardisation is a process where you try to ensure all your participants experience the research process in the same way.
For example, by having a list of steps and instructions to follow, which stays the same for all participants.

Randomisation

Sometimes having a standardised procedure can cause problems if the order in which things are done or presented could be an extraneous variable. In this case, researchers may choose to randomise parts of the procedure to remove any bias by making it all 'due to chance'.
For example, participants may do the conditions in a random order by having a computer decide what order to present material to them.

Pilot studies

A pilot study is a small-scale trial run of the experiment. This allows you to check that your design or method will work. It is useful as a practice to check timings and instructions and to identify any problems or where significant results may occur. Changes can then be made to ensure that the study runs smoothly and fewer errors are likely to occur in the procedure.

Now try this

1 Describe what is meant by a matched pairs design.
2 Outline **one** strength and **one** weakness of using an independent groups design.

Observational design

Observational research involves watching and recording behaviour that is relevant to a particular research aim. It is impossible to accurately record all relevant or target behaviour as it happens (unless you use video recording technology, and even then you still need to extract the target behaviour), so researchers use different methods to extract information from observing people. You need to know about constructing **behavioural categories** and data extraction using **time** and **event sampling**.

Behavioural categories

Before starting the observation, the researcher decides which behaviour is relevant to the research question and sets up a **tally chart** to record it. This consists of different **categories of target behaviour** that the researcher ticks when they see it occurring.

For example, if the research question is: *Do male children show more aggression than female children?*, the researcher will create categories such as punch, kick, push, verbal abuse. In separate columns, they then record the frequency of male and female aggressive incidents using either **event** or **time sampling** techniques.

Example of a tally chart used to measure acts of aggression

Boys			Girls		
kick	punch	verbal abuse	kick	punch	verbal abuse
IIII	I	I	I	II	IIII I

Event sampling

The observer watches for the target behaviours in the sample and simply records all instances of the behaviour in the appropriate column when they happen.

Time sampling

The observer watches and records all the occurrences of relevant behaviour at set, or randomly set, time intervals.

Establishing reliability of data collection

- Researchers should make sure that the tally chart works by conducting a **pilot observation** to check that the categories are easy to identify and nothing is missing.

- Observers should be **trained** in advance of the data gathering to ensure they know what they are looking for and can reliably identify it.

- Multiple observers should be used to watch the same behaviour and **inter-rater reliability** should be tested. This is where one observer's tally is compared to others who observed the same thing. If there is agreement between researchers, then the inter-rater reliability is high as there will be a positive correlation between their data. Look back at page 99 for a reminder about correlations.

Evaluation: behavioural categories

- 👍 These must be clear and objective so that anyone could easily identify when the target behaviour has happened.

- 👍 They should be comprehensive in covering all possible behaviour that is relevant to the research aim.

Event sampling

- 👎 This can be difficult to do accurately when there is a lot of action to record, therefore reducing reliability of the data.

Time sampling

- 👎 It is possible to miss important events because they happen outside of the time frame for recording behaviour.

Now try this

1 Construct a tally chart to measure pro-social behaviour in male and female pre-schoolers.

2 Outline **one** possible problem with this sampling technique.

Ethics in research

The **British Psychological Society (BPS)** provides guidance on the principles that underpin research ethics in psychology. This helps psychologists (including students) to ensure that their research is conducted in an **ethically acceptable** way. The rights of participants must be respected at all times, and any risk to them should be minimised as much as possible.

The British Psychological Society

Promoting excellence in psychology

The logo for the British Psychological Society

Informed consent

Participants should be aware of their involvement in the research and, wherever possible, know the full aim of the investigation *before* they take part. They should then formally agree to take part before the study begins.

Consent can be gained by getting participants to sign a form to say they know what is happening and they are happy to participate.

In the case of children under 16, parents should consent on their behalf. In other cases where a person cannot consent on their own behalf, for example someone who is mentally unable to understand the consequences of participation, the next of kin would be contacted.

Gaining consent

If informed consent is not always possible, consent can be gained through different means.

Presumptive consent can be gained by asking a group of people who are similar to the participants to see if they would consent to take part if they were asked.

Prior general consent can be gained by warning the actual participants that they will be deceived in some way before they take part. This then allows the participants to decide whether they still want to take part without knowing what is going to happen.

Retrospective consent can be gained at the end of a study when the true aim can be fully revealed to the participant, if it hasn't been already. Participants can then choose whether to allow their data to be included.

Deception

Participants should be aware of all elements of the investigation before they take part, and should not be lied to during the process of the research. However, sometimes telling participants everything will affect their behaviour. In this case, participants can be **deceived** if the deception has been justified to and agreed on by an ethics committee, but it must be addressed fully in the **debrief** later.

Confidentiality

The names and personal details of participants should not be revealed to others beyond the researchers.

This can be achieved by referring to all participants by a number or initial rather than a name, and not using locations when discussing the participants. In case studies, a popular strategy to maintain confidentiality is to use a **pseudonym** or fake name.

Protection from harm

Participants can be harmed by participating in research if they are put under stress, embarrassed, frustrated, hurt or exposed to anything that changes their mental or physical state. Researchers must avoid causing harm unnecessarily.

A way to avoid harm is to make it clear to participants that they can **withdraw** at any time, including at the end of the study when they can take their data with them. They can also be offered follow-up counselling or support if there is a need.

Debriefing

After taking part in research, the participants should be informed about exactly what the investigation is aiming to do. The participants should also be offered an opportunity to ask questions or even be offered support if they have been upset by taking part in the study. The debrief is especially important if participants have been deceived at any point in the study.

Now try this

Explain how researchers can keep participants' details confidential.

Peer review

Research becomes part of the psychological knowledge once it has been published in an academic, peer-reviewed journal. There are hundreds of psychology journals published across the world. You need to be able to describe and evaluate the **role of peer review** in the scientific process.

The peer review process

Once the research investigation is complete and has been written up as an academic paper by the researchers, they submit it to a suitable scientific journal. It then goes through the peer review process. This is an important part of the scientific method.

1 Editor sends copies to several expert reviewers (peers)	→	2 Reviewers independently read the paper	→	3 Editor decides what to do next

This can be: • single blind where the author is unaware who the reviewers are • double blind where neither the author nor the reviewers know who each other are • open review where everyone knows who is involved.	Whichever method is chosen, the reviewers go through the paper very carefully and check it for mistakes and issues of fraud. They then report back to the editor with their comments and suggestions.	This can be to: • accept and publish • accept but only if small revisions are made by the author • reject but suggest revisions and then resubmission • reject outright.

The peer review process

Evaluation

Over a million articles are submitted to scientific journals every year. Without peer review, there would be no control over what gets published and enters the public domain.

👍 Peer review acts as a barrier, stopping flawed, fraudulent and foolish research becoming part of the public understanding of psychology.

👎 It is impossible to ensure that all reviews are done in a totally unbiased way because the reviewers may have a vested interest in promoting or supressing some studies that agree with or refute their own research.

👎 There is a possibility that research that does not find a significant effect is less likely to be published so will not feed back to the theoretical framework, giving a biased view of the research area.

👎 Even when the process is properly carried out, some bad reseach still gets through. The system is not perfect.

Journal of Experimental Psychology: General

The *Journal of Experimental Psychology: General®* publishes articles describing empirical work that bridges the traditional interests of two or more communities of psychology.

 Peer review is part of the scientific process

Peer review attempts to ensure that only reliable and valid work is published. Once findings are published, other researchers can check them through replication. This leads to an essential part of the scientific process: **theory construction**.

Theories are changed and developed in light of research findings, and replication is necessary for this to happen. Without publication, however, it could not happen. Without peer review, there would be no control over what is published, making the process less efficient.

Now try this

Outline **one** advantage and **one** disadvantage of the peer review process.

Implications of psychological research for the economy

🌐 **Real world** According to the British Psychological Society, psychologists make a major contribution to our understanding of various issues that impact on the economy. For example, psychologists have made contributions to debates on the impact of diet on health, the causes and impact of adversity in childhood and the effective interventions for mental health issues that affect 25% of the population. Their work leads to change in health-related and other socially important behaviours. You need to be able to explain ways in which psychological research impacts on economic activity.

Clinical psychology

A major economic contribution of psychology is in dealing with mental health issues. The 2013 Annual Report of the Chief Medical officer estimates that mental health issues cost the UK economy £70–100 billion per year. This includes the cost of health and social care for sufferers, lost economic activity due to days off work and underperformance as a result of mental health issues. Psychologists work to understand the causes of disorders and to develop treatments, thus contributing to the economy. Research in psychology has produced effective treatments for many disorders, including:

- drug treatments
- talking cures
- cognitive behavioural therapies.

Such treatments have enabled people to continue to live independently, staying in the community rather than being admitted to institutions for long periods of time.

Occupational psychology

Psychological research has made big changes to the workplace. For example:

- Stress management programmes have been designed to reduce days lost through illness.
- Research into biorhythms has led to changes in the way shift patterns are organised, thus increasing productivity and reducing time off work.
- Managing human resources, for example developing effective recruitment strategies that ensure the right people are employed rather than those that will not benefit the company.

Health psychology

Health psychologists use theories and research to effect behaviour change that will lead to improved health and therefore less demand for health services, thus saving money. For example:

- treating addiction
- running health promotion campaigns.

Change4Life campaign banner

Developmental psychology

Research by Bowlby and others highlighted the importance of early childhood experience in the development of the child. Attachment theory led to the development of new working practices for parents, encouraging them to form strong emotional bonds with their children and leading to the introduction of parental leave. Look at page 42 for a reminder about Bowlby's influence.

It has also caused a change in the way children without parents are treated, encouraging early adoption and changing the way institutions that look after children operate.

Ultimately, this contributes to the economy as these children grow up to be psychologically healthy adults living independent lives, earning their own money and contributing to the economy.

Now try this

Explain how psychology can have a positive impact on the economy.

Validity and reliability

You need to demonstrate knowledge and understanding of **reliability** and **validity** across all methods of investigation, and ways of assessing and improving them.

Types of validity

This is the extent to which the research actually measures and tests what it claims to.

Internal validity

This is the extent to which the results of the study are due to the tested variable rather than extraneous or confounding variables.

External validity

This is the extent to which the results of the study can be generalised to other people (population validity), other settings (ecological validity) and across time (temporal validity).

Reliability

This is the extent to which the research is consistent. If the research is repeated in the same way and the findings are the same, the results are said to be reliable.

Internal reliability

This is concerned with internal consistency, and is demonstrated in the way that the procedure is applied and the measurements used.

External reliability

This is about how consistent a test is over time – does it consistently produce similar results?

Assessing validity

There are four ways of assessing validity:

1. **Face validity** is the most basic assessment of validity – simply look at the test to see if it seems to be testing what it claims.

2. **Concurrent validity** uses already validated measures for the variable being tested and correlates the measures from one test with measures using another.

3. **Predictive validity** checks validity by assessing how well it predicts future behaviour – for example, whether a test of IQ predicts school performance.

4. **Temporal validity** compares results over time by retesting – the findings are valid if they remain the same.

Assessing reliability

There are three ways of assessing reliability:

1. **The test–retest method** measures external reliability – give the test to the same participants on two (or more) occasions and correlate the results. It is reliable if they are the same.

2. **Inter-observer reliability** measures internal reliability – multiple observers (researchers) independently record the data and their records are correlated. If they agree, the measures are reliable.

3. **The split-half method** measures the internal reliability of tests or questionnaires – participants complete the test, which is then divided into two halves and each half is scored. If the test consistently measures what it is supposed to, the scores for each half will be the same.

Improving validity

Internal validity can be improved by employing tighter controls on extraneous variables and by ensuring high levels of reliability in the procedure and measurement.

For example, by carrying out a controlled laboratory experiment.

External validity can be improved by developing realistic tests and using natural settings for studies rather than artificial tests in highly controlled conditions.

For example, by conducting research in the real world.

Improving reliability

Increasing the **objectivity** of the measures will increase their consistency over time and between people. Such **operationalised variables** are essential to improving reliability. For example, by defining aggression (subjective) as pushing/kicking (objective and operationalised).

Standardising procedures with participants is another way to ensure a study is reliable internally and externally, as all participants have a consistent experience and the study can be replicated to test the reliability of the results.

Now try this

What is the difference between reliability and validity?

Features of science

You need to be able to demonstrate knowledge and understanding of the features of science, including **objectivity** and the **empirical method**, **replicability** and **falsifiability**, **theory construction** and **hypothesis testing**, **paradigms** and **paradigm shifts**.

Scientific method

This is a way of acquiring knowledge through observation, measurement and experiment.

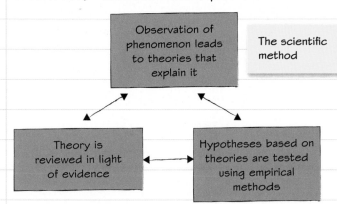

Observation of phenomenon leads to theories that explain it

The scientific method

Theory is reviewed in light of evidence

Hypotheses based on theories are tested using empirical methods

Empirical methods

These are data-collecting techniques based on sensory information. That is, actual **evidence** rather than thoughts and ideas.

For example, experiments to observe changes in the behaviour of a participant are recorded by the researcher.

Objectivity

This is achieved when the data and its interpretation are free from **bias**. This is essential for research to be considered scientific.

Empirical methods aim to produce objective data.

Replicability

To test the reliability of findings, research must be replicated (repeated exactly). Researchers replicate the procedure used and test it to see if the same results occur, otherwise findings could be the result of a flawed process.

Theory construction

Initially, theories seek to explain observed phenomena (**induction**).

Theories enable predictions (testable hypotheses), which are tested and the results are used to refine the theory (**deduction**).

Falsifiability

Theories should generate testable predictions which can be proven wrong. This means that the process used to test the hypothesis and the data must be objective and exist in a way that can be tested.

For example, Freud's view of unconscious processes motivating behaviour cannot be falsified as they cannot be objectively tested and measured to prove them wrong.

Hypothesis testing

A hypothesis is a testable prediction based on a theory. Empirical tests yield objective data that allows a decision to be made about accepting or rejecting the hypothesis. It is an essential part of the scientific process because it provides evidence that contributes to the judgement of theory as being valid or not.

Paradigms and paradigm shifts

A **paradigm** is a shared set of assumptions about the content and methods of a particular discipline.

For example, an early behaviourist paradigm was that behaviour can be explained in terms of learning from the environment and that this can be tested scientifically.

A **paradigm shift** occurs when the dominant paradigm is replaced with a new one.

For example, simple stimulus–response learning was challenged by social learning theory.

⬆ Extend Kuhn and Popper

Kuhn and Popper were philosophers of science and are credited with introducing these ideas to science.

Popper (1935) argued that all science is based on hypothesis testing, and that theories can never be absolutely proven right so must be continuously tested through the process of theory construction.

Kuhn (1962), on the other hand, argued that scientific knowledge evolves through paradigm shifts where the development of a minority position becomes more accepted by others.

Now try this

Explain why replication is an important feature of science.

Report writing

Psychological research is reported in a scientific format designed to communicate what was done, why it was done, what was found out and what this means. You need to demonstrate knowledge and understanding of the conventions of reporting psychological investigations.

Abstract

The purpose of the abstract is to summarise the research so other researchers can quickly decide if it is relevant without having to read the entire report.

The abstract briefly outlines the entire investigation so the reader can see what the aim of the research was, the theoretical background, the method, the results and the conclusions drawn from the results, all within one short paragraph.

Although the abstract is situated at the beginning of the report, it is written last.

Introduction

This section outlines **why** the study was done.

The beginning is general, an outline of the theoretical perspective being tested. This leads to a focus on the theory being tested.

Next comes a summary of research already done on the topic, getting more and more specific to the investigation.

The end section outlines the aims of the study, ending with the hypothesis.

A 'funnel' format, such as this, is used.

The method or procedure

This section details **what** was done. Several sub-sections provide detail to enable exact replication.

- **Method** – including design decisions and identification of variables.
- **Participants** – sampling method, sample size and breakdown, and allocation to conditions if relevant.
- **Apparatus/materials** – any technical equipment needed to run the study.
- **Standardised procedure** – step-by-step instructions, including when and where the study took place and instructions to the participants.
- **Controls** – details of how issues of bias were dealt with.

Results

The results section summarises the data in meaningful tables and charts, supported by written descriptions of the conclusions drawn from the data, including details of the findings of any inferential tests used (see pages 118–119).

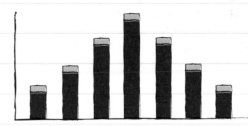

Clear charts are used to summarise the data gathered from the research.

Discussion

The discussion links the findings and conclusions of this study to the background theory and research.

It also explores the limitations of the research and suggests modifications that would improve it.

It then outlines the implications and applications of the findings and suggests ideas for future research.

References

This is a list of all the references cited in the writing of the report. It features a standard format known as the Harvard style of referencing and is applied to information gained from journals, books and specific chapters in books. Internet sites also need referencing appropriately. The references allow others to check the sources of information for accuracy.

Now try this

What is the purpose of the method/procedure section in a scientific report?

Types of data

Primary data

This is information gathered by the researcher first hand in order to answer their specific research question. Collecting primary data involves: designing a research study → piloting it → getting a sample → gathering data → analysis.

Evaluation

👍 It is likely to be more reliable and valid than secondary data due to high levels of control available.

👎 It costs a lot to do in terms of time and effort.

Secondary data

This is information that has already been gathered for other research purposes, including government statistics or studies done by other researchers.

The relevant data is identified and analysed in a way that enables the researcher to draw conclusions relevant to their research aim.

Evaluation

👍 It does not cost as much as primary research in terms of time and effort.

👍 Data is drawn from several sources so can provide greater insight into the research.

👎 It may be less reliable than primary data.

Meta-analyses

This is a method that combines data from several studies that have the same research aim. It uses **secondary data**.

The data from each study is pooled and re-analysed using statistical techniques that allow a conclusion to be drawn. This is useful as the large sample size that results from combining data allows trends and differences to emerge that may not when only small samples are used.

For example, the study by Van Ijzendoorn and Kroonenberg (1988) into cross-cultural patterns of infant attachment type used data from 32 different studies. Look at page 41 for a reminder about cultural variations in attachment.

Qualitative data

✓ This is data in the form of words and descriptions.

✓ Self-report methods such as interviews and questionnaires through the use of open questions are techniques used to collect data. Look at page 98 for a reminder about self-report techniques.

✓ Behaviour is not usually measured, just explored with an attempt to interpret and understand its meaning, providing a deeper insight into what people feel and think about things.

✓ It can be converted to quantitative data.

✓ Both types of data can be gathered in the same study.

Quantitative data

✓ This is numerical data.

✓ Experiments (page 96) and correlations (page 99) gather numerical data, as do observations (page 97) and closed questions in self-report methods.

✓ Behaviour is measured in terms of how much, and is quantified so comparisons can be made by analysing the dataset using appropriate descriptive statistics (page 113) and graphical representations (page 115). Inferential statistical tests can be done on quantitative data to determine the significance of any findings for the population being tested (page 118). It is therefore regarded as more scientific and objective than qualitative data.

Evaluation

👍 It is likely to provide in-depth exploration of a topic.

👎 It is time-consuming to gather and analyse.

Evaluation

👍 It is easy to analyse and make comparisons between groups.

👎 It is likely to only give superficial measures.

Now try this

Identify one method that uses secondary data.

Descriptive statistics

Maths skills You need to be able to analyse quantitative data using **descriptive statistics**, including measures of central tendency and measures of dispersion, percentages and correlations.

Describing measures of central tendency

These are averages that tell us about the middle value in a dataset. There are three:

1 **The mean** – add all the data items together and divide by the number of data items used.

Total = 67, **mean** is 67 ÷ 10 = **6.7**

2 **The mode** – this is the most frequently occurring data item.

Mode is 6 as there are three of them.

3 **The median** – rank all the data items from smallest to largest in size and pick the middle value. If you have an even number of data items then there will be two middle values; add these together and divide by 2.

> Scores on a recall test for a word list:
>
> 3, 5, 6, 6, 6, 7, 8, 8, 9, 9

The median is 6.5 as the 5th and 6th scores are 6 and 7.

Evaluation of measures of central tendency

	Strength	Weakness
mean	likely to be most representative as all scores used	harder to calculate than other measures; cannot be used on nominal data; can be affected by extreme scores
median	unaffected by extremes; easier to calculate than mean	less representative than mean as it does not use all the scores
mode	very easy to calculate; unaffected by extreme values	data is often multi-modal so meaningless; does not use all the scores

Measures of dispersion

These tell you about the variability within the dataset. There are two:

1 **The range** – this is worked out by subtracting the lowest value in the dataset from the highest value. The higher the range, the more variability there is likely to be in the dataset.

2 **The standard deviation (SD)** – this tells you the spread of data around the mean and allows you to see the relationships between scores. For more information on the SD and normal distributions, see page 116.

> You do not need to be able to calculate the SD, but you must be able to interpret what it shows.

Evaluation of range

👍 It shows the overall spread of the whole dataset.

👍 It is easy to calculate.

👎 It may not be representative of the data if there are extreme values at the top and/or bottom of the dataset.

Evaluation of SD

👍 It provides a representative measure of data spread as it takes all scores into account.

👍 It provides useful information about how individual scores relate to each other and to the mean.

👍 It gives a measure of the reliability of data as small standard deviations mean there was little variation in the scores.

👎 It is harder to calculate than the range.

Now try this

1 Work out the mode, median and mean of this dataset: 5, 3, 3, 7, 6, 9, 1, 10, 8, 11.

2 Which score is the most representative and why?

> Look at page 99 for an explanation of correlations and the use of correlation coefficients, and page 114 for percentages and how to calculate them.

Maths skills

🖩 **Maths skills** In your psychology exams, 10% of the total marks available will be assessing your maths skills. These include arithmetic, data handling, algebra and graphs. This page deals with some basic mathematical concepts.

Percentages

A percentage is the proportion of the total calculated out of 100. It is the only descriptive that can be used when you have nominal data, but percentages can be calculated for the other types of data.

To work out the percentage, you divide the number you wish to express as a % by the total score possible and multiply by 100.

For example, if you score 48 marks out of a possible 72 in an AS level psychology exam, you could calculate the percentage by:

$\frac{48}{72}$ = 0.666666 × 100 = 66.7% (rounded to one decimal place)

Fractions

A fraction is a part of a whole number. For example, $\frac{1}{3}$ is a fraction, meaning that the whole number has been split into three equal parts and one of those is being represented.

To calculate a fraction, you divide the score achieved by the total score, and represent this as:

$$\frac{\text{score achieved}}{\text{total possible}}$$

Continuing the exam mark example, $\frac{48}{72}$ can then be simplified by dividing both parts by the largest number they are both divisible by. In this case, that is 24, making the most simplified version of this fraction $\frac{2}{3}$.

Ratios

A ratio tells you how many of one thing there are in comparison to another thing.

There are two types of ratio:

- **Part to part** – the two numbers add up to the whole.
- **Part to whole** – the part is expressed in relation to the whole.

In the exam mark example:
- In the part-to-part ratio, for every 2 points you achieve you will miss one, expressed as 2:1 success.
- In the part-to-whole ratio, 2 out of every 3 points will be scored (2:3).

Mathematical symbols

= equal to	~ approximately equal to
< less than	≪ much less than
> more than	≫ much more than
≤ equal to or less than	∑ sum of

We might use symbols like these to show if results are significant. For example, $p \leq 0.05$ where p represents the probability of chance factors influencing the results. Look at page 118 to find out more about significance levels and probability.

Estimating results

When looking at data for the first time, it is useful to apply basic arithmetic to estimate what the results might show in a table. This can help you to quickly identify any trends in the data.

Participant	Score 1/20	Score 2/20
1	9	14
2	7	12
3	7	16

For example, using this data you can easily estimate that the mean average for score 1 is going to be lower than that for score 2, even without calculating the actual mean.

Order of magnitude

This is a way of expressing a number by focusing on its overall size (**magnitude**), where the number of decimal places moved is replaced by $10^{\text{number of places}}$.

For example, the figure 6 700 000 would be expressed as 6.7×10^6.

Significant figures

This is a way of rounding scores to make the figure easier to understand. The figure is rounded to the digit after the first 0, rather than just going to a certain number of moves AFTER the decimal point.

In the exam mark example above, you could round the 66.6666% to the nearest whole number as a significant figure (67%) to make it easier to express.

Now try this 🖩 **Maths skills**

Express $\frac{16}{32}$ as a fraction, as a ratio and as a percentage.

Displaying data

🖩 **Maths skills** Once you have gathered quantitative data, you will need to display the data in an appropriate way in order to begin analysing what you have found. You need to know how to construct **tables** and how to generate **bar charts**, **histograms** and **scattergrams**.

Data tables

These should contain **descriptive statistics** such as measures of central tendency and dispersions. For some data, it might be limited to percentage calculations.

All columns and rows need to be labelled.

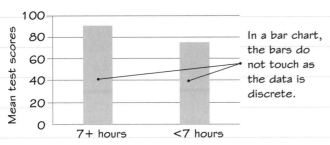

	7+ hours	Less than 7
mean score	90.44	75
modal score	85	82
range	29	20

Tables should be clearly labelled and have an appropriate title.

A table to show the test scores out of 100 for students who had 7 hours or more sleep on the night before the test.

Scattergrams

These are only used to display correlational data. Look at page 99 for an explanation of correlations and to see scattergrams of different correlations.

The two co-variables are plotted against each other, one on each axis.

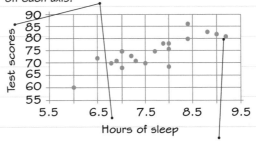

This is a positive correlation as both variables increase.

A scattergram to show relationship between hours of sleep and test score.

Bar charts

These consist of **categorical data** for comparison. The categories go on the x-axis (bottom) and the **frequency of occurrence** on the y-axis (side).

In a bar chart, the bars do not touch as the data is discrete.

A bar chart to show mean test scores of students who had different amounts of sleep on the night before the test.

Histograms

These are used when the x-axis is showing **continuous data** while the y-axis shows the **frequency of occurrence** of that data.

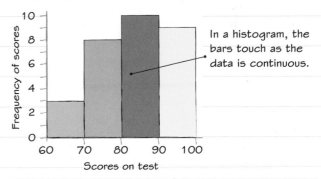

In a histogram, the bars touch as the data is continuous.

A histogram to show the frequency of scores on a test.

Other graphs and charts

These include **pie charts** and **frequency polygons** (line graph). Which one you choose to use should depend on the clarity with which it displays the data. The simplest is often the best choice.

1 **Pie charts** show the frequency of categories as percentages.

2 **Frequency polygons** are similar to histograms in that both have continuous data along the x-axis, but polygons can show the frequency of scores for two or more variables (as lines).

Now try this

🖩 **Maths skills**

1 Draw a scattergram to show a negative correlation and one to show no correlation.
2 Using the charts and graphs about the relationship between the amount of sleep and test scores (shown above), draw suitable conclusions based on the data.

Distributions

📱 **Maths skills** These show the frequency of something as it occurs in a population. Distribution graphs are histograms with the measured variable along the x-axis and the frequency on the y-axis. You need to know about the **normal distribution** and **skewed distributions**.

Normal distribution

If you take enough measures of a variable within a population you will get a **normal distribution**.

Key features:

* The mean, median and mode will be at the same point.
* The data is symmetrical about the mean.
* The shape of the line on the graph is bell shaped (bell-shaped curve).

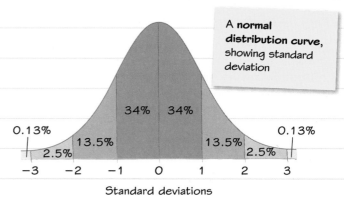

A **normal distribution curve**, showing standard deviation

Explaining normal distributions

In a normally distributed population, 68% of measures taken will fall close to the mean. Only a very small proportion (0.26%) will be at either end of the distribution.

This is marked by the **standard deviation**, which is a measure of the variance of scores around the mean. If a score falls 3 or more standard deviations from

the mean, then only a tiny proportion of the population will have that score.

For example, standardised measures of IQ have a mean of 100 and a standard deviation of 15. So, 68% of people will have an IQ score between 85 and 115, whereas only 2.5% will score 130 to 145 and even fewer (0.13%) above 145.

Skewed distributions

Some distributions are not normal, but are **skewed**. These are non-symmetrical because the scores are not distributed equally on either side of the mean. They are common when only a few measures have been taken.

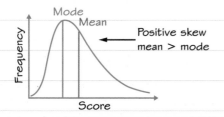

A **positive skew** results from scores that are mainly below the mean. This means that more scores are concentrated to the left of the graph.

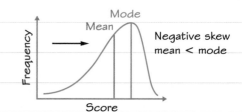

A **negative skew** occurs when most scores fall above the mean and the peak of the chart is to the right.

Application of normal distributions

The statistical definition of abnormality is based on the normal distribution (see page 50). Behaviour that is statistically infrequent, that is more than two standard deviations from the mean, is deemed **abnormal**.

This concept also underpins some inferential statistical tests (see page 118). Parametric tests such as the t-test work best on normally distributed data.

Now try this 📱 **Maths skills**

1 Describe the characteristics of a normal distribution.

2 Are these statements true or false?
  (a) In negatively skewed distributions most of the scores lie above the mean.
  (b) In a normally distributed population, 34% of scores lie within one standard deviation of the mean.

Levels of measurement

You need to be able to demonstrate knowledge and understanding of the different **levels** of quantitative data (**nominal**, **ordinal** and **interval**). This is important as each level allows for a more or less sophisticated analysis and is a crucial factor in the choice of **inferential tests**.

Nominal data

This is frequency data. It is gathered by counting the frequency of occurrence of the target behaviour. It is discrete data because it is not on a scale of measurement – it simply measures how many. Tally charts are used to record the data, which is summarised in a contingency table.

For example, the number of people who finish a half marathon.

Use and evaluation

This level of data is the most simple and only limited calculations can be made using it.

This means that analysis is also limited and quite superficial. Measures of central tendency, for example, are inappropriate. The best you can do is express differences as a percentage or proportion (see page 114).

Inferential testing is confined to fairly simple tests such as the **sign test** or **chi-squared** (see page 119).

Ordinal data

This data is continuous data because it represents scores along a scale. The scale of measurement has inexact quantities between points, so all you can tell from ordinal data is broadly how much of something there is. This allows you to rank order participant responses along the scale.

For example, the position people came in a marathon – first, second, third, fourth and so on.

Use and evaluation

This level of data supports a more sophisticated analysis, enabling comparisons using measures of central tendency such as the mean, median and mode, and calculations of range and standard deviation (see page 113).

Ordinal data enables more powerful inferential tests to be used such as the **Mann–Whitney** or **Wilcoxon test** (see page 119).

Interval data

This is also continuous data but the scale of measurement features exact and equal intervals between points on the scale.

Each point on the scale represents equal quantities of the measured variable, telling you exactly how much each measure represents.

For example, the times taken by competitors in a marathon as measured in hours, minutes and seconds.

Use and evaluation

This is the best type of data for analysis as it supports all types of calculation and is suited to the most powerful inferential tests such as the **t-tests** or **Pearson's r** (assuming it meets the other requirements for parametric tests, such as being normally distributed).

It is sometimes difficult to decide if data is ordinal or interval. If in doubt, say 'data that can be treated as interval'.

Now try this

Work out which level of data is represented in each of the following:

(a) Number of males who smile on entering college

(b) Attitude to a psychology revision programme as measured on a numerical scale

(c) Frequency of A, B, C, D and E grades achieved by male and female students

(d) Number of people who own a cat or who own a dog

(e) Number of items each person recalled from a word list

(f) Reaction time to spot a red dot on a screen containing green dots.

Inferential testing 1

Maths skills You cannot test all members of a target population so you take the data generated from a sample and **infer** that it is true of the population at large. You use **inferential tests** to be sure that what you found is not due to random error in your sampling or methodology.

Significance levels and probability

In order to accept that your results are true of the general population, you have to assess the probability that they occurred by chance factors rather than as a genuine effect measured in the study. You can never be 100% certain of this but need to be reasonably sure.

Probability levels

- The standard probability level accepted in psychology is 5%.

- If the probability (p) that your results happened by chance is 5% or below, then you accept that there is a genuine effect ($p \leq 0.05$).

- If the probability is greater than 5%, then you have to say that it is too risky and accept the null hypothesis ($p \geq 0.05$). Look at page 101 for a reminder about null hypotheses.

The process of inferential testing

1 Gather data and put it through the appropriate inferential test for Z, an observed or calculated value.

2 For every test, there is a **critical values table**. Using information on design (page 104) and hypotheses (page 101), find the critical value appropriate to your study.

3 Compare your observed value from the test to the critical value on the table. Decide whether your results are significant or not.

Level of significance for a two-tailed test			
N	0.05	0.025	
7	0	0	
8	1	0	
9	1	1	

An extract from a critical values table for s in the sign test

How to do a sign test

This is the simplest inferential test used when looking for a difference between variables with nominal data and a repeated measures design.

To calculate the sign test:

- For each participant, subtract their scores on measure 1 from measure 2.

- Add a plus or minus sign to indicate the direction of the difference (more or less).

- Omit data where there is no difference.

- Count the number of the least frequently occurring signs.

- This number is your calculated or observed value.

- This is called s.

Sign test example

Participants are asked how much they dream. They then have to eat cheese before they go to sleep and report whether they dream more or less. The hypothesis is that they will dream more.

Participant	Dreams	Sign
1	more	+
2	less	−
3	more	+
4	more	+
5	same	omit
6	less	−
7	more	+

In this example, $s = 2$ because minus (−) is the least frequent sign and there are two of them.

Using critical values tables

You need to know whether your hypothesis was **directional** (one-tailed) or **non-directional** (two-tailed), the number of scores (n) used to calculate s and the probability level you are aiming for. Look at page 101 for a reminder about directional and non-directional hypotheses.

The dream example is one-tailed, with 6 scores and we will accept a 5% risk ($p \leq 0.05$).

Interpreting the test result

You will find the critical values tables in your A level psychology textbook.

In the dream example, the critical value for $n = 6$, $p \leq 0.05$ and one-tailed is 0. To be significant, our observed statistic(s) must be equal to or less than 0. In this case, $s = 2$ so we must say there is no significant effect as we cannot rule out the probability of chance factors ($p \geq 0.05$).

Now try this

What is the standard level of risk that psychologists set to judge whether research findings are significant or not?

Inferential testing 2

Maths skills You need to demonstrate knowledge and understanding of inferential testing, including probability and significance, and be familiar with the use of different inferential tests as well as Type I and Type II errors.

Inferential testing and significance

- The purpose of an **inferential test** is to allow for generalisation beyond the sample to the rest of the target population, by finding out whether the observed difference or relationship is significant or not.

- It takes into account the type of hypothesis being tested (prediction of difference or relationship between variables, see page 101), the design of the study (see page 104) and the level of data gathered (see page 117).

- The right test is then selected and applied to the data in order to find the test statistic (observed or calculated value, see page 118).

- **Significance** is determined by comparing the test statistic to the critical value on that test's critical value table (see page 120) in order to calculate the **probability** that the results occurred by chance alone.

Probability

Researchers set the significance level they must meet in order for the hypothesis to be accepted. Typically, this is the 5% level. However, this does not always mean that the decision about whether the results are significant is valid.

Type I error

This is an optimistic decision leading to the rejection of the null hypothesis when in fact the results obtained were due to chance. This is more likely to happen if you set your significance level too high, as there is a higher risk of chance affecting the results, for example at $p \leqslant 0.10$

Type II error

This is where you are too cautious and accept the null hypothesis when the results are real. This is more likely if you set your significance level too low, for example at $p \leqslant 0.01$ or below.

When to use each inferential test

Level of data	Test of difference		Test of correlation
	Repeated measures	Independent measures	
nominal	sign test	chi-squared	
ordinal	Wilcoxon	Mann–Whitney	Spearman's rho
interval	related t-test	independent t-test	Pearson's r

Statistical tests

The **sign test** and **chi-squared** are used when nominal data has been gathered and you are testing for differences or associations between variables.

Mann–Whitney and **Wilcoxon** test ordinal data and test for differences between conditions.

The **t-tests** are used for interval or parametric data (normally distributed) and are the most powerful tests of difference.

Spearman's rho and **Pearson's r** are used to test correlational data. It is not possible to run a correlation on nominal data.

Now try this

Which test would you choose if you were measuring reaction times on the same group of people in the morning and again later in the day? The prediction was that they would be better in the morning.

Using critical value tables

Maths skills You need to be familiar with the use of **statistical tables** and **critical values** in interpreting significance.

Interpretation of significance

Statistical analysis using the appropriate inferential test produces an observed or calculated value. Different tests will have different names for this value.

For example, in the sign test it is s (see page 118) and in the Wilcoxon it is T.

Each test has an accompanying table of **critical values** which is used to determine whether the findings of the study are significant. This is done by comparing the observed value with the critical value on the table for the chosen level of significance.

For example, $p \leq 0.05$.

In each test, you need to know if the observed value has to be equal to or more than the critical value or equal to or less than the critical value (this will be stated under the table).

Using the critical value tables

- You need to know the type of hypothesis (see page 101), the level of significance needed and the number of participants.
- In a chi-squared test, you need the degrees of freedom (df) based on the make-up of the contingency table.

For example:

	Happy	Sad	Hungry
Boys			
Girls			

The table consists of rows and columns. The df value is worked out by:

(rows − 1) × (columns − 1)

For a table with three rows and two columns:

df = (3 − 1) × (2 − 1) = 2

Example of critical value table for the Mann–Whitney for a directional hypothesis at $p \leq 0.05$

n	1	2	3	4	5	6	7	8	9	10
1	–	–	–	–	–	–	–	–	–	–
2	–	–	–	–	0	0	0	1	1	1
3	–	–	0	0	1	2	2	3	4	4
4	–	–	0	1	2	3	4	5	6	7
5	–	0	1	2	4	5	6	8	9	11
6	–	0	2	3	5	7	8	10	12	14
7	–	0	2	4	6	8	11	13	15	17
8	–	1	3	5	8	10	13	15	18	20
9	–	1	4	6	9	12	15	18	21	24
10	–	1	4	7	11	14	17	20	24	27

To be significant, the observed value must be equal to or less than the critical value.

Example of critical value table for Pearson's product moment

Level of significance for a one-tailed (directional) hypothesis			
0.05	0.025	0.005	0.0005
Level of significance for a two-tailed (non-directional) hypothesis			
N	0.10	0.05	0.01	0.001
7	.669	.754	.875	.951
8	.621	.707	.834	.925
9	.582	.666	.798	.898
10	.549	.632	.765	.872

To be significant, the observed value must be equal to or greater than the critical value.

Now try this

The result of the Mann–Whitney test for N1 = 7 and N2 = 8 was 10. This was a directional hypothesis and the 5% level of significance is required. Should the null hypothesis be accepted or rejected? Explain your answer.

Exam skills 1

You will be assessed on your research methods knowledge on Paper 2 of the A level exam. The questions will usually follow from a description of some research and ask you to apply your knowledge to that study. The questions about this research continue on page 122.

Worked example

Read the item and then answer the questions that follow.

> Research has suggested that dancing can affect cognitive performance. Specifically, a structured dance can improve ability to recall and use knowledge, whereas free-style dancing can improve creativity. A psychology teacher wanted to test this, so she gathered all her students before they sat their mock exam for Psychology. She asked for volunteers to participate in the study and 28 students agreed. They were randomly allocated to an experimental group of 14 who were made to dance the Macarena, and a control group of 14 who stood in silence whilst the others danced. All students then sat the mock exam. The scores for the students who danced were compared to those in the control group.

As you read through the stimulus material, you should be working out the experimental design used, the sampling technique, the sample make-up, the variables tested and measured, and the level of data gathered. This will make it easier to demonstrate your understanding in the way you answer the questions.

(a) What is meant by *internal validity*? How might the random allocation of participants to the two conditions improve the internal validity of the study? **(3 marks)**

Internal validity is whether the results are actually due to the manipulation of the causal variable: in this case, whether the dancing influenced the students' mock exam scores. Random allocation stopped the teacher putting all the best students in the dance group to avoid biased results, making any difference more likely to be because of the dancing rather than other factors such as intelligence.

Note that this question is asking for two things. Start by giving a simple definition and make sure that the second part of your answer is clearly linked to the stimulus material.

A clear definition is supplied with good use of terminology. The answer consistently refers back to the study by talking about the teacher and the exam scores. This is good practice.

Worked example

(b) What is meant by *reliability* in research? **(2 marks)**

Reliability concerns the consistency of the data and the way it is gathered.

For 2 marks, a simple definition will suffice.

This is a clear and concise answer that identifies consistency in both the data and the research method.

Worked example

(c) Identify the dependent variable in this study. **(2 marks)**

The dependent variable is the scores the students got on their mock exam marked by the teacher.

A good answer. The mock exam scores are measurable and may depend on whether students danced or not.

Exam skills 2

You will be assessed on your research methods knowledge on Paper 2 of the A level exam. The questions here continue to use the research described on page 121. Reread the item before you look at these worked examples.

Worked example

(d) Briefly discuss any issues the dependent variable you identified in question (c) might cause in terms of the reliability of the data. Briefly outline how the teacher could have modified the study to increase the reliability of the measures. **(6 marks)**

Because the teacher is marking her own students, it is possible that the reliability of the marking might be low. She knows the students and might be inconsistent in the way the mark scheme is applied between the students, as her expectations affect how she marks the answer, making her marking subjective. The teacher should have employed an experienced independent marker, using a set mark scheme to mark the mock exams. This would have removed subjectivity and increased consistency, and therefore made the data more reliable.

 This question is likely to be marked according to bandings. To access the top bands, both parts of the question must be dealt with. So an explanation as to why the data might not be reliable is needed and useful suggestions as to how it could be improved. For all 6 marks, your answer should have some depth.

 An appropriate challenge to the reliability of the data is made here, with a good level of detail.

This is a sensible and well-explained suggestion, with a clear benefit for the study.

Worked example

Maths skills

(e) The teacher decided to use a Mann–Whitney inferential test to analyse the data. Give **two** reasons why this test was appropriate in this case. **(2 marks)**

She gathered data that could be treated as ordinal and it was an independent measures design.

 Note that two clear reasons are required. Always read the questions carefully.

 It is a good idea to memorise the table that summarises the choice of tests (see page 119).

Worked example

Maths skills

The result of the Mann–Whitney test was U = 65.

(f) Determine whether this is significant for a directional test at $p \leq 0.05$ using the data in Table 1. Explain your answer. **(2 marks)**

Table 1: Critical values table for the Mann–Whitney test

N2	N1			
	12	13	14	15
12	42	47	51	55
13	47	51	56	61
14	51	56	61	66
15	55	61	66	72

To be significant, the value of U must be equal to or less than the critical value.

These results are not significant at the 5% level because the observed value of U (65) is more than the critical value for N1 = 14 and N2 = 14, which is 61.

 Always read the table title and the information about whether the observed value should be more or less than the critical value. Review page 120 to remind yourself about using critical values tables.

 This answer effectively uses details from the table to explain the decision, which is correct.

Exam skills 3

Exam questions on Research methods are likely to be varied and will often be based on stimulus material. Before looking at these questions, you might find it helpful to revise experiments (page 96), sampling (page 103) and designs on page 104.

Worked example

Read the item and then answer the questions that follow.

> A psychology teacher is interested in finding out whether having more sleep affects students' performance in class. He decides to conduct an experiment to find out. He uses two classes. He asks one to go to bed early one night and the other to stay up late. Both classes learn the same material and do the same test of learning, which he marks.

(a) What sampling technique is the teacher using?   **(1 mark)**

(b) Write a suitable hypothesis for this research.   **(2 marks)**

(c) Is this a repeated measures, matched pairs or independent measures design?   **(1 mark)**

(a) The sampling technique is opportunity.

(b) Amount of sleep affects performance on a test.

(c) Independent measures.

This is a fairly simple study that can lead to some general questions. You must read the item carefully and **apply** your knowledge.

This may only be worth 1 mark, but try to avoid giving one-word answers; sentences are better.

The question does not specify what type of hypothesis. This answer, although brief, operationalises both variables so is appropriate.

As you are asked to identify the design from a list, this would get the mark.

Worked example

Read the item and then answer the question that follows.

> The results showed that students who slept more scored an average of 2 marks higher than the other students. He therefore wanted to advertise the benefits of sleep in the college newsletter. However, a colleague of the teacher thought that there were some issues with the way this research was carried out, and suggested that some improvements should be made to the design and procedure of the study first.

Outline **two** issues with the way the teacher conducted this research and suggest **one** way to improve this study.   **(4 marks)**

There may be problems with the independent measures design because students in one class could be more interested in the topic than those in the other class, and so would perform better on the test. This challenges the validity of the results.
A second issue is a lack of control as the teacher does not know if the students really slept for the length of time they were supposed to, making the findings unreliable.
One improvement would be to randomly assign the participants to the experimental conditions.

A 4-mark question requires you to spend about 5 minutes reading and then answering the question.

It is important to refer to the item/stimulus when answering this question, rather than give general criticisms.

Remember, this question calls for two issues **and** an improvement. Always read the question carefully and follow the instructions.

Exam skills 4

Maths skills You will be required to demonstrate an ability to handle data in the context of psychological research. Be sure to check exactly what maths skills you are expected to be able to use and practise these – especially if you do not use maths regularly. You are allowed to take a calculator into the exam with you.

Worked example

Read the item and then answer the questions that follow.

A group of students have been challenged to take a 20-mark test after no revision, and then another test after doing two hours of revision, using a new strategy devised by their teacher. Their results from the two tests are in the table below.

Table 1: Results

Participant	Marks, no revision	Marks, 2 hours revision
1	10	17
2	15	14
3	7	12
4	9	20
5	11	17

Maths skills (a) Calculate the mean score for each condition.

(2 marks)

Mean after no revision	Mean after 2 hours revision
10.4	16

Maths skills To work out a **mean**, you first need to add up all the scores in each condition, and then divide the result by the number of scores in each condition:

$$10 + 15 + 7 + 9 + 11 = 52 \div 5$$
$$= 10.4$$
$$17 + 14 + 12 + 20 + 17 = 80 \div 5$$
$$= 16$$

In this instance, the question does not ask you to show your working, so just giving the mean for each condition is correct. However, if the question asks you to show your working, make sure you do so to be sure you gain the marks available.

Worked example

Maths skills (b) Calculate the <u>percentage increase</u> for participant 5 in Table 1 above, giving the answer correct to one decimal place. **(3 marks)**

Percentage increase for participant 5 is 54.5%.

Maths skills To work out the **percentage increase**:

(a) calculate the difference between the two scores (in this case, 6 marks)

(b) divide the difference (6) by the original score the participant achieved (11) and multiply the result by 100 to give the percentage increase:

$$6 \div 11 = 0.545454 \times 100$$
$$= 54.545454\%$$

(c) then give the answer to one decimal place – round up or down as appropriate.

Worked example

(c) Describe what the data in Table 1 suggests about the influence of the revision technique used on test performance. **(3 marks)**

Four of the five participants showed an improvement in test score following two hours of revision using the new technique, suggesting that the technique can effectively help improve performance. However, one participant showed a minor decrease in score after the revision, so it may not work for everyone.

Interpreting the data is another important skill you should practise. In this case, you should state what the data tells you. You are not required to infer what could have caused it.

When asked to interpret data, use all of the data in your response. Here, you should comment on the fact that most people did better on the test after revision, but also that one person didn't.

Exam-style practice 1

Practise for Paper 2 of your A level exam with these exam-style questions. There are answers on pages 300–301.

1 Read the item and then answer the questions that follow.

> Twenty participants were given a list of 20 words to learn while music played. Some time later, they were randomly assigned to equal-sized groups for either the experimental condition where the same music played during recall, or the control condition where recall was conducted in silence. Their scores were calculated on the basis of how many of the 20 words on the list they remembered.

The following results were obtained in the experiment

Table 1:

	Recall with music	**Recall without music**
mean	15	11
range	8	12

(a) Write a suitable title for Table 1.   **(2 marks)**

> A good title should enable the reader to understand the results of the experiment without having to go back and read anything else. So both conditions should be mentioned, as well as the dependent variable.

(b) What type of chart would best display this data? Justify your choice.   **(2 marks)**

> Identify a suitable chart and briefly explain your choice.

(c) Write a suitable directional (one-tailed) hypothesis for this study.   **(2 marks)**

> No marks will be awarded for a non-directional or null hypothesis. You should include both the independent variable and the dependent variable.

(d) Why would the researcher choose to randomly assign the participants into each of the two conditions?   **(2 marks)**

> Look at the data and **analyse** what it tells us. Do not just state what is already on the table, but tell the examiner what you think it means.

(e) Draw **two** conclusions from the results in Table 1.   **(2 marks)**

2 Explain why a researcher might prefer to conduct a field experiment in preference to a laboratory one.   **(2 marks)**

> This question is looking for you to identify a strength of the field experiment that is not present when conducted in a lab. You need to give details of why the field experiment is better.

3 Outline **one** strength of opportunity sampling as a technique for selecting participants.   **(2 marks)**

> Focus on a clear strength but for both marks this should be elaborated: you could explain why this sampling method has this strength and another does not.

4 Outline **one** weakness of opportunity sampling as a technique for selecting participants.   **(2 marks)**

5 Evaluate the independent measures design as used in experiments.   **(4 marks)**

> In this answer you can cover one or more strengths and or weaknesses of this design. You could choose to do one in a lot of depth or more in less depth.

Exam-style practice 2

Practise for Paper 2 of your A level exam with these exam-style questions. There are answers on page 301.

6 Outline the purpose of a pilot study. **(3 marks)**

> You need to define the overall purpose of any pilot. It would be a good idea to use examples to illustrate what you mean.

7 Read the item and then answer the questions that follow.

> **Maths skills** A psychologist is interested in finding out whether people are more willing to help others when they have been exposed to a helpful message. People were approached in a shopping centre and were unaware this was a psychology experiment. Participants were first asked to give money to a charity and then were given a card thanking them for their donation, which explained how every penny counts. They were then asked to donate again, and the amounts given before and after the message were compared. Their hypothesis was that there will be a difference in the amount donated after they are given the card compared to before.

> The exam will often feature brief write-ups of studies as stem or stimulus materials. Use your knowledge of the different research methods to answer the questions. In this case, it is an experiment. In other cases, it might be an observation, a correlation or a survey.

Table 1 Participant donations

Participant	Donation 1	Donation 2
1	0.50	0.73
2	0.75	0.75
3	1.00	1.25
4	0.50	1.00
5	1.00	0.98
6	1.50	2.00

(a) Calculate the mean scores and the range for donation 1 and donation 2 in Table 1, and construct a suitably titled and labelled table summarising this data. **(6 marks)**

> **Maths skills** Use a calculator to work out the mean scores and the range, and show your working. The table should be clear – marks will be awarded for each element done correctly.

(b) Identify the experimental design used in this study. **(1 mark)**

(c) Outline **one** advantage and **one** disadvantage of this experimental design. **(2 marks)**

(d) Identify and explain how the psychologist should have addressed the ethical issues in the investigation. **(5 marks)**

> Rather than make a list of issues, you would do better to single out two and explain clearly how the psychologist could have resolved any ethical problems.

Table 2 Table of critical values for a sign test

	Significance level: two-tailed/non-directional		
	0.01	0.05	0.02
	Significance level: one-tailed/directional		
N	0.05	0.025	0.01
5	0	–	–
6	0	0	–

> **Maths skills** Show your working for the value of s (the observed/calculated value obtained from the test).

> Look at page 120 to find out how to use the critical values table. Remember to ignore any participant data that is tied to work out the number of participants (n). Always read the instructions at the bottom of the table to know whether the observed/calculated value needs to be equal to or more than or equal to or less than the critical value.

(e) Use the information in **Table 1** to perform a sign test. Then use the critical values in **Table 2** to decide if the null hypothesis is to be accepted or rejected at the minimum level of $p \leqslant 0.05$. **(4 marks)**

Exam-style practice 3

Practise for Paper 2 of your A level exam with these exam-style questions. There are answers on page 301. Before looking at these questions, it would be good to review case studies and content analysis (page 100), the role of peer review (page 107), the features of science (page 110), validity and reliability (page 109), inferential testing (pages 118–119) and levels of measurement (page 117).

8 Outline the scientific process as it is applied in psychology.

(6 marks)

> This is a straightforward question asking you to detail the process of science. The mark scheme for this question will be banded, so to reach the top band your account must be coherent. This means successfully and concisely linking the different elements of the process together, using appropriate terminology effectively.

9 Why is peer review an important part of science?　**(3 marks)**

> This is an explain question. You need to demonstrate your knowledge of what peer review is and apply it to what you know about the scientific process. The mark scheme for this question will not be banded, but for full marks you must elaborate your points appropriately.

10 One purpose of peer review is to assess the reliability and validity of the research study.

(a) What is the difference between reliability and validity?

(2 marks)

(b) Explain **one** way that the peer reviewer could assess the validity of a study.　**(3 marks)**

> The first part of this question is a simple statement of difference, calling for basic knowledge of reliability and validity.

> The second part is more complex as it asks you to apply your knowledge of assessing validity to the peer-review process.

11 Outline the key features of the case study method.　**(3 marks)**

> This question requires a clear description of more than one feature of a case study.

12 Explain **one** way that qualitative data can be analysed. **(2 marks)**

> Notice that the answer should be limited to one analytical technique. As it is only for 2 marks, it does not require much detail.

13 What is the purpose of an inferential test?　**(2 marks)**

> This question is about tests in general, not any one in particular. To answer it, you need to explain the function of inferential tests.

14 Explain the difference between nominal, ordinal and interval data.　**(3 marks)**

> You need to know about different levels of measurement to answer this effectively.

Gender bias

The term '**gender**' relates to characteristics that separate males and females (see page 156). In the past, psychological research was typically carried out by males on males, reflecting societal attitudes and resulting in **bias**. This research was then assumed to apply equally to both males and females. The idea that there were no differences between males and females is known as **universality** – behaviour that is found in one person is true for all.

Androcentrism

- Male bias
- Male behaviour is taken as the norm.
- Female behaviour that is different from this norm may be construed as unimportant or even deviant.
- Some women's behaviour is 'pathologised' (seen as being ill).

For example, premenstrual syndrome (PMS) is in the DSM-5 and is seen as a condition to be treated instead of a normal factor of women's behaviour.

Alpha bias

- Exaggerates gender differences
- A misrepresentation of behaviour that exaggerates the differences between males and females.
- Some theories have been used to devalue women.

For example, Freud's (1905) theory of psychosexual development suggested that girls do not identify so strongly with their mothers and therefore have a weaker superego (see page 266), suggesting they are less moral.

Beta bias

- Minimises gender difference
- A misrepresentation of behaviour that minimises the differences between males and females.
- Studies that use only men or women and then suggest that the findings should be applied to everyone are beta biased.

For example, Milgram (1963) used an all-male sample for his original obedience study (see page 5) but applied the findings to both males and females.

Evaluation

🗨 Although female psychology students outnumber males, at a senior level within universities there are more male psychology lecturers and researchers. This could lead to only researching questions in areas that affect men whilst ignoring areas that affect women.

👍 Awareness of gender differences has resulted in society questioning characteristic behaviours based on the male norm.

Evaluation

🗨 Psychological research sometimes reinforces gender stereotyping and discrimination. For example, studies suggest that females are more emotional and men are more logical.

👍 The emergence of feminist psychology to redress the balance has heightened the value of females.

Evaluation

🗨 Most experimental methodologies are based around standardised treatment of participants. This assumes that men and women respond in the same ways to the experimental situation, which could result in artificial differences being found.

👍 Recognising beta bias has had an influence on equality in education, for example.

Now try this

1 Briefly outline the problems associated with using alpha bias and beta bias studies in psychological research. Use examples in your answer.

2 Which term is used to describe a theory that uses male behaviour as the norm?

Cultural bias

A large number of psychological theories and studies that you have already looked at show evidence of **cultural bias**. That is, they take a **universal** viewpoint of behaviour and ignore cultural differences. The assumption that research can be generalised globally is known as **ethnocentrism**. In contrast, **cultural relativism** considers the cultural context.

Ethnocentrism

This occurs when a researcher assumes that their own culturally specific practices or ideas are 'natural' or 'superior'. The norm may be set as the researcher's own cultural background and anything seen as deviating from these norms may be classed as abnormal, rather than being an accurate reflection of behaviour.

Ainsworth's development of the Strange Situation (1969) is a good example. When carried out in other cultures, Van Ijzendoorn and Kroonenberg (1988) found that the methodology used to measure attachment in American children was not an appropriate method to measure children in other cultures, leading to erroneous (biased) classification of non-American children. For more information on this study, see page 41.

Early IQ testing used Western assumptions about intelligence (universality); this may have disadvantaged non-Westerners, resulting in poor performance. Thus non-Westerners could have been viewed as having inferior IQs.

Cultural relativism

Cultural relativism is a belief that cultural norms and values derive their meaning within a specific social context, suggesting that there is no global right or wrong. Social norms differ from culture to culture. Therefore, when looking at behaviour in any given culture, it is vital to examine the **cultural context** in which the behaviour is set, in order to explain it.

When looking at abnormality, for example, cultural relativism suggests that behaviour that is deemed normal and acceptable in one culture may be completely unacceptable and abnormal in another.

For example, we understand what depression is (see page 53), as classified by DSM-5. However, some countries such as China have no concept of depression, and diagnose neurasthenia (emotional disturbance) instead. The condition is concerned with somatic symptoms, which Chinese people would see as an imbalance of chi (energy), and therefore not a mental illness.

Evaluation

🚩 Sampling bias can reduce population validity. Participants from a specific culture may not be representative of all cultures.

🚩 Psychological research may reinforce cultural stereotyping and discrimination.

Evaluation

👍 To reduce cultural bias, greater use should be made of research conducted from within each culture by members of that culture. Otherwise, it is difficult to be completely objective. More cross-cultural or trans-cultural (using many cultures) research studies are now being carried out.

Now try this

1 What is meant by ethnocentrism?

2 What is meant by cultural relativism?

Free will and determinism

Free will is the belief that we have freedom of choice, and therefore behave in the way that we want to. However, in some approaches in psychology the belief is that our actions are determined, so we have little or no choice in how we behave.

Free will

Free will is the notion that we have choice over our own behaviour. Most of us consider that our behaviour and thoughts are of our own volition and that we are free to choose the decisions we make and have control over our actions.

Psychology questions this. As a science, psychology tries to examine causes of behaviour and thoughts. As humans are such complex beings, psychology seeks to find out which aspect of a person makes the decision. However, it is difficult to separate whether human behaviour is caused by free will or determinism.

Determinism

The opposite of free will is the idea that our behaviour and actions, even some of our thoughts, can be determined by other internal or external factors, such as biological, environmental and psychic influences.

Soft determinism acknowledges that some form of free will is present in human behaviour (it is partly but not fully controlled internally), soft determinism recognises that there are often other factors – such as role models – that may coerce or influence a person's behaviour.

Hard determinism proposes that free will is an illusion. This suggests humans are governed by forces over which we have no influence (behaviour is controlled externally).

Types of determinism

Determinism is a continuum (see page 75).

Environmental determinism says all behaviour is controlled by external influences such as our parents and the environment.

Biological determinism suggests human behaviour is determined by our biology, in particular our genes and chemicals in our brain.

The **humanistic approach** supports the idea of humans exerting their free will in behaviour. Rogers and Maslow (1943, 1954) stood firm on the notion that everyone is free to make their own choices in life (see page 74).

Free will ◄————————► **Hard determinism**

Soft determinism

The **cognitive approach** is an example of soft determinism as it acknowledges free will through 'rational processing' of information to direct behaviour.

Psychic determinism believes behaviour is controlled by unconscious fears and desires from traumatic past events and experiences.

Scientific emphasis on causal explanations

Psychology as a science uses methods from the natural sciences to explain causes of human behaviour and thought. In order to do this, psychologists must:

- generate a theory and hypothesis whereby cause and effect can be established
- use empirical methods such as laboratory experiments to test the hypothesis
- apply statistical analysis to see if their prediction is statistically significant or not.

Evaluation

- 🗨 Free will means that behaviour cannot be predicted or objectively measured.
- 👍 Free will emphasises the individual as responsible for behaviour.
- 🗨 Determinism leaves us with no responsibility for our own actions.
- 👍 The deterministic approach tries to predict behaviour under scientific conditions.

Now try this

Outline what is meant by free will and determinism.

Nature–nurture

This debate asks whether our behaviour is a product of our genes (**nature**) or environmental influences such as upbringing (**nurture**). You need to know about the relative importance of **heredity** and **environment** in determining behaviour, and the **interactionist approach**, which is positioned between the two extremes.

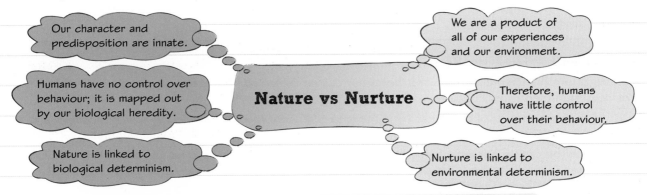

Our character and predisposition are innate.

Humans have no control over behaviour; it is mapped out by our biological heredity.

Nature is linked to biological determinism.

Nature vs Nurture

We are a product of all of our experiences and our environment.

Therefore, humans have little control over their behaviour.

Nurture is linked to environmental determinism.

Historically, each standpoint was viewed as being exclusive, but today the nature–nurture debate is regarded more as a continuum (see page 76).

Approach focus

 The **biological approach** supports the **nature** side of the argument – all behaviour is pre-determined by our genes and biochemistry. Twin studies are used to research **heredity**.

If an identical twin (monozygotic, MZ) develops a condition, such as schizophrenia, and the other twin also develops the condition, this would show support for the nature debate, as identical twins share 100% of their genes.

 The **behavioural approach** supports the **nurture** side of the debate – all behaviour is shaped by what people are exposed to. The use of twins in research can also be used to research **environment**.

When studying twins, a 100% concordance rate is never found with MZ twins for any condition. This could suggest that other factors, such as the environment, also influence behaviour.

Interactionist approach

Some approaches take an **interactionist** viewpoint. They see behaviour as being influenced by both nature and nurture. They would argue that, although a number of behaviours are influenced through the inheritance of a particular genotype, it is their interaction with the environment (phenotype) that causes a behaviour (see page 71).

Evaluation

👍 If we identify a genetic basis for a condition, then we do not blame the person for their behaviour. For example, criminal behaviour shown in Raine's (1997) study is due to brain dysfunction.

👎 It is difficult to separate the effects of heredity and environment. When studying the influence of genetics on schizophrenia, most participants also had a shared environment.

👍 Behaviour that is identified as being learnt can then be unlearnt. This would be useful for criminal behaviour and some forms of mental disorder. Behaviour would appear to be under the control of the individual (free will).

👎 It is difficult to separate out the effects of heredity and environment. For example, when looking at the influence of the family environment on anorexics, they also share genetics.

Now try this

A study found that men who had poor upbringings and low MAOA activity (the MAOA gene is associated with violent, aggressive behaviour) were four times more likely to have been convicted of a violent crime prior to the age of 24. Briefly explain these findings in relation to the nature–nurture debate.

Reductionism and holism

If something is **reductionist** it attempts to reduce complex human behaviour to a single, basic component whilst ignoring other factors that could play a role. The opposite concept is **holism**, which looks at an individual's behaviour as a whole, taking into account all factors. **Reductionism** is commonly used by students of psychology to criticise a particular approach, study or theory but it is not necessarily always a negative thing.

Levels of explanation

Levels of explanation are the idea that behaviour can be explained in degrees of reduction, in a hierarchy or continuum (see page 75).

✓ At the bottom level of the hierarchy is the idea that behaviour is explained by a single component. In psychology, for example, behaviour would be explained in terms of chemicals in the brain.

✓ At the top of this hierarchy is the holistic level, where there is no attempt to reduce the explanation of behaviour. All factors – for example, the environment and culture – would be taken into account. They see different levels of behaviour as being influential and it is therefore a more rounded view.

Reductionism

This argument suggests that we can explain behaviour and experiences by reference to only one factor, such as biology or learning.

- **Biological reductionism** explains behaviour purely from a biological approach such as genetics, biochemistry or the structure of the brain.

- **Environmental reductionism** simplifies behaviour into a response to a stimulus. For example, the behaviour of a person with OCD is a response to the modelling of that behaviour by a parent.

Holism

This side of the debate looks at the person **as a whole**.

- It looks at the **social context** of behaviour as being important, such as the family and culture, as well as biological factors.

- It could be seen as taking an **interactionist** viewpoint that suggests all factors have equal importance in explaining behaviour.

Evaluation of reductionism

👍 By breaking down a phenomenon to its constituent parts, it may be possible to understand the whole.

👍 The focus on a single aspect has led to some great discoveries in psychology.
For example, the cause of schizophrenia has been linked to excessive dopamine activity, which has led to improved treatment.

👍 This is consistent with a scientific approach in psychology.

👎 This is too simplistic because it ignores the complexities of human behaviour and experience.

👎 Behaviour often has a number of different causes; reducing possible explanations to one level can only provide a limited understanding.

Evaluation of holism

👍 A holistic approach may be more appropriate for psychology as it is looking at human behaviour, which has lots of aspects such as conscious thoughts and the context within which behaviour occurs.

👍 This approach looks at the person as a whole, which is important in therapeutic settings.
Jahoda's (1958) criteria of ideal mental health take a holistic view of what people should possess to be mentally well.

👎 Not isolating individual factors may make it difficult to discover causes of certain conditions or illnesses.

👎 It is more hypothetical and lacks the scientific rigour that other explanations of behaviour offer.

Now try this

With reference to reductionism and holism, how could researchers find out possible causes of OCD?

Idiographic and nomothetic

This debate examines which approach is appropriate when gathering data. An **idiographic** approach focuses on an individual and yields information that is rich and in depth. A **nomothetic** investigation studies a large number of people, from which general laws can be formulated. For more on comparing these approaches, see page 76.

Idiographic vs nomothetic

Idiographic approach (individual)	Nomothetic approach (applies to all)
It involves studying a particular individual.	It involves testing a large sample.
Data generated is detailed and extensive.	This would generate a large amount of data.
The sample will not be representative because of the uniqueness of the traits the individual possesses.	The sample should be representative of the larger population, such as through random sampling.
It uses methods such as the case study to investigate the individual.	It tends to use the experimental method or correlational procedures.
Analysis of data uses qualitative methods, such as thematic analysis.	Analysis of the data uses quantitative methods, such as statistical tests.
This approach is useful in generating new areas of research.	From this approach, general laws can be generated that are applicable to all.

Example of an idiographic approach

The psychodynamic perspective can take an idiographic approach to conducting research through the use of case studies, such as Freud's (1909) study of Little Hans (see page 163).

When interpreting Hans' dreams, Freud took an **idiographic** approach.

However, the psychosexual stages and the psyche (id, ego, superego) take more of a nomothetic approach, but the ways in which these aspects of development become apparent in the individual are unique.

The humanistic perspective also takes an idiographic approach to carrying out research, using qualitative methods such as **self-report**.

Example of a nomothetic approach

The biological approach takes a nomothetic stance to conducting research through the use of laboratory experiments. These help to establish cause and effect for behaviour. It is a useful approach when looking at developing treatments for mental illness.

Drug therapy for schizophrenia (see page 202) uses the nomothetic approach to research the effectiveness of the treatment.

The **learning/behaviourist** approach adopts a nomothetic view that all human behaviour is a result of what we learn, using research that gathers quantitative data, which helps to generate universal laws.

Evaluation of idiographic approach

- 👍 Detail from an idiographic approach is rich and often prompts ideas for further research.
- 👎 Research findings that are carried out on a single person lack population validity because of their uniqueness, and cannot be generalised to all.

Evaluation of nomothetic approach

- 👍 The detail gathered from a nomothetic approach is vast and enables researchers to generalise findings to the population.
- 👎 Because one size does not fit all, some explanations are not appropriate because of individual differences.

Now try this

Briefly outline **one** problem with using an idiographic approach and **one** problem with using a nomothetic approach in research.

Ethical implications of research

Research is not only concerned with the findings but with the impact of those findings. All research must consider the **ethics** of the process (see page 106) and the effect of the findings on the participants and on society in general. The **ethical implications** of research are therefore part of the research process.

Ethics

Guidelines by the British Psychological Society (BPS) and university ethics committees are in place to try to avoid any research causing difficulties for any of the people involved directly or indirectly. The guidelines have become more stringent to reduce potential problems for both the researcher and the participants.

Socially sensitive research (SSR)

Sieber and Stanley (1988) used the term 'socially sensitive research' to describe research that could have costs for the participants – directly or indirectly – or for the people or group of people they represent.

> SSR could create stigma for others, such as those with mental health problems, and may change the public view of such groups and/or social policy.

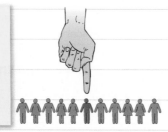

Research can be socially sensitive for a number of reasons:

- the research question
- treatment of participants
- the institutional context
- interpretation and use of findings.

Examples of SSR

Research carried out to explain mental illnesses and their potential cause may have a huge impact on the people affected by these disorders. For example, the family systems explanation of anorexia nervosa suggests the role of the family being implicit in the disorder.

- Raine's (1996) study on the 'killer brain' is considered socially sensitive as it suggested children could be identified as having a predisposition to violent behaviour.

- Humphreys' (1970) study 'Tearoom Trade' is considered socially sensitive as it investigated the sexual practices of gay men in public toilets at a time when homosexuality was not widely accepted. Humphreys' findings opposed many stereotypes, as only 14% were members of the gay community interested in primarily homosexual relationships. It therefore challenged society's views of homosexuals as being promiscuous and degenerate.

Evaluation

- 👎 It is not always possible to anticipate the effects of research on an individual, group or society. This makes it difficult to judge whether or not the research should be carried out.

- 👎 The guidelines are not always objectively decided as, ultimately, decision makers interpret them in respect of each piece of research presented for consideration. Therefore, subjective interpretation may be present.

- 👍 Scarr (1988) suggested that, regardless of the outcomes, there was a duty for psychologists to carry out SSR as it could be important in raising awareness of topics such as race, sex and gender inequalities and abuse.

- 👍 Aronson (1992) said that stopping research because of its sensitivity is taking a 'backward step'. He suggested it was better to educate people about sensitive topics rather than shy away from them.

Now try this

Researchers interested in finding out about eating disorders wanted to interview schoolgirls aged 16 at both a state school and an independent boarding school. They were interested in the number of girls who had signs of an eating disorder.

This would be an example of socially sensitive research. How could this have been addressed by the researchers?

Exam skills 1

In answering questions on issues and debates in psychology, you will be expected to illustrate your answers with knowledge and understanding of other topics you have studied in your A level course. Before you look at the worked examples, remind yourself about holism and reductionism (page 132) and the scientific emphasis on causal explanations (page 130).

Worked example

What is meant by 'reductionism' in psychology?

(2 marks)

Reductionism refers to reducing complex human behaviour to the simplest explanation, as it focuses on constituent parts whilst ignoring any other influences. For example, we may blame genetics for obsessive–compulsive disorder (OCD) whilst not taking into account a person's environmental influences.

 This answer shows a clear understanding of reductionism and provides an appropriate example.

Worked example

Here, you are required to describe what the term means and to show an understanding of its application. As a 4-mark question, the detail needed is more in-depth compared to a 2-mark question.

Explain what is meant by 'holism' in psychology.

(4 marks)

Holism is the opposite side of the debate to reductionism. It explains human behaviour by looking at the whole person, not just a single aspect, and explores a number of factors. It therefore takes an idiographic approach to explaining behaviour and uses a range of data collection methods, such as unstructured interviews and questionnaires. For example, a doctor may look at environmental influences (another family member with the disorder) as well as genetics for the cause of OCD.

 This answer demonstrates an understanding of the holism vs reductionism debate in psychology, and provides a good, succinct answer with an example.

Command phrase: Briefly outline

When asked to 'briefly outline' the meaning of something, provide a definition and include a brief example to show your understanding. You are not required to provide any evaluation.

Worked example

Briefly outline what is meant by the scientific emphasis on causal explanations of behaviour.

(2 marks)

Psychology uses methods from the natural sciences to investigate behaviour and thought. In using these methods, psychology can justify itself as a science. Psychologists use theories and testable hypotheses to generate conclusions about human behaviour. Through this, cause and effect can be established, as extraneous variables have been controlled for in a rigorous way.

 This question focuses on material that is new to this course. Make sure you know what it means and how you can apply it to other topics in your A level course, such as the approaches in psychology.

 You may find it useful to make a table for each issue and/or debate, with a reference to other topics and specific examples, and explain how they relate to each other.

Exam skills 2

In answering questions on issues and debates in psychology, you will be expected to illustrate your answers with knowledge and understanding of other topics you have studied in your A level course. Before you look at the worked examples, remind yourself about the nature–nurture debate (on page 131) and determinism (on page 130).

Worked example

Read the item and then answer the question that follows.

> A study into schizophrenia found a concordance rate of 50% for identical twins and 15% for non-identical twins.

Explain the outcome of this study in relation to the nature–nurture debate. **(6 marks)**

This study suggests that both nature and nurture play a part in the onset of schizophrenia. If the illness was innate, for example, due to genes (nature), then the identical twin pairs should have a concordance rate of 100%. As the concordance rate is only 50%, this suggests that nurture (environment) must also play a part, such as each twin's upbringing or their experiences. Equally, for the non-identical twins, the concordance rate is 15% but should be 50% if only nature was responsible. The use of twins in research is complex as they are usually brought up in the same environment. It is therefore difficult to separate nature and nurture. An interactionist approach would be the best approach to take here as it acknowledges the influence of both in behaviour.

Explain is an AO3 term, requiring you to set out the factors in this debate. As the question asks about the study, it also includes some AO2 marks, so you need to give theoretical or practical examples to support your points. Your answer should relate to the outcome of this particular study.

When a question refers to a stem or scenario, you must contextualise your answer. Make sure you refer to the study and also show a clear understanding of the nature–nurture debate.

This response has shown good engagement with the stem and has fully answered the question.

Worked example

What is the difference between hard and soft determinism in psychology? **(4 marks)**

Hard determinism is the view that people have no control over their behaviour because it is controlled by other factors. For example, a biological approach uses hard determinism and would suggest someone's genetic make-up was a factor in their behaviour. This is seen as an external force because there is nothing the person can do about it. Soft determinism takes the view that behaviour is determined but only to a point. It believes that people still have the ability to exert free will, so internal factors play a part in their actions.

You will have about 4 minutes in which to answer a 4-mark question. You should practise your timings when you attempt these types of exam questions.

When answering exam questions get straight to the point of what you are going to say, as this answer demonstrates. Timings are crucial for success.

Exam-style practice 1

Practise for Paper 3 of your A level exam with these exam-style questions. There are answers on page 302. Before looking at these questions, it would be good to review gender and cultural bias in psychology (pages 128–129), the nomothetic approach (page 133) and socially sensitive research (page 134).

1 Which of the following research biases result in the view that there are no differences between men and women, largely because such research is carried out using only male participants? Shade one box only.

A Alpha bias ◯

B Cultural bias ◯

C Androcentric bias ◯

D Beta bias ◯

(1 mark)

> Cultural bias is clearly related to a different concept so can be ruled out straightaway.

2 Which of the following **two** sentences relate to a nomothetic approach?
A The approach of studying the individual in order to find out about their uniqueness.
B The approach of investigating large groups of people in order to find general laws of behaviour that apply to everyone.
C The approach is unscientific.
D The approach is useful in predicting behaviour. **(2 marks)**

> Think about how a nomothetic investigation is carried out in order to rule out the two answers that relate to an idiographic approach.

3 Outline **one** problem associated with alpha bias in psychological research.

(4 marks)

> You need to know what alpha bias is. It is important to learn the meaning of the key terms in gender and cultural psychology so that you can correctly apply them to other topics.

4 Briefly outline what psychologists mean by 'cultural bias'. **(4 marks)**

> You need to provide a definition and use appropriate examples to show your understanding. No evaluation is needed.

5 Read the item and then answer the question that follows.

> To refuse to publish research because of its social implications is just intellectual cowardice. Our first responsibility is to the integrity of scientific knowledge. Publish and be damned. In the majority of cases, the social benefits of SSR far outweigh the potential negative consequences.

Discuss a cost–benefit analysis of carrying out socially sensitive research. Refer to research in your answer. **(8 marks)**

> The term 'discuss' requires both an outline and an evaluation. This question also asks you to include references to research. Raine (1996) and Humphreys (1970) could both be used here.

Exam-style practice 2

Practise for Paper 3 of your A level exam with these exam-style questions. There are answers on pages 302–303. Before looking at these questions, it would be good to review cultural bias (page 129), determinism (page 130), the nature–nurture debate (page 131) and the nomothetic approach (page 133).

6   What is meant by 'ethnocentrism' in psychology?   **(2 marks)**

> This question is an AO1 requirement so you need to write a short definition, in just two or three sentences. A 2-mark question should take no longer than 2 minutes.

7   The majority of Western views in psychology are likely to be ethnocentric because most of the research we look at comes from the US or the UK.

Discuss the problems faced in carrying out ethnocentric research.   **(6 marks)**

> The term 'discuss' is both an AO1 and AO3 assessment objective. Therefore, you need to **outline** what the problems are, **give examples** and also discuss what the **implications** might be. Try to present a balanced answer.

8   Read the item and then answer the questions that follow.

> Schizophrenia often runs in families, but many people with schizophrenia have experienced a major life event leading up to their first episode or have some dysfunctional family patterns of communication.

   (a) With reference to the item, explain what is meant by 'psychic', 'environmental' and 'biological' determinism.   **(6 marks)**

> This question requires you to explain what the three terms mean with some focus on explanations of schizophrenia.

   (b) With reference to the item, identify **one** influence of nature on our behaviour and **one** influence of nurture on our behaviour.   **(2 marks)**

> Again, referring to schizophrenia, you need to identify which explanation takes the nature side and which explanation takes the nurture side of the debate.

9   Read the item and then answer the question that follows.

> A psychologist wanted to find out whether she was correct in believing that an increase in the number of referrals to her eating disorders clinic was because of early childhood experiences. She decided to use an idiographic approach to study one girl and record her thoughts about her childhood and her eating behaviour in a diary over a period of four weeks. She carried out a content analysis on the diary. Analysis of the diary showed that the girl often thought about childhood events and believed that this had influenced her eating behaviour as she got older. Findings from studies like this are often used as a basis for other investigations.

> Make sure you engage with the stimulus to access the full marks, as the question asks about 'the above study'.

Explain how the psychologist might develop the above study through taking a nomothetic approach.   **(6 marks)**

Evolutionary explanations

Evolution is the process by which a species adapts to its environment through **natural selection**. Characteristics that aid the survival of the species are passed on in the genetic material from one generation to the next through **reproduction** as males and females select partners to improve their chances of reproductive success.

Human reproductive behaviour

Evolutionary theory states that males and females differ in their reproductive capabilities.

1   Males produce approximately 100 million sperm per ejaculation, meaning they have the potential to reproduce many times.

2   Females are born with a limited number of eggs, one of which is released per month for around 35–40 years, meaning they have fewer opportunities to reproduce.

Because of this difference, males may feel more competition with other males to find suitable fertile females, while females may be more selective over male partners who possess the best characteristics to pass on to her limited potential offspring. This means they use different strategies to select a partner.

Sexual selection

Sexual selection refers to characteristics that increase the chances of reproduction and therefore aid the passing on of genetic material.

1   A male's best chance of success is to have sex as often as possible with as many different females as he can to increase his opportunities to reproduce. He may seek out females who show signs of fertility to increase the chances of success even further.

2   A female, on the other hand, increases her chances of reproductive success by choosing mates who show signs of superior genetic fitness and who display signs of being able to provide resources to support her and any potential offspring.

Male strategies

- **Mate-guarding** – males may be protective of their mate to prevent other males having the opportunity of getting her pregnant and therefore leaving them using their resources to raise another male's offspring.

- **Sneak copulation** – males may have sex with other females in the absence of their partner to increase the chance of passing on genetic material to more offspring.

- **Size and appearance** – males evolved to be larger and some species developed physical attributes to increase the appearance of strength to females.

Female strategies

- **Sexy sons hypothesis** – females are thought to seek out attractive males so that any sons they produce will be equally attractive and will continue to pass on the genes to another generation.

- **Courtship** – females use courtship to select the most suitable male to reproduce with. By making a male spend time and resources in the build up to a relationship, the female can check his suitability for reproduction.

- **Handicap hypothesis** – Zahavi (1975) argued that females seek males with signs of handicap that indicate strength of genes over adversity.

Research evidence

✓ Davis (1990) found that in personal adverts males tended to seek out health and attractiveness, and females looked for high status and resources. This suggests that males and females may seek out different characteristics, supporting the evolutionary ideas.

✓ Buss (1989) found that males and females looked for different characteristics in marriage partners across a variety of cultures, supporting the claim that the difference stems from biology and evolution.

Evaluation

🗡 The evolutionary explanation ignores relationships that are not sexual and not aimed at reproducing, such as homosexual relationships. If mate choice is based on biological preferences surrounding reproductive success, any relationship not aiming to reproduce is difficult to explain and therefore ignored by this explanation.

👍 Evidence suggests that males may be more likely to engage in risky behaviours, which could be a strategy to indicate to females that they are physically strong and possess genetic strength.

Now try this

Explain how partner preference could be influenced by evolutionary factors.

Self-disclosure

Self-disclosure refers to the telling of personal information about oneself. At the beginning of a relationship, this may be an important signal that trust is developing between partners. It indicates attraction and is a starting point to intimacy in romantic relationships.

Self-disclosure and relationships

Self-disclosure may be important for two reasons:

1. We share more information as we get to know people and trust them more.

2. We feel closer to people and are more attracted to them *because* we disclose information to them.

Disclosing information about oneself is an important part of attraction.

Factors affecting the influence of self-disclosure

Gender – females may tend to disclose more and also place more importance on disclosures from a potential partner.

Content – what is disclosed could influence attraction from another person.

For example, telling a new partner very personal information about oneself at the start of a new relationship may be a violation of social norms.

Self-disclosure

Appropriateness – some kinds of disclosure may be seen as more or less appropriate.

For example, sharing very personal information on a first date could be seen as off-putting to a new partner.

Attributions – why a person discloses is important. We are more attracted to someone if they seem to especially want to disclose intimate information to us.

Evaluation

👍 Much research evidence supports the claim that self-disclosure is an important feature of attraction in romantic relationships. This suggests it is a valid explanation of a feature of attraction.

👎 Some of the research into self-disclosure does not differentiate between the type of relationship being studied. For example, self-disclosure may play a different role in attraction in a potentially long-term relationship than it would in a fling.

👎 The personality of the people involved in the relationship is not necessarily taken into account. Some people may disclose more than others, while some will place more emphasis on receiving self-disclosure from others.

Research evidence

☑ Altman and Taylor (1973) found that appropriateness of the disclosure was important. If someone disclosed lots of personal information at a very early stage of a relationship (on a first date), they were rated as less likeable and attractive. This could be because they were seen as having poor social skills.

☑ Kleinke (1979) found that when people were perceived as being selective over who they shared personal information with – so that the person receiving the disclosure felt 'special' as they had been chosen – the person making the self-disclosure was rated to be more attractive.

☑ Collins and Miller (1994) conducted a meta-analysis into the relationship between self-disclosure and attraction. They found people rated those who made more personal disclosures as more attractive and likeable. They also found evidence that individuals made more self-disclosures to people who they were attracted to. This would suggest that levels of self-disclosure are important in the initial attraction phase of a relationship.

☑ Kito (2010) found that self-disclosure was higher in romantic relationships than other types of relationship (friendships) in samples from both America and Japan, suggesting self-disclosure is an important factor in romantic relationships.

Now try this

1 Outline **one** factor that influences the effect of self-disclosure on attraction.

2 Explain what research has shown about the role of self-disclosure in attraction.

Physical attractiveness

Physical attractiveness is another element of attraction in relationships and is often the first thing that draws couples together. It occurs more quickly than getting to know someone's personality or sense of humour, and can immediately signal whether two people may wish to get to know each other better. A theory behind the effect of physical attractiveness on relationships is the **matching hypothesis**.

Physical attractiveness

What is seen to be physically attractive to one person is likely to be different to someone else, as physical attractiveness is a subjective factor. From an evolutionary point of view, there are certain characteristics that all men and women may find attractive (see page 139 for more detail on evolutionary explanations), and many people will agree on an individual's general level of attractiveness. A psychological phenomenon known as the **halo effect** (Dion, 1972) means that we tend to attribute positive characteristics to those who are physically attractive, making them more desirable partners.

The matching hypothesis

Walster et al. (1966) suggested that individuals are attracted to others who are of a similar level of attractiveness to themselves. Before approaching a potential partner, the individual will assess their own level of attractiveness in relation to others. They will then focus attention on others of the same or a similar level of attractiveness, as they see the threat of rejection as lower. The security felt in the relationship is likely to be higher if the couple are of a similar level of attractiveness. If one partner feels physically 'inferior' to the other, they may be concerned that their partner will be considering more attractive alternatives.

Research evidence: Walster et al. (1966)

Aim: To see whether matched attractiveness levels were a precursor to relationship formation.

Procedure: University students were rated for attractiveness by independent judges before being randomly paired with a partner of the opposite sex at a dance. Partners were asked to rate how much they liked their partner and whether they would like to see them again.

Results: Partners were most likely to 'like' the partner if they had a high level of physical attractiveness, regardless of their own level of attractiveness. Those who met up again after the dance were likely to be of a similar rating of attractiveness.

Research evidence: Taylor et al. (2011)

Aim: To see whether the matching hypothesis is supported in real-world dating behaviour.

Procedure: Four studies were conducted looking for evidence of matching in dates organised through a dating website. Evidence of matching based on attractiveness, popularity and self-worth was investigated using questionnaires and independent ratings from other people.

Results: Evidence suggested that most people made contact with more attractive partners for possible dates, regardless of their own level of attractiveness, refuting the matching hypothesis. They also found that replies were most likely to be sent to contacts who were rated similarly, suggesting actual dating may be explained by the matching hypothesis and not initial attraction.

Evaluation

👍 Walster and Walster (1969) told students that they had been matched by a computer program with a partner, even though matching was done randomly. They asked participants to rate their 'match' when they met, and found that those who were closer in matched physical attractiveness rated each other more favourably than those who were mismatched.

👎 In cultures where arranged marriage is popular, family members may spend time matching partners on factors like success and social standing while physical attractiveness might be less important. This shows that physical attractiveness may not have universal appeal in attraction.

Now try this

Outline the role of physical attractiveness in the formation of relationships.

Filter theory

Attraction at the start of a relationship depends on many things, but Kerckhoff and Davis (1962) put forward the **filter theory**. The actual people we could develop a relationship with comprise a huge array of individuals, so we 'filter' to narrow down all the possible matches we could make.

 Social demography – we will be attracted to those who we are most likely to encounter.

For example, those who live closest to us, work with us, socialise in the same places, etc.

We will also filter those who are from the same ethnic backgrounds, of a similar level of education and other similar 'social' variables.

 Similarity in attitudes – attraction is more likely to build in those who share similar beliefs and views.

For example, when meeting and getting to know new people, those who have similar attitudes to us will be seen as more attractive and therefore more suitable to develop a relationship with.

 Complementarity – this filter refers to seeking out those who provide us with emotional satisfaction. We will become most attracted to people who fulfil our emotional needs. This will then become the basis of long-term commitment, which can develop as the relationship progresses.

Research evidence

✓ Festinger et al. (1950) found that people were more likely to develop friendships with people who lived closest to them in an apartment building. The suggestion was that physical proximity increased liking, which then developed into friendships. A similar explanation may account for the development of relationships.

✓ Kerckhoff and Davis (1962) tested the theory in a longitudinal study of students in relationships for more than or less than 18 months. They found that up to 18 months the most important filter was attitude similarity; after 18 months, emotional complementarity became a more important factor in the relationship.

✓ Taylor et al. (2010) found evidence that of all the American couples who married in 2008, 85% of them married a person from the same ethnic group as them. This would support the claim that social demographic factors are important in attraction.

✓ Gruber-Baldini et al. (1995) found that couples who shared more similarities, such as education level, at the start of a relationship were more likely to be together 20 years later.

Evaluation

🏷 Filter theory can be criticised for being **gender biased** as it does not account for the fact that filters applied by males and females may be different.

For example, males may place less emphasis on complementarity than females when filtering potential partners.

🏷 Filter theory could also be considered **culturally biased** as it assumes that all cultures would use the same limiting factors to filter those to whom people are attracted. However, this makes the assumption that all relationships are based on personal choice and are voluntary.

For example, some cultures practise arranged marriage, or non-voluntary relationships, whereby family members will choose partners based on their own limiting factors. They may place less emphasis on proximity or complementarity when deciding to match partners than individuals with free will would.

🏷 The filters affecting relationship formation may change over time as attitudes change in society. For example, social demographic factors, such as ethnicity, may change in importance. In the 1960s, interracial relationships may not have been common, but evidence from Taylor et al. (2010) suggests that 15% of marriages in 2008 were interracial.

Now try this

Explain **one** limitation of filter theory as an explanation for attraction in relationships.

Social exchange theory

Social exchange theory (SET) claims that relationships are a series of exchanges between partners, with each person 'giving' certain things to the other, while also 'receiving' from their partner. As an **economic theory**, it states that provided each person feels they are in 'profit', the relationship will continue.

Social exchanges

Both partners in a relationship will gain certain **rewards** and will also give something back to the relationship, which are seen as **costs**.

Rewards
Relationships bring certain **rewards** such as sex, companionship and shared living space.

Costs
Relationships also bring **costs** such as time away from friends and family, sharing finances and arguments.

If both partners see they gain more than they put in, and are in profit, then the relationship will continue. Feeling they are at a loss may mean satisfaction is low and the relationship may end.

Four-stage model

Thibaut and Kelley (1959) suggested that relationships develop through four stages:

1 **Sampling** – Many relationships will be started while the person 'tries out' the potential rewards and costs associated with being a couple.

2 **Bargaining** – Once a potential partner is identified, all of the possible sources of profit and loss are assessed to decide whether to pursue a deeper relationship.

3 **Commitment** – The relationship continues when the costs are outweighed by the rewards, meaning that attraction will increase.

4 **Institutionalisation** – The couple settle into the relationship, setting an expectation for what rewards and costs will be tolerated for the continuation of the relationship.

Comparison levels

According to SET, both partners will assess their level of profit and loss regularly to determine their level of satisfaction. There are two **comparison levels**:

1 **The comparison level (CL)** assesses the number of rewards received and the amount of costs they give to the relationship.

2 **The comparison level for alternative relationships (CLalt)** assesses the profit offered by the current relationship against any potential profit from an alternative relationship.

Research evidence

✓ Rusbult (1983) gave participants questionnaires to complete over a seven-month period. They found that the beginning phase of relationships had little to do with perceived profit, but as relationships became more committed, the reward/cost comparison became more apparent. Satisfaction and therefore continuation of relationships was associated with perception of profit in the current situation.

✓ Rusbult and Martz (1995) found that abused women were more likely to return to their partners if there was no better alternative available. This suggests that even an abusive relationship could be profitable if the abused partner gains more from being in the relationship than from leaving, such as somewhere to live or financial security.

Evaluation

🖋 Many people criticise SET as it suggests that humans keep score in their relationships, making them appear selfish. While some individuals and/or couples may be the kind to 'keep score', many others will maintain relationships for other reasons, such as mutual respect and trust. This suggests that the theory does not apply to all relationships universally.

🖋 An alternative explanation was put forward to modify the economic approach to relationships by suggesting that rather than profit, couples seek to maintain relationships based on fairness. Equity theory (see page 144) assumes that both partners require the feeling that they are gaining equally rather than each seeking to maximise their own profit margin.

Now try this

Outline social exchange theory as it applies to relationships.

Equity theory

Equity theory states that relationships do not rely on equality to continue, but instead they depend on how much **fairness** is perceived by both partners. Motivation to maintain the relationship comes when each partner is happy and the relationship is fair.

Inequity in relationships

Walster et al. (1978) said that each partner in a relationship will 'put in' to a relationship, and will also 'take' from the other partner. So long as each partner remains satisfied that they are both giving and receiving in a fair ratio, they will continue with the relationship.

However, if either partner feels that they are giving more than they receive (**under-benefitted**) or receiving more than they put in themselves (**over-benefitted**), the level of satisfaction will decrease. This puts the continuation of the relationship under threat.

Motivation to maintain the relationship

When one or both partners feel an imbalance between what they give and receive in the relationship, it creates discomfort. This acts as a motivation to return the relationship to a state of **equity** or fairness. If one or both partners are not motivated to balance out the ratio of 'giving' and 'receiving', the imbalance may finally end the relationship.

For example, if one partner feels they give more financially to a relationship, but do not receive sufficiently in return for this, they may feel they are being taken advantage of and act to end things.

Four principles of equity

Walster et al. (1978) claimed that there were four principles of equity:

Principle	Explanation
1 Profit	Each partner seeks to gain more than they put in.
2 Distribution	Partners will negotiate to ensure the relationship remains equitable and fair.
3 Distress	When unfairness is perceived, dissatisfaction begins. Distress will increase in line with the amount of inequity.
4 Restoring balance	When inequity is detected, partners will be motivated to act to restore the balance.

Research evidence

☑ Stafford and Canary (2006) asked married couples to complete surveys on relationship satisfaction. They found that those who felt they were in equitable relationships were the most satisfied, followed by over-benefitted partners; the under-benefitted were the least satisfied. This supports the idea that equity increases the likelihood of relationship maintenance.

☑ Dainton (2003) found that people who were in romantic relationships perceived as 'unfair' were the least satisfied, but also the most motivated to improve the equity of the relationship. This supports the claim that equity is a leading factor in maintaining relationships.

☑ Moghaddam et al. (1983) found that partners in US relationships valued equity over equality, but in Europe, equality was more important. This would suggest that the theory is not applicable to all cultures in the same way.

Evaluation

🔖 Many people have criticised equity theory for claiming people are inherently selfish because they are judging relationship satisfaction on the basis of what they are gaining.

🔖 Some have criticised equity theory on the basis that much of what people put into a relationship is emotional, and emotion is difficult to measure. The claim that we balance input with gains is therefore problematic.

Now try this

Outline equity theory as an explanation of relationships.

Rusbult's investment model

Rusbult's **investment model** of relationships considers the factors associated with commitment in romantic relationships. The theory states that commitment levels will be related to three factors: **satisfaction** in the current relationship, lack of or comparison with **potential alternatives** and amount of **investments made** in the relationship.

 ## Satisfaction

This refers to the positive vs negative effects felt from being in the relationship. Each partner will assess how much the relationship fulfils their needs, whether they are emotional, sexual or other personal needs. If the positive effects outweigh the negative, then the level of satisfaction will be high. Rusbult felt that there was a correlational relationship between satisfaction level and commitment to the relationship – the more satisfaction is felt, the more commitment there is to maintain the relationship.

 ## Comparison with alternatives

Rusbult suggested that people are always considering other potential alternatives in comparison to their current relationship. When faced with any other possible mate, she felt that people make a very quick calculation regarding whether their needs can be met with a higher level of satisfaction with the 'new' partner. If the answer is 'yes', then the level of commitment to the current relationship will decrease. If the answer is 'no', then the level of commitment to maintain the current relationship remains high.

 ## Investments made

Every relationship involves investment of resources made by both partners into the joint partnership. Direct investments include the time and effort put into the relationship, while indirect investments include children, shared friends and possessions the couple may have bought together. The commitment in the current relationship will be highest when the perceived losses associated with ending the relationship outweigh any dissatisfaction felt.

Additional factors

Equity – Rusbult considered that satisfaction levels would be affected not only by how much the person has their needs met, but also by how *fair* the relationship is perceived to be.

Social support – commitment to a relationship may be influenced by friends and family. If such people have a positive view of an individual's partner, they may view them more positively and therefore remain committed to a relationship with them.

Research evidence

✓ Rusbult and Martz (1995) found that women in abusive relationships were more likely to stay in such relationships when the number of better alternatives was low, the amount invested in the relationship was high and the level of dissatisfaction felt (severity of abuse) was lower.

✓ Rusbult et al. (1998) found that high levels of commitment were associated with high levels of satisfaction, lower numbers of quality alternatives and high measures of investment in the relationship. This evidence supports all three variables associated with relationship commitment according to Rusbult.

Evaluation

👍 A lot of research evidence gathered to support the theory comes from real romantic relationships, meaning that the evidence has a good degree of external validity as it relates to commitment levels in existing relationships.

👎 Much of the evidence gathered to support investment theory relies heavily on **self-report methods** such as questionnaires. This could challenge the reliability of the data gathered as there are many reasons why people may not answer questions about their relationship honestly.

For example, they may feel uncomfortable admitting that they have considered alternatives to their current relationship.

Now try this

Compare the investment model and social exchange theory.

Duck's model of breakdown

Duck (2001) suggested that relationships generally end in **phases**. The length of the relationship will likely influence how quickly couples move through each phase of breakdown, but the phases are thought to be applicable to any and all relationship breakdowns.

Reasons for breakdown

Duck stated that there were three common reasons that relationships break down:

1 **Pre-existing doom** – where the end of a relationship is likely to be predictable from the start, due to issues such as lack of compatibility or serious differences in views.

2 **Mechanical failure** – the most common cause of breakdown, where a couple find that they cannot continue in a relationship any longer as the relationship itself does not work.

3 **Sudden death** – where an unpredictable event causes a couple to split, such as discovery that one partner has cheated, or a traumatic event that occurs between the couple.

Phases of breakdown

Duck proposed that relationships break down in four identifiable phases. Each has a threshold point which, when reached, spells the beginning of the new phase.

Intra-psychic phase
- Threshold - 'I cannot do this any more'
- One partner feels dissatisfied with the relationship and begins to consider how and when to end the relationship.
- The dissatisfied partner considers if and when to share their feelings with the other person.

Dyadic phase
- Threshold - 'I would be justified in walking away'
- The dissatisfied partner shares their feelings and the couple discuss the relationship's status.
- Resolutions can be discussed and attempts may be made to restore satisfaction in the relationship.

Social phase
- Threshold - 'I mean it'
- If a resolution is not possible, the couple make their split public and discuss dissatisfaction with people outside of the relationship.
- Blame-placing and gossip-spreading may be common in this phase.

Grave-dressing phase
- Threshold - 'It is inevitable'
- This marks the end of the relationship and this phase is about 'moving on'.
- Each partner will begin rebuilding their life out of the relationship as well as telling their version of events from the end of the relationship.

Research evidence

✓ Tashiro and Frazier (2003) surveyed students following a break up. They found that many reported not only feeling distressed following the break up, but also experiencing some personal growth after the relationship ended.

For example, many said they now felt they knew themselves better, or knew what they now wanted from a relationship, thus supporting the claim made by Duck that 'grave-dressing' is a key phase in relationship breakdown.

✓ Hatfield et al. (1984) supported the existence of the 'intra-psychic phase'; they found that when people feel dissatisfied with a relationship, they are likely to report increased social withdrawal while they decide what to do. This suggests that people need a phase of personal time to work out what to do next.

Evaluation

👍 This theory has good face validity as the phases described by Duck are often reported during the end stages of a relationship.

👎 Evidence has found that males and females may experience relationship breakdown differently, suggesting the theory is not universal. For example, Argyle (1988) found that women were more likely to state lack of emotional support as a reason for a relationship ending, while men stated reasons like 'lack of fun', suggesting that the reasons for breakdown differ depending on gender.

Now try this

Describe what occurs in the dyadic phase of Duck's model of breakdown.

Virtual relationships and self-disclosure

Virtual relationships are conducted online, often through a form of social media such as dating websites. Psychologists are interested in whether the information people give about themselves (**self-disclosure**, see page 140) differs in virtual relationships when compared to face-to-face relationships.

The 'up' side to anonymity

When partners meet online they are able to reveal information more easily to the 'stranger' due to the **anonymity** virtual relationships offer. This means that people will be more honest about their 'true' self and less worried about how they appear. The intimacy in the relationship may therefore build up more quickly than in a face-to-face relationship, where it may take months of meeting to reach the same level of honesty. This may be particularly true in people who have low self-esteem, or are concerned about their physical appearance.

The 'down' side to anonymity

One problem with the anonymity of virtual relationships is that people can lie more easily about who they are. This would allow some people to prey on vulnerable individuals, such as those with low self-esteem or poor social skills, for financial or sexual gain.

> Online profiles allow people to share information about themselves more freely, and also control exactly what information they choose to give.

Research evidence

✓ Scott et al. (2006) found that participants reported a higher level of intimacy in their face-to-face relationships than their online relationships. Also, those who had online romantic relationships reported lower levels of intimacy in their face-to-face relationships than participants who had only had face-to-face relationships.

✓ McKenna et al. (2002) found that participants who self-disclose more honestly online are more likely to have made friendships virtually and moved these from virtual to face-to-face. They also found that a lot of these friendships were still intact two years later.

Research evidence: Peter et al. (2005)

Aim: To investigate whether people classed as introverts and extraverts had different motivations for online relationships.

Procedure: A group of 493 adolescents completed self-report data on measures of extraversion/introversion, online self-disclosure, frequency of online communication and motives for communication.

Results: They found that introverts communicated online due to poorer social skills, and had more online friendships due to higher online disclosure than extraverts.

Conclusion: Personality may influence online disclosure in virtual relationships.

Evaluation

👍 Research suggests that virtual communication allows people with poorer social skills to communicate more effectively. This could help vulnerable people access help and support online if they find face-to-face discussions challenging.

👎 Although people may report high levels of intimacy in their online relationships, the self-disclosure shared online may represent a person's 'ideal self' rather than their real 'self'. Virtual relationships allow elements of a person to be hidden, and these may not become clear until later in a relationship if it eventually becomes face-to-face.

Now try this

Explain how self-disclosure may differ in virtual relationships compared to face-to-face.

Absence of gating

'Gating' refers to barriers that may prevent relationships from forming, due to limiting factors. In virtual relationships, there is an **absence of gating** as many of these factors can be hidden more easily.

Absence of gating

When we meet people face-to-face, there are certain characteristics that we take note of that may increase or decrease the likelihood of a relationship forming.

For example, if we do not find the person physically attractive this will become a **limiting factor** that will reduce the chance of us attempting to start a relationship with them.

Limiting factors create barriers to relationship formation. This is known as '**gating**'. Virtual relationships are not subject to the same limiting factors because some of these characteristics associated with face-to-face meeting are not obvious when talking online.

Why prevent gating?

Online relationships allow people to create a virtual persona where they can portray themselves however they want. Factors they do not like about themselves can be hidden easily until the relationship has progressed to a point where the person no longer worries that the **limiting factor** will have a negative effect on the relationship. In these circumstances, **self-disclosure** (see page 140) will also be important as getting to know the 'real person' will be the key to the limiting factor not being a barrier to the relationship.

♪Extend The dangers of preventing gating

The absence of gating may be open to abuse by some as they can deliberately hide elements of their true identity, allowing them to get close to people online who may otherwise not want to start a relationship with them. Similarly, many people who would favour virtual relationships may be more vulnerable due to personal characteristics they do not want to share with others. If someone wanted to deliberately prey on the vulnerable, meeting someone online would allow them to do so.

Research evidence

McKenna et al. (2002) conducted a laboratory experiment where participants were required to have two 20-minute conversations with other people on 10 different occasions. The control condition consisted of two face-to-face meetings, and the other two conditions began with an online conversation and a face-to-face meeting. Although all of the paired conversations were with the same person, in one of the online/face-to-face conditions participants thought they were talking to two different people. Results showed that when meeting a person online, they were rated as more liked than when they met face-to-face. This would suggest that when meeting in person, gating features may influence the quality of interaction between two people.

Evaluation

🖝 Much of the evidence into the effect of absence of gating relies on self-report data, which may be prone to social desirability. For example, people may not want to be seen as shallow and so may not be honest about how much they like a person when asked, affecting the validity of the findings.

🖝 Research does not seem to consider how the issue of gating may influence different groups of people, hence there may be gender or cultural bias in the application of the theory. For instance, absence of gating may have a different effect on the relationship formation of men and women.

Now try this

Explain how absence of gating may affect virtual relationships.

Parasocial relationships

Parasocial relationships are one-sided relationships – one person develops an emotional attachment to another person, usually a celebrity, who is unaware of the 'relationship'.

What are parasocial relationships?

They are often perceived to be abnormal – even obsessive – relationships that develop in people who are emotionally unstable.

Parasocial relationships may be a normal part of developing personality by modelling themselves on famous people, as suggested by social learning theory (see page 69).

Factors in parasocial relationships

- **Age** – They can occur in anyone at any age, but there seems to be an increase in occurrence during adolescence, when the adult personality is developing.
- **Gender** – Males are more likely to develop parasocial relationships with sports personalities, while females are more likely to develop them with entertainment celebrities.
- **Education** – People with a lower level of education are more likely to develop parasocial relationships with celebrities, possibly due to a lack of ability to reason that reality and fiction are distinct.

Celebrity Attitude Scale

McCutcheon et al. (2002) claimed there are three levels of parasocial relationships, which can be measured using the **Celebrity Attitude Scale.**

1 **Entertainment-social level** – social aspects: discussing the target of the emotional attraction (the celebrity) with friends and in social situations; enjoying the entertainment provided by the celebrity. This may be experienced by a number of 'fans' of celebrities.

2 **Intense-personal level** – strength of feelings: the feelings for the celebrity become more personal and border on obsessive. The person develops an emotional attachment to the target of the parasocial relationship.

For example, the fan may spend all their money following a star on tour around the world in a bid to stay physically close to them. These feelings are experienced by a small number of 'fans'.

3 **Borderline-pathological level** – level of uncontrollable feelings: a very small number of 'fans' will develop uncontrollable feelings for the target of the relationship, and will begin to behave in a more obsessive way as a result.

For example, at this level, the person might attempt to meet with the object of their desire and believes that the feelings they have might be reciprocated if they were to meet in real-life.

Research evidence

☑ McCutcheon et al. (2002) found that there was a negative correlation between level of education reached and interest in celebrities. Rubin et al. (1985) found that there was no correlation between measures of loneliness and parasocial relationships in TV viewers. This refutes suggestions that parasocial relationships develop as a substitute for 'real' relationships.

☑ Giles (2000) found that younger people show higher levels of attraction to celebrities than older people do, supporting the claim that age may influence parasocial relationships.

Evaluation

👍 Evidence that younger people show more attraction to celebrities than older people could be explained by the fact that younger people spend more time interacting with media sources.

👎 Much of the evidence into parasocial relationships relies on self-report data, which could be unreliable and/or lack validity. Participants may feel uncomfortable admitting to what could be perceived by others to be an 'abnormal' relationship and so downplay their feelings or behaviour.

Now try this

Describe the different levels of parasocial relationships.

Absorption addiction model

According to McCutcheon (2002), many people will be interested in celebrities because of the entertainment offered by 'keeping up' with the gossip from their lives. However, some people will take this interest a step further and will become **absorbed** or **addicted** to these celebrities, increasing the chances of a **parasocial relationship** developing.

Absorption

Some people may develop obsessions with celebrities to try to **absorb** the success they have achieved to make themselves feel better.

Addiction

Once the interest in the celebrity goes beyond absorption they may become **addicted** to the celebrity. This could lead to risky behaviours to try to 'build' the relationship, such as stalking or acting as if they are actually in a relationship with the celebrity.

The absorption addiction model

Giles and Maltby (2006) described in detail the three stages through which parasocial relationships may descend and through which the absorption-addiction model occurs.

1 **Entertainment-social level** – most people enjoy talking about celebrities and their lifestyles with their friends, and find this level of involvement in their life interesting.

2 **Intense-personal level** – for some people, a personal interest in one of these celebrities will intensify and may become obsessive. This may spark off a parasocial relationship as the individual feels an artificial closeness to the celebrity in question.

3 **Borderline-pathological level** – in a small number of people this interest in the celebrity develops even further and the behaviours associated with the relationship become abnormal and uncontrollable. They may fantasise about their life with the celebrity, and even stalk them to make direct contact. In some cases, they may believe they are in a real relationship with the celebrity, which justifies their behaviour.

Research evidence

☑ McCutcheon and Houran (2003) asked 600 participants to complete a personality test and then interviewed them about their attitudes to celebrities. They found that one-third had signs of Celebrity Worship Syndrome, with 20% of these stating entertainment-social reasons, 10% showing intense-personal attitudes and 1% displaying borderline-pathological behaviours. They claimed that this suggested a scale of parasocial relationships from normal to abnormal.

☑ Maltby et al. (2003) found that people with entertainment-social interests in celebrities were more extravert, while those with more intense-personal interests were more neurotic, suggesting that personality factors may be important in parasocial relationships.

Evaluation

👍 Understanding the thoughts and behaviours that could precede borderline-pathological tendencies may help to identify those at risk before their behaviour progresses into criminality. This can also help to develop treatments by better understanding the causes of behaviours such as stalking.

👎 Behaviour such as celebrity stalking, which is associated with parasocial relationships, is very complex and can have many triggers. This can make understanding the psychology behind it very difficult. As much of the research relies on self-report data such as interviews assessing attitudes to celebrities, it may be subject to social-desirability bias as some people will not be honest. Thus, the evidence lacks reliability and validity.

Now try this

Outline the absorption addiction model of parasocial relationships.

Attachment theory explanation

Attachment types are patterns of behaviour that become evident in infancy in response to separation and reunion with caregivers (see page 40). Evidence has suggested that the type of attachment a person has in childhood extends into adult relationships. Psychologists also believe that some attachment types are more likely to develop **parasocial relationships** than others.

Attachment types and parasocial relationships

Insecure-resistant attachment
People with insecure-resistant attachments may be quite clingy, as they become extremely distressed at the thought of separation from those they are attached to. They have a need to build attachments to others as they crave the closeness of a relationship, but the risk of rejection in real relationships is high.

This can mean that people with this attachment type are more prone to parasocial relationships because they can develop a close attachment to the celebrity without the chance that they will be rejected. As the celebrity is unaware of the relationship, the individual with the parasocial relationship is safe from the risk of being abandoned by the one they care about.

Attachment types and parasocial relationships

Secure attachment
Those with secure attachments value physical closeness and seek out relationships with others as they find it easier to trust others. They tend to find building face-to-face relationships with others easy. They therefore have little need to engage in parasocial relationships.

Insecure-avoidant attachment
People with insecure-avoidant attachments are untrusting of others and therefore tend to avoid trying to develop close relationships with other people. They will therefore be unlikely to engage in parasocial relationships.

Research evidence

✓ Cole and Leets (1999) gave 115 students a questionnaire measuring parasocial relationship traits as well as two different measures of attachment type. They found that those rated as insecure-resistant were most likely to develop parasocial bonds with TV personalities. Those least likely to develop this type of relationship were insecure-avoidants. Some securely attached individuals (those who reported higher levels of mistrust) were also quite likely to develop parasocial relationships, but not to the same extent as the resistantly attached.

✓ Cohen (2004) found that those who were categorised as insecure-resistant were more likely to predict more negative effects if their favourite TV characters were to be taken off-air. The stronger the parasocial bond to the character, the worse the negative effect was predicted to be.

Evaluation

👍 There are many similarities between parasocial relationships and attachment behaviour, suggesting that they are related.

For example, very intense parasocial relationships can lead to stalking. This can be likened to the seeking of 'close proximity', which is often seen in research categorising infant attachment types.

👎 The categorisation of attachment styles has often been criticised for a lack of validity.

For example, Ainsworth's original research (see page 40) categorised three types, but later research by Main and Solomon (1986) added another attachment type (Type D), suggesting the research may be incomplete.

👎 Research has suggested that, while attachment types evident in children have been well supported, the evidence linking this to adult behaviour patterns is inconclusive. It is possible that the attachment types for parasocial relationships are different to the standard types seen in children, therefore the explanation may not be fully valid.

Now try this

Identify which attachment type is more likely to develop parasocial relationships, and explain why.

Exam skills 1

Before you look at this worked example, remind yourself about the maintenance of romantic relationships (pages 143–146).

Worked example

Discuss theories of the maintenance of romantic relationships.

(16 marks)

Excerpt 1

Maintenance refers to the continuation of relationships, and one theory to explain this is social exchange theory. This theory suggests that all social interactions are a series of rewards and costs, and in a relationship the level of 'profit' achieved will affect satisfaction with the relationship. The companionship, financial security, support and sex associated with romantic relationships are all possible rewards, while costs might include spending time away from family and friends, arguments and sacrificing relationships with others. Each individual will weigh up the rewards and costs of their relationship – if they perceive a profit they will be motivated to maintain the relationship, but if they perceive a loss they may opt to end it. Each partner will also compare the current relationship to the potential profits achievable in alternative relationships and, provided the current relationship is seen as most profitable, it will continue.

Excerpt 2

Rusbult and Martz (1995) found that women in abusive relationships were more likely to stay if there was no better alternative. This would suggest that even a violent relationship might be viewed as favourable if there is nothing better available. The loss associated with leaving the relationship then outweighs the negative aspects of the current situation. Many people would argue that social exchange theory views humans as selfish, as they are seeking only the most profitable relationship for themselves. There are, however, many other reasons relationships continue, such as mutual respect. A better explanation might be equity theory, which suggests relationships continue when there is a state of 'fairness' rather than simply profit.

Command word: Discuss

Discuss means to both describe and evaluate. A 'discussion' means to develop an argument by introducing the content, demonstrating knowledge of the various theories of relationship maintenance, and then assessing the quality of these explanations. It would be good to compare different theories to create further discussion points, too.

The question asks about 'theories' of maintenance, which means that more than one will need to be discussed.

This paragraph gives quite a lot of detail on social exchange theory as an explanation of relationship maintenance. You are unlikely to have enough time to give this amount of detail describing another theory, and it would probably be unnecessary, but you must include a second theory. It is useful to include one in detail so you can go into depth, but then in your second (and possibly third) include less detail in your description to give you some breadth as well.

The next paragraph could describe equity theory or the investment model.

Essays should always include appropriate use of specialist terminology to speak the 'language' of psychology.

It is a good idea when doing an essay question to use a variety of evaluation points such as **evidence, limitations** and **comparison** to another theory. This gives a better discussion than just repeating the same points again and again. Show a clear line of argument by linking your points together and using research evidence to back up the points you make.

From here you could continue the evaluation to discuss equity theory and why this may be better (or not) as an explanation of relationship maintenance.

Exam skills 2

Before you look at these worked examples, remind yourself about attachment theory and parasocial relationships (page 151).

Worked example

Outline **one** strength and **one** limitation of attachment theory as an explanation of parasocial relationships.

(6 marks)

One strength of using attachment theory to explain parasocial relationships is that the evidence suggests that behaviours associated with parasocial relationships are very similar to those associated with attachment types. For example, extreme parasocial relationships can result in stalking where people try to be close to the person they have the parasocial relationships with. This could be seen as 'proximity seeking behaviour' similar to that seen in children in the Strange Situation Procedure with their attachment figures.

One limitation of using attachment theory to explain parasocial relationships is that the categorisation of attachment types may not be valid. People have criticised Ainsworth's (1978) attachment types, suggesting that they may not be completely accurate because another 'disorganised' attachment type was added several years later. If the attachment types are not valid, then any explanation of parasocial relationships based on these three types is also not valid.

The question refers to one strength and one limitation so you must make sure your answer covers each one in detail. For 6 marks in total you should be aiming for 3 marks on the strength and 3 marks on the limitation.

Try to use the PEE or PEEL method when creating evaluation points like this. This will encourage you to elaborate your point clearly, which will help you to achieve the 3 marks for each part of the question. With the PEE or PEEL technique, you make your initial **P**oint and then **E**laborate this by suggesting what it means. Then **E**xplain why this could be seen as a strength or limitation. Your final point can then **L**ink back the content that forms the basis of the question.

You can use research evidence as strengths and limitations of a theory. Any research that supports the claims of the theory would be considered a strength, while research evidence that contradicts the theory could be seen as a limitation.

Worked example

Explain what is meant by a 'parasocial relationship' in psychology.

(2 marks)

A parasocial relationship is a one-sided relationship where one person feels a connection to another person, but the other partner may not be aware of the relationship. For example, celebrity stalking could be a kind of parasocial relationship.

Although this is a 'define' question, and only offers 2 marks, to do well you need to give enough accurate detail about what a parasocial relationship is. Try to give a clear definition and then give an example to illustrate what this type of relationship is.

Exam-style practice 1

Practise for Paper 3 of your A level exam with these exam-style questions. There are answers on page 304. Before looking at these questions, it would be good to review evolutionary explanations (page 139), factors affecting attraction in romantic relationships (pages 140–142) and the investment model (page 145).

1 Explain **one** limitation associated with studying the influence of self-disclosure on relationships. **(2 marks)**

> Why might it be difficult to test the accuracy of the statements given as examples of 'self-disclosure'?

2 Briefly outline **one** feature of attraction according to filter theory. **(2 marks)**

> Select one of the elements of attraction that the theory identifies, such as similarity in attitudes, and then describe what it means and how it influences whether you are attracted to someone or not.

3 Read the item and then answer the question that follows.

> Melanie has been with her husband, Roberto, for 15 years and they have two young children. Melanie gave up work when their oldest daughter was born, and now that they have both started at school she has begun to work part-time in a local shop. Roberto owns his own business, which is very successful, but he has recently been very stressed due to the long hours. He does not like Melanie going out to work as he does not know where she is or who she might be talking to. During an argument, Roberto lashed out at Melanie and slapped her across the face. When she told her friends what had happened, they were surprised when she said she was not going to leave Roberto.

Explain why partners may stay in abusive relationships. Refer to Rusbult's investment model and Melanie in your answer.

(4 marks)

> Read questions like this carefully. There are clues in the stimulus material about Melanie to help you answer the question. Make sure you refer to Melanie in your answer as the question asks.

> Rusbult's investment model relates commitment to relationships to the amount that has been put into (or invested in) the relationship. Even in an abusive relationship, the amount of time and effort already given to the relationship may outweigh the possible risks of remaining with the abusive partner. For example, one clue they refer to in the stimulus about Melanie is the fact that they have two children, which is a considerable investment.

4 Discuss the influence of evolutionary factors on relationship development. **(16 marks)**

> Evolutionary explanations relate to survival and reproduction needs that motivate behaviour. In this case, how mate preferences are determined and what will ensure the best chances of survival and the greatest reproductive success.

> Begin with a general discussion about the various evolutionary motives for relationships. You could then discuss the difference in male and female strategies for mate choice based on the different motives of males (fertility) and females (stability and support).

> To evaluate the evolutionary explanation, provide research evidence to support or refute the claims made about mate preference. Also discuss issues such as reductionism – evolutionary explanations ignore the role of social or psychological factors in mate preference. Use research evidence in your answer.

Exam-style practice 2

Practise for Paper 3 of your A level exam with these exam-style questions. There are answers on pages 304–305. Before looking at these questions, it would be good to review distributions (page 116) and correlations (page 99) in Research methods, Duck's model of breakdown (page 146) and absence of gating (page 148).

5 Complete the following diagram to name the stages of Duck's theory of relationship breakdown. **(1 mark)**

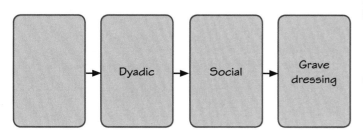

This kind of 1-mark question can still feature on your A level paper and can be a quick way to gain marks. Although they are often based on recall of information, they will not be easy and usually require detailed knowledge such as key terms. Make sure you are confident in your use of the language of psychology associated with the theories and research studied.

6 Read the item and then answer the questions that follow.

> A research study has shown that in a sample of 100 couples in arranged marriages, at the beginning of the relationship the ratings given by each partner of how much they 'loved' or 'liked' their partner were quite low. As the length of the marriage increased, so did the ratings of how much they loved or liked their partner.

The marks for graph questions in psychology are given for accurate labelling rather than the perfectly plotted graphs you are expected to draw in maths or science.

(a) Sketch a graph to show how the length of relationship relates to ratings of liking and loving their partner. **(3 marks)**

(b) What type of relationship does your graph show? **(1 mark)**

When asked to sketch a graph, a rough outline of what the graph would show is all that is needed. Do not worry about using rulers and measuring everything perfectly if you are running out of time. Make sure it shows the direction of the relationship and that the axes are clearly labelled with an appropriate title.

7 (a) Briefly outline why virtual relationships may feature an 'absence of gating'. **(2 marks)**

(b) Explain what effect the absence of gating may have on virtual relationships. **(6 marks)**

In research methods in psychology, studying a relationship is another way of saying 'doing a correlation', so make sure you understand this terminology.

This is a two-part question. Answer each part separately and be careful not to repeat yourself.

8 Read the item and then answer the question that follows.

> Zarah has recently separated from her husband after they both decided that the relationship was not working. She is talking to her best friend and tells her that at first she felt unhappy but did not want to talk to her husband until she felt it was really serious. After she told him how she felt she says they sat and discussed how they both felt and then decided that they should separate. It was not until they had made that decision that they told anyone in their family or their friends what was going on. Now that he has left their shared home, Zarah is contemplating decorating the house.

You must refer to Zarah's experience in your answer. The best way for you to do this would be to pick out statements from the scenario that illustrate elements of Duck's theory. For example, Zarah states that 'at first she felt unhappy but didn't want to talk to him …' which could relate to Duck's Intra-psychic phase as she is thinking of ending the relationship but has not yet shared her feelings with her husband.

Discuss Duck's model of relationship breakdown. Refer to Zarah's experience in your answer. **(16 marks)**

Sex-role stereotypes

Sex refers to a person's biological status as either male or female, while **gender** relates to their social and/or psychological characteristics of masculinity or femininity. We often assume that males will be masculine and females will be feminine, but this is not always the case. These assumptions about the qualities and characteristics of males and females can lead to **sex-role stereotypes**.

Sex-role stereotypes

These are shared beliefs regarding what is or is not appropriate behaviour for males and females. When these beliefs are accepted by the majority of people, they can become **norms**, or 'rules' that we expect people to follow. This, in turn, leads to pressure to conform. These sex-role stereotypes then become taught as part of the process of **socialisation**, where each generation learns how to behave in an acceptable way from the previous generation.

Female sex-role stereotypes

Females are often referred to as the 'fairer sex'.

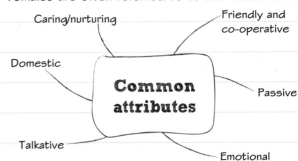

Caring/nurturing — Friendly and co-operative — Domestic — **Common attributes** — Passive — Talkative — Emotional

Male sex-role stereotypes

Males are often seen as the more 'dominant sex'.

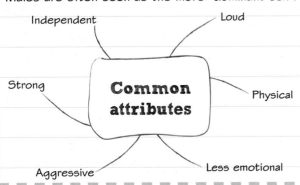

Independent — Loud — Strong — **Common attributes** — Physical — Aggressive — Less emotional

The influence of stereotypes on gender

Once the stereotypes have been accepted into the norms of society, each generation will be expected to live up to these stereotypes. The way people are treated will reflect these expectations.

For example, males will be encouraged to participate in sports, while females will be expected to complete the majority of domestic tasks.

Toy choices for children may also be influenced by stereotypes.

Research evidence

✓ Seavey et al. (1975) conducted a study where adults were introduced to 'Baby X' – a baby dressed in yellow who they were told was either a boy or a girl or the gender was not mentioned. When told the baby was a girl, all the adults gave her the doll to play with. Sex-stereotyped toys were used more often when they thought the baby was a girl.

✓ Eccles et al. (1990) found that parents often influenced their children's activity choices on the basis of gender-stereotypical encouragement, supporting the idea that socialisation may continue sex-role stereotyping.

Evaluation

👍 Sex-role stereotypes are likely to differ by culture, which supports the idea that gender roles are influenced more by external/social factors than biological factors.

👎 Sex-role stereotyping in society may place invisible 'barriers' to the expectations of children regarding the things they can and cannot do. If boys are encouraged to play sports more than girls, girls may think it is abnormal for them to want to take part in sports. Likewise, if a boy wants to become a nurse, he may worry about how society would view this as boys are not expected to be 'caring'.

Now try this

Explain how sex-role stereotypes can influence gender development.

Androgyny

Androgyny refers to a gender role characterised by a balance of both masculine and feminine traits.

Psychological androgyny

Society tends to assume that males are masculine and females are feminine. The two gender-role identities are therefore seen as mutually exclusive: a person cannot be both masculine *and* feminine. Psychologists have suggested, however, that some people are not influenced by these sex-role stereotypes – they will not be forced into the masculine or feminine gender role. Instead, they will develop high levels of both masculine and feminine traits as part of their gender-role identity, which will then categorise them as **androgynous**.

Research evidence

- ✓ Burchardt and Serbin (1982) found that there was a negative correlation between androgyny score and depression scores, suggesting a flexible gender role may protect against mental health problems.
- ✓ Flaherty and Dusek (1980) found self-esteem to be higher in those categorised as androgynous, suggesting a flexible gender role is a positive thing.

Measuring androgyny

Tests of gender-role identity used to assume that masculinity and femininity were opposite ends of the same spectrum of gender. Gender-role identity could be assessed as either high in masculinity or high in femininity.

Bem Sex Role Inventory (BSRI)

Sandra Bem argued that this was an outdated view and, in the 1970s, she developed the **Bem Sex Role Inventory (BSRI)** as a new way to categorise gender role. The survey consists of 20 stereotypical masculine statements, 20 that are stereotypically female and 20 that are gender-neutral.

From the self-report data, participants can be categorised as:

Masculine	High masculinity; low femininity
Feminine	High femininity; low masculinity
Androgynous	High masculinity; high femininity
Undifferentiated	Low masculinity; low femininity

Research evidence

- ✓ Bem (1974) presented data from a large-scale test of the BSRI and found that 34% of males and 27% of females tested as androgynous. This suggests that androgyny is not an uncommon trait and exists as a separate category of gender role to masculine and feminine.
- ✓ Peters and Cantrell (1993) used the BSRI and measures assessing the quality of relationships, and found that females who scored high on androgyny had the best relationships. They suggested that androgyny is a positive characteristic for some and could improve the way they interact with others.
- ✓ Holt and Ellis (1998) tested the validity of the adjectives used to assess masculinity and femininity on the BSRI. They found that all but two of the adjectives used on the original questionnaire in 1974 were still valid in measuring gender-role identity. This suggests that the BSRI has temporal validity even 20 years after its development.

Evaluation

- 🖝 Evidence suggests that the masculine elements of androgyny may relate to positive effects on mental health. However, this may reflect Western societal views that masculinity is more favourable than femininity as a gender-role identity, making this point ethnocentric.

- 👍 The Bem Sex Role Inventory has been shown to have good test–retest reliability (see page 190), suggesting that the categorisations made are consistent over time.

Now try this

Outline one criticism of the Bem Sex Role Inventory as a measure of psychological androgyny.

Chromosomes and hormones

A person's sex is determined by their biological status of being either male or female. This is usually categorised based on the genitals a person has, but the biology of 'sex' is determined by the **chromosomes** and **hormones** a person possesses.

Chromosomes

Humans have 23 **chromosome** pairs, with one of each pair inherited from each parent. Chromosomes carry genetic material that helps to make each person unique. The 23rd pair of chromosomes contains our sex chromosomes.

If the 23rd pair is XX, the person is female; if it is XY, they are male. This pair of sex chromosomes instructs the body in how to develop, and this will also influence which hormones the body is exposed to.

Hormones: testosterone

Until approximately 9 weeks into gestation, the only difference between the sex of developing embryos is their sex chromosomes. Then, around 9 weeks, the **gonads** of an XY foetus will become testes and begin to produce **testosterone**. The Y chromosome contains a gene called sex-determining region Y (SRY) that tells the sex organs (gonads) to become testes. The production of testosterone then informs the developing foetus to take on male characteristics, including a masculinised brain and a tendency to masculine characteristics such as aggression and competitiveness.

Hormones: oestrogen

The lack of a Y chromosome in the XX embryo will mean that there is no SRY gene, and therefore no instruction for the gonads to develop into testes. The developing sex organs will instead become **ovaries**. The ovaries will then produce hormones such as **oestrogen** (a group of steroid hormones including **oestradiol**, **oestrol** and **oestriol**) that will feminise the body. This will mean that the body develops female physical features, such as breast tissue. Oestrogen is also involved in changes associated with the menstrual cycle, as well as feminine traits such as sensitivity.

Hormones: oxytocin

Oxytocin acts in both males and females, although it has a much more significant effect in females by working in combination with oestrogen. Oxytocin is associated with reproductive behaviours. For example, it stimulates and regulates contractions during childbirth. It is also associated with breastfeeding, as it helps with the production and release of milk. In both males and females, oxytocin levels increase during sex to increase intimacy levels, but in males the levels drop rapidly after orgasm. Oxytocin is also closely linked to nurturing behaviour associated with child-rearing.

Research evidence

✓ Money and Ehrhardt (1972) found that girls whose mothers took medication containing testosterone during pregnancy showed more masculine traits.

✓ Albrecht and Pepe (1997) found that giving oestrogen to pregnant baboons reduced miscarriage, suggesting that oestrogen is associated with successful pregnancy.

 Application

Elbourne et al. (2001) found that giving oxytocin during the final stage of childbirth was associated with a lower risk of complications, supporting the idea that oxytocin is needed for successful birth.

Evaluation

🌷 Many studies of hormones have been conducted on animals. However, the behaviour of animals and humans is very different, as is the biology, making it problematic to assume that they can be explained in the same way, so generalisation is difficult.

🌷 It is often assumed that hormones are typically 'male' or 'female' when actually they are found in different concentrations in both males and females. The hormones are also part of complex physiological systems that control gender-specific traits and behaviours. This means that the hormonal sex differences between males and females are being treated too simply.

Now try this

Explain what research evidence has shown about the influence of hormones on sex differences.

Klinefelter's syndrome

First reported by Dr Harold Klinefelter in the USA in 1942, **Klinefelter's syndrome (KS)** is a disorder that leads to males having an extra X chromosome (XXY sex chromosomes). This is a type of '**trisomy**', where an extra copy of a chromosome is present in the cell nuclei. KS is not an inherited condition – it results from an error that occurs during **meiosis**. Approximately 1 in 600 male babies born in the UK will have KS (NHS, 2014).

Signs and symptoms

Males with KS are likely to have small testes that produce lower levels of testosterone. This results in a more feminised body shape and characteristics than are seen in normal males.

Infants with KS can be slightly developmentally delayed, reaching milestones slightly later than normal. There are also some psychological characteristics such as poor language skills, lower reading ability and being noticeably more passive/quiet than typical males. Fertility levels can be poor in males with KS.

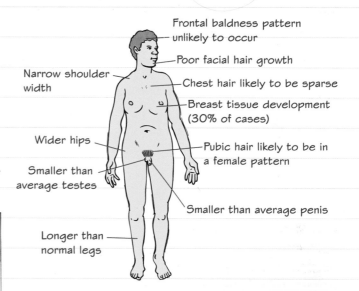

Frontal baldness pattern unlikely to occur

Poor facial hair growth

Narrow shoulder width

Chest hair likely to be sparse

Breast tissue development (30% of cases)

Wider hips

Pubic hair likely to be in a female pattern

Smaller than average testes

Smaller than average penis

Longer than normal legs

Other typical physical signs and symptoms associated with Klinefelter's syndrome.

Mosaic Klinefelter's syndrome

About 1 in 10 people with KS have mosaic Klinefelter's syndrome (MKS), which means that the extra X chromosome appears in some, but not all, of their cells. This often causes lesser symptoms than in patients with full KS.

Research evidence

☑ Simpson et al. (2003) found that males with KS responded well to treatment with male hormones, showing improvements in behavioural and language problems associated with the disorder.

☑ Ramasamy et al. (2009) found that microdissection testicular sperm extraction could be successfully used to take viable sperm from males with KS who had very low fertility due to lack of mobile sperm in the ejaculate. Using this technique, they found that such males were able to successfully father children, providing a useful treatment.

Evaluation

👍 Researching KS increases our understanding of the disorder, which means that better advice and treatments can be offered to patients suffering from KS.

👍 Studying people with abnormal chromosome patterns improves our understanding of the role of those chromosomes in normal development. By understanding the behaviour and gender development of males with an extra X chromosome, we can better understand the role of the X chromosome in the development of both males and females in the general population.

👎 Studying KS may be considered socially sensitive research as there could be implications associated with investigating males with an additional X chromosome. For example, some may argue that it suggests there is something 'wrong' with them.

Now try this

1 Explain the difference between Klinefelter's syndrome and mosaic Klinefelter's syndrome.

2 What behavioural effects are seen in patients with Klinefelter's syndrome?

Turner syndrome

First diagnosed by Dr Henry Turner in 1938, **Turner syndrome (TS)** is a chromosome abnormality that results in girls having only one complete X chromosome; the other X chromosome is either missing or incomplete. TS affects approximately 1 in 2000 baby girls born in the UK (NHS, 2015).

Up to 99% of cases of TS are thought to result in early miscarriage (often before pregnancy has been confirmed) or stillbirth, but if a baby is born with TS, the prognosis is positive.

Signs and symptoms

Babies born with TS often have swollen hands and feet caused by a build-up of fluid prenatally. Girls with TS will often have no periods and be infertile because of underdeveloped ovaries.

Some girls with TS will develop minor learning difficulties in childhood, although significant psychological problems are not common. They may also have problems interacting with others, often thought to be the result of reactions of others to their physical appearance.

Shorter than normal stature compared to others their age

Down-slanting eyes

Heart defects

Short neck with webbed-like flap of skin

Broad chest and nipples wider apart

Small amount of breast tissue/breast development

Abnormalities of the kidneys

Rudimentary ovaries

Brown spots or moles frequently seen over the body

Common physical signs and symptoms of Turner syndrome in females.

Mosaic Turner syndrome

Mosaic forms of TS are also possible (MTS), where the X chromosome is only missing or incomplete in some, but not all, body cells.

Research evidence

☑ Price et al. (1986) followed a group of 156 females with TS over a 17-year period. During that time, 9% (15) of them died, compared to only 3.6% in a matched sample without TS. Many of the deaths were the result of illnesses of the cardiovascular or circulatory systems, suggesting that the life expectancy of people with TS is lower than normal.

☑ Quigley et al. (2014) found that girls with TS who were given oestrogen therapy in childhood were likely to have earlier and greater development of breast tissue when they went through puberty which could offer positive psychological effects for the girls.

Evaluation

☛ TS can be diagnosed prenatally by looking at features of the developing foetus that are characteristic of the abnormality. This could be considered ethically questionable and socially sensitive by some, as labelling a foetus as abnormal could lead to parents seeking a termination of the pregnancy.

☛ Patients with TS often suffer early ovarian failure in their teens and become infertile, losing their eggs either before, or very early during, puberty. One treatment option is to freeze eggs from girls with TS before puberty to enable them to conceive later, but there are ethical implications of subjecting young girls to this kind of treatment.

👍 Research has found that providing treatment with oestrogen prior to puberty can help girls to develop slightly larger breasts. This could be an important psychosocial factor for girls with TS, as it may make them feel more 'normal' and therefore more accepted by society.

Now try this

Outline **one** common feature associated with Turner syndrome.

Kohlberg's theory of gender development

Kohlberg's (1966) **theory of gender development** comes from Piaget's **cognitive development theory** (see page 173). Kohlberg believed that children develop an understanding of gender as a result of **maturation** – as a child gets older, its understanding of the world changes. Children gain understanding of gender in three stages.

① Gender labelling/identity

Age: 18 months–3 years

During this stage, a child develops a basic understanding of the concepts of 'male' and 'female'. They begin to categorise people into male and female groups, but these labels are not always used accurately and they may be used interchangeably. The knowledge and understanding of gender labels is weak at this stage, but it is the first evidence that children understand these labels exist.

② Gender stability

Age: 3–5 years

By the age of about 4 years, children begin to show evidence that they understand that gender labels are fixed, so that boys become men and girls become women. However, the categorisation of gender is still based on superficial characteristics such as clothing and hair length. A boy who puts a dress on might be referred to as a girl, while a woman who has her hair cut short may be seen to have changed into a man. At this stage, obvious features of gender identity are detected, but subtle differences are ignored or not yet understood.

③ Gender constancy/consistency

Age: 6–7 years

By the age of 7, most children have acquired gender constancy, the understanding that gender remains consistent regardless of physical appearance or changes in clothing, hairstyle and so on. Instead, they become aware of what it means to be male or female, and that this label is something that remains constant across both time and different situations.

Research evidence

 Slaby and Frey (1975) questioned 2–5-year-old children to assess their level of gender constancy. Some questions related to gender labelling, some to gender stability and some to gender constancy. They were then classified as either high or low in terms of their understanding of gender constancy. Several weeks later, the same children were shown a short video of a male and a female performing gender-stereotypical activities on opposite sides of the screen. The amount of time children spent looking at each person was measured. In general, children with high gender constancy spent longer watching same-sex role models than children with low gender constancy. This suggests that the knowledge of gender precedes the watching of same-sex role models' behaviour.

 Thompson (1975) found that 2-year-olds were able to select same-sex people from a set of pictures, suggesting that they could accurately label their own gender. While 76% of 2-year-olds demonstrated gender labelling, 90% of 3-year-olds did. This supports Kohlberg's claim that knowledge of gender concepts is based on maturation.

Evaluation

 Munroe et al. (1984) found that children worldwide showed similar patterns of gender development, suggesting it is a natural process linked to age and stage of development.

 Kohlberg's theory suggests that gender-specific behaviour only appears after the child has developed gender constancy. However, many children prefer gender-stereotypical toys and games before the age of 7, suggesting that gender constancy is not the starting point for gender-specific behaviours.

 Kohlberg's theory is often criticised for describing the development of gender understanding rather than explaining how it influences gender-specific behaviour.

Now try this

Outline **one** criticism of Kohlberg's theory of gender development.

Gender schema theory

Gender schema theory (Martin and Halverson, 1981; Bem, 1981) is a **cognitive explanation** of gender. It claims that the development of gender-appropriate behaviour occurs alongside cognitive understanding, as the child's knowledge of their own gender will determine the type of behaviour they learn.

Gender schema

A **schema** is a small 'package' of information that is stored about a particular object or situation. In the case of a **gender schema**, information develops about what it means to be 'male' or 'female'.

According to Martin and Halverson (1981) and Bem (1981), the gender schema begins to develop at around 2–3 years old, when a child learns that the categories of male and female exist. As the child develops, they then **assimilate** new information into this schema as they experience more gender-specific information.

In-group and out-group schemas

As the child experiences more about gender and their schema develops, they begin to categorise themselves as one gender. Their perceptions about themselves will then be based on what they understand to be appropriate for their gender. They will categorise others as like them (their **in-group**) or not like them (their **out-group**) based on gender. Associated with this, they categorise objects, toys and activities as 'for boys' or 'for girls', and start to make choices based on what they think is appropriate.

Developmental changes in gender schema theory

Under 4 years	Children develop an understanding of the categories 'male' and 'female'; they develop strong gender stereotypes associated with these categories. Knowledge and understanding comes from watching the behaviour and attitude of others.
Next	Children will learn the more subtle differences between males and females – what they like to do, who they spend time with, and so on – focusing mainly on their own gender. Knowledge of the opposite gender is not as detailed.
Then	In- and out-group schemas become strengthened and children's knowledge of the expectations of their gender are seen as rules that should be followed.
Then	The schema for the opposite gender becomes as strong as the same-sex schema.
By adolescence	The 'rules' associated with gender schema knowledge are seen as more flexible and gender-appropriate behaviour can be overridden by personal preferences.

Research evidence

☑ Martin and Halverson (1983) found that, when shown images of people in different roles, children under age 6 recalled more **gender consistent** (e.g. a male firefighter) than gender inconsistent ones (e.g. a male nurse). This suggests that children under 6 judge gender schemas as 'rules' to be followed.

☑ Bradbard et al. (1986) found that children aged 4–9 years were more likely to explore objects labelled for their gender, and a week later were more likely to remember these objects over similar objects labelled for the opposite gender. This supports the view that the understanding of gender identity is a deciding factor in toy choice.

Evaluation

👍 Unlike social learning theory (see page 164), which states that same-sex role models will be imitated regardless of the type of behaviour shown, gender schema theory explains why same-sex role models demonstrating gender-appropriate behaviour are much more likely to be imitated.

👎 Many argue that gender schema theory is **reductionist** as it fails to account for the influence of biological factors on gender behaviour. Gender schema theory explains all gender behaviour through cognitive means and ignores the role of biology on differences in behaviour between males and females.

Now try this

Describe gender schema theory as an explanation of gender development.

Freud's psychoanalytic theory

Freud's theory of gender development is a psychodynamic explanation (see page 72). Freud believed that gender development was a product of internal conflicts occurring through the process of **psychosexual development**. According to Freud, children become aware of their gender and associated issues of sexuality in the third/**phallic stage** (3–5 years). Energy is centred on the genitals, and it is towards the end of this stage (5 years of age) that gender development occurs.

Oedipus complex

- At the end of the phallic stage, boys direct their increasing sexual energy towards their mother as the opposite-sex parent.

- The increasing feelings of love and desire are accompanied by feelings of resentment towards the father as he is the one who 'possesses' her.

- The boy will also have anxiety directed towards the father because he is worried that if his desire for his mother is discovered, then his father will punish him. Specifically, boys have **castration anxiety** related to this potential punishment.

Electra complex

- At the end of the phallic stage, girls direct their increasing sexual energy towards their father as the opposite-sex parent.

- They also develop resentment towards the mother as they think she has already punished them for these feelings by castrating them: they realise that boys have a penis and they do not.

- Because the girl feels that she has lost out, she is thought to develop **penis envy**. In the absence of being able to actually gain one, she instead focuses on wanting a baby.

Male identification and internalisation

In order to resolve the Oedipus complex, boys are thought to take on characteristics of the father's gender identity in a process known as **identification**. The boy will **internalise** elements of his father's identity in order to feel more able to attract a woman like his mother. Failure to successfully resolve the Oedipus complex was used to explain homosexuality.

Female identification and internalisation

In order to overcome the Electra complex, girls will **identify** with their mother by **internalising** elements of her personality, such as her gender-role identity. By doing this she may be able to attract a male partner like her father in future. Freud believed that identification in females was not as strong as in males because females think they have already lost their penis and therefore anxiety is less than males who fear castration.

Research evidence

Freud (1909) suggested that 5-year-old Little Hans' phobia of horses was displaced castration anxiety. Hans had a fear of horses that were wearing black bits around their face which was thought to symbolise Hans' father's glasses and moustache. The fear of being bitten by the horse was thought to symbolise castration anxiety, which would be associated with resolution of the Oedipus complex. The fear stopped when Hans reported dreams about marrying his mother and a plumber fitting him with a bigger penis, both of which could be signs of identifying with his father.

Evaluation

- The only evidence Freud had to support his concepts of the Oedipus and Electra complexes were from the study of 5-year-old Little Hans. One case study is clearly insufficient to support a theory and thus the evidence lacks validity.

- Freud's ideas are difficult to test scientifically because they are difficult to falsify. Many of the desires and thoughts associated with the Oedipus and Electra complexes are thought to be unconscious. As they are beyond conscious awareness, objectively testing their existence is very difficult.

Now try this

Define what is meant by the term 'internalisation' in the psychodynamic explanation of gender development.

Social learning theory

The social learning theory (SLT) approach to gender development emphasises the importance of other people in the learning of gender roles.

The process of social learning

According to SLT (see page 69), the understanding of gender roles is the product of **observational learning**, where we watch both males and females around us and learn what they do. Once aware of their own gender, children will then begin to imitate the behaviour they see as most appropriate to them. Children will **imitate** both gender-appropriate and gender-inappropriate behaviour, but the way this is **reinforced** by others will determine which behaviours they choose to imitate again later.

Vicarious reinforcement

Gender-appropriate behaviour can be **directly reinforced** by people who tell their children they are a 'big, strong boy' or a 'pretty girl' when they show gender-appropriate behaviour. But **vicarious reinforcement** is a key feature of SLT, as children are influenced by indirect reinforcement through observing others. Siblings and peers will be rewarded or punished by others for gender-appropriate or inappropriate behaviour.

For example, boys wearing dresses may be called names, which would encourage other boys not to copy this behaviour.

Role models

- **Role models** are the people children take the most notice of, as they are in some way similar to them and are seen as someone to look up to.
- **Parents** are important role models for children as they will actively shape boys' and girls' behaviour to be different. Children will observe and learn behaviour from their parents' gender roles, such as boys copying Dad doing the gardening, while girls help Mum bake a cake.
- **Peers:** children will observe the play of both boys and girls and decide what is appropriate for themselves.

Gender type behaviour – a boy copying his dad shaving.

Research evidence

✓ Fagot (1978) observed children at home playing with parents, and found that boys and girls were reinforced for different behaviours. Boys were positively reinforced for playing with 'male' toys like building blocks, but were punished for playing with dolls, while girls were positively reinforced for staying close to the parent and punished for rough play. This supports the claim that parents shape gender-appropriate behaviour.

✓ Langlois and Downs (1980) found that when children were playing with opposite-gender toys, same-sex friends were less tolerant than mothers. This was particularly the case with boys, where peers often made fun of them or encouraged them to play with other toys instead.

✓ Maccoby (1990) found evidence that young children often play together in same-sex pairs or groups and avoid mixing with the opposite sex during play. She suggested that sex segregation then becomes learned and extends beyond childhood. This would suggest that gender behaviour is likely to be influenced by the interactions with others that begin in play during childhood.

Evaluation

🌶 SLT fails to take into account **biological** influences on gender-role behaviour. For example, two same-sex children could be raised by the same parents but their gender-roles may not necessarily be the same. Therefore, theoretically, other factors must play a part in the gender role.

👍 SLT does take into account **cognition** in learning of gender role. People have some choice in not only who to imitate but also what to imitate, so there is an element of free will in the gender role chosen.

Now try this

1 Explain how gender-role development may occur through the process of social learning.

2 Outline **one** criticism of social learning theory as an explanation of gender.

Influence of culture

Culture can be defined as a set of beliefs, attitudes and behaviours that separates one group of people from another. Several aspects of gender identity and gender role can differ cross-culturally.

Culture and gender norms

In different cultures the expected behaviours of males and females are not necessarily the same. For example, Western cultures recognise two gender roles: masculine and feminine, whereas Samoan culture has a third gender role: **fa'afafine** – biological males who choose to adopt traditional Western 'feminine' roles.

According to the principles of SLT (see page 164), these norms pass to each generation of children.

Culture and gender stereotypes

Just as gender norms differ across different cultures, so too can the stereotypes associated with masculinity and femininity. Gender is seen by many to be a social construct, meaning that society creates many of the psychological differences between males and females by perpetuating sex-role stereotypes (see page 156). Stereotypes can differ by culture. For example, Cuddy et al. (2015) reported that American participants believed men were less interdependent than women, but Korean participants reported the opposite.

Research evidence

✓ Mead (1935) observed the behaviour of three tribes in Papua New Guinea and found some interesting differences in gender roles in comparison to Western norms. In the Arapesh, both genders displayed traditionally feminine roles, such as high levels of nurturing. In the Mundugumor, both men and women were highly aggressive and dominant – a trait we associate with the masculine gender role. In the Tchambuli, Western gender roles were reversed, with men being more feminine and women being more masculine. This suggests that gender roles are culturally determined.

✓ LaFromboise et al. (1990) found that in North American tribes, the roles of men and women did not always reflect Western traditional roles. For example, women would often take on aggressive roles and be involved in fighting, which we might traditionally think of as masculine traits.

✓ Talbani and Hasanali (2000) found South Asian girls growing up in Canada felt their families were disappointed if they didn't comply with the male-dominated expectations of their society, suggesting cultural pressure may encourage gender behaviour.

Evaluation

🗨 There can be a problem with cross-cultural research as there can be an **imposed etic** where the methods used to gather data are from one culture and are not necessarily applicable to the culture being studied. Using gender-based questionnaires designed in Western cultures may make assumptions about gender role that are then imposed on the culture being studied.

👍 Many similar views of masculine and feminine behaviour exist cross-culturally. This could be explained by the global saturation of Western media (see page 166) transmitting common norms.

Extend Universality of gender role

Some evidence suggests that elements of gender roles and gender attitudes are **universal** and do not vary cross-culturally, suggesting that, rather than being the product of cultural differences, gender-role behaviour may actually be the result of shared **biological factors**. Williams and Best (1990) studied gender stereotypes in 30 countries and found universal attitudes towards masculinity and femininity. For example, males were commonly viewed as dominant and autonomous, while females were seen as nurturing and sociable.

Now try this

Explain **one** way that culture may influence gender-role development.

Influence of media

The **media** is a powerful influence on our behaviour as we are exposed to it continually. Media comes in many forms, from books, to advertisements, to films, and from a very young age children see how these different forms of media portray males and females.

Portrayal of gender roles

Even at home, very young children will be shown books or TV programmes where male and female characters are likely to be presented in different roles and showing different behaviours. Many children's books and programmes have been criticised for showing males and females in stereotypical roles and, therefore, perpetuating these gender roles.

For example, adverts showing girls playing with dolls and boys conducting science experiments suggest this is the norm.

Media role models

Characters from books, films and TV are often early role models for children. In line with the SLT explanation of gender, children will identify with certain characters and begin to model themselves on their behaviour. If the character they choose is showing stereotypically male or female behaviour, they will not only take note of this and learn from it, but they will also begin to imitate what they have seen.

Real world **Textbooks**

checker · teacher · policeman · milkman · postman · elevator operator · typist · waitress · salesman · fireman

Schoolbooks have been criticised for depicting gender stereotypes for males and females in relation to particular occupations.

Reinforcement in the media

If parents demonstrate stereotypical gender roles in the home, the media may reinforce these further, portraying them as normal. If characters in books and on TV are shown to be rewarded for gender-appropriate behaviour, such as being referred to as 'quiet girls' or 'boisterous boys', these attributes are assumed to be positive and therefore may be more likely to be imitated.

Evaluation

👎 It is over-simplistic to assume that children passively learn their gender role from watching TV and reading books. They can choose which characters become their role models and do not simply absorb the roles portrayed by the media.

👍 Understanding the role of the media in continuing gender stereotyping has led to efforts to show more balanced gender roles in children's media. For example, research by England et al. (2011) showed that traditional Disney princess roles were very feminine, but more recently, Disney has produced princess roles that are more balanced and less stereotypically female. Children's media producers have also made a more conscious effort to show both males and females in non-stereotypical roles such as stay-at-home dads and female doctors.

Research evidence

✓ Williams (1981) reported evidence from a natural experiment conducted in a town in Canada. Prior to the introduction of TV to the town, the amount of gender-stereotypical views and behaviour were relatively low. Two years after TV was brought to the town, the difference between the behaviour of boys and girls had increased and there were significantly more stereotypical views related to gender. This would suggest the media influences gender-role behaviour.

✓ Bee (2000) found that children's books often showed males and females in stereotypical roles. Adverts were also often differentiated. Adverts aimed at boys were much faster paced with loud music or noises, while those for girls were much quieter and slower paced, and included gentler themes. This suggests that media aimed at children differentiates by gender.

Now try this

Outline evidence from one study that illustrates the influence of the media on gender-role identity.

Social explanations for GID

Gender identity disorder (GID), sometimes referred to as gender dysphoria, is an example of atypical gender development. Some psychologists claim that GID can be explained by social factors such as reinforcement and role models.

Gender identity disorder (GID)

GID, or gender dysphoria, is a disorder characterised by feelings that one's psychological gender is not the same as one's physical status of being male or female.

Individuals with GID may show early signs, such as an unwillingness to dress 'like a boy' or 'like a girl', and this can even extend to feelings of disgust with their own physical appearance. In a survey from 2012, it was estimated that GID affects up to 1% of the population to some extent.

Some people with GID may seek to change their physical appearance surgically. For example Caitlyn Jenner recently underwent gender reassignment to identify as a female.

Social explanations: operant conditioning

Some psychologists argue that GID can be explained by reinforcement by people such as parents. In early childhood, many children will experiment with gender roles as they learn what 'gender' is all about. If parents were to give praise in the form of positive attention to children while they were acting as the opposite gender, the behaviour may be more likely to be repeated at another time.

A boy playing at being a princess.

Social explanations: SLT

Some psychologists have argued that GID could be the result of a lack of suitable same-sex role models for a child to model themselves on. The normal process of observing the behaviour of these models to learn from them, and then imitating this behaviour themselves, therefore does not happen. SLT claims that these children may be observing and imitating opposite-sex role models, resulting in cross-gender behaviour and confusion of gender identity.

Evaluation

🌱 Referring to GID and gender identity 'disorder' suggests that this is a disorder or illness, and that there is a correct gender that men and women should be. This has led to a change in label to gender dysphoria.

👍 Many people with gender identity issues show signs in early childhood, suggesting a social explanation because children are likely to be very responsive to the behaviours of others around them. Small children could easily be shaped by parental reinforcement and role models, strengthening their gender confusion as they become more aware of social expectations for their physical sex.

Research evidence

✅ Rekers (1995) found that a common feature associated with gender dysphoric feelings in a group of 70 young boys was that they had a lack of male role models. This would support the idea of the importance of role models in gender role development and that the lack of same-sex role models could influence the gender role adopted by children.

✅ Gladue (1985) found that in samples of male participants, there was little difference in the hormone levels of those with cross-gender feelings, those who identified as homosexual and those who were heterosexual. This would suggest that hormones play little role, and therefore social factors may be more influential.

Now try this

Explain **one** social factor that could explain gender identity disorder.

Biological explanations for GID

Much of the research into biological factors associated with **gender identity disorder (GID)** focuses on **genes** and **hormones**. More recent evidence would suggest that GID is more likely to result from biological factors than from **social factors**.

Genetics

One explanation of GID suggests that those with the disorder inherit certain gene variants that make gender development happen slightly differently to normal. For example, there is evidence that some males with GID have inherited **androgen receptors** that are not sensitive to male hormones such as testosterone. This means that when these hormones are released, and masculinisation of the body is supposed to be triggered, the body does not respond. Other evidence has found that gender identity issues can be common in families, suggesting that it is genetic.

Brain differences

Post-mortem studies of people with gender dysphoria compared to 'normal' males and females have indicated that there are differences in an area of the **hypothalamus**, which suggest that gender identity could be related to activity in the brain.

Hormones

If the hormones released during prenatal development to aid gender development do not work effectively, then the developing foetus may not be masculinised or feminised in the normal way. As a result, the body's physical appearance and the brain of the child could actually have different gender identities. As the child grows up, the apparent mismatch between the way they look and how they feel could be the cause of their gender dysphoric feelings.

During prenatal development, there is a normal hormone surge at around 9 weeks if the foetus is developing testes, which masculinises the foetus (see page 158). Problems with this process could interrupt male development and result in more feminine behaviours. Other problems with hormone production during pregnancy could be a result of medication taken by the mother or issues with the mother's endocrine system. If the mother has an altered hormonal balance, this could affect the development of the foetus. This could also influence gender dysphoric feelings.

Research evidence

- ✓ Hare et al. (2009) found evidence that a variant of the androgen receptor gene that caused a reduced effect of testosterone was seen more often in male-to-female transsexuals than in non-transsexual males. This could support the claim that the body is not as masculinised during prenatal development.
- ✓ Zhou et al. (1995) found that in a small sample of male-to-female transsexuals there was evidence of brain activity more typical of females than males. As the brain's sex is influenced by sex hormones prenatally, it could suggest that hormones have prevented the brain from masculinisation.
- ✓ Garcia-Falgueras and Swaab (2008) found that in male-to-female transsexual participants there was an area of the hypothalamus that was more similar to the same area in female controls, suggesting that brain structure may resemble the gender they 'feel' they are.

Evaluation

- ☞ The biological explanation of GID ignores the role that social or psychological factors may play in the feelings of gender confusion. Assuming that something as complex as gender role confusion is purely accounted for by biological factors is **reductionist** and does not take into account the many other elements of gender-role identity.

- 👍 Most people who have serious gender-role confusion and choose to actually change their gender identity respond well to hormone therapy both prior to and following surgery. The fact that hormones can help people to transition from male to female, or female to male, suggests that hormones play a really key role in gender-role identity. If studying the influence of hormones on treating those with GID can help to make these therapies better, more people may be helped in future.

Now try this

Explain **one** advantage of research into a biological explanation of gender identity disorder.

Exam skills 1

Before you look at these worked examples, remind yourself about cognitive and psychodynamic explanations for gender development (pages 161–163), and social explanations for gender identity disorder (page 167).

Worked example

Describe the social explanation for gender identity disorder.

(4 marks)

Children may begin to show gender-atypical behaviour in childhood as a result of learning. Operant conditioning would claim that if a child had been reinforced with attention for acting as the opposite sex, this behaviour may well be repeated in the hope of gaining more attention. It could also be the result of social learning. If a child did not have a suitable same-sex role model in childhood, they could imitate the behaviour of an opposite-sex model having observed their behaviour. This could lead to cross-gender behaviour and confusion over gender identity.

> Read the question carefully. Here, it only asks about a 'social' explanation and so the answer must refer to the influence of factors outside of the individual, specifically how others can influence the development of gender identity disorder.

> It is important that your answer relates specifically to gender identity disorder and not gender development in general. Therefore, the explanation should centre on gender confusion and/or gender-inappropriate behaviour rather than typical gender development.

Worked example

Read the item and then answer the question that follows.

> Ella is 3 years old. A boy in her class at nursery has long hair and Ella keeps referring to him as a girl. When Ella's mum asks her why, Ella says 'Toby's a girl because he has long hair'.

Explain why Ella's statement suggests she has not yet achieved gender constancy.

(3 marks)

Gender constancy means that children have acquired the knowledge that gender identity remains consistent across time and situation, and they are no longer affected by superficial changes in appearance. Ella's statement that Toby is 'a girl because he has long hair' suggests she does not yet understand that a boy with long hair is still a boy.

> This kind of question has 2 parts – you are being asked to demonstrate understanding of the concept of gender constancy but in the context of a scenario about a young child. An answer should cover both of these elements.

> This answer begins with a clear outline of what gender constancy means, and the final sentence makes specific reference to the scenario about Ella and her comments about the boy with long hair.

Worked example

Outline **one** limitation of the psychodynamic explanation of gender development.

(2 marks)

One limitation of the psychodynamic explanation is the lack of scientific evidence to support the claims of the theory. The feelings and thoughts associated with the Oedipus and Electra complexes were described as being unconscious, meaning that they happen beyond conscious awareness. The existence of these thoughts and feelings would be impossible to falsify because even the people experiencing them are not aware they are happening.

> 'Outline a limitation' means that the answer should focus on an evaluation point, but to do well the point needs to be elaborated considerably.

> Falsification is a key feature of scientific research – it means that ideas, in theory, can be 'proved' to be wrong. Many of Freud's theories cannot be falsified because the claims relate to the unconscious mind, which makes it very difficult to prove it does not exist.

Exam skills 2

Before you look at these worked examples, remind yourself about the role of chromosomes and hormones in gender development (page 158) and atypical sex chromosome patterns (pages 159–160).

Worked example

Discuss the influence of biological factors, such as chromosomes and hormones, on gender development.

(16 marks)

Excerpt 1:
Gender development can be influenced by chromosomes. Everyone possesses 23 pairs of chromosomes, one in each pair from each parent. One pair of these will determine sex – you will always gain an X chromosome from your mother, but the father can give either an X or a Y chromosome, and this will determine the sex of the embryo. Sex chromosomes that are XX will result in female sex, while sex chromosomes that are XY will result in male sex. This gene pair will then be responsible for further biological changes in the developing foetus. For example, at around 9 weeks into prenatal development the presence of a Y chromosome will result in the sex organs developing into testes that will begin to produce testosterone ...

Excerpt 2:
... It is also possible that atypical sex chromosome patterns can occur, such as XXY, resulting in Klinefelter's syndrome. Males with Klinefelter's syndrome typically have smaller testes, lower testosterone levels and a more feminised body shape ...

Excerpt 3:
... The influence of hormones can be supported by evidence from Money and Ehrhardt (1972), who found that girls whose mothers took drugs containing testosterone during pregnancy had more masculine traits, suggesting that testosterone is associated with masculinity. However, the hormonal explanation is very reductionist as it ignores the role of other influences, such as social factors, on the development of masculine (or feminine) behaviours ...

Command word: Discuss

Discuss means you will need to describe what the biological factors are and how they influence gender development, and then evaluate the impact that these factors have.

Allow 20 minutes to complete a 16-mark essay and no more.

With the biological explanation, it is often useful to start at 'the beginning' in relation to the point in development when genes and hormones have the biggest influence. In this way we can treat the influence of biological factors as a sort of timeline through the biological development of males and females.

From Excerpt 1, it would be useful to move into a discussion of how testosterone and other hormones influence gender development, both in terms of physical appearance and behaviour.

This paragraph can further describe the influence of chromosomes and hormones on atypical gender development patterns.

A level questions will offer more marks for AO2/3 than AO1 in essay questions (for example, this essay would offer 6 × AO1 and 10 × AO3 marks). It is therefore important to focus on developing well-argued evaluation points that are clear and concise. Description needs to be accurate and detailed, but evaluation needs to provide a good-quality discussion, so it is not enough to simply list strengths and weaknesses. You could also add examples to support your points.

Exam-style practice 1

Practise for Paper 3 of your A level exam with these exam-style questions. There are answers on page 306. Before looking at these questions, it would be good to review androgyny (page 157), GID (pages 167–168) and the section on research methods.

1   Read the item and then answer the questions that follow.

> Kristina is 7 years old and has always been called a 'bit of a tomboy' by her parents as she is very active and enjoys sport. At weekends she plays football as well as going to ballet classes. Her parents describe her as very quiet and sensitive at times, but she can also be assertive and competitive.

With reference to Kristina, explain what is meant by the term 'androgyny'.   **(2 marks)**

> This question is asking two things: firstly 'what is androgyny?' and secondly 'why might Kristina be androgynous?'

> Make sure you have included a definition of androgyny, reference to the feminine traits Kristina has, and reference to the masculine traits she shows, stating how she demonstrates androgyny.

2   Jesse has been diagnosed with gender identity disorder. Explain what research has shown about the possible causes of gender identity disorder.   **(6 marks)**

> Remember that 'research' can include both theories and/or studies; as long as you focus on the causes of GID, you can't go far wrong.

> Questions like this are likely to be marked on 'bands'. Familiarise yourself with the mark schemes and look at what common themes appear in each mark band to help develop your skills at answering these questions.

3   Outline **one** strength and **one** limitation of the biological explanation for gender identity disorder.   **(4 marks)**

> One strength could come from a study supporting the fact that gender identity disorder is the result of biological factors. For example, the results of Hare et al. (2009).

> A limitation could focus on the argument that explaining gender identity disorder purely from a biological standpoint is reductionist. Debates are a useful way to create discussion in your answer when evaluating.

4   Read the item and then answer the questions that follow.

A researcher is investigating Freud's ideas about internalisation and identification of gender identity. She has decided to give a questionnaire to measure masculinity to a group of 20 boys and also to their fathers, and then she plans to look to see if there is a relationship between the two scores.

(a) Identify the research method used in this investigation.   **(1 mark)**

(b) If Freud's theory is correct, what kind of relationship should the researcher find in her data? Explain your answer with reference to the two sets of data she is gathering.   **(2 marks)**

(c) Sketch a scattergram to illustrate the direction of relationship described in (b), making sure you label both the x- and y-axes.   **(3 marks)**

> When identifying research methods, think of the aim of the research and about how this was achieved. This should help you to select the correct method.

> Read these questions carefully and try to visualise what is being done in the investigation to help you answer the questions.

> **Maths skills** Sketching graphs does not require you to be precise – you do not have the data to do this. From your knowledge of scattergrams, you should be able to illustrate different patterns of relationship. From the theory identified, work out what the direction of the relationship should look like.

Exam-style practice 2

Practise for Paper 3 of your A level exam with these exam-style questions. There are answers on pages 306–307. Before looking at these questions, it would be good to review explanations of gender development (pages 156–168).

5   Which **one** of the following statements is an accurate summary of the main claims made by gender schema theory?

A   Gender-appropriate behaviour is learned passively by watching the behaviour of others.   ○

B   Children will learn gender-appropriate behaviour by it being reinforced by parents.   ○

C   Gender roles are learned by actively seeking out information about a person's own gender.   ○

D   A child's gender identity is learned by identifying with the same-sex parent.   ○

(1 mark)

> Always check carefully to be sure you are not confusing explanations with one another. Sometimes the claim of one explanation might be similar to that of another, but there will be subtle differences between them that you need to be aware of.

6   Researchers into gender often use questionnaires to gather information about a person's gender identity. Outline **one** limitation associated with using questionnaires in psychological research.   **(2 marks)**

> This kind of question is quite generic, even though it appears in the gender section. Think back to your research methods knowledge and consider the issues of using self-report methods.

> Remember that 'discuss' questions require both description and evaluation of the focus of the question.

7   Discuss Kohlberg's explanation for gender development.   **(16 marks)**

> Kohlberg's theory is a cognitive explanation for gender development that focuses on how the understanding of gender role identity develops as a child matures. Start by describing how this process occurs (AO1) and then discuss the implications of this claim and provide evidence to support the explanation and limitations of the theory (AO3).

8   Describe and evaluate the psychodynamic explanation for gender development.   **(16 marks)**

> It can be tempting to spend a long time describing (AO1) the psychodynamic explanation as it contains a lot of complex and interesting ideas. However, your answer must have more evaluation (AO3) than description.

9   Discuss social learning explanations of gender development, making reference to comparison with the biological explanation in the evaluation.   **(16 marks)**

> The focus of this question is on social learning, which includes the observation of role models. Going through the social learning theory and mediational processes in relation to learning gender-role behaviour will be a good starting point.

> When comparing social learning explanations with biological explanations, a useful place to begin would be to compare their stance in the nature vs nurture debate.

> Good evaluation could be generated from the lack of evidence to support the claims made by the psychodynamic explanation, or issues with the small amount of evidence that does exist, such as the case study of Little Hans.

Piaget's theory of cognitive development

Piaget believed that thinking developed with age from simple reflexive behaviour to complex abstract problem solving. It is often called a **constructivist theory** because the child constructs their own representation of the world through stages of maturation. A child moves on when ready and cannot be accelerated. This concept is called **readiness**.

Piaget's stages of cognitive development

 Sensorimotor stage
- 0–2 years
- Knowledge is limited to the senses as they explore the world.
- Key concept: **object permanence**

 Concrete operational stage
- 7–11 years
- Child can now conserve but cannot think in the abstract.
- Still needs concrete things to help solve problems.

 Pre-operational stage
- 2–7 years
- Child has language but makes mistakes when classifying objects.
- Key concepts: **egocentrism, irreversibility** and **centration**

 Formal operational stage
- 11+ years
- Can use abstract reasoning.
- Can use hypotheses and hypothetical situations.
- Can understand theory.

For example, as we mature, we build on simple reflex **schemas**, such as sucking, to a fully developed schema of drinks and drinking (hot drinks, cold drinks, fizzy drinks, making tea, tea ceremonies and so on).

Piaget's terminology

Operations – strings of schemas in order

Object permanence – knowing that an object continues to exist even when it is out of sight.

Conservation – knowing that if nothing is added or taken away, a substance must remain the same.

Egocentrism – only being able to see the world from your own viewpoint.

Irreversibility – not understanding that you can undo an action, such as re-shape some playdough.

Centration – focusing on a small aspect of a task, not the whole thing.

Abstract reasoning – being able to think without the object in front of you, using your imagination.

Equilibration – finding a balance between assimilation and accommodation during cognitive development.

Piaget's cognitive mechanism

 1 A problem comes along which does not fit our existing schema. We are in **disequilibrium** which is uncomfortable.

2 If it is quite similar, we **assimilate** the difference and modify our schema, maintaining our equilibrium.

A **schema** is a set of information you have about an object, place or person

3 If it is very different, we **accommodate** or modify our schema until we are in equilibrium again.

According to Piaget, we develop schemas to build our knowledge of the world. We do this through a process of assimilation, accommodation and equilibration which are Piaget's functional invariants.

Now try this

1 Helen is a new driver. When she drives her parents' car for the first time, will she be accommodating or assimilating her schema to fit the new task?

2 If she went abroad and drove in France with a hire car, would she be assimilating or accommodating her schema for driving?

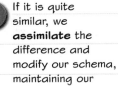

Piaget: Sensorimotor stage

Piaget studied his own three children intensively and noted that they all progressed through the same stages in an **invariant order** (they had to do one before the other). He also noted that children across the world were no different, which suggests that the stages are driven by a biological process of **maturation**. In the **sensorimotor stage (birth to 2 years)**, babies show remarkable progress, developing some key concepts and abilities.

Object permanence

This is a key characteristic of this stage and suggests that babies do not automatically realise that things are constant when out of sight.

Piaget hid objects under cloths and discovered that, below 7 months of age, babies quickly lost interest. He believed this showed they had no idea of the permanence of objects or even people.

🔍 Key study Piaget's Blanket and ball study (1963)

Aim: To investigate at what age children acquire object permanence.

Procedure: Piaget hid a toy under a blanket while the child was watching and observed whether or not the child searched for it. Searching for the hidden toy was evidence of object permanence. Piaget assumed that the child could only search for a hidden toy if s/he had a mental representation of it.

Results: Piaget found that infants searched for the hidden toy when they were around 8 months old.

Conclusion: Children around 8 months have object permanence because they are able to form a mental representation of the object in their minds.

The sensorimotor stage

Piaget believed that the stage could be divided into **six sub-stages**, which mirrored the developing skills of the baby.

1 **Reflexes (0–1 month)**
In this stage a child is merely showing reflexive responses such as the startle reflex or sucking reflex.

2 **Primary circular reactions (1–4 months)**
The baby repeats simple actions such as vigorously kicking, which it finds pleasurable.

3 **Secondary circular reactions (4–8 months)**
The baby will repeat actions with objects, not just their own body, such as shaking a rattle because it enjoys the sound.

4 **Co-ordination of reactions (8–12 months)**
This is the beginning of intentional action; the baby will reach out for things or crawl towards items s/he wants and begins to imitate people.

5 **Tertiary circular reactions (12–18 months)**
Babies are now capable of trying out actions and noticing their effect, so they can do shape-sorter puzzles and stack cups inside each other.

6 **Early representational thought (18–24 months)**
Babies can now form mental representations of objects and they have developed the ability to visualise things that are not physically present. Piaget called this the **general symbolic function (GSF)**.

Evaluation

👍 Piaget's theory is responsible for much of what happens in nursery and primary education. His ideas of the invariant stages help decide what a normal child should be achieving by a certain age. This will also help identify a child who is struggling.

👎 Piaget has been heavily criticised for his tests lacking rigour and being too difficult for children in this stage. Bower and Wishart (1972) used a laboratory experiment to study infants aged 1–4 months. They waited for an infant to reach for an object, and then turned out the lights. They then filmed the infant using an infrared camera. They found that the infant continued to reach for the object for up to 90 seconds after it became invisible.

Now try this

Briefly describe what Piaget meant by object permanence and explain why it is an important concept.

Piaget: Pre-operational stage

In the **pre-operational stage (2 to 7 years)**, the **general symbolic function** (GSF) develops further but children are still focused on the appearance of objects rather than logic or operations (strings of **schemas** in order). They are still building schemas and their thinking has several key characteristics which show the errors in their thinking.

 Key study **Piaget and Inhelder (1956)**

Aim: To see whether children under 7 years can decentre (understand that other people see things differently to them) and see the mountain scene from a different viewpoint.

Procedure: Children aged 4–8 years were shown the mountain scene on a table top and could walk around it. They then sat on one side while being shown 10 pictures of different views of the model. They had to choose the view that a doll placed at various sides of the table could see.

Results: Four-year-olds chose their own view. Six-year-olds showed some ability to decentre but made mistakes. Seven- and 8-year-olds were able to decentre.

Conclusion: Children under 7 years are still egocentric and fail to understand that there are different viewpoints in the world other than their own.

Piaget's three mountains are all clearly different to help the child choose the right view.

The pre-operational stage

Piaget divided the stage into **two sub-stages**, each with specific characteristics.

1 Pre-conceptual (2–4 years) characteristics

- **Centration** – children are unable to see more than one aspect of a situation at a time (they cannot decentre). This inability to decentre gives 2-year-olds difficulty in social relationships as well as with objects.

- **Transductive reasoning** – relationships between two things are based on a single attribute such as colour or shape but not both.

- **Animistic thinking** – the belief that inanimate objects are alive.

- **Seriation** – children find it hard to put items in order, seeing only the extremes (biggest and smallest).

2 Intuitive (4–7 years) characteristics

- **Egocentrism** – children only see things from their own point of view.

- **Conservation** – children are unable to conserve (see page 173).

Children do not understand that the amount of liquid remains the same whatever the shape of the glass.

Evaluation

👍 More useful *concepts* were described by Piaget in this stage, which help the teacher understand how children learn and plan lessons accordingly. It led to discovery learning and the idea of the 'child as a scientist' experimenting on their world. This is currently a very popular model of educational practice or pedagogy.

👎 Hughes (1975) found that using a more understandable task such as hide-and-seek meant that children were more successful and less egocentric at a younger age. He found that

90% of children between $3\frac{1}{2}$ and 5 years of age could hide a doll where a policeman doll could not see it. Thus, Piaget's methodology lacked mundane realism and ecological validity.

👎 Borke (1975) found that by using the 'mountains' model on a turntable, 3-year-olds selected a correct view 42% of the time and 4-year-olds 67% of the time. With other displays, using familiar toys rather than mountains, the 3-year-olds' accuracy increased to 80% and the 4-year-olds' to 93%.

Now try this

Discuss how the methodology used by Piaget may have meant that he was mistaken about the ages at which children could decentre.

Piaget: Concrete operational stage

An operation is an action performed mentally using schemas in a logical series. In the **concrete operational stage (7 to 11 years)**, children cannot do this yet and need concrete objects to help them, such as counters for maths and pictures to tell a story. The main development in this stage is **conservation** and during this stage problems that challenged a pre-operational child are gradually resolved.

Conservation types

Different conservation types occur at different ages and always in the same order (an invariant order).

1   **Conservation of liquid (by 6–7 years)**
Piaget (1952) poured liquid from a shorter, wider beaker into a taller, thinner beaker. When asked, 7-year-old children typically said there was more liquid in the taller glass until they could conserve (see page 175).

2   **Conservation of substance/number/length (by 7–8 years)**
Piaget (1960) laid out two identical rows of counters and pre-operational children agreed they were the same. Piaget then pushed one row together, shortening the line. When asked, the child thought there were more in the longer line.

3   **Conservation of weight (by 8–10 years)**
Children agree two balls of clay weigh the same on a balance scale, then one is squashed flat. When asked if they are still the same, children think the squashed one weighs less.

4   **Conservation of volume (by 11–12 years)**
Children see two identical balls of clay dropped into two glasses; the water level rises equally. One ball of clay is then re-shaped and they are asked if the water level will rise to the same level again or if one will rise more.

Research evidence

✓ McGarrigle and Donaldson (1974) found that by using a 'naughty teddy' who messed up a row of sweets, they could show that children could conserve number at a younger age than Piaget predicted.

> Taking away the adult from the experiment seemed to allow the children to conserve number more successfully.

✓ Rose and Blank (1974) pointed out that adults often repeat a question in order to hint that a child's first answer to a question was wrong. Piaget did this by asking children the same question twice in the conservation experiments, before and after the transformation. When Rose and Blank replicated this but asked the question only once, after the liquid had been poured, they found many more 6-year-olds gave the correct answer. This shows children can conserve at a younger age than Piaget claimed.

Horizontal and vertical décalage

Piaget believed that a child could conserve number before weight within the stage and this he called **horizontal décalage**. There is also **vertical décalage** where children have mastered conservation but still cannot classify objects as fish or animals.

Main developments

The concrete operational stage sees the end of **egocentrism** and the ability to **decentre** in social relationships as well as in tasks such as conservation.

Class inclusion also occurs in this stage, where children realise that there can be subsets of objects and that things can belong to two or more categories at the same time. For example, a cat is also an animal.

Evaluation

🖋 Piaget believed intensive coaching could not accelerate children through these stages, but it is clear that plenty of play in an enriched environment does speed up learning.

🖋 Piaget believed understanding came before language, but Vygotsky believed that language and social play were crucial to cognitive development. Piaget has been criticised for neglecting the social environment of the child.

Now try this

Describe **one** conservation task and give **one** criticism of Piaget's interpretation of the results.

Piaget: Formal operational stage

In the **formal operational stage (11+ years)**, children can now manipulate ideas without needing the object present. They can use imagination, logic and make hypothetical deductions. For example, they can perform mental arithmetic tasks at speed. They can apply rules to a problem and find successful solutions.

Piaget's experiments in the formal operational stage

In **the third eye problem**, Piaget (1970) asked children where they would put a third eye, if they were able to have one, and why. Schaffer (1988) repeated this test with 9- and 11-year-olds. The 9-year-olds all suggested that the third eye should be on the forehead. However, 11-year-olds were more inventive, suggesting, for example, that a third eye placed on the hand would be useful for seeing round corners.

In **the pendulum task** (Inhelder & Piaget, 1958), children were asked to work out which of three factors was the most important in determining the speed of the swing of a pendulum: the length of the string, the weight of the pendulum or the strength of the push.

Children could vary the length of the pendulum string and the weight, then measure the pendulum speed by counting the number of swings per minute.

To find the correct answer, the child had to grasp the idea of the experimental method – to vary just one variable at a time (e.g. trying different lengths with the same weight). Children in the formal operational stage approached the task systematically, testing one variable at a time to see its effect. Younger children typically tried out these variations randomly or changed two things at the same time.

Research evidence

Siegler (1979) asked children to predict which way a balance would go as weighted disks were moved along the arm closer to the fulcrum (centre) or further away.

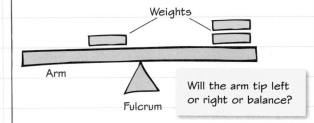

Weights

Arm

Will the arm tip left or right or balance?

Fulcrum

He studied the answers given by children from 5 years of age upwards, concluding that they apply rules, which develop in the same order as predicted by Piaget. He found that eventually the children were able to take into account the interaction between the weight of the discs and the distance from the central fulcrum, and so successfully predict balance. However, this did not happen until participants were between 13 and 17 years of age.

Evaluation

👍 This stage coincides with the change to secondary school where more abstract thinking and problem solving is required in the entire curriculum, supporting Piaget's contribution to the education system.

👎 Not everyone fully reaches this stage. Many people still need concrete diagrams to help them work out problems or still count on fingers into adulthood, which is quite normal. This calls into question whether it properly exists as a stage.

👍 Piaget's theory uses both biological and cognitive approach concepts and sees them working together. It is arguably more holistic as a result.

👎 Dasen (1977) suggests that the formal operational stage does not exist in all cultures, suggesting that this stage is more nurture than nature. For example, the Inuit do not develop operations for volume.

Now try this

Describe **one** challenge to the formal operational stage as described by Piaget.

Vygotsky's theory of cognitive development

Vygotsky was a Russian psychologist. He and Piaget had a common belief that children need to learn by being active and testing ideas. For Vygotsky, however, learning occurred in a **social** context, and children learned within the norms and attitudes of their own culture.

The influence of culture

Vygotsky believed that basic mental functions such as attention, perception and memory developed into more sophisticated and effective mental processes through interaction with the socio-cultural environment.

For example, memory in young children is limited by the biological maturation of the brain. However, we improve it in our culture by note-taking, mnemonics or mind maps. In other societies, rote-learning is the favoured strategy that children are taught.

These are all versions of Vygotsky's **tools of intellectual adaptation**.

Vygotsky suggested that thinking, even when carried out alone, is affected by the beliefs, values and tools of intellectual adaptation of the culture in which a person grows up, and is therefore **socio-culturally determined**.

The social influence

According to Vygotsky (1978), a lot of learning occurs through social interaction with a skilful tutor or **more knowledgeable other** (MKO).

An MKO could be a parent, teacher or older child.

The MKO may model behaviours and/or provide verbal instructions for the child. Vygotsky refers to this as **cooperative or collaborative dialogue**. The child seeks to understand the actions or an instruction provided by the MKO and then **internalises** the information, using it to guide and improve their own performance.

Internalisation

The ability to think and reason by oneself is called inner speech. For Vygotsky, cognitive development involves the process of internalising the problem solving taking place during the interaction of the child with its parent, siblings or teacher. Vygotsky sees the 'child as an apprentice', gaining skills and knowledge through collaborating with other people.

Comparing Piaget and Vygotsky

Vygotsky   Piaget

Child = apprentice

Language-driven cognitive development   Used in schools

Social environment

Stages of cognitive development

Child = scientist experimenting on the world

Semiotics

Semiotics means using signs and symbols to create meaning. For Vygotsky, this is the primary function of language development. He identified three stages:

1 **Social speech (0–3 years)** — pre-intellectual language, where language and thinking are not interdependent until around age 2 years.

2 **Egocentric speech (3–7 years)** — self-talk and thinking aloud.

3 **Inner speech (7+ years)** — self-talk becomes silent and internal, and language is used for communication only.

Research evidence

☑ Gredler (1992) found that in New Guinea, tribal people used fingers and arms when counting and this had limited their learning, supporting the idea of cultural influences on cognitive development.

☑ Berk (1994) found that children talked to themselves more when doing something difficult, supporting the idea of egocentric speech. Interestingly, even adults vocalise inner speech sometimes to help with problem solving.

Now try this

Explain what Vygotsky meant by inner speech.

Zone of proximal development

One of Vygotsky's key ideas was the zone of proximal development (ZPD). This is the gap between a child's current and potential ability. Scaffolding and the cultural environment of the child are the key factors to enable extra progress and maximise potential. Their absence would keep a child below their potential.

Scaffolding

A child's cognitive development is assisted by an MKO (see page 178) who guides by giving hints and tips to problems. This is known as **scaffolding**.

Scaffolding is the successful and supportive interaction between the MKO and the child

Current understanding – child can work unassisted

Child uses inner speech to work unassisted at their current level of understanding

Zone of proximal development – child learns through scaffolding

An MKO uses scaffolding to assist the child to progress

Tasks out of reach are stressful for the child

Out of reach

Zone of proximal development

As the child learns to master the problem, scaffolding is gradually withdrawn. Learning happens in a social relationship where the MKO and child do things together, then gradually the child does more on its own. This helps relieve the stress and tension of failure at a difficult task and maintains the child's self-concept and enjoyment of learning.

Concept formation

Vygotsky gave children puzzle blocks with nonsense syllables on them and they had to work out what the symbols meant. The children showed four stages of concept development depending on their age and maturity.

1 **Vague syncretic** – child uses trial and error to try to solve the problem.

2 **Complex** – child uses some strategies to try to solve the problem, but they are not successful.

3 **Potential concept** – now they are more systematic and look at one aspect of the problem at a time.

4 **Mature concept** – systematic and successful.

Research evidence

☑ Wood et al. (1976) assessed mothers who were supporting 4- and 5-year-old children to construct a pyramid of blocks. They found that 'sensitive guidance' worked best. Too much help frustrated the children.

☑ Freund (1990) got 3- and 5-year-old children to help a puppet decide what should go into a doll's house. Half the children had the support of their mothers and half worked alone. The children with guidance were more successful, indicating support for the idea of scaffolding.

Role of the teacher

Piaget	Vygotsky
Role of the teacher is important but not central. Child learns by discovery.	The teacher (as MKO) is seen as fundamental to cognitive development.
'Readiness' is a central concept in education – children need to be ready to progress to the next stage.	Children should be actively encouraged to move through the ZPD and do not need to be ready. They should be given the opportunity to stretch themselves.

Evaluation

👍 The concept of the ZPD is universal and works in every educational setting.

👍 Vygotsky's ZPD can explain the influence of culture and environment and supports the idea of enrichment in education.

👍 Language development comes before cognitive development so that sensitive guidance from MKOs can be used successfully.

👎 The theory has been criticised for ignoring biological factors and individual differences, but the concept of the ZPD is individual to each child.

Now try this

Using concepts from Vygotsky's theory of cognitive development, explain how a 4-year-old should be helped to do a jigsaw puzzle they cannot do by themselves.

Baillargeon: early infant abilities

Baillargeon's aim was to investigate **object permanence**, which Piaget had suggested was not fully formed until around 7 months (see page 174). To find out if younger babies had object permanence, Baillargeon came up with the **violation of expectation technique** (VOE).

 Key study **Baillargeon et al. (1985)**

Method: The child is repeatedly shown a new scenario/event until they look away. This indicates that it is no longer new to them. Then they are shown an alternative and impossible example of the scenario. For example, a solid object passing through another solid object. The length of time they look at it is compared with the possible scenario.

The key assumptions for this method are:

- a baby will spend longer looking at something it is surprised by (the basis of VOE)
- babies have an innate ability to understand the properties of objects.

habituation   impossible test   possible test

The drawbridge task

Method: Five-month-old babies are first familiarised/habituated with a drawbridge swinging through 180 degrees. A box is then placed in the way and the baby either sees a 'possible event', where the drawbridge stops when it reaches the box, or an 'impossible event', where the drawbridge carries on moving through the box. Their looking times are recorded by cameras focused on the baby.

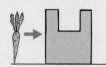 **Key study** **Baillargeon and DeVos (1991)**

The sliding carrot task

Method: Three and a half-month-old babies watch either a tall or a short carrot slide past a window in a screen. After a period of habituation, babies show surprise and look for longer when the tall carrot does not appear in the window.

Results: These results indicate that the babies:

- realised that each carrot continued to exist when out of sight
- assumed that each carrot retained its height behind the screen
- believed that each carrot pursued its trajectory behind the screen
- expected the tall carrot to be visible in the screen window and were surprised that it was not.

Conclusion: This supports the idea that babies as young as $3\frac{1}{2}$ months of age are aware that objects continue to exist when hidden. They therefore have object permanence.

Evaluation

👍 The VOE technique has become a paradigm or accepted method of testing the cognitive abilities of babies. Baillargeon conducted many more studies in support of her theory.

👎 Despite this, these are assumptions about what these babies are doing, and it is not entirely clear whether they are surprised or just find the impossible situations more interesting. Cashon and Cohen (2000) showed that 8-month-old babies looked longer at a block placed in the path of a rotating screen, even when this was a possible situation.

Now try this

Explain how the violation of expectation technique is used to investigate object permanence.

Note that this question is a general methodology question and not about Baillargeon's research specifically.

Social cognition: Selman

Social cognition refers to how an individual becomes aware of how they fit into a social world. To do this successfully, a person must be able to take another's point of view and understand that not everyone thinks in the same way as they do. Selman (1980) investigated this with role-taking **interpersonal dilemmas**. From this he established levels of interpersonal interactions or **perspective-taking**.

Selman's levels of perspective-taking

Interpersonal dilemmas are stories about people interacting together, which have different possible answers. From these answers, Selman developed **five levels of thinking**. Here is Holly's dilemma.

Holly is 8 and an expert tree climber, but one day she falls out of a tree. She promises her dad she will not climb trees again, but then she meets Shawn whose kitten is stuck up a tree. Only Holly can save him. Should she climb the tree?

The stages of Selman's five levels of thinking

Stage 0: Egocentric viewpoint (3–6 years)
A child can label other people's obvious feelings but do not see the cause of those feelings.
Holly's father will not mind her rescuing the kitten as he will think the same as she does.

Stage 1: Social informational role taking (6–8 years)
Children know other people have different information and may or may not agree with them.
If Holly shows her father the kitten, he will not be angry that she climbs the tree because he will have the same information.

Stage 2: Self-reflective role taking (8–10 years)
Children can see other people's viewpoints, but not at the same time as their own.
Holly will realise that her dad will not punish her as he will understand why she did it. Holly realises that her dad can see her viewpoint.

Stage 3: Mutual role taking (10–12 years)
Children can see the mutual and simultaneous viewpoints of each other.
Holly will understand why her dad thinks like he does when he sees her behaviour at the same time as seeing her own reasons.

Stage 4: Social and conventional system role taking (12–15+ years)
Children realise that society has a view and a set of values that should be obeyed.
The ethical concept that animals should be protected justifies Holly's actions.

Research evidence

- ✓ Gurucharri and Selman (1982) tested the interpersonal dilemmas in a longitudinal study over 5 years with 41 children. They found that 40 children developed perspective-taking as predicted by Selman's stage theory.

- ✓ Epley et al. (2004) used a cross-sectional design to test 4–12-year-olds using 5 × 5 grids of boxes placed back to back. The children had to move objects hidden in the boxes according to instructions, working out which objects were mutually visible and which were uniquely visible. To be able to do this, they had to decentre (see page 175). The results showed that egocentric errors declined with age, and older children were faster at disregarding the uniquely visible object.

Evaluation

- 👍 Selman's interpersonal dilemmas have become an accepted way (paradigm) of investigating the development of perspective-taking.

- 👍 Perspective-taking has a role to play in resolving conflicts between children to increase empathy and reduce anger.

- 👍 There are similarities with Piaget's theory of egocentric thinking in the pre-operational stage (see page 175), and the ability to decentre at around 7 years old coincides with Selman's stages 0 to 1.

- 🚩 Selman did not consider social factors such as arguments, which could promote perspective-taking and mediation.

- 🚩 Selman's sample were all Western and from middle-class economies, affecting generalisability.

Now try this

How could using an interpersonal dilemma be made an objective way of investigating social cognition in children?

Theory of mind

Theory of mind (ToM) refers to the ability to **decentre** (see page 175) and put yourself in someone else's place, understanding that they may be thinking and feeling differently to you. It is an essential ability for successful social interaction, and develops in normal children at around 4 years of age.

Preparation for ToM

Children are born pre-wired with the early skills that they will need to develop their ToM later on. These skills include the ability to:

- pay attention to people and copy them
- recognise others' emotions and use words to express them ('happy', 'sad', 'mad')
- know that people act according to the things they want
- understand the causes and consequences of emotions ('if I throw my toy, Mum will be cross')
- pretend to be someone else (such as a doctor or a cashier) when they play.

The false-belief paradigm

ToM is tested using the **false-belief method**. The child is shown a scene and is asked to interpret it from the viewpoint of one of the characters in the scene. If they can do this, then they have a ToM. If they use their own viewpoint, they are yet to develop ToM. One of the best known examples is the Sally-Anne task (see page 183).

Order of development

According to Smith (1999), amongst others, children develop ToM skills in the following order:

1 **Understanding 'wanting'** – different people want different things.

2 **Understanding 'thinking'** – different people have different, but potentially true, beliefs about the same thing.

3 **Understanding that 'seeing leads to knowing'** – if you haven't seen something, you don't necessarily know about it and you will need extra information to understand.

For example, talking to mum on the phone. When she is in a new place, she will have to give more information to help understanding.

4 **Understanding 'false beliefs'** – sometimes people believe things that are not true, and they act according to their beliefs, not according to what is really true.

5 **Understanding 'hidden feelings'** – people can feel a different emotion from the one they display.

Biological evidence

✓ Frith and Frith (1999) found that the amygdala, basal ganglia, temporal cortex and frontal cortex showed raised levels of activity when people had to consider other's mental states, suggesting these brain areas were involved in ToM.

Research evidence

✓ Perner et al. (1987) used a **deceptive box task** where children are shown a tube of chocolates that contains pencils rather than chocolates. Children are asked what another child, who has not seen inside the tube, will think is inside. In this task, 3-year-olds say that another child will expect there to be pencils in the tube. However, 4- and 5-year-olds normally pass the deceptive box task, indicating that they are able to distinguish between their own knowledge and that of another person. Therefore, Perner et al. argued that children exhibit an understanding of false belief at 4–5 years of age.

Evaluation

👍 Lack of ToM coincides with Piaget's conservation and occurs at the same age, increasing validity.

👍 ToM occurs in all cultures at around the same time, which supports the idea of underlying biology from nature, but good nurture can help it.

👍 ToM matters, because without it children have communication problems and find relationships difficult.

👎 There could be problems with the adult questioning used in these false-belief studies with very young children. They could be misinterpreting the questions, lowering validity.

👎 The false-belief tasks can be quite complex and require more concentration and memory than 3-year-olds possess, reducing reliability.

Now try this

Explain how the false-belief paradigm can be used to show whether a child has a theory of mind.

Theory of mind and autism

Autism spectrum disorder (ASD) is a developmental disorder occurring more frequently in boys, which is usually diagnosed around 3 years of age. ASD affects many aspects of a child's behaviour and it has been suggested that a **lack of a theory of mind** (ToM) may explain this. This is tested with a false-belief task.

Some key autism symptoms

Some children with ASD:

- do not babble, and language development is often delayed

- have problems making eye contact, facial expressions, body language and gestures, leading to problems with relationships

- may also lack awareness of and interest in other children, and tend to play alone

- do not demonstrate imaginative or pretend play, or will continually repeat the same pretend play

- like to stick to the same routine, and little changes may trigger tantrums, or may engage in repetitive activity such as opening and closing doors or lining things up.

🔍 Key study Sally–Anne study (Baron-Cohen et al., 1985)

Aim: To see if a lack of a ToM can explain the behaviours in autism.

Procedure: A natural experiment with three sample groups: 20 children with autism who were on average 12 years old with a mental age of 5.5 years; 14 children with Down's syndrome whose mental age was 3 years and chronological average age was 11 years; 27 children classed as 'normal' with an average age of 4.5 years and a mental age of 4.5 years.

Each child watched the researcher play a game of hide-and-seek with two dolls, called Sally and Anne, and a marble hidden in a box or a basket. To check understanding there are four questions:

1 The naming question (*to check they know which doll is which*)

2 Where is the marble really? (*reality question*)

3 Where was the marble in the beginning? (*memory question*)

4 Where will Sally look for her marble? (*false-belief question*)

Findings: All the children passed the naming, reality and memory questions; only 20% of the children with autism passed the false-belief question compared with 86% of the children with Down's syndrome and 85% of the normal children.

Conclusion: Most children with autism do not have a ToM and find it hard to attribute beliefs to others. Being unable to use ToM helps explain some of the deficits that children and people with autism show. It would seem to be specific to the autistic sample as the children with Down's syndrome were able to play the game.

The Sally–Anne task explained

1 Sally has a marble. She places her marble in her basket.

2 Sally goes out for a walk, leaving her marble in her basket. Anne remains behind whilst Sally is out.

3 Anne removes Sally's marble and places it in her own box.

4 Sally returns later and wants to play with her marble.
Will she look in the basket or in the box for her marble?

Evaluation

👍 Leslie (1987) suggested an innate theory of mind mechanism (ToMM) that matures in normal children at around 2 years of age, but physiological damage before or after birth affects its development in children with autism.

👍 Replications of the Sally–Anne task have supported Baron-Cohen et al.'s (1985) findings and explain some – but not all – ASD symptoms.

👎 Not all children with autism lack ToM. It is also possible to improve ToM through expert tuition, so it is unlikely to be innate.

👎 Validity is questionable when using dolls that do not have minds as the characters in the story.

Now try this

The Sally-Anne task involves dolls making decisions. Evaluate the use of dolls to test theory of mind.

Mirror neurons

Mirror neurons fire when a person observes the same action performed by another – the neuron 'mirrors' the behaviour of the other, as though the observer were itself acting. This is called **motor resonance**. This function is thought to be involved in ToM. For example, if you observe someone vomiting it is hard not to feel nauseous yourself.

Biological evidence

Rizzolatti et al. (1996) found mirror neurons by accident.

It is tentatively suggested that a problem in this system could account for the inability of people with autism to empathise or 'read' other people, and why they lack a ToM.

Cheng et al. (2006) found, using a magnetoencephalography (MEG) study, that female brains show a stronger motor resonance than male brains, possibly accounting for superior performance in **social referencing** where we look at others to read their emotions and then know how to respond.

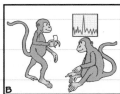
An example of Rizzolatti's monkeys: A monkey does action, B monkey sees action

Rizzolatti noticed that the macaque monkeys he had wired up to electrodes showed the same firing pattern when they watched other monkeys pick up food as when they did so themselves. He then coined the term 'mirror neurons'.

Research evidence

✓ Rizzolatti and Craighero (2004) looked for the mirror neuron in humans. It is not yet possible to test single neurons in humans, so they used EEGs, PET and fMRI scans (see page 89). They found a network in the frontal and parietal brain regions that appeared to work as mirror neurons.

✓ Iacoboni et al. (1999) showed, using fMRI, that the human inferior frontal cortex and superior parietal lobe are active when the person performs an action and also when the person sees another individual performing an action. It has been suggested that these brain regions contain mirror neurons. They have been defined as the human mirror neuron system.

Problems for the hypothesis

✓ Jarrett (2012) says we are clearly capable of understanding actions that we are unable to perform, such as slithering like a snake, without needing mirror neurons for it.

✓ Hickok (2014) thinks the function of mirror neurons is not about understanding the actions of others, but about using others to make our own choice of how to act. Seen this way, mirror neuron activity is just as likely a consequence of action understanding as a cause.

✓ In a meta-analysis of 25 studies, Hamilton (2012) concluded that there was little evidence for a global dysfunction of the mirror system in autism.

Evaluation

👍 The evidence for a biological basis for the mirror neuron system seems more prevalent in social animals, which live in groups, and it may serve a survival function.

🗨 There is a chance this system could be in some way faulty in autism but this is not conclusive.

🗨 Heyes (2012) says that we do not know whether mirror neurons have evolved to help us understand each other's actions or whether they are the after-effect (the brain's response).

🗨 More work needs to be done to find any certainty that a specific neuron system exists to help us understand each other's behaviours.

For example, people with damage to Broca's area, which is used to produce speech, can still understand speech (see page 86).

But this research is difficult, costly and highly reductionist, possibly meaning a loss of validity.

Now try this

Discuss the evidence for the function of mirror neurons in helping us understand each other's behaviour.

Exam skills 1

As well as knowing the content of the A level topics, you could be asked about the methodology used by the researchers, and you will be expected to be able to evaluate it. When the question is focused on a topic area, your response should be specific to that area. Before you look at these worked examples, remind yourself about observational techniques (page 97) and cognitive development (pages 173–184).

Worked example

Researchers such as Piaget (1956) and Baron-Cohen (1987) conducted a series of controlled observations to investigate the development of thinking in children. Explain what is meant by a controlled observation and give two limitations of the use of controlled observations for studying cognitive development.

(6 marks)

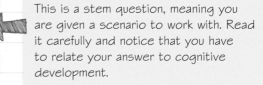 This is a stem question, meaning you are given a scenario to work with. Read it carefully and notice that you have to relate your answer to cognitive development.

In a controlled observation, the researcher sets up a task or situation for a child or adult to do and then watches how they deal with it. Nowadays, the child would usually be video recorded and the researcher would then be able to watch the recording with another researcher to see if they agreed.

This question is worth 6 marks and you have to explain and give limitations. Therefore, keep the explanation short so that you have time for the limitations.

As well as inter-rater reliability there must be a standardised procedure between the observers. This could mean that the task was very limited and therefore lacking in mundane realism. For example, Baron-Cohen restricted his participants to just watching the Sally-Anne task.

Several methodology points are made, demonstrating knowledge of the application of science. You should try to use all knowledge gained over both years of your course to give depth to your answers.

Another limitation could be that validity can be lowered because the children will know they are being observed and may act differently or answer questions differently than they would in natural play. Despite this, the fact that we cannot see what someone is thinking means we have to rely on observation of behaviour and do it as rigorously as possible.

Worked example

Read the item and then answer the question that follows.

Jonny and Sammy are getting thirsty, so Jonny's mum gets them a drink. She opens two cans and pours them into two glasses, one of which is taller and thinner than the other. Sammy starts to complain that he has got less in his glass but Jonny says no, they are both the same.

Which one of the following is correct?

(1 mark)

First, rule out the answers that must be wrong. In this case, Jonny and Sammy cannot both be in the same stage.

A Jonny is in the concrete operational stage and Sammy is in the pre-operational stage

B ~~Both Jonny and Sammy are in the pre-operational stage~~

C ~~Both Jonny and Sammy are in the concrete operational stage~~

In order to answer this apparently simple question you need a good understanding of Piaget's stage theory.

D Sammy is in the concrete operational stage and Jonny is in the pre-operational stage

Exam skills 2

Before you look at the worked examples, remind yourself about Piaget's theory (page 173) and Vygotsky's theory (pages 178–179) of cognitive development.

Worked example

Briefly outline Vygotsky's concept stages.

(2 marks)

Vygotsky had four concept stages. The first was the vague syncretic stage in which the child uses trial and error to solve problems. Next was the complex stage where the child has developed some strategies to help them but they are not very effective. Third was the potential concept stage and finally the mature concept stage. The difference between these last two was how well developed was the ability to systematically work through problems, finally using multiple strategies to succeed in a task.

> To be successful here, you need accurate knowledge. You could use flashcards to help you revise this sort of information.

Worked example

Discuss how Piaget and Vygotsky's views on the cognitive development of young children can be applied to education.

(16 marks)

Piaget saw the child as a scientist experimenting on the world because he believed that children learned by discovering things for themselves. He felt that children had to be ready to move on and could not be forced. They had to mature into the next stage of development. On the other hand, Vygotsky felt that children could be pushed to achieve more than they could alone if they had a more knowledgeable other (MKO) to help them. He said that interacting with MKOs using language and cultural tools would expand the child's zone of proximal development. In Piaget's world the child is self-driven but in Vygotsky's they are motivated by the social world in which they live.

> The child as scientist is explained and coupled with the concept of readiness. The idea of biological maturation is also introduced to make a clear difference from Vygotsky.

> Here the key concepts of Vygotsky's theory are clearly compared and a final comparison is made.

The teacher in a Piagetian classroom has to let the children learn by discovery. This means that they should set up tasks and problems and provide the necessary materials but should allow the child to make progress according to their own pace. On the other hand, the teacher in the Vygotskian classroom should provide scaffolding for the child because they are the MKO for the child. Scaffolding is providing helpful hints and tips to support the child in moving forward in their thinking. The Piagetian teacher has to look out for readiness in the children. For example, noticing them starting to ask questions about time would be the right point to introduce the clock and calendar. The Vygotskian teacher should look to the layout and seating plan and place children next to those who can help them progress by talking through problems...

> This time the emphasis is on what the teacher is doing, so you would need to think about what these two classrooms would be like.

> It is a good idea to use examples to show your understanding. For 16 marks this answer needs some evidence – refer to pages 177 and 179 for examples. Finally, write a conclusion.

Exam-style practice 1

Practise for Paper 3 of your A level exam with these exam-style questions. There are answers on pages 308–309. Before looking at these questions, it would be good to review the research on autism (page 183) and mirror neurons (page 184), and Baillargeon's explanation of early infant abilities (page 180).

1 Briefly outline the symptoms of autism. **(2 marks)**

This 'outline' question should be straightforward and requires knowledge of the key features of autistic spectrum behaviour.

Note that the question asks for an outline, which requires description, not just a list of the symptoms.

2 Read the item and then answer the question that follows.

> For Sport Relief 2016, Eddie Izzard ran 27 marathons in 27 days in South Africa to raise money and commemorate Nelson Mandela's 27 years in prison. As we watch his pain and suffering we feel empathy and donate willingly to the fund.

This is a question based on a stem to get you thinking. Even if you did not see Eddie Izzard's efforts, you should be able to imagine what it was like for him.

Discuss the extent to which mirror neurons could explain our behaviour. Refer to Eddie Izzard's efforts in your answer.

(16 marks)

In your answer, you should consider the following points.

- Focus on the empathy and then our action. You should be able to outline how mirror neurons could explain this.
- Next, you need to consider the evidence for and against the mirror neuron explanation. Turn the evidence to focus on this particular question if you can.
- Refer to the marathons and the act of donation throughout.
- At the end, you should come to a reasoned conclusion either way.
- Support your points with real life or theoretical examples.

3 (a) Briefly outline how Simon Baron-Cohen believes a lack of the theory of mind explains autism. **(2 marks)**

   (b) Explain **two** limitations of the theory of mind as an explanation for autism. **(6 marks)**

This is a pair of questions on autism. Pairs of questions often appear and there may be other sections relating to methodology, too. It is a good idea to read ahead through each section of the paper to see what is coming so that you avoid repetition.

4 Discuss how Baillargeon's research sheds doubt on Piaget's belief in object permanence. **(16 marks)**

Question 3 (b) looks at problems or limitations only. The classic mistake to avoid is doing just one limitation because you will usually have your marks capped however well you do it. Make sure you include research evidence in your answer.

This question restricts you to one researcher, so you need depth of knowledge.

- Baillargeon conducted several studies, so you should use your wider knowledge here.
- Use at least two of her studies to answer this question.
- You will briefly need to outline how Piaget did his research so that you can draw comparisons.

Exam-style practice 2

Practise for Paper 3 of your A level exam with these exam-style questions. There are answers on page 309. Research method questions could be applied to any part of the course. Before looking at these questions, it would be good to review measures of central tendency (page 113) and distributions (page 116) in Research methods, and the many criticisms of Piaget's theory (pages 173–180).

🔢 **Maths skills**

5 Read the item and answer the questions that follow.

> A researcher decided to test whether 6-year-old children could learn the skill of drawing a 3D 10 cm cube more accurately if they worked with an older, 8-year-old child. He set up an experiment with two groups, 10 children in each group. Those in the experimental group were paired with an older child. The control group had the same amount of time and materials but no extra support. He measured the difference in millimetres between the finished drawing and a perfect drawing (the total outline for the template = 900 mm).

The researcher found the following results.

Participant	Experimental condition: difference in mm	Participant	Control condition: difference in mm
1	9	11	14
2	11	12	12
3	13	13	9
4	7	14	7
5	5	15	13
6	6	16	12
7	8	17	6
8	10	18	15
9	11	19	14
10	3	20	12
Total	**83**	**Total**	**114**

(a) Find the mean, median and mode of the experimental condition. **(3 marks)**

(b) Sketch a graph to show the most likely distribution curve for the error scores in the experimental condition. Label the axes of your graph and mark on it the positions of the mean, median and mode. **(3 marks)**

(c) What sort of distribution does your graph show? **(1 mark)**

6 Outline **one** of Piaget's contributions to classroom education. **(2 marks)**

7 Describe and evaluate Piaget's theory of cognitive development. **(16 marks)**

> Your graph does not need to look perfect; it is a sketch. The most important things are to correctly label the axes and mark the mean, median and mode with the right skew.

> As this is an outline question, you need to give a little more detail than just naming an application.

> This question needs thorough preparation.
> - You need to have the evaluation points ready with the matching research. As part of your revision, a table of points and research is well worth learning.
> - You have many critical researchers at your disposal who all make different points. Use them to support your evaluation.
> - Timing is vital. This question could eat up your time so be ready for it. Aim to spend a maximum of 20 minutes on it.

Classification of schizophrenia

Schizophrenia is a common but much misunderstood mental disorder with a worldwide prevalence of 1% of the population. Males and females are equally at risk but it tends to occur earlier in males.

Types of schizophrenia

Clinicians see schizophrenia as being one of two types:

- **Type I** is more acute, has more of the **positive symptoms** but responds better to treatment.
- **Type II** is chronic, has more of the **negative symptoms** and is less responsive to treatment. It affects mood, thought processes and the ability to determine what is reality.

Symptoms used for diagnosis

A diagnostic system such as **DSM-5** is used to diagnose schizophrenia. This recognises groups of symptoms that create a disorder.

- **Positive symptoms** – these are additional to normal life experiences and concern losing touch with reality.
- **Negative symptoms** – these detract from normal life experiences. They include **anhedonia** (loss of pleasure in life), **disturbances of affect** (inappropriate emotional responses to situations), **thought process disorders** and **psychomotor disturbances** such as pacing up and down.

Symptoms

For a diagnosis, two or more symptoms must be present for more than a month.

Positive symptoms	
Perceptual disturbances	**Hallucinations** are visual and/or auditory (hearing voices). Voices are typically abusive or critical of the person.
Cognitive symptoms	**Delusions** – false beliefs which defy logic. **Delusions of grandeur** – thinking they are kings or queens. **Paranoia** – belief they are being persecuted. **Delusions of control** – thinking other people are controlling them.

Negative symptoms	
Social symptoms	**Withdrawal** from social contact.
Cognitive symptoms	**Language impairments** such as **alogia** (excessively brief replies), jumbled, incoherent speech and **echolalia** (copying sounds). A person finds it hard to maintain a train of thought.
Affective symptoms	**Avolition** – fatigue-like symptoms with a lack of personal care and ability to make plans. **Lack of emotion** or inappropriate emotional responses, such as laughing when at a funeral.
Behavioural disturbances	**Stereotyped behaviours** – moving oddly with no obvious purpose. **Psychomotor disturbance** – not having control of your muscles, or staying in one position for a long time (catatonia).

The clinical interview

To get a diagnosis, the client would typically self-report symptoms in a clinical interview with a psychiatrist. The observations of a family member or friend would also be taken into account. Questions would be about everyday functioning, early life and childhood. It is usually several months before a diagnosis can confidently be made.
If the onset is sudden and severe, the client may be admitted to a mental hospital for their own safety and occasionally may be sectioned under the Mental Health Act (2007).

Now try this

Outline the clinical characteristics of schizophrenia.

Choose a few points from both positive and negative symptoms.

Had a look ☐ Nearly there ☐ Nailed it! ☐

Reliability of diagnosis

The reliability of a diagnosis reflects how **consistently** the symptoms of patients are used to make the same diagnosis. It is very important that diagnoses of mental illnesses are reliable because the patient needs to receive the right treatment.

Types of reliability

1 Test–retest reliability – on separate visits, the diagnosis remains the same.

2 Inter-rater reliability – this occurs when two different clinicians make the same diagnosis of the patient independently of each other.

Criteria for diagnosis

Two or more of the following groups of symptoms must be present for at least a month (see page 189):

☑ delusions

☑ hallucinations

☑ disorganised speech

☑ disorganised or catatonic behaviour

☑ negative symptoms such as alogia or avolition.

Research evidence

☑ Read et al. (2004) found a 37% concordance rate in test–retest reliability for schizophrenia. In this case, a concordance rate is an agreement rate between two clinicians.

☑ Jakobsen et al. (2005) found a concordance rate of 98% from a sample of 100 patients in Denmark, using the ICD-10 classification system produced by the World Health Organization (WHO).

☑ Söderberg et al. (2005) found a concordance rate of 81% using the DSM-4 classification.

These more recent studies seem to suggest that reliability has improved over time, as clinicians use diagnostic criteria which have become more detailed.

Causes of unreliability of diagnosis

Ward et al. (1962) identified three types of factors which affect the reliability of diagnosis.

1 Client/patient factors

- Clients may not be able to talk about their mental state clearly. They may feel ashamed and leave out information.

- The person (a relative) speaking on the client's behalf may have a vested interest in the diagnosis being made and minimise or maximise the severity.

- Atypical presentations mean that not all clients present with the textbook symptoms and they may not exactly fit the DSM criteria.

2 Clinician factors

- How well the clinical interview is conducted depends on the rapport with the client and how the semi-structured nature of the interview unfolds.

- How well the clinician is trained and where they were trained.

- What approach in psychology they follow.

- How much they rely on observation or tests.

3 Classification factors

- Differences between DSM and ICD (the WHO system) descriptors of the illness and which is used by the clinician.

- The use of DSM criteria for billing purposes in private medical bills may lead to a bias in use.

Evaluation

👍 Using a classification system improves diagnosis and, over time, this has become more refined as both DSM and ICD have been updated.

👍 Classification systems provide a common language for clinicians to communicate with their teams.

👍 Clients get the help they need through the correct treatment programme.

👎 The three sets of factors outlined by Ward et al. (1962) show that diagnosis is easily flawed.

👎 Getting the wrong psychiatric label could be devastating to the client, as a diagnosis of schizophrenia is often misunderstood by the general public and has employment implications.

Now try this

What is the difference between test–retest and inter-rater reliability when referring to the diagnosis of schizophrenia?

Validity of diagnosis

Validity is concerned with the **accuracy** of the diagnosis: is it the correct diagnosis?

Assessment of validity

1   **Predictive validity** will correctly predict the likely prognosis of the illness.

2   **Descriptive validity** refers to the symptoms of an illness being unique and distinct from another illness.

3   **Aetiological validity** refers to all the people with an illness appearing to experience it in a similar way.

🔍 Key study   On being sane in insane places

The **Rosenhan** (1973) study is a test of the validity of diagnosis. In 1973, the system in use was DSM-II which Rosenhan believed was not a valid measure for diagnosing schizophrenia.

Aim: To test the validity of DSM-II in identifying schizophrenia.

Procedure: Eight pseudo-patients presented at 12 mental hospitals in America, claiming to hear voices saying 'empty', 'hollow' and 'thud'. Once admitted, they acted normally. Time taken to release them and how they were treated was recorded as the DV.

Later, in a second study, a hospital was told to expect more pseudo-patients. The DV this time was how many 'fake patients' were identified. There were none.

Findings: The 8 pseudo-patients were admitted for between 7 and 52 days. On release, the diagnosis was schizophrenia in remission. Normal behaviour on the ward was seen as part of their illness. However, 35 out of 118 actual patients suspected that the pseudo-patients were sane.

In the second study, 83 out of 193 patients were thought to be fake when they were genuine.

Conclusions: The diagnosis of schizophrenia lacked validity at the time. The treatment of mental patients reflected an attitude that they were depersonalised. The label they were given at the start stuck, and this was reflective of society's attitude towards schizophrenia.

Evaluation

🔹 When the pseudo-patients turned up at the mental hospital, they were assumed to be ill as no-one would normally want to be admitted. This created an expectancy effect amongst the staff, so it is not really surprising they got admitted.

🔹 The study was unethical because the staff believed the patients. In addition, in the second study, patients with genuine needs were doubted or turned away.

Research evidence

☑ DSM-5 reflects the shift in the opinion of clinicians that it may not be possible to diagnose schizophrenia as a separate disorder because clients present with such different groupings of symptoms. This was supported by Jansson and Parnas (2007), who reviewed 92 studies that applied different definitions of schizophrenia to the same patient samples. They found that both ICD-10 and DSM-IV had reasonable reliability but only low validity, which suggests schizophrenia may not be a separate condition.

☑ Mason et al. (1997) followed 99 patients with schizophrenia over 13 years to see if the predictive validity of the main classification systems worked. They found that if they used the symptoms that were present over six months, there was good predictive validity.

☑ Jablensky (2010) concluded in his review paper that, for the time being, the clinical concept of schizophrenia is valid and supported by empirical evidence. Its multiple features form a broad syndrome with reasonable internal cohesion and a characteristic evolution over time.

Now try this

Discuss why it is difficult to reach a valid diagnosis of schizophrenia.

Co-morbidity

Co-morbidity refers to the **co-existence** of two separate conditions or illnesses at the same time. This complicates the diagnosis of mental illness and may mean that different treatment programmes are needed side by side. It also adds to the difficulty of making valid and reliable diagnoses.

Schizophrenia and OCD

It is common for someone with schizophrenia to also experience depression and/or obsessive–compulsive disorder (OCD). See page 54 to remind yourself about OCD.

The incidence of schizophrenia is 1%, while for OCD the prevalence rate is 3% of the population. In the population with schizophrenia, the reported prevalence of clinically significant obsessive–compulsive symptoms (OCS) ranges from 10–52%, and for OCD from 7.8–26%. This is far higher than chance and suggests it is a recognisable sub-group called **schizo–obsessive disorder** (Hwang and Hollander, 1993).

There is a strong suggestion that clozapine, one of the drugs used to treat schizophrenia, could be responsible for some of this. See page 202 for more on drug treatments.

Schizophrenia and depression

As depression shares some of the negative symptoms of schizophrenia, there is symptom overlap. See page 53 to remind yourself about depression. However, someone with major depression or bipolar disorder may also have psychosis, which overlaps with the positive symptoms of schizophrenia. This makes the descriptive validity of the conditions very difficult. It can also affect the predictive validity, because the primary diagnosis could be wrong and the treatment therefore also not ideal.

Buckley et al. (2008) reported that around 50% of clients with schizophrenia also had depression; 15% had co-morbid panic disorder and 29% had co-morbid post-traumatic stress disorder. An additional 47% had substance misuse problems.

Levels of risk

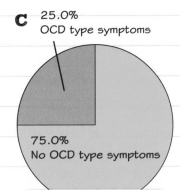

A 12.1% OCD type symptoms
87.9% No OCD type symptoms

B 17.1% OCD type symptoms
82.9% No OCD type symptoms

C 25.0% OCD type symptoms
75.0% No OCD type symptoms

This diagram shows the normal incidence in the population for OCD type symptoms.

Once a patient has experienced an episode of schizophrenia, the level of risk increases.

In full schizophrenia, levels reach 25%.

Evaluation

🖋 Jeste et al. (1996) point out that clients with co-morbid symptoms are in the majority and yet are left out of studies to try to control the sample. This will affect the generalisability of the studies because the findings will be limited to those with no co-morbid symptoms.

🖋 The high levels of co-morbid symptoms seen in schizophrenia suggest it is not a clearly defined mental illness, and there are problems with the validity of the diagnosis (see page 191).

🖋 The biggest challenge in schizophrenia diagnosis is telling it apart from bipolar disorder (manic depression). The latest DSM-5 has moved to make it a spectrum disorder, rather like autism, and has tried to remove the subtypes, which it suggests had become unhelpful.

🖋 Clearly there is some confusion in the diagnosis. This is compounded when clients also overuse alcohol or cannabis, which also leads to lower levels of functioning and a worse outcome for the client.

Now try this

Explain how experiencing a co-morbid illness could affect the diagnosis of schizophrenia.

Culture bias

Culture bias refers to the tendency to over-diagnose members of other ethnic groups as having schizophrenia because their typical behaviours might be seen as abnormal by clinicians. There could be, for example, communication issues because of how the client describes their symptoms and lifestyle.

Culture bias in the UK

In the UK, people are more likely to be diagnosed with schizophrenia if they are of African-Caribbean descent.

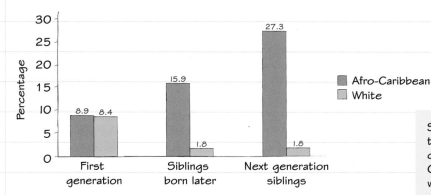

Sugarman and Craufurd (1994) found that, as successive generations came and settled in the UK from the Caribbean, their risk of being diagnosed with schizophrenia increased.

This data suggests that schizophrenia among the African-Caribbean population is no less genetic than for the remainder of the population, but that the increased frequency of the disorder is either due to environmental stress factors, which are more common in the African-Caribbean community, or there is bias in diagnosis from one culture to another.

Research evidence

✓ Kirkbride et al. (2008) contest the idea of bias because of the consistent pattern that has been found over successive generations, as in the study above. They concluded that migratory factors may be important.

✓ Whaley (2004) believes that it is cultural bias because each culture has a different way of expressing their symptoms, which could lead to misinterpretation by clinicians from another culture.

Evaluation

👍 The DSM-5 has a section that acknowledges there has been cultural bias in diagnosis in the past and calls attention to the clinician to understand that different cultures describe their illnesses in different ways. This should mean that diagnosis is fairer in future.

👍 In many cultures it is normal to claim to have heard voices or seen people who have recently died. Rack (1982) suggests that people showing this behaviour in the West are more likely to be seen as psychotic and diagnosed with schizophrenia.

👎 Cochrane and Sashidharan (1995) argue that racism and social deprivation experienced by immigrants are likely to affect mental health but that clinicians wrongly attribute this to their ethnicity.

👎 This does not explain why it is African-Caribbean people who stand out amongst immigrant populations as having a higher risk. Cochrane (1983) suggests that mothers in immigrant families to Western Europe may have caught influenza when they became pregnant. 'Flu is not a common illness in the Caribbean. The mothers would have had low immunity and it is now known that 'flu in pregnancy increases the risk by at least a quarter. Pregnant women are now routinely offered a 'flu vaccine to prevent this risk.

Now try this

Outline some factors that could explain why there is a much greater incidence of schizophrenia in the African-Caribbean population.

Gender bias

Schizophrenia was originally believed to have equal incidence in the male and female population. **Gender bias** is the tendency to ignore or exaggerate symptoms in both men and women, so that the true picture could become distorted. It is thought that gender bias could have masked the fact that women have a very different experience of schizophrenia than men.

Research evidence

Most recent studies are finding an increasing incidence of schizophrenia in the male population compared to the female one.

Incidence

✓ Castle et al. (1993) found that the male incidence was twice that of females using clearer diagnostic criteria from DSM-IV.

✓ Lewine et al. (1984) found that if clearer criteria were used, fewer females were diagnosed, suggesting that there may have been earlier bias towards women.

Age of onset

✓ There are clear differences in the age of onset, with males typically showing symptoms around their late teens and females in their mid-to-late 20s.

Hormones

✓ Female experience of schizophrenia in late onset (late 50s) is likely to be chronic and mild rather than acute. This could be linked to the menopause and indicates that oestrogen may protect women until the levels drop at menopause.

✓ Kulkarni et al. (2001) found that oestradiol (from oestrogen) added to anti-psychotic medication helped women more than the anti-psychotic alone.

Female
Less severe experience
Late onset
Atypical features experienced
Depressive symptoms
Favourable prognosis

Male
More severe experience
Earlier onset
Typical features experienced
Negative symptoms
Chronic experience of the illness

Castle et al. (1991) argue that these differences suggest there could be two separate conditions, questioning the validity of a schizophrenia diagnosis in women.

Evaluation

👍 Angermeyer and Kuhn (1988) in a review of 50 studies found that women had fewer re-hospitalisations, fewer admissions and shorter hospital stays. In their own study, Angermeyer et al. (1989) confirmed these impressions of a male–female difference.

👍 Seeman (1986) reviewed the early-1980s literature concerning gender differences in the social outcome of people with schizophrenia. She concluded that overall, women with schizophrenia live better lives than men with schizophrenia. A number of more recent studies (such as Goldstein, 1988) concur.

👎 The fact that there are clear differences in age of onset and how the illness is experienced by men and women suggests that there are problems with the validity of the diagnosis. Castle and Murray (1991) suggests that women experience 'affective psychosis' not schizophrenia.

👎 The differences between men and women in their experience of schizophrenia have been ignored until recently. It is now clear that women respond better to the medication and have a better outcome because they are typically in relationships and have support on onset of the condition.

Now try this

Consider the evidence for gender bias in diagnosing schizophrenia.

Symptom overlap

Symptom overlap occurs when the symptoms of two mental illnesses are very similar. It is particularly problematic between schizophrenia and bipolar disorder (see page 53). It can also occur with major depression, intoxication through drugs and autism (see page 183).

Schizophrenia and bipolar disorder

Schizoaffective disorder

Genetic influence

Shared genetic determinants

Genetic influence

Schizophrenia (negative symptoms)

Overlap (psychotic symptoms, chronic course, cognitive deficits)

Bipolar disorder

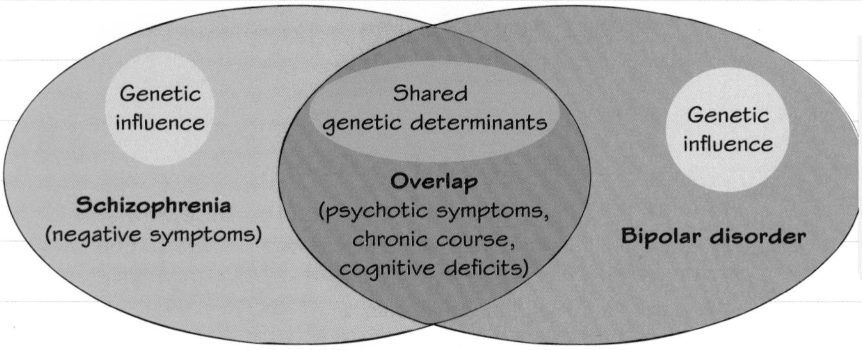

This diagram shows the extent of the symptom overlap with the positive symptoms of schizophrenia and the mania in a bipolar cycle. It is suggested that there may be a common genetic basis for this overlap.

Research evidence

Ripke et al. (2011) looked at 50 000 patients' genetic material. They found that of seven gene locations on the genome associated with schizophrenia, three were also associated with bipolar disorder, which suggested there was a genetic overlap between the two disorders.

Schizophrenia and autism

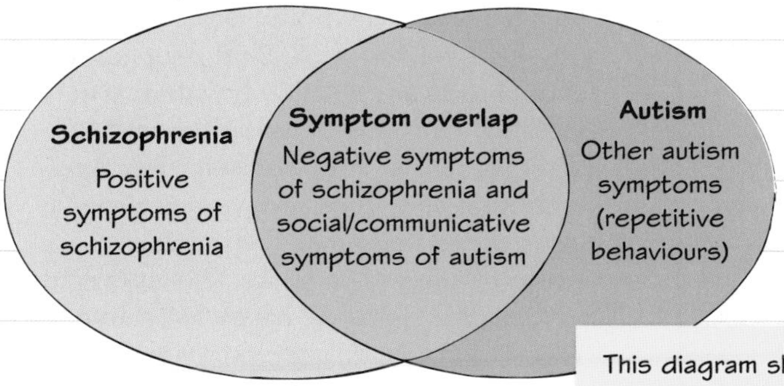

Schizophrenia
Positive symptoms of schizophrenia

Symptom overlap
Negative symptoms of schizophrenia and social/communicative symptoms of autism

Autism
Other autism symptoms (repetitive behaviours)

Research evidence

Konstantareas and Hewitt (2001) compared 14 people with autism and 14 people with schizophrenia. None of the people with schizophrenia had symptoms of autism but seven of the people with autism had symptoms of schizophrenia.

This diagram shows the overlap between the negative symptoms of schizophrenia and the social and communicative problems in autism. The positive symptoms are not shared.

Evaluation

- Genetic overlap between the conditions suggests that clusters of genes may one day be discovered to be responsible, opening the possibility of gene therapy.

- Neuroscience is showing clear differences in the brains of sufferers of schizophrenia, which are not shown in the other conditions or with drugs. As this is better understood, it is possible that scanning technology may ultimately help in diagnosis and there will be less symptom overlap.

- Ketter (2005) points out that misdiagnosis due to symptom overlap could lead to the wrong treatment and needless suffering or even suicide.

- The stickiness of labels and the negative association with a diagnosis of schizophrenia may make clinicians especially cautious. It is not uncommon for a client to have two possible diagnoses for a while until, over a period of months, the picture becomes clearer. This can cause frustration and worry.

Now try this

Explain the difference between co-morbidity and symptom overlap.

Genetic explanation for schizophrenia

Biological explanations for schizophrenia focus on genetics, abnormal dopamine functioning (see page 197) and neural correlates (see page 198). According to the **genetic explanation**, schizophrenia can be passed on through the genes.

Genetic influence

The risk for the general population of developing schizophrenia is less than 1%. If you have a close relative with schizophrenia, the risk increases to between 6 and 17%.

If you have an identical twin with schizophrenia, then your risk rises to 48%. This is suggestive of a genetic influence in developing the condition.

 ## Key study Gottesman and Shields (1976)

Aim: To review twin and adoption research over the previous 10 years.

Sample: 711 participants in the adoption studies; 210 monozygotic (identical, MZ) and 319 dizygotic (non-identical, DZ) twin pairs in the twin studies.

Procedure: A review article studying the incidence of schizophrenia in adopted children and MZ twins across several studies.

Results: There was an increased incidence of schizophrenia in adopted children with a biological parent with schizophrenia. One study by Kety (1968) found that siblings of children with schizophrenia showed a much higher percentage of schizophrenia. All twin studies found a higher concordance rate for schizophrenia in MZ than in DZ twins. In Gottesman and Shield's own study, the rate was 58% for MZ twins, and 12% for DZ twins.

Conclusion: There is a strong genetic input into the onset of schizophrenia. Concordance rates of less than 100%, however, show there must be some interaction with the environment, raising questions of nature vs nurture.

Research evidence

✓ Varma and Sharma (1993) reported a concordance rate of 34.78% in first-degree relatives (FDR) of people with schizophrenia and 9.2 in FDRs of controls. This suggests that there is a genetic component in schizophrenia.

✓ Kety et al. (1994) using an adoption study in Denmark and a sample of 155 families, found schizophrenia in nine adopted children, eight of whom had biological mothers either with schizophrenia or psychoses of some kind. This further supports the genetic evidence.

✓ The Schizophrenia Working Group (2014) analysed the DNA of 36 989 people with schizophrenia and 113 075 without and identified 128 genetic variations at 108 locations on the chromosomes implicated in schizophrenia. The associations were higher where the genes had a role in tissues relating to immunity. This supports the idea of a biological cause but also a link between the immune system and the condition.

Evaluation

👎 If genes were the sole cause of the condition, concordance rates would be 100% and they are not, so clearly there are other influences involved. Also, the wildly differing concordance rates suggest some caution is needed in accepting the results.

👎 Problems with twin studies mean that we cannot be certain that environment is not playing a part. For example, epigenetic modification means that some twins share the placenta and some do not, so from conception there are differences in environment.

👍 Findings from the genetic studies provide evidence for the diathesis-stress model (see page 206) which suggests that a predisposition to the illness is switched on by stress in the environment.

👍 Boklage (1977) found that when MZ twins were right-handed, the concordance rate for schizophrenia was 92%. If one was left-handed and one right-handed, the concordance rate fell to 25%. This shows a genetic influence but also that it is hard to compare studies 'like for like' as not all researchers will have controlled for handedness.

Now try this

Explain **two** challenges to the genetic explanation of schizophrenia.

The dopamine hypothesis

The **dopamine hypothesis** links the neurotransmitter **dopamine** to the onset of the condition.

The hypothesis

Dopamine works in the brain to stimulate the action of neurons at the synapse (see page 84). Some researchers believe that too much dopamine causes the onset of schizophrenia. They point to the fact that antipsychotic drugs that block dopamine via D2 receptors are effective in reducing the positive symptoms. Also, L-dopa – a drug which converts to dopamine and is given to patients with Parkinson's disease – creates schizophrenia-like symptoms. Hallucinogenic drugs such as LSD also create psychotic-type symptoms and they also work on the dopamine circuit.

Research evidence

✓ Davis et al. (1991) suggested that high levels of dopamine are not found in all individuals with schizophrenia. Clozapine, an antipsychotic drug which is effective in treating schizophrenia, does not block very much dopamine activity, shedding some doubt on the hypothesis. Davis further suggested that high levels of dopamine in the mesolimbic pathway are associated with positive symptoms, and high levels in the mesocortical pathway are associated with negative symptoms. This could therefore explain why not everyone is helped by the antipsychotic drugs.

✓ Javitt (2000) found that glycine, a glutamate receptor agonist, reversed drug-induced psychosis in rats and improved the symptoms of people with schizophrenia, suggesting that glutamate and dopamine have a connection in the condition.

An agonist is a substance that acts like another substance and therefore stimulates an action at the synapse.

✓ The suggestion is that glutamate normally prevents too much dopamine being released but in schizophrenia this action is not working as it should.

The dopamine mechanism

This is the brain's pleasure pathway (known as the mesocorticolimbic pathway). Dopamine is released whenever we do anything that makes us feel good and can lead to euphoria. This could possibly link with some of the symptoms of schizophrenia and bipolar disorder.

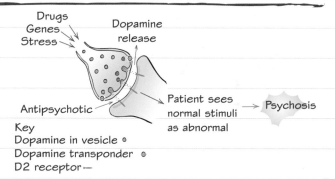

Key
Dopamine in vesicle ∘
Dopamine transponder ⊙
D2 receptor —

Howes and Kapur (2009) proposed that drug misuse, stress and genes could all increase levels of dopamine being released by the presynaptic vesicles at the synapse. The postsynaptic receptors are blocked by antipsychotics but the levels of dopamine are still too high in the synapse, creating the psychosis in which the person with schizophrenia interprets normal stimuli as abnormal.

Evaluation

👍 The dopamine hypothesis has generated huge amounts of research and driven drug treatments that have had some success in treating people with schizophrenia.

👍 It is now possible to indirectly measure dopamine levels through scanning technology, using radiolabelled L-dopa to compare healthy people with those with schizophrenia.

👎 It has been criticised as over-simplistic and inconclusive. We now know that more than just dopamine is involved in the condition. And this does not explain the negative symptoms of schizophrenia.

👎 Healy (2000) suggested that drug companies have a vested interest in promoting the dopamine hypothesis because they stand to make huge profits from the antipsychotics.

Now try this

To what extent can excess dopamine levels explain the symptoms of schizophrenia?

Neural correlates

A third **biological explanation** for schizophrenia focuses on **neural correlates**. New advances in scanning technology have allowed the brains of individuals with schizophrenia to be scanned and certain differences have been noted between their brains and the brains of healthy individuals. These are neural correlates and, as the name suggests, this is correlational data and not causal data. The cause-and-effect relationship has still to be established.

Ventricular differences

Post-mortem research has identified differences in the ventricles of the brains of people with schizophrenia.

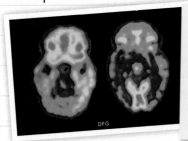

Andreasen et al. (1990) conducted a controlled CAT scan study and found significant enlargement of the ventricles in those with schizophrenia compared to controls.

Enlarged ventricles suggest damage to the central brain areas and prefrontal cortex. This could account for the negative symptoms of people with schizophrenia.

Wernicke's area differences

Hoffman and Hampson (2012) have attempted to explain auditory verbal hallucinations (AVHs). This study suggests that the core mechanism producing AVHs involves a complex functional loop. Components of this loop include Wernicke's area (see page 86), the left inferior frontal cortex and the putamen. The putamen appears to play a critical role in the generation of spontaneous language, and in determining whether auditory stimuli are registered consciously as real or not. Excessive activity seen in the Wernicke's region in people with schizophrenia could, therefore, generate an overabundance of potentially conscious language representations, explaining the voices.

Amygdala differences

Li et al. (2010) showed in a meta-analysis that the bilateral amygdala and right fusiform gyri were less active in schizophrenia patients. This area of the brain is used for processing faces and the lower activity could explain the difficulties experienced by the patients in this respect.

This image shows the gradual diminishing of cortical activity as the patient experiences the negative symptoms and often becomes less active. Early medication can slow this thinning of the cortex as the patient maintains a more active lifestyle.

Grey matter differences

Grey matter differences are found in schizophrenia patients over time.

Earliest deficiency

5 years later

Low deficiency
0%
-5%
-10%
-15%
-20%
High deficiency

Evaluation

🔍 Not all people with schizophrenia show enlarged ventricles, which again raises doubts that it is a single condition.

🔍 The effect of medication needs considering. Antipsychotic drugs are typically sedative and taken for life. While this means patients are more able to have a normal life, they have damaging long-term side effects, which could be seen in the brain imaging studies. The research does not usually mention this.

🔍 Co-morbid factors such as addiction and stress need to be considered as confounding variables in many patients. These will also affect brain tissue.

🖊 Ho et al. (2003) have shown, by re-scanning patients, that brain differences increase over time as symptoms worsen – despite being on medication. This helps establish a stronger causal relationship.

🖊 The evidence is building to find a more complete explanation for schizophrenia. It is possible that more certainty over diagnosis and treatment is coming.

Now try this

What does the research evidence suggest about the neural correlates and structural differences in schizophrenia?

Family dysfunction explanation

Psychological explanations for schizophrenia focus on **family dysfunction** and **cognitive explanations** (see page 200). This page considers family dysfunction.

Family dysfunction

The family dysfunction explanation is concerned with sources of **stress**, which can bring on problems with people who have a genetic predisposition to schizophrenia. This is called the **diathesis-stress model** (see page 206). Sometimes the source of the stress is within the family. In addition, having a child with schizophrenia is very upsetting to the family. This makes it difficult to be certain of which comes first.

Why stress is harmful

Stress releases cortisol, a hormone that causes multiple effects on the body through the fight-or-flight response (see page 227). In the long term, these effects are harmful physically and mentally – they cause stress, anxiety and depression, which could be the forerunner for the prodromal or pre-symptom phase of schizophrenia.

Research evidence

Patino et al. (2005) conducted a cross-sectional study with 3426 children and adolescents looking at family dysfunction and migration history. They recorded family dysfunction when at least three of the following problems were reported:

- ✓ poor relationship between adults in the household
- ✓ lack of warmth between parents and child
- ✓ overt disturbance of father–child relationship
- ✓ overt disturbance of mother–child relationship
- ✓ overt disturbance of sibling–child relationship
- ✓ parental overprotection
- ✓ child abuse.

The presence of both migration history and family dysfunction was associated with a fourfold (95% confidence interval) risk of psychotic symptoms compared with their absence or either on their own, suggesting a cumulative effect when they interact. Migration history alone approximately doubled the risk.

Other studies

Tienari et al. (2004) found that 36.8% of high-genetic risk adoptees living in a dysfunctional family environment developed a schizophrenia-spectrum disorder, compared to only 5.3% of those in a healthy family environment. This suggests that people with a high genetic risk for schizophrenia-spectrum disorders receive a protective effect from a healthy family environment.

Bateson's double-bind hypothesis

A double bind is a set of contradictory positions, both of which have a negative consequence.
For example, a mother tells her child that she loves him/her, while at the same time turning away in disgust (the words are socially acceptable; the body language is in conflict with it). The child does not know how to respond to the conflict, so he/she is in a quandary.

Bateson (1972) hypothesised that growing up in this high negative-emotion environment could lead to psychosis.

Kavanagh (1992) conducted a review of 26 studies of schizophrenia patients who returned home after hospitalisation. Those returning to high-emotion families had a mean relapse rate of 48% compared to 21% in low-emotion families. This supports Bateson's hypothesis.

Evaluation

- 👎 Having a person with schizophrenia in the family is very stressful and can create high emotional states and conflicts. Therefore, it is difficult to establish which comes first – the dysfunctional family or the dysfunctional child.

- 👎 This explanation fails to explain why not all children in dysfunctional families develop schizophrenia.

- 👍 Family therapy has been shown to be effective in achieving a more positive outcome in patients with schizophrenia, which supports the theory.

- 👍 Expressed emotions (EE) is a communication style that involves criticism, hostility and emotional over-involvement. A patient returning to a family with high EE is about four times more likely to relapse than a patient whose family is low in EE (Linszen et al. 1997).

Now try this

Describe what is meant by a dysfunctional family and explain how it could affect the development of schizophrenia.

Cognitive explanations

Cognitive explanations of schizophrenia focus on faulty thinking as an explanation for the symptoms. Voices, for example, are seen as misperceptions instead of 'inner speech', which we all experience. Hallucinations are seen as biased information processing, while negative symptoms are seen as control strategies to try to manage the high levels of mental stimulation being experienced.

Research evidence

Much research has investigated the idea of cognitive deficits underlying the difficulties faced by schizophrenia patients, particularly in memory, attention, motor skills, executive function and intelligence.

Elevag and Goldberg (2000)

- Cognitive explanation assumption
- Cognitive deficits are caused by faulty thinking by the patients, which could have an underlying biological cause.

We are normally able to filter information but this appears to be difficult for people with schizophrenia.

- Schizophrenia is better explained by cognitive deficits rather than symptoms.
- Memory and attention are the main core deficits, providing support for the theory.

- Takahashi et al. (2013) got people with and without schizophrenia to listen to tones and to try to tell them apart.
- Schizophrenia patients found this very difficult.

This could be because they find it hard to rapidly encode new information or selectively attend to information.

Beck and Rector (2005) proposed a **cognitive model** in which there is an interaction of environmental, neurobiological, behavioural and cognitive factors that lead to cognitive deficits.

In support, Bowie and Harvey (2006) found that cognitive impairments were a core feature of schizophrenia, mainly affecting attention, working memory, verbal learning and executive function.

These impairments are present before the illness progresses and are always found. Further support came from the fact that, once treated, some of these deficits were seen to reduce.

Evaluation

- Cognitive theories do not explain the cause of schizophrenia or what has led to the deficits.

- If the explanation for hallucinations is biased information processing, it ought to be possible to persuade a person with schizophrenia of the reality. In fact, it is extremely difficult to shift their thinking.

- It can explain both positive and negative symptoms, which is a strength.

- In combination with biological treatments, it can lead to an effective therapy.

- Harvey et al. (2004) argue that a possible unifying factor for effective treatment is cognitive functioning, which is impaired in people with schizophrenia. Treatment of cognitive dysfunction may have a central role in increasing the breadth of effective treatment for schizophrenia. They speculate that new drugs will be found that improve cognitive functioning and therefore the outlook for people with schizophrenia.

Now try this

1 Suggest a suitable method and design for a study to investigate differences in memory between patients with schizophrenia and healthy participants.

2 Suggest a suitable task for your study and justify it.

Dysfunctional thought processing

Dysfunctional thought processing is an important part of the **cognitive explanation** of schizophrenia. Healthy people are able to use **metacognition** to guide their thinking and problem solving. Metacognition is a person's awareness of how they are thinking and feeling and their knowledge of when they have made an error. In schizophrenia, people lose this awareness resulting in **cognitive dysfunction**. This particularly presents itself in the positive symptoms, where they lose touch with reality.

Research evidence

☑ Joshua et al. (2009) used the **Hayling sentence completion task** (see opposite) to compare people with bipolar disorder and schizophrenia against healthy controls. They found that the people with schizophrenia were slower to respond and also slower in suppressing the inappropriate responses when compared to healthy control participants. They also made more errors. There were some differences with the bipolar group. The bipolar disorder group did not differ in performance compared to the healthy control group. Performance of the people with schizophrenia was associated with higher ratings of cognitive disorganisation. Performance was not related to age, gender, predicted IQ or any other clinical characteristics.

☑ Evans et al. (1997) used **BADS** (see opposite), IQ tests and memory tests on 31 people with schizophrenia, 35 brain-injured and 26 healthy participants. The individuals with schizophrenia and brain damage had impaired executive functioning. Those with schizophrenia showed problems in memory as well. This provides more evidence that schizophrenia disrupts thinking.

☑ Brune et al. (2011) found evidence in a meta-analysis over 20 years of research that supported the idea that schizophrenia impaired metacognition, leaving patients with impairments in social functioning, self-reflection and empathy.

Hayling sentence completion task

In the test, the participant has to provide the final word of a sentence as fast as they can.
For example, 'He mailed the letter without a … (participant says) stamp.'

In the second part, participants are required to verbally generate a word that was inappropriate and unconnected to the sentence in every way.
For example, 'The captain wanted to stay with the sinking … (participant says) banana.'

Therefore, participants had to first suppress or inhibit a strongly activated response (*ship*) before they could generate a new, unconnected one (*banana*). Participants' response times for both sections were collected using a stopwatch. As a result, this test has high inter-rater reliability and test–retest reliability (see page 190) and is believed to be a valid measure of cognitive performance.

BADS

The Behavioural Assessment of the Dysexecutive Syndrome (BADS) test is a set of tasks that assess the skills and demands involved in everyday life. It shows up difficulties with frontal lobe damage.

The client will do seven different activities as part of the test, ranging from estimating the length of a dental appointment to using a zoo map to find a circuit which would view a selection of animals, to solving a practical problem of getting a cork out of a narrow bottle.

Evaluation

👍 If a clear idea of the problems with metacognition can be established, then patients can be treated and helped to overcome these deficits. As usual, the research shows a variety of responses in many areas of functioning, which makes this difficult.

👎 Metacognition is invisible. It is investigated by observing a participant's behaviour on various tests such as the two above. This raises the question of how valid and reliable the tests are.

Now try this

Briefly discuss the difficulties of investigating dysfunctional thinking in patients with schizophrenia.

Drug therapy

People with schizophrenia are usually offered **antipsychotic** medication, which helps with the positive symptoms, such as hallucinations and delusions. Antipsychotic drugs fall into two types: first-generation **'typical'** older drugs, which were developed in the 1950s, and second-generation **'atypical'** newer drugs, developed since the 1990s. Their use is controversial but essential for many patients to remain out of hospital.

Typical vs atypical antipsychotic drugs

	Typical	Atypical
Examples	Chlorpromazine Fluphenazine Haloperidol	Clozapine Quetiapine Olanzapine
Mode of action	Blocks dopamine receptors and reduces levels of excitation via dopamine in the synapse. It also affects the cholinergic system, causing a variety of side effects.	Acts on serotonin and dopamine systems (in the case of clozapine).
Effectiveness	Works to reduce the levels of hallucinations and delusions in some people. Does not affect negative symptoms.	Works on positive and negative symptoms (with clozapine).
Key side effects	Dry mouth and blocked nose Urinary problems Problems with sexual function Tardive dyskinesia (facial twitching)	Weight gain, diabetes, cardiovascular conditions such as stroke and myocarditis. Agranulocytosis is a risk with clozapine (reduced white blood cell count requiring regular blood tests).

Overall effectiveness of antipsychotics

Smith et al. (2010) point out that antipsychotic medication can reduce the positive symptoms of psychosis in about 8–15 days. However, they often fail to significantly improve the negative symptoms and cognitive dysfunction. Which drug to use for a specific patient is based on benefits, risks and costs. Both typical and atypical drugs have equal subject attrition and symptom relapse rates when used at low to moderate dosages. There is a good response in 40–50% of patients, a partial response in 30–40% and treatment resistance (failure to respond satisfactorily after six weeks to two of three different antipsychotics) in the remaining 20%. Clozapine is an effective treatment for those who respond poorly to other drugs, but it has the potentially serious side effect of agranulocytosis in 1–4% of patients and has to be constantly monitored through blood tests.

Evaluation

👍 Davis et al. (1989) found that antipsychotics were more effective than placebos in a meta-analysis of over 100 studies: 75% of patients improved against 25% on the placebo.

👍 Marder (1996) found that clozapine was as effective as typical antipsychotics for positive symptoms, helping 30–61% of patients who were resistant to typical antipsychotics.

👎 Lieberman (2005) found that 74% of 1432 individuals discontinued treatment within 18 months because of the side effects. Typical drugs caused muscular disorders whereas atypical drugs caused more weight gain.

👎 This is socially sensitive research. Some argue that these drugs are used to sedate people as a measure of social control to make them easier to manage and deprive them of free will, instead of working more actively with them, which would be more costly and time-consuming.

Now try this

How do antipsychotic medications work to help people with schizophrenia?

Cognitive behaviour therapy

Recent research has suggested that psychotic disorders could be seen as distortions of a person's perceptions and so could have a cognitive explanation. If this is true, it should be possible to help individuals logically deal with their hallucinations and delusions, to see them for what they are and live with them under control. This is done using **cognitive behavioural therapy** (CBT).

CBT treatment applied to schizophrenia

The **ABC model** of treatment was first created by Ellis (1957) for people suffering with depression (see page 59). Applied to people with schizophrenia, it follows six stages.

1 Assessment – patient expresses his/her own thoughts about their experiences while the therapist listens actively. The use of rating scales – both specific and general – is encouraged to monitor progress.

2 Engagement – the use of Socratic questioning (drawing out understanding) and empathy creates a therapeutic relationship.

3 ABC model – the use of the model allows the patient to organise their thoughts and feelings.

Activating event	Beliefs	Consequence
Voices	'Voices are constantly mean and hostile' 'You will never believe what I say' 'I will never be able to do what I want to again'	Emotions Sorrow Depression Loneliness Desperation Behaviour Isolation

The ABC model applied to schizophrenia by Kingdon and Turkington (2006).

4 Goal-setting – realistic goals for therapy are discussed with the patient early in their treatment, using the distressing consequences (C) to fuel the motivation for change. It is the therapist's job to ensure that the goals are measurable, realistic and achievable. The goals are revisited both during and at the end of treatment.

5 Normalising – de-catastrophising psychotic experiences. Psychotic experiences are placed on a continuum with normal experiences, making the possibility of recovery seem less distant.

6 Critical collaborative analysis – Once trust is formed, gentle questioning is used to help the patient appreciate maladaptive beliefs.

7 Developing alternative assumptions – the patient should develop their own alternatives to previous maladaptive assumptions, preferably by looking for alternative explanations and coping strategies already present in his/her mind.

 Key study **A comparison study by Sensky et al. (2000)**

Aim: To compare CBT with non-specific befriending interventions.

Method: A randomised controlled trial with 97 patients in the UK who were non-responsive to medication. They received a mean of 19 sessions over 9 months.

Procedure: The CBT group experienced the above seven stages. The befriending group had the same time with a therapist who was empathetic but did not try to treat them, talking about daily activities and hobbies instead. Patients were assessed by 'blind' raters at baseline, at the end of the 9 months of treatment and 9 months after that, using recognised scales.

Results: Both groups improved in both positive and negative symptoms and there was no difference at the end of the treatment phase. However, at follow up, the CBT group showed great improvement whilst the befriending group had lost some benefits.

Conclusion: CBT has significant and lasting benefits for both positive and negative symptoms of schizophrenia.

Evaluation of functional recovery

👍 Works in combination with drug therapy and is more effective than either treatment on its own. NICE guidelines recommend the combination for suitable patients.

👍 Requires a skilled therapist who is used to working with patients with psychosis.

👎 CBT is not suitable for all patients. People with extreme agitation will not be able to rationalise or empathise with a therapist.

👎 Trower et al. (2004) suggest that CBT provides strategies for dealing with schizophrenia rather than treating the symptoms.

Now try this

What is meant by a randomised controlled trial as used by Sensky et al. (2000)?

Had a go ☐ Nearly there ☐ Nailed it! ☐

Family therapy

One of the psychological explanations for schizophrenia is dysfunctional families (see page 199). Returning home to a high expressed emotion (EE) environment causes more relapses in the schizophrenia patient. **Family therapy** attempts to combat this and help the family find more positive ways of dealing with the stress of life with a family member with schizophrenia.

Goals of family therapy

Give the family all the information they need to understand the illness.

Help the family understand they are not to blame for the illness.

Help the family come to terms with the behaviour of the patient, which can be frustrating or frightening.

Goals of family therapy

Encourage discussion about what it is like to live with a family member with schizophrenia to share support.

Help the person with the illness move forward and stay as normal as possible.

Get everyone's voice heard to reduce tension in the family.

Family therapy takes place over many sessions, usually in a patient's home, but it can be done in a group session with several families taking part.

Research evidence

✓ Pilling et al. (2002) compared family therapy to other types of treatment in a meta-analysis of 18 studies with 1467 patients. They found that patients who experienced family therapy had the fewest relapses and hospital admissions and the best compliance with their medication, supporting the view that treating the whole family is beneficial.

✓ A recent meta-analysis conducted by Bird et al. (2010) showed that family interventions in early psychosis significantly reduced relapse and readmission rates.

✓ Caqueo-Urízar et al. (2015), in a review article, highlighted the burden placed on the family when caring for the patient with schizophrenia. Without support, the caregivers frequently experience stress and isolation. However, with family intervention and support there are some positives gained by the experience.

Evaluation

👍 Families need to be involved with the treatment of schizophrenia. Frequently they provide the most valuable information to the clinician whereas the patients may deny they are ill.

👍 Younger patients will still be at home and so their parents will be the caregivers and will benefit from the support of family therapy.

👎 The cuts in hospital beds and shortage of clinicians with long waits for appointments can place an intolerable burden on a family where the patient is very ill.

👎 Although there is evidence that drug therapy with family therapy is very effective, it is often the case that patients get drug therapy alone because it is cheaper and can be managed by GPs.

Now try this

Briefly discuss the effectiveness of family therapy for treating schizophrenia.

Token economies

Token economies are based on the behaviourist philosophy of Skinner's (1936) theory of operant conditioning, which states that behaviour can be shaped by the use of positive and negative reinforcers. These could be primary reinforcers such as food and drink or secondary reinforcers such as a token or money which can be exchanged for a primary reinforcer (see page 269). They are used in hospitals to help institutionalised people with schizophrenia to gain more control over their daily lives and increase positive behaviours.

An example of a token economy

In the Meadowview Unit in Clinton Valley Center, Michigan, USA (1988–91), a token economy point system provided an organised and structured programme that emphasised and reinforced positive behaviour. The staff's primary focus was to observe and reinforce desired behaviour although patient participation was voluntary. Points were only given (never taken away) and the participants were never threatened with losing points. Rewards for specific criteria were given only when met, and included verbal praise, points and backup reinforcers from the token store.

Getting up within 10 minutes
of being called . . . . 5 points

Showering using soap, drying
off and leaving the shower area
clean and in a reasonable time . 5 points

Shaving on a daily basis . . . . . 5 points

Brushing teeth twice a day . . . 5 points

Combing hair so that it looks tidy 5 points

Points award system examples

Ice cream	25
Puzzle books	75
Yogurt	35
Deodorant	75
Shampoo	75
Canned drink	30
Toothpaste	30
Crisps	30
Soap	30
Socks	25
Chocolate bar	15
T-shirt	75

A few examples of exchange values in the token store

Research evidence

✓ McMonagle and Sultana (2000) conducted a meta-analysis of token economy programmes and found some evidence for progress with the negative symptoms of schizophrenia.

✓ Dickerson at al. (2005) found further support for token economies helping patients to become more independent when they were used with other treatments such as drug therapy.

Evaluation

👍 All staff can award tokens for participation and attendance as well as other activities of achieving daily independence and subsequent progress within the hospital community. There is no need for specialist training.

👍 The token system provides a positive means for motivating and at times controlling behaviour.

👍 From a psychiatric perspective, token systems provide a means of monitoring the progress of the patient. The patient may also get some indirect intrinsic satisfaction with their progress.

👍 Token economies are behaviourist programmes that work best with institutionalised patients in long-term psychiatric care.

👎 The programme is staff intensive and demands resources and sufficient time to fully establish and use statistics.

👎 The patients become dependent upon receiving points to perform daily tasks, thus coupling point reinforcers with secondary reinforcers such as praise and attention is essential. Reinforcement is only extrinsic and does not change a person's internal state.

👎 The token programme requires continuous ongoing dedication, cooperation and scheduling of all disciplines on all three shifts, which at times is not easy to consistently obtain and does not exist outside of the hospital.

👎 A token economy is always used in combination with other treatments and is not a treatment programme in itself.

👎 They can be seen as demeaning and there is an issue of social power with a risk of abuse of power and withholding of basic needs if the staff is so inclined.

Now try this

Describe some limitations of token economy programmes used for patients with schizophrenia.

Interactionist approach

An **interactionist approach** explains schizophrenia through a combination of factors, including psychological, biological and social. Similarly, interactionist treatments combine biological and psychological or psychosocial therapies. It is normally referred to as the biopsychosocial perspective.

Interactionist explanations of schizophrenia

According to the **diathesis-stress model**, many factors interact to explain schizophrenia. A diathesis is an inherited risk or condition.

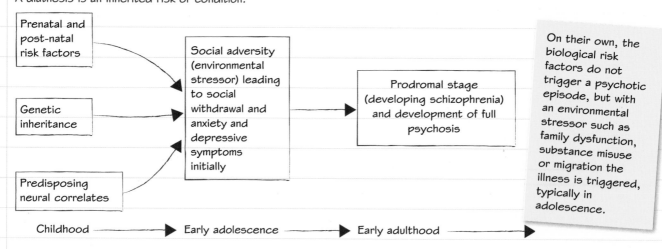

On their own, the biological risk factors do not trigger a psychotic episode, but with an environmental stressor such as family dysfunction, substance misuse or migration the illness is triggered, typically in adolescence.

Interactionist treatments for schizophrenia

Research has shown that where two or more treatments are used together the effectiveness is increased, which is not surprising with such a complex illness with many symptoms.

Mindfulness (training in meditation) for treating the positive symptoms

Anti-depressants for treating the negative symptoms – this is called combination therapy

Assertive community therapy for getting patients back to work and into the community

Antipsychotics with…

Family therapy for those with dysfunctional family problems

CBT for treating the positive and negative symptoms

Drug therapy is usually the first course of treatment and is given before the others to stabilise the patient.

Research evidence

✓ Murray and Lewis (1987) proposed a neurodevelopmental model to explain schizophrenia. It puts life events at its heart and ties in with the research evidence on migration and childhood abuse in dysfunctional families, which is known to multiply risk.

✓ Barlow and Durand (2009) found support for the diathesis-stress model with the diathesis being the genetic inheritance and the stress being the dysfunctional family.

✓ Hogarty et al. (1986) looked at relapse rates of schizophrenia patients: drug therapy alone had a relapse rate of 41%, but with family therapy it improved to 19% and with social support therapy to 20%.

✓ Sudak (2011) found that compliance with antipsychotic medication improved when patients were also given CBT, which helped them to see benefits.

Now try this

Evaluate the diathesis-stress model of schizophrenia.

Exam skills 1

Before you look at the worked examples, remind yourself about the diagnosis and classification of schizophrenia (pages 189–195). Mind-map all the topics that could come into the answers to these questions.

Worked example

Briefly outline the clinical characteristics of schizophrenia. **(4 marks)**

The symptoms of schizophrenia can be divided into positive and negative. The positive symptoms are additional experiences which a normal person would not have, such as delusions and hallucinations. The negative symptoms describe a lack of normal experiences, such as social withdrawal, anhedonia, apathy, personal neglect and flattening of emotional response. Delusions are experiences where the patient has a loss of control over their own thoughts, possibly feeling paranoiac. Hallucinations can be auditory (hearing voices) and/or visual (seeing things that are not there).

It is a good idea to look at the language used by examiners on past papers. 'Clinical characteristics' means **symptoms**, which makes this a straightforward question if you recognise it as such.

You have been asked to 'outline' so you must do more than list the symptoms. The level of detail here is about right.

Worked example

Explain why schizophrenia is difficult to diagnose. **(4 marks)**

Schizophrenia is difficult to diagnose for a variety of reasons, including co-morbidity and symptom overlap. Quite often a patient has more than one illness at the same time such as schizophrenia with obsessive–compulsive disorder (OCD). This makes it very difficult to clearly identify a set of symptoms that are unique to the illness.

In the population with schizophrenia, the reported prevalence of clinically significant obsessive compulsive symptoms (OCS) and of OCD ranges from 10–52% and from 7.8–26% respectively. This is far higher than chance and suggests that there could be a sub-group called schizo–obsessive disorder (Hwang and Hollander, 1993). Similarly, symptom overlap occurs with other mental illnesses. For example, Konstantareas and Hewitt (2001) compared 14 people with autism and 14 patients with schizophrenia, finding that none of the people with schizophrenia had symptoms of autism but that seven of the people with autism had symptoms of schizophrenia. The symptoms that overlapped were the negative ones. In addition, the positive symptoms of schizophrenia overlap with the mania of bipolar disorder. All this makes a single diagnosis very difficult.

To answer an 'explain' question, you need to provide some detail and examples.

Focus on the difficulties only, and remember your time limits – spend no more than 5 minutes on a 4-mark question.

There is potentially a lot of choice for the difficulties of diagnosis. For example, you could discuss reliability, validity, and gender and culture bias. In this answer, two others are used – co-morbidity and symptom overlap. A mind map of the topic would be helpful for selecting your final choice of factors on which to focus.

Exam skills 2

You could be asked to apply your knowledge of methodology anywhere in the paper. You could also be asked to interpret data and apply knowledge of how science works. Before you look at the last worked example, remind yourself about drug therapy for schizophrenia (page 202).

Worked example

Gottesman and Shields (1976) reviewed five twin studies and found a concordance rate among identical twins of between 75 and 91%.

(a) What is a concordance rate?   **(2 marks)**

A concordance rate tells us what level of agreement there is between a set of twins who have identical genetic risk of schizophrenia. The higher the concordance rate, the more likely it is that the condition is inherited.

For 2 marks, make a point and briefly expand it.

Worked example

(b) If schizophrenia was an entirely hereditable condition, the concordance rate would be 100%.

Suggest **two** reasons why not all twins inherit the disorder.

(4 marks)

This question is all about application of your knowledge, both of factors that are known to explain schizophrenia and also the problems of twin studies.

Not all twins inherit schizophrenia equally because there are always some environmental variations in their lives. Firstly, even in the womb, monozygotic foetal twins often share a common maternal circulation, which may disadvantage one as compared to the other, and lead to increased discordance in these twin pairs. Typically, twins are born premature and birth complications might affect one twin more than the other. These are known to have an influence. Secondly, individual variations in personality could also be a factor. One twin may be less anxious than the other and therefore respond more robustly to stress and expressed emotion in the family while the other feels the strain.

Worked example

Briefly outline a difference between typical and atypical antipsychotics for the treatment of schizophrenia.   **(2 marks)**

In this question, there are many possibilities. Use a simple example and save your thinking time for longer questions.

One difference between typical and atypical antipsychotics is that typical antipsychotics primarily target dopamine receptors and the other systems such as the cholinergic systems, causing a range of unpleasant side effects. Atypical antipsychotics, on the other hand, work on dopamine and serotonin production and seem to be more effective against the negative symptoms.

Knowing how antipsychotics work is very useful for many question styles.

Exam-style practice 1

Practise for Paper 3 of your A level exam with these exam-style questions. There are answers on page 310. Some questions require more extensive prose and more thought and application of knowledge. Try to keep these answers strictly timed. You will always get the most marks by attempting every question on the topic.

1 Discuss the reliability and validity of diagnosing schizophrenia.

(16 marks)

> Note that this question is about diagnosis and not explanations or treatments, so keep your answer relevant.

2 Read the item and then answer the question that follows.

> Some researchers have suggested that teaching people with schizophrenia to meditate would help them control their auditory and/or visual hallucinations. They have already obtained a sample of 40 volunteers who are all currently medicated with antipsychotic drugs but still experience the unpleasant symptoms.

Outline a procedure for a study to investigate the effectiveness of meditation for treatment of the positive symptoms of schizophrenia.

(8 marks)

> Procedures tell us what the participants actually have to do once they are part of a study, so you can assume that you already have your sample, even if it is not stated, as in this example.

> To answer this question, think about the following.
> - How will you allocate participants to the meditation condition, and what will be your control?
> - How many sessions, how long and will they be in a groups?
> - How will you assess the baseline condition and then the change you hope to see?
> - How will you control for extraneous variables?
> - How will you avoid experimenter bias?

3 Read the item and then answer the question that follows.

> Our psychological well-being depends on a huge array of things in addition to our genes and our parents, from how our classmates treated us at school, to whether or not we encounter abuse and trauma in our lives, to government economic policies … As the British Psychological Society recently put it …: 'The precise combination of causes will be different for each person. No professional can ever say with certainty what has caused one particular individual to have certain experiences.' We would do well to remember that before attributing blame to either genes or parents.

Briefly outline and explain why parents have been blamed for their children developing schizophrenia.

(8 marks)

> Aim to write a clear argument, with good use of psychological terms and the correct citation of research.

4 Read the item and then answer the questions that follow.

> 'There is increasing reason to doubt the usefulness of the diagnosis "schizophrenia". The term has been used as a catch-all for an assortment of unusual thoughts and feelings that often have no intrinsic connections, and aren't qualitatively different from those experienced by the general population.' (Daniel and Jason Freeman, *The Guardian*, 7 March 2014)

> For relevant research to include in your answer, look at family dysfunction (page 199).

(a) Briefly explain **one** limitation of an accurate or useful diagnosis of schizophrenia.

(2 marks)

> Think about what prevents an accurate diagnosis. There are many different ways this could be answered, but the quote is directing you towards the more recent idea that schizophrenia is a syndrome and not a single condition or that there is symptom overlap.

(b) Briefly explain **one** limitation of taking a biological approach to treating schizophrenia.

(2 marks)

5 Discuss the nature–nurture debate in relation to schizophrenia.

(16 marks)

> This question gives you a clear focus. Aim for balance, include research evidence and come to a reasoned conclusion. There is no need for lots of description; concentrate on the findings and conclusions of the research.

> This question leads you to think of problems in drug therapy, which is the biological approach.

Exam-style practice 2

Practise for Paper 3 of your A level exam with these exam-style questions. Several types of questions are covered to help you. There are answers on page 312.

6   The graph shows the results of a double-blind drugs trial.

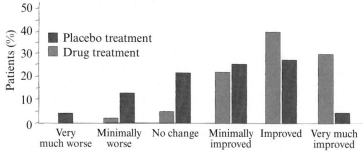

Patients (%) vs Very much worse, Minimally worse, No change, Minimally improved, Improved, Very much improved

Placebo treatment / Drug treatment

> Improvement in patients with schizophrenia following treatment with an antipsychotic drug or placebo during a six-week period.

7   **(a)** Briefly explain why double-blind drug trials use a placebo.

(2 marks)

> Remember that a double-blind trial is a trial where neither the clinician nor the patients know what they are taking – the antipsychotic drug or the placebo.

(b) Outline **two** conclusions you can draw from the graph about the effectiveness of the drug compared to the placebo.   **(2 marks)**

> Using the graph, look for the pattern in the two groups. Use the scale to assess the amount of change.

(c) Briefly explain why the placebo drug allowed more than 20% of the sample to improve.   **(2 marks)**

> You need a good grasp of the dopamine mechanism, so review it on page 197.

8   Explain the link between the dopamine hypothesis and antipsychotic medication.   **(8 marks)**

9   Briefly outline and explain the neural correlates of schizophrenia.   **(8 marks)**

> When you **outline** the neural correlates, you describe what they look like. When you **explain** them, you explain how they function to cause or explain schizophrenia.

10 Explain the cognitive explanation of schizophrenia, and outline **one** strength and **one** limitation of this explanation.   **(8 marks)**

> Try to balance the strength and limitation equally, and use evidence to support your points even though the question does not ask for it.

11 Compare **two** explanations for schizophrenia.   **(16 marks)**

12 Discuss **two** examples of bias in the diagnosis of schizophrenia.

(16 marks)

> 'Compare' questions require you to find similarities and differences. The easiest way to do this is by choosing a series of issues and using them to make your comparisons and contrasts.

The graph shows the results of trials in the community of cognitive behavioural therapy (CBT) with schizophrenia.

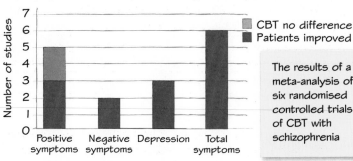

Number of studies vs Positive symptoms, Negative symptoms, Depression, Total symptoms

CBT no difference / Patients improved

> The results of a meta-analysis of six randomised controlled trials of CBT with schizophrenia

> You have explicitly learned two types of bias so this is a straightforward question. Before attempting it, look at pages 193 and 194.

(a) Briefly explain how effective CBT was in helping the positive symptoms of schizophrenia.   **(2 marks)**

> Be careful to read labels on graphs. In this case the vertical axis refers to number of studies not amount of change.

(b) Using the results in the graph, would you advise use of CBT for treating negative symptoms of schizophrenia? Explain your answer.   **(2 marks)**

(c) Overall, is CBT effective in treating schizophrenia from these results? Explain your answer.   **(2 marks)**

> Also read the title carefully. In this case you are informed these patients are out in the community.

Food preferences: evolutionary explanations

Individuals who adapted to their environment in terms of what they ate had a greater chance of survival, allowing them to reproduce and pass on their genes to their offspring. Preferences for certain foods facilitated this **evolutionary** advantage.

Food preferences

Meat preference for savoury foods can be traced back to our **environment of evolutionary adaptation (EEA)**. This protein-rich diet contributed to the growth of the brain in humans.

Bitter/sour are associated with food that has gone off or is potentially poisonous. We have an innate ability to detect these.

Salt is essential for neural and muscular activity and water balance.

Neophobia (fear of the new) – we avoid food we have not encountered before. In the EEA, we stayed safe as we ate foods we already knew and avoided foods that might have been harmful.

Taste aversion – foods that make us sick will be avoided in future. Associations with the foods help survival as a form of biological preparedness, to ensure we learn through experience to not eat the same food again.

Research evidence

Taste aversion	Garcia et al. (1955) found that rats given radiation after eating saccharin were sick and then showed an aversion to saccharin. The rats associated saccharin with being sick, so they learned to avoid it. This makes **evolutionary sense** – we have an **innate predisposition to avoid foods** that could potentially threaten our survival.
Neophobia	Birch et al. (1998) found infants who rejected new vegetables accepted the food over time. This shows that we tend to eat foods we know and only eat new foods after repeated exposure.
Sweet foods	Desor et al. (1975) investigated three-day-old babies' food preferences based on facial expressions. They appeared to innately prefer sweet-tasting foods and reject bitter tasting ones.
Meat	The relationship between meat-eating and brain growth is mixed. Fossil evidence does show our ancestors ate animal organs, which were rich in nutrients, but it is not innate as infants have to be introduced to eating them.
Bitter and sour	Steiner et al. (2001) found that the look of disgust is universal when tasting bitter and sour foods. This suggests it is innate and a sign that the food has gone off.
Salt	Beauchamp (1987) reported that people with a deficiency of salt eat it in higher quantities than others, suggesting an **innate drive** to maintain optimal levels for survival.

Evaluation

👍 There is good research support for the approach, which explains innate preferences for certain foods.

👍 We show similarities to other species for food preferences; the same innate mechanisms for survival appear to be in place.

👎 Evolutionary explanations are post-hoc: food preferences are explained by events that happened many years ago. This makes the explanation difficult to falsify.

👎 It ignores other influences, such as culture, that play a big part in contemporary food preferences and therefore is an incomplete explanation of eating behaviour.

Now try this

Outline **one** evolutionary explanation of food preference.

Food preferences: learning experiences

The impact of other people, whether in the context of the family environment or cultural eating practices, is seen as an important influence on people's food preferences.

Culture influences

Culture can influence food choice through the transmission of various restrictions, such as not eating pork or beef. These practices are often driven by religious beliefs or norms, which can also encourage the eating of certain foods at a particular time of the year.

For example, turkey is eaten at Christmas.

The cultural norms of a group can also influence the groups of foods that are encouraged.

For example, Western society sees being thin as the ideal shape and therefore eating less sugar and carbohydrate is supported.

Social influences

The behaviour of the family strongly influences what we eat. Mothers, in particular, play an important role due to their eating habits while pregnant, as the flavours are transmitted to the baby through the amniotic fluid and also via breastfeeding. Both can influence a child's food choices and flavour preferences.

Social learning theory (SLT – see page 69) plays a prominent role through vicarious learning, imitation and modelling.

Operant conditioning (see page 68) can also influence children's food preferences if food is used as a reward.

SLT says younger siblings may watch (vicarious learning) their older siblings (model) and what they eat, and then eat the same foods (imitation).

Research evidence

✓ Research on the Pima Indians of New Mexico found those who remained in the community had low levels of obesity, whereas those who moved to areas influenced by American culture and diet developed high levels of obesity. This suggests that the culture in which people live encourages their eating and they become acclimatised to new foods and diets.

✓ Xie et al. (2003) reported a correlation between income and diet. The higher socio-economic status of the family, the better their diet in terms of a bigger intake of protein, calcium, iron, fruit and vegetables. Poorer families eat more potatoes, sugars and fewer fruits and vegetables.

Research evidence

✓ Baker et al. (2003) looked at a sample of 279 teenagers from a Catholic girls' school and an American public school and showed that they were less likely to have a positive attitude regarding healthy eating if their parents and peer group did not value these behaviours.

✓ Harper and Sanders (1975) concluded that a child's food preferences were influenced by a role model, usually the mother, highlighting SLT as an important factor.

Evaluation

🚩 Food availability worldwide and increased population mobility means cultural influences are not as prominent as they once were and are environmentally reductionist – eating is based on the environment and nothing else.

👍 Cultural influences on food choice can be as a result of seasonal weather and availability of certain foods.

Evaluation

🚩 Social influences are not the only factors affecting food choice and therefore are environmentally reductionist.

👍 Research supports the suggestion that families do shape a child's eating preferences and habits.

Now try this

Outline learning theories of food preferences.

Neural and hormonal mechanisms

Biological **explanations** of eating behaviour involve two areas of the **brain**, together with a number of **hormones**, including **leptin** and **ghrelin**. Together, they control our food intake.

Lateral hypothalamus (LH)

This is part of the dual centre model of feeding. This area of the brain responds to the release of hormones, which the brain detects, and initiates eating by telling the person they are hungry. Time elapsed since the person has last eaten causes a drop in glucose in the blood whilst a hormone, **ghrelin**, is released when the stomach is empty. This is proportional: the less food there is, the more

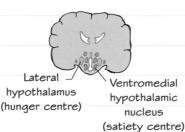

Hypothalamic nuclei

Lateral hypothalamus (hunger centre)

Ventromedial hypothalamic nucleus (satiety centre)

Ventromedial hypothalamus (VMH)

Once the person has started to eat, the levels of ghrelin reduce as the stomach becomes fuller. Rises in glucose in the blood, together with fat cells releasing **leptin**, signal the VMH, which signals satiety (fullness). The person then stops eating.

Set point theory

A balance of these two areas, known as the **set point theory** maintains the body's weight and eating. This should result in **homeostasis** – body weight regulated at a preferred level by a feedback mechanism in which your body is programmed to function optimally. It is thought if a person over or under eats over a period of time the body develops a new set point.

Dual centre model of feeding

Ventromedial hypothalamus activated – person is now satiated – individual stops eating

Leptin released from fat cells activates VMH

Ghrelin no longer released as stomach full

Time elapsed

Individual eats

Blood glucose level is low

Empty stomach releases **ghrelin**

Lateral hypothalamus responds to these two and signals hunger

The homeostatic perception of hunger and fullness

Research evidence

Lutter et al. (2008) used two groups of mice. They fed one normally and starved the other group for four days. They found an increased level of ghrelin in the hungry mice compared to the control group of mice.

👍 This research could help doctors treating people with anorexia, for example, who may not respond appropriately to ghrelin, or whose LH is not activated. Successful trials on animals allow doctors to extend research findings to human participants.

👎 However, this explanation could be said to be reductionist. There are multiple hormones involved in eating, and isolating one to explain complex patterns of behaviour whilst ignoring the role of other influences is too simplistic.

Zhang (1994) used mice that had the obesity gene; they completely lacked leptin. They continually ate because their brains perceived them as starving. When given leptin injections, the mice lost weight because their eating decreased.

👍 This research has helped doctors treat obese people through undertaking leptin therapy. This could help people who have failed to control their weight through dieting.

👎 However, some obese people do not lack leptin but appear to be leptin resistant.

👎 Studies using animals present difficulties in extrapolating findings to humans.

👎 This explanation is also reductionist. Both explanations ignore the importance of **free will**: humans have conscious thoughts and should be able to override their biological drives.

Now try this

Outline the neural and hormonal mechanisms in eating behaviour.

Anorexia nervosa

Anorexia nervosa is an eating disorder characterised by severe weight loss, fear of being fat and refusal to maintain body weight. It is predominantly a female disorder as some 85% of people with the condition are women and 15% males. Biological explanations for anorexia include **genetic** and **neural explanations**.

Genetic explanation

This explanation suggests that that there is an inherited component of the disorder transmitted through a person's genes. It proposes that if a person inherits the gene it makes them more vulnerable, but other factors possibly trigger the onset.

Extreme weight loss results in protruding bones.

Neural explanations

Structural abnormalities of the brain may influence the disorder. Damage to prominent areas such as the hypothalamus was influential in early research but recent studies have attempted to isolate more specific areas. For example, dysfunction in the lateral hypothalamus could prevent hunger (see page 213). The **insula** brain area has also been investigated as it contains more neural connections than any area of the brain. In people with anorexia, this area has been shown to develop differently. Dysfunction in any area could implicate the insula because of its multiple connections to other areas.

Research evidence

Bulik et al. (2006) studied 31,406 Swedish twin pairs and found the heritability of the disorder to be 56%. This supports earlier research by Holland et al. (1988), who found concordance rates for monozygotic (MZ) twins of 56%, showing there is a genetic component to anorexia.

🚩 Twin studies do not isolate nature from nurture. If anorexia was due to genetics only, we would expect a 100% concordance for the MZ twins and 50% for the DZ twins.

Research evidence

Oberndorfer et al. (2013) compared 14 recovered females who had had anorexia with 14 non-anorexic females. FMRI scans measured their response to repeated tastes of sucrose (caloric) and sucralose (non-caloric) to separate neural processing of each. The anorexic-recovered women had reduced responses in the anterior insula, where taste and reward are processed, compared to the control group. This may reflect the altered regulation of signals related to sweet taste to which people with anorexia may have less sensitivity, which leads to their disorder.

Evaluation

👍 Identifying genetic factors could lead to risks for development of the disorder being highlighted and further research could be continued.

🚩 Genetic explanations cannot explain why in twin studies concordance rates are not 100% for MZ twins, which would be expected if it was only genetics that influenced the disorder.

🚩 If biological explanations are valid, they do not explain the increased incidence of the disorder nowadays.

🚩 Biological explanations can be considered determinist.

Evaluation

👍 Biological explanations can lead to the development of treatments, such as drugs to address brain mechanism abnormalities.

🚩 No brain area has been completely isolated because of the complexity of the brain and interaction of all of the systems.

🚩 Most research is on females, which may not explain the 15% of males who develop the condition. However, this figure may not be a true reflection of male sufferers as many may go undiagnosed.

🚩 Biological explanations can be considered **reductionist**, where the focus is on a single factor being solely responsible for anorexia.

Now try this

Discuss whether biological explanations of anorexia could be considered reductionist.

Anorexia: family systems theory

Family systems theory (FST) is a psychological explanation for anorexia nervosa. FST looks at patterns of behaviour that are deemed dysfunctional in the family. These include **enmeshment**, **autonomy** and **control**.

Enmeshment

Minuchin introduced the term in the 1970s and explained anorexia as resulting from a family that is over-involved in each other's lives. Although these families are very loving and show a lot of affection to each other, they also become overprotective of their children and stifle any independence the child wants to exert. This hinders the child's social development as they become reliant on the family. This is particularly true of mother–daughter relationships.

Research evidence

Minuchin et al. (1978) looked at 45 families: 11 contained a child with anorexia and 34 did not. Using self-report, each family was rated on four characteristics: enmeshment, overprotectiveness, rigidity and avoidance of conflict – all factors associated with FST. They found that the families that were rated high on dysfunction, such as high levels of enmeshment, tended to be the families with anorexia, supporting FST.

Autonomy and control

The lack of **autonomy** away from parents, specifically the mother, is often found in the beginnings of females with anorexia, according to FST. The disturbance in the establishment of this autonomy is demonstrated in distortions of self, such as their body image. This lack of independence can lead to the person with anorexia seeking ways of exerting autonomy and so starving themselves is a way of doing this. This establishes self-identity and is unique to them and no one else in the family. Developing anorexia is then exerting control in their food intake through excessively controlling their body size and weight.

Research evidence

Karwautz et al. (2003) compared 31 pairs of sisters, where one had anorexia, on test scores of their family relationships. Using self-report, the Subjective Family Image Test showed differences in perception between the sisters. The sister with anorexia, compared to the sister without, had scored lower in the level of autonomy she felt she had in the family. This was more prominent in relation to their mothers. This research supports the role of autonomy and control in anorexia.

Evaluation

🖛 The FST takes a **reductionist** view by only looking at psychological factors whilst ignoring further important factors such as biology.

🖛 Problems with FST include testing and falsifying the evidence. FST lacks use of the scientific method, which has negative implications for psychology as a science.

🖛 Anorexia has an incidence of 85% in females compared to 15% in males. This is difficult to explain if FST was an exclusive explanation of the complex disorder as it looks in particular at the mother–daughter relationship.

👍 These explanations focus on nurture, but a more comprehensive explanation may come from looking at the interaction of both **nature** and **nurture**.

👍 The development of family therapy in response to FST has enabled people with the condition, and their families, to try to manage how the family deals with the condition. This is a practical way of aiding recovery and avoiding potential relapse after successful treatment.

🖛 The use of questionnaires may reduce the validity of the findings in some research because of the risk of socially desirable responses.

Now try this

What is meant by an 'enmeshed family', and what features are seen in such a family?

Anorexia: social learning theory

The social learning theory (SLT) of anorexia nervosa is an extension of the **behaviourist** approach (see pages 67–68), whilst it also acknowledges the role of **cognition** (see pages 70 and 217). It suggests the disorder is learned through observing other people's behaviour and then imitating them (see page 69).

SLT of anorexia

Modelling

This suggests that females in particular learn behaviours through **observation** of role models.

For example, if they saw their mother or friends dieting (**paid attention**), observation of the experience would be **retained**, which increases the likelihood of them **reproducing** or imitating the behaviour at a later stage because of the **motivation** to be slim.

Media

Women are more likely to develop anorexia than men and the influence of the media could explain this. Women are targeted more – for example, in fashion magazines showing thin models – compared to males and therefore may see these photos and imitate the models they see.

Social learning theory

Reinforcement

Vicarious reinforcement may also occur: seeing someone else being rewarded for their weight loss, for example, being complimented. When this occurs, individuals may imitate the weight-loss behaviour through dieting, which in turn can then be reinforced externally, such as getting compliments themselves. It can also be reinforced internally when the individual feels good about themselves.

Research evidence

✅ Fearn (1999) made a study of young women living on the island of Fiji. Prior to 1995, there was no Western television on the island. By 1998, after the introduction of television, 74% of the participants said they were 'too big or fat'. Prior to this, there had been no reports of eating disorders but they then began to appear. This supports the role of imitating the behaviour of models and being influenced by the media. The cultural values changed after the islanders saw Western models who were thin and admired, highlighting **vicarious reinforcement**. In non-Western cultures such as China, fewer role models exist and anorexia is not so prevalent. However, there has been an increase in Chinese students studying in the West developing anorexia nervosa, which would also support the model.

✅ Goresz et al. (2001) reviewed 25 studies that showed the media ideal of thinness caused body dissatisfaction and contributed to the development of eating disorders. The effect was most prominent in girls under 19 years of age.

✅ Eysenck and Flanagan (2000), however, pointed out that while a majority of young women in the West are exposed to the media, only a small percentage (3–4%) develop an eating disorder.

Seeing Western models increased the incidence of eating disorders in Fijians (Fearn 1999).

Evaluation

👍 Social learning theory is useful in explaining why anorexia predominantly affects females, because of the influence of the media images targeted at women, and – for similar reasons – why it is more predominant in Western culture.

👎 However, it fails to explain why not all women subjected to the same media images develop the disorder. Nor does it explain male cases of the disorder who are not targeted in the same way, yet still develop the condition.

Now try this

1 Most research on eating disorders considers females only. Why?

2 The social learning theory of anorexia is environmentally deterministic (see page 130). Explain why this is the case.

Anorexia: cognitive theory

Cognitive theory looks at the thinking patterns of the person with anorexia, which are believed to be **distorted** and **irrational**. People with anorexia believe they are fat and overestimate their actual size; these are known as **cognitive biases**.

Distortions

People with anorexia have negative perceptions about their body whereby they have distorted thoughts about themselves – all based on their weight and eating. These are due to errors in thinking and a breakdown of rational thought processes. The individual with anorexia nervosa may also have misperceptions about their bodies and have unrealistic body ideals.

I'm so useless because I'm fat

I'm so fat - why does no one else see it?

I'm a faliure; I ate food; I can't do anything right

Distorted thoughts may lead to strict eating behaviour and guilt about eating.

Irrational beliefs

The irrational beliefs held by people with anorexia lead to the development and maintenance of the disorder. They see themselves as fatter than they are and their thinking is maladaptive. Examples of errors in thinking include:

- **All or nothing beliefs**: 'I ate one crisp … I can feel the weight going on.'
- **Overgeneralising**: 'If I can't control my eating I'm a failure.'
- **Magnifying/minimising**: 'Being size 8 is unacceptable … If I reach size 4 then my life will be perfect.'
- **Magical thinking**: 'If I can lose more weight, I will be so happy.'

Research evidence

✓ Williamson et al. (1993) asked a group of patients with anorexia (AN) and a control group without to adjust a 'stretched' photograph of themselves back to what they actually looked like. The AN group significantly overestimated real size as they did not readjust the photograph enough. The non-AN group, however, flattered themselves by representing themselves as leaner than they really were. This shows people with anorexia cognitively misrepresent their own body image, that is, they have distorted perceptions.

✓ McKenzie et al. (1993) found that females with anorexia judged their ideal weight to be lower than a comparable control group. After a sugary snack, they judged their body size to have increased whereas the control group did not. This shows that just eating one thing activates fear of weight gain and highlights the irrational thinking patterns of people with anorexia.

Evaluation

👍 Cognitive behavioural therapy has been developed as a treatment for a number of disorders, including anorexia nervosa. It has a high rate of success, which is supportive of the theory that faulty cognition can underlie the condition, as the therapy involves challenging the irrational thoughts, and changing them into rational ones.

👎 The approach does not establish cause and effect. It does not state whether faulty cognition causes the anorexic behaviour or the irrational thinking is as a result of the condition.

👎 The cognitive approach does not acknowledge the role of other approaches such as social learning theory (see page 216), which might be a better explanation of the increased number of people with the disorder. The cognitive explanation cannot explain this.

Now try this

Identify **one** strength and **one** weakness of the cognitive theory of anorexia.

Obesity

Obesity refers to an excess of body fat and can be measured using the Body Mass Index (BMI). A person is considered obese if their BMI is 30 and above. In England, 24.8% of adults are obese, according to NHS statistics. **Biological** explanations see obesity as caused by **genetics** and **neural functioning**.

Genetic explanations

1 The basal metabolic rate (BMR) theory shows a genetic basis for a mutated version of the protein KSR2. Carriers of this mutation show **hyperphagia** (overeating) in childhood with a reduced BMR. Depletion of KSR2 in mice results in obesity.

2 The incidence amongst family members is looked at to see the vulnerability of developing the condition.

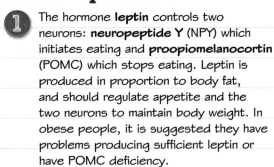

If one parent is obese a child has a 40% risk of also being obese; if both parents are obese the risk factor is 80% (Hetherington and Ranson, 1942).

3 In the **environment of evolutionary adaptiveness (EEA)**, storing body fat at times when food was plentiful would have increased the chances of survival for our ancestors in times of famine.

Neural explanations

1 The hormone **leptin** controls two neurons: **neuropeptide Y** (NPY) which initiates eating and **proopiomelanocortin** (POMC) which stops eating. Leptin is produced in proportion to body fat, and should regulate appetite and the two neurons to maintain body weight. In obese people, it is suggested they have problems producing sufficient leptin or have POMC deficiency.

2 The ventromedial hypothalamus (VMH) (see page 213) is implicated as it should inform the person when they are full to stop eating. In obese people, the VMH may not be functioning properly, so they continue to eat.

Research evidence

✓ Stunkard et al. (1986) compared the degree of obesity of adoptees and their biological and adoptive parents. They found a correlation with the biological relatives but not the adoptive parents, suggesting a genetic link.

✓ Chamala et al. (2007) found that modern Pima Indians had high levels of obesity due to a genetic metabolic efficiency. In the EEA, their metabolism was an advantage in the desert conditions in which they lived, where food was scarce. Today, this works against them as they eat readily available, high-calorie foods.

Research evidence

✓ Friedman (2005) found it was the inability of leptin to block POMC that influences obesity development, as appetite is not suppressed and therefore weight gain occurs.

✓ Wickens et al. (2000) found that when injecting NPY into rats that were satiated, they began to feed again, supporting the role of this neuron in eating and obesity.

✓ Reeves and Plum (1969), during a post-mortem on an obese woman, found a tumour on her VMH, suggesting that this had impaired the sensation of satiety (fullness), and therefore that the VMH influences obesity.

Evaluation

🖒 A lot of the research has been carried out on animals. This is a problem because humans can think about their eating behaviour, which animals cannot. Therefore we may not be able to extrapolate the findings from research to humans.

🖒 Biological explanations could be **determinist**, suggesting that a gene could cause the person to overeat and become obese, and ignoring free will.

👍 Biological explanations are useful as they can help to develop appropriate drug treatments to help people to lose weight, when dieting alone has failed.

👍 Research evidence on the role of leptin strongly supports the biological approach, but its role is complex and includes other hormones and neurons.

Now try this

Outline **one** problem of using animals in research into obesity.

Obesity: psychological explanations

There are a number of psychological explanations for obesity, including **restraint**, **disinhibition** and the **boundary model**.

Restraint theory

People with obesity try to limit their eating through dieting in order to lose weight. Around 80% of these people will fail because the **restraint** they put on their food intake is unrealistic. The opposite usually occurs in that they overeat. Our body has a **set point** for weight, which is determined by **homeostasis** – a biological mechanism (see page 213). We try to maintain this through what we eat. In restrained eaters the control is:

- cognitive regulation rather than biological. (What the person thinks they should or shouldn't eat in their own minds not what their body tells them.)

- the widening gap between homeostasis and the cognitions, when people change from overeating to dieting. (They are hungrier because they have been used to larger quantities of food.)

Around 80% of obese people will fail in their attempts to diet.

Disinhibition

This is a lack of control and the tendency to overeat, which could cause obesity. Once the **cognitive boundary** is crossed the dieter feels that they have 'blown it' for the day (Herman and Mack 1975). This leads to **disinhibited** eating and the dieter puts off the diet for another day. They therefore often remain at risk of obesity.

Boundary model

The boundary model (**Herman and Polivy 1984**) suggests that hunger motivates an individual to consume food above a set minimum level. Satiety motivates them to keep intake below a set maximum level. The distance between the two is set by psychological factors and determines how much a person will eat.

🔍 Key study Herman and Mack (1975)

Aim: To see if dieters would overeat if given a high calorie preload (milkshake).

Procedure: 45 female students participated and were told they were taking part in a taste preference test. They were separated into three conditions:

1. no preload
2. preload = one milkshake – asked to rate the taste
3. preload = two milkshakes – asked to rate the taste

They were then given three tubs of different flavoured ice cream and asked to rate the taste in a ten-minute limit, whereby they could eat as much of the ice cream as they wanted. They were assessed as being restraint/non-restraint eaters. It was found that:

- non-dieters ate less ice cream in condition 3 than in condition 1 and 2.

- dieters ate significantly more ice cream in conditions 2 and 3 than in condition 1.

This showed what Herman and Mack termed the 'what the hell' effect because they had already indulged in either one or two milkshakes prior to eating the ice cream. The restraint people felt they had gone over their boundary. Restraint does appear to make people more vulnerable to disinhibited eating (Ogden 2009).

Evaluation

👍 The explanations have helped the medical profession to identify why diets fail for people with obesity. Because too much restraint in eating has been shown to negatively affect diets, a better approach would be to have a less restrained diet.

👎 Psychological explanations do not explain how disinhibition occurs, only that it results in overeating – but not why.

👎 It is determinist as it suggests that people break their cognitive boundary for eating, then show disinhibited eating, but it ignores free will.

Now try this

Why could research into obesity be considered socially sensitive?

Success and failure of dieting

Dieting is a big industry in the Western world, perhaps because of the influence of Western ideals to be slim. Many factors may influence whether a diet is successful or not.

Successful dieting

Psychological explanations have been shown to be good predictors of successful dieting. Success is often a result of factors such as motivation, exercise and social support.

Weight-loss programmes help dieters to stay motivated through the network of meeting other dieters weekly; they offer **rewards** for weight loss (for example praise), which **reinforces** the dieting.

> Weight-loss programmes also give diet plans that are not totally restrictive but are varied and healthy, which allows restrained eaters to see dieting as positive.

Interventions that combine group therapy, health advice and exercise have been shown to produce moderate but sustained weight loss that tends to be more successful.

Failure

Failure in dieting can also be explained from a psychological perspective. People often fail because the limit they put on themselves cognitively is far lower than their body would expect to eat normally, and therefore the diet is **unsustainable**. Low restrainers often find dieting far easier than high restrainers because their diets are more sensible and **achievable**. High restraint can lead to unpleasant side-effects such as low energy and dizziness, which make it harder to maintain the diet. Thus **negative reinforcement** occurs; the dieter breaks their diet to avoid the unpleasant stimulus of hunger.

Dieters can become demotivated because they feel the weight loss is too slow. They then give in to temptation, leading to thoughts that diets do not work, and it is pointless them trying to lose weight; it becomes self-fulfilling.

Research evidence

✓ Miller-Kovach et al. (2001) found Weight Watchers to be superior in maintaining weight loss over a two-year period compared with personal regimes. This was possibly due to the social support it offered.

✓ Bartlett (2003) reported that a weight-loss programme of 1–2 pounds per week was motivational while also being realistic.

✓ Rodin et al. (1977) studied psychological predictors of successful dieting. They found that belief in a behavioural model of obesity was key. In other words, a person had to accept they were responsible for their obesity in the first place and therefore they could control it through dieting.

Research evidence

✓ Jeffery (2000) found that dieters who did not maintain their behavioural changes – such as their belief in having control over their weight – often regained the lost weight within six months.

✓ Cummings et al. (2002) suggested that a combination of psychological and biological factors cause diets to fail. Low calorie diets stimulate the appetite by increasing ghrelin production by 24%, which encourages dieters to eat, and therefore the diet fails. Gastric bands work by shrinking the stomach, so it produces less ghrelin and the person feels less hungry.

Evaluation

👍 Research findings can assist with identification of successful dieting strategies in order for health workers to address the growing issue of obesity.

👎 Research is gender biased as it mainly focuses on females, who are more likely to diet, so cannot be applied to male dieting. It is also culturally biased as dieting is a more Western behaviour.

Now try this

Outline **one** strategy that might help a dieter to lose weight and to maintain the weight loss.

Exam skills 1

You need to be able to demonstrate a variety of skills in your exam answers to meet the assessment objectives. Make good use of exemplar questions to practise these skills while also being organised in terms of timings. Before you look at these worked examples, remind yourself about the evolutionary explanation for food preferences (page 211), neural and hormonal mechanisms in eating behaviour (page 213) and cognitive explanations of anorexia (page 217).

Worked example

Outline the role of ghrelin in the control of eating behaviour.   **(2 marks)**

The hormone ghrelin is secreted from the stomach into the bloodstream, and the amount released is proportional to the emptiness of the stomach. An empty stomach sends signals to the brain to initiate hunger and stimulate eating.

Command word: Outline

Outline requires you to describe what ghrelin does in a couple of sentences.

- It does not require any evaluation.
- Write in full sentences.
- Use relevant key terms, such as ghrelin, initiate, stimulate.

Worked example

Outline the role of hormonal mechanisms in the control of eating behaviour.   **(4 marks)**

Leptin is a fat hormone that is secreted into the bloodstream to signal to the brain (via the hypothalamus) that calorie storage is high. It tells the brain that the body has sufficient fat stored and to stop eating. When people don't eat enough food, fat is used up and so the fat cells cease to secrete leptin. The opposite is true of ghrelin. As the time from the last meal increases, so ghrelin secretion is increased and we feel hungry.

This AO1 outline question requires a description of *both* ghrelin and leptin as the question is plural. These hormones must be explicitly linked to the neural mechanisms of satiety and hunger.

More detail is required here than the first question as the answer is worth more marks; marks are an indicator of the time you need to spend per question. Think about spending a minute per mark.

Worked example

What is meant by the term *neophobia* in relation to evolutionary food preferences?   **(2 marks)**

Neophobia means fear of the new. The reluctance to try novel food is based on an adaptive process to ensure survival and to avoid eating unfamiliar foods that could harm us.

You need to give the definition here in the context of the evolutionary approach.

Worked example

Briefly explain **one** limitation of the cognitive explanation of anorexia nervosa.   **(2 marks)**

A lot of people have distortions in their thinking surrounding their weight but don't go on to develop AN, suggesting there are other factors that play a role.

Identify one limitation and explain the point you make.

Had a look ☐   Nearly there ☐   Nailed it! ☐

Exam skills 2

Anorexia nervosa has multiple explanations. Before you look at the worked examples, remind yourself about the cognitive explanations (page 217).

Worked example

Discuss the cognitive theory of anorexia nervosa.   **(8 marks)**

The cognitive theory for anorexia nervosa suggests that it is due to faulty or irrational thinking by the sufferer. Such people hold schemas that distort their perceptions about their weight, which lead them to misperceive how their body really looks. This weight-based schema makes them think they are fat when looking in the mirror, when they are not, and so they begin to lose weight in order to deal with the threat of being overweight. There is also a correlation between low self-esteem and anorexia, based on their perceived physical appearance. People with anorexia also have irrational thoughts linked to their weight, such as if they are thin people will like them more.

Research has shown that sufferers have distorted thinking. Mackenzie (1993) found that women with anorexia estimated their body size to be bigger than it actually was compared to women without anorexia. This highlights the irrational thinking patterns people with anorexia have. Williamson et al. (1993) asked a group of patients with anorexia and a control group without anorexia to adjust a 'stretched' photograph of themselves back to what they actually looked like. The group with anorexia significantly over-estimated their real size as they did not readjust the photograph enough. The group without anorexia, however, flattered themselves by representing themselves as leaner than they really were. This shows that people with anorexia cognitively misrepresent their own body image, supporting the cognitive explanation. Seeing themselves as bigger than they actually are could encourage the extreme dieting behaviour.

However, the way the brain processes information is far more complex than this approach proposes. It also takes a determinist viewpoint as it suggests that if our thinking is irrational around our weight we will develop anorexia. This ignores the role of free will as to whether we choose to starve ourselves or not. The approach also fails to establish cause and effect; it does not state whether the faulty cognitions cause the anorexic behaviour or the irrational thinking is a result of the condition. Nevertheless, the cognitive approach has led to the development of cognitive behavioural therapy, which has been used successfully in helping people with anorexia see that their thoughts are irrational.

Command word: Discuss

This requires you to **outline** and **evaluate** the cognitive approach to anorexia nervosa. There is no requirement to say what anorexia nervosa is.

Consistent effective use of appropriate psychological terminology in your answer is key.

The answer shows an understanding of the cognitive explanation of anorexia nervosa, using appropriate terminology.

Research can be outlined in an AO1 question as shown here in this answer. The student has not attempted to evaluate it but used it to emphasise the point about distortions.

Exam-style practice 1

Practise for Paper 3 of your A level exam with these exam-style questions. There are answers on pages 313–314. Before looking at these questions it would be a good idea to review explanations of food preferences, including evolutionary (pages 211–212), and obesity (pages 218–219).

1   Outline the psychological explanations of obesity.   **(16 marks)**

> Questions on Paper 3 will include different assessment objectives: AO1 outline your knowledge of the topic; AO2 apply your knowledge to a scenario given in the exam question; and AO3 evaluate the explanation or theory in the question.

> To build up the skills necessary for a 16-mark question you need to be able to outline the theory first, because the AO1 marks will be a maximum of 6. The rest of the marks will be made up of AO2 and/ or AO3.

2   Evaluate psychological explanations of obesity.   **(10 marks)**

> Evaluate the theory and use research evidence in your answer to support the points you make.

3   Briefly outline the evolutionary explanation of food preferences, with reference to neophobia and taste aversion.   **(4 marks)**

> The specification asks for evolutionary food preferences, including neophobia and taste aversion. In another question, you could be asked about each component separately. For example, a question could ask you to outline neophobia or taste aversion.

4   Outline the role of learning in food preferences.   **(4 marks)**

> The specification includes cultural and social influences. Therefore a question could ask you to outline each component separately.

5   A lot of the research into the area of obesity only shows a correlation. What are the problems with the conclusions of these types of studies?   **(2 marks)**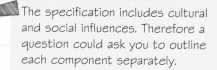

> This type of question is testing your knowledge of research methods embedded in the topic of eating.

6   Read the item and then answer the question that follows.

> Molly is getting married in three months' time and is desperate not to put on any weight as she is worried that her dress will not fit. She complained to her friends that the more she tries to stop eating, the more she eats.

> When you have this type of question in the exam, it is important to engage fully with the stimulus, as some – or in some cases all – of the marks are for the application to the stem (AO2).

If you were a friend of Molly, what would you advise? Refer to research studies in your answer.   **(4 marks)**

Exam-style practice 2

Practise for Paper 3 of your A level exam with these exam-style questions. There are answers on pages 314–315. Before looking at these questions, it would be good to review the topics of anorexia (pages 214–217), obesity (pages 218–219) and research methods.

7   Outline the social learning theory of anorexia nervosa.

(4 marks)

> 'Outline' means describe how the theory explains anorexia nervosa.

8   Outline the cognitive theory of anorexia nervosa.   **(2 marks)**

> There are three psychological explanations of anorexia. You can use the others as evaluation.

9   **(a)** A psychologist believes that anorexic behaviour is often seen with characteristics of obsessive compulsive disorder (OCD). She wants to find out if this belief is valid. How would she investigate this?

(4 marks)

> This requires you to apply your knowledge of research and decide which would be an appropriate study to use.

(b) After carrying out her research, the psychologist now wants to see if her results are significant or not. How would she do this?

(2 marks)

> **Justify** means explain or defend why this test would be suitable.

(c) With reference to your answer to (b), justify the use of this test.

(2 marks)

(d) With reference to anorexia nervosa, what would these results **not** tell us?   **(2 marks)**

> These types of assessment may come up in any of the sections even though they are really research methods questions. This assesses whether you can transfer your knowledge and understanding of research methods into any scenario or context.

10 Discuss the genetic explanation of anorexia nervosa.   **(8 marks)**

> The term 'discuss' is both an AO1 and AO3 assessment. Therefore, you need to both outline and evaluate for these types of questions.

11 Identify **one** strength and **one** weakness of the family systems theory.

(4 marks)

> The term 'identify' requires you to name a strength and a weakness and expand on each. Think about development of treatments. What weaknesses are there with the supporting research? If a theory has research evidence that has flaws, then this weakens the theory.

12 Which gender bias is seen in the family system theory?   **(2 marks)**

> Review gender bias on page 128.

General adaptation syndrome

Stress is a physical and emotional reaction to some kind of **stressor** or threat. People generally feel stress when the demands placed on them outweigh their perceived ability to cope. When we are stressed, we have a **physiological response**.

General adaptation syndrome

Selye (1936), a Hungarian endocrinologist, first explained the body's physiological response to stress. He described three distinct stages in the way the body reacts when a stressor is detected, which he referred to as **general adaptation syndrome (GAS)**:

Alarm reaction
An initial reaction to stress where the body reacts with a fight-or-flight response.

Resistance
If stress is prolonged, the parasympathetic nervous system reduces fight-or-flight responses, but cortisol production increases.

Exhaustion
If stress continues, the body cannot maintain normal function, making a person vulnerable to illness.

Research evidence

✓ Selye (1936) discovered GAS by accident when studying the effects of various stressors on hormone levels in rats. He found that rats suffered many negative health problems from the stress of the multiple procedures they endured. For example, they were subjected to extreme cold, high levels of physical exercise and surgical cuts, and over time they showed increasing negative effects. This led to the development of Selye's theory of GAS, which he then applied to humans.

✓ Miodrag and Hodapp (2010) conducted a review of research that suggested that parents of children with intellectual and learning difficulties experience high levels of stress and also have increased health problems. They suggested that there may be a causal link between the stress of their situation and their health problems, which could be an example of exhaustion.

Evaluation

👍 Selye was the first person to describe a relationship between stress and physical illness. More recent research has continued to investigate this further.

👎 Selye's research on rats could have serious ethical issues due to the unpleasant procedures used. Many would argue that the experimental procedures used were invasive and were known to cause physical harm to the rats. In some of Selye's later studies, the rats were deliberately made to endure stressful events such as intense light and sound, which would have been very unpleasant.

👎 Selye's explanation of general adaptation is quite limited as it focuses only on physiological effects. Many of the reported effects of stress are quite complex. For example, stress can be associated with changes in mood, issues with concentration and reduced motivation. This suggests that we need to consider other effects rather than just the physical ones.

👎 The original research was conducted on rats and there may be problems when extrapolating the results of animal research to explain human behaviour. While humans and animals share many similar structures and functions in the nervous system, the physical stressors the rats were made to endure were different from the likely psychological stressors humans may face.

Now try this

1 Explain the effects of general adaptation syndrome (GAS) on the body.

2 How might we criticise the concept of GAS?

Sympathomedullary pathway

If a **stressor** occurs only for a short duration, it is referred to as an **acute** stress. The hypothalamus detects a stressor, sending a message to the adrenal medulla, which will trigger the release of adrenaline and noradrenaline into the bloodstream. The body's response to acute stress is often referred to as the **fight-or-flight response** (see page 85).

 The hypothalamus

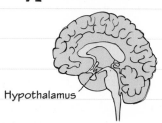

Hypothalamus

The **hypothalamus** in the brain will first detect that there is a stressor present, and that this stressor is acute.

 The adrenal medulla

Cortex
Medulla
Kidneys
Adrenal glands

A message is then sent from the hypothalamus to the **adrenal medulla** located in the centre of the adrenal glands above each kidney. The adrenal medulla releases the hormones **adrenaline** and **noradrenaline** into the bloodstream.

Fight or flight

This response from the body gives the body the energy needed to fight the threat or run from it. This is thought to be an evolutionary reaction hardwired into humans to aid survival.

 The sympathetic nervous system

The **sympathetic nervous system** (SNS) is activated in response to the presence of an acute stressor (see page 83). This branch of the nervous system is aroused by the increase in adrenaline in the bloodstream, which will activate the **fight-or-flight response**. The SNS will increase blood pressure and heart rate, dilate pupils, increase respiration and reduce non-urgent functions such as digestion and bladder contraction.

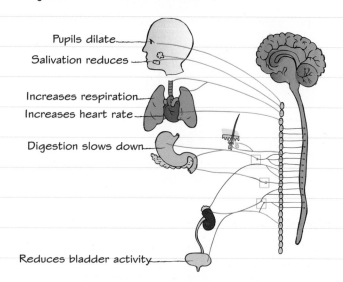

Pupils dilate
Salivation reduces
Increases respiration
Increases heart rate
Digestion slows down
Reduces bladder activity

The sympathetic nervous system

Research evidence

✓ Some research suggests that there are gender differences in responses to acute stress. Taylor et al. (2000) published evidence that, while males experience fight or flight, the increased level of oxytocin in females (a hormone associated with care and nurturing) during acute stress means that the response in females is more like 'tend-and-befriend'. Evolutionary psychologists may assume this is due to females wanting to protect their offspring from threat, rather than just themselves (see page 239).

✓ Mason (1975) found some evidence of individual differences in the amount of adrenaline and noradrenaline secreted by different individuals. This would suggest that the biological explanation of responses to acute stress by the sympathomedullary pathway could differ for individuals.

Now try this

What is the role of the sympathetic nervous system in responding to stress?

Hypothalamic-pituitary-adrenal system

When **stressors** are present over a prolonged period, for example, in the case of someone who works in a stressful environment every day, we would describe the stress as **chronic**. This type of stress activates the **hypothalamic-pituitary-adrenal system (HPA)**, which creates a response that is different from the fight-or-flight response seen in acute stress responses.

Hypothalamic-pituitary-adrenal system

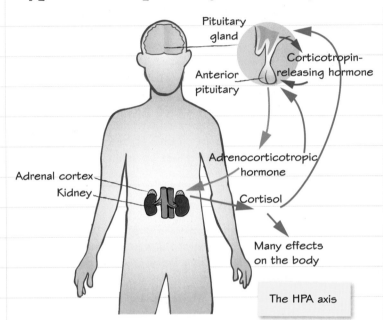

The HPA axis

Hypothalamus
When the hypothalamus detects a chronic stressor, it releases **corticotropin-releasing hormone (CRH)** into the bloodstream.

Pituitary gland
This hormone then stimulates the anterior **pituitary gland** to release **adrenocorticotropic hormone (ACTH)**.

Adrenal glands
This travels in the blood down to the adrenal gland where the **adrenal cortex** then releases the hormone **cortisol** into the blood.

The role of cortisol

Cortisol is a hormone that naturally increases and decreases throughout the day. In the case of chronic stress, the level of cortisol in the blood increases and remains high because the 'threat' from the stressor does not go away. In the short term, high levels of cortisol in the blood are not problematic.

For example, cortisol helps to provide the body with a steady flow of energy by converting glucose into energy.

Over a long period, however, high levels of cortisol can cause:

- high blood pressure
- immunosuppression
- sleep disruption
- impairment of cognitive skills
- slow wound healing
- increased fat around the abdomen.

These effects can have implications for a person's general health.

Research evidence

✓ Clarke et al. (1994) found that infant rhesus monkeys whose mothers were deliberately exposed to stress during pregnancy showed enhanced stress responses in the HPA system. These increased levels of reactivity in the HPA system continued throughout the life of the rhesus monkeys.

✓ Vgontzas et al. (2013) found that chronic insomniacs showed an overall increase in arousal of the HPA system, leading to an increase in the levels of ACTH and cortisol present in the blood. They suggested that the increased levels of these hormones could be causing the sleep disturbances, rather than the other way around. This supports the idea that one role of cortisol is in causing sleep disturbance.

Now try this

Explain the role of cortisol in responding to stress.

Immunosuppression

One of the effects of a prolonged, high level of cortisol in the bloodstream due to stress (see page 227) is a reduction in the functioning of the **immune system**, or **immunosuppression**.

How the immune system works

Our immune system produces billions of cells that travel around the body in the blood so they have easy access to different parts of the body. They defend against antigens, such as bacteria, viruses and cancer cells. White blood cells (leukocytes) are the major group of immune cell, and one type of these (lymphocytes such as B- and T-cells) produce antibodies that bind to and destroy antigens.

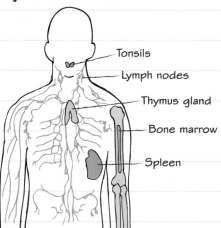

- Tonsils
- Lymph nodes
- Thymus gland
- Bone marrow
- Spleen

Where cells are produced in the immune system

Stress and the immune system

In the short term, one of the roles of cortisol in the blood is to help the body respond to invasion from pathogens. However, if the levels of cortisol remain high for a long period, they can interfere with how your immune system works. Chronic stress is associated with an increased risk of many illnesses due to reduced immune function, for example, cancer, flu and even more minor illnesses such as the cold virus. It has also been shown that people under high levels of chronic stress may find that wounds take longer to heal.

🔍 Key study Kiecolt-Glaser (1984)

Aim: To see if the immune system is compromised during periods of high stress.

Procedure: Two blood samples were taken from 75 medical students (49 male, 26 female) one month before their final exams, and again on the first day of exams. Levels of T-cells in the two samples were compared. They also gave questionnaires to the participants to measure symptoms of stress.

Results: The blood samples from the first day of the exams contained lower levels of T-cells. The lowest levels were seen in those reporting the most symptoms of stress.

Conclusion: Exam stress seems to disrupt normal immune functioning.

Evaluation

- 👍 Using blood samples is objective as it involves counting the number of T-cells present, which is a factual measure of the effect of stress.

- 👍 Comparing the students' blood samples over two different time periods is an example of a repeated measures design, meaning that there is no issue of participant variables influencing the results.

- 👎 The study only used medical students, meaning that there is sampling bias as they do not represent all students, let alone the whole population affected by stress.

- 👎 When under stress, many people partake in 'unhealthy' lifestyle choices such as less exercise and more alcohol consumption. Researchers did not investigate whether these factors could have played a part in the results obtained.

Research evidence

- ☑ Kiecolt-Glaser et al. (1995) found that wounds inflicted on participants who were caring for family members suffering from Alzheimer's disease took longer to heal than the same wounds in a sample of matched controls.

- ☑ Cohen et al. (1993) found that patients exposed to the common cold virus were more likely to be infected by the illness, and show symptoms sooner, when they reported high levels of psychological stress symptoms.

Now try this

1 What has research shown about the effects of stress on the immune system?

2 Explain **one** criticism of the supposed link between stress and the functioning of the immune system.

Cardiovascular disorders

Long-term exposure to stress can put pressure on the heart, which can then lead to an increased risk of developing **cardiovascular diseases** (CVD) such as high blood pressure, hardened arteries and coronary heart disease.

Stress and risks to the heart

During **acute stress**, the heart is put under pressure from adrenaline increasing the heart rate and blood pressure, while blood flow to the heart itself decreases. This puts **direct** pressure on the heart by causing increased risk of blood clots and potential for irregular heartbeats to occur. In the short term, the risk of having a heart attack increases, and there is a risk of repeated damage over time causing problems in heart functioning.

Plaques in the artery build up over time

If stress continues and becomes a **chronic** problem, the blood vessels may become damaged. Fatty deposits or **plaques** can build up in the blood vessels, narrowing them over time. This has a **direct** impact as the heart cannot pump effectively, and blood flow is disrupted. This can cause chest pains and angina, as well as increasing the risk of heart attacks over time.

Risk factors for cardiovascular diseases

Being stressed can cause **unhealthy lifestyle** choices, which can damage the heart **indirectly**. People may feel that they do not have time to exercise or to cook healthy meals, and they may rely on smoking and drinking alcohol to help them relax. Lifestyle changes can cause a build-up of plaques in the arteries, which increase the risk of heart attacks and angina.

🔍 Key study   Melamed et al. (2006)

Aim: To review data on causes of CVD associated with 'burnout' (long-term stress leading to exhaustion).

Procedure: They conducted a literature review of evidence showing causal links between extended periods of stress and risks of CVD.

Results: A number of contributory factors were highlighted in the physical effects of burnout, including impaired immunity and poor health behaviours, both associated with CVD.

Conclusion: Behaviours associated with high levels of stress and 'burnout' were associated with increased risks of CVD.

Research evidence

✓ Orth-Gomér et al. (2000) found that marital stress was a predictor of poor prognosis in women diagnosed with coronary heart disease (CHD). For example, the risk of heart attacks was three times higher in women facing marital stress compared to other women without this type of stress.

✓ Krantz and McCeney (2002) presented a review of evidence and concluded that acute and chronic stress were among five psychosocial risk factors associated with developing coronary artery disease (CAD).

Evaluation

👍 Many studies into stress use levels of cardiovascular problems as a measurement for stress levels, indicating the amount of evidence there is linking the two things together.

👎 Certain personality characteristics may make some people more vulnerable to negative effects of stress, making research evidence difficult to interpret. For example, see page 234 for information on Type A personality.

👎 The evidence relating stress to heart disease is correlational and therefore we cannot tell cause and effect. While it may be found that people who are stressed are more likely to suffer from CHD, we would find it very difficult to work out exactly which element of their 'stress' is the variable that increases the risk of CHD. For example, stress often causes lifestyle changes so it may be these causing CHD rather than stress itself.

Now try this

What has research shown about the relationship between stress and cardiovascular problems?

Life changes and daily hassles

These are general events in life that cause people to feel unable to cope with the demands placed on them at a given time.

Life changes

Life changes or 'life events' are large-scale changes to a person's life that do not happen very often. These might include adjusting to a bereavement, unemployment or even the birth of a baby. Life events can be positive (getting married) or negative (becoming seriously ill). Adjusting to these events can result in stress.

Daily hassles

Daily hassles are minor irritations that people encounter all the time, which can be a constant source of stress. These include losing your keys or waking up late for school/work. Daily hassles tend to be encountered regularly, and it is a build-up of these that cause stress. On a daily basis, we also have a number of **uplifts** – little events that cheer us up every day and reduce the stress felt.

 Rahe (1972)

Aim: To investigate the effects of life changes on the health of US sailors while away at sea.

Procedure: 2664 male sailors were given a questionnaire to assess the number of life changes they had experienced in the previous 6 months (see page 232 for information on the SRRS questionnaire). Their health was then monitored while they were away at sea for between 6 and 8 months.

Results: A positive correlation of +0.118 was found between life events experienced and number of illnesses reported.

Conclusion: Life events may increase the risk of suffering illness as a result of the stress caused.

 Kanner et al. (1981)

Aim: To see if daily hassles were a good predictor of health problems associated with stress.

Procedure: A questionnaire was given to 100 middle-aged US adults to measure the number of daily hassles and uplifts they had experienced in the past month (see page 232 for more details on the hassles and uplifts questionnaire). They also completed a questionnaire assessing their psychological health. This was done once a month for 10 consecutive months.

Results: Daily hassles were correlated with symptoms of psychological ill-health, such as anxiety and depression.

Conclusion: Hassles may be a better predictor of stress-related illness than life events.

Evaluation

- Most of the evidence relies on questionnaire data where the responses from participants may not be reliable. For example, they may have to report **retrospectively** and may have forgotten details of how they felt.

- Much of the research suggests life events are negative and thus cause a negative effect. But many life events are also positive, such as having a baby. Likewise, not everyone will experience life events in the same way, as we all view events differently. This makes it difficult to relate life events to stress levels.

- Many life events cause a number of daily hassles, so separating out the source of stress may be difficult.

- People may receive a lot more support to deal with a life event, while daily hassles are likely to be 'ignored' as a serious source of stress. This may explain why illness is more associated with daily hassles than with life changes.

- There may be individual differences in the way people cope with daily hassles, thus making it difficult to assess the impact they have on stress and illness.

- It is useful to know that daily hassles may be a significant cause of stress-related illness because society may tend to ignore these 'minor annoyances' when discussing stress. For those who treat people suffering with stress, research would suggest that they should discuss both life events and daily hassles.

Now try this

Explain the difference between a daily hassle and a life change.

Workplace stress

Psychologists tend to focus on two key sources of stress in the workplace – **workload** and level of **control** over the work done.

Workload

This refers to the number of tasks a person is required to complete in a given timeframe. The more a person is expected to do, and the shorter the time to do it, the bigger the **workload**. Evidence has linked high levels of stress with a large workload.

Job demands-control model

Karasek's (1979) theory claims that while workplace demands can be stressful, having control can help to 'buffer' these effects by giving people more freedom to change elements of the job to suit them. This explains why people doing the same job can have the same workload, but only one feels the negative stress – the other has more control over how and when the work is done.

Control

This refers to the amount of influence a person has over the nature and timescale of their own work. This could include many different factors.

Psychologists generally believe that the more **control** you have, the less stress you feel.

For example, it could relate to the amount of **control** a person has over when their work needs to be completed by, or the method they use to complete the work.

 Key study **Krantz et al. (2005)**

Aim: To investigate whether total workload was related to symptoms of stress in males and females from Sweden.

Procedure: Questionnaire data was gathered from 743 women and 595 men who worked at least 35 hours per week. Information was gathered about workload (including paid work commitments, unpaid work at home and child care responsibilities) and signs of stress and illness.

Results: Females showed higher levels of symptoms of stress when they had high workplace demands and higher home workload demands, while males had more symptoms associated with longer working hours.

Conclusion: There may be gender differences in the stress response to total workload.

Key study **Marmot et al. (1997)**

Aim: To see whether level of job control was related to stress-related illness.

Procedure: A longitudinal study on 10000 civil servants in London. Data was gathered over a 5-year period using different methods: employee questionnaires, observations by the researchers and reports carried out by personnel staff on the roles and responsibilities of staff. Information about participants' health was also gathered.

Results: Those with low job control were four times more likely to die from a heart attack than those with high control. They were also more likely to suffer other stress-related illnesses such as digestive problems and cancer. Those with more control (and therefore responsibility) were less likely to suffer negative effects of stress.

Conclusion: Low job control was associated with high stress levels.

Evaluation

👍 If employers are aware of potential workplace stressors, they can take steps to try to reduce stress in employees. For example, teaching unions have been tackling issues associated with increased teacher workload. So the evidence can be applied to real life.

👎 It is difficult to isolate the causal variable in this kind of research. There could be other workplace factors associated with stress that have nothing to do with workload or control. For example, stress from hours worked rather than actual workload. Plus, people who feel stressed may exaggerate their workload, so the data may lack reliability and/or validity.

Now try this

Explain how **one** factor associated with the workplace may cause stress.

Self-report scales

In order to understand the effects of stress on individuals, we need to be able to **measure the stress** they are under as well as the potential **sources** of that stress. One way this can be done is using **self-report data**, most usually **questionnaires**.

Social Readjustment Rating Scale (SRRS)

Holmes and Rahe (1967) developed the SRRS as a way to measure life events and how they might be related to stress levels. They looked at medical records of 5000 patients and compiled a list of the 43 most commonly experienced life events in the months before becoming ill. The list was then given to a group of judges who assigned scores to each event based on how much 'change' was needed to adjust to the event. The higher a person's scores on the SRRS in the previous year, the higher their risk of stress-related illness is thought to be.

Rank	Life event	Score
1	Death of spouse	100
2	Divorce	73
4	Prison term	63
10	Retirement	45
12	Pregnancy	40
16	Change in financial state	38
24	Trouble with in-laws	29
30	Trouble with boss	23
32	Change in residence	20
42	Christmas	12
43	Minor violations of the law	11

A few of the items included on the SRRS. People who scored 150–300 points in a given year had a 50% chance of developing health problems the next year; over 300 points, an 80% chance.

Daily hassles and uplifts scale

The daily hassles and uplifts scale was devised in the early 1980s as a way to measure daily stress. It contains 117 negative items and 135 positive items that participants are asked to rate in terms of how much of a hassle (negative effect) or an uplift (positive effect) they felt they were. The more hassles that are reported, the more at risk of stress-related illness a person is thought to be. However, the uplifts on the scale counteract the effects of the hassles, so the uplifts can cancel out the hassles.

Life event	Severity		
Misplacing or losing things	1	2	3
Inconsiderate smokers	1	2	3
Concerns about owing money	1	2	3
Too many responsibilities	1	2	3
Problems getting on with work colleagues	1	2	3
Laid off or out of work	1	2	3
Having to wait	1	2	3
Inability to express yourself	1	2	3
Too many meetings	1	2	3

Examples of some of the daily hassles participants are questioned about on the hassles and uplift scale, where 1 = somewhat severe, 2 = moderately severe and 3 = extremely severe

Evaluation of SRRS

👍 The SRRS is a way to measure the life events experienced in a quantitative way, meaning scores can be reliably compared from person to person.

👎 The resulting data can only give a correlation between life events and likelihood of illness, but the cause and effect may be unclear. For example, unemployment could be the result of a long-standing illness causing a person to miss a lot of work for a long time.

Evaluation of daily hassles/ uplifts scale

👍 By quantifying the daily hassles and uplifts experienced by a person, researchers are able to more easily analyse the results in relation to how likely it is that the person will suffer from stress-related illness.

👎 The judgements made by each participant on a particular day could be affected by how they feel on that particular day in general. A person may perceive more hassles and fewer uplifts if they are in a bad mood one day, for example.

Now try this

Outline **one** criticism of using self-report data to investigate stress.

Physiological measures of stress

Physiological measures of stress involve taking measurements from the body, looking for signs of stress. Physiological is another word for **biological**, so all the methods used to measure stress in this way involve looking at the body's response to stress.

Types of measure

Physiological measures of stress could involve looking for evidence of either acute or chronic stress. Measures could be taken of heart rate and blood pressure to look for increases that might indicate stress. Blood or urine samples could also be taken to look for high levels of the stress hormones adrenaline or cortisol, which could indicate that the body is under stress.

One of the most interesting physiological measures of stress is the **skin conductance response**, also called galvanic skin response.

Skin conductance response (SCR)

SCR is the skin's resistance to electric impulses. When we are under stress the skin sweats more, meaning that it can conduct electricity more easily. Conversely, when we are not stressed, the lack of sweat means that the skin does not conduct electricity as easily.

An SCR monitor can be attached to the fingers and then an electric current passed through the skin to take a measure of conductivity.

 The polygraph test

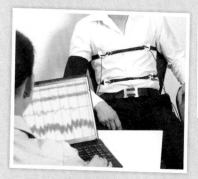

Polygraph tests use SCR to measure stress caused by lying, among other measures.

One way that physiological measures of stress have been applied is in the use of **polygraph tests** or 'lie-detectors'. Polygraph tests take a number of measures from an individual including heart rate, blood pressure, breathing rate and SCR. A baseline measure is taken of the individual to see what their 'normal levels' of each of these are. The same participant will then be asked questions and measures will be taken while they respond to see if they show any signs of stress. Signs of stress will be taken as a sign of lying.

Key study Storm (2000)

Aim: To see if SCR can be used to measure responses to stressful stimuli in preterm infants.

Procedure: A group of 20 preterm infants had their SCR measured for 3 minutes before, during and after being given a heel prick.

Results: Measurements of skin conductivity increased during heel prick and then returned to normal/baseline level.

Conclusion: Stress responses in preterm infants can be measured using SCR, which could be useful for neonatal care in alerting staff to pain or stress in the babies.

Evaluation

👍 A useful application of physiological measures like SCR is in measuring stress responses in people who may not be able to report them, such as in the case of Storm's research on preterm infants.

👍 Using physiological measures of stress is more objective than using self-report measures to gather data on stress levels.

👎 SCR measurements can be affected by external stimuli such as temperature, so the measures taken may be unreliable and inconsistent.

👎 A person's SCR measurements can be different for different stimuli and on different occasions with the same stimuli, so they are not necessarily a useful way to measure stress levels.

Now try this

Explain **one** useful application of biological methods of measuring stress.

Types A, B and C personality

Personality traits can separate people into different 'types' which would account for individual differences in how people respond to stress. Research has established three distinct types of personality associated with a vulnerability to negative effects of stress – **Types A, B** and **C**.

Type A personality

People with Type A personality traits are:

- **time urgent** – they are very impatient and constantly doing new things
- **competitive** – constantly want to win, even when there is no prize
- **hostile** – easily irritated and get angry quickly.

Type A personality types may be more likely to suffer from coronary heart disease (CHD) or high blood pressure.

Type B personality

People with Type B behaviour patterns take a more measured approach to life than Type As. Although they may share the same ambitions, they do not perceive urgency or competition in trying to achieve them.

People with Type B personality are:

- **more relaxed**
- **self-confident**.

They are much less likely to perceive events as stressful, and consequently suffer fewer stress-related health problems than type As.

Type C personality

Those with Type C personality traits are:

- **introverted** – they like to keep to themselves
- **meticulous** – they like to complete work to a high standard, focusing on the details
- **dependable** – they will please others even when it may disadvantage themselves.

Because they often do not share their emotions with others, and are easily stressed due to their high level of perfectionism, they are prone to some types of cancer as well as depression associated with stress.

Extend Type D personality

An additional type has been added since types A, B and C were first discovered. People categorised as Type D are often referred to as 'distressed' or 'disease-prone'.

People with Type D traits are:

- **irritable** – they worry often and become agitated quickly
- **pessimistic** – they often think negatively, although they do not often share this with others for fear of rejection
- **obedient/conformist** – they like to do what is expected of them.

This type of person may be prone to depression and/or anxiety, as well as cardiovascular disease.

Research evidence

✓ Friedman and Rosenman (1974) studied 3200 American males for 8.5 years and found that Type A personality traits were associated with higher rates of heart problems. In total, 257 developed CHD over the time period. Of these, 70% had Type A personalities. Twice as many Type As as Type Bs died from heart attacks over the 8.5 years, although some Type Bs did still suffer heart attacks. Also, many Type As recover well after non-fatal heart attacks because of their increased likelihood of being more determined to improve their health.

✓ Morris et al. (1981) found evidence that Type C females showed higher rates of cancer than other personality types. They suggested this could be the result of poor immune function, which could be caused by repressing emotions.

Evaluation

👍 By understanding that certain personality traits may make a person more vulnerable to the negative effects of stress, psychologists may be able to identify people who are high risk and help to advise them on behaviour patterns that could protect them from the stress.

👎 People do not easily fall into one 'type' of personality, and may show different behaviour patterns or traits in different situations or at different times. This makes the usefulness of this research problematic because the categories themselves may not be that reliable.

Now try this

Explain how personality type may be related to effects of stress.

Hardiness

Hardiness is a set of personality traits defined by Kobasa (1979). The traits are felt to protect a person from the negative effects of stress and explain individual differences in how people cope with stressful situations. Hardiness is a way of perceiving stressful situations so that the person may actually be able to turn the stress into a more positive thing in their mind.

Hardy personality

Kobasa (1979) compared two groups of middle-aged executives on responses to recent stressful life events. Both groups had a similar level of 'stress' in terms of recent events, but while one group became ill afterwards, the other group did not. After analysing the data, she found that the only major difference between the two groups was that the 'ill' group showed fewer characteristics of the personality type she referred to as '**hardiness**'. According to Kobasa, someone who is '**hardy**' demonstrates **commitment**, **control** and **challenge**.

Commitment

Having a strong sense of purpose, and viewing tasks in relation to the effort they take to complete effectively. Showing **commitment** to getting things done.

For example, someone with high levels of hardiness might be **committed** to getting an A grade in Psychology, and will recognise that to achieve this they will need to work really hard all the way through the course.

Challenge

Viewing change as a **challenge** to be mastered, rather than a source of stress. They recognise that change is a normal part of life, and it is not something to be feared.

For example, a person with a high level of hardiness who finds themselves facing redundancy from work may welcome the **challenge** to seek out new career opportunities rather than worrying about being out of work.

Features of hardiness

Control

Feeling that they have the ability to take **control** of any situation, and that they can influence the outcome of a situation.

For example, someone with a high level of hardiness could be described as having an internal **locus of control** (see page 9). They are likely to take personal responsibility for what happens to them, meaning that they will not give up easily when faced with potential stressors.

Research evidence

✓ Wiebe (1991) found that participants high in hardy personality traits had a higher level of tolerance frustration, perceived stressful tasks as less threatening, and were more likely to approach tasks with a positive rather than negative attitude when compared to participants low in hardiness. She also found that males with high hardiness showed a lower level of physiological arousal in response to stressful tasks.

✓ Maddi et al. (2002) compared two groups of university students deemed 'high risk' for drop-out or failure. The experimental group were given hardiness training during their first semester, while the control group were not. At the end of the first year the retention rate for the experimental group was higher, and they showed a much higher increase in assessment scores than the control group. This suggested that being trained in hardiness may make people cope better with stressful situations such as starting university.

Evaluation

🖒 The concept of hardiness has a useful application to real life; hardiness training can help people cope with stress in their everyday life by buffering the negative effects.

🖒 Most research into hardiness is conducted on stress that occurs in people's natural life, meaning that it is ecologically valid – and more ethical – than deliberately exposing people to artificial stress.

👎 Some would argue that 'hardiness' does not exist as a personality type, but rather it reflects a positive way of thinking. So rather than being 'hardy', these people may just adopt positive thinking styles that help them deal with stress more easily.

Now try this

Outline **one** criticism of the relationship between hardiness and stress.

Drug therapy

If stress has a serious impact on a person's health, **drugs** can be used to manage the symptoms or stop the negative effects of stress on the body. There are two main categories of drugs used to treat stress: **benzodiazepines** and **beta-blockers**.

❶ Benzodiazepines (BZs)

Anxiolytic (anti-anxiety) drugs, such as **benzodiazepines**, can be used to treat chronic stress. These work in the brain to stop the body being aroused by stressful stimuli. BZs increase the action of the neurotransmitter **GABA** (gamma-aminobutyric acid), which occurs naturally as a 'calming' chemical in the brain (see page 84). BZs boost the action of the GABA that already exists, so the brain feels calmer and less aroused by stressful stimuli. BZs also dampen the excitatory effects of **serotonin**, so the nervous system activity is slowed down, increasing feelings of calmness.

❷ Beta-blockers (BBs)

These drugs act in the nervous system to block **beta-adrenergic receptors** found in various parts of the body such as the heart and blood vessels. These receptors are stimulated by adrenaline, which is released from the adrenal medulla when we are scared or threatened by a stressful stimulus (see page 85). BBs block the beta-adrenergic receptors from being stimulated by adrenaline. This reduces the physical effects of stress in the fight-or-flight response.

Research evidence for BZs

Zandstra et al. (2004) compared a group of short-term and a group of long-term users of BZs. They found that those most at risk of long-term use (and therefore more problems with dependence) were those who were older, poorly educated and had little social contact with other people. Their research suggests that anyone prescribed BZs who is in this 'group' should be more closely monitored, or should be encouraged to use other treatments for stress.

Research evidence for BBs

Alexander et al. (2007) set participants up in a stressful situation (public speaking) and then tested their cognitive performance in a mental arithmetic task. The participants were tested several times, including under the influence of BBs, and also after being given a placebo (a 'drug' with no clinical effect, though the participant is not aware of this). They found that stress impaired performance on the maths task, but this effect was reversed if the participants took BBs, suggesting BBs may improve cognitive impairments caused by stress.

Evaluation of BZs

👍 Drugs like BZs are a cost-effective way of treating effects of stress because patients can be given the drugs to take in their own time, meaning they do not need supervision.

👎 BZs are only suitable for short-term treatment of stress because they can be addictive. Over time the brain can develop tolerance, meaning that they become less effective the longer they are taken.

👎 Some patients experience severe side effects from BZs, such as memory problems and reduced concentration span.

Evaluation of BBs

👍 BBs are a useful way to treat some of the symptoms of stress that can be dangerous, such as increased heart rate and blood pressure. Because they work very quickly they are a favourable treatment for stress.

👍 Drugs are a familiar form of treatment, so patients are more likely to stick with this than attend therapy sessions regularly.

👎 The drugs only treat the immediate symptoms of the stressful situation, so while they are useful as a short-term solution, they do not help in the long-term.

👎 They can have side effects, including hallucinations and fatigue.

Now try this

Explain the negative effects of using drugs to treat stress.

Stress inoculation training

Stress training (therapy) (SIT), developed by Meichenbaum and Cameron (1972), is a form of cognitive behavioural therapy (CBT) used to treat stress. The name 'inoculation' is applied because it can provide a long-term resistance to the effects of stress.

Stress inoculation training (SIT)

This type of treatment programme is based on CBT and involves tackling the thought processes that could be leading to problematic behaviours. By acknowledging 'faulty' thought processes, changes can be made to then bring about a change in behaviour, thus resulting in less problematic behaviours.

Three stages of SIT

SIT is a three-stage process that involves making the client aware of their own stressors, giving them skills to deal with these in a positive way and then putting these skills into practice.

Conceptualisation
- Patients are encouraged to talk about the stressors they face and how they currently deal with them.
- Negative thought patterns are discussed, such as 'I am a failure at work because I keep missing deadlines'.

Skills acquisition and rehearsal
- New skills are discussed to help the patient deal with the stressors in a more productive way. This could include relaxation techniques.
- More positive thought patterns may be discussed, such as 'I need to get organised to avoid missing deadlines'.

Application and follow-through
- The skills they have learnt will be put into practice through role plays of stressful situations.
- Gradually, the patient will work up to real-world practice in increasingly stressful situations, until eventually they feel able to use the skills independently.

Research evidence

Jay and Elliot (1990) looked at the effectiveness of SIT to help parents of children receiving treatment for leukaemia deal with the stress of the situation. They compared parents given SIT with those given another therapy, and found that the SIT group reported lower levels of anxiety and better coping skills than the other group. This suggests that SIT may be a useful treatment for dealing with real-life stressors.

Evaluation

- 👍 Unlike drug treatments for stress, SIT has no negative side effects. Because the biology of the individual is not being affected by the therapy, there can be no impact on their physiology such as cognitive impairments or hallucinations.

- 👍 The skills acquired during SIT provide the patient with a long-term coping strategy to deal, not only with current stressors, but also with all future stressful situations.

- 👍 CBT can help soldiers to confront the trauma they have faced, and challenge the blame or other negative thoughts that may accompany the memory of the events witnessed. This helps them to deal with the trauma and develop coping strategies to use long-term.

- 👎 SIT is only effective if the patient is motivated and capable of spending time considering their own stressors and practising the skills taught. Some people experiencing high levels of stress may be too impatient to take time to 'treat their own stress', meaning it may be ineffective for some.

One specific application of SIT is in the treatment of post-traumatic stress disorder (PTSD) in soldiers returning from conflict.

Now try this

Outline the process used in stress inoculation training.

Biofeedback

Biofeedback is a method of stress management that aims to make people aware of their body's responses to stress and then learn how to counteract them and control their stress levels in any future situations.

Types of biofeedback

Monitors can be attached to different areas of the body to alert the patient to subtle changes in their biology brought on by stress (see page 233). The type of biological change targeted will depend on what problems the patient has that are associated with stress. For example, sensors (like galvanic skin response monitors) can be applied to feedback on:

- **breathing rate** – attached to the chest and abdomen
- **heart rate** – attached to the fingers, neck, chest or wrist
- **muscle tension** – attached to skeletal muscles

How biofeedback works

The patient is attached to a monitor, which will give a visual or auditory indication that the body is responding to stressors in an undesired way.

For example, the patient may have a monitor that sounds a buzzer when the heart rate becomes too high. Or a light may flash when the muscles tense up.

When the patient is told by the monitor that their biology is responding to the stress they are then taught techniques to reduce the biological response. This could include relaxation methods to reduce muscle tension, or breathing techniques to slow down respiration.

The biofeedback loop

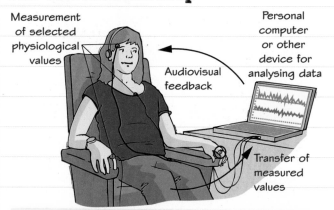

Measurement of selected physiological values

Audiovisual feedback

Personal computer or other device for analysing data

Transfer of measured values

The individual is given constant feedback to enable them to consciously control their biological response to stress.

🔍 Key study Lemaire et al. (2011)

Aim: To see if biofeedback could help to reduce stress in a group of doctors.

Procedure: A group of 40 doctors were placed in either the biofeedback group or the control group. All participants were given twice-weekly support visits from the researchers over a 28-day period, but half of them were also trained in how to use a biofeedback device three times a day during the same time period.

Results: Doctors in the biofeedback group showed a significant reduction in reported stress at the end of the 28 days.

Conclusion: Regular biofeedback can help to reduce stress in doctors.

Evaluation

👍 Biofeedback is less invasive than drug treatments with less risk of side effects or possible addiction. Thus it is more suitable for long-term treatment and will be suitable for more people.

👎 This treatment may be more costly than drug therapies as patients require specialist equipment and training in how to use it. However, new equipment is being developed all the time, such as wearable devices and apps you can download. This means eventually the treatment may become cheaper and more easily available.

👎 Although evidence suggests it is effective, little is understood about how biofeedback works. Some would argue that the effects seen are merely the result of the relaxation techniques taught and not necessarily the actual biofeedback itself. It could also be a placebo effect caused by people expecting to feel better because they are told biofeedback will work.

Now try this

Evaluate biofeedback as a method to treat stress.

Gender differences

The way people **cope with stress** can be influenced by many things, one of which is their **gender**. Males and females may perceive stressful situations differently, or simply react differently to stress.

Biological differences

Males and females differ in their biological make-up, and this could mean that they respond differently to stressful situations.

For example, a male who feels threatened may react aggressively or may actually run away (fight-or-flight response) as they produce higher levels of **noradrenaline** and **cortisol** in response to stress. Women, on the other hand, produce higher levels of the hormone **oxytocin** which makes them prone to caring and nurturing behaviour. When threatened they may be more likely to try to use reasoning to avoid stress, or seek out friends to help them cope.

Research evidence

Taylor et al. (2000) presented a paper that suggested that the 'fight-or-flight' response is a typical male response to acute stress, while the same response in females is better described as a 'tend-or-befriend' response (see page 226). They argued that experiencing a stressor triggers the release of **oxytocin** in females – a hormone associated with the attachment relationship and nurturing behaviour. The paper describes how female biology may have meant that, in the evolutionary past, females would be unable to 'run or fight' when under stress because of having offspring with them. As a result, the tendency for females is to 'protect' during times of stress, or make friends in order to reduce the stress felt in the situation.

Evaluation

👍 Understanding that gender differences may exist in the type and amount of stress experienced, and how this may be dealt with, could have useful implications. For example, businesses could be made aware of possible gender differences that exist to better support employees.

👎 By reporting gender differences in coping with stress, psychologists could be creating a 'self-fulfilling prophecy' where men and women begin to act in line with expectation and the gender differences become more exaggerated.

Social differences

Men and women differ in their social relationships, which could explain why their response to stress is different. Males generally have many friends, but don't use them for social support, while females often have a small group of close friends whom they rely on for social support in times of need. Females may be more open to discussing their stresses than males, so their response to stress may be more social than males.

Males and females may also use different strategies to deal with the source of stress.

Males often use problem-focused coping strategies, such as discussing issues at work with their boss.

Females may use emotion-focused coping strategies, such as going shopping with friends when stressed.

🔊 Key study   Matud (2004)

Aim: To investigate gender differences in stress and coping strategies.

Procedure: In total, 2816 participants completed questionnaires assessing their levels of stress, including life events and daily hassles (see page 232), as well as common coping strategies. The results of the male and female participants were then compared.

Results: There were no differences in number of life events experienced by males and females, but females scored more highly on daily hassles and chronic stress. Females reported more physical and psychological symptoms. Women also used more emotion-focused coping strategies than men.

Conclusion: There are gender differences in the amount of stress and how this is dealt with.

Now try this

Compare ways in which men and women have been shown to respond differently to stress.

Social support

Social support refers to the amount of help, time and resources offered to an individual by others in order to help them cope with stress. Family, friends, colleagues, teachers and even doctors or therapists can all be a source of social support when dealing with stressful situations.

Types of social support

Stroebe (2000) identified five main types of social support people can receive.

Appraisal support – help to understand the stressful situation and the effect it is having on the individual. Sometimes people can benefit from an objective view of the situation from someone else.

Informational support – support by providing information and ideas on how the person could cope with stress, or simply comment on how they think the person is coping to help them reflect on the situation.

Social support

Emotional support – when others can provide comfort for the stressed individual by offering sympathy or care in some way. This can help them to feel better while they cope with the stress.

Instrumental support – providing tangible help to cope with the stressful situation. This could be **indirect**, such as helping out with housework while a person adapts to and copes with a bereavement to give them more space and time to grieve. Or it could be **direct** such as lending money to help a person financially following loss of employment.

Esteem support – support in making the person feel valued and capable while they cope with a stressful situation. If others can 'big them up' by demonstrating all the positive things they are doing, it may help them to feel more in control and actually make coping seem easier.

Improving social support

Not everyone has a wide social circle to draw on when stressed. Psychologists have suggested how social support networks can be sought out in times of need. For example:

1 **Support groups** are set up for people who share a similar situation. Spending time with people facing similar stressors can be helpful.

2 **Social media** can be a useful way to connect with people when it is difficult to do so face-to-face. Relying heavily on online communication, though, can cause more problems.

3 **Joining clubs or starting hobbies** can be a good way to meet like-minded people. This way, you are surrounding yourself with people and making more connections with others.

Key study — Bolger and Amarel (2007)

Aim: To investigate whether **visible** (obvious) or **invisible social support** (indirect) is more effective in helping people cope with stress.

Procedure: A group of 257 female participants were made to give a public speech as a stressor. Each was paired with a female researcher who provided either visible support (including advice on what to do) or invisible support (including an audible discussion with another researcher about good tips on public speaking). Following the speech, the participants reported back on their stress levels.

Results: Visible support seemed to increase emotional reactions to stress, while invisible support reduced stress levels.

Conclusion: It is possible that visible stress may make people feel judged as unable to cope.

Evaluation

👍 Understanding different types of social support is useful as some may be more useful in certain situations than others. For example, the type of support needed to deal with work stress is very different to the type of support needed to deal with bereavement.

👎 The effects of social support are difficult to measure as it is unclear what – if in fact anything – helps to reduce the stress. It could simply be an increase in self-esteem from feeling valued that makes people feel better, rather than an actual decrease in stress.

Now try this

Identify **two** types of social support and explain how they differ.

Exam skills 1

Before you look at these worked examples, remind yourself about methodological issues in the study of stress (pages 232–233).

Worked example

Explain **one** limitation of using questionnaires to study stress.

(2 marks)

Read questions carefully and look for the hints given by the exam board regarding how much content they expect you to cover.

Questionnaires are prone to social desirability bias where people answer questions in a way to make themselves look better in the eyes of someone else. Certain people might feel they would be judged if they admitted to high levels of stress so they 'play down' their real stress levels in order to look more in control. This would reduce the validity of the findings from the research.

Questionnaires are covered as a research method (see page 98). Here you are being asked to make a point regarding a limitation that is relevant to studying stress. That means general limitations such as social desirability need to be made specific to the study of stress.

Worked example

Explain **one** limitation of the Social Readjustment Ratings Scale as a tool to study causes of stress.

(2 marks)

This is similar to the question above, as the SRRS is an example of a specific type of questionnaire to study stress. The difference here is that your elaboration of the point you make must relate directly to the use of the SRRS.

The SRRS often relies on retrospective data because people are asked to recall events they have faced in the last year that could have caused them stress. Because they are having to think back, they may forget events that happened that could be possible life events to cause stress.

Using key terms such as 'retrospective data' or 'social desirability' (used in the previous answer) is really important to show you can use the language of psychology, but you must be sure to explain what the term means to demonstrate understanding.

Worked example

Which **two** of the following statements could be seen as strengths of the use of physiological measures of stress?

Always read multiple choice questions carefully. This question asks for **two** statements to be identified. Only providing one answer would mean marks would be lost.

A   They are conducted in controlled environments making them less prone to extraneous variable interference.   ⬭

B   They give an objective measure of stress levels.   ⬤

C   They provide correlational data meaning that cause and effect can be inferred from the data.   ⬭

D   They are not influenced by individual differences in the way people report and respond to stress.   ⬭

E   They allow participants to report their stress levels in their own way.   ⬤

(2 marks)

Do not assume that multiple choice questions are going to be easy. Often the answers given will all sound as if they could be true, but only by reading them carefully and matching them against your understanding of the content of the question will you be able to work out the correct answers.

Exam skills 2

Some of the exam questions will require you to read a short scenario and then refer to it in your answer. Before you look at these worked examples, remind yourself about immunosuppression and stress (page 228).

Worked example

Read the item and then answer the questions that follow.

> Saraya started university almost a year ago and has found living away from home and starting a new course in a different city very stressful. She is about to sit her first end-of-year exams and has a cold that does not seem to go away. Saraya's friend is studying psychology and has told her about some research that suggests that stress can affect the immune system.

(a) With reference to the results of one study into the effects of stress on the immune system, explain why Saraya has a cold all the time.

(5 marks)

(a) One study into the effect of stress on the immune system is by Kiecolt-Glaser (1984). Blood samples taken from 75 medical students on the first day of their exams showed much lower levels of T-cells than the samples taken one month before. This would suggest that the immune system was functioning less well when the exams started because of the additional stress. She also found that the T-cell levels were lowest in the students who reported the highest number of psychological symptoms of stress. Because Saraya has been feeling stressed since she started university and is now starting her exams, her number of T-cells might be quite low, meaning she is less able to fight off a virus, which would explain why she has a cold that won't to go away. Her body is unable to fight it off because of the stress.

(b) Outline **one** limitation of the research study you used in (a).

(3 marks)

(b) Kielcolt-Glaser only used medical students in her study and the type of stress they suffer may be different from that of other people, even other students. They are likely to be working long hours while also studying, and the work they do has very serious consequences as they may be making life-or-death decisions with very little experience. This will mean their stress levels may be significantly higher than for the majority of people, making the study unrepresentative of the general population.

Always read the scenario before attempting the question. Often the scenario will offer some clues that might help you answer the question, or the question that follows is likely to require you to use some information from the scenario in your answer.

Stress can influence health in many ways. The specification indicates that you must be able to talk about immunosuppression and stress, as well as stress and cardiovascular disease. This question clearly asks for research into stress and the immune system, so make sure a suitable study is selected.

Question (a) only asks for results from a suitable study. Do not waste time outlining the procedure before you discuss the results of a study. It is a good idea to read the question carefully and make sure you answer it in the most efficient way possible, which here would mean only focusing on the results.

The reference to the results will need to be quite detailed. Make sure that when revising you cover depth of knowledge about relevant studies as well as breadth, by covering more than one suitable study.

If you look at question (b), there is no requirement to make the answer relevant to the scenario. You therefore do not need to mention Saraya or the scenario. Instead, get straight to the point and discuss the limitation of the study.

Exam-style practice 1

Practise for Paper 3 of your A level exam with these exam-style questions. There are answers on pages 316–317. Before looking at these questions, it would be good to review the section on stress (pages 225–240).

1 (a) With reference to hardiness as defined by Kobasa, outline what is meant by 'control'. **(2 marks)**

   (b) Briefly explain what is meant by 'workload' as it relates to workplace stress. **(2 marks)**

   (c) Briefly explain what is meant by 'skin conductance response' as a measure of stress. **(2 marks)**

> Key terms are a common focus for short exam questions, so spending time making sure you can accurately define the terms is useful. Make sure you can also elaborate these terms. Giving examples is a good way to do this as it shows understanding.

2 Explain what research has shown about the effect of workplace factors on stress. **(4 marks)**

> The question refers to 'what research has shown', which means you must focus on the results and conclusions from research studies. Do not go into detail about the procedures used as these are not relevant to the question.

3 Discuss research that has investigated life events as a cause of stress. **(8 marks)**

> 'Discuss' means you must both describe the research and evaluate it. You could focus on one study into life events as a cause of stress and describe and evaluate this in detail, or you could choose two or three studies and briefly discuss each one. As long as you provide some clear explanation and evaluation in your answer, either strategy would be appropriate.

4 Explain **one** limitation of research into the relationship between stress and cardiovascular disease. **(3 marks)**

> Questions that simply ask you to 'explain **one** limitation' of research do not require any description of the study/studies. This can be difficult for students at first – to evaluate something without first describing what it is – but the more you practise this, the easier it will become. No marks will be given for any description you give on this kind of question, which means beginning with a lengthy description is wasting time.

5 Discuss **at least two** methods of stress management. **(16 marks)**

> Planning out essay questions like this is a really good way to keep you focused while you write your answer and stop you forgetting your points when you are midway through. You should spend a total of 20 minutes writing a 16-mark essay, so within that time allow at least 2 minutes to plan before you begin to answer the question.

> Here, you are required to cover a *minimum* of two methods. Some students find it easier to go into **depth** and detail on two methods of stress management, while others prefer to cover **breadth** by discussing more than two methods in less detail. Practise your answers and decide which strategy would work better for you in the exam.

Exam-style practice 2

Practise for Paper 3 of your A level exam with these exam-style questions. There are answers on page 317. Before looking at these questions, it would be good to review the sections on general adaptation syndrome (page 225), biofeedback (page 238) and social support (page 240).

6 Using an example, briefly explain what is meant by 'emotional support' as a type of social support.   **(2 marks)**

This kind of question requires a 'brief' explanation of a key term, and also an example that should clearly illustrate what this key term means.

7 Read the item and then answer the question that follows.

> A group of 20 students have been participating in a study at their college into the effects of biofeedback techniques on dealing with exam stress. Half of the group have been shown how to use a galvanic skin response monitor to identify when they are beginning to feel stressed, and then given training in how to reduce their physiological response to the stress. The other half have not been given the training. The study began 6 weeks before their AS level exam for Psychology. The biofeedback group had biofeedback sessions twice a week for the full 6 weeks, while the control group did nothing. Each participant was given a questionnaire to measure the general level of stress they felt at the beginning of the study, and then again on the morning of the exam. The mean average score from the questionnaire for each group is shown in the table below.

There is a lot of stimulus here which must be read before attempting the question. Make sure you read the stimulus material carefully as it will probably help you to answer the question that follows.

Table 1: Stress questionnaire responses for a group trained in using biofeedback compared to a control group

Group	Average stress score 6 weeks before the exam/100	Average stress score on the day of the exam/100
Biofeedback group	63	69
Control group	65	84

Using your knowledge of biofeedback techniques, explain the data shown in **Table 1**.   **|4 marks|**

Look at the data in the table carefully and plan out what you want to say before you start writing. Questions like this will expect you to use all of the data presented in some way, but the exam injunction in the question is to 'explain' the data, so do not simply repeat the data from the table in sentences.

8 (a) With reference to general adaptation syndrome, briefly explain what is meant by 'exhaustion'.   **(2 marks)**

Some words in psychology have different meanings depending on where you use them. For example, 'exhaustion' means something very specific when related to GAS, so you must make sure you give the correct definition of the term in the context of the question.

   (b) Explain **one** limitation of research into general adaptation syndrome.   **(2 marks)**

Although you may be able to think of many limitations of the research, here you need to elaborate on your answer of just **one** limitation, so choose something you are sure you can explain clearly and in depth.

Neural and hormonal mechanisms

The structure of the brain and the biochemistry of the body are thought to play a significant role in **aggression**. You need to know how the **limbic system**, **serotonin** and **testosterone** are involved in aggressive behaviour.

Limbic system

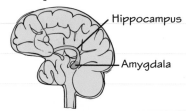

Hippocampus

Amygdala

> The **limbic system** includes the hippocampus and amygdala, and is one of the circuits in the brain that is involved with emotions, including aggression.

The **amygdala** appears to process emotions and plays a part in aggression. Removal of the amygdala reduces aggression in previously violent individuals, who then also show a loss of emotions. Damage or malfunctioning of the amygdala is associated with testosterone levels increasing, leading to a rise in aggressive behaviour.

Serotonin

Serotonin is a neurotransmitter involved in mood and impulse control (see page 84). The results regarding the role of serotonin in aggression are mixed. Some studies show that low levels of serotonin are associated with increased susceptibility to impulsive behaviour and aggression, whilst others have found the opposite – that high levels are involved in aggressive behaviour. As serotonin regulates mood and facilitates an individual's emotional state to a situation, it would make sense to assume that low levels of serotonin would hinder that response and may result in the individual behaving more aggressively.

Testosterone

This is a predominantly male **hormone**, although some is produced by females. It is known as an androgen because it generates male characteristics (see page 158). High levels of **testosterone** are shown to play a role in aggressive behaviour, which is why aggression is often thought to be a male trait. It acts on areas of the brain that control aggression from puberty onwards. Reduced levels of the enzyme **aromatase** (found in the amygdala), which processes testosterone, have been shown to affect aggression levels, resulting in a lack of an emotional response, making aggression more likely.

Research evidence

✓ Raine et al. (1997) compared 41 murderers to 41 non-murderers to see if there were brain differences. Murderers had abnormal activity in the amygdala and lower metabolism of glucose in the prefrontal cortex, which is associated with loss of control. This suggests that aggression is caused by biological processes.

✓ Scerbo and Raine (1993) carried out a correlational analysis and found consistently lower levels of serotonin in people described as aggressive. No cause and effect was shown.

✓ Wagner et al. (1979) found that castrated male mice showed lower levels of aggression, but if given testosterone their aggression increased. This suggests that testosterone plays a part in aggressive behaviour.

Evaluation

👍 Finding a biological cause for aggression could help discover treatments, particularly for violent criminals.

👎 Research carried out on animals makes it difficult to extrapolate to human aggression. Some areas of the brain do differ in animals and this could be a problem applying it to humans.

👎 Each of the three aspects is determinist as they suggest that having the abnormalities will cause aggression, without acknowledging free will.

Now try this

Briefly outline **one** study that looks into the role of testosterone and aggression.

Genetic factors

Researchers are interested in whether aggression is an **inherited behaviour** and therefore a product of nature (**genes**) rather than nurture (environment). You need to know the key aspects of genetic explanations, including the **MAOA gene** (see page 131).

MAOA gene

The MAOA gene (monoamine oxidase A) regulates an enzyme (also called MAOA), which is linked to the breakdown of neurotransmitters – serotonin and dopamine – in the synapses (see page 84). Genetically, a mutation on this gene can cause low or high MAOA enzyme activity.

Lower levels of the enzyme can result in higher than usual levels of the neurotransmitters, because they are not broken down. In some individuals, this is displayed as increased aggressive behaviour, highlighting a correlation between low levels of MAOA and aggressive behaviour.

However, not all men with the gene mutation show aggressive behaviour. The environment also plays a role, as males with low-activity MAOA are more at risk of committing a violent crime if they have suffered abuse as a child (Caspi et al. 2002). This shows the interaction of nature and nurture.

Research evidence

Brunner et al. (1993) studied a Dutch family, five male members of which possessed a shortened version of the MAOA gene. They consequently had abnormally low levels of the MAOA enzyme and were not able to break down all the neurotransmitters. The men had behavioural problems. They were aggressive, showed borderline mental retardation and some had been in prison for attempted rape and assault. This study shows how the MAOA gene affects behaviour and that the condition is sex-linked and carried on the X chromosome. However, as the men were all brought up in the same environment, nurture may also have played a role in their aggressive behaviour.

The MAOA gene has been linked to aggressive behaviour.

XYY genotype

Whilst most people have 46 chromosomes (23 pairs), it is possible for a male to have an extra Y chromosome, making them XYY. Research has shown a link between an extra Y chromosome and aggression. Males with this extra chromosome are taller than average, have a low IQ and display behavioural problems.

Research evidence

Price et al. (1966) studied males in hospitals for the criminally insane. They discovered that 28% of the patients had the extra Y chromosome compared with under 0.1% of the general population. This suggests that this extra chromosome correlates with aggressive behaviour.

Twin studies

Twin and adoption studies suggest an important role for genetic factors and aggression.

McGuffin and Gottesman (1985) examined concordance rates of aggression in twins, finding an 87% concordance rate in the monozygotic (MZ identical) twins and a 72% concordance in the dizygotic (DZ non-identical) twins. This indicates that genetics could play a role in aggression, although it is not the only factor.

Research evidence

Rhee and Waldman (2002) carried out a meta-analysis of anti-social behaviour (operationalised as psychiatric diagnoses, delinquency and behavioural aggression) in 51 twin and adoption studies. They found the genetic component of antisocial/aggressive behaviour was 40% and the environmental contribution was 60%. This suggests that it could be a combination of both nature and nurture that influences aggressive behaviour.

Evaluation

- 👍 The research into aggression can be considered reductionist, which is usually used as a negative point of evaluation. However, if a single gene can be isolated and found to be the root cause of aggression, this could lead to the people affected getting the appropriate treatment.

- 👎 The research could be considered socially sensitive and have harmful consequences for particular groups of people. For example, if aggressive people are judged to be inferior, some rogue leaders could look to extinguish them (e.g. Galton's eugenics motivated the Nazi holocaust).

Now try this

Evaluate genetic explanations of aggression.

Ethology

Ethology is the study of animals and their behaviour. It is used to explain some human behaviour, such as aggression, by looking at animals in their natural habitat. This has helped us to understand human aggression in the process of evolution.

Lorenz (1966)

Lorenz, an ethological theorist, suggested that humans show comparable behaviour to other animals. Ethological research could therefore be generalised to humans because similar driving forces lie behind any behaviours: fear, hunger, reproduction and aggression.

Innate releasing mechanisms

Lorenz suggested that animals use an **innate releasing mechanism (IRM)** or drive, which acts as a release for aggression in response to a **stimulus**. Once the aggression has been spent, the drive builds up again until a stimulus triggers it once more and the aggression is displayed. The stimulus is known as a '**releaser**'.

Cats when confronted with a dog (stimulus) release aggression through an IRM. The IRM allows the release of aggression through a **fixed action pattern**.

Fixed action patterns

This is the behaviour that **results** from the IRM. A **fixed action pattern** (FAP) is a sequence of behaviours that is the same for all animals in that species. As such, FAPs are innate and adaptive.

Male sticklebacks are aggressive towards any other male members of the species that encroach on the territory around their pre-prepared nest. However, they encourage female sticklebacks to stay and lay their eggs in the nest.

Research evidence

✓ Sackett (1966) reared monkeys in isolation and showed them pictures of monkeys playing, exploring and in threatening poses. As the infant monkeys got older, they reacted to the pictures of infant monkeys and threatening stimuli, showing an innate releasing mechanism to respond to a stimulus and detect a threat.

✓ Tinbergen (1952) devised replicated models of stickleback fish, with red bellies for the males and swollen bellies for the females. Male sticklebacks attacked the male models, replicating the pattern of aggressive behaviour seen in the natural world when the female is nesting to lay eggs. This shows the behaviour is innate and a fixed action pattern.

Evaluation

👎 Ethology when applied to human aggressive behaviour is both **determinist** and **reductionist**. It oversimplifies the complex differences between humans and animals. It also suggests that even if humans experience the innate releasing mechanism it does not always **determine** their behaviour; not all humans act upon it as some people exert **free will**.

👎 The idea of generalising ethological research on aggression to humans is problematic. In humans, aggression is used with intent to inflict harm, whereas in ethology it is used as a ritual. Human females do not want an aggressive male as her partner – this would not be considered an adaptive behaviour.

👍 Lorenz's research has remained a key part of the evolutionary theory of aggression.

Now try this

1 Explain how the innate releasing mechanism works.

2 Explain what is meant by a fixed action pattern.

Evolutionary explanations

Aggression can be seen as an **adaptive response** as it helped us in the **environment of evolutionary adaptiveness (EEA)** to procure resources, secure mates and punish/deter infidelity. Humans were more likely to survive if they could achieve those things.

Aggression in males

Evolutionary psychologists believe all behaviour is linked to **reproduction**, including aggressive behaviour. Competition between males to achieve status in attracting females gives the men better access to potential mates, which could lead to successful reproduction.

The status achieved as a result of displays of aggression appeals to females who consider their strength a sign that they are able to provide for them and any offspring.

Aggression in females

In evolutionary terms, a female is crucial to her offspring's survival, as she protects and raises them. Females choose a mate according to how well he can provide for, protect and nurture any offspring they may have. In order to survive to carry out her role as caregiver, females have evolved to be less aggressive than males and are more likely to ostracise others in any disputes. The adaptive and functional benefits of aggressive behaviour must outweigh the possible costs.

Symptoms

The role of jealousy, infidelity and cuckoldry in the EEA.

	Males	Females
Infidelity and jealousy	**Jealousy** may have occurred as an adaptive response as males were at risk of the females going off with someone else. This would put their gene pool at risk. Therefore, jealousy was a result of suspecting **female infidelity**, which could help prevent **cuckoldry** (where another male gets their partner pregnant).	In evolutionary terms, females have the problem of keeping a mate to provide resources for themselves and any offspring. If **emotional infidelity** occurs, such as an affair, they may lose this. **Jealousy** may trigger acts of aggression, including threats of violence towards other women, and mate guarding – watching and staying close to their partner (see page 139).
Cuckoldry and jealousy	Males are at risk of cuckoldry because they are always uncertain of the paternity of any offspring they have. In evolutionary terms, if this has occurred it makes no sense for him to stay in the relationship as he is then investing resources in genes that are not his.	Females are never at risk of cuckoldry as they are always sure the baby is theirs. However, infidelity by their partner poses a different risk for women – the loss of the man's time, parenting, investment and resources.

Research evidence

✓ Buss and Shackelford (1997) found that men used far more aggressive tactics than women to keep their partner if they feared infidelity. They used strategies such as threatening violence against her and the male, especially if his partner is younger. This supports the evolutionary theory that a younger partner would be more fertile and could put the man at risk of cuckoldry.

✓ Miller (1980) found that 55% of battered wives claimed their husbands' jealousy of suspected infidelity was the reason for their assaults, even though it was often without substance. This supports the evolutionary approach of aggression as men used it as a preventative measure against the wife cheating.

Evaluation

🔹 EEA explanations of male aggression suggest that males have no free will and are innately driven to act in this way to attract and retain a partner, and are therefore determinist.

🔹 EEA explanations are considered socially sensitive research as they almost excuse male aggression on females as being justified.

🔹 Male-on-female assaults vary culturally, which suggests it is not universal. It therefore lacks validity, as other explanations must be involved.

🔹 It is difficult to test evolutionary explanations as they are all after the event (post-hoc).

Now try this

Outline the roles of infidelity and jealousy in evolutionary explanations of aggression.

Deindividuation and frustration

Social psychological explanations for human aggression include **deindividuation**, the **frustration–aggression hypothesis** and **social learning theory** (see page 250 for more on SLT). They focus on the environmental influences on aggression while ignoring any biological, innate explanations.

Deindividuation

This is the loss of both public and private self-awareness (Prentice-Dunn and Rogers, 1982). This notion of aggression originated from LeBon (1896) who suggested that, as a result of being in a large crowd, an individual's behaviour changes. Deindividuation causes people to lose their **self-identity** so they no longer **feel responsible** for their own behaviour because they become anonymous in the crowd. Responsibility for their behaviour is diffused across the group.

Crowds tend to show more aggressive behaviours than individuals on their own.

Frustration–aggression hypothesis

Dollard et al. (1939) suggested that aggression occurs as a result of a person feeling frustrated. Frustration is felt when a person is prevented from reaching a goal. If the individual is close to achieving their goal, their aggression will be increased if they are thwarted in their attempt.

Aggression → successful = catharsis.

For example, a footballer fouling an opponent to stop him from scoring.

Aggression → unsuccessful = more frustration.

An angry driver shouts at other drivers in the traffic jam, which makes no difference to the hold-up, and then hits the steering wheel in frustration.

Research evidence

Mann ('Baiting crowd', 1981) analysed 21 incidents of suicide (reported in American newspapers). He found that in 10 of the 21 cases where there was a crowd, baiting had occurred whereby the crowd urged the potential suicide to jump. This more often occurred at night. Other factors were the distance of the crowd from the person jumping and the size of the crowd. Mann explained this as deindividuation. He suggested that key features – such as darkness and a large group – had caused the deindividuation and led to individuals becoming anonymous, making aggression more likely.

Research evidence

☑ Harris (1974) used confederates to generate frustration by pushing into queues at a bus stop, cinema or supermarket. They either stood in front of the second person (high frustration) in the queue or the twelfth person (low frustration). Harris found much higher levels of verbal aggression in the first condition compared to the second, showing evidence for the hypothesis that frustration can lead to aggressive behaviour.

☑ Miller (1941) suggested that aggression is only one of a number of responses to frustration, and people also find other ways to deal with the frustration.

Evaluation

👍 The deindividuation theory has helped to reduce aggression. For example, using CCTV cameras at football matches has been shown to reduce levels of violence.

👎 Only a minority of people lose their moral codes when in a crowd.

Evaluation

👍 The frustration hypothesis is a good explanation when applied to aggression in sport. For example, more aggression is seen in a team that is losing.

👎 Not all frustration leads to aggression.

👎 Aggression can be learnt (see page 250).

Now try this

Outline **one** social psychological theory of aggression.

Social learning theory

Social learning theory (SLT) is a social psychological explanation of aggression. It is an extension of **behaviourism** as it believes aggression is learned but it also acknowledges **mediating cognitions**. These will decide if the behaviour that has been observed will be imitated.

 Attention

The individual has to pay **attention** to the modelled aggressive behaviour.

 Retention

The individual has to store that memory and **retain** it until they want to retrieve it.

 Reproduction

The individual must have the confidence and capabilities to **reproduce** the aggressive behaviour.

 Motivation

The individual has to be **motivated** to imitate the aggression through being rewarded.

You can remember this as the **long ARRM!** – **A**ttention, **R**etention, **R**eproduction, **M**otivation.

Social learning theory (SLT)

SLT suggests that aggression is learnt through **observation** of **role models**, such as parents or peers. If a person sees aggression being reinforced (**vicarious reinforcement**) then they are likely to **retain** it, which increases the likelihood of them **reproducing** the behaviour at a later stage. The individual has to feel they are capable of imitating the behaviour. They then have to be **motivated** to repeat the behaviour – this is the cognitive part of the theory. This explains why some people who see acts of aggression choose not to replicate it because they feel unhappy doing so: they are not motivated to do so.

Evaluation

👍 SLT can explain individual differences in aggressive behaviour, including cultural variations. Some countries such as America have a lot of violent crime (e.g. guns) whereas the !Kung San people of the African Kalahari Desert show little signs of aggression as it is not their norm to behave in that way. SLT can explain aggression in this way, as children living in these respective places would see modelled behaviour and act accordingly.

👎 SLT was based on research using children. It was laboratory based and so may lack ecological validity in applying findings to real-life aggression in adults.

👎 SLT ignores biological factors and so is environmentally determinist.

 Key study ## Bandura's (1961) Bobo doll experiments

Aim: To see if children would learn and imitate aggression from watching adult role models.

Procedure: Bandura used children from the Stanford University nursery (see page 69).

Results: He reported that the children who observed a model behaving aggressively towards an inflatable Bobo doll were more likely to **imitate** the behaviour when they could play with the doll at a later stage. The probability of replication was increased when the model (adult) was **rewarded** for their aggressive behaviour. Replication was also dependent on the sex of the model. For example, boys were more likely to imitate male aggressive models.

Conclusion: This supports SLT in that vicarious reinforcement influences aggressive behaviour.

A child imitating aggressive behaviour on a Bobo doll.

Now try this

Briefly explain social learning theory as an explanation of aggression.

Institutional aggression

You need to know about **institutional aggression** in the context of **prisons**. The two different explanations for aggression in prisons are: the **disposition** of the person and the **situation** in which they are put.

Dispositional explanations

This explains prisoners' aggression as the characteristics they have brought into prison with them. It may explain why the rate of violence in prisons is so high. Irwin and Cressey (1962) called it the **importation model**. This suggests that because of their already aggressive ways the prisoner will engage in further acts of aggression whilst in prison. Factors that could lead to violence in prison include prisoners' lives before prison, their home life and genes, which could predict the type of prisoners most likely to be aggressive while in prison, based on their norms from outside.

Prison sub-cultures

Irwin and Cressey (1962) identified three sub-cultures and offender types:

Sub-culture	Offender	Norms/values
criminal	repeat offender	follows criminal norms; does not betray others
convict	familiar with gangs	believes in the hierarchy of power and uses aggression on other prisoners
conventional	one-off	not usually aggressive; maintains a low profile

Situational explanations

This explains aggression as a product of the prison environment, which causes individuals within it to become violent. Contributory factors include the rules in the prisons, the physical conditions and the characteristics of the prison officers. Sykes (1958) called this the **deprivation model** as he claimed prisoners become aggressive because of the deprivation they suffer whilst in prison.

Deprivation model

Sykes (1958) said there were five types of deprivation, causing stress and frustration for prisoners and leading to aggression:

liberty	loss of freedom and privacy
autonomy	unable to make their own decisions about day-to-day living
goods and services	no mobile phones, restricted internet use (education only)
sexual relationships	intimacy that would come with partner in the outside world
security	prisoners often feel under threat

Research evidence

Allender and Marcell (2003) found that gang members, once in prison, disproportionately engaged in acts of prison violence. This supports the importation model as the disposition of the person predicts their aggression once inside.

Research evidence

Haney, Banks and Zimbardo (1973) showed in the Stanford Prison experiment (see page 4) that mentally healthy young men (guards) carried out acts of non-physical aggression while in a mock prison environment. Zimbardo claimed that many of the same psychological processes were found at Abu Ghraib, (see page 3), suggesting situational factors had a major impact on behaviour.

Evaluation

🍗 Research is correlational so we cannot assume cause and effect; individual norms cause a continuation of aggression in prisons.

👍 A lot of research evidence supports the importation model, suggesting outside norms will continue inside prison.

Evaluation

🍗 Many studies do not support the deprivation model. Disposition was the biggest predictor of inmate aggression regardless of the institution.

👍 Real-life prison riots in response to poor conditions or reduced privileges support the situational model.

Now try this

Evaluate the role of situational and dispositional factors in explaining aggression in prison.

Media influences

The **media**, including films, television and computer games, may influence people's aggression through observations of different role models (see SLT on page 250). You need to know about the three underlying mechanisms: **desensitisation**, **disinhibition** and **cognitive priming**.

Effects of computer games

Computer games have become increasingly violent. Players of these games get increasingly **desensitised**, and may even get **positive reinforcement** from using violence. This may then **reinforce** aggressive behaviour in everyday life or lead to **disinhibition**. Computer games may also be beneficial, as a way of venting anger or relieving stress.

Underlying mechanisms

1 **Desensitisation** – the more media violence we see or play, the less we respond to it emotionally – we are **desensitised** to it. Initially, gamers playing violent games may have a negative emotional reaction, which inhibits them from engaging in a violent act. As they become more desensitised they are more likely to act aggressively in the real world.

2 **Disinhibition** – people may act in a **disinhibited** or uncharacteristic way when playing a game. Suler (2004) explained it in three ways: the gamer becomes **anonymous**, they take on a character in the virtual game (**solipsistic introjection**) and they play out the criminal behaviour as there is no law enforcement (**minimisation of authority**) in the virtual world.

3 **Cognitive priming** – cognitive priming is the **storing** of aggressive scenes, which may be **activated** later in a similar situation. Aggressive **cues** can **trigger** aggressive feelings and thoughts.

For example, violent computer games or television shows can provide 'scripts' that players act out later. Shooting simulation games can develop the skills to use a real gun and if in a situation with one then be cued to use it in real life.

Research evidence

✓ Drabman and Thomas (1974) found that young children shown a violent film clip were slower to respond (by seeking help) when they saw other children fighting than those shown a neutral film. This suggests that the clip had made the children **desensitised** towards the violence.

✓ Suler (2004) found that when the responsibility of the computer gamer was removed through being anonymous, they then played in a way that was uncharacteristic of them (aggressively). This supports the process of **disinhibition**.

✓ Josephson (1987) carried out a study on 396 boys aged 7–9 years who played floor hockey. They were split into two groups and watched either a violent or non-violent film. Impartial observers rated aggressiveness in their next match. The behaviour of the boys who had watched an aggressive film was rated as more violent while playing hockey (tripping, shoving) than those who had watched a non-violent film. This supports **cognitive priming** – the aggressive cues of the film triggered the aggression.

Evaluation

👍 As most of the research is experimental, it is well controlled and results will be valid.

👎 The findings of research are mixed and sometimes correlational. This means the cause and effect of media on aggression cannot be established. There are numerous other influences that need to be considered, such as home environment.

👎 A lot of the research on media and aggression is carried out in laboratory conditions and may lack ecological validity. The behaviour shown may not reflect how they might behave in real life.

👎 Aggression is not operationalised as meaning the same thing in the studies, which is another flaw – there is no one measurement of what aggression is defined as.

Now try this

Outline the strengths and weaknesses of research into the influence of media on aggression.

Exam skills 1

Before you look at these worked examples, remind yourself about genetic factors in aggression (page 246) and the influence of media on aggression (page 252).

Worked example

Outline and evaluate **one** study on genetic factors in aggression.   **(4 marks)**

Brunner et al. (1993) studied males in a Dutch family and found five males who had the defective MAOA gene and had problems with behaviour, such as aggression. They had also spent time in prison for aggressive crimes, including attempted rape and assault. Other family members who did not have the defective gene did not show the behavioural problems, which therefore suggests the role of genetics. This study shows how the MAOA gene affects aggression, although it is difficult to separate the role of nurture as they were all from the same family and environmental influences could have affected the men. Therefore, it may not just be the role of genetics influencing the aggression. The sample size is extremely small and lacks population validity as they are from Holland and all males. It would be difficult to apply these results to other people as the study is both androcentric and ethnocentric. However, it did contribute further understanding of the role of the MAOA gene in aggressive behaviour, and may be useful in helping to develop appropriate treatments for people with extreme aggressive behaviour.

This question requires you to both outline and evaluate. In an exam, the credit will be for AO1 and AO3 material in your answer.

For a 4-mark question, such as this, you should allow just over four minutes to answer it.

The answer clearly outlines one piece of relevant research (Brunner et al., 1993), providing detail about what they did, the findings and a short succinct evaluation.

If you mention more than one piece of research you will not get credit for both, so make sure you read the exam question properly. Don't waste time writing about things that are not required.

Worked example

Explain what is meant by cognitive priming in relation to the effects of computer games on aggression.
                                                              (2 marks)

Cognitive priming is the idea that aggressive cues can trigger aggressive schemas of feelings and thoughts previously associated with antisocial behaviour. This can cause someone to behave in an antisocial way. Players who hold or have learned aggressive responses may be more likely to show aggression after playing violent computer games, which could trigger the response.

As this question is only for 2 marks, you need to focus on a short answer that is only two or three sentences long, with some brief detail and the use of appropriate terminology.

The answer includes a clear and correct definition of cognitive priming.

The concept of cognitive priming has been correctly linked to computer games and aggression, and how this plays a role.

Exam skills 2

Before you look at these worked examples, remind yourself about the role of neural and hormonal mechanisms in aggression (page 245).

Worked example

Describe and evaluate the role of neural and hormonal mechanisms in aggression.   **(16 marks)**

In humans, the surgical removal of the amygdala (part of the limbic system) reduces aggression in previously violent individuals. If the amygdala is damaged, levels of the hormone testosterone increase. Higher levels of testosterone have been associated with aggression. Other neural mechanisms – such as the neurotransmitter serotonin – have also been linked to aggression. Neurotransmitters are chemicals that allow electrical impulses to transmit messages from one area to another across the synapse. Serotonin helps to regulate mood, and low levels of serotonin have been associated with aggressive behaviour. Serotonin, at normal levels, exerts a calming inhibitory effect on neural firing in the brain. Also implicated is cortisol, which under normal circumstances inhibits testosterone, but lower levels of cortisol could result in more testosterone, causing aggression.

Research evidence in support of the testosterone theory comes from Wagner et al. (1979). Castrated male mice showed lower levels of aggression, but when given injections of testosterone their aggression increased, suggesting that testosterone is influential in aggression. However, humans are more complex than mice as they have higher order thinking and can choose to exert their free will over their behaviour.

Further support was provided by Dabbs et al. (1995) who measured testosterone in the saliva of criminals and found that those with the highest levels had a history of violent crime. As the research is only correlational, cause and effect cannot be established as there could be other factors causing their aggression, such as their environment. A further weakness is the issue of gender bias. Most research into this relationship is based on studies of males, as males produce far more testosterone than females. This means the theory and research are alpha biased as it exaggerates the difference between men and women in terms of aggression. Females may be aggressive but show different types. For example, they could be seen as more verbally aggressive rather than physically aggressive.

Support for the serotonin explanation comes from Mann et al. (2000). They gave 35 participants a drug known to deplete serotonin. Using a questionnaire to assess hostility and aggression, they found that this drug led to increased aggression and hostility scores in males but not females...

A banded scheme will be used to mark the answer to this question. A total of 6 marks will be awarded for the AO1 content and 10 marks for AO3. Therefore, make your description brief and to the point to allow you to spend more time on the evaluation.

The answer also outlines what a neurotransmitter is. Although this detail is not strictly necessary, it does show a good understanding of the mechanisms.

The answer provides an accurate and balanced description of both neural and hormonal mechanisms, mentioning the three you are required to know: limbic system, serotonin and testosterone. Each mechanism is then clearly linked to explaining aggressive behaviour.

Each point of evaluation is clearly explained in full and linked back to the question.

Evaluation points are extended to include any ethical issues or debates such as the use of animals. The answer includes an explanation as to why using animals could be a problem.

Methodological weaknesses are highlighted and explained here.

Exam-style practice 1

Practise for Paper 3 of your A level exam with these exam-style questions. There are answers on pages 318–319. Before looking at these questions, it would be good to review neural and hormonal explanations for aggression (page 245), evolutionary explanations (page 248), institutional aggression (page 251) and the influence of media on aggression (page 252).

1 Explain how dispositional factors may affect institutional aggression.
(4 marks)

> There are two explanations of institutional aggression in the context of prisons. You could use the other as part of an evaluation.

2 Explain how situational factors may affect institutional aggression.
(4 marks)

> Be prepared to be tested on any of the neural or hormonal mechanisms named in the specification. If you know the material, outlining the differences is no more challenging than a more straightforward question, such as being asked to outline both.

3 Outline the differences between the role of testosterone and the role of serotonin in aggression. **(4 marks)**

4 Briefly outline the role of the limbic system in aggression. **(2 marks)**

> The limbic system involves a number of components. You should know about one of these in detail, for example, the amygdala, and maybe another one to a lesser extent.

5 Explain the role of disinhibition in the effects of computer games on aggression. **(4 marks)**

> There are three roles you have to know about in this part of the topic: anonymity, solipsistic introjection and minimisation of authority. Make sure you know about all three.

> In this extended writing question, planning is essential. You need to use a few minutes to jot down the areas for your AO1 material and what you will use for your AO3 section. You should spend no more than 20 minutes planning and writing your essay.

6 Discuss evolutionary explanations of aggression. **(16 marks)**

> Aim to give an accurate and detailed answer. You need to make sure you discuss the points you make effectively; don't just write a shopping list of points without discussing why they are important, what they show and how they support the theory.

> Do not 'name drop', that is just mentioning a researcher or a piece of research without **explaining** its relevance. Think about its relevance and what it adds to the discussion of the theory. Specialist terminology needs to be used appropriately and effectively. For example, for this question: adaptive, survival, reproduction, mate retention, cuckoldry, genes and defending resources.

> The question is quite broad so you can include any of the evolutionary explanations. For example, you could include explanations in relation to infidelity and/or jealousy.

Had a go ☐ Nearly there ☐ Nailed it! ☐

Exam-style practice 2

Practise for Paper 3 of your A level exam with these exam-style questions. There are answers on page 319. Before looking at these questions, it would be good to review the research methods section and deindividuation and frustration (page 249).

🖩 **Maths skills**

7 Read the item and then answer the questions that follow.

> The government employed a team of researchers to investigate acts of aggression in males and females in prison. The hypothesis was that there would be an association between the number of aggressive acts (operationalised as physically hitting another prisoner) and length of time spent in the cell. They carried out a time sampling observation at two different prisons: one for men and the other for women. The results are shown in Table 1 below.

Table 1: The number of acts of aggression in males and females in prison

	Males	Females
Locked up for > 20 hours	50	10
Locked up for < 20 hours	35	5

(a) Which statistical test is appropriate to analyse the results? Justify your choice. **(4 marks)**

(b) They found $\chi^2 = 48.66$.
What value of degrees of freedom should be used? **(1 mark)**

> The degrees of freedom refer to the fact that the table is a 2 × 2 contingency table. The formula for working out degrees of freedom is: (number of rows − 1) × (number of columns − 1).

Table 2: Levels of significance for a two-tailed test

DF	0.10	0.05
1	2.71	3.84
2	4.60	5.99
3	6.25	7.82

> The table is for a two-tailed test because the hypothesis was non-directional. In the exam, you could be given both a one- and a two-tailed table to test that you know which would be an appropriate one to use.

Rule: the observed value has to be equal to or greater than the critical value to be significant.

(c) Using the information in Table 2, state whether the results are significant or not at the 0.05 level. Explain your answer. **(4 marks)**

> To look up the values in the table, you have to compare the observed value, in this case 48.66, against the tabled or critical value.

> Questions like this integrate knowledge of research methods and the topic material.

8 Briefly outline the frustration–aggression hypothesis. **(4 marks)**

> Outline questions are good to practise, to ensure you can use specialist terminology.

9 Describe **one** piece of research on deindividuation as an explanation of aggression. **(4 marks)**

> To do well, include all details of the study, such as number of participants, what they did, what the findings were.

Defining crime

A **crime** is any action that breaks the law. However, defining crime in real life is not so simple. You need to understand the problems in defining and measuring crime, including official statistics, victim surveys and offender surveys.

Problems in defining crime

What is and is not a crime depends on many factors, which makes it difficult to consistently and objectively decide when a crime has been committed. There are four main issues:

- **Age:** the age of criminal responsibility varies over time and across cultures. In the UK, it currently stands at age 10, but was previously age 8 years. The same act, therefore, committed by people of different ages would be defined differently as a crime or not.

- **Culture:** the social norms of what is criminal vary between cultures, making a universal identification of criminal behaviour difficult.

- **Historical context:** even within a culture, the law is continually being updated, rendering acts that were once criminal legal and vice versa. For example, homosexual acts were illegal in the UK until 1967.

- **Circumstance:** for an act to be a crime, the person must be shown to have committed the act and also intended to commit the act. The same behaviour in different circumstances could be criminal or not criminal.

Ways of measuring crime

Official statistics
Data is gathered from several sources by the Office of National Statistics on the amount of crime committed in England and Wales. It is published every year to show headline figures and trends in the types of crime recorded.

Police recording of crime
Data is taken from the police computer systems that log reports of crime and is used to measure the amount of crime committed. It feeds into the Office of National Statistics figures.

Measuring crime

Victim surveys
The Crime Survey for England and Wales conducts annual face-to-face surveys with around 40,000 people of different ages asking about their experiences of specific crimes. This is used to track the total amount of crime and changes in trends of crime.

Offender surveys
The Offending, Crime and Justice Survey 2006 gathered longitudinal self-report data on offending behaviour over a 3-year period. This aims to collect data of otherwise unreported crime.

Evaluation of statistical measures

- 👍 These measures are objective and should be reliable as a result.

- 👎 Many crimes are not reported to the police, leading to a serious under-estimation of the amount of crime committed, suggesting this measure is not valid.

- 👎 Laws and definitions change over time so it is difficult to say whether crime rates are rising or falling.

Evaluation of surveys

- 👎 Self-report measures in both types of survey may lack reliability as people may give socially desirable responses.

- 👎 They may not even realise or remember that they have been a victim of crime so there is likely to be an under-estimation of the amount of crime committed.

- 👍 The crime survey is carried out every year so is useful as it identifies changes in offending behaviour and can inform police resourcing.

- 👍 The offender survey is the only data gathered from the criminal perspective.

Now try this

Explain **two** problems associated with defining crime.

Offender profiling: top-down

Offender profiling is an investigative tool used to help catch criminals. It involves narrowing the search for a perpetrator by providing the police with insights into their likely qualities based on an analysis of the behaviour required to commit the crime. It is most often used in violent crimes such as murder and rape.

Top-down profiling

This was developed by the FBI in the USA during the 1970s and 80s. Based on interviews with 36 convicted murderers, a database was compiled to pick out characteristics of the types of person that committed the crimes.

Today, this information is applied to new crimes to help identify the perpetrator. It is called a '**top-down**' approach because it starts with a theory about the type of person that committed the crime and evidence from the crime scene is used to profile the criminal. A key classification in offender profiling is **organised** versus **disorganised** criminals.

Crime scene analysis

1 The **type** of crime – for example, is it one of a series? If murder, was it deliberate?

2 The amount of **premeditation** involved.

3 Type of **victim** – high risk (easy to victimise) or low risk (more likely to fight back).

4 The amount of **risk** taken by the perpetrator.

5 How it fits with previous crimes – for example, signs of **escalation**.

6 The **time** of the crime.

7 The **location** of the crime.

Organised vs disorganised typologies

Organised	Disorganised
Leads an orderly life and kills/attacks after a critical event.	The offender is more likely to have committed the crime in a moment of passion.
Planning and control are evident from the crime scene analysis – for example, leaves little physical evidence behind.	No evidence of pre-planning – for example, uses whatever is available as a weapon and leaves DNA or other physical evidence behind.
Offender is likely to be of average or higher intelligence.	Offender is likely to be of below average intelligence.
Offender is likely to be socially competent – for example, has 'normal' family relationships.	Offender is not socially competent and probably lives alone.
Offender is more likely to be employed in a skilled job.	Offender will have a poor work history.
Probably the eldest child in the family, who experienced inconsistent discipline as a child.	Likely to have a low birth order, often the youngest in family, and may have suffered harsh discipline as a child.

Evaluation

👍 The method was developed by the FBI who use it to help identify perpetrators. This means it has ecological validity as it arose out of actual practice.

👎 It is not scientific as it lacks a clear theoretical basis, and is difficult to test as it relies on the subjective interpretation of the crime scene and the unique experience of the profiler.

👎 It is mostly only useful in cases of murder and rape, especially when these are part of a series, so is a limited way of investigating crime as most crime is not as serious as these.

👎 Canter (2004) tested the organised/ disorganised typology and found no evidence that crime can be categorised in this way as all crimes contained elements of both typologies. Instead, it would be better to investigate personality differences between offenders.

Now try this

Outline what is meant by top-down offender profiling.

Offender profiling: bottom-up

In the bottom-up approach, the profiler uses **investigative psychology** and **geographical profiling** to inform the search.

Bottom-up profiling

The profiler makes no initial assumptions about the perpetrator until a **statistical analysis** of the data from the crime scene has been compared to a database of similar crimes. It is called 'bottom-up' because a profile of the offender is built from the data rather than imposed by the investigator at the outset.

Bottom-up profiling is a **cognitive social approach** as it analyses the interactions between the perpetrator and others in order to understand their behaviour. The profiler then applies theories of human behaviour to the evidence that has emerged.

This type of profiling is data driven and uses **investigative psychology** and **geographical profiling** to narrow the search for the offender.

Investigative psychology

This was developed in the UK by Canter et al. (1990) and has five key ideas that are used to analyse the crime.

1 **Forensic awareness** – if they leave little or no physical evidence then they may have committed a crime before and been through the system.

2 **Time and place** are useful for understanding the lifestyle of the criminal, for example, where they live/work.

3 **Criminal career** looks at how experienced they are and what they might do next.

4 **Interpersonal coherence** assumes that the behaviour shown in committing the crime is behaviour that they would show in their normal lives.

5 **Criminal characteristics** help police by putting offenders into a category.

Geographical profiling

Geographical profiling was developed by Canter (2008). This method analyses the timing and place in which the crime took place. It uses geographical information to find a crime pattern: where the offender originally encountered the victim, attacked them and (in murder cases) disposed of the body.

Looking at the pattern of locations tells the investigator about the perpetrator's familiarity with the area. This leads to a decision about whether the perpetrator is a 'commuter', travelling in to an area to commit a crime, or a 'marauder', setting out from a base central to the crime locations.

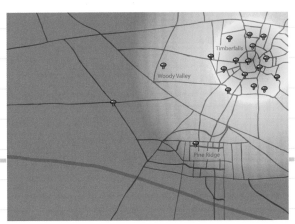

A map is drawn to show the key locations of criminal behaviour to see whether hotspots emerge, indicating potential bases for the criminal.

Evaluation

👍 Canter's 1986 profile of the 'Railway Rapist' using the bottom-up approach directly led to the capture and conviction in 1988 of John Duffy. Canter gave 17 suggested characteristics of the criminal and 12 were found to be accurate, suggesting the method has a useful application.

👎 It is not possible to generalise from case studies such as this, and there is only limited evidence that the method works.

👍 The bottom-up method is based on data – it relies on statistical analysis and the use of databases. This makes it objective and scientific.

👍 Geographical profiling is not limited to very serious crimes; it can be effective in investigating property crime, too.

Now try this

Evaluate the use of bottom-up offender profiling.

Historical explanation for crime

Criminal behaviour features across cultures and across time periods but there was no real attempt to explain *why* people became criminals until the work of **Cesare Lombroso** in late 19th-century Italy. His was one of the first recorded systematic studies of criminals, from which he developed an **atavistic theory of crime**, proposing a biological basis for criminal behaviour.

Lombroso's theory (1876)

According to Lombroso, criminal physiology was qualitatively different from that of non-criminals. Specifically, he believed that criminals represented a form of primitive human – they were some sort of 'biological throwback', unsuited to living in a civilised culture and therefore more likely to commit crime. In addition, because of the **biological** nature of the criminal behaviour, criminals would have **biological markers** that identified them as criminals. In other words, there were specific physical features associated with being a criminal.

Lombroso's studies

Throughout his career, Lombroso used his medical training to conduct scientific measurements of the skulls of convicts. He took data from criminals in Italian prisons and from the skulls of deceased criminals. In this way, he identified common features across the criminals.

This work spanned many years. From it, he believed he could identify '**born criminals**' and distinguish them from occasional criminals, such as those who commit opportunistic crime.

Physical features of a criminal

Jaw lines are often strong and sometimes described as 'lantern'.

Criminals have a heavy brow, often with a sloping forehead and a monobrow.

Large ears feature in a criminal type.

Atavistic features of a 'born criminal' identified by Lombroso

Evaluation

- Lombroso did not include a control group in his research, so it is difficult to establish that the atavistic features were only to be found amongst criminals.
- Goring (1913) applied Lombroso's theory to a population of prisoners in London and also to a control group, and found no link between criminal behaviour and physical appearance.
- Lombroso's sample is questionable as he did not screen out people with learning difficulties, which may lead to being convicted of crime and may also have linked physical characteristics.
- This theory is extremely reductionist, arguing that criminal behaviour results entirely from your biological make-up.
- It is also very deterministic as it proposes that, depending upon biological make-up, some people are destined for a life of crime.
- It could be that someone with the features identified by Lombroso became a criminal as a result of reduced social opportunities because of their appearance. The direction of causality is unclear.
- Overall, this approach is outdated and has been discredited as it had no valid or reliable evidence to support it.

Now try this

Outline and evaluate a historical approach to explaining crime.

Genetic explanation

Another biological explanation for crime looks at **genetics**. The genetic explanation proposes that there may be genes that run in families or that occur randomly within the population, pre-disposing those with the genes to engage in criminal behaviour.

Super-male syndrome

Males with this genetic condition have an extra Y chromosome on chromosome 23. So, instead of the usual XY formation, they have XYY. This is a **genetic mutation** that happens randomly at conception in about 1:1000 males.

Such males are typically taller than average with lower intelligence, and some may have behavioural problems.

Price et al. (1966) linked this abnormality to violent crime by suggesting that these men may lack empathy and become aggressive.

Evaluation

🔱 There is some research evidence that connects XYY with crime. Theilgaard (1984) found a higher proportion of XYY men than expected in a prison population, but this could be due to lower intelligence contributing to their criminal acts.

🔱 Limiting the explanation to a simple gene sequence and suggesting that this automatically causes criminal behaviour is **reductionist** and **deterministic**.

🔱 Many men with XYY do not commit crime, and most criminals do not have XYY genes.

Crime runs in families

Farrington et al. (1996) conducted a longitudinal family study of 411 males from 397 families over 24 years. The study found that:

- 6% of families accounted for 50% of convictions recorded in the sample
- 75% of families where the parents were convicts had a convicted child
- 75% of families with one child convicted also had another convicted.

This suggests that criminal behaviour is transmitted in families.

Twin studies

Twin studies typically show a higher concordance rate for offending behaviour between MZ (genetically identical) twins than DZ twins (who share 50% genes). For example, Raine (1993) found MZ to have 52% concordance for crime compared to only 21% in DZ.

Twins, whether MZ or DZ, share the same birth order and family circumstances. If the concordance rate for MZ differs from that of DZ, it can be assumed to be a result of the different proportion of genes in common.

Adoption studies

These look at behavioural correlations between adopted children and their biological parents compared to their adoptive parents. They allow for the relative role of nature vs nurture in the formation of behaviour to be investigated.

For example, Hutchings and Mednick (1975, 1994) found that in a sample of male adoptees, 86% of those with a criminal conviction had a biological father who had also been convicted, whereas adoptees who had not been convicted had a convicted father 31% of the time.

This suggests a strong genetic influence on criminal behaviour.

Evaluation

🔱 It is hard to disentangle nature from nurture. For example, in **family studies** the children could have learnt criminal behaviour rather than been genetically disposed towards it.

🔱 **Adoption studies** remove the effect of learning from biological parents. However, the age of adoption or the amount of contact with the wider family cannot be controlled, so it is still not possible to rule out social transmission of offending behaviour.

🔱 **Twin studies** control for social transmission as only the amount of genetic relatedness changes between the types of twin. Studies show that those with identical genes share more behaviour. However, identical twins are generally treated more similarly than non-identical twins, so it is still not possible to draw a definitive conclusion. If crime were genetic, the concordance rate would be 100%.

Now try this

Briefly outline **one** limitation in studying the genetic influence on criminal behaviour.

Neural explanation

As the brain is the organ of behaviour, we might expect criminal brains to be different from those of non-criminals. As a third biological explanation, research has focused on **neurochemical** and **structural differences**.

Neurochemical differences

Noradrenaline is associated with the fight-or-flight response (see page 85). Raised levels may increase the likelihood of an aggressive reaction.

Serotonin is involved in mood and impulse control. Changes in serotonin levels could increase the chances of an impulsive response in a person.

Dopamine is released in the reward pathways when we do something pleasurable. For some people, this could be an aggressive act. It is also associated with substance misuse. Drugs affect dopamine levels and lead to addiction. Addiction makes a person more vulnerable to criminal behaviour.

Evaluation

👍 Brunner et al. (1993) found evidence from a case study of a family of violent criminals that showed differences in the way serotonin was metabolised. For more about Brunner's et al. study, see page 246.

👎 Research into neurochemical effects on behaviour cannot definitively prove cause and effect, so it lacks clear experimental validity. The chemical imbalance may be caused by a pre-existing mental health disorder, which may be the reason for crime.

👎 Much of the research has been done on animals for ethical reasons. This lacks generalisability due to the increased complexity of the human brain.

Structural differences

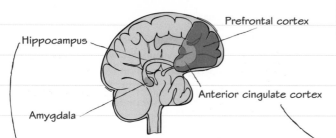

Prefrontal cortex

Hippocampus

Anterior cingulate cortex

Amygdala

As the amygdala and the prefrontal cortex are linked, information from one affects the other.

The **limbic system** includes the hippocampus and amygdala, which processes emotional information. The amygdala is implicated in psychopathic behaviour. A smaller than average amygdala is linked to a lack of empathy, for example, a lack of guilt when harming someone else. This may lead to crime.

The anterior cingulate cortex links the limbic system to the prefrontal cortex, the area responsible for impulse control and social interactions. Damage to the prefrontal cortex has been shown to be associated with criminal behaviour.

Evaluation

👍 Raine (1997) found lower activation in the prefrontal cortex of murderers compared to matched controls when doing a task in a PET scanner, suggesting that there are differences in the brains of those who do and do not commit crime.

👎 It is impossible from this to demonstrate causality as other factors may be responsible for brain differences such as diet and damage during birth.

👍 Further research by Raine (2000) shows that people with psychopathic personality characteristics have reduced frontal lobe volume, so the evidence is consistent.

👍 The use of advanced scanning techniques increases the scientific validity of the research and makes the conclusions more objective and reliable.

👎 Not everyone with this type of neurology will go on to commit crime, which challenges the deterministic conclusions that could be drawn from the research. Some become successful in business, by using the traits associated with psychopathic personalities in a legal way.

Now try this

Identify and explain **one** neurological cause of criminal behaviour.

Eysenck's theory of the criminal personality

According to Eysenck (1964), criminal behaviour may be influenced by **personality characteristics** that are linked to **biological differences** between people. Eysenck's theory of the criminal personality is regarded as a **psychological explanation**.

Eysenck's theory (1964)

Personality consists of three dimensions that can be measured.

1 **Extraversion–Introversion** where extraverts are sensation-seekers and introverts prefer to avoid sensation.

2 **Neuroticism–Stability** where neurotics are those who are emotionally unstable and very reactive.

3 **Psychoticism** – people high on this scale lack empathy and sensitivity.

Eysenck believed these dimensions have a **biological basis** and that the predisposition to certain traits was inherited.

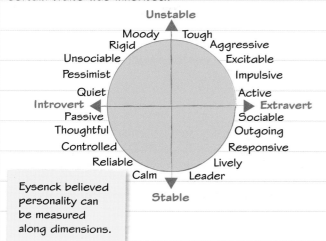

Unstable

Moody　Tough
Rigid　　　Aggressive
Unsociable　　Excitable
Pessimist　　　Impulsive
Quiet　　　Active
Introvert ◄———————► Extravert
Passive　　Sociable
Thoughtful　　Outgoing
Controlled　　Responsive
Reliable　　Lively
Calm　Leader

Stable

Eysenck believed personality can be measured along dimensions.

Biological basis of personality traits

Extraversion

- The ascending reticular activating system (ARAS) is responsible for the general arousal levels in the nervous system.
- It is connected to the cerebral cortex.
- It governs arousal of the brain.

Neuroticism

- The limbic system, which controls our emotional reactions, is easily triggered.
- Neurotic people will react to emotional stimuli quickly.

Psychoticism

- Hormone levels are implicated.
- High levels of testosterone are associated with increased aggression.
- Issues with the metabolism of serotonin means levels are affected.

Link to crime

Eysenck proposed that people who were high in psychoticism (P), extraversion (E) and neuroticism (N) – the **PEN personality** – would be more likely to commit crime due to a combination of personality characteristics. For example, the risk-taking behaviour of the extravert, the impulsivity of the neurotic and the lack of guilt of the psychotic.

Evaluation

🟐 There is some support for this theory but the research evidence is mixed. Heaven (1996) found that high P levels were predictive of offending behaviour. The evidence for high E leading to criminality is inconclusive, with some studies supporting high E and others finding no effect.

🟐 There are issues with how offending behaviour is measured and defined, which may affect the findings from research, as Farrington (1992) found. Convicted offenders tend to be high in

N and low in E, but from self-report data of non-convicted people the reverse is true. This suggests the theory has limited validity.

🟐 The theory is very **deterministic** as it suggests that criminal tendencies result from biological differences between people, which then results in a criminal personality. This may give offenders an excuse for failing to take responsibility for the choices they make. It also suggests that such people will continue to offend as they have limited free will.

Now try this

Explain how personality characteristics might lead to offending behaviour.

Had a look ☐   Nearly there ☐   Nailed it! ☐

Cognitive explanations for crime

Cognitive explanations centre on the way we **process information** and how this affects our behaviour. Offending behaviour is directly influenced by our habitual thought processes. Kohlberg's (1958) theory explores how these change through childhood and how this affects our moral reasoning.

Developmental theories of crime

Piaget (1932) believed that cognitive ability develops over time and that children think qualitatively differently from adults. This impacts on their ability to understand right and wrong. He said there were three stages in which the child focuses on different aspects of the environment in order to understand its moral implications. These stages become more sophisticated as they get older: **stage 1** focused on *rules*, **stage 2** on *responsibility* and **stage 3** on *justice*. Piaget believed that stage 3 would develop by around age 9.

Kohlberg's theory (1958)

Kohlberg thought that Piaget's stage model was too simple. He conducted extensive research using the **moral dilemma paradigm**. This uses narrative stories that feature a person committing a 'crime', and participants are asked who was right and who was wrong, and why. Kohlberg's research led him to propose **three levels of moral reasoning**, with each level featuring two stages. He also suggested that some people never achieve the final stages, and that these people are more likely to commit crime.

Kohlberg's levels and stages of moral reasoning

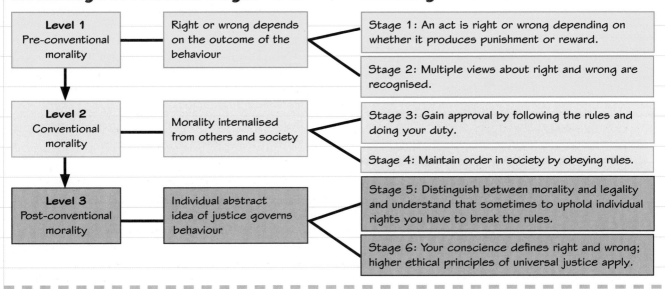

Level 1 Pre-conventional morality	Right or wrong depends on the outcome of the behaviour	Stage 1: An act is right or wrong depending on whether it produces punishment or reward.
		Stage 2: Multiple views about right and wrong are recognised.
Level 2 Conventional morality	Morality internalised from others and society	Stage 3: Gain approval by following the rules and doing your duty.
		Stage 4: Maintain order in society by obeying rules.
Level 3 Post-conventional morality	Individual abstract idea of justice governs behaviour	Stage 5: Distinguish between morality and legality and understand that sometimes to uphold individual rights you have to break the rules.
		Stage 6: Your conscience defines right and wrong; higher ethical principles of universal justice apply.

Evaluation

- Kohlberg's theory has been criticised for being an artificial way to investigate moral reasoning, as there is no real consequence for the decisions being made. Thus it lacks ecological validity.

- The sample on which his theory is based was all male, suggesting an issue of **beta bias** (see page 128). Gilligan (1977) challenged the validity of applying the theory to females, suggesting that female morality was centred on caring behaviour rather than notions of justice. Kohlberg's theory is therefore **androcentric** as it suggested that women have lower levels of moral development than men.

- Walker (1989) showed that moral development happens over time, thus supporting Kohlberg.

- The theory is also supported by statistics, which show the peak age for antisocial behaviour is young adulthood.

- Ashkar and Kenny (2007) found that a sample of juvenile delinquents showed pre-conventional levels of morality when interviewed about their specific crime, but conventional levels when asked about crimes other than their own, suggesting that it is not as simple as Kohlberg's theory proposes.

Now try this

Apply Kohlberg's theory of moral reasoning to explain offending behaviour.

Cognitive distortions

Criminals make **attributions** for their crimes that allow them to reduce their feelings of guilt. **Biases** in thinking – or **cognitive distortions** – can make some people more likely to commit crime because of the way they process the information. Others may learn to become criminals through social interactions (**differential association theory**).

Hostile attribution bias

Attribution bias is about how you explain your own and other people's actions. It allows offenders to place the blame for what they do on other people, such as the victim. Through their attitudes and motivation, the victim somehow caused the offender to behave the way they did.

For example, if the offender believed that the victim was disrespecting them, then they might respond with violence in order to regain respect.

Evaluation

👍 Holtzworth-Munroe and Hutchinson (1993) showed a potential link between hostile attribution bias and domestic violence, with the perpetrators claiming that the victims' negative attitudes or behaviours contributed to the crime.

👍 Gudjonsson and Bownes (2002) found that violent criminals and offenders showed a strong consistency in the way they attributed blame for their crimes.

👎 Most research in this area uses hypothetical situations or vignettes, which lack ecological validity as there are no consequences for using a hostile attribution in these cases.

Minimalisation

This cognitive bias operates to **minimise** the guilt offenders feel for their actions by letting them think that their actions were 'not that bad', that the victim did not suffer any harm, or that the victim in some way deserved it. They manage their own emotions by rationalising their actions in a way that fails to recognise the impact they have on other people.

For example, an offender could justify shoplifting by saying that it was a victimless crime.

See page 269 on restorative justice.

Evaluation

👍 Kennedy and Grubin (1992) found that a majority of a sample of convicted sex offenders blamed their crime on the victim or said that the victim benefitted.

👍 Cognitive explanations offer a potential treatment for crime, as changing cognitions should change behaviour. This has been attempted through restorative justice, where offenders meet their victims.

👎 Minimalisation does not explain the cause of offending behaviour, but rather is used to justify it and remove guilt. It is a coping strategy.

Differential association theory

This takes a different view and argues that criminal behaviour is learned through interaction with others. Criminals learn how to commit crime, they learn the motives and drivers for crime and the rationale and attitudes of criminals. Crime is socially easy because of whom they mix with. Crime becomes a career.

For example, children who grow up in a criminal family and live in a high-crime area are likely to view antisocial activity as more normal than being law abiding.

Evaluation

👍 This theory has been shown to have some validity. Alarid et al. (2000) found that differential association could explain convicts' offending as a product of their social associations.

👎 The theory is lacking in detail and ignores isolated criminal acts.

👍 It has face validity as an explanation for gang-related crime, as gang members learn from each other, so it can account for this kind of crime.

Now try this

Explain how cognitive distortions can lead to offending behaviour.

Psychodynamic explanations

Based on the theories of Freud (1933), psychodynamic explanations for offending behaviour propose that **unconscious motivations** developed during childhood are responsible for criminal tendencies.

Superego

The superego is the final part of personality that develops in the phallic stage of childhood (see page 163). It is a product of **nurture** as it develops through interaction with parents. It represents the morality principle (concerned with knowing what is right and wrong) and is linked to crime in one of three ways:

1 **Underdeveloped or weak superego** – a lack of identification with the same-sex parent produces a superego unable to control the id's desires for instant gratification. Lack of punishment by the superego equals no guilt for offending.

2 **Overdeveloped or strong superego** – the person feels guilty all the time and so engages in crime in order to be punished. Alternatively, the superego is so over-controlling it stops even trivial behaviour that it regards as immoral, resulting in a build-up of pressure in the person until it overwhelms them and they erupt into violence.

3 **Deviant superego** – the superego develops normally as a result of internalising the parent's moral values, but if those moral values are deviant, the child's values will also be deviant. This increases the likelihood of offending.

Defence mechanisms

According to Freud (1936), thoughts and desires that cause us anxiety or guilt are managed by the ego. Offending behaviour results from ego defences being engaged.

For example, in **rationalisation**, the offender justifies their negative acts by creating positive reasons for it such as stalking someone in order to 'protect' them.

Another example is **sublimation**, a strong but socially unacceptable desire is expressed in an alternate form of behaviour. A desire to kill a sibling, for example, might be sublimated to animal cruelty.

Maternal deprivation

Bowlby (1951) proposed that disruption of the attachment relationship with the mother (or primary caregiver) in early childhood led to the development of 'affectionless psychopathy' characterised by a lack of both empathy and guilt.

It is suggested that this affects the child's internal working model, as without empathy they become less caring towards other people, do not see the victims' perspective and so do not mind hurting them. See page 42 for more on maternal deprivation.

Evaluation

🍂 Whilst these theories seem to have face validity in being able to retrospectively explain some criminal acts by some individuals, they lack predictive validity, as they are unable to forecast who will offend and how it will happen.

🍂 Bowlby's (1944) juvenile thieves study supports the maternal deprivation hypothesis. Boys who had experienced separation from their primary caregiver in early childhood were more likely to show characteristics of affectionless psychopathy. These boys were also more likely to have committed antisocial behaviour than others not separated from their primary care-giver.

🍂 The evidence is limited to case studies and studies such as Bowlby's, which have small samples and are therefore not generalisable, lending only limited validity to the theory.

🍂 Psychodynamic concepts in general are difficult to test scientifically because they concern unconscious motivations. These can only be assumed to exist rather than demonstrated experimentally, so the evidence is very limited and the theory lacks validity.

🍂 Some cases do fit with the theory, such as Megargee's (1966) description of over-controlled violent offenders who have no history of anger or offending but suddenly explode and engage in violent angry outbursts. This fits with the overdeveloped superego theory.

Now try this

Explain how the superego might influence offending behaviour.

Custodial sentencing

Once an offender is convicted of a crime, various sentences are applied, including going to prison. Dealing with offending behaviour is an important part of the criminal justice system. You need to know the aims of **custodial sentencing** and its **psychological effects**.

Custodial sentencing

Custodial sentencing is when an offender is sent to prison. The aims of doing this include:

- acting as a **deterrent** through social learning and vicarious punishment, by showing the negative consequences of crime and stopping others becoming criminals
- **retribution** for the crime, making the criminal pay for what they have done
- **confinement** of criminals to reduce the amount of crime as they are locked away from society
- **rehabilitation** of the criminal so they do not reoffend once released.

One aim of prison is to keep dangerous people away from society.

Evaluation

- The prison population in the UK is rising, suggesting it is not an effective deterrent to those considering committing crime.
- Prison is expensive, costing £37,648 per year per prisoner in 2012. Other types of sentencing such as community orders are cheaper and may be cost-effective. One study by the UK Ministry of Justice in 2012 found that there were lower recidivism rates (reoffending) following a court-ordered community sentence rather than prison.
- According to the National Audit Office, there is no correlation between the number of people in prison and criminal offences, suggesting that confinement is not working.
- Rehabilitation is not currently effective within prisons as the recidivism rate is high (see page 268).
- For some people who are a danger to society, it is the only option.

The psychological effects of custodial sentencing

Institutionalisation	Mental health problems
Some prisoners become dependent on the institution for their routine. In prison you are told when to wake, sleep and eat with very little choice involved. People become used to this and find it difficult to take control of their own lives once released. They become dependent on the prison system.	According to a Ministry of Justice survey, many prisoners have pre-existing mental health problems (26% of female and 16% of male prisoners) and many more develop them in prison. Estimates show that 49% of female prisoners and 23% of males suffer from anxiety and depression, possibly because of the stress caused by overcrowding and the loss of liberty.

Evaluation

- People can become institutionalised in prison. The Stanford Prison Study (Haney et al., 1973) showed how quickly being locked up led to a change in behaviour (see page 4).
- Hollin (1992) found that some prisoners felt prison was preferable to their home life due to the regular meals and routine, suggesting it is not effective as a deterrent.

- The self-harm and suicide rates in prison are high, especially amongst the younger inmates and those on remand (Dooley, 1990). This supports the view that mental health is affected by imprisonment.
- Snow (2006) found that prisoners displaying mental health issues such as depression were at higher risk of suicide and self-harm.

Now try this

Evaluate how effective custodial sentences are in meeting their aims.

Recidivism

Recidivism is the relapse into criminal behaviour after being convicted and punished for a crime. It is a key measure of the effectiveness of the criminal justice system.

Rates of recidivism

- UK Ministry of Justice statistics (2013) show that 47% of prisoners will reoffend within a year of release from prison.
- This increases to 59% for those who served a sentence of less than one year.
- 73% of under 18s convicted of a crime will reoffend within a year of release.

> This is why it is sometimes referred to as a revolving door policy, as no sooner are they released than some offenders are back in jail.

Impact on economy

Reoffending by all recent ex-prisoners is estimated to cost the UK economy between £9.5 and £13 billion per year (Source: National Audit Office, 2012). This reflects loss of earnings, the cost of criminal activity, increased welfare benefits to the families of prisoners and the cost of keeping people in prison.

At such a cost, it is very important that sentencing has a rehabilitative function.

Explaining recidivism

There are various reasons why prison is not effective.

Institutionalisation	• For some prisoners, the routine of life in prison is better than their life outside. They are not supported in the same way when released.
	• This means they cannot cope on the outside and reoffend in order to go back to prison.
Ineffective punishment	• Prison should act as a punishment and so ought to stop the offending behaviour that led to them being imprisoned.
	• There is usually a long delay between the commission of the crime and being admitted to prison, which stops it being effective.
Mental health issues and substance abuse	• Many people sentenced to prison have pre-existing mental health disorders and/or addictions, which were part of the reason they committed the crime.
	• For many prisoners these issues are not treated and so when they are released, they reoffend.

Evaluation

- 🔖 The data on recidivism may be unreliable as only those who are caught reoffending are included. In reality, the figures are likely to be higher.
- 🔖 The data on the causes of recidivism may not be valid – when asked why they reoffend, many offenders lack insight into their own motivations, blaming the system rather than themselves.

Application of research

Equipping offenders for life after prison is a major challenge for the criminal justice system. This means that, before release, mental health issues are treated and inmates are prepared for employment so they can support themselves in a legal way. Gillis et al. (2005) found a 15% drop in recidivism rates when prisoners were given training and support to enter the workplace on their release from prison, showing how planning for release and support can effectively tackle reoffending.

Now try this

Outline the impact of recidivism on the economy.

Behaviour modification and rehabilitation

One of the aims of custodial sentences is to provide rehabilitation for prisoners. This includes **behaviour modification** such as **token economy** programmes. Other forms of rehabilitation include restorative justice programmes and anger management (see page 270).

Token economies

Based on operant conditioning (see page 68), a token economy system aims to **positively reinforce** desirable and extinguish undesirable behaviour.

- Tokens (secondary reinforcers) are issued by the prison staff when the prisoner exhibits target behaviour.

- Tokens are then exchanged for things the prisoner values such as cigarettes or phone cards.

- Tokens can be removed when undesirable behaviour is exhibited (punishment). The threat of losing tokens acts as negative reinforcement for the target behaviours.

Tokens can be exchanged for extra time with visitors.

Evaluation

👍 Hobbs and Holt (1976) tested young offenders in institutions and found that the behaviour of prisoners improved on a token economy programme compared to control groups.

👎 Rice et al. (1990) found that this only worked on some prisoners and that improvements were short term.

👎 It does not work in everyday life as there is no one to issue the tokens, so it lacks ecological validity.

👎 To be effective it must be administered fairly and consistently. Reppucci and Saunders (1974) found that often it was not.

👎 It could be argued that this breaches the human rights of prisoners by only giving them the things they want when they perform appropriately.

Restorative justice

Restorative justice aims to get the criminal to empathise with the victim and understand the human consequences of crime, thus changing their cognitions. It gives the victim a voice with which to express their feelings.

Restorative justice can be done in several ways, including face-to-face communication or through a mediator where the victim asks the perpetrator questions and tells them about their experience. It happens in a controlled, neutral setting.

Evaluation

👍 It is relatively cheap and easy to administer compared to custodial sentencing.

👍 Sherman and Strang (2007) in a large-scale multi-cultural study found that it changed the offender's perspective and reduced recidivism for most – but not all – offenders across a range of crimes. They also found that the victim's mental health benefitted through a reduction in post-traumatic stress.

👎 The evaluation of such programmes depends on self-report data from victims and offenders, which can be unreliable as they may give socially desirable answers about the value of the intervention.

👎 There is a high participant attrition rate so it only works where both victims and perpetrators are highly motivated to complete the programme.

Now try this

Explain how a token economy programme could be applied to modify criminal behaviour.

269

Anger management

Anger management is an intervention aimed at reducing recidivism by using **cognitive behavioural therapy (CBT)** to tackle violence. It is often used with offenders in prison.

Anger management

Anger management aims to modify the effect of anger and decrease the likelihood of offending by changing how the perpetrators of violence respond to the physiological changes they experience that lead to angry outbursts.

This technique was developed by Novaco in the 1970s and has become widely used to combat the effects of anger by breaking it down into cognitive, emotional, physiological and behavioural components.

Fight-or-flight response

The autonomic nervous system responds to threat by increasing **adrenaline** levels, which causes a physiological response in the body, preparing the person to run away from danger or attack (see page 85). This physiological response leads to an emotional reaction. In aggressive people, this is anger. The anger then leads to physical violence. By damping down the physiological response and changing how it is interpreted, it is possible to stop the anger turning to violence.

Cognitive preparation

Through talking with a therapist, the person identifes triggers that make them feel angry. These are environmental stressors, such as being disrespected.

They are encouraged to think about whether the thoughts are rational and how other people would see the situation.

Skills acquisition

The person is taught coping strategies and skills that allow them to control their anger and handle the emotions differently. This can involve relaxation training or assertiveness training. Specific techniques include thought stopping, fogging and the broken record.

Application practice

In a safe environment and usually in small groups, the person role-plays situations that have triggered anger in the past. They try out the skills they have learned and get feedback from others about how they handled the situation.

Evaluation

- 👍 Ireland (2004) tested the programme on a prison population and found a 92% improvement in behaviour compared to a control condition, suggesting that it is an effective treatment.

- 👎 The data relied on self-report and therefore it may be inaccurate and lack internal validity as the prisoners might exaggerate their improvements.

- 👎 It is hard to measure whether it produces long-term benefits as this data would be based on recidivism rates, which depends on the perpetrators of violence being caught and convicted.

- 👎 Anger management will only be effective in reducing hostile aggression – aggression that stems from anger. Not all aggression is hostile. For example, holding up a shop with a gun.

In order to be effective, the practitioner must have received effective training and be experienced. This makes it a more expensive option than other behaviour modification techniques.

Now try this

Explain the process of anger management.

Exam skills 1

Before you look at the worked examples, remind yourself about custodial sentencing (page 267), recidivism (page 268) and rehabilitation (pages 269–270).

Worked example

Explain what is meant by recidivism. **(2 marks)**

Recidivism happens when a convicted offender reoffends after serving their sentence. For example, on coming out of prison, the offender is caught carrying out a crime.

For 2 marks a clear definition is required with suitable expansion.

The definition is clear and detailed, with an appropriate example.

Worked example

What are the aims of custodial sentencing? **(4 marks)**

One of the main aims of custodial sentencing is rehabilitation, where the criminal is encouraged to change their behaviour through training and counselling. For example, they can learn skills that would enable them to gain employment when they leave, thereby supporting themselves and not reoffending. Another aim is deterrence. Other people will see criminals being sent to prison and will avoid committing the same acts. It should also punish those who have committed crime and stop them reoffending.

There are several aims to custodial sentencing. In answer to this question, you could choose to briefly outline four or you could decide to do two aims in more depth. Note, though, that it must be more than one aim.

This answer covers two aims, both of which are explained well and in sufficient detail to gain all the available marks.

Worked example

Jason has been given a custodial sentence following his 3rd conviction for violent assault. He attacked and badly injured a man in a pub after he lost his temper. The judge gave him 3 years in prison with a recommendation that he undergo anger management training.

Explain why the judge recommended anger management training in this case, and briefly outline the treatment Jason might receive in his training. **(6 marks)**

Jason 'lost his temper' and attacked someone, indicating that he was angry when he committed the crime. Anger management aims to help people control their anger by changing the person's perception of threat and their emotional and physiological responses to threat.

Jason will initially spend some time with the therapist identifying the triggers for his anger, and will try to change his perception of them so that they are less threatening to him. He will then learn some key skills to deal with the triggers in a non-violent way and designed to dampen down his fight-or-flight response that led to angry aggression in the past. Finally he will practise these skills in role play and group work sessions until they become well learned, thereby reducing his risk of reoffending for anger-related violence.

This is an application question requiring you to use the information in the source material in your answer.

It is also a split question, where you must explain the judge's reasoning for anger management and then go on to explain what Jason might experience in anger management training.

This clearly links the source material to the question with the use of the criminal's name and the reference to losing his temper.

The detail and depth in these examples are about right, and there is consistent reference to the case in the source material and a brief but relevant account of all three stages in anger management.

Exam skills 2

Before you look at the worked example, remind yourself about offender profiling (pages 258–259).

Worked example

Discuss offender profiling as a method of identifying criminals.

(16 marks)

Offender profiling aims to help the police narrow down the search for offenders. There are two types of offender profiling: top-down and bottom-up. Top-down profiling is usually done by trained investigators with experience and knowledge of criminal behaviour. The Behavioural Analysis Unit of the FBI profiles in this way. Crime scene analysis leads to the profiler making an educated guess as to characteristics of the perpetrator, because the behaviour needed to commit the crime will be reflected in other traits that the criminal has. They will look at the victimology and modus operandi and use this information to work out what kind of person would commit this crime. This would include working out if the perpetrator was organised or disorganised. An organised crime scene implies an intelligent person who has planned ahead, perhaps by taking a weapon with them and by clearing up evidence afterwards. A profile of a disorganised criminal would reflect the randomness of the crime and victim, the opportunistic method used and physical evidence left at the crime scene, indicating a person of average or below average intelligence who is likely to live alone and have a poor work history.

In evaluation, this method can be accused of being subjective as it relies on the past experience and expertise of the profiler. This makes it an unreliable method of investigation as each profiler will make different deductions. The method has limited usefulness as it really only works with serious and serial crime because it requires data from several crime scenes to build a picture of the perpetrator. However, it has proven successful in some cases. For example, in the Unabomber case, the profile was found to be accurate and led to his arrest in 1996. Furthermore, the organised/disorganised typology is simplistic and criminals will show features of both types of behaviour. For example, someone could plan a crime well but an unexpected event might cause them to leave physical evidence behind.

Bottom-up profiling is different because it does not start with pre-conceived ideas about the type of person the perpetrator is. Instead, it focuses on the logistics of the crime, its location and timing to provide a picture of the person's routine. Geographical profiling is one aspect of this. Developed by Canter (2008), it looks at the locatedness of the crime(s) and examines the choices the perpetrator made. It also suggests two types of offenders: those that commute to commit crime away from where they live and those who commit crimes close to home. Using a database, profilers look for similar crimes to see if a pattern emerges that helps deliver a profile, based on where the person lives and works...

It is always a good idea to plan long answers. AO1 description of the techniques will account for 6 marks and the rest will be AO3 evaluation or AO2 application and AO3 evaluation. If you break down the AO1 component to both types of profiling, it makes the challenge less daunting. This also applies to the evaluative components, which if separated to top-down or bottom-up paragraphs, make it more manageable.

This first paragraph summarises top-down profiling well, it covers the organised/disorganised typology in enough detail and includes crime scene analysis. It is accurate and focused.

This paragraph is evaluative, covering several issues in a detailed and organised way.

This paragraph describes bottom-up profiling, including details of geographical profiling, which is required on the spec.

To complete this essay, provide more evaluation of the bottom-up method to include examples of its successful use, such as Canter's profile of the 'Railway Rapist'.

Exam-style practice 1

Practise for Paper 3 of your A level exam with these exam-style questions. There are answers on pages 320–321. Before looking at these questions, it would be good to review defining crime (page 257), psychological explanations of crime (pages 263–264) and rehabilitation (pages 269–270).

1   Outline **two** issues that make measuring crime problematic.

             (2 marks)

> For 2 marks, this question does not need a lot of detail, but the answer must be more than a simple identification of an issue.

2   Describe **one** or more ways in which crime is measured.

             (4 marks)

> Although this question allows you to give more than one way to measure crime, it is usually better to focus on one way if you have enough information.

3   Outline **two** or more ways that offenders are treated in order to rehabilitate them.   **(6 marks)**

> This question is descriptive, so no evaluation or explanation is needed. There are three named options on the specification to choose from: restorative justice programmes, anger management and behaviour modification in prison. You must cover at least two.

4   Briefly explain **one** limitation of Kohlberg's theory of moral development.   **(2 marks)**

> To answer this well you must give detail when focusing on a problem with the theory, so identify the issue and then expand your answer to really explain what the problem is.

5   Read the item and then answer the question that follows.

> Carole is worried about her daughter Amy. Amy is often in trouble at school for cutting class to hang around with older girls and for being rude to teachers who challenge her behaviour. Carole thinks this is just a phase. Amy's older sister disagrees and thinks that it might indicate a criminal personality. She points out that Amy has always engaged in risky behaviour, that she has a quick temper with frequent mood swings and does not show any remorse when she is badly behaved.

> You must use the information in the source material provided here to answer the question, as well as your knowledge about Eysenck's theory.

Using concepts drawn from Eysenck's theory of the criminal personality, explain why Amy's sister thinks that this is not a phase that Amy will pass through.   **(4 marks)**

> Your answer must be detailed and should feature the accurate and appropriate use of terminology.

Exam-style practice 2

Practise for Paper 3 of your A level exam with these exam-style questions. There are answers on page 321. Before looking at these questions, it would be good to review explanations for crime (pages 260–266) and research methods.

6 According to the atavistic theory of crime, what are the physical features associated with criminal behaviour? **(2 marks)**

> For 2 marks, it is acceptable to list the main features drawn from Lombroso's theory. As long as each list entry is written as a coherent sentence, it would not be necessary to explain or develop your answer.

7 Evaluate the atavistic explanation for crime. **(4 marks)**

> In this answer, you should not waste time describing the theory. You would be expected to write a paragraph.

8 Explain ways researchers investigate genetic links to crime. **(4 marks)**

> This question is not directly about forensic psychology but is related. The focus of the answer needs to be on methods used to investigate genetic influences. The command word is 'explain', so it is not enough to just describe the methods, you must explain how they work and link it all to crime. There is no need to evaluate the methods.

9 Evaluate the psychodynamic explanation for criminal behaviour. **(4 marks)**

> To do well here it would be good to focus on two issues and develop each one in detail.

10 Read the item and then answer the question that follows.

> Morgan has just been convicted of shoplifting. Both of his parents have long criminal records and his brother is currently in prison for burglary. Morgan shows no remorse for his crime, stating that the shop is covered for its loss by insurance and his shoplifting really does no harm at all. At his trial, Morgan's lawyer argued that Morgan was destined to be a criminal.

> There are two clear theories that suggest Morgan is predetermined to be a criminal. These are genetic and differential association. You could focus on one theory and provide a lot of depth or do both in less detail.

Using concepts drawn from one or more theory of criminal behaviour, explain why Morgan's lawyer made this argument.

(8 marks)

> Even though the question does not explicitly require you to use the source material, it would be wise to refer to the information in the question to explain the lawyer's beliefs.

What is addiction?

An **addiction** can be seen as a lack of control, a compulsion to carry out a behaviour or a dependence on a behaviour. Addictive behaviours produce physical and psychological dependence, tolerance and withdrawal syndrome.

Physical dependence

A smoker, for example, finds it physically difficult to not engage in the addicted behaviour. Abstinence from it starts to lead to physical/bodily effects. There is a need rather than a want to engage in the behaviour. Physical symptoms differ for different addictions.

For example, someone with a dependency on gambling who has not gambled for a number of hours could show their physical dependency by tremors, increased heart rate and sweating. These physical signs are similar for addictions to physical substances, as well.

Psychological dependence

Someone with a dependency on a behaviour will feel they **need** to engage in the behaviour for their psychological well-being; they **think** they cannot cope without it and have a mental and emotional compulsion to continue with the behaviour. Psychological dependence can occur **without** physical dependence. For example, a smoker who is unable to smoke for any length of time starts to think about cigarettes the longer the time lapse since their last cigarette. They may start to feel anxiety or become irritable, evidence of a psychological dependence.

Tolerance

The effect of the behaviour decreases over time. The first time someone gambles, for example, they may feel euphoria as they play the fruit machines. However, the more they engage in the behaviour the less effect it has on them. The initial feelings have now disappeared and the individual needs to engage in the behaviour more frequently, perhaps gambling with higher stakes, to get the same feelings. They have built up a **tolerance** to the substance or the behaviour and need to take more/do it more in order to feel the same effect.

Withdrawal syndrome

The most common withdrawal symptom is physical, where an individual will need to take more of the substance or carry out more frequent behaviour to avoid **withdrawal** symptoms. The bigger the time lapse between engaging in the behaviour, the more depressed and anxious they feel. They **crave** the substance, experiencing body tremors and nausea, making it difficult for the individual to refrain for too long because of how unpleasant they feel, and so they seek to carry out the behaviour again to avoid this.

Research evidence

☑ Walters (1999) defined the four Ps in addiction:

- **progression** – as the addictive behaviour progresses, so do the tolerance levels

- **preoccupation** – the behaviour dominates the thoughts of the individual

- **perception** – the individual feels no control over the behaviour, it controls them

- **persistence** – the person continues the behaviour despite the problems of tolerance, dependency and withdrawal.

☑ Kuss and Griffiths (2011) wanted to highlight that addictions could include certain behaviour as well as substance abuse. They reviewed literature over an 11-year period, looking at participants between the ages of 8 and 18. They found that gaming produced the same effects as substance abuse – such as tolerance in the participants – supporting the idea that gamblers can show the same side-effects of abstinence as a person who has a substance addiction.

Evaluation

👍 Through investigating addiction and its impact, appropriate treatments may be developed. For example, awareness that gambling can have the same effects as a substance on individuals has led to its inclusion on the DSM-5 so people can be treated appropriately for their addiction.

👎 The term addiction is difficult to define as it incorporates a number of factors, such as physical and psychological dependency, as well as withdrawal and tolerance.

Now try this

What is meant by the term psychological and physical dependence in relation to addiction?

Risk factors

Risk factors in the development of addiction include **genetic vulnerability, stress, personality, family influences** and **peers**.

Genetic vulnerability

Family studies by Merikangas et al. (1998) suggested that first-degree relatives of addicts are at higher risk for an addiction. Some genes may make a person more or less sensitive to the effects of dopamine, for example. The less sensitive may seek out addictive behaviours to compensate for this. A variation of DRD2 (a dopamine receptor gene) is found more commonly with people who have addictions to alcohol, nicotine and cocaine compared to non-addicts. Comings (1996) found just under half of smokers and ex-smokers carried the A1 variant of DRD2. They had fewer D2 receptors, which may make them more vulnerable to developing an addiction.

Stress

People use substances such as nicotine and alcohol to relieve stress in their lives. Children and young people are most at risk of using these negative coping strategies. The use of these strategies is puzzling, as the addiction that can occur as a result actually causes the individual even more stress. Research has linked the number of negative life events and drug use, especially if the life event occurred before adulthood. However, a cumulative effect can also occur as the number of years of stressful life events is correlated with drug or alcohol dependency (Lloyd and Turner, 2008). Also, Driessen et al. (2008) found a third of drug addicts also suffered from PTSD, showing severe stress may increase vulnerability to addictions.

Personality

Eysenck's (1958) personality questionnaire (EPI), designed to measure personality type, has been used to support the idea that certain personalities could be more prone to addictions. Those deemed to be more neurotic (anxious) and psychotic (tendency to be cold and aggressive) are more at risk than introverts and extraverts. Smokers were seen to have scored higher on neuroticism, using the EPI, compared to non-smokers. People who had smoked but quit smoking scored somewhere between the two groups (Terracciano and Costa, 2004).

Peers

Social identity theory (Tajfel and Turner, 1979) proposed an increase in popularity as a reward for engaging in group behaviour. This may explain the influence of peers to develop addictive behaviours. This explanation also links to social learning theory (SLT) processes of observation, imitation and reproduction of rewarding behaviour. NIDA (2005) in the USA found that 90% of smokers started in adolescence, mainly due to observing and imitating peers, supporting the role of SLT.

Family influences

Children often model their behaviour on parents. If parents have relaxed attitudes towards drug use or there is family discord, the children are more likely to start taking drugs. Fisher (1999) found that teenage gamblers are more likely to have a parent with gambling problems who is unconcerned about their children's gambling. This supports the role of family influences on addictions.

Peers can be influential in smoking.

Evaluation

🔎 A lot of the research is carried out on restricted samples and therefore results may not be generalisable. For example, a majority of the studies were carried out on Western populations so there may be other factors that influence people from different parts of the world.

👍 As most of the research has been carried out on people with addictions, the research has high external validity in terms of how true to life the findings are.

👍 For all the influences, there is plenty of supporting evidence suggesting that results are valid. But there could be a number of influences occurring at once, so isolating one factor is difficult.

Now try this

Evaluate research into the risk factor of genetic vulnerability in the development of addiction.

Nicotine and neurochemicals

Nicotine addiction can be explained by the effect it has on the biology and chemistry of the brain.

Dopamine release

Nicotine increases feelings of pleasure by altering the neurotransmission of **dopamine**. Nicotine binds to specific receptors on the presynaptic neuron and excites the dopamine-containing neuron. The nicotine then fires more electrical signals, causing more dopamine to be released. This provides a positive, rewarding feeling which leads to maintenance of the addictive behaviour, as the smoker wants to repeat the pleasurable experience.

Tolerance develops, and the smoker has to smoke more to get the same initial pleasure. The dopamine overstimulates the reward pathway, which then becomes desensitised, thus tolerance occurs. If the levels of nicotine are not sustained, withdrawal symptoms follow.

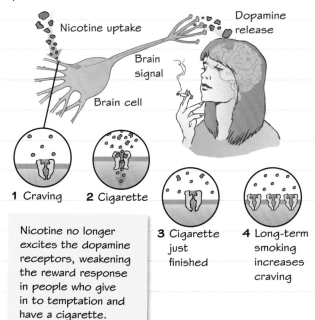

Prefrontal cortex

Dopamine release

Nucleus accumbens
Ventral tegmental area

Stimulation of nicotine receptors

Nicotine enters the brain

The dopamine reward system is part of the limbic system (see page 245).

Nicotine uptake

Dopamine release

Brain signal

Brain cell

1 Craving **2** Cigarette

Nicotine no longer excites the dopamine receptors, weakening the reward response in people who give in to temptation and have a cigarette.

3 Cigarette just finished

4 Long-term smoking increases craving

Research evidence

Corrigall and Coen (1991) found that rats would self-administer nicotine into the reward centres of their brains unless their dopamine release systems were inhibited. This suggests that nicotine addiction is maintained because of the rewarding effects produced from increased dopamine levels. In humans, this would produce continued smoking behaviour.

Fixed action patterns

Comings et al. (1996) found a link between a variant of a dopamine gene and smoking. People with the gene variant had *fewer* dopamine receptors in the pleasure centres of the brain. This suggests they may be more likely to become addicted to nicotine, compared to others without the variant, as the nicotine would increase activity in the few dopamine receptors they did possess and compensate for their deficiency.

Evaluation

🖒 Evidence for a chemical change in the brain from smoking is strong. This provides an objective explanation of nicotine addiction, and has been validated through brain imaging.

🖒 The dopamine explanation for nicotine addiction could explain why there may be a genetic influence (Comings et al. 1996).

🖓 Neurochemical explanations are reductionist, ignoring other complex factors and free will.

🖓 Use of animal research weakens the generalisability of the findings as we cannot be sure that results would extrapolate to humans, due to the differences in physiology between species.

Now try this

Outline which side of the nature–nurture debate the biological explanation of nicotine addiction takes.

Nicotine and learning theory

An alternative explanation for nicotine addiction is **learning theory**, which includes the principles of **social learning theory** (see page 69) for the initiation of smoking and explains the use of **operant** and **classical conditioning** (see pages 67–68) to maintain the behaviour.

Social learning theory (SLT)

SLT states that we copy behaviours from **role models**, such as our peers or people we deem to be similar to us, for example, someone of the same gender. Thus, in smoking behaviour, we would **imitate** our peers through **observing** them smoke.

This shows others as being more popular from their smoking behaviour.

Smoking occurs through the process of **vicarious reinforcement** – reinforcement received **indirectly** by seeing others smoke.

Operant conditioning

This explains that adolescents continue to smoke for **peer approval** (reward). The **pleasurable** feelings produced by the boost of popularity in a group positively reinforce the behaviour.

The smoker may lack confidence and the smoking boosts their self-esteem, through becoming more popular.

The smoker **avoids withdrawal** symptoms through continuing to smoke, thus **negatively reinforcing** the behaviour.

Classical conditioning

This suggests that people smoke as it becomes **associated** with other activities or people. Smokers associate even the suggestion of the group with a cigarette (**cue reactivity**). The smoking behaviour is increased if the individual is confronted with 'cues' that remind them of their addiction.

It could be a group of friends associated with the smoking behaviour.

Classical conditioning is useful to explain maintenance rather than initiation of smoking.

Research evidence

- ✓ DiBlasio and Benda (1993) found the initiation of smoking was heavily influenced by peers and group association, suggesting that cues and SLT both play a role.

- ✓ Robinson and Berridge (2003) suggested that many people take potentially addictive substances but few become addicted, suggesting that there are other psychological factors involved in nicotine addiction (not just reinforcement).

- ✓ Carter and Tiffany (1999) have supported the theory that exposure to smoking-related cues such as ashtrays increases the urge to smoke and produces a range of physiological effects such as raised heart rate. These may contribute to the smoking behaviour, suggesting the role of biological factors as well as psychological ones.

Evaluation

👍 There is a lot of research evidence to support the role of SLT. As a result, improved smoking prevention programmes could target adolescents (those most vulnerable to influence of peers) to inform them of the social influences.

👎 Learning theories suggest that addictions occur because of positive reinforcement or consequences of the behaviour. However, in real life the potential pleasure derived from smoking is only intermittent, not consistently rewarding. For example, smoking does not always remove a negative mood, which therefore suggests that learning theories are only partial explanations.

👎 Learning theories support nurture (the environment) but ignore nature (biological causes).

Now try this

Identify **one** strength and **one** limitation of learning theory in relation to addiction.

Gambling and learning theory

Gambling is unlike many of the other addictions you will have looked at – in particular smoking – as it is not a substance and therefore does not **directly** alter chemical transmission in the brain. This results in a strong case being made for **psychological explanations**.

Operant conditioning

This explains gambling through the principle of **positive reinforcement**, which increases the chance of the behaviour being repeated. Winning money would be the positive reinforcement along with the excitement of the win. Operant conditioning also explains that the short-term pleasure gained from gambling gives more immediate positive reinforcement (e.g. winning) than the long-term effect of punishment (e.g. debt), and thus maintains the addictive behaviour.

Winning money reinforces gambling behaviour.

Partial and variable reinforcement

Partial reinforcement is an example of operant conditioning whereby gambling is explained as a reward only occurring some of the time. Therefore, a person playing a fruit machine will keep playing it in an attempt to get the jackpot. It is expected that a fruit machine will pay out occasionally or on the principle of **variable ratio reinforcement schedules**. For example, payouts could occur anywhere between one and twenty attempts, after certain ratios of putting in money, and a gambler is never sure when the machine will pay out. Therefore, fruit machines and playing lottery scratch cards are both good examples of a reward based on a variable ratio.

Addictions such as gambling, which may be initiated in this way, are more difficult to overcome.

Classical conditioning

This suggests that environmental cues present during the gambling may become **associated** with the pleasure provided by the addiction. For example, the lights and sounds of a fruit machine may be associated with the pleasure of gambling. This explanation is weaker than operant conditioning for gambling as there may be no cues but they still gamble.

Social learning theory

This suggests that children learn gambling behaviour through **observation** of **role models** such as parents or peers, if they saw them win money (**attention**). Observation of the experience would be **retained**, which increases the likelihood of them reproducing or **imitating** the behaviour at a later stage because of the **motivation** to win.

Research evidence

✓ Moran (1970) suggested that it was the size of the reward (reinforcement) that encouraged gambling. Blaszczynski and McConaghy (1989) suggested that winning money temporarily removed some of life's problems (negative reinforcement).

✓ Sharpe (2002) claimed that while variable reinforcement schedules contribute to social gambling they do not fully explain pathological gambling, as consistent losses should cause the individual to stop. For gambling to become pathological, large payouts – in particular a 'big money win' early in a gambling career – can establish an addiction. This can distort future expectations of the outcomes of gambling, where losses can be expected in the pursuit of another big win.

Evaluation

🕈 Operant conditioning does not explain why gamblers continue with their behaviour when they continually lose or they get into financial difficulty.

👍 Operant conditioning is appropriate to explain the maintenance of gambling because of the intermittent reward of winning.

👍 Partial and variable reinforcement help explain the addiction as the gambler will always be thinking if they gamble one more time their big win will come.

👍 Social learning theory takes into account the role of cognitions – thought processes involved in learning behaviour – which is a good explanation of addictive behaviour running in families.

Now try this

Evaluate learning theory in relation to gambling.

Gambling and cognitive theory

The **cognitive approach** looks at the role of people's **interpretations** and **irrational thoughts** towards gambling. This theory looks at how the individual develops a belief system around the gambling that suggests they misinterpret the causes of their wins and losses; gamblers believe in the role of luck.

Social learning theory (SLT)

low mood → leads to addiction (gambling)

↑   ↓

financial, medical, social problems

> Vicious circle of addiction

Beck et al. (2001) devised the cognitive model of addiction, indicating that addicts find themselves in a '**vicious circle**': they have a low mood so gamble to alleviate it. Gamblers only focus on the winning and how happy that makes them **feel** while ignoring the losses they incur. These **cognitive distortions** take many forms such as '**hindsight bias**' where, after gambling, they claim they expected the win or loss, further supporting their irrational thinking – that they can control the outcomes of their gambling.

Research evidence

- ✓ Delfabbro and Winefield (2000) found that 75% of game-related thoughts during gambling were irrational and encouraged further risk-taking. These irrational cognitions could maintain arousal during gambling episodes and cause further gambling to occur.

- ✓ Wohl et al. (2007) tested 82 adult gamblers for symptoms of addictive gambling, their enjoyment of gambling and their perception of dispositional luck (the belief that they were lucky). The participants were divided into two groups: recreational gamblers and disordered gamblers. The disordered gamblers enjoyed gambling more than the recreational gamblers and saw themselves as luckier, illustrating cognitive biases in high-risk gamblers.

🔍 Key study Griffiths (1994)

Griffiths studied the role of skill and cognitive bias in fruit machine gambling. One of three hypotheses was 'That there are significant differences in the thought processes of regular and non-regular gamblers'. They were a volunteer sample.

> I don't think the machine wants to pay me as it's not in a good mood

- The participants were given £3 each to put into a fruit machine.

- The objective was to stay on the machine for 60 gambles and win back the original £3.

- Regular gamblers made more irrational verbalisations, demonstrating cognitive biases.

This research is important because it could help gamblers to get treatment in modifying their behaviour and thoughts – to see the irrational patterns behind their thinking.

Evaluation

- 👍 Identifying the thought processes behind gambling is a positive step in helping the gambler overcome their addiction. Cognitive behavioural therapy (CBT) can be used to challenge their irrational thoughts and get gamblers to think in a more realistic way.

- 👍 Research uses a quasi-method where participants are already gamblers. This provides valid results as to how gamblers behave and think.

- 👎 It is difficult to establish cause and effect; the cognitive bias may be a result of the gambling and not a cause of it.

- 👎 As participants usually know they are taking part in research they may display demand characteristics or give socially desirable responses in questionnaires. This can lead to findings that lack internal validity. In Griffith's research, participants may have used verbalisations because they knew they were being observed.

Now try this

Describe research evidence for the role of cognitions in explaining gambling behaviour.

Reducing addictions: drug therapies

Drug therapies are used to reduce addiction. They aim to block the biological effect of the addictive behaviour and to replace the feeling they get from the addictive behaviour. There are a number of drug therapies available for various addictions.

Agonist substitute

Drugs known as **agonist substitutes** attempt to restore neurotransmitters to their normal level to avoid the highs that addictive behaviours can cause, for example, the pleasure felt by smoking. These types of drug therapies provide a safer drug similar to the addictive one. In the case of **gambling**, it has been shown to have similar effects on the brain as **amphetamine** use, so well-controlled doses of amphetamines can reduce the gambling behaviour.

Safer sources of **nicotine**, such as patches, gum and nasal sprays, are some of the ways in which nicotine replacement therapy is given. The nasal spray and gum give an instant hit of nicotine.

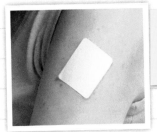

Nicotine patches slowly release nicotine so the addict no longer craves an actual cigarette.

Antagonist substitution

Antagonist treatment uses a drug that blocks receptors so neurotransmitters cannot fit into them. This in turn reduces nerve impulses (**antagonists**) so that if any of the substance is taken it will have no effect.

Naltrexone has been found to be effective in antagonist treatment.

It has been suggested that some **gamblers** feel the same 'rush' that drug addicts feel – this may be due to the rewarding effects drugs have through stimulation of neurotransmitters in the brain. Blocking the rewarding feeling with naltrexone is successful in reducing the compulsion to gamble. **Varenicline** is a drug that blocks the effects of any nicotine added to the system. Clinical trials have shown varenicline to reduce relapse in smokers who had been abstinent for 12 weeks after initial therapy.

Research evidence

Fiore (1994) carried out a meta-analysis of the effectiveness of nicotine patches. When compared to participants who wore a placebo patch, the nicotine patch wearers were twice as likely to stop smoking.

This suggests that the nicotine patches work by still providing the smoker with lower doses of nicotine without them craving a cigarette.

Research evidence

Kim and Grant (2001) carried out a six-week trial of naltrexone, which works on dopamine production, on 17 compulsive gamblers; 14 completed the trial. Most had stopped gambling by the sixth week. Two gamblers relapsed when medication stopped. This suggests that the gambling stopped as a 'real' response to the drug and not a placebo effect.

Evaluation

👍 Drug treatments and replacement therapies have good results for reducing the addiction. The treatments provide evidence for biological explanations.

👎 Drug therapy is not always suitable as it could exchange addiction from one drug to another. For example, heroin users can get addicted to the heroin substitute methadone. This raises the ethical question of harming a person by giving them another drug that could cause them further problems.

👎 Biological therapies do not address any underlying psychological problems that may have triggered the addiction. Therefore, a combination with a psychological therapy is likely to achieve the best outcome.

Now try this

Outline **one** strength and **one** limitation of drug therapies.

Behavioural intervention

The two types of behavioural intervention, **aversion therapy** and **covert sensitisation**, work on the principle that all behaviour is learnt and therefore people should be able to unlearn behaviours. Behavioural interventions can be used for a number of addictions, including smoking and alcohol.

Aversion therapy

This is based on classical conditioning. The therapy involves making negative associations with the addictive behaviour.

NS + Antabuse US → UR

eventually

CS + → CR

For example, Antabuse, an emetic drug (an **unconditioned stimulus, US**) is given to make alcoholics feel sick (an **unconditioned response, UR**). Paired with the alcohol (the **neutral stimulus, NS**), avoidance occurs because people do not want to feel sick (**conditioned response, CR**) and the alcohol then becomes the **conditioned stimulus** that makes them feel sick, which is now the **conditioned response**.

Covert sensitisation

This is also based on the principles of classical conditioning. The treatment differs from aversion therapy because of the covert nature. The patient does not experience the stimulus, for example, taking a drug. Instead, they **imagine it**. In the case of an alcoholic, they would have to imagine having a drink at home. The alcohol makes them feel very nauseous. For example, they are asked to imagine actually being violently sick within the room where they have had the drink. Over time, the person **associates** the **unpleasant effects** with the **addictive behaviour**. Once they have completed this stage, they would be asked to imagine the same place and being offered a drink. This time they have to imagine refusing the drink and therefore they avoid the nauseous feeling and the vomiting. This should remove their feeling of wanting a drink. This therapy requires a vivid imagination, which is why it may not work for everyone. With prolonged therapy, the unwanted behaviour should be weakened, if not eliminated.

Research evidence

- ✓ Meyer and Chesser (1970) found that aversion therapy worked for at least a year in 50% of the patients who undertook this therapy.

- ✓ Howard (2001) used an emetic on 82 hospitalised alcoholics and found that this changed their attitudes towards drinking. Over a 10-day period, they reduced their positive alcohol-related beliefs.

Research evidence

- ✓ Gelder (1989) reported that covert sensitisation is a preferred treatment because it raises fewer ethical concerns than traditional aversion therapy. However, it was not more effective, so the only benefit was the moral aspect.

- ✓ Ashem and Donner (1968) found the results were more favourable for treatment of alcoholics; 40% who used this treatment were still abstaining after six months compared to a control group.

Evaluation

- 🖋 It ignores the reasons as to why a person develops an addiction in the first place. It only treats the symptoms, not the cause.

- 🖋 Drug treatments have potential side effects.

- 👍 There is research support for the effectiveness of the treatment.

- 👍 Pairing something unpleasant can be used with any addiction. For example, mild electric shocks have been used with gamblers.

Evaluation

- 🖋 It does not treat the cause of the addiction.

- 🖋 People who are not highly motivated will not benefit, nor will people who lack the ability to imagine the unpleasant effects.

- 👍 The patient is in control of how bad they make the imagined effects. This protects them from real harm.

- 👍 No side effects.

Now try this

Outline criticisms of behavioural-based interventions.

Cognitive behavioural therapy

Cognitive behavioural therapy (CBT) challenges both the cognitions and thoughts behind the behaviour while also seeking to change the behaviour itself.

How does CBT work?

CBT assumes that the behaviour has been learnt and can therefore be unlearnt, and that correcting the faulty thinking will help the addict overcome their behaviour. It is usually offered over a 12-week period in order to promote abstinence and stabilise the addictive behaviour. The main focus is to analyse the individual's thoughts and feelings and the circumstances around the behaviour, while tailoring a programme of support.

1 Relapse prevention

The triggers for engaging in the behaviour are identified in order to identify strategies that could be used to avoid relapse. The therapist will ask the client to think about both positive and negative implications of relapse.

For example, a gambler could be asked to think about what would happen if they entered a betting shop or, alternatively, walked past the shop. Perhaps the benefits they may feel would be the feelings of engaging with the addiction, but the negatives could be losing more money.

The training also challenges the attitudes the person may hold about the behaviour, as some beliefs will be unhealthy. This part of the therapy is important in getting the person to feel **in control**.

2 Relaxation skills

The person needs to use alternative relaxation to that previously used.

For example, they may have an alcohol addiction, in which case their way of relaxing and dealing with stressful situations in the past was to drink alcohol. This unhealthy method of relaxation needs to be replaced with a healthier physiological method such as breathing techniques.

Therefore, the client is taught appropriate relaxation techniques for them to use instead of their addictive behaviour. In using these methods, it gives the person time **to relax** in a more appropriate way, and gives them time to realise they may be at risk of relapse.

3 Cognitive restructuring

This is the most difficult aspect of the therapy as it requires the addict to look at their thought processes related to the behaviour and change them. The therapist may challenge them to think of alternative ways to cope that do not involve their addictive behaviour.

For example, challenging someone with an alcohol problem to think more positively about not drinking and more negatively about the alcohol.

This can be difficult as they may use alcohol to boost their self-esteem. So this part of the therapy has to get them to think more positively about themselves without using alcohol.

Research evidence

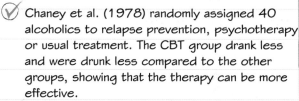 Chaney et al. (1978) randomly assigned 40 alcoholics to relapse prevention, psychotherapy or usual treatment. The CBT group drank less and were drunk less compared to the other groups, showing that the therapy can be more effective.

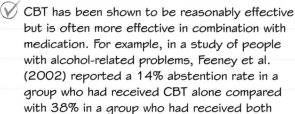 CBT has been shown to be reasonably effective but is often more effective in combination with medication. For example, in a study of people with alcohol-related problems, Feeney et al. (2002) reported a 14% abstention rate in a group who had received CBT alone compared with 38% in a group who had received both CBT and medication.

Evaluation

👍 There is a lot of research evidence to support CBT for addictions. However, as it is usually combined with other treatments it is difficult to isolate its true effectiveness.

👎 CBT is not for everyone as it relies on the person's motivation to engage with the therapist. The client must also trust the therapist, and maintaining both of these aspects can result in high attrition rates. Group CBT sessions may work better to encourage individuals who find the intensity of individual sessions daunting.

👎 There are possible ethical implications, as the therapy could cause psychological harm through challenging their way of thinking.

Now try this

Outline some of the techniques used in cognitive behavioural therapy in reducing addictions.

Theory of planned behaviour

The **theory of planned behaviour** (TPB) is a model of **behaviour change** developed by Ajzen (1985). It is a **cognitive theory** that looks at the way in which health beliefs lead to health behaviours.

The theory of planned behaviour

The theory explains the factors that lead to a person's decision to engage in a particular behaviour. It can be used with any health behaviour to predict the intention to carry out the behaviour or applied to the intention to stop.

> **Behavioural attitude** – for example, 'I am losing a lot of money through gambling.' 'My health is suffering from smoking.'

> **Subjective norms** – for example, 'I know my family wants me to stop gambling or smoking.'

> **Perceived behavioural control** – for example, 'I believe I am in control, therefore I can stop.'

> **Intention** – 'I will attend therapy to help me stop.'

> **Behaviour** – the person begins therapy to stop gambling or smoking.

The model predicts that behaviour stems from the individual's attitude, social pressure and their perceived control. These elements predict the intention of the behaviour.

Control – how much an addict believes they have control over their behaviour is probably the most important aspect of the model. If they lack this, their behaviour will probably continue.

Research evidence

☑ Godin et al. (1992) examined the extent to which TPB could explain smoking intentions and behaviours. Data was collected using questionnaires and trained interviewers. Participants were questioned at the start of the study and 6 months later. Researchers found that the three elements helped to explain intentions, but **perceived behavioural control** was the most important predictor of ultimate human behaviour, as predicted by the model.

☑ Oh and Hsu (2001) studied gambling behaviour. They used a questionnaire to assess gambling behaviour, participants' social norms and attitudes, perceived behavioural control (perceived gambling skills and levels of self-control) along with behaviour intentions. Actual behaviour was positively correlated with attitudes and behavioural intentions.

Evaluation

🖢 As the model uses self-report to gather data, it could lack validity as participants may give socially desirable responses.

🖢 People may not always act as they say they will.

👍 The model has good practical application as therapists can use it to help them decide if an addict is likely to adhere to the intervention programme to help them overcome their addiction.

Now try this

How could a therapist apply all stages of the TPB model to someone giving up smoking?

Prochaska's model of behaviour change

Prochaska's (1997) model explains behaviour change in addiction.

Prochaska's six-stage model

The model illustrates the stages people go through to bring about a change from unhealthy to healthy behaviour. Any successful intervention depends on the motivation of the individual to change. This is a major problem for people with addictive behaviour because they often refuse to admit that they have a problem. If they come forward for help, the type of intervention will depend on the stage that their addiction has reached.

6 Termination
The person is no longer tempted by their addiction, and relapse won't occur, but some never reach this stage: *'I cannot even stand the smell of smoke.'*

1 Pre-contemplation
Friends and family think the person's behaviour is a problem but not the person themselves: *'I'm okay.'*

2 Contemplation
The person knows they need to do something about their addiction but still does nothing: *'I will stop smoking tomorrow.'*

PROCHASKA'S SIX-STAGE MODEL

5 Maintenance
The person needs to keep motivated and realise the benefits of changing their behaviour but relapse is still possible: *'Since stopping smoking six months ago, I have saved a fortune!'*

4 Action
The person puts the plan into action: *'I have not had a cigarette for a month.'*

3 Preparation
The person starts to plan how to stop their behaviour, such as avoiding situations that may tempt them: *'I won't go to the pub so often because I smoke when I have a drink.'*

Progress across the stages is not straightforward and individuals can switch backwards and forwards. This reflects how people in real life think about their addictions: attempting to give up and then relapsing and starting the behaviour again. They call this the 'revolving door phenomenon'.

Research evidence

✓ DiClemente et al. (1991) found that if a person made it to the preparation stage, they were more likely to attempt to quit smoking at 1- and 6-month follow ups, compared to those in the contemplation stage. This shows support for the model as it suggests that once people know they need to do something about their addiction they prepare themselves to do so.

✓ Aveyard et al. (2006) found that even when intervention programmes were personalised at each stage for a smoker, there was no increase in effectiveness for the person quitting.

Evaluation

👍 Research evidence suggests that the model can successfully explain changing unhealthy behaviours to healthy ones.

👍 The model has been tailored to specific addictions. This makes intervention programmes easier to administer, depending on what stage the addict is at.

👎 The model only explains how the change occurs, not why. It may not work for everyone, and factors such as motivation to change and support are important for success.

Now try this

Name the stage of Prochaska's model that is likely to apply in **each** of the following examples.

(a) Sam is really pleased with herself. She used to have a gambling problem, but has refrained for a year.

(b) Billy is aware that he has a drink problem, but puts off doing something about it.

(c) Maria has decided to do something about her smoking. She has bought nicotine patches to help.

(d) Adam stopped gambling a month ago but still attends Gambling Anonymous to help him through.

Exam skills 1

Before you look at the worked examples, remind yourself about vulnerability factors for addictive behaviour, including genes, stress, personality, family influences and peers (page 276).

Worked example

Outline the role of peers in the development of addiction. Refer to research evidence in your answer.
(4 marks)

Research suggests that young people are influenced by peer pressure. Using the principles of social learning theory (SLT), the addictive behaviour is observed and imitated, and peer approval is a reinforcing factor. The behaviour is seen as being rewarding and so develops. McAlistair (1984) found that increased levels of smoking were linked to peer encouragement and approval to smoke, whilst Sussman and Ames (2001) found that peer use of drugs is a strong predictor of drug use among teenagers due to role modelling. However, they also looked at other factors and found the family influence, such as poor supervision and parents' drug taking, also had an effect on addiction. This shows that several factors could influence addictions and peer pressure is just one of these.

The first part of the question requires you to provide an outline of how peers influence addictions.

This answer correctly uses the principles of social learning theory to support the role of peers in the development of addictions.

The answer then gives the findings of research to support this risk factor.

When asked to include research in a question, particularly for a short one, you only need to talk about the relevant findings that support the point you are making.

This answer covers both requirements of the question, outline and research.

Worked example

Explain **two** risk factors in the development of addiction.
(4 marks)

A **certain personality** type could influence addictions. Eysenck (1958) suggested that personality was a risk factor and people with certain traits were more vulnerable. He found that those with neurotic traits (e.g. depression), psychotic traits (e.g. aggression) or extraverts (e.g. risk-takers) were more vulnerable to becoming addicted. Research has shown strong correlations between these aspects of personality and addictions such as smoking. People with low self-esteem are also more prone to addictions as some substances can boost their confidence, such as alcohol.

Stress has also been shown to be linked to addictions, as people use behaviours such as smoking or drinking as a way to deal with stressors. Smokers may smoke to deal with stress, but as the addiction takes hold they smoke to avoid more stress from withdrawal. People who have experienced very stressful situations are more vulnerable to developing addictions.

As the command word is **explain**, no evaluation is needed.

The answer gets straight to the point and identifies the first risk factor in the first sentence, which is always a good technique to use.

No details of the research are necessary, although mentioning Eysenck (the person who developed the theory) demonstrates good knowledge.

Relevant information from Eysenck's theory is used regarding addiction.

The second factor is identified clearly and made immediately relevant to addictions.

This is a succinct answer that identifies the two risk factors involved with addiction, with elaboration on each.

Exam skills 2

Before you look at the worked examples, remind yourself about neurochemical explanations of nicotine addiction (page 277).

Worked example

Discuss the neurochemical explanation of nicotine addiction.   **(16 marks)**

One explanation of nicotine addiction is brain biochemistry, which emphasises the role of neurochemical factors such as **dopamine**. The theory proposes that nicotine increases feelings of pleasure by altering the neurotransmission of dopamine in the brain's reward system. The nicotine binds to specific dopamine receptors on the presynaptic neuron and excites the dopamine-containing neuron. As the smoking behaviour continues, it fires more electrical signals, causing more dopamine to be released. This provides a positive, rewarding feeling of euphoria, which leads to maintenance of the addictive behaviour. As the smoker increases their smoking, the nicotine can no longer excite the dopamine receptors at the same level; this causes the addiction as the smoker attempts to get the same rewarding feeling, resulting in smoking more cigarettes. Gradually, the smoker becomes addicted as they develop a tolerance, which results in a craving for nicotine...

Discuss questions require both outline and evaluation.

The first sentence starts to answer the question immediately by identifying the neurotransmitter dopamine. In the exam you have no time to waste – you have approximately one minute per mark.

Appropriate terminology is used throughout the answer.

This extract covers the first part of the essay, the AO1 material, and ends with explaining how tolerance occurs, resulting in the addiction. To complete this essay, evaluation is needed. You would then need to:

- Include research that supports the theory, for example, Corrigall and Coen (1991).
- Discuss the use of animal research and the problems when generalising to humans.
- Mention that the research used is scientific and carried out in controlled laboratory conditions, which improves the validity of findings.

Any weaknesses identified need to be linked back to the question. For example, if animals are used to support the dopamine theory, you could suggest that humans do not develop addictions to nicotine in the same way, which weakens the dopamine explanation.

Worked example

Briefly outline **one** weakness of the neurochemical explanation of nicotine addiction.   **(2 marks)**

One weakness is that the explanation is reductionist, as it suggests that addiction can be explained in terms of its smallest constituent parts (dopamine activity) and that no other factors influence the behaviour. However, factors such as hereditary influences have been shown to play a role in addictions. Therefore, it oversimplifies human behaviour by isolating one neurochemical factor and ignoring other complexities in how the mind works.

For a 2-mark question, just a few sentences are sufficient.

One weakness, reductionism, is identified and clearly explained.

The answer shows understanding of reductionism and applies it to the neurochemical explanation of addiction.

The answer concludes well, without being repetitive.

Exam-style practice 1

Practise for Paper 3 of your A level exam with these exam-style questions. There are answers on page 322. Before looking at these questions, it would be good to review descriptions of addiction (page 275), reducing addiction (page 282) and the theory of planned behaviour (page 284).

1 Complete the diagram to show the theory of planned behaviour model of behaviour change. Add labels A–D.   **(4 marks)**

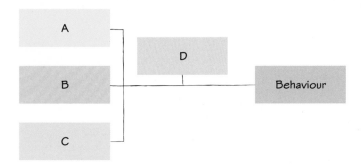

> If you know the model, this question is straightforward. When revising the model, colour-code the diagram and your revision notes listing what each part of the model predicts about behavioural change.

2 Briefly outline what is meant by tolerance and psychological dependence in relation to substance addiction.   **(2 marks)**

> Make sure you make reference to substance addiction in your answer and do not just define the terms.

3 Explain **one** behavioural intervention aimed at reducing addictive behaviour.   **(4 marks)**

> Read the question carefully. Only outline one intervention.

4 Aversion therapy has been used to treat addictions. Which **one** of the following statements is true of aversion therapy?

   A The aim of aversion therapy is to establish an unconditioned response to a conditioned stimulus. ☐

   B The aim of aversion therapy is to establish a conditioned response to a previously neutral stimulus. ☐

   C Aversion therapy involves establishing an association between a voluntary response and a voluntary consequence. ☐

   D Aversion therapy is based on the theory of operant conditioning. ☐

> Knowing the basis of both operant and classical conditioning and understanding the principles behind each will enable you to identify which one is the correct answer.

5 The government wants to run a television campaign aimed at reducing smoking amongst teenagers. Using the theory of planned behaviour, outline how they could do this.   **(6 marks)**

> This is an applied question, so the emphasis is on applying your knowledge of the model to a campaign that could discourage smoking.

Exam-style practice 2

Practise for Paper 3 of your A level exam with these exam-style questions. There are answers on pages 322–323. Before looking at these questions, it would be good to review descriptions of addictions (page 275), vulnerability factors for addictive behaviour (page 276), gambling and cognitive theory (page 280), reducing addictions (page 281–282) and Prochaska's model of behaviour change (page 285).

6   Outline Prochaska's model of behaviour change in relation to smoking addiction. **(4 marks)**

> You could be asked to apply your knowledge of behaviour change to one of the addictive behaviours named in the specification. Make sure you describe the model and apply it to the smoking addiction.

7   Read the item and then answer the question that follows.

> Mark has smoked since he was fourteen. His friends smoke, as do his parents. He feels that without smoking he wouldn't be so confident, and would not be able to cope with his upcoming A level exams.

> You must outline a minimum of two, but you do not need to outline all five named in the specification (genes, stress, personality, family influences and peers).

Outline **two** or more risk factors in the development of Mark's smoking addiction. **(6 marks)**

> Marks are available in questions such as this for the outline (AO1) and engagement with the stem (AO2), so make sure you give examples to support your points.

8   Which **two** of the following statements are true of tolerance?

   A   The behaviour is carried out over longer periods of time than previously.   ◯

   B   The individual experiences low mood and nausea in the absence of the substance.   ◯

   C   Larger doses or more of the target behaviour is needed to get the same feeling.   ◯

   D   The individual is restless and irritable when not engaging in the behaviour.   ◯

> The two correct choices could be used as part of an answer to describe what tolerance is.

9   Outline and evaluate drug therapies for reducing addiction. **(16 marks)**

> A number of drugs can be described for the treatment of any addiction. However, as you will have already covered material on smoking and gambling, it is easier to keep the material confined to treating those two addictions.

10   Read the item and then answer the question that follows.

> Dayna has always thought she was 'lucky' since she used to play and win frequently on the penny slot machines while on holiday with her family. She began buying scratch cards once a week when she turned 18 as she was sure she would win a top prize because of how lucky she was. After winning £50 on one she began to buy them daily. She has now got into debt but she feels the big win is just a scratch card away.

> Ensure you include key terms for these types of questions on the approaches, along with examples of the addictive behaviour in context.

Briefly explain Dayna's addiction to gambling from the cognitive approach. **(6 marks)**

> Make sure you outline the cognitive approach (AO1) to contextualise your answer.

11   Discuss how covert sensitisation is used to treat addiction. **(8 marks)**

> You need to outline what covert sensitisation is and evaluate it as a treatment.

Answers

The answers provided here are examples of possible responses. In some cases, other answers may also be possible.

1. Types of conformity

the informational social influence

2. The Asch study

B, D

3. Variables affecting conformity

any two from: group size, social support and task difficulty

4. The Stanford Prison experiment

The study lacks ecological validity or mundane realism. The fake set-up was obvious and much less imposing than a real prison. The high level of control and total observation were also more than would happen in a real prison. However, it was good enough for both prisoners and guards to play along with the role play.

The ethical guideline of protection has been questioned. The guards became hostile quite quickly and made the prisoners do degrading tasks. This behaviour was not stopped by Zimbardo and it caused a lot of anxiety and distress. However, this is what happens in real prisons and so it could be argued that it was legitimate to observe it.

5. Milgram's study of obedience

An autonomous state is a state in which you remain responsible for your own actions. It would lower obedience because the person would remain unaffected by the presence of an authority figure. The autonomous state is affected by personality characteristics and the presence or absence of others who are showing autonomous behaviour.

6. Explanations for obedience

The head teacher has greater legitimacy of authority than the classroom assistant, as perceived by the pupil. Hofling et al. (1966) showed that the hierarchy in a hospital led to nurses obeying a doctor even though they did not know him, therefore we could assume that the head teacher in a school would have similar power.

7. Situational variables

Increased obedience would come from making badly behaved students sit nearer the teacher, increasing proximity. The school should look smart and be well maintained to increase the perception of the location as a place of high expectations. Having teachers formally dressed increases their legitimate authority. Having a uniform means that the individual autonomy of students is reduced, making them more likely to be in an agentic state.

8. Obedience: dispositional explanation

Being brought up in a family where parents are very strict and do not allow discussion and debate over a child's actions creates unconscious hostility towards authority figures, but this remains suppressed in the presence of authority where the person is submissive. If told by an authority figure to harm someone they will do so, especially if the victim is seen as weak or as a minority, because the repressed hostility emerges as prejudice and discrimination.

9. Resistance to social influence

Through experience, getting older and passing through education, a person has the chance to learn from their mistakes and observe other people who are more successful by showing an internal locus of control. Once a person is aware of how they think and learn they can consciously change it, by using more effective study skills, perhaps. Once a person gains success in this way they will continue to be more internal locus as they have been rewarded for their greater effort.

10. Resisting social influence through social support

These participants have a low commitment to the study by receiving just the $10 fee. They are meeting in a hotel. This is an anonymous setting and the company has no legitimate authority over them. There is no real pressure to comply once the experimenter leaves the room. The task is also easy to resist as no real harm has been done to the company by the employee, so it becomes a question of moral judgement, which is strongly affected by individual differences.

11. Minority influence

Minority influence is exerted by one person or a small number of people over the majority. It works best when the minority has new information, remains consistent but flexible and is not dogmatic. An example would be climate change, which is now widely accepted but used to be thought of as a crank's view.

12. How social influences affect social change

Social change is the slow adoption of a new belief or way of behaving by a section of society, which eventually becomes accepted as the norm.

16. Exam-style practice 1

1 B

2 Asch found a conformity level of 31.8% once he got to three confederates. After this, increasing the number made very little difference. After nine confederates, conformity started to fall. It is possible that more than three confederates makes the naïve participant increasingly suspicious.

3 *Answer could include:*
Strength: Using scales allows for the collection of quantitative data, which means that statistical analysis can be undertaken to test the findings. This can increase the credibility of his research.

Weakness: Correlational data does not imply cause, so Adorno could not conclude that having an authoritarian personality causes obedience in people. His scale statements were very strongly worded and leading, so he was being subjective rather than objective in his methods.

4 Change in society caused by minorities usually begins with informational social influence. The minority might start to talk about something new, for example, climate change was once a minority view. Over a long period the minority gives a consistent message, and this is one of the characteristics that makes them successful in bringing about change. The second characteristic is commitment to their cause, where they show determination to stick to their viewpoint but without being inflexible. For example the climate change scientists stuck to their view despite challenges. The majority become gradually influenced by the innovative idea and more and more people convert to the minority view.

5 Social influence affects social change through the influence of the majority and the minority, and one of the most obvious examples is fashion trends. Fashion is a social influence which is culturally determined by what is popular with the majority, and wearing jeans is a cultural norm in western cultures. In general, people feel the need to follow the majority through their need to belong to their social group, therefore they conform to the current fashion. However, it is the minority influence which pushes the boundaries and moves fashion forward. This is often led by a celebrity who follows a designer who promotes more extreme versions of clothes, pushing the boundaries of technology and textiles. In this case, very skinny jeans have been designed and modelled by a minority who had influence over their admirers at a point in time. After a while, the minority fashion becomes mainstream and another new idea is needed. This is called reaching a critical mass. The majority influence keeps social groups together, and people learn to recognise what is expected of them so that they are not seen as outsiders.

6 (a) It is normal to hold a door for someone carrying a large item.
(b) It is normal to shake hands on first meeting a stranger.

17. Exam-style practice 2

7 The two explanations to cover are social support and locus of control (LoC). For LoC, quote research evidence from Holland (1967), Avtgis (1998) and Twenge et al. (2004). Make it clear how the research evidence supports the explanation – don't just list it. For social support, quote Gamson et al. (1982) and Asch's and Milgram's variations, where they had a fellow dissenter. You should also apply to examples in real life. To evaluate, consider how well they explain individual differences and here you could contrast idiographic versus nomothetic explanations. People who dissent from the

majority are unusual and over generalised nomothetic explanations do not work. Another good evaluative point would be the validity of the research in supporting the explanation. In A level answers you would be expected to be able to relate your answer to the approach in which it sits and to the issues and debates surrounding psychology as well. This opens up points about ethnocentrism and determinism to add further depth to the evaluation.

8 Conformity can be helpful to allow large groups of people to live alongside each other in harmony. Supporting the majority generally leads to peaceful and orderly societies.

9 Unanimity is when everyone agrees with each other.

10 Asch used 123 male student volunteers who were tested one at a time with between seven and nine confederates. When they arrived at the laboratory they were told they were taking part in a study of visual perception and seated within the group either in a line or round a table. They were told to look at lines on two cards and say which of the comparison lines matched the stimulus line. On 12 out of 18 trials (the critical trials) the naïve participant heard the confederates give incorrect answers before answering last or last but one. There was also a control group of 36 who were tested individually with no confederates.

11 C, B, A

12 One limitation of agency theory as described by Milgram is that it tends to be determinist and cannot explain why not everyone gets into the agentic state. Individual differences in personality make some people more resistant than others to being agents of others. It also depends on the role and the context. For example, Hofling found a lot of evidence for agency theory in his study of nurse obedience, in which 21 out of 22 nurses obeyed the instruction to give the unknown drug Astroten to their patients. This is not surprising, because nurses are expected to obey doctors who are their superiors and seen as a legitimate authority. In this context we can see that nurses are in the agentic state. However, where people are more equal in status, such as within a team, there will be more questioning of authority. In Milgram's own study, around a third of his participants refused to obey and maintained their autonomy, reflecting the individual differences amongst his participants.
One limitation of agency theory is that it has been applied to justify atrocities by soldiers, who have used the defence that they were just obeying orders. Blind obedience is created when a group is socialised to give up their autonomy, which happens in highly organised hierarchical social systems. The Nazi soldiers who exterminated the Jews saw themselves as agents of the Third Reich, and did not question what they were told to do. However, the law deems that there is no such thing as blind obedience and that these acts were committed out of free will and were therefore tried as war crimes. Nowadays, blind obedience is not encouraged, and soldiers are expected to remain autonomous and responsible for their actions.

13 Locus of control can be internal or external. Internal locus individuals see themselves as responsible for what happens to them, and they know they are in control of their own successes and failures. External locus individuals believe that they are subject to luck, and trust other people to do the right thing for them. In Milgram's experiment, 25 out of 40 participants went all the way to 450 volts. These 25 who obeyed were likely to have an external locus of control, and trusted the authority figure when he asked them to continue. However, the 15 who refused to obey are more likely to have an internal locus of control and feel responsible for what happened to the victim of the shocks. As we mature we tend to have a more internal locus, as we realise we can influence the direction of our own lives.

18. The multi-store model

To support the multi-store model there should be evidence for the importance of rehearsal and the existence of separate stores. One piece of evidence comes from neuroscience, where Talmi et al. (2005) found that different brain areas were involved when participants were recalling words from the beginning or end of a list. For STM it was the right inferior parietal lobe and for LTM it was the medial temporal lobe. Another piece of evidence comes from patients who have damage in one area of the brain, then lose either their STM or LTM. HM lost his hippocampus in an operation, leaving him unable to learn new things in LTM while retaining the ability to remember short strings of digits in STM, indicating that there are two separate stores. To test rehearsal, Peterson and Peterson (1959) used trigrams (a set of three consonants) to test retention in STM. They got participants to learn the trigrams and then count backwards from a three-digit number until told to stop (to prevent rehearsal). They tested after 3, 6, 9, 12, 15 or 18 seconds, which they called the retention interval. They found that STM declined rapidly without the benefit of rehearsal.

19. The sensory register

Coding is the format by which information is stored in memory stores in the brain. Infomation is coded through synaptic activity and the stimulation of various neurotransmitters. **Capacity** is how much information can be held in our memory stores. **Duration** is how long information can be held in store.

20. Short-term memory

for example, catch and match

21. Long-term memory

Frost (1972) showed that participants used both visual and semantic coding, depending on whether they were expecting to recall or recognise visually or semantically categorised pictures or picture names in a free recall task. He found that parallel access of visual and semantic memory codes occurred. When recognition is expected, a visual cue provides faster access, and when expecting recall, verbal access is more efficient. This demonstrates that separate coding occurs.

22. The working memory model

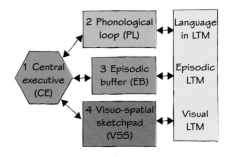

23. Types of long-term memory

Clive Wearing has retained his procedural memory for playing the piano as this is unaffected by the damage to the hippocampus. The procedural memory is used for automatic actions. However, in order to remember that he has played a piece, he needs his STM to be intact, and the loss of the hippocampus has stopped him forming memories for more than a few minutes.

24. Explanations of forgetting: interference

proactive interference (PI)

25. Cue-dependent forgetting

state dependent

26. Misleading information

In the response-bias explanation, when a person gets a leading question, it biases their response but the memory has not changed. In the memory substitution explanation, when a person gets a leading question, it actually changes the stored memory.

27. Anxiety

No effect of anxiety: in a study by Christianson and Hubinette (1993), 110 witnesses of 22 real-life bank robberies in Sweden were interviewed 4–15 months after the robberies. Some had been onlookers or customers (low anxiety), and others were bank employees who had been directly threatened or subjected to violence during the robberies (high anxiety). The findings were that the victims were 75% accurate in their recall of the robbers' clothing and behaviour, and that the accuracy was still evident 15 months later. There was no difference between rated degree of emotion and number of details remembered. **Anxiety reduces accuracy: Pickel (1998)** suggested it was the unusualness of the gun that caused the weapon focus effect. Participants were shown a man using scissors, a gun, a wallet or a raw chicken either in a place they were expected to be or in an unusual place. Participants' recall of the man was poorest in the most unusual conditions. The unusual items would have increased arousal, causing a narrowing of focus away from the perpetrator.

28. The cognitive interview

The cognitive interview uses memory enhancement techniques to improve witness recall over the standard police interview.

32. Exam-style practice 1

1   C

2   B

3   There are many ways the research method could affect the result of eyewitness testimony studies. Examples include:
   - Laboratory experiments are artificial and restrict the actions of the witnesses, forcing them to respond in just one way to isolate the independent variable and measure the dependent variable. In real life, witnesses could act in many different ways to help them remember the event.
   - Laboratory experiments increase demand characteristics so the witnesses could be aware of what the experimenter wants and so behave as the experimenter wants.
   - If a mock crime scene is set up, it has to be less threatening than a real crime because the researcher must consider the ethics of protecting the participants.
   - If the researcher tries to make the witnesses anxious again, there may be ethical issues, and doing this often involves medical procedures, which are not criminal activities.
   - Field experiments never isolate the independent variable completely, and so there are often confounding variables that interfere with the witnesses' recall, such as the passing of time while a crime is processed.
   - Case studies of witnesses to crimes have the problem of generalisability.
   - The type of crime chosen for the study will also affect the results, as more violent crimes create more anxiety.

4   Mahima can expect the interview to have four components. First she will be asked to recall the event in her own words, giving as much detail as she can. This will allow the interviewer to devise some strategies for further questions and get the basic narrative. Next, she will be asked to mentally reinstate the context she was in at the time of the robbery, such as her mood, what she was thinking about and where she was going. Then she might be asked to change perspective and imagine the scene from the perpetrator's viewpoint. Finally, she will be asked to change the narrative order and recall events from back to front. Doing this enhances memory by maximising the chances of cueing memories that have been stored but are inaccessible.

5   The echoic store receives and stores sounds, and the iconic store receives images.

33. Exam-style practice 2

6   One criticism of the methods used to investigate STM is that they lack mundane realism. In order to measure the capacity of STM, researchers such as Miller (1956) used the digit span method, in which gradually increasing lists of digits are read to the participants who have to recall them until they make mistakes or fail to recall them. By this means it was found that the capacity was between five and nine items. However, in real life we would hear more complex items but they would have more meaning and readily fit our existing schemas, meaning that we could retain more information. A second criticism is that in laboratory experiments the participants are sitting there expecting to recall something. Usually the task is deliberately meaningless, such as recalling nonsense trigrams (Peterson and Peterson 1959), so extra effort would be needed. This creates demand characteristics which limit the application of the findings.

7   An example of proactive interference is learning French before learning Italian, and then remembering French words when you want to recall Italian ones.
   An example of retroactive interference is being unable to recall the name of a student you taught two years ago because new names interfere.

8   The encoding specificity principle states that memory is superior for items when they are recalled in the same place as they were learned. For example, we often find lost items when we retrace our steps, whether mentally or physically.

9   (a) sensory memory (or register)
    (b) short-term memory
    (c) long-term memory
    (d) rehearsal loop
    (e) forgetting

10 One advantage of using laboratory studies to investigate memory is that we can find a cause and effect relationship by eliminating extraneous variables and limiting the participant's responses to the dependent variable. This allows us to rigorously test our hypothesis using a standardised procedure so that we can replicate the research to establish a body of knowledge.
    A disadvantage of using laboratory studies is that they lack generalisability. Often the samples are university undergraduates of psychology earning extra credits for their exams. This sample is likely to be homogeneous and will not reflect the huge variety of memory ability in the population at large. Older and younger people will not be represented and university undergraduates are likely to have better memories than most.

11 Two factors that affect the accuracy of eyewitness testimony are anxiety and the cognitive interview. Anxiety has been well researched because most crimes will involve some stress on the part of witnesses. The question is: does eyewitness testimony remain accurate? There are conflicting views on this. On the one hand, Yuille and Cutshall (1986) in a field experiment with real witnesses to a multiple shooting, showed that the witnesses were remarkably accurate despite rating themselves as quite stressed on a seven-point scale. The witnesses who were the most stressed were 88% accurate compared with 75% who said they were not particularly stressed, showing that anxiety had not affected memory and indeed, the stress response may have led the witnesses to being more focused on the incident they were watching, potentially increasing their ability to store the memory and recall accurately later. On the other hand, Christianson and Hubinette (1993) interviewed 110 witnesses of 22 real-life bank robberies in Sweden 4–15 months after the robberies. Some had been onlookers or customers (low anxiety), and others were bank employees who had been directly threatened or subjected to violence during the robberies (high anxiety). The findings were that the victims were 75% accurate in their recall of the robbers' clothing and behaviour, and that the accuracy was still evident 15 months later. There was no difference between rated degree of emotion and number of details remembered. In this case, anxiety had not made much difference to accuracy either in terms of improving or decreasing consistency over time. These two studies are high in ecological validity as they use real events and witnesses, and they demonstrate that in a real world setting there may be unexpected results because the 'participants' are subject to extraneous variables that might either exacerbate or decrease any anxiety experienced.

In a meta-analysis, Deffenbacher (2004) attempted to find a definite conclusion to the argument about the effects of anxiety on witnesses. He found that witnesses were consistently inaccurate (effect size –0.31) with identification of faces and other details of crimes when they were very anxious, but it depended on how the research had been conducted. More life-like reconstructions of crime scenes had worse recall than studies that had used apprehension of an injection as the way of creating anxiety and this may be because fear of an injection is a known quantity to the participant as they will expect to experience pain in a controlled way, whereas fear of a crime scene is likely to be higher due to fear of the unknown and not being in control. More research is therefore needed to come up with a final view on the effect of anxiety.

The cognitive interview is so named because it used cognitive psychological concepts about memory to improve recall. According to Tulving (1973) both context and state-dependent cues are involved in witnessing an event. Creating a mental picture enacts the encoding specificity principle, which states that recall is better when learning and recall states are similar. To help the witness get back into a similar state the interview follows four stages and each has a psychological rationale designed to cue the person into remembering extra details. For example recalling the event in reverse is very helpful as anyone will know who has lost keys and the retraces steps to find them. Using a laboratory experiments and raters who were 'blind ' to the witnesses interview type, Fisher and Geiselman (1985) found that the Cognitive Interview achieved more accurate detailed memories than the standard police interview. Most police forces now use the technique as standard practice, therefore suggesting that it has real world applications beyond the laboratory. However, it does not always work with all crimes and would be unsuitable in a rape case for example, because this would be too traumatic for the victim of the crime. Furthermore, in a meta-analysis of 55 studies, Kohnken et al. (1999) found that cognitive interviews produced both more accurate and less accurate details than the Standard Police Interview (SPI). Time passing also reduced its effectiveness so it works best when the witness has close involvement in the crime scene and they are interviewed soon afterwards.

34. Caregiver–infant interactions

Interactions between caregiver and infant lead to attachment because a bond develops through communication. Interactional synchrony works through the infant and the caregiver taking account of what the other is offering, and showing understanding of the other's needs. For example, they have a two-way communication where each waits to respond to the other. Similarly, reciprocity leads to a relationship being built between the caregiver and the infant as they develop expectations about how each should contribute to their communication, enabling patterns of communication to develop. For example, when one smiles there is an expectation of a smile in return. In this way a relationship is built.

35. Stages of attachment development

Initially infants are in the pre-attachment stage where they show no preferences for specific people, but at around three months they enter the indiscriminate attachment stage when they begin to prefer specific people, usually those who are looking after them the most. However, they don't mind other people interacting with them. At about seven months they get fussier about who is with them. This is the discriminate attachment stage, and they are anxious around strangers and become upset when their primary caregivers are not there. At nine months, infants develop multiple attachments beyond the primary caregiver to others they have come into contact with, such as grandparents and older siblings.

36. The role of the father

One way that fathers have different roles from mothers in caregiving is nurturing. In most cases, mothers are found to be more nurturing whereas fathers are more associated with play. For example, Hardy (1999) found that dads were not as good as mums at detecting distress in children, suggesting lower nurturing abilities.

37. Animal studies of attachment

Harlow's study shows the importance of contact between infant and mother monkeys. He found that infant monkeys would always prefer to cling to a surrogate wire mother covered in soft towelling than to a wire mother that had no covering but had food. This shows that physical contact was important to the monkeys because whenever they were distressed they immediately went to the cuddly surrogate.

38. Learning theory of attachment

Learning theory suggests that infants attach to their caregiver due to conditioning. Babies learn to associate their caregiver with food. Hunger is an unpleasant experience that can be removed by food. Food is an unconditioned stimulus that leads to the unconditioned response of satisfaction of hunger. The caregiver provides the food. Although initially the caregiver does not cause a response in the baby, with enough pairings of caregiver and food, the caregiver becomes a conditioned stimulus, leading to a conditioned response of satisfaction.

39. Bowlby's monotropic theory

Sensitive responsiveness involves how quick the caregiver is to detect a need in the infant and to respond to it appropriately.
Critical period is the period of early

infancy (up to 3 years old) during which an attachment relationship must develop for the infant to develop normally.
Monotropic relationship is the one relationship of central importance to the development of the attachment, usually with the primary caregiver.
Social releasers are biologically programmed behaviours shown by infants that are designed to attract a caregiver's attention, such as smiling or crying.
Internal working model is the template for all future relationships. It is based on the monotropic relationship with the primary caregiver and goes on to affect how the child interacts with others.
The continuity hypothesis suggests that the attachment relationships that occur during infancy go on to affect future relationships.

40. Ainsworth's 'Strange Situation'

The procedure used is quite artificial and so the babies might be responding to the artificiality rather than to the separation and reunion with mother, suggesting that the procedure lacks ecological validity. However, the strict controls used that make it more artificial also make the measures more objective and reliable, allowing replication of the procedure. It can also be criticised as culturally biased as it assumes that some behaviours are more indicative of a secure attachment, which may be true only in a certain culture, which means that the SSP should not be used as a universal measure of attachment. It has been shown to have good predictive validity, as the infant attachment style determined by SSP in infancy persists through early childhood.

41. Cultural variations in attachment

The UK had 25% more type B (secure) attachments than China. Levels of type A (insecure-avoidant) attachments were similar, with China having 3% more. China had 22% more type C (insecure-resistant) attachments than the UK, which only had 3% of children in this category compared with China's 25%.

42. Bowlby: maternal deprivation

The judge would have to consider the care of the child. Bowlby suggests that the child needs to form a monotropic relationship with its primary caregiver. This means that the baby should stay with its mother in order to avoid later development of emotional problems. Therefore, the mother should not receive a custodial sentence, or should be sent to a mother and baby unit. If this is not possible, then care for the child should be organised to provide continuous care from one specific person.

43. Romanian orphan studies

Procedure: Rutter (1998) conducted a longitudinal study.
- He tracked the development of 165 Romanian orphans adopted into UK families; 111 of them were under 2 years old at the time of adoption, the rest were under 4.
- He recruited a comparison group of 52 British children adopted before the age of 6 months.

- He assessed the children's physical and cognitive progress at the outset and then every four years.
Results: At the outset, the Romanian children were behind the UK children on all measures. Four years later, he found that most of the Romanian children had caught up physically and cognitively (especially those adopted by the age of 6 months).

44. The influence on later relationships

There is a lot of research that suggests childhood attachment relationships affect relationships in later life. For example, Sroufe (2005) found that securely attached infants were more socially confident than others, meaning that they find it easier to make friends. Hazan and Shaver (1987) found a link between early attachment type and the type of adult relationships people had. However, this study may be biased because the sample was self-selected and perhaps only people who were insecure with their attachments volunteered because this made them more interested in the topic. Other research such as Steele (1998) on adult relationships could be mentioned.

48. Exam-style practice 1

1   B
2   This study found that the most common attachment type across all cultures was secure (Type B), with the UK having the highest levels (75%) and China the lowest levels (50%). The highest level of insecure-avoidant was in West Germany (35%) and the lowest in Japan (5%). Only three countries showed moderately high levels of insecure-resistant: Japan (27%), Israel (29%) and China (25%). The conclusions drawn from this is that attachment is broadly universal.
3   (a)   A controlled observation is where the researcher sets up a situation, usually in a laboratory setting, in order to carefully record the behaviour of the participants. This is to control for extraneous variables that could affect what happens and distract from the main aims of the study.
    (b)   One issue that might arise from the use of a controlled observation is a loss of mundane realism, as the participant is aware that they are being observed and their behaviour could be affected by the unnatural setting in which it is being observed.
4   (a)   A securely attached infant will show distress when the primary caregiver leaves them and joy on reunion, and stranger anxiety when an unfamiliar person interacts with them. They will use their caregiver as a secure base from which to explore the world.
    (b)   An insecure avoidant infant will not show distress on being left alone and will not show emotion on their return. They interact as easily with strangers as with attachment figures and do not seem to need the carer as much.
    (c)   This type of attachment leads to behaviour such as being distressed when the carer leaves them but not taking comfort from them on their return. They are wary of strangers and seem to both need and reject the carer's attention.

5 Van Ijzendoorn and Kroonenberg (1988) conducted a meta-analysis using the Strange Situation Procedure (SSP) to measure attachment styles in eight different cultures. They found that the most common attachment type was secure, although there were differences between countries in the percentages that occurred. For example, the highest level was found in the UK (72%) and the lowest in China (50%). The type of insecure attachment each culture had was very different, with only China showing an equal number (25% for each). Only Japan (5% insecure-avoidant and 27% insecure-resistant) and Israel (7% and 29% respectively) showed higher levels of resistant than avoidant. These findings support the idea that attachment behaviour is universal, but suggests that culture plays a small part in the type of attachment formed. Both individualistic cultures, such as the UK, which value independence and competition, and collectivist cultures, such as Japan, which value sharing and interdependence, were considered in the research, suggesting a representative sample of cultures. That said, most of the countries used in the meta analysis were western and the majority of the studies used had occurred in western settings. Using the SSP across these different cultures may be culturally biased because of the way attachment was measured. For example, in Japan there are differences in child rearing practices especially amongst the middle classes where Japanese children are never left alone, so to put them in a situation where they are alone causes great distress, which is interpreted as showing high levels of insecure-resistant attachment. Furthermore, Japenese children are raised to be polite and interested in strangers and thus tend not to exhibit the stranger anxiety that was seen in the American children in Ainsworth and Bell's original study. This may also lead to the children being classified as insecure resistant. This suggests that the SSP is not a valid tool for use in other cultures because it fails to take account of child-rearing practices and assumes that all children are raised in similar environments with the same rules. So, to employ the SSP in this way also encourages an ethnocentric bias, whereby western researchers may judge cultures like Japan in a negative way because the infants are being classified into a 'type' that may be viewed as less desirable. It could be argued further that the characteristics of insecure-avoidant attachment reflect the values of an individualistic culture. In Germany, for example, the level was 35% because again there are different child rearing practices where the child is trained to show less dependence on their caregiver, so they are not as affected by their mother's presence or absence and can fend for themselves. Van Ijzendoorn and Kroonenberg found that there was more variation within cultures than between them, suggesting that subcultural differences are more important than culture in influencing attachment types. To suggest that culture and nationality are the same is therefore inappropriate.

49. Exam-style practice 2

6 (a) **Event sampling** is the tracking of specific target behaviour by the participant.

(b) **Time sampling** is the recording of the behaviour being tracked at set time intervals during the observation.

(c) **Covert observation** is a situation in which the participants are unaware that they are being watched for research purposes.

7 (a) Longitudinal research involves the tracking of individual participants over a period of time. In this case, Schaffer and Emerson studied mother–baby attachment relationships over a period of 18 months.

(b) The researchers measured separation protest by observing what happened when the infant was left alone. They measured stranger anxiety by the researcher approaching the child at the start of each home visit and recording their reaction.

(c) One strength of self-report data is that it allows the researcher to gather data about things that have not been or cannot be directly observed, such as attitudes and opinions or, in this case, what happens when the observer is not present.

One weakness is that it may not be as accurate and reliable as other methods, because the participant might not choose to share their views honestly or may not remember all the details of an event they are reporting.

8 Very young infants are unable to communicate their internal thought processes and so the researcher has to infer from their behaviour what is happening. This makes the data less objective as the researcher may interpret their behaviour wrongly. Also, young infants have particular needs that have to be met, so a carer needs to be with them to ensure no distress occurs and that the child's needs are met quickly to avoid any harm occurring.

9 Bowlby suggested that humans are genetically programmed to form an attachment relationship with a caregiver in order to survive. For normal psychological development to occur, the child needed to develop an internal working model of relationships which was based on the primary attachment relationship formed in infancy with the main caregiver. If the relationship was insecure or missing, the child would not develop normally. The continuity hypothesis stems from this because it suggests that the relationship formed in the critical period of infancy (the first 3 years) is a predictor of later relationships. This is supported by research. For example, Hazan and Shaver (1987) found a link between childhood attachment type and adult relationships. Bowlby suggested that if the relationship is disrupted in the critical or sensitive period (up to age 5), it will have serious effects on the child's psychology, and the child can become an affectionless psychopath as a result of long-term separation from the caregiver.

50. Definitions of abnormality (1)

Deviation from social norms means that the person is not behaving in a way expected by the society he or she lives in. This has become noticeable to others and the person is probably not able to function fully as a family member or worker. It is having a negative effect and is not improving. The person gets classed as mentally ill when they can no longer function normally.

51. Definitions of abnormality (2)

Two from:
• It is subjective and not well-defined – what is a realistic view of the world?
• It changes over time and over cultures. For example, we see independence as a healthy sign, whereas collectivist cultures such as the North Koreans do not.
• Most people do not self-actualise but we would not say they are abnormal.

52. Phobias

cognitive and emotional characteristics

53. Depression

With a classification system such as the DSM-5. This manual lists the symptoms and provides guidelines according to how long the client has suffered the symptoms. In order to decide on the severity of the depression, the clinician would look at how many of the symptoms the client has and decide accordingly. The more symptoms, the more severe the depression.

54. Obsessive compulsive disorder

Obsession – the house will burn down. Compulsion – I need to check the gas has been turned off. The obsession is the thought and the compulsion is the behaviour.

55. The two-process model of phobias

Biological preparedness is another explanation from an evolutionary perspective. This idea sees us as being prepared to avoid those things that could have harmed us in our evolutionary past such as snakes and spiders. These ancient fears or instincts are still within us today. Hence, we are far more likely to develop phobias of creatures rather than cars, although cars are more likely to hurt us. Part of this idea is that having a fear is actually useful for our survival.

56. Behavioural treatments for phobias

Over several weeks of treatment the client works with the therapist through a number of stages.
Step 1: The client is taught progressive relaxation techniques (working round muscle groups and relaxing them one by one).
Step 2: The therapist and client construct a hierarchy of fears about the object from the least to most feared representation. These are then imagined by the client.
Step 3: The client starts with the least feared representation and uses a fear thermometer to indicate how they feel as they relax in its presence.
Step 4: The client moves up the hierarchy, slowly relaxing at each stage.
Step 5: The client faces the most feared representation successfully.

57. Beck's negative triad

Beck's diagram (on page 57) would be acceptable with commentary: Beck believed that depression could be explained through a cognitive triad of negative thinking.

As the person got depressed, their self-schemas would become more negative and they would enter a cycle where they saw the world from a bleak standpoint. Ultimately, they then see the future as no better and can't see a way out of their illness.

58. Ellis's ABC model

One similarity is that both models explain depression through faulty thinking patterns which then keep the negative cycle going and maintain the depression.
One difference is that Beck sees depression in a triad of automatic thoughts that perpetuate the illness, whereas Ellis sees activating events as having consequences that in turn are affected by our beliefs.

59. Treating depression

Ellis identifies 11 musturbatory beliefs that are emotionally damaging, such as 'I must be good in all my A levels'. Trying to live up to these ideals is stressful. A therapist challenges these beliefs through reframing. That is, suggesting more realistic and positive ways of looking at life events. Clients practise positive and optimistic thinking over approximately 12 sessions. In this education phase, clients learn about the links between their thoughts, emotions and behaviour. This is followed by behavioural activation and pleasant event scheduling to get the client out and about again, such as planning a trip to the cinema. Goals are set to boost self-esteem where the therapist is confident the client will succeed. These involve challenging negative beliefs such as thinking they could not manage a bus journey by actually doing one.

60. Biological explanations of OCD

Criticisms of the genetic explanation – **one** from:
- There are so many genes implicated as 'candidates' for OCD that there is unlikely to be a clear picture of genetic influence.
- Twin studies can be flawed because MZ twins usually share a lot of similar environments as well as genes, so it is hard to separate the genetic influences from the environmental ones..

Criticisms of the neural explanation – **one** from:
- We do not know whether brain and neural changes cause OCD or are the result of OCD.
- We do not know how genes may interact with neural transmission to cause the symptoms of anxiety and OCD. This research is still in its infancy.

61. Biological treatments of OCD

One problem with using drug treatments for OCD is the side effects. These are serious for some, with an increase in suicidal thoughts in the initial few weeks of the treatment, particularly in young people. Some people experience weight gain, heart arrhythmias and a loss of libido, causing them to stop taking their medication.
By contrast, non-biological, cognitive CBT sessions of two hours over 10 weeks produce better remission (NICE guidelines evidence 2014).
However, treatment-resistant cases are offered anti-psychotic drugs in combination with SSRIs. This appears to help.

Drug therapy is quick and easy to administer, unlike waiting for CBT. It is also cheaper and a GP can administer it. It is not a cure, but it manages the symptoms so that the patient can resume normal life.

64. Exam-style practice 1

1 (a) The emotional characteristics that the person will experience include fear and anxiety around needles or even pictures of needles, and a feeling of panic and anxiety when they imagine having an injection. This will increase when they have to go to the doctor, and may become a full panic attack. The behavioural characteristics will include difficulty breathing and a need to run away or avoid the situation. Some people may faint or freeze to the spot. These emotional and behavioural responses are caused by adrenaline in the body triggering the fight-or-flight response. This is thought to be an evolutionary response helping us escape from danger.

   (b) One weakness of this treatment for needle phobia is that it is actually painful to have an injection, so a fear of syringes or needles is not unjustified. The 'cure' is going to involve some pain, unlike other phobias that are less rational such as a fear of balloons. Systematic desensitisation is therefore not appropriate for all phobias.

   (c) An alternative treatment would be flooding. This is worse than desensitisation because it involves facing the fear head on. This would mean having injections until they became less frightening. There are big ethical issues with this as it could create an even worse fear through trauma. However, it would be more cost-effective and quicker if it worked. Sometimes overcoming the phobia can happen naturally if a person is seriously ill and is forced to have injections or has to inject themselves. Eventually, most people can cope with it.

2 Behavioural characteristics of OCD involve compulsions, which are repetitive behaviours such as hand-washing, counting and praying. Sufferers feel that they have to perform them or something terrible will happen. This creates anxiety. Compulsions reduce anxiety, so carrying out the behaviour is repeated over and over again. The behaviours intrude on normal life, and when bad can prevent a person carrying out daily activities.

3 (a) The two-process model explains phobias through classical and operant conditioning. First, classical conditioning explains how the phobia is formed, perhaps through a single unpleasant experience such as a dog bite. Then a fear of dogs is maintained through operant conditioning using positive and negative reinforcement. Escaping from or avoiding dogs becomes positively reinforcing. The sight of a dog coming towards you is a negative reinforcer, making you take action.

   (b) The two process model has research by Watson and Raynor (1920) with Little Albert, Pavlov (1903) with his original work on dogs and Skinner's

(1950s) work with rats and pigeons to support it. The research shows how behaviour can be formed and shaped, and has become accepted theory. More recently, other researchers have found that people also acquire phobias from traumatic experiences such as car crashes (De Gallo 1996). This gives the theory scientific credibility and reliability. On the other hand, not all phobias are acquired through trauma and some are started by observation of a role model.

An alternative explanation is that we are biologically prepared to become phobic towards things that could harm us through evolution. When we lived more dangerous lives, the people who spotted the danger were the ones most likely to survive, so they bred and passed down the genes for fear and phobias of things like snakes and spiders. However this is irrational in the modern world where we are not afraid of cars or electricity, which are more likely to kill us, but are more likely to fear a spider that is harmless.
Overall, the two process theory has more weight, especially as phobias can be overcome through systematic desensitisation which uses classical conditioning.

4 Joe could have been offered CBT as an alternative to drugs. Beck's cognitive therapy attempts to identify the automatic thoughts which drive depression. Abnormal behaviour is seen as being caused by disordered thinking processes relating to the negative triad. Beck saw the triad as relating to a person's dysfunctional negative view of themselves, their life experience and their future. It is usual to offer a number of sessions over a period of time (between 3 and 6 months) with a therapist and often patients continue to take chemotherapy at the same time. Over about twelve treatment sessions, Joe would be encouraged to identify irrational thoughts with the therapist called cognitive biases. These include overgeneralisation (sweeping generalisations that one failed relationship means constant failure) and minimising successes while maximising failures. The therapist could have offered Joe alternatives and challenges to the automatic thoughts. For example, the therapist might have asked: 'Where is the evidence for the belief? Is it logical to think like that and is it helpful to think like that?' Then Joe would have been set tasks to record when he enjoyed something or when someone gave him a compliment. Joe would be given homework to challenge his beliefs and to change his behaviour. This is to give Joe a more rational view of his life. Joe would be encouraged to take small steps to increase his level of enjoyable activities.
The advantage of CBT over drug therapy is that Joe would not have experienced the unpleasant side effects he found so difficult to deal with when taking medicines. Furthermore, drug treatments (usually SSRIs) are not usually a cure in themselves but can improve mood, so that talking therapies such as CBT are more effective. March et al. (2007) compared CBT to antidepressant drug therapy alone and then together. They found that after 36

weeks, 81% of the CBT group, 81% of the antidepressant group and 86% of the combined group of 327 depressed adolescents were significantly improved. This would suggest that using the two treatments together was best but an improvement of 81% is impressive for CBT alone.

Another advantage for Joe is that CBT works relatively fast, whereas drug treatments with SSRIs take over 10 days to show effects. Therefore it is cost-effective, but relies on well trained therapists to work well. Joe would need to establish a strong client-to-therapist relationship of trust for it to work. This is not necessary with drug treatments alone, which can be taken in isolation.

However, one difficulty of CBT is that therapists who follow the treatment of Albert Ellis advocate a strongly challenging approach, but not all patients can take this. Joe might find the sessions too challenging and therefore stop going before the treatment is finished. However, David et al. (2008) found that 170 patients with major depression treated with REBT (Ellis's Rational Emotive Behaviour Therapy) had better outcomes than those with the drug fluoxetine six months after treatment. This suggests that REBT is better in the long term than drug therapy and could be another alternative treatment that Joe could undertake. Ellis sees depression as being caused by an activating event, perhaps Joe's girlfriend ended a relationship, the beliefs about that event (Joe thinks there must be something wrong with him) and the consequences which is an emotional response to the event (his grief and depression). And this could be dealt with in the therapy sessions.

Another difficulty is that we don't really know whether irrational thinking is the cause or the effect of depression. Joe may have had depressed thinking which made him a negative person to be around and led to the breakdown of his relationship, rather than the relationship breakdown causing his depression.

Embling (2002) showed that not all depressed patients benefitted from CBT. Personality factors such as perfectionism and external locus of control hindered its effectiveness, so its effectiveness for Joe would depend on what sort of person he is and how prepared Joe is to become fully immersed in the type of therapy offered to him. Certainly, any therapy is much more likely to have a positive impact on him and to be better for him than no therapy or sporadic treatment using medication.

65. Exam-style practice 2

5 **One** from:
- It does not explain all types of depression such as bipolar disorder.
- Someone with major depression may not feel sad and may experience psychosis, which suggests another cause.
- The evidence linking negative thinking to depression is correlational. There is a relationship between inventory scores and the level of depression but this is not causal evidence. There could be an inherited biological or genetic predisposition to depression in the family, for example.

6 (a) $n = 10$ means there are 10 participant scores (in each gender group, in this case).

(b) means: males 5.9 ($59 \div 10$) and females 5.5 ($55 \div 10$)
medians: males 6.5 and females 6. To work out the median, find the middle value by sorting from smallest to largest.

	Males	Female
	2	1
	3	3
	5	3
	5	5
median –	6	6
	7	6
	7	6
	8	7
	8	9
	8	9

modes: males 8 and females 6 (the mode is the most frequently occurring)

(c) range: males = 6 and females = 8 (take the smallest value away from the biggest) so its 8–2 for males and 9–1 for females

(d) Males have a smaller range, indicating that they are more similar in their fear of dogs, whereas females show more extreme responses to fearing dogs.

7 One methodological problem with studying people with mental illnesses is that it could be difficult to find a control group to match them on all variables except their illness, so that the cause of their illness or effectiveness of their treatment could be identified. For example, if a researcher wanted to study people with depression, there are many variables that would need to be matched in the control group, such as age, gender, marital status, education level, religious beliefs and addiction to substances, which are all implicated in depression.

A practical problem is that people with mental illnesses are difficult to access. Many people might resent their GP or hospital doctor agreeing to their names being put forward for research. If they were approached through a support group and asked to volunteer, the sample would be biased because many people with mental illnesses might not be active members of any group or of society generally. Making hospital patients part of a research project might lead to resentment, or demonstrate exceptional willingness to be helpful which would create demand characteristics.

66. Origins of psychology

1 Introspection means to investigate human behaviour by asking people to report their own inner thoughts, feelings and beliefs behind their behaviour. One criticism of introspection is that the information by each individual is likely to be different, meaning that the information is highly subjective and cannot be generalised to other people.

2 Over time, the methods used by psychologists have become more scientific. The use of introspection was criticised for lacking objectivity, but with the rise of behaviourism came the use of more controlled laboratory experiments. As other approaches have become part of psychology, there has been a greater emphasis on the use of methods such as laboratory experiments, developing new hypotheses and adapting previous research, which has positioned psychology as a scientific discipline.

67. Classical conditioning

1 Classical conditioning is a process of learning whereby a stimulus that produces an automatic response is paired with another stimulus that produces no response. The association that develops between the two stimuli means that eventually the neutral stimulus will become a conditioned stimulus and will lead to the conditioned response on its own.

2 The behaviourist approach assumes that all behaviour is learned as a product of the environment within which we live.

68. Operant conditioning

Classical conditioning is learning as a result of associations made between two different stimuli, where one produces an automatic response, while operant conditioning is learning as a result of the consequences of a particular behavioural response.

69. Social learning theory

Vicarious reinforcement is the concept that we learn from the consequences of other people's behaviour. For example, seeing another person being rewarded for something gives the impression that this is a good thing, and may influence us to copy the behaviour. On the other hand, if we see someone else being punished it would encourage us to avoid copying the behaviour ourselves.

70. The cognitive approach

1 The cognitive approach emphasises studying the mind by investigating the observable behaviours of people and then interpreting the mental processes behind the behaviour. Another assumption is that the human mind works in the same way as a computer, with input, processing and output in the form of behaviour.

2 Cognitive neuroscience is emerging as an area of study where mental processes are being investigated in order to associate parts of the brain with certain functions. For example, brain scans can help researchers see which parts of the brain are involved in what kind of processes. Brain scans have shown that London taxi drivers have larger hippocampi than other people due to memorising the extensive street system in London.

3 One criticism of the cognitive approach is that most of the research takes place in laboratories and is often thought to lack validity because the tasks used may lack realism. Another criticism is that cognitive psychologists ignore the role of factors such as emotion and motivation in human behaviour, whereas approaches take such factors into account.

71. The biological approach

Genotype is the term used to describe the actual genetic material each person possesses, while the phenotype refers to how these genes are actually expressed in the development of the human body. Therefore the genotype is purely biological, while the phenotype is a biological component that can also be influenced by the environment.

72. The psychodynamic approach

One contribution is the development of a useful therapy for mental health disorders. This focuses on uncovering issues repressed in the unconscious mind that are affecting the well-being of the person, and bringing them into consciousness to allow the person to deal with them and move on.

73. Humanistic psychology

1 Free will is the subjective feeling of choice in life, where the person is able to choose their pathway through life.

2 Determinism is the opposite of free will – it is the view that a person's pathway through life is determined for them by factors out of their control.

74. Humanistic therapy

Congruence is an important part of therapy, which aims to help the client to achieve personal growth by understanding themselves better and balancing their self-concept, ideal self and real self so they are the same or similar.

75. Comparison of approaches 1

The biological approach is very different to the humanistic approach in terms of whether there is free will. The biological view suggests that much of our behaviour is predetermined by our genes that programme our brain and neurotransmitters, whereas the humanistic approach disagrees and proposes that we have free will to behave as we wish.

76. Comparison of approaches 2

The learning approach is perhaps the most nomothetic of the approaches as it proposes general laws of learning that apply to all species, such as classical conditioning. On the other hand, the humanistic approach is the most idiographic as it does not propose any commonalities between people, though it could be argued that Maslow's hierarchy of needs is generally applied to all people.

80. Exam-style practice 1

1 (a) Dylan may be more aggressive because he enjoys playing violent video games. Shooting games may offer points for aggressive play that would act as reinforcement for these kinds of actions. Operant conditioning suggests that if the behaviour is rewarded it will be more likely to be repeated, which may explain why he is fighting at school. According to operant conditioning, behaviours that are punished are less likely to be repeated. The school is planning to punish him, but his parents are not. This may make Dylan think this kind of behaviour is acceptable, making him less likely to stop doing it. Dylan also has an older brother who is quite violent. He may be a role model to Dylan. According to social learning theory, role models will have an influence on our behaviour. If Dylan looks up to his older brother, he may be paying attention to this type of behaviour and will be more likely to retain this. When he finds himself in a similar situation, such as an argument with another boy at school, Dylan may imitate the behaviour he has seen in his brother.

(b) Negative reinforcement is the rewarding of a behaviour by removing something unpleasant to make the consequence of the behaviour pleasant, so that the behaviour will be repeated. For example, Dylan started the fight over comments Bartek made about his sister. His violence towards Bartek could be negatively reinforced if he thinks that his actions have stopped the comments. He may feel he needs to repeat it again if someone makes comments he doesn't like in future.

2 A schema can be described as a little 'package' of information that is stored about a particular object or situation. It is useful as it helps us to understand the world around us and predict what might happen. For example we have a schema about 'restaurants' which enables us to behave appropriately, such as by paying the bill before leaving.

3 Skinner devised a cage referred to as a 'box' that he placed small animals into, such as rats and pigeons. He had apparatus in the box that would deliver different consequences in response to behaviour shown by the animals. For example, in one version, rats had a lever in the cage that would deliver food pellets when pressed as a type of positive reinforcement. In another version, the floor of the cage was electrified, and once the lever was pressed by the rat the electric current would be turned off.

4 Introspection could be said to be subjective due to the fact that each person may explain their own thought processes in a different way. Research using introspection requires people to verbalise their own thought processes, but there may be many things people either can't or won't share with others, so that the information shared is incomplete and personalised to the individual. This means it is of little use to help explain and understand the behaviour of others.

5 A

81. Exam-style practice 2

6 B

7 A

8 Once criticism of social learning theory is that it ignores the role of biology in explaining behaviour, as it claims that we are influenced by the experiences and observations made in our environment. This would suggest that a person's biological make up has little or no effect on their behavioural traits. However, one strength of social learning theory is that there is a wealth of evidence to support these explanations of behaviour. For example, Bandura found that children exposed to aggressive adult models were likely to copy the behaviour seen. Nevertheless, much of this evidence was gathered in laboratory settings immediately after exposure to the aggressive model, and therefore the evidence may not necessarily relate to real-life learning of aggression where exposure to aggression may be much more prolonged and delayed. Another advantage of social learning theory over other behaviourist explanations is that it takes into account cognitive components in learning of behaviour rather than claiming behaviour to be the result of simple stimulus – response pairings.

9 Bandura conducted a series of experiments in laboratories to help understand how children may learn aggressive behaviour from watching adults. He designed a procedure where children between 3 and 6 years old were made to watch adults displaying either aggressive or non-aggressive acts towards an inflatable 'Bobo doll'. Afterwards, they spent time in a room with many toys which they were instructed not to play with, to raise their level of frustration. Then they were taken to another room with toys they could play with that included a Bobo doll. They found that many of the children who had seen the adults acting aggressively went on to copy this behaviour on the Bobo doll themselves, suggesting they had learned this behaviour.

10 To make an inference, the researchers make an assumption about human behaviour based on the evidence they have gathered in their study. For example, if one group scores more highly on a memory test after being taught a memory improvement technique than a group that didn't learn the technique, the psychologist could infer that the memory technique helped to improve their memory.

11 The core assumptions of the biological approach relate to the concept that all human behaviour can be explained by looking at biological factors such as genetics, chemicals in the body and the functions of the central nervous system. Firstly, the approach assumes that behaviour can be explained by looking at a person's genotype and phenotype. The genotype is the unique (unless you have an identical twin!) genetic material each person possesses that determines key characteristics about a person. The phenotype is the result of the interaction between the genotype and the environment. For example, a person's genotype may determine their natural body shape, but their level of nutrition and exercise will interact with this to create their actual physical size. So, an individual could have a very petite body shape naturally but by eating high fat/high calory foods and avoiding exercise they may put on excess weight and become obese. Behaviours can also be inherited through genes because each parent donates 50% of their genes to each of their offspring. This means that parents and their children may share similar characteristics, such as symptoms of a mental illness addiction tendencies, etc. Behaviours may also result from the process of evolution, where the genes that control characteristics that give a species an advantage in their natural environment are more likely to be passed on to the next generation of the species. For example, a female with a nurturing nature may mean that her offspring are more likely to survive. One thing that genes will determine is the structure and function of the brain. This can have a big influence on a person's behaviour. The brain passes messages to the rest of the body through the nervous system in order to control behaviour. The messages are passed through chemical messengers known as neurotransmitters. These chemicals are thought to influence behaviour. For example, high levels of dopamine have been linked to symptoms of schizophrenia, whereas low levels of serotonin are routinely associated with depression.

One advantage of the biological approach is that the research conducted tends to be very scientific, as it is often done in laboratories where variables can more easily be controlled. This allows objective measures to be taken. For example, biological psychologists can use brain scans to detect the levels of different neurotransmitters in different areas of the brain, such as PET and fMRI scans. This allows them, for example, to see which parts of the brain are active when a participant undertakes tests whilst in the scanner and can show the different functional areas, such as those linked to memory, emotion, anger etc. The approach also has many practical applications, such as the development of drug therapies to treat mental health conditions. For example, drugs used to treat anxiety disorders such as OCD have been shown to be highly effective at reducing symptoms.

However, the biological approach focuses only on biological factors influencing behaviour, and does not take into account the many other factors that can influence human behaviour. For this reason, the biological approach is reductionist – it is too simplistic to assume that all behaviours can be boiled down to simple biological factors. For example, a behaviour as complex as schizophrenia could be explained in multiple ways. To assume that the various different symptoms are due to an increase in one neurotransmitter in the brain is probably naïve. However, by isolating the biological factors involved in the development of disorders such as schizophrenia, and understanding these more fully through detailed research, it may be possible to better identify exactly what causes them. The advantage of this is that a better understanding of the causes of abnormal behaviours like mental illnesses can lead to more effective treatments being developed in the future.

82. Exam-style practice 3

1 (a) Ananda had a bad experience in a small space when she got stuck in the cupboard. Because of this, she could have made an association between small spaces and the fear/anxiety she felt being stuck. Being stuck is the unconditioned stimulus, and her unconditioned response is being afraid, as this is the unlearned behaviour. Small spaces and closed doors would have been a neutral stimulus, as they do not automatically create the fear response. However, once the association has been created, small spaces and closed doors become a conditioned stimulus that now cause a conditioned fear response, meaning Ananda now avoids them.

(b) Negative reinforcement refers to a positive outcome as a result of something negative being prevented or removed as a result of behaviour. In Ananda's case, by avoiding small spaces and closed doors she avoids anxiety, which makes her feel better.

2 Introspection is the study of the functions of the mind by asking people to describe their own thoughts, feelings and experiences. Wundt (1870s) used introspection to study the human mind. Introspection could be seen as an inaccurate way of studying human behaviour. Our own personal views will shape the way we report back on what we think we have 'uncovered' about our behaviour, meaning that the conclusions

we draw are subjective to us and cannot be generalised to anyone else.

3 The biological approach in psychology ignores the role of the environment in behaviour. Biological psychologists assume that all behaviour is controlled by biological factors such as genes, hormones and neurotransmitters, and is determined even before birth in some cases. This means that the approach is reductionist, as it fails to account for how environmental factors such as upbringing or the media can influence behaviour.

83. Divisions of the nervous system

1 The sympathetic branch of the nervous system is the body's 'alert system' to prepare it for dealing with stress in the environment.

2 The central nervous system is the body's way of communicating with the brain. It allows information from the environment to be passed to the brain, and then messages to be passed to the body to influence behaviour.

84. Neurons and synaptic transmission

1 Synaptic transmission is the process by which messages are passed around inside the nervous system. A message is passed from one neuron to another across a small gap between them, known as a synapse. An electrical impulse starts inside one neuron and passes along the axon of the neuron, where it pushes vesicles filled with neurotransmitters to the terminal button. Here, the neurotransmitters are released into the synapse and are then absorbed by the receptors on the adjacent neuron.

2 Sensory neurons take messages to the brain from the environment as a form of input, while motor neurons pass messages from the brain to the muscles to produce actions (output).

85. Endocrine system

The endocrine system is a group of glands in the human body that produce and release hormones into the bloodstream. These hormones can then influence the behaviour of the person. For example, an increase in adrenaline triggers the fight-or-flight response.

86. Localisation of function in the brain

Localisation of function is the idea that different cognitive abilities are processed in different areas of the brain. Brain sites are identified for specific tasks such as language functions, which have discrete areas (Broca's and Wernicke's) in the left hemisphere of most people's brains.

87. Lateralisation and split-brain research

Lateralisation of function is the division of cognitive functions between the two hemispheres of the brain, where the left hemisphere will perform tasks that the right hemisphere does not. It can be tested in studies of split-brain patients, who have had their hemispheres surgically separated, by presenting objects so that only one side of the brain can perceive them, and finding out what the patients experience.

88. Plasticity and functional recovery

Brain plasticity can be seen in case studies of functional recovery after brain injury, where the brain rewires itself to compensate for the loss of function in the damaged area. Evidence for plasticity can be seen in Rosenzweig et al.'s study of rats (1962), where rats raised without a lot of stimulation had a much reduced cortical volume compared to rats raised in an enriched environment, showing that the brain adapts to the environment and is not set after birth. Maguire et al.'s study of London cab drivers (2000) provides support that this happens in humans, as the area of the brain responsible for spatial memory was bigger and more developed in the cabbies compared to matched controls, showing how the brain adapts itself to environmental learning.

89. Ways of studying the brain

Both methods use the same equipment to measure electrical activity in the brain. However, while EEGs measure general activity, ERPs are looking for specific activity related to specific functions; they aim to see which area is activated while doing a particular task.

90. Biological rhythms

The time length of the cycle is the key factor that differentiates between these two rhythms. The ultradian rhythm repeats more than once a day, for example, when we sleep we pass through a repeating 90-minute cycle of brainwave activity until we wake. The infradian rhythm takes longer; it repeats less than once a day, for example, the human female menstrual cycle takes an average of 28 days to repeat.

91. Endogenous pacemakers and exogenous zeitgebers

Endogenous pacemakers set the rhythm for sleep and wakefulness through the action of the suprachiasmatic nucleus (SCN). This is situated to receive signals from the optic nerves. When activity levels on the nerves are low, the SCN stimulates the release of the hormone melatonin from the pineal gland. Melatonin causes the brain to become less active, thus causing drowsiness and eventually sleep. An increase in light the next morning will increase the firing rates of the optic nerves, which causes the SCN to switch off the production of melatonin, thus increasing brain activity and waking up the person. The SCN will work in the absence of daylight, but will operate on a cycle of about 25 hours for most people.

94. Exam-style practice 1

1 Alessio is feeling stressed because he got up late and so his hypothalamus has sent a message along his sympathetic nervous system to alert his body that there is a threat of some sort. The message is then picked up by his adrenal medulla, which will produce and release adrenaline (hormone) into his bloodstream. The adrenaline will cause his body to react with the fight-or-flight response. When he is talking to the deputy head, he feels shaky, sweaty and has a racing

heart because the adrenaline causes an increase in muscle tension, increased heart rate and an increase in sweat in preparation to fight the threat or to run away from it.

2　1 = peripheral nervous system; 2 = brain; 3 = autonomic nervous system; 4 = sympathetic nervous system.

3　Synaptic transmission refers to the passing of messages from one neuron to another across a tiny gap called a synapse. An action potential is triggered in the nucleus of one neuron, which results in an impulse passing down the axon to the terminal button. In the terminal button are vesicles containing neurotransmitters which will be 'pushed' towards the outer membrane of the terminal button, and once the vesicle touches the membrane they 'fuse' together, releasing the neurotransmitter into the synapse. The receptor sites on the next neuron then bind to the neurotransmitter, receiving the chemical message which could either stimulate a further action potential, or inhibit one.

4　D

5　The pituitary gland is sometimes referred to as the 'master gland', as part of its function relates to controlling the production and release of hormones from other glands in the system. For example, in the body's response to stress, if stress becomes a long-term factor, the pituitary gland stimulates the adrenal cortex (outer layer of the adrenal gland) to release cortisol.

95. Exam-style practice 2

6　Age is a factor that can affect functional recovery after brain injury. The older you are, the less plasticity the brain has, which means it is less able to adapt to the damage by rewiring around it. Marquez de la Plata et al. (2008) found that patients under 40 years of age recovered more function than did those over 40 years. Another factor is educational experience, where the number of years spent in education increases the chance of recovery following brain trauma. This may be because the brain has developed a richer network of connections because of their enriched experience of the environment, providing more opportunities for diverting around the area of damage.

7　Localisation of function involves identifying the area of the brain responsible for a specific cognitive ability, for example, the localisation of language production to an area in the left hemisphere.

8　George's stroke may have damaged Broca's area, situated in his left frontal lobe. Broca (1861) found that this area of the brain was associated with the production of language after doing a post-mortem on his patient 'Tan', so called as this was the only word that Tan could say. It would seem that Wernicke's area is undamaged in George's case. This area is responsible for language comprehension. It is also in the left hemisphere, but further back. As George can understand spoken language, it seems likely that this was not affected by the stroke.

9　Rosenzweig et al. (1962) found that the brains of rats raised in a stimulating environment had greater cortical mass than those of rats raised in an impoverished environment. This suggests that environmental experience moulds the brain, showing that it is plastic. Maguire et al (2000) demonstrated that the

hippocampal areas of the brain in London cab drivers adapted to the learning of spatial knowledge when they memorised routes around London compared to the hippocampal areas of people that did not memorise routes. This shows how the brain changes as a result of experience.

10　An EEG aims to measure the electrical activity across the brain surface. This is done by attaching electrodes to the scalp. These are wired to a computer that records the activity as a pattern of brainwaves.

11　There is strong evidence that the suprachiasmatic nucleus (SCN) is an endogenous pacemaker in control of the sleep/wake cycle. Morgan (1995) found that the removal and transplantation of the SCN in hamsters removed and reinstated the sleep/wake pattern, showing a strong cause-and-effect relationship experimentally. However, this study may not apply to the same degree in humans, who do not rely on instinct as much as other mammals. Siffre (1975) conducted a free-running body clock study on himself where all exogenous pacemakers were removed. He found his sleep/wake rhythm settled to 25 hours, showing that endogenous factors also control the rhythm in humans. As humans have a SCN, it is logical that this is the controller.

96. Experiments

Laboratory experiments take place in controlled environments where the experimenter controls the setting, making them more artificial. In contrast, field experiments take place in the participants' natural setting, making them more realistic to the participants and increasing their ecological validity.

97. Observational techniques

1　All observations involve the systematic watching and recording of behaviour.

2　The main issue with covert, naturalistic observations is that people will be unaware they are being observed, so fully informed consent cannot be gained. The researcher must also be careful not to break the privacy guideline and ensure that the observation happens in a place where people would normally expect others to observe them. They must ensure that the observation is done in an ethically acceptable way.

98. Self-report techniques

Self-report data consists of people's own answers to questions based on the aims of the research rather than observational or behavioural data where the researcher records the data.

99. Correlations

1　One psychological example of a positive correlation would be that the more genes you share in common with someone who has schizophrenia, the more likely you are to develop symptoms.

2　One problem with correlations in psychological research is that they cannot give you information regarding cause and effect. They can only tell you whether two variables are related, but not in what way or whether one is causing the other to change.

100. Case studies and content analysis

Case studies are good because of the amount of detail they include. This allows for an in-depth and probably valid conclusion to be drawn. However, they lack population validity because they tend to be on unique individuals who are not representative of other people.

101. Aims and hypotheses

1　An aim states the purpose of the research from the outset. This is what the study has been designed to investigate. The hypothesis is a statement of prediction regarding the likely outcome of the study. This would take into account any data gathered from previous research studies.

2　A directional hypothesis is one that states the direction of effect that is likely to be seen. For example, in a correlation, a directional hypothesis would state whether the correlation is likely to be positive or negative.

102. Variables

To reduce demand characteristics, the researchers could conduct their experiment using an independent groups design. Each independent group of participants takes part in only one condition, so they are less likely to be able to work out the aim of the experiment than if they did both conditions. Therefore they cannot change their behaviour to suit what they think the researcher wants, or deliberately act in a different way to skew the data.

103. Sampling techniques

Opportunity sampling uses whoever happens to be available at the time and place of the study, so is quick and easy to do and does not add time and expense to the research. Random sampling means that every member of the target population has an equal chance of being selected, so it is likely that the sample will be quite diverse and therefore representative.

104. Experimental design and control

1　In a matched pairs design, one group from the sample is matched to another group based on key characteristics such as age, gender and level of educational attainment. Each group is allocated to a condition. By doing this, issues related to individual differences between participants in each condition can be minimised.

2　One strength of an independent groups design is that there are no order effects because the participants doing each condition are different. This means that performance on a task from one condition cannot interfere with the performance on a task in another condition, so fatigue or practice cannot confound the results. One weakness of using independent groups is that, because there are different people in each condition, the results from each condition are from different people. This means that the data may have been affected by individual differences that may not have been immediately apparent to the researcher.

105. Observational design

1

	boys	girls
smiling		
sharing		
cooperating		
supporting		
helping		

2 In event sampling, it can be quite difficult to record what is going on accurately when there is a lot of behaviour happening. In this case, for example, it might be hard to see whether a child is sharing or cooperating.

106. Ethics in research

Participants' details should not be shared at any point in the report, including names or locations. Participants can be referred to by numbers, initials or pseudonyms to protect their identity.

107. Peer review

For: Peer review increases the chances that the findings are valid and that mistakes are not made.
Against: It is not always value-free – the reviewers may be biased for or against the research and this may affect their judgements.

108. Implications of psychological research for the economy

Psychological research can usefully be applied to understanding and changing human behaviour in a way that benefits the individual, society and the economy. Health psychology can be applied to campaigns aimed at changing habits that lead to poor health; developmental psychology can be applied to ensure infants get the best start in life to help them become productive citizens. Occupational psychologists can improve productivity by helping with stress management. Perhaps the biggest contribution comes from clinical psychology, where the explanations for mental health disorders have led to successful treatments for many disorders that have had a negative impact on the economy.

109. Validity and reliability

Reliability is concerned with the consistency of the study, whereas validity is about whether it is a genuine measure of the aims of the study.

110. Features of science

Replication is important because it allows for the checking of data in order to determine its reliability, and also to enable theory construction to take place by constantly checking and rechecking the evidence on which it is based.

111. Report writing

The function of the method section in a scientific report is to provide enough detail to allow an exact replication of the study to take place. Replication is essential to test the reliability of the findings and therefore is important for the scientific process.

112. Types of data

meta-analysis

113. Descriptive statistics

1 mean = 6.3; mode = 3; median = 6.5
2 The mean score is most representative as it includes all the scores in the dataset.

114. Maths skills

fraction = ½; ratio = 1:2 (part to whole), 1:1 (part to part); percentage = 50%

115. Displaying data

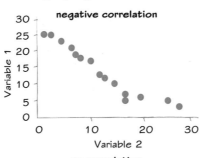

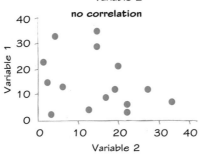

2 The conclusion that can be drawn from the graphs/charts is that the amount of sleep someone has affects their ability to perform on a test. The more sleep, the better the performance, as there is a strong positive correlation between these two variables. Furthermore, the mean scores of people who sleep for more than 7 hours is higher than those of people who sleep for 7 hours or less.

116. Distributions

1 A normal distribution is symmetrical about the mean, all measures of central tendency are the same and the curve is bell shaped.
2 (a) True – they lie above the mean.
   (b) False – 68% of the scores lie within one standard deviation (above or below) the mean.

117. Levels of measurement

(a) Nominal – as it is counting the frequency of people in a category, in this case smilers.
(b) Ordinal – each person's score is placed along a sliding scale, but the points on the scale are not quantifiably exact.
(c) Nominal – this may seem ordinal but it is counting the number of people in each category, in this case grades.
(d) This is also nominal – it is categorical data.
(e) Ordinal – each person has a score that can be measured against other people's scores.
(f) Interval – it is possible to ascertain exactly how much more or less each person scored than every other person, as time is an exact scale with quantifiable differences.

118. Inferential testing 1

It is $p \leq 0.05$, which means that the risk of the results being due to chance must be 5% or less, otherwise they are regarded as insignificant.

119. Inferential testing 2

As I am looking for a difference in performance and that difference is measured on an interval data scale, I would use the related t-test, because I have a repeated measures design. However, you could argue for using a Wilcoxon if you were unsure that the data was parametric, and then state that you are treating the data as ordinal.

120. Using critical values tables

Reject the null hypothesis. The critical value for N1 = 7 and N2 = 8 is 13 at the 5% level for a directional hypothesis. To be significant, the observed value had to be equal to or less than 13. As the observed value is 10, it is significant, so I reject the null hypothesis.

125. Exam-style practice 1

1 (a) Table 1: The mean number of words recalled when the background music heard during learning is or is not heard during recall.
   (b) A bar chart would be suitable to display this data because there are two discrete conditions that can be plotted on the x-axis with the average number of words recalled on the y-axis.
   (c) Word recall will be greater when the music played during learning is also played during recall.
   (d) Randomly allocating them to each condition means that everyone has an equal chance of being in either condition. In this study, the memory ability of the participants could confound the results if one group were naturally more able to remember information than the other group. Randomly allocating them should give a higher chance that the group in each condition will be unbiased.
   (e) Those who recalled with music recalled more words from the list of 20 than the participants who recalled without music. The results in the 'recall with music' condition were also more consistent, as the range was lower than in the 'recall without music' condition.
2 A field experiment is likely to be higher in ecological validity than a lab experiment because it is carried out in the situation where the behaviour being tested would happen naturally, so should suffer less from demand characteristics as the participants behave as they would normally.
3 Opportunity sampling is generally quick and easy to do therefore does not add time and expense to the research process, unlike random sampling which would take a long time to set up for a large target population.
4 Opportunity sampling is less likely to produce a representative sample than other methods such as random sampling because it chooses the people who happen to be present at the time of the research, who are unlikely to represent a wide range of people.
5 A strength of the independent measures design is that it reduces the chance of demand characteristics affecting the results,

as the participants only take part in a section of the study, therefore there is less time and information to allow them to work out what is being tested. However, unless the allocation to conditions is done properly, a certain type of participant may be allocated to only one of the conditions, thereby affecting the validity of the data.

126. Exam-style practice 2

6 A pilot study is used to test the procedure of a study to see if it needs adjustment before gathering the real data. For example, it could be used to check if the timing allowed for participants to carry out a task is too long or too short, and if the task is too easy or too hard for any meaningful data to be gathered.

7 (a) $0.50 + 0.75 + 1.00 + 0.50 + 1.00 + 1.50 = 5.25 / 6$, so the mean for donation 1 is 0.875
$0.73 + 0.75 + 1.25 + 1.00 + 0.98 + 2.00 = 6.71 / 6$, so the mean for donation 2 is 1.12
range for donation 1 is $1.50 - 0.50 = 1.00$
range for donation 2 is $2.00 - 0.73 = 1.27$

Table to show summary data for amount of monetary donations given before and after participants were given a card reminding them that every penny counts

Amount of money given	Before card	After card
mean	0.875	1.12
range	1.00	1.27

(b) This is a repeated measures design.

(c) One advantage is that it controls for participant variables affecting the data. One disadvantage is possible order effects where the participant's response in the second condition is affected by knowledge of condition 1.

(d) The psychologist could not get fully informed consent in this study as it would have caused the participants to behave unnaturally. In cases like this where deception is involved, they could ask for presumptive consent, where similar people are asked whether they would be upset by the procedure. If they are happy with it, then the study has gained consent. However, they must be sure that a full debrief is provided that covers the aims of the study and offers participants the chance to ask questions and to withdraw their data if they wish to. The study must also ensure that the participants are protected from psychological harm, so they must not be made to feel bad about the size of their donation or about not making a donation at all. Participant data must be kept confidential and they must not be identifiable.

(e)

Participant	Donation 1	Donation 2	Sign of difference
1	0.50	0.73	+
2	0.75	0.75	= (disregard)
3	1.00	1.25	+
4	0.50	1.00	+
5	1.00	0.98	−
6	1.50	2.00	+

total number of + is 4
total number of − is 1
disregard tie, so n = 5
least frequently occurring sign is minus (−), so s = 1
Critical value of n = 5 is 0 for a two-tailed hypothesis. To be significant, the calculated value has to be equal to or less than the critical value, therefore the null hypothesis is accepted.

127. Exam-style practice 3

8 The scientific process is a method of developing theories that explain phenomena through the gathering of empirical evidence. Observations of behaviour are made and psychologists develop theoretical explanations for the behaviour that can generate falsifiable hypotheses, which can then be objectively tested using empirical methods. Research is subjected to stringent examination to ensure that it is reliable and valid, for example through replication. It is then applied to the theory, where it can support the theory or contradict it, in which case the theory is revised.

9 Peer review ensures that the conclusions of investigations are reliable and valid before they are published and become part of our knowledge on a topic (elaborated point to earn 2 marks). They also spot errors in the report to ensure that mistakes are not published (basic point worth 1 mark).

10 (a) Reliability is an assessment of consistency in the research, whereas validity is an assessment of whether it truly tested what it claims to have tested.

(b) They could look for concurrent validity (1). This is where they find other studies that tested a similar aim and compare the results – if they are very different they might challenge the validity of the study being reviewed (2).

11 A case study is usually limited to a sample of one or a few individuals, chosen because they are in some way interesting or unusual. It gathers data using different methods such as interviews and medical records, and will be an in-depth investigation of the person/s.

12 Thematic analysis can be used to analyse qualitative data. The data is summarised into key themes by reading it, identifying themes and then coding the data according to the themes in order to draw a conclusion about the meaning of the data.

13 The purpose of inferential testing is to establish the probability that the results were due to random or chance factors and therefore whether they are significant or not.

14 Nominal data is discrete data as it consists of how many items are in each category. It is simpler than ordinal data, which is continuous along a scale but does not have exact intervals between points. Interval data is also continuous but features exact intervals between points on the scale.

128. Gender bias

1 The problem with alpha- and beta-biased research is that they are not representative of the whole population. They both take all-male or all-female samples and generalise findings to everyone (beta bias), or they take findings of research and exaggerate the differences between males and females (alpha bias). An example of alpha-biased

research is Freud's (1905) theory of psychosexual development. Freud suggested females do not develop such a strong superego compared to males and therefore could be less moral as a result. An example of beta-biased research is Milgram's (1963) original obedience research. He used a male-only sample, but findings were generalised to both genders as an explanation of why people obey orders.

2 Androcentrism refers to the use of male behaviour as the norm to measure all behaviour.

129. Cultural bias

1 Ethnocentrism is the idea that one culture is superior to another and that their behaviour is the norm.

2 Cultural relativism is the understanding that, when looking at behaviour in any given culture, it is vital to examine the cultural context in which the behaviour is set. This is because behaviour will differ from culture to culture.

130. Free will and determinism

Free will is used to explain behaviour as being controlled by the individual. It suggests that humans have responsibility and are free to choose how to behave. The opposite of free will is determinism. This explains behaviour as being a result of other influences such as our genes, chemicals in our brain or the environment. Therefore, we have no choice and – to an extent – are not responsible for our behaviour.

131. Nature–nurture

The men's behaviour has been influenced by having low MAOA activity, which implies that their violent behaviour is due to their genetics – taking the nature side of the debate. This could suggest that they have no free will in how they behave, as their criminal behaviour is determined through their biological heredity. However, it is too simplistic to only look at their genetics, as they also had poor upbringings, which could have influenced their aggressive behaviour. It has been found that children who grow up in criminal, violent households frequently continue with the same cycle of behaviour. Therefore, these men could have been influenced by their nurture. An interactionist viewpoint would suggest that it is the influence of both nature (genes) and nurture (poor upbringing). They may have had a biological predisposition for violent and aggressive behaviour but it needed the poor environmental conditions to trigger it.

132. Reductionism and holism

Researchers who want to investigate the genetic influence on obsessive–compulsive disorder (OCD) may miss something vital if only looking at participants' genes. Isolating the genes as an explanation could overlook any biochemical explanation; this is a weakness of taking a reductionist approach. However, the strength of a reductionist approach is that isolating one factor could help discover the cause of the disorder. As a result, a more appropriate treatment may be discovered. Researchers who take a more holistic view by interviewing people with OCD could discover a more complete explanation. There may be a genetic component but also an environmental explanation, which they could discover from a questionnaire. This could also help shape treatment programmes. A weakness of the holistic approach is that it is very difficult to build a complete picture of the causes of any disorder as there could be so many variables to take into account.

133. Idiographic and nomothetic

One problem with an idiographic approach in research is that, because it looks in great detail at an individual case study, it lacks generalisability. One problem with a nomothetic approach in research is that findings are often used as a 'one size fits all'. For example, where a treatment for schizophrenia may suit most people, it may not work for all.

134. Ethical implications of research

The researchers should have been fully aware of the possible impact of their research. The girls in the study could be affected by the findings, particularly the ones from the independent school. They may have felt that the school or their peers at the school were to blame for their eating behaviour. It could become a self-fulfilling prophecy that attending a school such as the one in the study could result in girls developing an eating disorder. The wider picture could indicate that the boarding environment could be bad for girls who are vulnerable to eating disorders, which could have negative implications for similar schools and their reputations. The researchers could have dealt with this by ensuring the confidentiality of all participants and the schools they attended. They would have to sensitively debrief the girls and assure them and the schools involved of their privacy. Disclosure and publication of results would also have to be carefully disseminated with assurances that no one involved would be identifiable.

137. Exam-style practice 1

1 C
2 B and D
3 Alpha bias is a misrepresentation of the behaviour seen in participants in research, whereby the differences between the genders are exaggerated. One problem could be that one gender is seen as superior to the other. For example, Freud (1905) overestimated the sex differences in males and females when he developed his psychosexual stages of development. He claimed boys had a better developed superego than females due to the Oedipus complex, which occurs in boys during the phallic stage. This results in boys identifying with their father to ensure a more successful moral development compared to girls. This resulted in girls being seen as less moral, supporting the prevailing views of the era that undervalued females.
4 Cultural bias can be defined as the act of interpreting and judging the behaviour and psychological characteristics of another culture by the standards of your own. This could be as a result of a majority of the researchers and universities who carry out studies being predominantly from a white, Western background. Other cultures are typically unrepresented and the findings of

such research is therefore only applicable to that culture. However, findings are usually generalised to all, which means that psychologists are unable to separate the truth about any cultural differences that might have been present from the way the research has been conducted, meaning it is culturally biased. For example, in Milgram's (1963) study of obedience, participants were all *white American males* and the rates of obedience found (65% of all participants going to 450 volts) were applied to all people. Milgram concluded that *people obey a figure of authority under certain conditions and show blind obedience*. He did not just apply the findings to American men, showing a cultural bias.
5 Carrying out socially sensitive research is a risk whereby researchers have to carry out a cost–benefit analysis to see if the sensitive nature of the research could do more harm than good to the population represented in the study, such as by increasing discrimination and perpetuating stereotyping. However, some may argue that the scientific knowledge gained from carrying out such research is more important than the harm it could cause. One piece of research by Humphreys (1970) investigated the sexual practices of gay men in public toilets. This was controversial as, at that time, same-sex relationships were not widely accepted and homosexuality was still considered a mental illness until 1973, when it was removed from DSM-II. This research used participant observation and structured interview to find out about the background of the men who used the facilities. Humphreys' findings opposed many stereotypes, as only 14% were members of the gay community and interested in primarily homosexual relationships. It therefore challenged society's views of homosexuals being promiscuous and degenerate, when in fact a number of the men were married and considered upstanding members of the community. This supports the idea that socially sensitive research should be carried out, because the benefits of it could ultimately challenge stereotypes. Even though ethics were broken, Humphreys claimed it was worth it because of the findings. In contrast, Raine (1996) studied the brains of violent criminals and found that in each case an area in the frontal cortex was damaged. This could explain their disposition to violence. He suggested that children could have brain scans to identify those at risk. However, this suggestion calls into question the ethics of such findings. It could cause a lot of anguish and also labelling if a programme was rolled out and some children showed the same brain abnormalities. Another area that could have far-reaching consequences is research on relationships. Some participants take part regarding their own relationship and this could have implications for the couples involved. Individuals who participate may not benefit from taking part, but science could. Although people will have agreed to take part, no one can predict the future problems caused by participating. Therefore, there may be wider implications of studies such as these that are not immediately obvious, and not all socially sensitive research benefits will outweigh the negative consequences.

138. Exam-style practice 2

6 Ethnocentrism is where people see things from their own or a similar point of view and measure the behaviour of all others against those norms. The assumption is that one ethnic group is superior to all other groups.
7 We must try to understand someone else's world to avoid bias and be aware of our own biases. For example, it is important to be aware of ethnocentrism when diagnosing disorders. Hearing voices may indicate schizophrenia in the West, but in other parts of the world it is considered to be a spiritual experience. This could lead to misdiagnosis of a serious mental illness, which is a problem for the patient. The DSM has been updated in an attempt to recognise cultural-bound syndromes, but it is still diagnosed far more in some cultures than in others, suggesting ethnocentrism. There are also differences in language that researchers may encounter when carrying out research in other cultures. Because of this, researchers may not have full understanding of the customs and traditions nor fully understand what is being said. This could lead to problems in interpretation, and findings may lack validity. Even if researchers attempt to immerse themselves in a different culture to study them, these problems may still be evident. The data may be interpreted differently because of the cultural background of the researcher, for example, the idea that secure attachments are 'best' in the US but not in Germany because German culture has different ideals for raising their children. This can lead to biased findings. The advantage of carrying out research that is not confined to Western society is that it can show whether characteristics are universal or unique to a particular culture. However, certain methodologies may be more suited to a particular culture. For example, the 'Strange Situation' was only suited to American culture. When it was carried out on Japanese children, the study had to be stopped because the distress of the infants when left alone was too much. Therefore, the study was ethnocentric and should only have been used on other American children to assess their attachment type.
8 (a) Determinism is an understanding that behaviour is determined by factors over which we have no control. In humans it suggests we have no free will or choice over our behaviour. Biological determinism is one type of determinism and is shown here as the schizophrenia behaviour being controlled by a person's biology (their genes, chemicals and so on), as the stem suggests the condition 'runs in families'. This therefore suggests a person will inherit the condition and have no control over it as it is passed on through inherited behaviour. The next type of determinism suggested in the stem is environmental determinism, where behaviour is controlled by external influences, for example, parents – as suggested in the statement 'dysfunctional family patterns of communication'. The person's environmental conditions may determine the development of the disorder. The last type of determinism

– psychic determinism – is where behaviour is controlled by unconscious fears. That schizophrenia may be a result of 'major life events in the past' implies that it may be as a result of traumatic past experiences, for example, the death of a close relative or spouse. All three types of determinism could be influential in the development of schizophrenia.

(b) Nature is where we inherit certain traits or behaviours through our genes and is shown in the stem as schizophrenia 'runs in families'. Nurture is where we develop traits or conditions because of the environment that we live in or because of the influences of the people around us. For example, in the stem it suggests that schizophrenia could be as a result of 'dysfunctional family patterns of communication'.

9 Taking a nomothetic approach would involve the psychologist testing a larger sample of girls. It could be argued that only studying females is justified, as eating disorders are significantly more prominent in females compared to males. The sampling should involve a method of sample selection to give representativeness of a larger population, for example, random sampling of a number of eating disorder clinics in different areas. For the control group, a random sample of females from other clinics that do not have an eating disorder could be used. The researcher would probably use a testable experimental hypothesis, such as 'females aged 14–16 years having treatment for an eating disorder have more negative thoughts about childhood than 14–16 year olds who do not have an eating disorder'. Taking a nomothetic approach would involve collecting a large amount of data and the analysis would probably involve quantitative methods. A content analysis could also be used. They would identify themes present in the diaries, such as the girls talking about aspects of their childhood experiences with their parents, and then the number of times the themes came up. For example, they may talk about parents' controlling behaviour or feelings that they had to be perfect to please their parents. These themes, once tallied, would generate quantitative data, which could be analysed with a statistical test, making it easy to draw conclusions. The results and conclusions could then be applied to a wider population, making them more generalisable.

139. Evolutionary explanations

Males and females will look for different partner characteristics in relationships to aid reproductive success. For example, males may seek out fertile females because males can reproduce successfully many times, but females cannot. To give them the best chance of reproduction, the female they choose should be fertile, and therefore they may look for traits such as youth and health. Females, however, need to be choosier about their partner because they have limited opportunities to reproduce. Therefore, the male who impregnates them needs to be able to provide for her and her offspring. To this end, they may seek out successful males with adequate resources to support her and her offspring should she become pregnant.

140. Self-disclosure

1 One factor is appropriateness. While self-disclosure might be seen as important in a relationship, the type of information shared, or the point at which it is shared, might affect how attractive it appears. For example, sharing very intimate information about oneself on a first date could be off-putting to some people.

2 Research generally shows that self-disclosure increases attraction in a relationship. For example, Collins and Miller (1994) found that those who shared more personal information were rated as more attractive and likeable by others. However, Altman and Taylor (1973) found evidence that when information was shared at an inappropriate time, such as at a first meeting, this could have a negative effect on their perceived likeability.

141. Physical attractiveness

Generally, people assume that more attractive people are more attractive mates as they are assumed to have other positive characteristics. This means people may seek out more attractive partners to have relationships with. However, Walster et al. (1966) suggested that, rather than just seeking out the most attractive mate, people actually strive to find a partner who is similar to them in terms of level of attractiveness. They assumed that couples who were mismatched in terms of their physical attractiveness were more likely to suffer jealousy or insecurity. By looking for a partner 'in their league', people run less risk of being rejected by the partner who may want a more physically attractive mate.

142. Filter theory

One limitation of filter theory is that it could be seen as biased. Males and females are likely to filter potential partners differently, as they may place different levels of importance on certain limiting factors. For example, females may place more emphasis on similarity in attitude as they are more concerned with emotional connections. The theory may also be culturally biased because not all cultural groups will see the filters as equally important. For example, in some cultures where communities are very remote, there may be practical reasons why similarities in demographic variables such as location are limiting factors in attraction in relationships. This means that we cannot reliably apply the theory to all relationships.

143. Social exchange theory

Social exchange theory states that relationships continue when both partners perceive that they are gaining a profit in their current relationship. Each partner will assess the rewards gained in the relationship, and also what the relationship costs them. From these they can each assess their level of profit. If they feel they are in profit, they are likely to remain in the relationship. The couple will also each assess how the current relationship compares to other alternatives that may be available. As long as the current relationship is more profitable than the alternatives, it will continue.

144. Equity theory

Equity theory claims that relationships are maintained when they are perceived to be balanced in terms of what is being invested and what is being gained from the relationship. This is an economic theory of relationships that states that each partner weighs up how much they put into their relationship and then assesses what they gain from it as well. Rather than simply seeking the most 'profit', equity theory states that we feel dissatisfied with relationships that seem to be unfair or imbalanced. This inequity is then the motivation for the relationship to either change to rebalance things for both partners, or end the relationship if renegotiation is not possible.

145. Rusbult's investment model

According to the investment model, relationships are maintained when there is a high level of satisfaction, which is similar to the social exchange theory's concept of maintaining relationships that are the most profitable. However, one element that is different between the two explanations is that the investment model suggests that satisfaction is not just about profit, as claimed by social exchange theory, but also about the amount of fairness perceived in the relationship. For example, if one partner felt that they were contributing a lot less to the relationship than their partner then they may feel guilt, which will decrease the amount of satisfaction felt even though they are actually in profit. The investment model also differs from social exchange theory as it claims that, as well as the level of satisfaction with the relationship in its current state, partners are also motivated to maintain the relationship when the investments made in the relationship are highest. This would suggest that a relationship does not need to be profitable all the time for a person to remain with a partner, but the previous investments made will determine the overall satisfaction level.

146. Duck's model of breakdown

During the dyadic phase, the dissatisfied partner opens up to their partner and shares the fact that they are not happy with the current relationship. At this time, both partners can discuss their feelings and they may try to resolve the issues with the relationship. They now have the chance to negotiate and make changes to improve the level of satisfaction in the relationship. If they make the decision not to try to resolve the issues, or attempts at resolution fail, then the relationship continues to break down and the couple enter the 'social phase'.

147. Virtual relationships and self-disclosure

In virtual relationships people may feel more comfortable sharing personal information and intimate details about themselves with a potential new partner than if they met them, because virtual relationships offer more anonymity. This may be particularly true for those who lack the social skills to meet strangers face-to-face. However, some people could find it easier to lie when meeting a partner virtually rather than face-to-face, which means that the self-disclosure for some may be less honest in a virtual relationship.

148. Absence of gating

Absence of gating may make relationships more likely to form for people who have many limiting features that make it difficult for them to meet people face-to-face. For example, someone who stutters badly may find speaking to someone very challenging and may therefore avoid conversation with strangers, making relationships difficult. However, the absence of gating offered by virtual relationships means that the same person has more opportunities to meet people online where the stutter can be hidden until the relationship has developed far enough that it is no longer a limiting factor. The lack of face-to-face interaction means they can get to know people and build a level of intimacy that will help the relationship to progress.

149. Parasocial relationships

The first level is known as entertainment/ social, where the interest in the celebrity is mainly focused on the entertainment value of what they do, and they are often the basis of discussion between the person and their friends. The next level is intense-personal whereby the feelings become stronger and almost obsessive in nature. Finally, there is the borderline-pathological level, where the individual begins to act out their obsessions and may even try to make contact with the object of their affections. They are likely to think that the feelings will be returned should they meet the person face-to-face.

150. Absorption-addiction model

The absorption-addiction model of parasocial relationships states that the development of such relationships occurs in a series of stages, from normal interest in celebrities to abnormal obsessions. People begin with an interest in a certain celebrity and enjoy discussing them with their friends. They then develop intense-personal attitudes towards the celebrity, possibly as a way of absorbing some of their perceived success. Finally, this may develop into borderline-pathological behaviour if the person becomes obsessed with the celebrity. They may even start to think that a genuine relationship exists between the two of them, or they could seek out ways to meet the celebrity, which could lead them into criminal behaviour such as stalking.

151. Attachment theory explanation

Insecure-resistant or insecure-ambivalent. People with these attachment types are likely to seek out closeness in relationships, but fear rejection. Consequently, they may seek out parasocial relationships where they feel they are close to someone, but there is no chance they will be rejected as the celebrity partner has no idea that the 'relationship' exists.

154. Exam-style practice 1

1 Statements labelled as 'self-disclosure' cannot easily be tested for accuracy. While someone may claim they are telling the truth about

themselves, it is not always possible to test the validity of the information they have shared.

2 One feature is similarity in attitudes. For example, if you share the same views as another person – such as your attitudes towards marriage – then you are more likely to view them favourably because they are 'like you'.

3 Rusbult's investment model claims that relationships continue when the investments that have been made into the relationship outweigh any negative effects of being in the relationship. In the case of Melanie, she has been with Roberto for 15 years, which means they have invested a lot of time into the relationship already, and they also have two children – another joint 'investment'. For Melanie, leaving the relationship would mean that the time and energy invested in those 15 years and two children were for nothing. So for her, leaving the relationship would be considered wasting her investment. Therefore, even though Roberto hit her, she may choose to stay to honour those investments.

4 Evolutionary factors that influence relationships are those that ensure the best chance of reproductive success and survival for a particular species. For example, in humans, males produce a high number of sperm, and a good number of sperm are released in each ejaculation, meaning that males have many, many opportunities to reproduce. From this perspective, for males, promiscuity and seeking out many casual partners would give the best chance of them reproducing many times. On the other hand, females are born with a limited supply of eggs, and only one is released each month during the menstrual cycle, so their possibility of reproducing is significantly reduced compared to males. From a female perspective, seeking out partners with the best genetic qualities would be beneficial as it means their limited number of offspring are of good 'quality'. So, for women, being more choosy over sexual partners and looking for signs of genetic and physical fitness would be preferential.

Other possible points to include for AO1 include:
* *Male strategies: mate-guarding, sneak copulation, size and appearance*
* *Female strategies: sexy sons hypothesis, courtship, handicap hypothesis*
For AO3 you could include:
* *Davis' (1990) findings*
* *Buss' (1989) findings*
* *Issues of bias – relationships not based on reproductive strategies cannot be explained, for example homosexual relationships or non-sexual romantic relationships*
* *You may also wish to discuss other general criticisms of this approach to relationships, such as the view that males are more promiscuous and do not want monogamous/ long-term relationships.*

155. Exam-style practice 2

5 Intra-psychic
6 (a) The graph should look something like this:

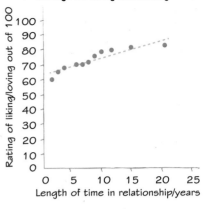

Graph to show the relationship between length of relationship and ratings of liking and loving

(b) Positive correlation
7 (a) Limiting factors are features of a person that may prevent us from being attracted to them and therefore wanting to start a relationship with them. In effect, these limiting factors are 'gates' that close to prevent a relationship occurring with someone you might not like. Virtual relationships may have an absence of gating because, when you do not meet someone face-to-face, there are certain things about them that you will not know, meaning that a relationship can develop that may not have had you first met face-to-face.

(b) In virtual relationships, people can hide elements about themselves that they are embarrassed about or that may not be 'attractive' to potential partners during the initial phase of the relationship. As a result, relationships have time to develop and people can get to know each other more personally before these features are revealed. In people with low self-esteem or extreme shyness, the absence of gating might give them sufficient time to get to know their partner online before they meet, so that when they do finally meet they feel more relaxed. If they had first met face-to-face, their shyness or low self-esteem may have prevented them from getting to know each other, making a relationship very unlikely to form. Absence of gating could also be open to abuse in virtual relationships, as some people may deliberately hide aspects about themselves to get close to people who may be vulnerable.

8 Duck's theory of relationship breakdown is divided into four phases, each with its own threshold which, once reached, sparks the move into the next phase of the breakdown. Relationships may progress through some stages but be rescued before the relationship actually ends if the partners can agree to a solution.
The four phases are:
* Intra-psychic
* Dyadic
* Social
* Grave-dressing
To complete the AO1 part of the question, you should go on to describe each phase briefly.
Zarah is demonstrating the four phases of breakdown. For example, when talking to her friend she says she felt unhappy at first but did not tell anyone, which is an example

of the intra-psychic phase. She then states how she discussed this with her husband and they shared how they felt, demonstrating the dyadic phase of the breakdown.

Add in another two examples of what Zarah did that illustrate what the theory claims.

Evidence supporting Duck's theory comes from Tashiro and Frazier (2003) who found that when asking students about their breakdowns, many reported an element of personal growth after their relationships ended, which would support the concept of the grave-dressing phase. Likewise, Hatfield et al. (1984) found that many people socially withdraw during periods of unhappiness in their relationships while they decide what to do. This would support the idea that there is an intra-psychic phase at the start of a relationship breaking down.

One strength of Duck's explanation is that there is good face validity, as many people report these clear stages during the breakdown of a relationship, suggesting that they are a good reflection of what many people experience. One criticism, however, is that the theory may not be a good representation of how both males and females experience breakdown. For example, Argyle (1988) found that men and women often reported different reasons for relationships breaking down, which may mean that the four phases are not universally experienced in the same way for both males and females.

To continue this, you could find other research evidence that may support or contradict the claims made by Duck. You might also find it useful to consider other generic evaluation points such as the reliability of the findings upon which this theory is based, or the ethical concerns raised by studying relationship breakdown.

156. Sex-role stereotypes

Sex-role stereotypes are expectations that society has of males and females based on generally accepted ideas about what males and females should be/do. These sex-role stereotypes can become 'norms', which are then transmitted to the next generation through the process of socialisation. Parents may encourage their children to participate in certain activities because they are stereotypically 'for boys' or 'for girls', and this then teaches children about what society expects of them. Boys may be encouraged to take part in rough-and-tumble play, while girls might be given toy kitchens to play with. Both tell children about what they are expected to do, and therefore influence their views of how they should behave based on their gender.

157. Androgyny

The Bem Sex Role Inventory is based on Western gender-role characteristics. The masculine element may therefore be seen as more favourable than the feminine characteristics, as masculine traits – such as dominance and lack of emotion – may be perceived as more positive than passivity and high levels of emotion. Consequently, the research that supports the idea that masculine traits associated with androgyny may be more closely related to good mental health may be culturally biased. The BSRI could therefore have traits of bias within it.

158. Chromosomes and hormones

Evidence has found that hormones have influences on gender-specific behaviours. For example, Money and Ehrhardt (1972) found that girls whose mothers had taken medication containing testosterone during pregnancy were more likely to show higher levels of masculine behaviour, suggesting that testosterone is associated with more male-typical traits. Another study by Elbourne et al. (2001) found that mothers given oxytocin during the final stage of childbirth were much less likely to face complications such as blood loss. This would suggest that oxytocin plays an important role in successful childbirth, which may explain why it is often found in higher levels in females than in males.

159. Klinefelter's syndrome

1 Klinefelter's syndrome is a chromosomal abnormality where males have an additional X chromosome, making all of the cells in their body contain XXY sex chromosomes. In patients with mosaic Klinefelter's syndrome, the additional X chromosome is found in some, but not all, of the body's cells. This means patients with mosaic Klinefelter's syndrome often have fewer signs of the disorder than patients with full Klinefelter's syndrome.

2 Klinefelter's syndrome can cause slight developmental delay in infants, meaning that they may reach milestones such as speaking, sitting and walking later than other children their age. Language deficits can be seen in patients with Klinefelter's syndrome, and they may be much more passive, quiet and emotional than males in the general population.

160. Turner syndrome

One common feature in girls with Turner syndrome is fertility problems. Girls with Turner syndrome are likely to have underdeveloped ovaries and therefore may not ovulate or menstruate each month, rendering them infertile. Sometimes the disorder will only become apparent when the girl fails to go through puberty or when a woman cannot get pregnant after years of trying.

161. Kohlberg's theory of gender development

One criticism of Kohlberg's theory is that it provides a description of the different stages of a child's understanding of the concept of gender, but it does not explain how this process of development actually happens. Nor does it effectively explain how this influences gender-specific behaviour in males and females. Consequently, the theory may be seen as incomplete and lacking in detail.

162. Gender schema theory

Gender schema theory is a cognitive explanation of gender that makes the assumption that a child's understanding of gender role is a product of learning and assimilating new information into a basic schema. A basic gender schema will exist in children by the age of 2–3 years old, when they can categorise people on the basis of being male or female. This schema will then develop as the child experiences

more examples of males and females, and the typical behaviour they show. All of this information is assimilated into the schema, which then gradually builds throughout childhood. By the age of 5 or 6 years, children will have a good understanding of their in-group gender role, but they will view this quite rigidly. By the time they reach 8–10 years old, their knowledge of gender schemas is solid for both the in- and out-group.

163. Freud's psychoanalytic theory

Internalisation refers to the process by which a child takes on the gender identity of the same-sex parent as a way to resolve the sexual feelings they have developed towards their opposite-sex parent.

164. Social learning theory

1 Social learning states that gender-role behaviour is learned through the process of observation, imitation and reinforcement. Children will see same-sex models and learn what they do, giving them knowledge of behaviour associated with that gender-role identity. After choosing which models they are most influenced by, they will then go on to imitate the behaviour they have seen. Some of this will be gender appropriate, while some will be gender inappropriate. The actual behaviour of the child can then be shaped through the process of reinforcement. Parents and peers will reinforce behaviour they see as appropriate to the child's gender, while gender inappropriate behaviour will be punished. Over time, this will shape the child's gender-role identity to be male or female.

2 One criticism of social learning theory is that the role of biology in gender-role behaviour is ignored. For example, higher levels of testosterone in males can account for the higher levels of aggression seen in males just as well as observing aggressive male role models can. Some evidence has found that gender roles can differ in same-sex siblings raised by the same parents and therefore subjected to similar observations and reinforcements. If one brother is more masculine than another, their biology could be the reason.

165. Influence of culture

Every culture will have their own set of cultural norms regarding the gender roles of males and females. These norms will be shared with children by their parents and these parents will then reinforce and punish behaviour to shape the child's gender role to meet the expected behaviour. For example, if girls are expected to be quiet and demure in a culture, parents are likely to punish loud behaviour in girls, and reward girls for being quiet and sensible.

166. Influence of media

Williams (1981) found that two years after TV was first introduced to a town the difference in behaviour between boys and girls had increased, suggesting that the media may have influenced how boys and girls behaved. It was also found that the stereotypical views of the children in the town regarding gender had increased after the introduction of TV, suggesting that their exposure to TV had changed their views of typical male and female behaviour.

167. Social explanations for GID

One social factor could be a lack of same-sex role models in childhood when the gender role is developing. During early childhood, social learning theory claims that children identify role models with whom they share important characteristics. They then observe them, learn from their behaviour, and go on to imitate this themselves. If a child has no one of the same sex to serve as a role model for their gender identity, psychologists believe this could cause the child to develop cross-gender tendencies.

168. Biological explanations for GID

Investigating the biological factors associated with gender identity disorder can help with the development of treatments. Many people who choose to change their gender role because of feelings of gender confusion respond well to hormone therapy, which has been developed as a result of research into biological influences on gender-role identity.

171. Exam-style practice 1

1 Androgyny means to display a balance of both masculine and feminine characteristics. Kristina displays both masculine and feminine personality traits. Sometimes she is quiet and sensitive, which are often considered to be feminine traits, while at other times she is assertive and competitive, which are things we would associate more with masculinity.

2 One explanation for gender identity disorder (GID) is that it is genetic, as some males with GID have been found to inherit a gene that makes them less sensitive to androgens. For example, Hare et al. (2009) found evidence that a variant of the androgen receptor gene that reduced the effect of testosterone was seen more often in male to female transsexuals than in non-transsexual males, suggesting that in some males with GID there has been a disruption of 'normal' male development, which could explain their feelings. Another explanation could be a lack of exposure to the hormones that determine gender development. For example, if a female foetus is exposed to high levels of male hormones during prenatal development, her developing brain may be masculinised, resulting in slightly more masculine behaviour than feminine. This could result in confusion for the girl when growing up if her behaviour resembles her male peers more than typical females. However, a contradicting view would be that GID has a social cause. For example, Rekers (1995) found that a common factor in a group of 70 boys with GID was a lack of a significant male role model when growing up. This might suggest that they did not get the chance to learn masculine behaviours from observing male role models and therefore have not been able to imitate them themselves.

3 One strength of the biological explanation of GID is that there is a wide range of scientific evidence supporting the explanation. The evidence is often

conducted in laboratories gathering objective data, which means there is a high level of reliability. For example, studies looking at genetic markers are taking a measure of the markers seen, rather than simply inferring that this may be the case from looking at the behaviour shown by the participant.
One limitation of the biological explanation of GID is that it ignores the role of social factors and is therefore reductionist. GID is a complex disorder that is experienced very differently by different people, and simply stating that this is the result of genetic markers or abnormal hormone exposure does not take into account the many other possible reasons for developing GID, such as a lack of same-sex role models when growing up.

4 (a) Correlation
(b) A positive correlation. The higher the boys' masculinity score, the higher their fathers' masculinity scores will be.
(c) Something like:

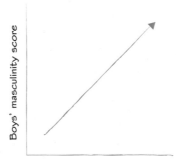

172. Exam-style practice 2

5 C

6 One limitation of using questionnaires is that people may not be honest in their answers, making the data invalid. They may answer questions giving socially desirable answers because they want to make themselves appear better, meaning that responses are not reflecting their true thoughts.

7 Kohlberg's theory is an example of a cognitive explanation of gender, as it discusses the development of gender in relation to maturation processes. As the child grows, their knowledge and understanding of the world changes. Alongside this, their knowledge of gender also changes over time.
From here you could then go on to describe the three stages of Kohlberg's theory:
1. Gender identity/gender labelling
2. Gender stability
3. Gender constancy
One piece of evidence supporting Kohlberg comes from Slaby and Frey (1975) who found that children in the gender constancy stage (over 6 years old) spent longer watching models who were the same gender as themselves, compared to younger children who spent equal amounts of time watching both same-sex and opposite-sex models. This would suggest that once in the gender constancy stage, children are actively seeking out role models of the same gender to learn from their behaviour. There is also evidence that the stages outlined by Kohlberg have been shown in different cultures, which could suggest that his theory is universal (for example, Munroe et al., 1984). However,

Bussey and Bandura (1992) suggested that they had evidence that children who should not yet have reached 'gender constancy' had strong awareness of 'gender-appropriate' behaviour. Here, children as young as 4 years were found to rate themselves more positively when playing with 'gender-appropriate' toys than with toys seen as for the opposite gender.
From here you could go on to compare Kohlberg's theory to gender schema theory as an alternative cognitive explanation. From Bussey and Bandura's evidence you could make the linking point that while the study refutes the claims made by Kohlberg, the evidence may actually support gender schema theory. Other relevant discussion points about Kohlberg's explanation include:
• *that it takes into account biological influences on gender development by focusing on the child's natural maturity;*
• *that much of the theory was developed from evidence gathered using self-report methods, which may not be reliable, especially when dealing with children.*

8 The psychodynamic explanation of gender development comes mainly from Freud's psychoanalytic theory that sees gender role developing during the phallic stage of development. Up to the age of about 3 years old, Freud argued that a child's development was centred on other elements of their life and they have very little understanding of, or interest in, gender. However children at the age of 3 years old enter the phallic stage of development and become aware of the differences between boys and girls because their libido is now focused on the genitals. As a child nears the end of the phallic stage, at around 5 or 6 years old, Freud believed that they will go through either the Oedipus complex if they are a boy, or the Electra complex if they are a girl. In the Oedipus complex, young boys develop sexual feelings towards their mother and at the same time become jealous of the father's relationship with her. They will also become fearful of the father, as they worry about what he may do to the boy if he discovers how he feels about his mother. This fear is often referred to as 'castration anxiety' because the increasing understanding of anatomical differences between males and females leads boys to fear that the father will castrate him. For girls, the Electra complex refers to sexual feelings developing towards the father and therefore jealousy towards the mother, but rather than fearing castration by the mother they will blame her for their lack of a penis – almost as if she has already castrated them. Girls then develop 'penis envy', which some have argued is more a jealousy of male dominance in society, rather than actual envy over her lack of a penis. In order to resolve the internal conflicts caused by the Oedipus or Electra complex, children identify with their same-sex parent, internalising their gender identity, apparently in the hope that, in future, they will be able to attract a partner who is similar to the opposite-sex parent they have desired.
One major criticism of Freud's explanation of gender development is the lack of scientific research evidence to support the theory. Freud presented evidence from a case study of 5-year-old 'Little Hans' who had a fear of horses, which Freud felt was

symbolic of Oedipal conflict – with the fear of being bitten by the horse symbolising the boy's castration anxiety. However, this was the only case study offered to provide support for the theory. As much of the evidence was gathered through conversations with Hans' father rather than from Freud's direct observations of Hans himself, many have argued that the evidence is unreliable. Many feminists have criticised Freud's theory for failing to provide a full account of female gender development. Freud himself gave very little discussion to the development of the female gender role, instead focusing on the idea that females develop their identity, in part, through envy of males. This means that the theory is very androcentric and does not take into account the more equal role of females in modern society. Another major criticism of Freud's explanation of gender identity is the failure to account for the development of children's gender identity in families where a same-sex parent is available for the child to identify with and then internalise the gender role from.

From here you should be able to consider other possible discussion points, or elaborate on those already presented. For example, you could discuss:

- *the lack of falsifiability in Freud's research*
- *research evidence from 'non-typical' families, for example homosexual parents and single parent families*
- *criticisms over Freud's 'sexualising' of child development*
- *lack of temporal validity in Freud's theory that is over a century old.*

9 *The opening part of your essay should describe the social learning explanation of gender development. This means including references to:*

- *observational learning*
- *the influence of role models*
- *the imitation of behaviour*
- *mediational processes involved in social learning: attention; retention; motivation and motor reproduction.*

Evidence supporting social learning theory as an explanation of gender development comes from Seavey et al. (1975), who showed that adults would interact differently with a baby when they were told it was a girl, compared to if they were told it was a boy. This included giving different toys to play with and talking to the child in a different way. Fagot (1978) found that children were reinforced differently during play at home according to their gender. Boys, for example, were positively reinforced for playing with trucks and building blocks, but punished for playing with dolls, while girls were positively reinforced for staying close to parents but punished for rough-and-tumble play. These studies illustrate that parental or adult influence is a powerful transmitter of gender-appropriate behaviour. Langlois and Downs (1980) also found that peers can influence gender-role behaviour as they are less tolerant of friends playing with opposite-gender toys/games, often teasing or making fun of them. This would suggest that gender-role behaviour is influenced by the behaviour of peers as a form of motivation.

In comparison to the biological approach to gender development, the social learning explanation places very little emphasis on the role of genes and hormones in the development of gender-role identity. For example, the biological explanation might claim that two children of the same sex from the same family would have a good chance of having a similar gender-role identity because they share a lot of the same genetic material. And in the case of identical twins, from a biological viewpoint their gender-role identity should be the same because their genes are. However, in many cases there are likely to be differences in the gender-role identity of same-sex siblings even if they share the same genes. In this case, social learning theory would account for the differences. For example, even identical twins will have had different experiences, different friends, seen different television programmes and been reinforced slightly differently by others. All of these factors could explain why one child may be slightly more feminine than another, which the biological approach might struggle to explain.

173. Piaget's theory of cognitive development

1 This would be assimilation because it would not require much change.
2 This would be accommodation because she would have the driving seat on the opposite side of the car and be driving on the right-hand side of the road.

174. Piaget: Sensorimotor stage

Object permanence is a concept Piaget believed developed in babies at around 7–8 months of age. It is the knowledge that an object or person continues to exist even when out of sight. This is an important concept because, without it, the child's world would be a series of comings and goings, which would make attachment to people or objects impossible.

175. Piaget: Pre-operational stage

Piaget used quite informal methods to test children, based on his own environment and observations. The Swiss mountain study has been criticised for being too difficult and abstract for most children, suggesting that they showed egocentrism when, in fact, with a simpler, more understandable task such as hide-and-seek used by Hughes (1975) in the policeman doll study, they were able to decentre and see a different viewpoint. Similarly, Borke (1975) got children to rotate the mountains display on a turntable to practise looking at the different views until they were familiar with the idea. She also used familiar toys to test the children and found a far higher level of ability than Piaget did, suggesting that his methodology was to blame. However, no one suggests he was wrong about the concept of egocentrism.

176. Piaget: Concrete operational stage

To test conservation, Piaget (1960) asked children to agree that two lines of counters were the same prior to transforming their appearance. After they watch one of the lines being pushed together they are then asked, 'Are they still the same number?' McGarrigle and Donaldson (1974) challenged this method and said that the child was being confused and intimidated by the adult making changes, which they do all the time in the child's life. Instead, they used a 'naughty teddy' to mess up the lines of counters in the conservation of number task. This then enabled the children to answer more freely that the two lines still had the same number of counters without feeling that they might upset an adult and, as a consequence, much younger children were able to conserve.

177. Piaget: Formal operational stage

Biological maturation does not seem to explain the formal operational stage, as not everyone demonstrates formal operational thinking by the age of 11, and it is not seen cross-culturally according to Dasen (1977). This goes against Piaget's ideas of an invariant biologically or even genetically driven sequence of stages.

178. Vygotsky's theory of cognitive development

Vygotsky referred to inner speech as the final part of his three stages of language development. He saw it as internalising the problem-solving solutions the child learned by interacting with other people. In this stage, egocentric speech, whereby the child thinks aloud while solving problems, has become silent and language is now only used to communicate with other people.

179. Zone of proximal development

Vygotsky introduced two concepts that could be used here, namely the idea of the zone of proximal development (ZPD) and the idea of scaffolding. When a child is in the ZPD, they can do some things by themselves but need the support of someone who knows more (an MKO) to help them reach their potential. In this case, the child's mother could be the MKO, and she should give hints and tips rather than place the pieces in the puzzle. For example, she could suggest that the child look for all the red pieces or the corner pieces and use them first. This is what Vygotsky means by using scaffolding to assist the child.

180. Baillargeon: early infant abilities

In the violation of expectation technique, a baby is seated in front of a screen on which objects move in a predictable way, such as a swinging drawbridge. Once the baby has habituated to the scene, the researcher changes it to show something that should be impossible if the objects remained the same height or solidity. If the baby shows surprise at the impossible event (violation of expectation), it suggests they have knowledge of the properties of the objects and their permanence, and in this way very young babies can be tested.

181. Social cognition: Selman

Using an interpersonal dilemma could be objective as part of a standardised procedure with careful recording of the children's responses. The recording should then be watched back by at least two researchers who are blind to the aim of the study. This would give inter-rater reliability. They would then code the responses according to what they saw and heard. If the aim is to investigate the development of social cognition, either a longitudinal or a cross-sectional design could be used.

182. Theory of mind

The false-belief paradigm tests whether a child can imagine what another character would think when returning to a scene where something has been hidden while they were away. If the child has not developed a theory of mind (ToM), they will say that the character gives the same answer as themselves, even though they know where the item was hidden because they saw it being moved, but the character did not. If they have a ToM, they will be able to see that the returning character will mistakenly think that the hidden item is in its original place because they were away when it was moved. The false-belief task gives an objective yes/no measure, which is usually based on toys and the game of hide-and-seek, which children understand.

183. Theory of mind and autism

Using dolls is in some ways an advantage because very young children will not be intimidated about saying what they think is happening. Whereas if it was replicated by adults hiding things, they might not want to say what adults were doing. Also, actors would show non-verbal as well as verbal behaviour, which would be another variable, and so the task could be lacking validity. However, using dolls could be criticised for lacking validity because dolls do not think, and we know that a key deficit in ASD is lack of pretend play, so maybe using this task was overly challenging as well as lacking in validity.

184. Mirror neurons

Rizzolatti et al. (1996) discovered mirror neurons and suggested that they had a function in helping us understand each other's behaviour. They used a sample of macaque monkeys whose mirror neurons became active when they watched other monkeys pick up food. This probably helped us survive because it helped us to imitate the successful members of our groups. Cheng et al (2006) found that females appeared to be able to use the mirror neuron system more effectively, perhaps explaining their superiority in reading emotional states in other people. It has also been proposed that a lack of mirror neurons or a fault in the system could explain the communication problems faced by people with autism, particularly the lack of a ToM. However, Rizzolatti and Craighero (2004) have been unable to find a single mirror neuron in the human brain. Instead, using scans, they have found networks in the frontal and parietal lobes which become active when a person watches another person's behaviour. Unfortunately the picture is not that clear. Jarrett (2012) said that we are clearly capable of understanding actions that we are unable to perform, such as slithering like a snake, without needing mirror neurons, thereby challenging the concept.

Hickok (2014) considered that the function of mirror neurons is not about understanding others' actions, but about using others to make our own choice of how to act. Seen this way, mirror neuron activity is just as likely a consequence of action understanding as it is a cause. Finally, Hamilton (2012) assessed the results from 25 relevant studies of the mirror neuron system in people with autism, and concluded that there is little evidence for a global dysfunction of the mirror system in autism.

187. Exam-style practice 1

1 Some classic symptoms of autism are that language development is often delayed and children are less vocal, so do not babble at the usual time. They can also have problems making eye contact and reading facial expressions, body language and gestures, leading to problems with relationships. They may also lack awareness of and interest in other children. They tend to play alone. When they do play, they do not demonstrate imaginative or pretend play, while others will continually repeat the same pretend play. Another feature is their preference for routine; they like to stick to the same routine and little changes may trigger tantrums. Others may engage in repetitive activity, such as turning light switches on and off, opening and closing doors, or lining things up.

2 When we watch someone like Eddie Izzard running through pain to complete his marathons, we feel empathy with him because we know how painful it is and how much effort is involved in running quite short distances. The ability to put ourselves in other people's shoes is called having a theory of mind (ToM). Researchers believe that we feel this empathy because we have mirror neurons which activate when we watch him, giving us a similar awareness of what he is going through. This is called motor resonance.
Rizzolatti et al. (1996) found mirror neurons by accident. They noticed that the macaque monkeys they had wired up to electrodes showed the same firing pattern when they watched other monkeys pick up food as when they did so themselves. They then coined the term 'mirror neurons'. It is tentatively suggested that a problem in this system could account for the inability of people with autism to empathise or 'read' other people, and why they lack a ToM. Cheng et al. (2006), using a magnetoencephalography (MEG) study, found that female brains show a stronger motor resonance than male brains, possibly accounting for superior performance in social referencing where we look at others to read their emotions and decide how to respond. By this logic, females should have greater empathy for others, and in the case of Eddie Izzard, they might donate more money to his appeal.
However, there are challenges to the idea of mirror neurons. Jarrett (2012) says we are clearly capable of understanding actions that we are unable to perform, such as slithering like a snake or running 27 marathons in 27 days without needing mirror neurons for it. Rizzolatti and Craighero (2004) looked for the mirror neuron in humans. It is not yet possible to test single neurons in humans, so they used EEGs, PET and fMRI scans, and found a network in the frontal and parietal brain regions that appeared to work as mirror

neurons. Iacoboni et al. (1999) showed, using fMRI, that the human inferior frontal cortex and superior parietal lobe are active when the person performs an action or sees another individual performing an action. It has been suggested that these brain regions contain mirror neurons. Even though actual neurons have not been found, they have been defined as the human mirror neuron system. Hickok (2014) suggested that the function of mirror neurons is not about understanding others' actions, but about using others to make our own choice of how to act. Seen this way, mirror neuron activity is just as likely a consequence of action understanding as a cause of it, and so it can only explain our behaviour to a limited extent.

3 (a) Simon Baron-Cohen believes that normal people have a theory of mind or ToM. This enables them to read other people's faces and therefore their emotions, so that they can respond appropriately to someone who is happy or sad. They also understand that other people have their own thoughts. This makes friendships easier. People with autism are thought to lack this ability, thereby causing them relationship problems and communication difficulties. He demonstrated the effect with the Sally-Anne task, showing that children with autism could not, on the whole, understand that other people (in this case represented by a doll) would not respond in the same way as they did when they saw a hidden marble moved from one hiding place to another.

(b) One limitation of the ToM for explaining autism is that some children with autism showed a ToM in the Sally-Anne task, and the ToM cannot explain some of the other key deficits in children with autism, such as the delay in speech. It is also possible to improve the deficit through practice, suggesting that it is not a biological process. Another limitation is that children with autism are very capable in other ways such as mathematics, and one would expect a thinking deficit to affect problem-solving skills, but it does not.

4 Object permanence is the idea that objects and people continue to exist even when out of sight. Piaget believed this developed at around 7 months. He tested it by hiding objects under cloths to see if the child showed surprise when it was revealed, or would try to get it from under the cover. Baillargeon et al. (1985) developed the violation of expectation technique to investigate object permanence with very young infants of just 5 months. Propped in a baby seat, they watched a new scenario/event until they looked away, which indicated that it was no longer new to them. Then they were shown an alternative and impossible example of the scenario, for example, a solid object passing through another solid object. The length of time they looked at it was compared with the possible scenario. The key assumptions for the method are that a baby will spend longer looking at something it is surprised by, and that babies also have an innate ability to understand the properties of objects.
In a series of studies, Baillargeon and DeVos (1991) showed that babies did show

object permanence by showing surprise at what happened. One example is the sliding carrot. Three and a half-month-old babies watch either a tall or a short carrot slide past a window in a screen. After a period of habituation, babies show surprise and look for longer when the tall carrot does not appear in the window. These results indicate that the babies realised that each carrot continued to exist when out of sight and assumed that each carrot retained its height behind the screen. They also believed that each carrot pursued its trajectory behind the screen and expected the tall carrot to be visible in the screen window, showing surprise when it was not.

This supports the idea that babies as young as three and a half months of age are aware that objects continue to exist when hidden. They therefore have object permanence. However, this conclusion was challenged by Cashon and Cohen (2000), who proposed that it was the novelty of the new appearance that caused the babies to look for longer. As it is very difficult to be certain what young babies are reacting to, there is room for doubt, but it is clear that Piaget's belief about the age at which object permanence occurred was probably wrong.

188. Exam-style practice 2

5 (a) mean = 8.3, median = 8.5, mode = 11
  (b) Credit any negative skew diagram given with correct labels.

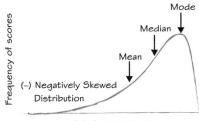

  (c) Negative skew

6 One way Piaget's theory could be applied to the classroom is to look at the concept of readiness. Piaget believed that learning was most effective when the child was ready to move up in their understanding and therefore ready to learn more. An example could be learning to tell the time when children first start noticing time passing.

7 *You could begin by outlining Piaget's stages of cognitive development.* Piaget believed that a child learns by interacting with its environment. He described the child as a scientist experimenting on the world, so he saw the child as an active learner. He believed that learning took place through a process of assimilation and accommodation, which increases knowledge by creating and adapting schemas (our packets of knowledge). When we assimilate we make small changes to existing knowledge, but when we accommodate we have to make big leaps, and we temporarily feel uncomfortable or what Piaget called 'in disequilibrium'. So, to learn best, we have to be challenged.

Other key ideas were that development happened through maturation and in fixed stages. During these stages, the child learns key concepts such as object permanence and conservation. Object permanence occurs when the child understands that people and things have a permanent existence and do not come and go when

out of sight; conservation refers to the ability to understand the constancy of volume, mass and number even when it changes appearance. Piaget believed that these concepts occurred at set ages and in a precise order.

Piaget's ideas have been heavily criticised, but one idea that is accepted is the development of the schema through assimilation and accommodation, and this is adapted into teaching practice in schools. Teachers are encouraged to stretch and challenge students in every lesson to create disequilibrium and the best learning.

The main criticism is that Piaget was wrong about the ages at which the key concepts occurred. This may be because he had no special techniques other than observation, and set quite difficult tasks for the children and babies. Researchers such as McGarrigle and Donaldson (1974), in the 'naughty teddy' replication of Piaget's (1960) conservation of number study, showed that children are able to understand the task at a much younger age when the task is child-friendly and the adult is replaced by a much less intimidating glove puppet.

Similarly, Hughes (1975) and Borke (1975) have demonstrated that children were not as egocentric as Piaget supposed, by making the three mountains task far simpler. They used, instead, a policeman doll to find another doll that was hiding, and placed the three mountains on a turntable so the child could turn it around and look at it from each side.

Finally, other theorists, such as Vygotsky, suggested that Piaget neglected the role of language and also social learning when he explained cognitive development. Instead, Vygotsky proposed that language was needed for learning to progress, and scaffolding by a more knowledgeable other was very important to draw the child on. Nevertheless, Piaget's ideas have had a major influence on education and still inform curriculum developments today.

189. Classification of schizophrenia

The clinical characteristics of schizophrenia are varied but fall under positive and negative symptoms. The positive symptoms in some way are additional to normal life, so the client may experience hearing voices, which typically are critical and destructive. The client may also experience hallucinations and imagine seeing creatures or people who are not really there. The negative symptoms take away from normal functioning and lead to a withdrawal from everyday life. The client may experience a range of symptoms that affect their emotions, speech and behaviour. An example might be showing incoherent speech, starting to ramble and talk about random ideas. Or they may show speech poverty and give very brief replies to questions. Emotionally they may be very flat or inappropriate. For example, laughing when in a sad context.

190. Reliability of diagnosis

Test–retest reliability occurs when a client with schizophrenia visits their clinician more than once and the clinician arrives at the same diagnosis both times. Inter-

rater reliability occurs if the clinician asks a colleague for a second opinion and they both agree the client has schizophrenia.

191. Validity of diagnosis

Schizophrenia is diagnosed by looking at symptoms that a client presents with at the clinic. There will be a mixture of positive and negative symptoms, and for every person this balance will be different. The length of time a client will suffer the symptoms also varies, with some people being affected for life and some having just one episode. This variety of experience calls into question whether it is actually one illness. Jansson and Parnas (2007) found limited validity in their review of 92 studies, finding that different definitions of schizophrenia were given to the same patients.

However, it depends on the type of validity, because Mason et al. (1997) found good predictive validity in their 99 patients, who were followed for 13 years. Finally, in a more recent review, Jablensky (2010) concluded that, despite the problems, there was enough empirical evidence from studies to suggest that there is a broad set of symptoms that makes a valid diagnosis and the predictive validity is good enough to make a prognosis.

192. Co-morbidity

If a client presents at a clinic with symptoms of both bipolar disorder and schizophrenia, for example, it is difficult to identify definite symptoms of schizophrenia because they overlap. In both illnesses there are psychotic features and depressive features. The clinician will have to wait and watch what happens over several months to come to a final diagnosis.

193. Culture bias

Sugarman and Craufurd (1994) showed that successive generations of immigrants had an increased risk of developing schizophrenia compared to white British controls. As their risk was the same at the start, it seems likely this was not genetic but environmental, such as the stress of coming to a new country and living in poor conditions. Cochrane (1983) suggested it could be due to the mothers contracting influenza when they arrived here. African-Caribbean countries do not have much immunity to 'flu, and it is well known that it can significantly increase the risk of schizophrenia.

194. Gender bias

The evidence for a gender bias in schizophrenia dates back to earlier versions of the diagnostic criteria before DSM-5. In these classification systems, the risk of developing schizophrenia was thought to be the same for men and women, and ignored the clear differences in women's age of onset and experience of the illness. More recently, the evidence has shown that men and women have very different experiences of the illness and rate of recovery from episodes. Castle (1991) suggests that women experience 'affective psychosis' rather than schizophrenia. It has also been said that a female experience of schizophrenia with late onset around the late 50s is likely to be chronic and mild rather than acute. This could be linked to the menopause, and indicates a hormonal element to the illness that protects women until their hormone levels drop at menopause. In support of this, Kulkarni et al. (2001) found that oestradiol (a female hormone) added to antipsychotic medication helped women more than the antipsychotic alone. Now that the gender differences are understood, there is less likelihood that there will be a bias in diagnosis.

195. Symptom overlap

Co-morbidity occurs when a client suffers from two illnesses at the same time. For example, someone might have schizophrenia and drug addiction. Symptom overlap occurs when some of the symptoms of two concurrent mental illnesses are very similar. For example, some of the symptoms of schizophrenia overlap with autism and bipolar disorder.

196. Genetic explanation for schizophrenia

The evidence for schizophrenia being a heritable biological condition is heavily based on twin studies. However, the problems with twin studies mean that we cannot be certain that environment is not playing a part. For example, epigenetic modification means that some twins share the placenta and some do not, so from conception there are differences in environment. A second challenge comes from research by Boklage (1977) who found that when MZ twins were right-handed, the concordance rate for schizophrenia was 92%. If one was left-handed and one right-handed, the concordance rate fell to 25%. This shows a genetic influence but also that it is hard to compare studies 'like for like', as not all researchers will have controlled for handedness.

197. The dopamine hypothesis

Excess levels of dopamine can explain some but not all of the symptoms of schizophrenia. Evidence from Owen et al. (1978), using post-mortem studies of people with schizophrenia, show a higher density of dopamine receptors in the cerebral cortex than those without schizophrenia, suggesting that they were more sensitive to the action of dopamine. However, Davis et al. (1991) pointed out that high levels of dopamine are not found in all individuals with schizophrenia, and clozapine (an antipsychotic drug which is effective in schizophrenia) not only blocks dopamine but also affects glutamate levels (glutamate usually blocks dopamine release). This sheds some doubt on the hypothesis. Davis (1991) further suggested that high levels of dopamine in the mesolimbic pathway are associated with positive symptoms, while high levels in the mesocortical pathway are associated with negative symptoms. This could therefore explain why not everyone is helped by antipsychotic drugs, because the drugs are not designed to affect both pathways, which have different receptors. In conclusion, the dopamine hypothesis is only a partial explanation of the symptoms.

198. Neural correlates

Research suggests that there are several critical differences in the brains of people with schizophrenia. Andreasen et al. (1990) conducted a controlled CAT scan study and found significant enlargement of the ventricles in people with schizophrenia compared to those without. Scans of twins where one is unaffected and the other is affected have shown the difference in the ventricles, which become enlarged in schizophrenia. This central area of the brain is involved in our basic emotions, and this could explain the negative symptoms of flattened emotion and lack of drive. Li et al. (2010) showed in a meta-analysis that the bilateral amygdala and right fusiform gyri were less active in people with schizophrenia. This area of the brain is used for processing faces, and the lower activity could explain the difficulties faced by patients in this respect. It is also known that grey matter diminishes over time in schizophrenia patients. Grey matter is made up of nerve cells, which are capable of adapting with use. Schizophrenia patients often withdraw from active life and it is possible that the retreating grey matter corresponds to a lack of mental stimulation.

199. Family dysfunction explanation

A dysfunctional family is one where the relationships are difficult, often tense and lacking in warmth. This could be for many reasons such as poverty, addiction, abuse, overcrowding and poor housing. All this creates stress, which is thought to act as a trigger for schizophrenia in a person who has a genetic predisposition. This is called the diathesis-stress model. Stress releases cortisol, a hormone that causes multiple effects on the body through the fight-or-flight response. In the long term, these effects are harmful to the body, and in the mind they cause stress and anxiety, which could be the forerunner of the prodromal phase of schizophrenia. Linszen et al. (1997) showed that high expressed emotion (EE) families are about four times more likely to have the family member relapse than a person whose family is low in EE, because these families have a communication style that involves criticism, hostility and emotional over-involvement.

200. Cognitive explanations

1 A laboratory experiment with an independent measures design.
2 Any suitable idea, such as word lists/pictures/faces.
  Justification could relate to accuracy of measurement, lack of bias, practical and ethical considerations, and reliability and validity.

201. Dysfunctional thought processing

Patients with schizophrenia are thought to lose the ability to think logically and problem-solve successfully as their illness progresses, unless successfully treated. To investigate this, researchers use tests such as the Hayling sentence completion task as part of an assessment. The tests aim to measure processing speed and ability to suppress inappropriate responses. These tests are standardised and have high inter-rater and test–retest reliability. However, they are not like the patient's day-to-day problems, so lack validity. As it is hard for a patient with schizophrenia to use metacognition to self-analyse, it is very hard to pinpoint exactly which parts of their thinking are faulty. To try to test this, Evans et al. (1997) used a Behavioural Assessment of the Dysexecutive Syndrome (BADS) test, which is a collection of more valid tasks with which to test reasoning.

202. Drug therapy

Antipsychotic drugs work by restricting the action of dopamine at the synapse by blocking its receptor sites. This means that the patient cannot create the high levels of excitation of the receptors that cause hallucinations and delusions, so the drug relieves the positive symptoms.

203. Cognitive behaviour therapy

A randomised controlled trial is one where patients are allocated at random to one of two conditions without them being aware of it. The trial is then assessed by a clinician who is unaware or 'blind' to which patient is in which condition. One condition is usually the active or test condition and the other is a control condition. In Sensky's (2000) study, the control was the befriending condition, and CBT was the active condition.

204. Family therapy

Family therapy has been found to be very effective in treating schizophrenia. Two meta-analyses by Pilling et al. (2002) and Bird et al. (2010) showed convincing support that it reduced relapses and helped keep patients out of hospital. It was especially useful with the early onset of psychosis in younger patients. This is linked to the evidence of family dysfunction where high expressed emotion (EE) families are known to increase the risk of developing schizophrenia, possibly because the stress in the family acts like a trigger and switches on a latent underlying genetic risk in the patient. However, caring for these patients places a large burden on the family and can increase any stress that is already there. The family therefore needs a lot of support for the therapy to be effective.

205. Token economies

The main limitations of a token economy for patients with schizophrenia is that it can only be effectively used in a hospital setting, where all the patient's behaviours are observed and rewarded. Once the patient leaves the hospital, the behaviours tend to be extinguished, as predicted by operant conditioning theory. In other words, they do not generalise. In addition, staff need to be very consistent across all three shifts that create 24-hour care and this is difficult to achieve. It is likely that some behaviour will be missed in the general busyness of a ward. Finally, the patients can become dependent on the points for good behaviour, which can seem to be demeaning and dehumanising them. It is easy to see how they could be abused and threatened by unprofessional staff, who could humiliate them.

206. Interactionist approach

The diathesis-stress model sees schizophrenia as being caused by the interaction of inherited factors and environmental stressors. The model has support from research by Barlow and Durand (2009), which has shown that inherited variations in the genes, coupled with stress from living in a dysfunctional family, predispose a person to developing schizophrenia. Murray and Lewis (1987) created a model that brought together these factors with the environmental stressors that increase levels of the stress hormone cortisol. They monitored this from childhood to adolescence and suggested that stressors in adolescence acted as triggers to developing psychosis.

On the other hand, not everyone who develops schizophrenia has a genetic predisposition, as we know from twin and adoption studies, and not everyone who develops it has a stressful upbringing. For some, it is switched on by substance misuse. At the present time, it is uncertain what the relative contributions are from genes and the environment, and so it remains a hypothesis rather than absolute fact.

209. Exam-style practice 1

1   In order to diagnose schizophrenia, clinicians will give the person with symptoms a clinical interview. In the interview the client will be asked questions about all aspects of their functioning and everyday life. It is also likely that a parent will be involved, as symptoms often appear in late teenage years. Ward et al. (1962) identified three ways that the diagnosis could be unreliable. First, clients may not be able to talk about their mental state clearly; they may feel ashamed and leave out information. If they are in an acute episode they may be incoherent and unable to self-reflect in any way. The person (a relative) speaking on the client's behalf may have a vested interest in the diagnosis and minimise or maximise the severity because they either want or do not want them to be sectioned and hospitalised, or they are ashamed themselves. Atypical presentations mean that not all clients present with the textbook symptoms and may not exactly fit the DSM criteria.

Second, a lot depends on the skill of the clinician and the personal relationship they make with the client. The interview is free-flowing around the questions. Each clinician will have a background in a particular approach depending on where they were trained, and this can take the interview in various directions. While they are asking the questions, they are also observing the client, and how well they do this can influence the accuracy of the diagnosis.

Third, the two main diagnostic systems, DSM-5 and ICD-10, have different descriptors of the illness, which could lead to problems where there is symptom overlap with other illnesses such as bipolar disorder. When these three weaknesses combine, it is easy to see how inter-clinician and test–retest reliability could be lacking. However, through many revisions of both classification systems and the gradual increase in the development of other medical tests, the diagnosis is becoming more reliable.

The validity of the diagnosis of schizophrenia was tested most famously by Rosenhan in 1973 in his study of mental hospitals, when pseudo patients pretending to have schizophrenia were all admitted, thus demonstrating poor understanding of the illness and low validity of diagnosis at that time. Since then, the diagnostic criteria have been refined, and Mason et al. (1997) found that the predictive validity of the two classification systems was good if clinicians used the symptoms present over six months. Jablensky's (2010) review concluded that, for the time being, the clinical concept of schizophrenia is valid and supported by empirical evidence. Its multiple features form a broad syndrome with reasonable internal cohesion and a characteristic evolution over time. Finally, the DSM-5 reflects a shift in the opinion of clinicians that schizophrenia may be better diagnosed as a syndrome rather than as a separate disorder because clients present with such different groupings of symptoms.

2   This would be an independent measures design. I would allocate 20 volunteers at random to the meditation group and 20 to a control group who would meet for the same amount of time each week and just chat. Both groups will continue with their medication. Before the study began, I would assess how troublesome the positive and negative symptoms were in each person by means of a self-report and a questionnaire to the carers of the volunteers, asking how they were functioning.

The experiment would run for 8 weeks and each session would last an hour, led by the meditation expert in a suitable room in the university where the volunteers feel relaxed. The other volunteers (the control group) will meet for a coffee in the university coffee shop. The sessions will all be group sessions, with all 20 taking part together.

After all the sessions, each group would be asked to complete a follow-up self-report and the carers to complete another questionnaire. These would be analysed to see if there had been improvement. Six months later I would check again to see if the improvement was maintained.

To avoid experimenter bias, I would ask a colleague to do the random allocation and also to collect the responses. One control would be to check that none of the volunteers had previously done meditation and to ask them to only use the meditation in the sessions. Another control would be to ask all the volunteers to come to the same place at the same time each week in case getting out of the house and meeting others was going to make an improvement on its own.

3   Parents have been blamed for their children developing schizophrenia because of evidence that growing up in dysfunctional families is damaging. For example, in a longitudinal study in Finland, Tienari et al. (2004) found that 36.8% of high-genetic risk adoptees living in a dysfunctional family environment developed a schizophrenia-spectrum disorder, compared to only 5.3% of those in a healthy family environment. The reason for the effect is described by the diathesis-stress model. Stress is known to bring on latent or underlying symptoms of schizophrenia where there is a genetic risk. In addition, Bateson (1972) hypothesised that growing up in a family that said positive things to the child while using negative body language put children in a double bind. This high negative-emotion environment could lead to psychosis. Kavanagh (1992) conducted a review of 26 studies of schizophrenia patients who returned home after hospitalisation. Those returning to high-emotion families had a mean relapse rate of 48% compared to 21% in low-emotion families. This supports Bateson's hypothesis. A high expressed emotion is a communication style that involves criticism, hostility and emotional over-involvement. A patient returning to a family with high EE is about four times more likely to relapse than a patient whose family is low in EE (Linszen et al. 1997).

4   (a)   One limitation of getting an accurate or useful diagnosis is symptom overlap between schizophrenia and other conditions. Ripke et al. (2011) looked at 50,000 patients' genetic material. They found that of seven gene locations on the genome associated with schizophrenia, three were also associated with bipolar disorder, which suggested a genetic overlap between the two disorders. Konstantareas and Hewitt (2001) compared 14 people with autism and 14 people with schizophrenia. They found that none of the people with schizophrenia had symptoms of autism but that seven of the people with autism had symptoms of schizophrenia. When two illnesses are co-morbid, it makes a clear diagnosis very difficult.

     (b)   One limitation of taking a biological approach to the treatment of schizophrenia is that it relies on drug therapy to alter dopamine levels. This is a reductionist approach, which has been very useful in finding more effective drug combinations that help positive symptoms. In support, Smith et al. (2010) point out that antipsychotic medication can reduce the positive symptoms of psychosis in about 8–15 days. However, they often fail to significantly improve negative symptoms and cognitive dysfunction, which have been better supported through CBT. In summary, the partial effectiveness and problems with side effects make a solely biological treatment less effective.

5   The nature–nurture debate looks at whether schizophrenia occurs as a result of inherited genes. Biological processes may start through misuse of substances such as cannabis, and the nurture side looks at dysfunctional families, migration and environmental stressors.

For this very straightforward question, choose evidence to support the following points.

In support of the nature:
* *genetic explanation*
* *dopamine hypothesis*
* *neural correlates in the brain.*

In support of nurture:
* *dysfunctional families*
* *diathesis-stress model*
* *cognitive dysfunction.*

There is an interactionist position between the two, which would make a good conclusion.

6 (a) Double blind trials use a placebo to provide baseline data against which to test the effectiveness of the active drug. The patient is unaware of which they are taking and so the effectiveness of the genuine drug can be fairly tested. The clinician is also unaware who is getting the active drug so that there can be no accidental bias from cues they might give to the patient.

(b) One conclusion is that nearly 30% of people improved with the placebo or inactive drug, showing that just the belief of taking an effective medication was enough to show improvement. A second conclusion is that no one got significantly worse on the active drug, unlike with the placebo. In fact, with the drug, everyone showed some improvement and some were very much improved.

(c) Placebo drugs look like the drug they are replacing and so the patients have faith that they are going to work. This creates an expectancy effect. When the drug is given by an authority figure backed up by the authority of science and modern medicine, the effect is powerful. In this case, you could surmise that part of the effectiveness of the antipsychotic was the placebo effect.

7 Dopamine works in the brain to stimulate the action of neurons at the synapse. Some researchers believe that too much dopamine causes the onset of schizophrenia and this is called the dopamine hypothesis. They point to the fact that antipsychotic drugs that block dopamine via D2 receptors are effective in reducing the positive symptoms. Also, L-dopa – a drug which converts to dopamine and is given to patients with Parkinson's disease – creates schizophrenia-like symptoms. Hallucinogenic drugs such as LSD, which create psychotic-type symptoms, also work on the dopamine circuit.

However, Davis et al. (1991) suggested that high levels of dopamine are not found in all individuals with schizophrenia. Clozapine, an antipsychotic drug which is effective in treating schizophrenia, does not block much dopamine activity, shedding some doubt on the hypothesis. Davis further suggests that high levels of dopamine in the mesolimbic pathway are associated with positive symptoms, while high levels in the mesocortical pathway are associated with negative symptoms. This could therefore explain why not everyone is helped by the antipsychotic drugs.

8 New advances in scanning technology have allowed the brains of individuals with schizophrenia to be scanned, and certain differences have been noted between their brains and the brains of healthy individuals. These are neural correlates and, as the name suggests, this is correlational data and not causal data. The cause-and-effect relationship has still to be established. For example, Andreasen et al. (1990) conducted a controlled CAT scan study and found significant enlargement of the ventricles in those with schizophrenia compared to controls. Enlarged ventricles suggest damage to the central brain areas and prefrontal cortex. This could account for the negative symptoms of people with schizophrenia. Li et al. (2010) showed in a meta-analysis that the bilateral amygdala and right fusiform gyrus were less active in schizophrenia patients. This area of the brain is used for processing faces, and the lower activity could explain the difficulties encountered by the patients in this respect. Not all people with schizophrenia show enlarged ventricles, which raises doubts about it being a single condition rather than a syndrome.

Hoffman and Hampson (2012) have attempted to explain auditory verbal hallucinations (AVHs). This study suggests that the core mechanism producing AVHs involves a complex functional loop. Components of this loop include Wernicke's area, the left inferior frontal cortex and the putamen. The putamen appears to play a critical role in the generation of spontaneous language, and in determining whether auditory stimuli are registered consciously as real or not. Excessive activity seen in Wernicke's region in people with schizophrenia could, therefore, generate an overabundance of potentially conscious language representations, explaining the voices.

9 Cognitive explanations of schizophrenia focus on faulty thinking as an explanation for the symptoms. Voices, for example, are seen as misperceptions of 'inner speech', which we all experience. Hallucinations are seen as biased information processing, while negative symptoms are seen as control strategies to try to manage the high levels of mental stimulation being experienced.

One strength of the cognitive explanation of schizophrenia is that Bowie and Harvey (2006) found cognitive impairments to be a core feature of schizophrenia, mainly affecting attention, working memory, verbal learning and executive function. These impairments are present before the illness progresses and are always found. Further support comes from the fact that, once treated, some of these deficits were seen to reduce.

One weakness of the explanation is that cognitive theories do not explain the cause of schizophrenia or what has led to the deficits. If the explanation for hallucinations is biased information processing, it ought to be possible to persuade a person with schizophrenia of the reality. In fact, it is extremely difficult to shift their thinking. The cognitive explanation does not account for the improvements people experience from antipsychotic medication, and cognitive treatments often rely on controlling the biological levels of dopamine before cognitive treatments can be put in place.

10 Two explanations for schizophrenia could be any from genes, the dopamine hypothesis, neural correlates, family dysfunction, cognitive dysfunction or an interactionist approach. Ideally, choose two clearly contrasting explanations for a compare question.

Once you have chosen two explanations, consider using the following points in your answer to make your comparisons and contrasts:
- *nature vs nurture*
- *reductionism vs holism*
- *usefulness of the explanation in relation to diagnosis and treatment*
- *the weight of evidence in support of the explanation*
- *free will vs determinism*
- *the scientific nature of psychology.*

11 Two examples of bias in the diagnosis of schizophrenia will be culture bias and gender bias.
For your discussion, here are some points to think about:
- *What is ethnocentrism?*
- *How does culture/gender bias affect validity and the evidence?*
- *How does gender/culture bias affect reliability and the evidence?*
- *How has the diagnostic manual responded to the allegations of bias?*
- *Why it is important to recognise cultural differences in the way people express emotions and symptoms?*
- *What is the argument that in males and females these could actually be different conditions?*

12 (a) The picture is mixed for the relief of positive symptoms, with three studies finding that it helped and two that it did not. For the negative symptoms it was more effective and it was similar to CBT in effectiveness for depression.

(b) From the graph only two studies found it to be effective for the negative symptoms, so it would not be a convincing treatment from these results. Four studies did not find a positive effect.

(c) Overall from these results, CBT is effective in treating schizophrenia because all six studies found some improvement in the symptoms, and as these were randomised controlled studies, they have good credibility because they will be free from bias. They were also done in the community and so would have good validity because the patients were carrying on with their lives.

211. Food preferences: evolutionary explanations

It was adaptive for humans to learn which foods would be a threat to their survival, hence the need for taste-aversion learning. This innate mechanism meant that humans who learned which foods were safe to eat were the most likely to survive. Food sources that caused sickness were quickly eliminated as humans developed an aversion to them to avoid future illness. Avoidance of foods that were bitter or sour tasting also evolved as a way to detect poisons in plants.

212. Food preferences: learning experiences

The first role is social. Social learning theory (SLT) states that we learn eating behaviours from observing other people and copying them. For example, children acquire eating behaviours by observing their parents. Correlations between parents and their children in the type of food eaten, eating motivations and body dissatisfaction have been found. A mother's attitude to food will affect her child's preferences, as Harper and Sanders found. Parents use operant conditioning, giving rewards for eating disliked food, for example by offering the children ice cream if they eat their vegetables. Peers also play a role, as it was found that children expressed preference for foods they saw advertised when children similar to them were shown eating them. Culture also influences our preferences. For example, different cultures and times have different food preferences, based on learning. People have schemas of what is food and what is not, based on cultural norms. Some religions believe that eating certain foods is wrong and also observe feasting days and times of fasting as religious practices. These all influence what people eat, as they learn what they should or should not eat based on their cultural norms.

213. Neural and hormonal mechanisms

The neural and hormonal mechanisms in eating behaviour involve a main area of the brain, the hypothalamus. Both the lateral hypothalamus (LH) and the ventromedial hypothalamus (VMH) are implicated. The LH is thought to be the feeding centre, the area involved in initiating eating. The VMH is thought to be the satiety centre, which tells the person when they are full and need to stop eating. These two areas respond to a number of hormones that signal the appropriate part. For example, when the stomach is empty, the hormone ghrelin is released which stimulates the LH so the person knows they need to eat. Leptin is released from fat cells when the body has sufficient food. This stimulates the VMH and therefore eating should stop. The LH also responds to other signals such as levels of glucose in the blood; when low, this also stimulates the LH.

214. Anorexia nervosa

Biological explanations could be considered reductionist as they isolate a particular aspect of the brain or a gene and use that to explain the disorder. This can be problematic as, while focusing on only one thing, they could be ignoring other explanations. As the disorder is complex it would be erroneous to rule out a number of possible explanations. For example, the genetic explanation looks at genes and uses twin studies to highlight the genetic link to the disorder. However, although they show an increased risk of developing the condition if somebody else in the family has the disorder, even for identical twins the concordance rate is never 100%, indicating there is more to the disorder than just genetics. Similarly, with neural explanations it is almost impossible to assume that one particular area is faulty in people with anorexia, as the brain has multiple connections to a single area, as seen in the insula area of the brain. However, it is useful to consider reductionist explanations, such as biological reasons for anorexia, as by isolating one particular factor this could lead to an appropriate treatment. If a particular gene is discovered then gene mapping could provide future treatments, which are beneficial to both the patient and the NHS. It could help treat the person more appropriately and save money for the NHS. Similarly, identifying a specific area of the brain could lead to understanding the role a particular area plays in eating, such as the lateral hypothalamus, which may lead to the development of treatment programmes. This saves time and money.

215. Anorexia: family systems theory

Enmeshed families occur where parents are over-involved in their daughters' and family's lives. They are affectionate but also overprotective, not allowing autonomous relationships within the family.

216. Anorexia: social learning theory

1   The disorder affects more females than males, and therefore a focus on females would be justified as the research attempts to explain the incidence. By studying mainly females, research may help doctors understand the risk factors for females. Only around 15% of people with the disorder are males. Researching males may therefore detract from explanations of the majority of sufferers.

2   The social learning theory (SLT) explanations can be criticised as being environmentally deterministic because they suggest that the environment shapes and influences behaviour. It says that someone who is exposed to role models, such as those seen in the media, will develop the disorder in an attempt to look like the models. It proposes that a female may see someone else diet and imitate that behaviour to extreme lengths in order to look like they do. This dismisses the free will of a person who can choose to ignore those external influences. A large majority of females do ignore such influences, as only a small percentage of the population develop anorexia.

217. Anorexia: cognitive theory

One strength of the theory is that the treatment used – cognitive behavioural therapy (CBT) – has a good rate of success in treating the disorder, as it helps people with anorexia to challenge their irrational thoughts. However, a weakness is distorted thinking or irrational beliefs have not been shown to cause anorexia. They may develop as a result of the disorder.

218. Obesity

Using animals to explain obesity has its problems as it is difficult to extrapolate animal behaviour to humans. Although animals share similar physiology to humans, they do not possess the higher level ordered thinking that humans do, such as cognitions, that should tell humans that they have eaten too much or that they must know their weight is causing them health problems. Therefore we must treat such evidence with caution.

219. Obesity: psychological explanations

Research into obesity could be considered socially sensitive because it could have a negative impact on the group of people who participated in the study and the groups they represent. For example, a majority of participants are females and this could have a detrimental effect on the public image of women who have weight problems. Showing disinhibited eating, for example, may be seen as a sign that they have little control over their food intake (or gluttony) and this could be seen as a negative.

220. Success and failure of dieting

A group-based social and practical support group would be a good strategy to use, for example, joining a weight-loss group meeting such as Weight Watchers. These types of programmes have been shown to be more successful than individual regimes as they encourage small, sustained weight loss per week, which is realistic to achieve. Dieters can become demotivated when they attempt to restrict their eating too much. The diet plans are varied and healthy so that dieting is seen as a positive thing. A dieter can continue to attend the support group even after achieving their target weight as this offers further reinforcement through reward (praise) that would ensure the weight loss is maintained.

223. Exam-style practice 1

1   The boundary model by Herman and Polivy (1984) suggests that we have a biological and cognitive limit for food intake so that we eat when we are hungry and stop eating when we are full. Obesity occurs when there is a mismatch between the limits of these two factors. People who are obese and may be trying to diet put a psychological/cognitive boundary on their food intake. However, if they go over this boundary through overeating, they develop a 'what the hell' effect and continue to eat, as they feel that they have ruined their diet for that day. This then increases the likelihood of becoming or staying obese. This can lead to disinhibited eating – overeating – because the individual shows little or no restraint. It often occurs when the individual is suffering from anxiety and distress, which could in itself be a result of their weight problems. Research has shown that anxiety is linked to disinhibited eating and a high body mass index (BMI). Food can be used as a comfort, and so more overeating occurs.
Research has shown that restrained eaters often overeat, which then leads to obesity; attempting not to eat actually increases the probability of overeating. Research has shown that dieters eat more than non-dieters. Restrained eaters try to reduce their food intake, but 80% of people who restrain their eating actually put on weight, which could lead to obesity. Because the level of restraint is idealistic but often not realistic, it leads to eating more. Therefore, obesity occurs through a self-imposed restricted food intake that fails, and the individual shows disinhibited eating.

2   Support for this theory comes from Herman and Mack (1975) who tested the role of disinhibition and overeating. They used 45 female students, in an independent groups design, who were put into one of three conditions. It was found the participants who were considered to be dieting ate more after a high-calorie 'pre-load' than did the participants who were not dieters. This showed what Herman and Mack termed the 'what the hell' effect. The restraint people felt they had gone over their cognitive boundary and showed disinhibited eating. This means that although disinhibition may explain obesity, a number of research findings, such as those of Herman and Mack, still fail to fully explain the reasons for disinhibition. Some people clearly

show restraint and do not develop obesity or disinhibited eating when trying to diet. This is a problem because it is a limited explanation. The idea of disinhibition has implications for obesity treatment as restraint is often recommended as a solution to excessive weight problems. However, if people with obesity try to diet and fail, this can leave them feeling depressed and lead them to display disinhibited eating. There could be a variety of reasons why people with obesity eat in this way, such as stress and emotional factors through to learned behaviours. Disinhibition proposes an association between food restriction and overeating, but it is only an association. It is also determinist as it suggests that if a dieter tries to restrain their eating, they will show disinhibited behaviour leading to obesity. This ignores the role of free will, which would suggest that we can override these desires to overeat.

Many psychologists also argue that it is very difficult to separate out the influences of nature and nurture when trying to explain obesity. For example, the biological boundary takes the nature side that is innate, but this has been combined with a cognitive factor that may be influenced by nurture and the environment. It is positive that the model is taking a multi-dimensional approach rather than the over-simplified approach of many other explanations.

3 Evolutionary explanations of food preferences are based on the environment of evolutionary adaptation and the need for a diet that ensured our survival. In an environment that was harsh in terms of food sources, it made sense for our ancestors to develop a preference for high-energy foods and reject poisonous ones or bitter-tasting foods that could be a sign that the food is 'off'. This gave them a selective advantage over those who did not reproduce these traits and preferences. Food preferences would be passed on through generations. As an adaptive trait, neophobia – in this case a fear of new foods – would have aided survival for our ancestors. This taste aversion is an adaptation to avoid possible toxic foods and therefore ensure we do not eat things that could make us sick. The evolutionary approach assumes that preferences have evolved, along with our environment, as social and cultural influences have altered the availability of food in contemporary advanced cultures.

4 The first role is social. Social learning theory (SLT) states that we learn eating behaviours from observing other people and copying them. For example, children acquire eating behaviour by observing their parents. Correlations between parents and children in terms of the type of food eaten, eating motivations and body dissatisfaction have been found. A mother's attitude to food will affect their child's preferences as Ogden (2003) found a significant correlation between the diet of the mum and child. Parents use operant conditioning, giving rewards for eating disliked food, for example, giving the child an ice cream if they eat their vegetables. Peers also play a role, as it was found that children expressed a preference for foods they saw advertised when children similar to them were shown eating them. Culture also influences our preferences.

For example, different cultures and times have different food preferences, based on learning. People have schemas of what is and is not food, based on cultural norms. Some religions believe that eating certain foods is wrong and also have feasting days and times of fasting in observation of religious practices. These all influence what people eat, as they learn what they should or should not eat based on their cultural norms.

5 Correlations cannot establish cause and effect, only a relationship. Therefore, in eating behaviour, biological explanations only show that there is a link between genetics and the onset of obesity. However, the fact that most families adopt similar eating patterns as they share the same environment means that this could be a third variable contributing to their obesity.

6 Molly needs to look at how many calories she is trying to stick to. Showing too much restraint has been shown to lead to risk of obesity through disinhibited eating (Ogden 2009). Molly has to use a more sensible eating plan. She has to identify risks factors for overeating that could lead to the 'what the hell' effect. If someone is showing restraint in eating they put a cognitive boundary on their food intake, which is less than the body's natural biological one (Herman and Mack, 1975). If they go over this boundary, they show disinhibited eating because they think they have ruined their diet. Although Molly is not dieting, she is trying to restrain her eating, which results in her showing disinhibited eating and may end up with her actually putting weight on.

224. Exam-style practice 2

7 Anorexia can be explained in terms of social learning theory. This suggests that anorexia develops as a result of observation of role models, such as parents or peers. For example, if they see their mother or friends (role models) dieting, they could remember it and reproduce the behaviour at a later stage because of the motivation to be slim. As the dieting behaviour develops, reinforcement occurs as the dieter is rewarded through compliments about the weight loss. This can encourage the individual to continue with the weight loss, and the initial dieting behaviour could then develop into anorexia. The media can also be influential, as females in particular see role models in magazines and in the media. The models tend to be extremely thin and girls can observe this and again be motivated to imitate this by dieting.

8 The cognitive explanation for anorexia suggests that it is the role of faulty or irrational thinking schemas that distort people's perceptions and interpretations of experiences that cause them to misperceive their own body size. The rigid thinking patterns and negative self-beliefs are transferred into extreme dieting behaviour, resulting in their self-worth being dependent on the maladaptive thoughts. These cognitive distortions about the way they think they look – rather than how they actually look – causes them to become extremely underweight as they still perceive themselves as fat.

9 (a) The psychologist could carry out a questionnaire to see if people with anorexia nervosa also have OCD

symptoms. Using a closed questionnaire with ratings, she could use a correlational analysis on the results.

(b) She would need to carry out a statistical test, Spearman's, to find out if her results are significant.

(c) This test is appropriate because it is a test for correlations using ordinal data (ranked data from the scores on the questionnaire).

(d) As the results are correlational, we cannot establish cause and effect; we cannot say that being anorexic causes OCD or that having OCD causes anorexia, only that the two co-occur frequently.

10 Genetic explanations of eating disorders show that anorexia can appear across generations in the same family. Holland et al. (1988) found that concordance rates for anorexia nervosa were significantly higher for monozygotic (MZ) twins than for dizygotic (DZ) twins (56% and 5%) with many reviews concluding that the genetic contribution is between 50% and 80%. This could conclude that genetics play a role in anorexia. However, the role of nurture cannot be discounted, as families share similar environments and so the behaviour could be learned. Also, as anorexia is not a common disorder, the studies are based on very few numbers of participants, which can result in a lack of reliability. Additionally, the studies assume that environmental influences are the same for both types of twin and that the only difference is in their genetics. However, it is possible that MZ twins are treated more similarly than DZ twins while growing up (for instance they are always the same sex, they look the same and are often dressed the same and confused with each other). This extra similarity may result in them being treated more similarly than DZ twins, which may contribute to the higher concordance rates. In addition, most of the research has focused on populations in Europe and America and therefore lacks population validity, as we cannot be sure that the same results would be found in non-Western cultures such as Africa and Asia. We also do not know what genetic component is being inherited, as no single gene has been identified as an anorexic gene, so it is not clear what exactly is inherited. For example, the behaviour of starvation is accompanied by body image dissatisfaction, and it would be difficult to propose that this aspect was inherited. Genes cannot be the only factor in the disorder as the concordance rates in MZ twins, while higher than in DZ twins, are never 100%. If genes were the only factor, we would see 100% concordance in MZ twins and 50% in DZ, but no study has found this. This suggests that it is too simplistic to say it is only a genetic condition. It could suggest a genetic predisposition that influences the risk factor of developing the disorder, but other things such as environmental triggers also need to be present. Connan et al. (2003) suggested an integrated model of both biological and psychological factors. It is therefore due to both nature and nurture.

11 Strengths of the family systems theory are that they have helped to develop an effective treatment in the form of family therapy. This therapy has been shown to be very

effective in helping to prevent relapse of the disorder as it encourages the whole family to alter their behaviour. The limitation of this theory is that the supporting research often uses self-report. This means the responses could be open to unreliable or socially desirable responses, which could reduce the validity of the findings.

12 A female bias is seen in these theories so they are beta biased as they ignore the differences between the genders and only focus on female behaviour to explain anorexia nervosa.

225. General adaptation syndrome

1 The first stage of GAS is 'alarm reaction' where the sympathetic nervous system responds with the fight-or-flight response to deal with the stressor, so the heart rate will increase along with blood pressure, while digestion will decrease. If the stress continues the body enters the 'resistance' phase, where the parasympathetic nervous system counteracts the effects of fight or flight, and cortisol production begins to increase. If stress still continues, then the body enters a phase of 'exhaustion' where it struggles to maintain normal functioning, and energy levels will be low. During this stage, the body is prone to illness because the immune system will be suppressed.

2 Selye (1936) developed the general adaptation syndrome (GAS) hypothesis following research using rats. Although there is some evidence of similar reactions in humans, there is a problem in extrapolating from rats to humans. Human stressors may be far more complex than the injections and procedures the rats were subjected to, so the two are not comparable. GAS is also a limited response to stress as it only focuses on the physiological effects and does not take into account the psychological effects. For example, many people find they have mood changes, they struggle to concentrate and they begin to lose motivation during periods of significant stress, which cannot easily be explained by GAS.

226. Sympathomedullary pathway

The sympathetic nervous system (SNS) is responsible for creating physiological arousal in response to acute stress. The name for the overall response is the fight-or-flight response. The SNS responds to an increase in adrenaline in the bloodstream. When activated, the body responds with an increase in heart rate, increased blood pressure, increased respiration, decreased digestive activity and pupil dilation, among other things. This physical response is a survival instinct that prepares the body to fight the stressor or run away from it.

227. Hypothalamic-pituitary-adrenal system

Cortisol is produced in response to chronic or long-term stress. It helps the body to convert glucose into energy, and therefore helps to maintain energy levels while the person deals with the stress they face. If cortisol levels in the blood remain high for a long period, they can reduce the function of the immune system, disrupt sleep patterns, impair cognitive functioning and increase blood pressure.

228. Immunosuppression

1 Kiecolt-Glaser (1984) studied medical students sitting exams. She showed that, in the blood sample taken when the exams started, the level of T-cells was lower, suggesting that immune functions were not as efficient. She also found the level of T-cells was negatively correlated with symptoms of stress reported in the questionnaires. This suggests that as levels of stress increase, the amount of T-cells active in the blood may decrease, reducing the effectiveness of the immune system. Cohen et al. (1993) also found that people who were stressed were more likely to develop symptoms of the cold virus after being deliberately infected with it, compared to people who did not report high levels of stress. This would suggest that the immune system is compromised by high levels of stress.

2 One criticism is that the relationship between stress and the functioning of the immune system is correlational. This means that we cannot establish that the stress is the cause of the immunosuppression. For example, during times of stress people may adopt many unhealthy lifestyle choices such as poor diet and increased alcohol intake. These other factors could be causing the immunosuppression rather than the stress itself.

229. Cardiovascular disorders

Many studies have linked stress to heart problems such as cardiovascular disease (CVD) and coronary heart disease (CHD). Evidence from Orth-Gomér et al. (2000) suggested that marital stress was related to poorer outcomes for women who had been diagnosed with CHD. This might tell us that stress at home increases pressure on the heart, which is why the women were more likely to have long-term negative effects after diagnosis. Melamed et al. (2006) found that people diagnosed with 'burnout', an extreme form of long-term work-related stress causing exhaustion and affecting their ability to cope with day-to-day demands, were highly likely to show physical signs associated with increased risks of cardiovascular disease, suggesting that burnout may well be associated with CVD.

230. Life changes and daily hassles

A daily hassle is a relatively minor stressor that occurs frequently, such as losing your keys or struggling to find a parking space at work, while a life change is a serious event that disrupts a person's life in a big way but only happens a few times in a lifetime, such as losing your job, or a bereavement of a close family member. While life changes cause a significant disruption – and therefore stress – on their own, daily hassles cause stress cumulatively by building up together over the course of every day/week/month.

231. Workplace stress

One factor in the workplace known to increase stress levels is workload. This refers to the amount of work people need to complete and the timeframe within which it is expected. The more a person is expected to do, and the shorter the time frame, the greater the workload. If someone is given a lot of work to do in a short space of time, this will increase their stress levels. For example, Krantz et al. (2005) found that females reported higher levels of overall stress than males. The main factor that seemed to explain this was that the females in the study reported a higher overall workload when both paid work and home work demands were taken into account. This suggests that overall work demands increase stress levels, and it is a combination of both paid and unpaid work that is important.

232. Self-report scales

Using self-report data may lack reliability as the information given by people about their own stress could be biased. For example, people may differ in their perceptions of stress – what one person perceives as very stressful, another person may see as a minor irritation. When reporting on stress, they may be relying on retrospective data, describing stress that has happened previously. This may be recalled inaccurately, or perceived differently depending on the person's current mood and situation. For example, someone who is currently under a great deal of stress is likely to recall lots of previous stressors, while someone who is currently very relaxed may struggle to recall the last time they felt stressed.

233. Physiological measures of stress

One application of the use of skin conductance response is in neonatal care. Preterm infants may spend much of their time asleep after birth, but while hospitalised they may require a significant number of medical and/or surgical procedures. Because they are often so visibly unresponsive (for example, they may not cry or try to move away when in pain), the use of skin conductance response is a useful way for medical staff and parents to judge any stress the infant may be feeling. This could help to identify pain or discomfort the baby feels, which may not be obvious, leading to better care.

234. Types A, B and C personality

Type A personalities have traits that make them highly strung and prone to the negative effects of stress, such as competitiveness and hostility when faced with a stressor. Type B personalities are more relaxed and self-confident, which means that they often do not respond negatively to stressors. Finally, Type C personalities are introverted and careful, and may bottle up their emotions when under stress. This personality type has been linked to higher rates of cancer and depression as a result of stress.

235. Hardiness

Most of the research into hardiness and stress has found a correlation between this type of personality trait and a healthier response to stress. However, the concept of hardiness has been criticised because it is unclear exactly what this type of personality is. The description of hardiness merely relates to three thinking styles adopted by certain people when faced with stressors. We are unsure whether this actually constitutes a personality type, or whether it is simply a positive way of thinking about stress that prevents people from being negatively affected by the stress they face.

236. Drug therapy

By giving drugs to treat stress the symptoms may be controlled – for example, the blood pressure may decrease – but the actual cause of the stress will not be dealt with. Because drug treatment is seen a short-term solution to stress, it may not offer a long-term solution for those struggling with stress. Drugs are not suitable for long-term treatment as many have side effects that can be quite unpleasant. Beta-blockers can cause hallucinations and fatigue, while benzodiazepines can cause memory problems and issues with concentration. Benzodiazepines can also be highly addictive so doctors would be reluctant to allow patients to take them for long.

237. Stress inoculation training

The first stage in stress inoculation training (SIT) is to discuss and understand the cause of the stress for the individual. This phase is called 'conceptualisation'. During this stage patients are also encouraged to discuss how they usually deal with these stressors and their thoughts related to the stressful situations. During the next phase, 'skills acquisition and rehearsal', the patient is shown alternative coping strategies and given time to rehearse these with the therapist. They may be taught relaxation techniques and thinking skills to change the way the stress affects them. The final stage, 'application and follow-through', gives the patient an opportunity to try the skills out in role plays until they feel competent in being able to use them in real situations. They will then be encouraged to use these in real situations and report back on their success.

238. Biofeedback

Evidence from Lemaire et al. (2011) found that doctors' stress levels decreased after training using biofeedback, suggesting it is effective in the real world. However, little is understood about how or why biofeedback actually works to reduce stress, and some have argued that it could be a positive effect of the relaxation techniques taught rather than the biofeedback itself. It is a less invasive treatment without the negative effects associated with drugs so is more suitable for a larger group of people. Because of the specialist equipment and training time involved in using biofeedback, it is a very costly form of treatment, much more so than prescribing medication, for example.

239. Gender differences

There are social differences in the reactions of men and women when they are stressed. For example, females may be more likely to reach out to talk to close friends and discuss how they are feeling, while males may be more likely to avoid spending time with friends as they do not feel as comfortable discussing their stress with others. Females may also be more likely to seek out emotion-focused strategies to cope with stress, such as distractions to make themselves feel

better, while males may seek out a more problem-focused approach by trying to tackle the source of stress.

240. Social support

One type of social support is emotional support; another is instrumental support. Emotional support means that someone is providing the stressed individual with an opportunity to discuss how they feel, or helping them to cope with the emotions associated with the stress, such as by comforting them to make them feel better. Instrumental social support, on the other hand, means that someone is doing something to actually help deal with the source of the stress. These two types of social support differ because emotional support may make them feel better in the short term, but is not actually helping change the situation, while instrumental support is helping to do something practical which could, at least partially, solve the problems causing the stress.

243. Exam-style practice 1

1 (a) Kobasa (1979) suggested that control was an important feature of hardiness as she believed this was about people feeling able to change (and control) their own situation. She suggested that those with a hardy personality strongly believed they can actively influence the outcome of a stressful situation, rather than allowing themselves to be passive 'victims' of stress.

   (b) Workload refers to the amount of work a person has to do (or feels they have to do). This can be both 'overload', that is feeling that they have too many things to do, as well as 'underload', where they feel that they don't have enough to do, or the tasks they are doing are too easy and don't use their skills.

   (c) Skin conductance response refers to the ease by which the skin can conduct electricity. For example, when we are stressed we produce slightly more sweat, and the sweat on our skin allows electricity to be conducted more easily. This can be measured by a galvanic skin response monitor that will then report back how stressed a person is at that time, by measuring the speed it takes for an electrical message to be passed along the skin.

2 Evidence suggests that people who have a high workload are more likely to suffer negative effects of stress. For example, Krantz et al. (2005) found that females who had high workload demands – at work as well as at home – were most likely to suffer from the negative effects of stress. This would suggest that the overall workload, in the workplace and at home, combines to create the negative effects of stress. Other research has also found that a lack of control over the pace and type of work completed causes stress at work. For example, Marmot et al. (1997) found that those with low job control were four times more likely to suffer heart attacks and also had a much higher chance of developing other stress-related illnesses, such as cancer and digestive problems.

3 Rahe (1972) studied the effects of life changes on a group of US sailors while they were

away at sea. He surveyed 2664 male sailors using the Social Readjustment Rating Scale (SRRS) to measure the number of life events they had faced in the previous 6 months. They then had their health monitored regularly while they were away at sea for 6–8 months. He found a significant positive correlation (+0.118) between the number of life events experienced and the number of illnesses reported while at sea. This would suggest that life events may influence stress levels, which in turn can impact on health. One problem with this study is that the SRRS was used to gather information on life events, and participants may not give an accurate account of the number of life events they have faced. They may forget things that have happened, or they may not see an event as a 'big deal' and not include it, meaning that the data may not be valid. There may also be issue with reliability as each participant's experience of a 'life event' may be different. One person who got married may have found it very stressful, while someone else who got married may have really enjoyed the whole experience. This means the comparisons between participants may not be reliable. It is also difficult to infer cause and effect from this data. Although more life events were related to more health problems, it is not clear whether the stress of the events is what made them ill. There could be many other variables that were not measured that may have influenced their health, such as their diet and how much exercise they do.

4 One limitation of research into the link between stress and cardiovascular disease is that much of the research is correlational and therefore we are unable to infer cause and effect from the data. For example, Marmot et al. (1997) found that stress caused by a lack of control in the workplace was associated with a significantly higher incidence of heart attacks in staff. While this would suggest that the stress caused the high risk of heart attack, other variables such as alcohol use, diet and exercise levels could all be the causal variable rather than simply the stress levels themselves.

5 One method of stress management is the use of drug therapy. Drugs such as benzodiazepines (BZs) and beta-blockers (BBs) can be given to patients as ways to reduce the negative effects of stress. BZs help to enhance the effect of GABA in the brain, as well as reducing the excitatory effects of serotonin. In combination, these two effects make the person feel very calm and prevent them from being aroused by stressful events. While BZs work in the brain, BBs act in the body by sitting in beta-adrenergic receptors to prevent them from being stimulated by adrenaline and noradrenaline when the person becomes stressed. By doing this, they can prevent the effects of adrenaline and noradrenaline under stress, such as increased heart rate and blood pressure.

Evidence has suggested that long-term use of BZs can be problematic as patients can become dependent on them. Zandstra et al. (2004) found that those most at risk from long-term use (and increased risk of dependence) could be identified by doctors as they are often older, lack social contact and are more poorly educated. This means that doctors could closely monitor patients falling into these categories to check for signs of dependence. BZs can also cause some serious side effects for patients, such as memory problems and issues with concentration, which may affect the patient's quality of life. While BBs provide a safer drug treatment for the effects of stress in the short term (as they do not have the same problems of developing dependence as BZs), BBs do not provide long-term treatments for stress and its effects. The use of BBs is also not recommended for some people as their use can slow down the heart rate and lower blood pressure if the dosage is not quite right, and for some patients this may be dangerous. *From here you should continue the answer by describing and evaluating a second (and possibly a third if you have time) method of treating stress. You could go on to describe the three stages of stress inoculation training, and then evaluate its usefulness. It would also be good to draw some comparisons between using stress inoculation training (SIT) rather than drug therapy to treat stress. For example, SIT might provide a better long-term solution to stress than drugs can offer. Providing some research evidence for the effectiveness of SIT would also be useful for evaluation of that treatment option. If you have time, you could also bring in the use of biofeedback methods to treat stress, but remember you would only have 20 minutes in which to complete the whole answer.*

244. Exam-style practice 2

6 Emotional support means to provide somebody with warmth, comfort or empathy to make them feel better about the situation they are stressed about. An example of this type of social support would be someone giving you a hug and telling you they are 'there for you' when you need them.

7 Both groups of participants began with very similar stress scores in general (63 and 65 out of 100, 6 weeks before the exam). However, after 6 weeks of biofeedback the experimental group only had an average rise of 6 points on the stress questionnaire, while the control group, without biofeedback, saw an increase of 19 points on the questionnaire. This would suggest that those trained in using biofeedback may be better able to control their stress levels, and although the day of the exam did make them a bit more stressed than before, this was not by very much. Biofeedback is a way of learning to recognise the physiological signs of stress, and then using techniques to control these and change the body's response to stress. This may explain why the biofeedback group did not show much increase in stress levels – they had learned how to control their response to stress, which helped to keep their stress levels lower than the group who had not had the training.

8 (a) Exhaustion refers to the final stage of general adaptation syndrome (GAS) where the stressor is still present after some time, meaning the stress is now chronic. At this point, the body becomes tired as it cannot continue to respond to the stress with high levels of arousal, and you will become physically affected. For example, the immune system will not function properly, making you vulnerable to illness.

(b) Selye (1934) first discovered GAS through his research with rats, where they were made to endure repeated stressful procedures such as surgical cuts and prolonged loud noises. This research deliberately caused suffering to the rats, which many would argue is inhumane. These aversive procedures were deliberately unpleasant in order to cause stress, and as such they may be considered unethical.

245. Neural and hormonal mechanisms

Wagner et al. (1979) castrated male mice under laboratory conditions to look at the impact. After castration, the mice showed decreased levels of aggression, suggesting it was the lower levels of testosterone that influenced the behaviour. The mice were later injected with testosterone and their levels of aggression increased once more. This study showed the relationship between testosterone and aggression.

246. Genetic factors

Genetic explanations support the idea of psychology as a science. The evidence used in research is scientifically driven with the use of laboratory experiments, controlled conditions or genetic testing that can all be validated. The explanations all take the nature side of the nature–nurture debate, focusing on the innate biological make-up of individuals. However, the research appears to suggest the role of both nature and nurture. One piece of research evidence to support the role of the MAOA gene by Caspi et al. (2002) suggested that aggressive individuals displayed different kinds of aggression dependent on their environment. Males with low-activity MAOA genes are more at risk of committing a violent crime if they had suffered abuse as a child, showing an interaction of nature and nurture. This suggests that males with the low-activity gene are not biologically determined to act aggressively, but are more likely to if something triggers it environmentally. However, Brunner et al. (1993) studied a Dutch family, five male members of which possessed a shortened version of the MAOA gene. They consequently had abnormally low levels of the MAOA enzyme and were not able to break down all the neurotransmitters. The men had behavioural problems such as aggression, showed borderline mental retardation, and some had been in prison for attempted rape and assault. This study shows how the MAOA gene affects aggression, although it is difficult to separate the role of nurture, as they were all from the same family and environmental influences could have affected the men. In support of a partial role of genetics, Rhee and Waldman (2002) did suggest that nature by itself (e.g. genes) was not a good enough explanation and that nurture (environment) had also to be acknowledged. In their twin and adoption studies, they found that the genetic component of anti-social/aggressive behaviour was 40% and the environmental contribution was 60%. Further support for genetics comes from a study by Price et al. (1966). They looked at males in hospitals for the criminally insane, finding cases

of an abnormality in some of the males' chromosomes. They discovered that 28% of the patients had the extra Y chromosome compared with under 0.1% of the general population. This suggests that this extra chromosome correlates with aggressive behaviour, thus supporting the role of genetics in aggression. However, this research had a limited sample as the men were already deemed to be 'criminally insane' and may not be representative of the general population. In the general population, finding such a high number of males with the XYY chromosome would be small. Evidence to support theories for aggressive behaviour tends to suggest there is more than one cause of aggression. It is reductionist to accept that aggression is due to a single biological gene, and a number of factors have to be considered.

247. Ethology

1 The innate releasing mechanism (IRM) is a drive, such as aggression, that acts as a release in response to a stimulus. Cues in the environment trigger the aggression, and once the aggression has been spent, the drive builds up again until a stimulus triggers it once more and the aggression is displayed again. This behaviour is instinctual and inherited. For example, cats when confronted with a dog (stimulus) release aggression through an IRM.

2 A fixed action pattern (FAP) is a sequence of behaviours that is the same for all animals in that species. This behaviour results from the innate releasing mechanism. As such, FAPs are inherited and adaptive. Aggression can be seen in a number of ways that are seen as fixed actions, such as the male stickleback fish, which protects the nesting female from other predatory males by attacking the males.

248. Evolutionary explanations

The threat of infidelity triggers aggression to different degrees in both men and women. Males have the evolutionary problem of cuckoldry, never being sure of the paternity of any offspring. Therefore, evolutionary theory suggests that the human emotion of jealousy has evolved to help prevent this. By using tactics to deter their partner from being unfaithful, men use aggression as a threat against other males – or even the females – to prevent them from cheating. Winning any such threat to them also makes the males more attractive to the females, as they will be seen as being strong enough to protect them and their offspring. Women use mate-guarding to warn off other females, such as putting more effort into their appearance and even verbal, but not physical, threats of violence; in men it can often be both. According to evolutionary theory, these behaviours make sense so that men do not invest in offspring that are not theirs, and females get to keep their mate so he can continue to invest resources in her and their offspring. These aggressive behaviours are adaptive as they ensure the survival of males' particular genes.

249. Deindividuation and frustration

Deindividuation can lead to behaviours that are usually inhibited by personal or social norms, such as aggression. Two factors present are the loss of public self-awareness, where an individual loses the sense that that they are identifiable to others, and also loss of private self-awareness, where the individual loses awareness of themselves. This can occur as a result of being in a large crowd, where anonymity is increased, and also if they are in a state of altered consciousness, for example, drunk. Being in a large crowd has a psychological consequence of reducing self-awareness because of the anonymity, and therefore the person feels less responsible for their actions. Individuals are more likely to show aggression as they become part of the group and lose their sense of having a separate identity. They therefore behave in a way that is not their normal way because they feel that responsibility for their behaviour has shifted from themselves to the group. This would explain aggression at football matches, for example, where (usually) young males do not feel personally responsible for their acts of aggression as they have lost their sense of self-identity. Their public self-awareness has also been lost.

250. Social learning theory

Aggression is learned through observing others (models) acting aggressively. People are more likely to imitate aggression if they see the model being rewarded for the behaviour (vicarious reinforcement). For example, if someone sees their peers successfully taking money from another using force, in future, if they feel they can do the same successfully and get money, they may repeat the action. They need to be able to identify with the role model – such as being of the same sex or status as the model. Learning can be retained for future replication in a similar situation, but only if the individual feels confident that they can do so. Bandura (1977) said these four processes had to be present for the behaviour to be imitated: attention, retention, reproduction and motivation. The observer needs to be self-confident in their ability to replicate the behaviour.

251. Institutional aggression

Situational factors can affect aggression in prison because of the loss of privileges prisoners must endure, such as freedom and privacy. This can build up into frustration and lead to aggression. Inmates who had no previous history of aggression could display outbursts or behaviour deemed to be aggressive. For example, Haney, Banks and Zimbardo (1973) showed in their Stanford Prison experiment that mentally sound men who went into a mock prison showed acts of aggression, although not physical. This ended up affecting the 'prisoners' in their study, whereby some had a form of breakdown because of their treatment. This shows a situational explanation could be applicable to aggression, as the guards had no known history of aggressive behaviour prior to the study. This was a laboratory experiment and could be criticised for lacking ecological validity as it was not a real prison, so in a real-life prison the men may not have acted in this way. However, the participants in the study did say they felt the conditions were real enough.

Better explanations come from the disposition of the prisoners. Irwin and Cressey (1962) said it was the characteristics that were imported into the prison that caused the aggression. They suggested that the prisoners' behavioural norms on the outside were brought into the prison environment and they continued with their usual behaviour, thus behaving aggressively once in prison. Research by Allender and Marcell (2003) found that members of gangs, once in prison, disproportionately engage in acts of prison violence. This shows support for the dispositional explanation of aggression. In further support, Fischer (2001) found that when gang members were isolated once sentenced, the rates of violence in prison reduced by 50%. The research in this area shows gender bias, however, as most of the participants are males. We do not know if the same explanations are valid for women, as they may behave aggressively for different reasons. The findings are also correlational, so we cannot know for sure why people display aggression in prison, only that there is a relationship between their previous aggression and subsequent behaviour in prison.

252. Media influences

The research used to support media effects are often laboratory-based experiments. This means they have high control and therefore should have valid results. For example, Josephson (1987) got boys to watch a film and then observed them playing hockey. However, because of the controlled conditions, the research often lacks ecological validity, as watching a film and then being observed playing hockey, for example, may not show aggression in real life. The boys knew they were taking part in an experiment and could have shown demand characteristics, so the results would lack validity.

Some studies used different kinds of media, for example, games and television, but they were not comparing like for like. Watching a film may be completely different from playing a computer game in terms of individuals becoming aggressive; it may depend on how realistic the form of media is to them. This can also affect the validity. Aggression is not operationalised as meaning the same thing in the studies, which is another flaw – there is no common definition or measurement of aggression. There have also been conflicting findings, as some research has found no influence of the media on aggression. For example, the Charlton (2000) St Helena study found that after the introduction of television on the island, no increase in aggressive behaviour. If research does show an influence of more aggressive behaviour, we do not know how long the effect lasts, as most research does not follow up on findings. However, Huesmann et al. (2003) did a longitudinal study and found after 15 years there was a correlation between viewing aggressive television programmes and later aggressive behaviour. As it is correlational, cause and effect cannot be established, as other influences in the environment could have impacted on their behaviour, such as an aggressive upbringing. Drabman and Thomas' (1974) research has some ethical

issues, as children were shown a violent film clip and timed to see how long it took them to help children who were fighting. Using children and showing them unsuitable media and testing their response to an aggressive situation is a concern as it could cause them potential psychological harm. Again, in real life, we are not sure if the children would behave in the same way and show desensitisation. The theory of media influences is environmentally determinist as it states that individuals become aggressive due to what they watch on television, in films or on the computer games they play. It disregards their home or other situational environment, such as prison. These factors could also influence people's aggression, as everyone is different and can respond to things in various ways.

255. Exam-style practice 1

1 The importation model states that aggression occurs in prisons because of the dispositional personality traits and social histories of the inmates, which they bring into prison with them. Many normative systems developed on the outside are imported into the prison system, leading to aggression. For example, some may have come from sub-cultures where violence is seen as a way of earning respect, and this would influence their behaviour while in prison. Pre-prison gang members may also join gangs while imprisoned, which results in increased violence due to ongoing gang disputes. Research has found that pre-prison gang members are ten times more likely to commit assaults in prisons compared to non-gang members.

2 The deprivation model explains institutional aggression as a result of the environmentally oppressive conditions inside. Inmates develop aggression in response to their surroundings. Boredom and a lack of privileges and privacy may cause prisoners to feel angry and result in aggression. Deprivation of seeing loved ones can also trigger an aggressive outburst. Aggression may also be seen as a means to gain resources such as cigarettes, or a result of a constant state of arousal, due to fear of the environment. This arousal easily leads to aggressive acts. Overcrowded prisons have higher rates of aggression, which suggests that it is the poor environment that influences the violence.

3 Testosterone, a predominantly male hormone, acts on areas of the brain that control aggression from puberty onwards. Reduced levels of an enzyme that processes testosterone, found in the amygdala, has been shown to affect aggression levels, resulting in an increase of testosterone and consequently a lack of an emotional response, which makes aggression more likely. As testosterone is produced in higher quantities in males than females, it could provide a good explanation for aggression in males. In contrast, serotonin is a neurotransmitter involved in mood and impulse control. It works in the frontal cortex to inhibit activity in the amygdala, and thus has a calming effect on mood. Reduced levels of serotonin are thought to be involved in aggressive behaviour, although research has also shown the opposite to be the case. Serotonin is found

equally in males and females, so could help to explain both male and female aggression.

4 The limbic system is one of the circuits in the brain that is involved with emotions, including aggression. It connects the spinal cord to the brain and controls a number of essential functions. It is made up of a number of components including the amygdala. The amygdala appears to process emotions and play a part in aggression. Removal of the amygdala reduces aggression in previously violent individuals, who then also show a loss of emotion. Damage or malfunctioning of the amygdala is associated with increased levels of testosterone leading to a rise in aggressive behaviour.

5 People may act in a disinhibited or uncharacteristic way if they get caught up in the moment of playing a game. Suler (2004) suggested three ways in which disinhibition occurs. Firstly, the gamer becomes **anonymous** and therefore they feel no responsibility for their actions. With the responsibility of the computer gamer removed, they played in a way that is uncharacteristic of them, for example, aggressively. Also, **solipsistic introjection** occurs. This is when the gamer takes on a character in a virtual game and acts as the character would, not as themselves. Lastly, **minimisation of authority** is seen. Most games lack any authority, so criminal behaviour in the virtual world is played out as it goes unchallenged.

6 Evolutionary explanations are difficult to test and therefore do not support psychology as a science. This is because the explanations are post-hoc, based on events that have already occurred potentially millions of years ago. Therefore, explanations for aggression are based on assumptions, not actual facts. Evolutionary theories are also based on comparing human behaviour to animal behaviour, suggesting it is an instinctive behaviour, which makes it determinist. When applying this to humans, it ignores the role of free will in whether or not to behave aggressively. It suggests males are innately driven to act aggressively to attract a partner, or to keep a mate – which may not be true today. Humans possess higher order thinking that animals do not; humans know that acts of aggression are wrong, so this could also influence their aggressive behaviour and override their instincts. The evolutionary explanations of male aggression seem to excuse the aggressive acts towards females as justified because of the risk of cuckoldry. Buss and Shackelford (1997) found that men used far more aggressive tactics than women to keep their partner if they feared infidelity. They used strategies such as threatening to beat up the other male, particularly if their partner was younger, and violent threats against her and the male. This supports the evolutionary theory as the younger partner would be more fertile and could put the man at risk of cuckoldry. This reduces aggression to a simple, basic response to threats of infidelity, and assumes that this is how all males would respond and that females may all cheat. Miller (1980) found that 55% of battered wives blamed their husbands' jealousy over suspected infidelity, even though it was often without

substance, for their assaults. This supports the evolutionary approach of aggression, as men used it as a measure to prevent the wife cheating. This weakens the explanation considerably as we know this is not the case. It may have been true for our ancestors but most people remain faithful and do not cheat. Also, male on female assaults vary culturally, suggesting it is not universal. Therefore, other explanations must be involved. A lot of the research explains male aggression while ignoring female aggression. Evolutionary explanations appear to struggle to explain female acts of aggression as easily as male aggression, which would appear to show that it is only men who are aggressive when that is simply not true. It could be said that it lacks temporal validity as, although female aggression was perhaps uncommon for our ancestors, it is more common today and this theory fails to explain this. Therefore, as an explanation, the evolutionary theories appear too simplistic to explain complex human behaviours seen today.

256. Exam-style practice 2

7 (a) Chi-squared is an appropriate test as the data was nominal (in categories) and it was looking for an association using an independent groups design.
   (b) The degrees of freedom needed is 1 as it is a 2×2 table. The formula is:
   (number of rows $- 1$) $\times$ (number of columns $- 1$)
   so $df = (2 - 1) \times (2 - 1) = 1 \times 1 = 1$
   (c) The results are significant because the observed value (48.66) has to be equal to or greater than the critical value of 3.84 using the 0.05 level of significance. Therefore the hypothesis is supported that there was an association between the number of aggressive acts and length of time spent in the cell.

8 Dollard et al. (1939) suggested that aggression was as a result of a person feeling frustrated. Frustration occurs when a person is prevented from reaching a goal. If the individual is close to achieving their goal, then aggression will be increased if they are thwarted in their attempt. If the aggression is successful they achieve catharsis, that is, their aggression is released. For example, a footballer fouling an opponent to stop him from scoring relieves the frustration of nearly conceding a goal. If, however, the aggression is unsuccessful and cannot alleviate the frustration, it leads to more aggression. For example, a driver frustrated in traffic shouts at other drivers, which makes no difference to the hold-up, and then hits the steering wheel in frustration.

9 Mann ('Baiting crowd', 1981) analysed 21 incidents of suicide (reported in American newspapers). He found that in 10 of the 21 cases where there was a crowd, baiting occurred whereby the crowd urged the potential suicide to jump. This more often occurred at night. Other factors were the distance of the crowd from the person jumping and the size of the crowd. Mann explained this as deindividuation. He suggested that key features, such as darkness and a large crowd, had caused the deindividuation. They had led to individuals becoming anonymous and so aggressive behaviour was more likely.

257. Defining crime

One major problem is the circumstance in which the crime is committed. It is hard to be able to objectively state that the perpetrator fully intended to commit the criminal act. For example, someone experiencing a psychotic episode may behave illegally but without intending to. Another problem is that an act that is criminal in one culture may not be in another. For example, in some cultures it is acceptable to have more than one spouse; in others, this is a criminal offence known as bigamy.

258. Offender profiling: top-down

Top-down profiling is a method of crime investigation where the investigator uses the crime scene to create a profile of the type of person that committed that crime. They use typologies and classify the likely perpetrator as being disorganised or organised. This then gives the police a broad idea of what kind of person they are looking for. For example, they might look at whether there was evidence of planning and the choice of victim to deduce the characteristics of the offender.

259. Offender profiling: bottom-up

Bottom-up profiling has been demonstrated to help catch serious offenders such as John Duffy, the Railway Rapist; the profile developed by Canter in 1986 was found to be very accurate and directly led to Duffy's identification. However, single case studies lack generalisability as this may be a unique case, or Canter might have got lucky – he was wrong about five characteristics he generated about Duffy. This method is also much more objective than top-down processing as it relies on data and statistical analyses rather than the subjective experiences and intuitions of a profiler. Furthermore, geographical profiling has more usefulness as it can be effectively used for less serious crimes such as burglary.

260. Historical explanation for crime

One of the earliest theories of criminal behaviour proposed that there was a criminal type of person based on their biological make-up. Lombroso (1870s) studied prison populations and found that they had physical features in common, such as large ears, jaws and foreheads. From this he suggested that such people were primitive versions of humans and as such were uncivilised, which resulted in their criminal behaviour. They were 'born criminals'. This theory was based on scientific measures and, at the time, was highly regarded. However, it has been criticised, as the study on which it was based lacked a control group, so whether the criminal features existed in non-criminals was not tested. Subsequent research by Goring (1913) in London with a control did not find a link between physical appearance and criminal behaviour. The theory is highly reductionist as it proposes a purely biological cause for complex behaviour. However, people with these features may be socially disadvantaged because they are generally unattractive, and social exclusion may have led them to crime rather than their biological make-up.

It is also very deterministic, suggesting that people with these characteristics are destined to become criminals, which allows them to surrender responsibility for their actions.

261. Genetic explanation

One limitation is the problem of removing the effect of environment in shaping behaviour. The children of criminals may become criminal because they learn from their parents rather than because they share their parents' genes.

262. Neural explanation

One neurological cause for criminal behaviour involves the limbic system, in particular the amygdala. This area is associated with emotional processing and will lead to feelings of guilt when harming another person. Criminals may have a smaller amygdala, or have reduced input to it, causing a lack of empathy towards their victims, and an increased chance that they will commit a crime.

263. Eysenck's theory of the criminal personality

According to Eysenck (1964), people who are very extravert and who are high on the neuroticism and psychoticism scales are more likely to be criminal because they are seeking sensation and might make risky decisions. If they are also high in neuroticism they are probably impulsive, so might be overreactive to situations and could become aggressive. This would be further exacerbated if they were high in psychoticism because they would feel no guilt for their actions; they are therefore more likely to commit crime.

264. Cognitive explanations for crime

Kohlberg's theory explains offending behaviour as a result of low levels of moral development. Children's cognitive ability affects their reasoning and this affects their moral judgements. Those who have not developed cognitively will be less able to distinguish between right and wrong, and so are more likely to commit crime. The way we think about rules and justice impacts on our willingness to engage in antisocial behaviour. For example, someone in the pre-conventional stage might focus on the reward they would gain and balance that against the likelihood of being caught. In contrast, someone in the conventional stage would think about the effect their behaviour would have on other people and society.

265. Cognitive distortions

Cognitive distortions affect how people process information about criminal or antisocial behaviour, making it more likely to happen. For example, they may have a hostile attribution bias, where they assume that the victim has a problem with them, and therefore react with violence towards them. This would explain acts of impulsive aggression towards others. Minimalisation is a bias that allows an offender to find excuses for what they did. They re-frame the crime in order to make out that it was not so bad or that the victim did not suffer or even benefitted from what happened. This

suggests that people commit crime because of a lack of guilt due to this kind of thought pattern.

266. Psychodynamic explanations

The superego is the part of personality concerned with moral behaviour. A weak superego, for example, might result in more immoral behaviour because it cannot control the id (the part of the personality that demands instant gratification). The person therefore acts on impulse and does what they want without feeling guilt. Alternatively, the superego might be strong. This results in a constant need for punishment, so the person engages in criminal acts in order to gain the punishment. Another way a strong superego affects behaviour is that it may be over-controlling and inhibits normal ways that the id can gain gratification. Eventually, this 'boils over', resulting in uncharacteristic and explosive anger and violence. Finally, a deviant superego developed by identifying with a parent who has deviant moral values will produce criminal behaviour, as they do not have the same standards of morality as other people, so will transgress.

267. Custodial sentencing

Some would argue that custodial sentences are ineffective in meeting any aim other than confinement, as criminals who are locked away cannot commit further crimes, although many of them still engage in criminal behaviour in prison through the abuse of drugs. Keeping someone in prison is expensive, costing around £40,000 per year, yet the rate of re-offending on release is high, suggesting that rehabilitation is not effective either. Another aim is to deter other potential offenders. However, figures show that the number of people in prison is very high and has risen dramatically over the last 20 years, suggesting that it does not effectively stop crime. Justice can be seen to be done, however, so that society and the victims of crime achieve retribution. But many would argue that prison simply encourages crime and acts as a training school for criminals.

268. Recidivism

The cost of recidivism in the UK has been estimated to be up to £13 billion a year. This includes the cost of keeping someone in prison, their loss of earnings and the cost of supporting families where the breadwinner is in prison. It also includes the economic impact of the crimes committed and the use of the criminal justice system to catch and convict reoffenders.

269. Behaviour modification and rehabilitation

Token economy programmes can be applied in prisons to manage the behaviour of inmates using the process of operant conditioning. Initially, a list of desired behaviour is drawn up and prisoner behaviour is monitored by prison staff. Whenever a desired behaviour is displayed, the prisoner receives a token. This is a secondary reinforcer for the desired behaviour. They can build up their tokens

and eventually exchange them for something they really want, such as extra visiting time, phone cards, cigarettes and access to television. Behaviour is also controlled by the removal of tokens when the inmate does something antisocial. In this way, the inmate's behaviour is shaped to be more law abiding.

270. Anger management

Anger management is a three-stage process. First, the offender undergoes cognitive preparation where they identify triggers for their anger by talking about it with a therapist. They then are trained in skills that allow them to change their response to the triggers and react differently, for example, by being assertive but not aggressive. Finally, they practise the skills in role-play settings where they feel safe to try out what they have learned.

273. Exam-style practice 1

1 People might under-report crime to the police because they do not think it is worth the trouble or serious enough, so the police have unreliable data on which to base their measure of crime.
   In victim surveys, the respondent might under-report crime because they have forgotten about being a victim of minor crimes.

2 The crime survey for England and Wales is a victim survey. An interviewer contacts participants and asks them individually about their experience of crime in the last year. The sample is large, consisting of over 30,000 adults and 3000 children aged 10–15. The survey changes over time, reflecting changes in criminal behaviour, for example, to include online offences such as identity theft. The figures are compiled and used by the authorities to track trends in crime and plan resourcing.

3 Restorative justice programmes aim to rehabilitate offenders by getting them to empathise with their victims through a face-to-face meeting or through a mediator. The victim has a chance to ask questions and to tell the offender how their criminal actions impacted on their life. This is usually done in a neutral setting. It can be in prison or somewhere else. A facilitator will be present. Anger management programmes are used to help violent criminals change their habitual response of anger by getting them to identify the triggers that make them angry. They are then taught skills to deal with future situations, such as relaxation and thought stopping. Finally, they engage in non-threatening role-play situations to practise these skills and gain feedback. In this way, the negative thoughts that lead to anger can be challenged and the behavioural responses that cause violence are changed.

4 One limitation of Kohlberg's theory is that it is androcentric. Gilligan (1977) pointed out that female morality develops in a different way from that of males, and so females do not achieve the same level as males do. This may be due to Kohlberg developing his theory from studies that only had male participants.

5 Amy's sister thinks that Amy has a personality that might lead her to criminal behaviour because it seems that she is an extravert. Her sister says that she has always

shown risky behaviour, which is consistent with the sensation seeking associated with extraversion. Furthermore, Amy has frequent mood swings and a bad temper, indicating that she might be highly neurotic and her apparent lack of empathy for those she hurts suggests that she may also have psychopathic tendencies. According to Eysenck, people who are extravert, neurotic and psychotic are more likely to become criminals.

274. Exam-style practice 2

6 There are several features associated with criminality. These include a large chin, asymmetrical face, a big sloping brow, big ears, extra digits and a third nipple.

7 This theory is outdated and based on limited and poorly conducted evidence. For example, Lombroso (1876) failed to test a control group in order to compare the known criminals to those who had not committed crime. Subsequent studies that did use a control (Goring, 1913) found no support for the theory. The theory is highly deterministic, suggesting that a person is a 'born criminal', and reductionist as it ignores other causal explanations for crime, such as low IQ, which is also associated with the features identified by Lombroso.

8 Twin studies are used. These consist of a comparison between twin pairs. Monozygotic (MZ) twins share 100% the same genes whereas dizygotic (DZ) twins share only 50% genes. Twins in both types of twin pair will share environmental influences, so any differences in the shared behaviour between the different types will be due to genes. Studies such as Raine (1993) compared the concordance rate for crime between the different types of twin and found higher concordance in the MZ twins.
Adoption studies measure the number of behaviours adopted children have in common with their biological parents (whom they do not live with) and their adoptive parents, with whom they share an environment.

9 The psychodynamic theory of criminal behaviour lacks validity because it is difficult to research its claims objectively: it claims that the superego is the root cause of criminality. As the superego is a hypothetical and unobservable concept, it cannot be proven scientifically, meaning that the theory has limited evidential support. However, Bowlby's (1944) 44 Thieves Study provided findings consistent with the claims of the psychodynamic theory. He found that boys who had a disrupted relationship with their primary caregiver in their early childhood, and so might have an underdeveloped superego, went on to show signs of affectionless psychopathy and were more likely to commit crimes.

10 Morgan's lawyer believes that Morgan has no free will regarding his criminal behaviour and that this could be because of either nature or nurture. On the nurture side of the debate, he could use differential association theory to explain why Morgan is destined to be a criminal – his family have a history of crime, so as Morgan grew up he learned the behaviour and motives of criminality from his family. He is likely to have witnessed them gaining positive reinforcement for their criminal behaviour and so would be likely to imitate their actions. The criminal way of

life became normal for him and so he would not see anything wrong with what he did. On the other hand, it could be due to nature rather than nurture. It is possible that Morgan was genetically predisposed to become a criminal as he would share the same genetic material as his parents and brother, all of whom are career criminals. Family studies such as Farrington (1996) found that 50% of the crimes recorded in a longitudinal study were committed by only 6% of the families in the sample, suggesting that in some families there is a strong tendency towards crime.
If the theories are combined, then there seems little chance that Morgan would not be a criminal, thus justifying his lawyer's comments.

275. What is addiction?

Abstinence from the addictive behaviour starts to produce physical, bodily effects. There is therefore a need rather than a want to engage in that behaviour. The physical symptoms can differ for different addictions. For example, someone with a dependency on gambling who has not gambled for a number of hours could show their physical dependency through tremors, increased heart rate and sweating. These physical signs are similar for addictions to physical substances. Someone with a dependency on a behaviour will feel they need to engage in the behaviour for their psychological well-being. They think they cannot cope without it, and have a mental and emotional compulsion to continue with the behaviour. Psychological dependence can occur without physical dependence. For example, a smoker who is unable to smoke for any length of time starts to think about cigarettes the longer the time lapse since their last cigarette. Psychologically they may start to feel anxiety or be irritable, which is evidence of a psychological dependence.

276. Risk factors

The family studies by Merikangas et al. (1998) suggested that first-degree relatives of addicts have a higher risk factor for addiction, thus highlighting a genetic influence on addictions. However, it is unknown what exactly is inherited – whether it is a single gene or a variant of a particular gene. A variation of the DRD2 (a dopamine receptor gene) has been found to be more common in people who have addictions to alcohol, nicotine and cocaine, compared to non-addicts, suggesting that this gene could play a part and is what is inherited. Comings (1996) found just under half of smokers and ex-smokers carried the A1 variant of DRD2; they had fewer D2 receptors, which suggested it made them more vulnerable to developing an addiction, showing it could be a single gene responsible. However, this is reductionist, as it is extremely difficult to isolate a single gene without it being influenced by anything else. It is also determinist, as it suggests that people who carry the gene variant will become addicted, but the theory ignores the role of free will. People still have a choice whether or not to smoke, for example, which this does not take into account. The research is correlational and so cause and effect is not established, as genetics are not the only thing that could

influence or cause an addiction. If the smokers carried the genetically transmitted variant gene from their family, it could also suggest they were at one point living in the same household. The influence of their environment could have also led them to smoke, and so it is impossible to draw firm conclusions from the research findings.

277. Nicotine and neurochemicals

The biological approach takes the nature side of the debate. It suggests behaviour is determined by our biological make-up over which we have little control. It ignores nurture, for example, any environmental influences such as peers or family members who smoke.

278. Nicotine and learning theory

One strength of learning theory to explain smoking addiction is that there is a lot of research evidence to support it. As a result, improved smoking prevention programmes could target adolescents (those most vulnerable to the influence of peers) to inform them of the social influences. This could help prevent young people from taking up smoking. However, learning theories suggest that addictions occur because of positive reinforcements or consequences of the behaviour, whereas in real life the potential pleasure derived from smoking would only be intermittent, not consistently rewarding. For example, smoking would not always remove a negative mood, which therefore suggests that learning theories are only partial explanations.

279. Gambling and learning theory

One strength of learning theories in explaining gambling is social learning theory (SLT), which takes into account the role of cognitions (thought processes) involved in gambling. It provides a good explanation of how a person may think about the behaviour before imitating it. For example, the family environment would provide role models on which the gambling behaviour would be modelled. Another family member may see someone else gambling and then winning, and this would provide them with a role model. They would retain that memory of seeing the other person win, and when they are motivated to imitate that behaviour, they too would gamble. However, some aspects of learning theory do not provide suitable explanations for gambling. Operant conditioning does not explain why gamblers continue with their behaviour when they continuously lose or get into financial difficulty. This aspect of learning suggests that the behaviour should be extinguished in the absence of reward, which it is not. However, the use of partial and variable reinforcements would appear to overcome this limitation, as they would suggest the big win will come if the person continues to gamble, because they have no idea when the win will occur.

280. Gambling and cognitive theory

One piece of research by Delfabbro and Winefield (2000) found that 75% of game-related thoughts during gambling were irrational and encouraged further risk-taking. These kinds of irrational cognitions could maintain arousal during gambling episodes. Wohl et al. (2007) illustrated cognitive biases in high-risk gamblers. They tested 82 adult gamblers for symptoms of addictive gambling, their enjoyment of gambling and their perception of dispositional luck (the belief that they were lucky). The participants were divided into two groups: recreational gamblers and disordered gamblers. The disordered gamblers enjoyed gambling more than the recreational gamblers and saw themselves as luckier, showing that they held cognitive biases. Griffiths studied the role of skill and cognitive bias in fruit machine gambling using volunteers. One of three hypotheses was that 'there are significant differences in the thought processes of regular and non-regular gamblers'. The participants were given £3 each to put into a fruit machine. The objective was to stay on the machine for 60 gambles and win back the original £3. Regular gamblers made more irrational verbalisations, demonstrating cognitive biases in gamblers.

281. Reducing addictions: drug therapies

Drug treatments and replacement therapies have good results for helping with addiction. The treatments provide evidence for biological explanations. However, biological therapies do not address any underlying psychological problems that may have triggered the addictions. Therefore, a combination with a psychological therapy is likely to achieve the best outcome.

282. Behavioural intervention

Behavioural-based treatments do not get to the root cause of the behaviour. They ignore why the addiction has started, so they treat the symptoms but not the cause. Covert sensitisation is not suitable for people who lack the required imagination to make the treatment a success. In using aversion therapy, there can be side effects, for example, with taking a drug to combat the addiction. This can also raise ethical issues of presenting an addict with more problems to overcome.

283. Cognitive behavioural therapy

The triggers for engaging in the behaviour are identified in order to think about strategies that could be used to avoid relapse. The therapist will ask the client to think about both positive and negative implications of relapse. The training also challenges the attitudes the person may hold about the behaviour, as some beliefs will be unhealthy. This part of the therapy is important in getting the person to feel in control of their behaviour. The person needs to use alternative relaxation to those previously used – the client is taught appropriate relaxation techniques in place of their addictive behaviour. Using these methods gives the person time to relax in a more appropriate way, and time to realise when they may be at risk of relapse. The therapy gets the addict to look at the thought processes they hold towards

the behaviour and then change it. The therapist may challenge them to think of alternative ways to cope that do not involve their addictive behaviour. For example, challenging someone with an alcohol problem to think more positively about not drinking and more negatively about the alcohol. This can be difficult as they may have used the alcohol to boost their self-esteem and so this part of the therapy has to get them to think more positively about themselves without using alcohol.

284. Theory of planned behaviour

A therapist examines the behavioural attitude. For example, a smoker admits that their health is suffering as a result of their smoking. The therapist discusses subjective norms with the client. For example, the client says they are aware that their family want them to stop smoking for health reasons. The most important part is when the therapist uncovers the perceived control the individual thinks they have over their behaviour. For example, a smoker has to believe they have the willpower to stop smoking. This can predict the intention of the behaviour. For example, the person will use nicotine patches to help them stop smoking. Finally, the outcome is the behaviour as the person is using nicotine substitutes and no longer smoking.

285. Prochaska's model of behaviour change

(a) Sam is in the termination stage.
(b) Billy is in the contemplation stage.
(c) Maria is in the action stage.
(d) Adam is in the maintenance stage.

288. Exam-style practice 1

1 A   Attitude and behavioural beliefs
   B   Subjective norms and normative beliefs
   C   Perceived behavioural control
   D   Behavioural intentions
2 Tolerance means an increased amount of the substance is required in order to experience the same effect, thus the individual becomes addicted.
   Psychological dependence is a mental and emotional compulsion to keep taking the substance or a belief that the substance needs to be taken: signs that an addiction has started.
3 Aversion therapy is a behavioural intervention used to reduce addictions. It is based on the principles of classical conditioning. The therapy introduces an unpleasant response to the addictive behaviour so that the addict would then associate the unpleasant or negative association with the behaviour. For example, people who have an addiction to alcohol can be given a drug called Antabuse (UCS). This is an emetic drug that would make the person sick (UCR). The alcohol (NS) – which was originally pleasurable – then becomes a conditioned stimulus producing a conditioned response of vomiting. The person associates the alcohol with being sick and therefore the behaviour should be extinguished. Even in the absence of the Antabuse the person will still feel sick when presented with alcohol. The therapy can also be used effectively with different addictions that have a chemical agent, such as drugs and nicotine.

4 B
5 The government would need to introduce a campaign to persuade the person who is addicted to smoking that they can be successful in quitting. They would need to focus on the **attitude and behavioural beliefs** of teenagers towards this habit and promote the fact it is a good idea to give up, for example, promoting awareness that it is damaging their health and could cause a number of diseases in the future. Therefore, the advert could begin with showing a teenager dreaming about themselves in the future with breathing problems. Secondly, the **subjective norms** of the group the smoker belongs to are important, and the government would need to show in the advert that their family and friends support them quitting. So when the teenager wakes up and tells their family about the dream they could be shown the family encouraging them to give up smoking so that their dream does not come true. The next part is the **perceived control** the smoker thinks they have over their smoking. The campaign could show things that need to be avoided, that may encourage the behaviour to occur. For example, being among other smokers may prove difficult so the teenager is shown keeping away from situations that may impact negatively on giving up. The end of the advert could show the teenager speaking positively to the camera saying 'I can do it and so can you', which shows the b**ehavioural intentions**. If these are not positive, the behaviour is likely to continue.

289. Exam-style practice 2

6 **Pre-contemplation** is the first stage of behaviour change for smokers, although at this point they have no intention of stopping smoking. They know others are concerned with their smoking but they don't see it as a problem. **Contemplation** is the next stage, where the smoker now thinks they need to stop but puts it off, saying things like 'I'm stressed today so I need to smoke, but I will stop tomorrow'. **Preparation** is the next stage, where the smoker will start to plan how they are going to stop and may make preparations, such as seeing their doctor to get nicotine patches to help them quit. **Action** is the fourth stage, where the smoker has quit smoking for a period of time and changed aspects of their life to suit being a non-smoker, such as putting the money they are saving to better use. In the **maintenance** stage the smoker is still working hard to prevent relapse, as they still feel vulnerable to starting again. This stage can be testing as they need to ensure they stay motivated to refrain from smoking, e.g. 'I feel much healthier every day since stopping'. The last stage – termination – is defined as when the person no longer feels at risk from smoking again. They are confident that they will no longer be a smoker.

7 Mark may be at risk of addiction to smoking because his genes may make him more or less sensitive to the effects of dopamine, which is involved with the reward area of the brain. His parents also smoke, which suggests the smoking could be a genetic risk factor. In addition to these genetic factors, families also influence children in other ways, for example, through the process of social learning theory, as

Mark may have modelled his behaviour on his parents. Parents who have relaxed attitudes towards smoking – such as Mark's, who both smoke – could also have influenced him. He could also be vulnerable as the stem suggests that Mark uses substances such as nicotine to relieve stress in his life. He appears to use nicotine when stressed as he feels he could not cope with his exams without smoking. Peer pressure can be influential in the development of addiction. This explanation links to SLT processes of observation, imitation and reproduction of rewarding behaviour, and Mark may have started smoking in the first place due to these influences.

8 A and C

9 Agonist substitutes, which are drugs that attempt to restore neurotransmitters to their normal level to avoid 'highs', are used to reduce addictions. These types of drug therapies provide a safer drug similar to the addictive one. In the case of gambling it has been shown to have similar effects on the brain as amphetamine use, so giving well-controlled doses of amphetamines can reduce the gambling behaviour. Safer sources of nicotine such as patches, gum and nasal sprays are some of the ways in which nicotine replacement therapy is given to reduce smoking addiction. The nasal spray and gum give an instant hit of nicotine. Patches slowly release nicotine so the addict no longer craves an actual cigarette. Antagonist treatments are another drug therapy that uses drugs to block receptors so neurotransmitters cannot fit into them, which reduce nerve impulses (antagonists) so that if any of the substance is taken it will have no effect. Naltrexone is one such drug that has been effective. It has been suggested that some gamblers feel the same 'rush' that drug addicts feel – this may be due to the rewarding effects drugs have via stimulation of neurotransmitters in the brain. Therefore, blocking the rewarding feeling with drugs such as naltrexone appears to work. Fiore (1994) carried out a meta-analysis of the effectiveness of nicotine patches. When compared to participants who wore a placebo patch they found the nicotine patch wearers were twice as likely to stop smoking. This suggests that nicotine patches work by still providing the smoker with lower doses of nicotine without them craving a cigarette. This research is good as it looked at a number of studies, so findings should be high in validity. It shows that nicotine patches could be superior to other treatments for the cessation of smoking. However, gradual withdrawal of the nicotine patches is necessary to stop completely, and results of follow-up studies are not as clear about the use of patches for the long-term cessation of smoking. Support for drug therapy for gambling comes from Kim and Grant (2001). They studied 17 compulsive gamblers who underwent a 6-week trial of naltrexone; 14 completed the trial. Most had stopped gambling by the sixth week. Two gamblers relapsed when the medication stopped, suggesting that the gambling stopped as a 'real' response to the drug and not a placebo effect. The sample size of this research is small so may not be generalisable to other gamblers because it may be unrepresentative of the gambling population.

Also, drug therapy is not always suitable as it could be exchanging addiction to one drug with another. For example, heroin users can get addicted to the heroin substitute methadone. Therefore, it may not work for all, and this is a weakness of the therapy. In addition to this, it is a chemical treatment and there could be unwanted side effects, which could raise ethical issues of harm. In support, drug treatments and replacement therapies have good results for helping with the addiction. Combined with a psychological therapy, it is likely to achieve the best outcome. This means the individual can get on with their lives without the demands of having an addiction and the impact this has, such as poor health and financial difficulties. This is beneficial to the individual and so could be seen as worth suffering the side effects for.

10 Beck et al. (2001) introduced the cognitive model of addiction indicating that addicts find themselves in a vicious circle, and that gamblers only focus on winning and how happy that makes them feel, while ignoring the losses they incur. For example, gamblers have cognitive distortions, which maintain the behaviour as their losses are minimised. Dayna has developed cognitive distortions towards her gambling. The evidence of this is that, from an early age, she has believed in luck in her winning, which has resulted in her developing an addiction to gambling. Dayna has not focused on how much she may have lost on scratch cards, a sign that her cognitive biases are only focused on the positive side of the behaviour (winning) while ignoring the negative side (the losses). Her mood and thought processes are dependent on her gambling behaviour. As Dayna is in debt she feels unhappy, so by repeatedly gambling and buying more scratch cards, she thinks it will lift her mood. She thinks that because she is lucky she will eventually achieve a big win, which could be an illusion of control, as the odds of this are heavily against it happening, and it is not something she has any control over. These cognitive biases perpetuate Dayna's gambling behaviour. Therefore her patterns of thinking are irrational.

11 Covert sensitisation is a particular type of aversion therapy and is based on the principles of classical conditioning. However, the treatment differs from aversion therapy because it is covert by nature – the patient does not experience the stimulus (taking a drug), rather they imagine it. In the case of an alcoholic, they would have to imagine having a drink and then feeling sick, and then eventually being very sick with the associated feelings. Over time, the person associates the unpleasant effects with the addictive behaviour, and with prolonged therapy, the unwanted behaviour should be weakened if not eliminated.

Support for the treatment comes from Gelder (1989) who reported that covert sensitisation is a preferred treatment because it has fewer ethical concerns than traditional aversion therapy. However, it was not more effective, so the only benefits were for moral reasons. However, Ashem and Donner (1968) did find more favourable results for treatment of alcoholics. In total, 40% who used this treatment were still abstaining after 6 months compared to a control group. This shows that the treatment is effective and it also has no side effects, which makes it more ethical than traditional aversion therapy. The patient is in control of how bad they make the imagined effects, which therefore protects them from real harm. However, this treatment may not work for everyone, as those who are not highly motivated will not benefit, nor will people who lack the ability to imagine the unpleasant effects they have to visualise. The success of the treatment may depend on the patient themselves rather than how good the treatment actually is. This type of treatment does not target the cause of the addiction, but only the symptoms, and after the treatment is over the person may revert to their old habits if the cause has not been addressed.

Published by Pearson Education Limited, 80 Strand, London, WC2R 0RL.

www.pearsonschoolsandfecolleges.co.uk

Text and illustrations © Pearson Education Limited 2017
Produced, typeset and illustrated by Cambridge Publishing Management Ltd
Cover illustration by Miriam Sturdee

The rights of Sarah Middleton, Anna Cave, Susan Harty and Sally White to be identified as authors of this work have been asserted by them in accordance with the Copyright, Designs and Patents Act 1988.

First published 2017

20 19 18

10 9 8 7 6 5 4 3 2

British Library Cataloguing in Publication Data
A catalogue record for this book is available from the British Library

ISBN 9781292111216

Printed in Slovakia by Neografia

Acknowledgements
The publisher would like to thank the following for their kind permission to reproduce their photographs:

123RF.com: 284; **Accord Healthcare Ltd:** 281tr; **Alamy Images:** ALANDAWSONPHOTOGRAPHY 249l, blickwinkel 247r, CAVALLINI JAMES / BSIP SA 158, Chronicle 260, epa european pressphoto agency b.v. 167tr, FURGOLLE / BSIP SA 133, Guillem Lopez 117, Henrik Kettunen 26, Iain Masterton 211, INTERFOTO 66, Marmaduke St. John 97, 269tr, 270, Phanie 89b, pictureline 267, Radius Images 34, 39, Reuters 149, Terry Whittaker 90, Vadym Drobot 246l, View Stock 38t; **American Psychological Association:** 107; **Reproduced with permission from © The British Psychological Society:** 106; **Change4Life:** 108; **Fotolia.com:** 9nong 52t, alexandro900 247l, Andrey Burmakin 233tr, 233cl, Andrey Popov 147, BillionPhotos.com 269bl, dalaprod 281cl, DragonImages 140, freshidea 129r, hsun337 19, JackF 212r, Jezper 246r, Monkey Business 3, 10, 36, Oksana Kuzmina 164, Oleg_Zabielin 237, photobar 56, PointImages 231, pololia 196, sabphoto 276, shaftinaction 248, william87 1t; **Getty Images:** Arunas Klupsas 174, Bettmann 12, Digital Vision 219, Donald Iain Smith / Moment 55, Maskot 167cl, Romano Cagnoni / Hulton Archive 43; **Pearson Education Ltd:** Pearson Education Ltd 201, Studio 8 98; **Press Association Images:** Barry Batchelor 1b; **Rex Shutterstock:** © IFC Films / Courtesy Everett Col 4; **Science Photo Library Ltd:** 229, Dr P. Marazzi 54, Science Source 37, SOVEREIGN, ISM 198; **Shutterstock.com:** Aletia 21, Andresr 71, Andrew Lever 52b, beltsazar 44, catwalker 216, Ivan1981Roo 220, Jaguar PS 53, Levent Konuk 89t, Lucky Business 279, Monkey Business Images 129l, 212l, oliveromg 178, sniegirova mariia 214, Vladimir Mucibabic 249r; **Sozaijiten:** 38b

All other images © Pearson Education

We are grateful to the following for permission to reproduce copyright material:

Figure on page 18 adapted from R.C. Atkinson and R.M. Shiffrin, Human memory: A proposed system and its control processes in *The Psychology of Learning and Motivation*, Vol. 2, pp. 89–195, Published by Elsevier Inc., Reproduced with permission from the author. Figure on page 22, reprinted from *Psychology of Learning and Motivation*, Vol. 8, Alan D. Baddeley, Graham Hitch. Copyright (1974), with permission from Elsevier.

Note from the publisher
Pearson has robust editorial processes, including answer and fact checks, to ensure the accuracy of the content in this publication, and every effort is made to ensure this publication is free of errors. We are, however, only human, and occasionally errors do occur. Pearson is not liable for any misunderstandings that arise as a result of errors in this publication, but it is our priority to ensure that the content is accurate. If you spot an error, please do contact us at resourcescorrections@pearson.com so we can make sure it is corrected.